Under the editorship of John E. Horrocks,
The Ohio State University

Mind in Evolution

An East-West Synthesis of Learned Behavior and Cognition

Gregory Razran

Queens College of the City University of New York

Houghton Mifflin Company · **Boston**

New York · *Atlanta* · *Geneva, Illinois* · *Dallas* · *Palo Alto*

Of physiology from top to toe I sing

. . . .

The Modern Man I sing
WALT WHITMAN
Leaves of Grass

All moving toward their own truths
Each bravely in his own path
Worms crawling lowly ruts
Men charting parabolas

ANDREY VOZNESENSKY
A Parabolic Ballad

Printed in the U.S.A.

Library of Congress Catalog Card Number: 73-141668

ISBN: 0-395-05085-5

FOREWORD

The history of man is characterized by his fascination with his own nature and by his attempts to understand its essence. In his eighties, near the end of a distinguished career as a neuroanatomist, Charles Herrick wrote, "Human nature interests me because it is my nature," and went on to say that it is man's unique capacity to look at his own nature as a spectator whose position is "inside the works." But man is capable of more than observation from a privileged spectator's position. Evolution has brought the level of his nervous activity to a point where, as the thinking-symbolizing animal, he is capable of making and explicating his observation in planned scientific terms susceptible to proof or disproof. Pascal put man's relative position in nature well when he wrote, "L'homme n'est qu'un roseau le plus faible de la nature; mais c'est un roseau pensant."

Over a quarter of a century ago, Sir Charles Sherrington wrote a book to which he gave the felicitous title, *Man on his Nature,* thus taking his place in the long line of those remarkable products of evolution who have developed to a point where they can do what no other can, consider their own nature. The present volume joins that company, for it is written by a man of insight who as a scientist has considered the nature of man and whose lifetime of study and research on the topic has given him much to say. He speaks not only from "inside the works" in Herrick's sense but also from "inside the works" as a laboratory researcher who has himself contributed to the knowledge the synthesis of which forms the *raison d'etre* of his book.

In *Mind in Evolution* Professor Razran deals with those central aspects of man's nature involving learned behavior, higher nervous activity, and cognition. He approaches this tripod by means of a comparative analysis and synthesis of three systems of mind, namely American behaviorism, Russian Pavlovianism, and Western "cognitionism." As written, the book is not in the main a presentation of a personal theory, but rather a comparative Russian-American literature presentation of the development of the mental processes in the form of a sequential topical analysis in which a theoretical position emerges.

Professor Razran's fluency in the Russian language and his personal acquaintanceship with leading figures in both Russian and American psychology enable him to present a view that is as novel as it is interesting. As might be expected, a very large amount of the Russian literature remains

v

untranslated, and a considerable amount is in general not available even in the original in the United States, with the result that much that appears in this book is no doubt new to American psychologists. Certainly its scope takes it far beyond any previous attempts to integrate or relate the research and point of view of Russian and American psychology. Of particular interest is Professor Razran's point that Russo-Soviet and American psychology have been growing apart for years not only because of a language barrier but also because of a thought barrier. He makes particularly explicit the wide experimental base and predominantly evolutionary approach of the Russians as compared to the unevolutionary approach of the Americans. Professor Razran's historically based discussions serve to give flesh and life to what could easily become the bare bones of a catalog of research findings based on "tens of thousands" of research findings. One cannot fail to be impressed throughout this book by the author's resolution of the problem he faced of drastic selection and integration, of what to use and what to eliminate. In writing a book such as this it is particularly difficult for an author to keep his selections and interpretations relatively free of his own personal bias, and this is particularly true when the author has been an active research participant over a great deal of the history of the area about which he is writing. Professor Razran has made a real effort to retain a catholic and objective position. In the main he has succeeded, but no one can be entirely free of looking at evidence in terms of his own interpretation.

This is a distinguished contribution to World psychology and one that should be of particular value to American psychologists as again and again points are made that, in all fairness, American psychology needs to have made—even if such points do occasionally make a few evolutionary egalitarians a bit unhappy.

John E. Horrocks

PREFACE

In large measure, the present book is a ramified outgrowth of my long interest in what is termed, in Pavlovian tradition, "evolution of higher nervous activity." This interest has in the last decade been buttressed by a grant from the National Institutes of Health which permitted me to spend four summers visiting Soviet research institutes and laboratories and to peruse in Soviet general and medical libraries tens of thousands of Russian titles of published experiments and discussions of Pavlov-launched research and thought. I was able to examine, and in differing degrees digest, approximately 90 per cent of the Russian publications—partly in Soviet libraries, but mostly in my own collection of some 1500 volumes, supplemented by the holdings of the National Library of Medicine and the Library of Congress.

In the mid-fifties, American knowledge of advances in the Pavlov system beyond the contents of the Anrep and Gantt translations of his two books was, however, so extremely limited that it seemed best to codify, first, the essence of new systematic and methodologic developments in *specific* areas. Interoceptive conditioning, compound-stimulus conditioning (including "dynamic stereotypes"), semantic conditioning, the "second-signal system," and the orienting reflex were singled out. But attention was given also to such relative "unknowns" as the Soviets' special grasp of operant conditioning, chimpanzees' ideation, and two-way and backward conditioning. The full ethos of burgeoning Soviet Pavlovianism was bared only briefly and summarily in the thirty-two articles—which vary in length from two pages to an entire issue of the *Psychological Review* (March, 1961)—published between 1957 and 1968.

Yet, all along my search and analysis it was quite clear to me that the chief character of this ethos had come to correspond more and more to my own "long interest." Since Pavlov's death, and to some extent during the last years of his life, the overall and overriding general systematic distinctness of Soviet higher nervous activity vis-à-vis American behavior or learning theory has inhered in its strong commitment to an evolutionary view of the learning mind and a wide concern with experimental validation of that view. "The evolution of higher nervous activity, that is, phyletic and ontogenetic differences in conditioning, has always been a dominant portion of [current] Soviet research and thought" (Razran, 1961a, p. 138).

The statement is incomplete in that this research and thought have involved wide evolutionary variations not only of conditioned species and subjects but also, as already indicated, of conditioned reactions and experimental designs. Interoceptive, compound-stimulus, and semantic conditioning were set forth not merely as illustrations of the scope of conditioning but as revelations of levels of its evolutionary ascent: respectively, an unconscious level, a level related to sensory integration or perception, and a level immanent in thinking. Moreover, the unconditioned system of orienting reflexes is held up as a more recent evolutionary acquisition than the appetitive and aversive reflex systems; one that Soviet theoreticians not uncommonly equate with the advent of cognition (cf. the American "expectancy" formulation of it). And evolutionism putatively comes to light in comparative analyses of the developmental dynamics of the Pavlovian conditioned-reflex paradigm in general. If, for instance, spinal mammals or primitive animals such as amphioxi manifest learned sensitization but not true associative conditioning, and if such sensitization is commonly a preliminary stage of true conditioning, then do not the two learning processes disclose a Darwinian kinship of evolutionary continuity and evolutionary novelty?

On the other hand, I should like to note that my original leaning toward an evolutionary conception of the learning mind has taken its departure not from Pavlov but from the work and views of early British and American comparative psychologists—C. Lloyd Morgan, L. T. Hobhouse, J. Mark Baldwin, R. M. Yerkes—and from general philosophic and scientific considerations. "It would really be a curious freak of organismic evolution the outstanding feature of which is the evolution of the brain and that special modifiability called learning capacity, if the laws of this modifiability remained fixed and did not evolve" (Razran, 1935, p. 7). Pavlov's *Wednesdays* had not yet been published and his formal writings differed only little from American counterparts in evolutionary concern—both were engrossed in the study of the experimental fundamentals of mind (or higher nervous activity) as such, rather than of evolving minds.

Later on, however, a continually diverging bifurcation developed. In both basic theoretics and parametric empirics, evolutionism has expanded in Soviet study of higher nervous activity and declined in correlative American experimental psychology, a quandary to my mind ever since. Hence, the present book and ambitious attempt to mobilize fully and to pit against each other germane East and West evidence—and logic. Roughly, 43 per cent of the evidence cited is Russian, 43 per cent American (including Canadian), 12 per cent European (East and West), and 2 per cent scattered (Japanese, Australian, and Latin American). Because of the language barrier, I have given the Russian portion the wider coverage; at the same time, no other significant systematic contribution is bypassed.

My first professional publication was a review of V. M. Bekhterev's 1926 *General Principles of Human Reflexology,* in the January 1927 issue of the *Journal of Philosophy, Psychology,* and *Scientific Method.* And since then my articles have been almost equally divided between surveys and analyses of Soviet psychophysiology and psychology and my own experimental and theoretical excursions. This, however, is my first book, and it is tempting to acknowledge briefly those whose writings and teaching influenced my thinking. I. P. Pavlov, of course, comes first. His influence was not only primal but progressive and accelerating. While I was originally critical of his special cortical dynamics and was the first, I believe, to demonstrate the specificity of salivary conditioning in adult human subjects through the role of cognitive attitudes, I learned later, from *Wednesdays,* that Pavlov's view on the effects of the "second-signal system" on human conditioning (1949, Vol. 1, pp. 335, 337-338; Vol. 2, p. 246; original dates, May 17 and 24, 1933, and February 21, 1934) differed from my own conceptions of the like role of cognitive attitudes only in that his was a system of human-animal dichotomy whereas mine eventually became a trichotomy of man, higher animals, and lower animals. And still later, as techniques for direct probings of neural correlates of conditioning have been discovered, I have come to feel more and more that Pavlov's behaviorally derived basic neural assumptions of mind mechanisms are for the most part correct, and thus prescient.

I read Sechenov after I had read Pavlov and Bekhterev and Watson. Hence, my appreciation of his genius could only be in the main historical. Yet, strikingly, more than once I have found some of his "objectifications" of mind more advanced and more sophisticated than those of his successors. Consider, for instance, his tenets that "association is effected through contact of consecutive reflexes" (that is, a linkage of reactions rather than of stimuli and reactions and a sequential linkage at that); that "ideas of objects" [read: perception] emerge from centrally integrated learning of such reflexes (in contrast to peripheralistic views); and that "the essential psychophysiology of truncated noneffector receptor-adjustor neural reactions is no different from that of neuromotor effector reflexes" (note the present-day equivalence of neural and effector conditioning). More could be cited. I continue reading Sechenov for "insight," allowing for some fallacies of fact and judgment common in his period.

J. S. Beritoff, P. K. Anokhin, and A. A. Ukhtomsky are three other Russian scientists who have influenced my thoughts on the learning mind. Beritoff's concept of two-way or reversible conditioning, developed in 1924, became an integral part of my own systematic endeavors, as did his 1932 treatment of compound-stimulus conditioning as an "afferent behavioral integration leading to individually-acquired activations of supplementary neural centers." His later view of image-directed behavior corresponds in some respects to my own interest in the relation of perception to conditioning; and while I must hold in abeyance my estimate of his claims of specific anatomical localization of imagery, I am surely in sympathy with his search.

I first came across Anokhin's "functional system" of integrated uncon-ditioned-conditioned interaction in 1949. I had been pondering the prob-lem earlier while reading E. B. Holt and L. Carmichael, and Anokhin's ex-periments and formulations pointed up a crucial and concordant East-West behavioral generalization: *The unlearned contains and models all that is learned even as the learned effectuates and modifies all that is un-learned.* Anokhin's early (pre-cybernetics) emphasis on the wide role of feedback—what he came to call "acceptor action"—in regulating behavior (in a sense akin to early American motor theories of consciousness) has also impressed me strongly, even if I have not followed the full swing of all of his theses. Finally, Ukhtomsky's "Principle of Dominance" was the basis of my first theory of conditioning, published in 1930 in the *Psycho-logical Review* while I was a graduate student at Columbia University—and it has been with me in some fashion ever since.

At Columbia, the prime molders of my psychological thinking as a student were, each in his own way, Robert S. Woodworth and Gardner Murphy. My earlier thinking was so global, deductionistic, and general-ized that it took Woodworth some time to reverse it to ordered exactness of facts, methods, and particulars. A seminar in "Contemporary Problems of Psychology" in which seven of fifteen sessions were devoted by Wood-worth to settling the status of eye movements seems to have done most of the reversing. Murphy, on the other hand, had a penchant for broad categories and thus tended to re-reverse the Woodworth influence; indeed, he did so to the extent that while I came to distrust deductionism in psy-chology, I did not become an all-out inductionist, but rather, invested my theoretics with what philosophers call "inductive jumps." Murphy has, furthermore, always encouraged my ideas, and, like me, he became a votary of "dominance" as a fundamental of psychobiology.

Karl S. Lashley and Clark L. Hull taught at the Columbia University summer session in 1927 and 1929, respectively. I took Lashley's two courses and assimilated avidly the essence of his experiments and his special behaviorism, which from that time forward substantially modified but by no means uprooted my Pavlovian engrossment. Indeed, Lashley's specific failure to obtain salivary conditioning in adult human subjects instigated my research in the area. I later corresponded with him and largely agreed to some of his criticisms of neo-behaviorists and myself groped sedulously in all directions to reconcile some of the basics of Pav-lov and Lashley. My contact with Hull was not so constructive. I had several private sessions with him and he explained to me in some detail the imposing essentials of his future system. But I, unfriendly to the deductive approach and inflated by the fact that my own article on con-ditioning theory had been accepted for publication by the *Psychological Review,* was very critical, and unwisely told Hull so in no uncertain terms —a breach that "naturally" made me *persona non grata.* Later, I was both affected and nonplussed by the massive influence which the Hull system came to exert on American psychology for several decades. *"Zeitgeist,"* I enlightened myself, and did not join.

I read German almost as well as Russian and English and have thus all along been familiar with the full framework of the experiments and theory of Gestalt psychology. However, while the school has influenced me in the problems that it posed, the answers that it offered penetrated the suggestive rather than the solutional strata of my core thinking. Gestalt "direct experience" postulates seemed to me, to begin with, appropriate only to the summit of mind and not to its basic hierarchical structure of hundreds of millions of years of ascending evolution. And when I noted later that even at the summit specific postulates were often unverified—or, because of vagueness, hardly verifiable—the Gestalt system appeared to me also more and more a hyperbole of a particular *Zeitgeist*. Its rightful problems of patterning and meaning demanded, I came to think, a behavioral and neurobehavioral objectification of a type that transformed association into conditioning.

Equal scrutiny of American and Soviet experiments of the learning mind have, to a considerable extent, made my own learning views unlike either tradition and likely unclear to both, particularly since hitherto these views and their rationales have been scattered among approximately 100 articles and not pooled into a book. Yet the integration of my earlier avowals is only one of the two basic efforts of the book. The other is a *new* systematization in the wake of intensive study of *new* East and West evidence—and logic—in the last half decade.

Gregory Razran

ACKNOWLEDGMENTS

John E. Horrocks, Leonard Carmichael, and Robert C. Rooney have been vitally encouraging in their kindest evaluation of the manuscript sent to them serially in the course of four years. Joseph P. McMurray, the president of Queens College, and Deans Robert F. Hartle, Sidney Axelrad, David A. Krinsley, and David H. Speidel have gone out of their way to free me of administrative duties in an exacting period, even as William N. Schoenfeld, William S. Battersby, and Gad Hakerem have done their utmost to lighten my teaching schedule. Diane Faissler and Jackie Leonard have most competently and sedulously guarded the clarity of my style and idiomaticalness of lexicon and expressions. Without this aggregate of cooperative help and assurance, the arduous task of putting the book together would surely have been much more difficult, if not impossible. I am grateful and appreciative.

The sources of the 70 figures in the book are 37 Russian publications (including one article of my own), 25 American (including 3 of my own), 3 British, 2 German, and one Uruguayan, with 2 new figures of my own making. I am deeply indebted to the non-Russian authors and publishers for their permission to reproduce this documentary crux of my various arguments. Permission was not requested of authors and publishers in the Soviet Union. However, past experience bears witness that it would have been gladly granted and that our Soviet colleagues fully welcome my making known their germinal scientific contributions to English readers. May they receive here my very special thanks.

Finally, I am happy to acknowledge that my research has been supported since 1957 by Grant MH 02196 from the National Institute of Mental Health, Department of Health, Education, and Welfare.

Gregory Razran

CONTENTS

CHAPTER ONE

Problem and Approach

THE PROBLEM

Evolution and No Evolution in Systematic Experimental Psychology

Mind in Evolution is the title of a book by L. T. Hobhouse published at the turn of this century, in 1901. Hobhouse was an English philosopher and sociologist and with that a pioneer in experimental animal psychology. He antedated Köhler in testing learning through tool-using techniques—including box-stacking and raking in food and other objects with sticks and ropes—and in delineating such learning in apes and monkeys as a near-human mastery of concrete perceptual relations which he called "Practical Judgment." But, unlike Köhler (1917), and in part following C. Lloyd Morgan (1894) and Thorndike (1898), Hobhouse acknowledged in lower animals a primarily nonperceptual "primitive type of learning" of "simple Confirmation and Inhibition," which he termed "Assimilation and Readjustment." And he further postulated two advanced "stages" of learning specific to man: acquisition of concepts through language and systematic thought through concepts.

Hobhouse was not, of course, a modern behavioral scientist—ultimately, indeed, he was a subjectivist and teleologist. However, as he himself stated, his inquiry was concerned "not so much with the inner nature of Mind as with its function, not so much with what Mind is felt to be by its possessor, as with its operations as apparent to an onlooker" (p. 5). The tenets of his first two stages of learning rested on whatever experimental (not anecdotal) animal data he could muster in his time, and all four stages were "correlated"—a key term in his conception of the function of mind—within a hierarchical framework of evolutionary continuity and evolutionary novelty. "Orthogenic" mental evolution was the guiding principle of Hobhouse's systematization of psychology. And he surely was not alone in upholding the principle. That mind (however looked at) evolves in Darwin's sense of "descent [or rather ascent] with modifications," and that such modifications are cumulated and selected to give rise to qualitatively newer and higher mechanisms and manifestations, was the consensus of the age.

Tens of thousands of experiments have been performed since the days of Hobhouse in the areas of learning, perception, and thinking. Yet, to date, there has been no replication of his nascent endeavor—no comprehensive evolutionary systematization of the three areas and none, notably, of even the most frequently studied area, learning. Unlike other life sciences and some social sciences (e.g., anthropology), modern psychology has lost almost all commerce with evolution as integrator and arbiter of its research and thought. Learning and perception and thinking do continue to be the core categories of the field—but scarcely as an integrated phylogenetic and ontogenetic hierarchy. Quite the contrary, the penchant has for years been toward a widely nonorganic, egalitarian fragmentation of the categories, combined with what might be called a "universalization of particulars." Learning, ultimately conceived as conditioning, and perception and thinking, jointly thought of as cognition, and each of their several divisions has come to claim for itself all of nature's mind. And each, in its own way, has come to discern but little between the mind principle in rats and men—indeed, between that in planaria, pigeons, Platyrhina (American monkeys), and Plato. (Freud and Piaget are, to be sure, evolutionary in their core thinking. However, inasmuch as their systems bear only on the human mind, and particularly inasmuch as Freud's is wholly detached from experimental psychology and Piaget's is only loosely anchored to its total enterprise, they are, as it were, outside the pale of the present book. In-group nonconformists—that is, evolution-bound experimental animal psychologists—in the United States are few and far between: Beach [1950], Bitterman [1965], the late Nissen [1951], and the late Schneirla [1952].)

Thorndike, Yerkes, and Early Behaviorists

Historically, the beginning of the uniquely unevolutionary character of most modern American systematic experimental psychology could no doubt be traced to Thorndike—to his view that all learning, from fish to man, is ultimately nothing but a trial-and-error selection and connection of reactions through a mechanical "law of effect," implied in 1898 and promulgated in 1913. Actually, however, Thorndike's organic egalitarianism had in the first several decades of the century only dented but by no means demolished the field's evolutionary commitments. For one thing, the psychology of the time was rather slow in accepting—or even realizing—the full import of his promulgation; indeed, the "law of effect" was sometimes regarded as a "law of affect" or even a "law of knowledge." For another, the promulgation itself was not so radical as to bid all learning to converge on studying one organism by one very simple method. Thorndike's own main learning technique, the problem box which he invented, was in all quite complex, and he did experiments with cats, dogs, chickens, and, later, children. In point of fact, a most salient feature of American psychology in the first decades of the century had been the probing of learning by methods ranging from the most rudimentary to the most intricate throughout the phyletic scale and, to some extent, all along human ontogeny.

Moreover, subjectivistic learning psychologists of the period, not in consonance with Thorndike, held fast to full-scale mental evolutionism. Consciousness and ideation had not yet been put through the egalitarian wringer of Gestalt psychology. Consider R. M. Yerkes, America's leading comparative psychologist of the time. He assumed that consciousness existed at the very dawn of life but maintained that it had evolved in the animal kingdom into five distinct ascending "levels," which he attempted to correlate specifically with the animals' bodily and neural evolution (1905a) and diagrammed as a "psychophylogenetic tree" (1911, p. 242). And, studying learning from earthworms to "great apes" by means of a wide gamut of ingenious methods, he thought that clear-cut existence of "almost-human" "ideational learning"—basically akin to what Köhler later inaugurated as "insightful learning"—was evident only in primates (1916a, 1916b). The phyletic compass of the learning experiments of Yerkes and his co-workers is very impressive—earthworm (1912), crawfish (Yerkes and Huggins, 1903), crab (1902), frog (1904, 1905b), turtle (1901), crow (Coburn and Yerkes, 1915), dancing mouse (1907), pig (Yerkes and Coburn, 1915), monkey (1916a, 1916b), gorilla (1927a, 1927b, 1928; Yerkes and Yerkes, 1929), chimpanzee (Yerkes and Learned, 1925; Yerkes and Yerkes, 1928, 1929), and orang-utan (1916a, 1916b; Yerkes and Yerkes, 1929). And so is the range of apparatus which he devised: a T-maze for earthworms, a conditioned-reflex apparatus for frogs, and boxes for simple discrimination learning, on the one hand, and on the other, the Yerkes multiple-choice apparatus, which could be set to tax the mind of a highly intelligent human adult. Margaret F. Washburn, author of America's first textbook of animal psychology (*The Animal Mind,* 1908) and Yerkes' avowedly subjectivistic contemporary in the field, was likewise wholly under the aegis of a mental evolution approach to mind.

Considerable evolutionary orientation persisted, in fact, among early behaviorists unswayed by Watson's view that all learning is simple conditioning and all thinking learned subvocal speech. Mind as behavior was not uncommonly embraced without this Watsonian simplism. Leaving out detailed documentation, we may note that as late as 1935 two significant, essentially behavioristic textbooks in the area—Warden, Jenkins, and Warner's three-volume *Comparative Psychology* and Maier and Schneirla's *Principles of Animal Psychology*—were fundamentally imbued with evolutionary professions.

Neo-behaviorists, Gestaltists, and Cognitionists

Total dislodgement of evolutionism from the main establishment of American psychology came to pass, it appears, only after neo-behaviorism and its antinome, Gestalt psychology, penetrated the field with full force and, we might say, joined in a common anti-evolution front. English translations of four books, two Russian and two German, seem to have effected most of the dislodging. I. P. Pavlov's *Conditioned Reflexes* (1927b) and *Lectures on Conditioned Reflexes* (1928b) showed American neo-behaviorists, irrespective of brand, what might be done with learning confined to the study of one organism by one simple method: (1) the vast amount of interrelated (parametric) information that could be obtained, and (2) the vast opportunity to systematize—or extrapolate—this information. As is known, no American neo-behaviorist had verified the work of Pavlov with the method and organism that he had used, but all were quick to parallel him. B. F. Skinner (1938) did the paralleling by replacing salivation with lever-pressing; C. L. Hull (1937), by substituting a behavioral system of intervening variables for a neural system of hypothetical constructs; and both Skinner and Hull, and all others, did it by using white rats instead of mongrel dogs—the rat, an old minion of American learning laboratories (Small, 1899). Learning in other species, including man, has been used by neo-behaviorists only as an auxiliary proving ground—a sort of a colonial possession of rats' minds. ("Go to the ant, thou sluggard, consider her ways and be wise.")

The two influential German books were Koffka's *The Growth of Mind* (1924) and Köhler's *The Mentality of Apes* (1925). These books, together with the earlier writings of Wertheimer (1912), offered consciousness-loving American psychologists a new look into its essence and presumed novel laws of its organization and action—the code of Gestalt psychology that the crux of mind is a ubiquity of meaning inherent in organisms' unique governance by organized wholes, or *Gestalten,* and not an amorphous awareness of sense data transformed through associations and synthesis into perception and ideation (nor, of course, that it is behavior concatenated of component conditioned or trial-and-error selected reflexes or reactions). The code's specific laws—e.g., closure, good continuation—were too vague to be definitely tested through experiments. Yet its cardinal message of meaning and "figure-ground" organization appears to have instilled enough new mettle into psychologists of the inness of mind to regroup them into a system that, appropriately, took on the name cognitive or cognition psychology. Brunswick (1957) defined cognition as "the acquisition of knowledge," while Krech (1932) stretched "insight" in apes to " 'hypotheses' in rats," and Krech and Crutchfield (1948) came to define all learning as "a reorganization of the cognitive field"—that is, to conclude, one supposes, that since lower, and even the lowest, animals learn, they, too, are possessors of cognition or knowledge. ("The earth shall be full of the knowledge of the Lord, as the waters cover the sea," said Isaiah; to which Ecclesiastes parried with: "Man has no preeminence above a beast: for all is vanity.")

In fine, the main establishment of present-day American psychology is sharply severed into two antagonist, yet in one sense allied, camps: unevolutionary conditioners, for whom the minds of worms and men are the minds of rats, and unevolutionary cognitionists, to whom the minds of worms and rats are the minds of men.[1]

Pavlov and Post-Pavlovians

In large measure, evolutionism became from its very inception a sort of invariant ethos of Russian science, more than that of science in any other country. *The Origin of the Species* (1859) was hailed enthusiastically by Mendeleyev, Mechnikov, Sechenov, Baer, Timiryazev, Chebyshev, the brothers Kovalevsky, with nothing like the opposition of Owen in England, Agassiz in the United States, Quatrefages in France, and Virchow in Germany. *The Variations of Animals and Plants* appeared in Russian a year earlier (1867) than in English (1868)—translated from proof—and *The Descent of Man,* the same year as in English (1871), in three separate translations, one by Marya A. Sechenova, pupil and wife of Pavlov's renowned predecessor. The evolutionary tradition continued unabated despite theologists' animadversions and government restrictions—Darwin's books were never banned, although pamphlets defending them often were —and Pavlov was, of course, within that tradition: an advocate of Darwin's ethos.

Pavlov's evolutionary mind view is reflected in both the methods and the principle phases of his conditioned-reflex system, otherwise known as "higher nervous activity (behavior)." He systematically broadened his conditioning design to include compound-stimulus conditioning, conditioned "dynamic stereotypes," higher-order conditioning, conditioning to stimulus relations, conditioning of associations (American equivalent: sensory preconditioning), and imitative or observational conditioning. And he thereby put forth not only a most serviceable means for testing the evolution of associative capacity in phylogeny and ontogeny but also a highly effective technique for analyzing the underlying mechanism of the evolving capacity in terms of continuity and novelty. By 1927, he began

[1] "Evolution" is seldom found in subject indexes of American textbooks of psychology, and very few items—most of them foreign—are listed under that heading in *Psychological Abstracts.* There are no articles by psychologists in the quarterly *Evolution,* the international journal of organic evolution, in publication since 1946. Hilgard, participating in a symposium of twenty-two leading scientists on "The Evolution of Man," as part of the University of Chicago Darwin Centennial, discussed evolution *of* psychology rather than evolution *in* psychology. Nor were the contributions of several American psychologists to the 1958 symposium of twenty-three scientists on "Behavior and Evolution" (Roe and Simpson, Editors) evolutionary in a special psychological sense.

to proffer his classic tenet that conditioning comprises two signal systems: a first-signal system common to both animals and men, and a second-signal system, language, unique to man, for which he later postulated "evolved operation of a *new* [extra] neural principle" (1933, p. 293).[2] Yet it should be noted that, with very few exceptions, Pavlov experimented only with dogs; and his second-signal system principle was launched as a general thought and elaborated almost solely on the basis of clinical demonstrations in the Leningrad Neuropsychiatric Clinic, which he attended assiduously for five years (1931-1936; *Clinical Wednesdays,* 3 volumes, 1954-1957). The evolutionary progression of mind from organism to organism in terms of conditioning continuity and novelty concerned him greatly (*Wednesdays,* 1949, Vol. 1, pp. 30, 77, 90, 154, 337; original dates, December 18, 1929-May 24, 1933—to cite only one of the six volumes of *Wednesdays,* three general and three clinical). But he simply did not manage to realize the specific experiments which his theory and methods had implicated. Indeed, he left a glaring gap in his very theory, failing to explicate in some way how the first-signal system had evolved into the second. To quote L. A. Orbeli, Pavlov's immediate successor in his Institute and staunchest evolutionist: "The second-signal system did not just drop from heaven" (1950, p. 15).

In the last three years of his life, Pavlov did, however, study directly learning and problem solving in two chimpanzees, Rosa and Raphael, the interpretive accounts of which allow another look—more restricted but also more distinct—at his evolutionism. Pavlov verified fully the empirical results of Köhler and others, even adding new stunts to the apes' wisdom repertory. However, he plainly declared that "insight is nothing but put-to-use prior associations"; that "associations form *Gestalten* and not *Ges-*

---

[2] The title of Pavlov's first book on the formation and disruption of conditioned reflexes was: *Twenty Years of Objective Study of the Higher Nervous Activity (Behavior) of Animals. Conditioned Reflexes. A Collection of Articles, Lectures, and Addresses.* It was published in 1923 and, with nine articles added, was translated into English in 1928 by W. Horsley Gantt as: *Lectures on Conditioned Reflexes. Twenty-Five Years of Objective Study,* etc. A second book, combining a series of lectures delivered in 1924 at the Petrograd Military Medical Academy, appeared in 1927 under the name *Lectures on the Work of the Large Hemispheres of the Brain* and was translated in the same year by G. V. Anrep as: *Conditioned Reflexes. An Investigation of the Physiological Activity of the Cerebral Cortex.* The last lecture of this book, first brought out the view of the unique-to-man second-signal system, developed in later articles and particularly in the "Protocols and Stenograms of Physiological Colloquia" and "Stenograms of Sessions in Neurological and Psychiatric Clinics," published posthumously (1949-1957) as three volumes called *Wednesdays* and three called *Clinical Wednesdays.* Thus, "higher nervous activity," augmented by the second-signal system, may be thought of as (*a*) the Pavlovian way of studying the physiological basis of learning, perception, and thinking, or, since its physiology is primarily deduced from behavior, as (*b*) the equivalent of American "fundamentals [or theory] of learned behavior and cognition." It is a separate teaching and research discipline in the Soviet Union.

talten, associations"; and that "perception is ultimately a conditioned reflex [which] Helmholtz not knowing of conditioning called 'unconscious inference' " (*Wednesdays,* 1949, Vol. 2, pp. 567, 580, Vol. 3, p. 46; original dates, November 28 and December 5, 1934, and January 23, 1935). Apes, Pavlov pointed out, possess highly advanced orienting-investigatory reflexes and thus, unlike dogs, may be conditioned on the basis of their manipulatory and curiosity-invoked activities without recourse to food or noxious stimuli (*Wednesdays,* 1949, Vol. 2, pp. 68, 166; original dates, October 18 and December 20, 1933; cf. Harlow, Harlow, and Meyer, 1950, and Berlyne, 1960). But, he continued, since apes, like dogs and unlike human beings, possess no second-signal system, no new principle of conditioning—or learning or thinking or intelligence—governs the ape mind. ("Man has preeminence above a beast, but ape has no preeminence above a dog—and all may not be vanity.")

Leaving aside the status of insight and *Gestalt,* it is nonetheless quite clear that Pavlov adhered to an unanalytic view of perception, egalitarian and not evolutionary. Devoted wholly to pondering the *evolving* mechanisms of change and becoming, he seems to have lost sight of the *evolved* essences of specific being. In a personal interview in the summer of 1934, Pavlov told me that his evolutionary outlook on mind and conditioning was only a first step which others must develop through experimentation, observation, and inference.

Post-Pavlovian students of Pavlov have gone much beyond him to "evolutionize" his system: (1) inducting programs of phyletic and ontogenetic comparisons of conditioning (Beritoff, 1959, 1968a; Karamyan, 1956; Kasatkin, 1951, 1952; Kol'tsova, 1958, 1967; Volokhov, 1951, 1968; Voronin, 1948a, 1957); (2) complicating the conditioning design through bilateral, "transswitched" (reversal), truncated, and situational conditioning, and expanding the studies of the specificities of the conditioning of compound stimuli (Anokhin, 1949b, 1961; Asratyan, 1953, 1961a; Beritoff, 1932, 1937; Kupalov, 1963, 1964; Voronin, 1948a, 1965); (3) uncovering the new, presumably evolutionarily lower level of interoceptive conditioning (Ayrapet'yants, 1937, 1952; Bulygin, 1959, 1966; Bykov, 1932, 1943; Makarov, 1949, 1959); (4) amassing a large body of experimental data on the special attributes of the second-signal system, by itself and in interaction with the first system—general data as well as data comparing subjects differing in maturity, capacity, and organic and functional normalcy (Ivanov-Smolensky, 1935a, 1965; Kol'tsova, 1958, 1967; Krasnogorsky, 1931, 1958; Pratusevich, 1960, 1964; Traugott, 1957); and (5) stressing in general the merit of the evolutionary approach (Orbeli, 1941, 1942, 1947, 1949, 1958).

Moreover, post-Pavlovians have, by and large, relinquished traditional "monoeffector" (one-reaction) conditioning techniques for a wide gamut of "polyeffectors," and, in addition, have availed themselves fully of newly-developed techniques of (*a*) direct neural and chemical probing of the basis of conditioning (Anokhin, 1949b, 1958c; Beritoff, 1940, 1969; Kogan, 1936, 1960; Kostyuk, 1960a, 1960b; Livanov, 1940, 1960a, 1960b; Rusinov, 1953, 1965a; Vladimirov, 1953, 1957; and others) and (*b*) minute quantifications of the orienting reflex (Sokolov, 1958a, 1964b; Vinogradova, 1959, 1961; and others), which Pavlov observed only grossly. And they have become very much involved in studying the relation of conditioning to ecology (Biryukov, 1960, 1963; Slonim, 1961, 1962; and others), on the one hand, and in experimenting with decorticate and subliminal conditioning (Belenkov, 1950a, 1965; Gershuni, 1946, 1957; Pshonik, 1948a, 1952; and others), on the other. The cortex is no longer considered the exclusive organ of conditioning, and, incidentally, Pavlov himself gave up his earlier supposition that the frontal lobes are the organs of the second-signal system.

With all that, however, present-day Soviet Pavlovians have not arrived at an evolutionary systematization of learning—and perception and thinking—not even of learning alone. They do possess a proper evolutionary spirit and a multitude of pertinent basic facts, but not an integrated evolutionary system—not yet, anyhow. As is known, there exists in the Soviet Union not only a Pavlovian physiologists' psychology of conditioning or higher nervous activity but also a psychologists' psychology of what we may call cognition, defined as "the science of psychic phenomena as functions of the brain reflecting reality"—with both disciplines professing that mind means conditioning *and* cognition. Perception, thinking, and complex phases of learning as such fall within the domain of the latter discipline (Kovalev, Stepanov, and Shabalin, 1966; Smirnov, Leont'yev, Rubinshteyn, and Teplov, 1956), whereas the fundamentals (typically termed "the physiological basis") of conditioning and learning, and—by extension— also of perception and thinking, are the concern of the former (Kogan, 1959; Voronin, 1965).

In other words, although the two Soviet psychologies adhere to one mind view and the one American psychology is split into two views, integrating the mind's core categories of learning, perception, and thinking is a more arduous task for a Soviet physiologist—or psychologist—than it is for an American psychologist. Or, to put it differently: While the two Soviet mind disciplines, unlike American behaviorism and cognitionism, no longer abnegate each other in theory, they are not in fact adequately integrated —at least not yet. Think of the wide gulf between Pavlov's view of perception "as ultimately a conditioned reflex" and the customary definition in textbooks of psychologists' psychologies as "awareness of an object or event" (Kovalev et al., 1966; and Smirnov et al., 1956).

As I noted in the Preface, the present book's probe of mind rests most predominantly on experimental evidence—and logic—of both Russo-Soviet higher nervous activity and psychology, and American psychology. The two have now for years grown apart, not only because of a language barrier but also because of a thought barrier, and the merit of bringing them together for English readers hardly needs emphasis—particularly in an area in which Soviet scientists command a very wide experimental base and their predominantly evolutionary approach is arguably more sound than the modern American predominantly unevolutionary tradition. Aspects of Soviet psychophysiology have been reviewed by me for the last thirty-five years, but with no total compaction of its fundamentals and, generally, little precise coordination with American and European counterparts. Past experience has been salubrious in redressing common Soviet unconcern for adequate statistical inference and frequently inadequate reportage and in ameliorating stressful feelings of American overly exacting concern with them.

An Evolutionary Prologue

Little of a general nature needs to be added to explicate the evolutionary intent of the book, and specific arguments must, obviously, be held in abeyance. However, two simple general questions might well be posed.

1. In recent years, well-controlled experiments in both East and West have demonstrated unmistakably the fundamental equivalence of the main characteristics and even the efficacy of *simple* conditioning in fish and monkey and, for that matter, man. That is to say, *simple* conditioning— essentially all that Pavlov divulged in his formal books (excluding *Wednesdays*) and Skinner in his—was already in full bloom on this planet some 500,000,000 years ago in organisms with no cortex, very little forebrain and, indeed, comparatively, not much brain altogether. What, then, one may well ask of an unevolutionary neo-behaviorist, is the specific role of cortex and brain in the operation of the mind, if the mind's governing principle is, as he posits, ultimately nothing but the mechanism of simple conditioning? And is it likely that in half a billion years the brain has not evolved for the mind some extra principle of action and change of action?

2. How, in general, could an unevolutionary, egalitarian view of mind and learning be reconciled with the striking multifarious evolution of the brain and nervous system, one that is the crowning example of all of evolution? The pertinent facts here are in the main too numerous and too generally known to warrant more than a bare mention. (1) *Communication* (nerve conduction)—for a velocity of 25 meters per second, the diameter of the nerve fiber in a squid *(Loligo)* is 650 micromillimeters, in a frog 1 micromillimeter and in a cat .35 micromillimeters, a 34,000-fold economization in biological material for equal work. (2) *Increase in units and relative mass*—over 12,000,000,000 neurons in the nervous system of modern man; the brain of a fish normally weighs less than its spinal cord, that of a cat is four times the weight of its cord, of a monkey eighth times, and of a man fifty times. The brain of a modern man at birth weighs more than that of most adult large apes and, presumably, only a little less than the brain of an adult Australopithecus, which is one-half the weight of that of Peking man and one-fourth that of modern man. (3) *Differentiation and*

specialization—structural and functional variegation of neurons, from pro-toneurons to most advanced stellate varieties; variegation of lobes and layers in the developing cortex: in mammals from order to order, in pri-mates from lemurs through monkeys and apes to man, and in man in the course of his million years or so of evolution (the rapid increase of short-axon neurons in the third and fourth layers of modern man's cortex merits special notice). (4) *Reorganization, integration, and hierarchization*—from syncytial nerve nets to synaptic directedness; structural cephalization and centralization and functional encephalization; evolutionarily older neuron units and neuron organization in lower animals existing as subsys-tems in the nervous systems of higher animals and man.

Plainly, the all-out quantitative and qualitative evolution of the nervous system and brain, comprehending evolutionary continuity as well as novelty and hierarchization, could not but be significantly reflected in correspond-ing evolutions of basic mechanisms and dynamics of mind, whether con-ceived as behavior and conditioning or as Gestalt and cognition.

THE MIND APPROACH

The mind approach (or, if you will, the mind-body approach) of the pres-ent book predicates a two-pronged caveat: (1) that the science of mind as behavior not unchurch altogether "raw" phenomenal feels (or, to use Hobhouse's expression, that "Mind as it appears to the onlooker" not dis-card "Mind as felt by the possessor"), and (2) that it make the most of the guidelines of its progenitor, the science of neural action.

Mind as Behavior

It may well be said that I. M. Sechenov, Russia's top nineteenth-century physiologist, was the first to induct, in full, the view that only the systematic study of behavioral manifestations—reflex manifestations, in his terms—of mind could ever constitute a science of mind. In a series of essays begun in 1863—*Reflexes of the Brain* (1863), *By Whom and How Should Psy-chology Be Studied?* (1873), *Elements of Thought* (1878), and others—Sechenov boldly declared that *"all* animal and human acts are reflex in es-sence," i.e., reactions to stimuli mediated by the nervous system; that "asso-ciations are effected through series of contacts [presumably neural contacts] between [such] consecutive reflexes" (1863, p. 498); that "ideas of objects, i.e., elementary knowledge, are outcomes of involuntary learning of con-secutive reflexes—integrated reflexes in the central element of the reflex ap-paratus" p. 481); and that, in general, the study of psychology should be turned over to physiologists (1873).

After Sechenov came I. P. Pavlov to proffer a plethora of conditioned-reflex data as a full-scale experimental validation of the mind-as-behavior or mind-as-reflex system that Sechenov ideated. The swoop of Pavlov's ob-jective credo and strategy was surely no less far-reaching than that of his predecessor. "The naturalist has no right to speak of higher animals' *psychic* processes without deserting the principles of natural science— which is the work of the human mind directed to nature through studies that derive their assumptions and interpretations from no other source than external nature itself," declared Pavlov in his 1906 Thomas Huxley Lecture (p. 911). Similarly, in 1903: "Vital phenomena that are termed psychic are distinguishable from pure physiological phenomena only in degree of complexity. Whether we call these phenomena psychical or complex-nervous is of little importance, as long as it is realized and recognized that the naturalist approaches them and studies them only objectively, leaving aside the question of essence" (p. 121). And in 1904: "The physiology of the higher nervous system [Read: psychology] of higher animals can be successfully studied only if one completely renounces the indefinite formu-lations of psychology and stands wholly upon a pure objective ground" (p. 135).

The core of the mind-as-behavior systems of American early Watsonian behaviorists and later neo-behaviorists is too well known to be specifically quoted here. However, two statements, one historical and one systematic, relating the American to the Russian mind revolution are in order. His-torically, there is the fact that although the Russian enterprise obviously preceded the American, the American was actually not cognizant of the existence of the Russian. Watson in *1913* knew nothing of Sechenov's essays—they were first translated into English in 1935—and he familiar-ized himself with the Pavlov (and Bekhterev) system only after he had developed the basics of his own system independently (Razran, 1965a). Systematically, the consideration is: How far apart are American mind-as-behavior and Russian mind-as-reflex? Two distances, or differences, need to be marked off. One: Created by physiologists, the Russian mind-as-reflex system identifies itself more with the neural aspect of behavior than does the American mind-as-behavior system—indeed, it might more exactly be considered a neurobehavior system. Two: Brought into being by psycholo-gists, the American system cannot help but be beleaguered by its ancestral concern with consciousness and lured by the lore of the linguistic trans-forms of logical positivism, a philosophy which the Russians eschew.

In essence, however, the Russian and the American mind enterprises are very close to each other and the differences between them are in no sense all-pervading. A noted early behaviorist, Max Meyer (1911), long ago de-fined psychology as the "science of nervous behavior," and such leading contemporary neo-behaviorists as Donald Lindsley, Neal Miller, and Carl Pfaffmann are, in fact, also neurobehaviorists—while what to do with the consciousness is, after all, largely a semantic problem. Pavlov himself bracketed his "Higher-Nervous-Activity" discipline with "Behavior" in the title of his first book in the area (1923), and, except for some disputes with Guthrie and Lashley (Pavlov, 1932b), he more than once equated his core approach and views with those of American behaviorists (1927a, pp. 15-16, 22; 1927b, pp. 5-6; *Wednesdays,* 1949, Vol. 2, p. 571; and elsewhere). And, in turn, American behaviorists have seldom disavowed the ultramarine and tramontane Sechenov-Pavlov-Bekhterev paternity. Note a statement in the most recent American *History of Psychology* (Esper, 1964): Sechenov "wrote the first 'objective' psychology and became the first 'behaviorist' of modern times . . . the main features which characterized American behaviorism of the twentieth century also characterized Sechenov's writings [and] he was more modest and less dogmatic than the early American behaviorists" (pp. 324-325). And note the titles of the first three chapters of a 1967 American volume, *Foundations of Conditioning and Learning* (G. A. Kimble, 1967a): (1) "Sechenov and the Anticipation of Conditioning Theory," (2) "Pavlov and the Experimental Study of Conditioned Reflexes," and (3) "The Objective Climate: Bechterew, Watson and Tolman." (A chapter by Hull follows—but, regrettably, there is none by Thorndike, Lashley, or Skinner.)

Behavior Is Not Enough:
The Return of Indestructible Consciousness

There is, of course, no doubt that the mind-as-behavior philosophy of twentieth-century experimental psychology has, on the whole, gained wider and wider ground in both East and West and that the trend is irreversibly forging ahead with full force. Yet in more recent decades this philosophy has become palpably concerned in both East and West with what we might call the indestructibility of consciousness and the need for making some concessions to it. As early as 1924, Pavlov wrote: "Certainly psychology, in so far as it deals with the subjective state of man, has a natural right to existence; our subjective world is the first reality with which we are confronted" (1924, p. 43; 1928b, p. 329). By 1930, he expressed regret that Ivanov-Smolensky, experimenting with conditioned bulb-pressing by school children, had not also obtained the children's subjective reports. "Human subjects, not being dogs, should be questioned about the conditioning experiments they undergo. . . . My earlier practice of not using subjective terms in order to avoid conceptual confusion is now, with full development of our field, valid only for our younger coworkers," he stated (*Wednesdays,* 1949, Vol. 1, pp. 61, 97, 98). And, a few years later, Pavlov expressly recommended that "psychiatrists become familiar with empirical psychology and not just rest on knowledge of conditioned reflexes" (*Wednesdays,* 1949, Vol. 2, p. 415). Post-Pavlovian students of Pavlov followed, for the most part, his path of concessions to consciousness, while Beritoff (1947, 1961, and elsewhere), a junior compeer rather than a student, went as far as to posit in higher animals an image-directed level of acquired behavior arising, he thinks, in the short-axon stellate neurons in the third and fourth layers of the cortex.

The course of American behaviorists' readmission of consciousness after Watson's resolute ban of it has been in part irregular and is also incomplete:

one system of neo-behaviorism, that of E. C. Tolman (1932), retrieved all of it through the inferring of consciousness from external behavior; another, that of B. F. Skinner (1959), adheres largely to the original ban. Yet when one views the entire behavioristic manifold with special regard for the "multi-successor" system of C. L. Hull (1943), the widening return procession of apparitions of consciousness is quite evident. Whereas Hull's own writings are as devoid of consciousness as those of Watson, Spence has in recent years (1963) acknowledged the role of cognition in human conditioning, Mowrer (1960a) has accorded vent to images and "hopes" and "fears" in his reformulated conditioning theory, Miller (1959) is all for stimulus-response liberalization, Osgood for extra studies of meaning (Osgood, Suci, and Tannenbaum, 1957), and brain behavior researchers not uncommonly relate their findings to pain and pleasure and attention and awareness—not to mention the behavioristic perception and ideation of Hebb (1949) and of Tolman-induced formulations (MacCorquodale and Meehl, 1953). Moreover, by all tokens, the procession of returning consciousness is continuing.

Critique of the Return, and Emendation

It cannot be said, however, that the American return of consciousness is proceeding in organized fashion or that its import is adequately comprehended. Communicative convenience and global "operationalism" seem to be the overriding motives and philosophy of the return. The ontologic difficulty of assuming that imagery, expectancy, or even awareness is operative in conditioning of lowest and decorticate animals and of deeply unconscious visceroviseral reflexes (Razran, 1955a, 1961a, 1965c) is ignored. And on the other hand, exclusive *operational* commitment extrudes unnecessarily the known subjective quale of the conscious categories.

For conscious categories do have specific essences and bear information on the nature of the stimulus or event that produces them. A taste of honey or quinine water informs more than does secretion of saliva and an image of food or fire more than an approach or withdrawal. To borrow a term from Gestalt psychology, but use it much less specifically, conscious reactions are in some way isomorphic with their environmental antecedents. Or, to put it in simple evolutionary terms: Sensations and images, as organism-environment levels of interactions higher than those of pure motor and glandular acts, are not just reactions wrung out by the environment but in some way reproductions of it. And, admittedly, they are based on higher-level neural action.

This position does not, of course, constitute a call for a conversion to an omniscient phenomenology nor in any sense a disowning of the usual assertion that subjective information as such merits no more than the status of a "private, raw feel." Indeed, it is hoped—and believed—that with increase of concomitant neural knowledge, methodologic recourse to cognitive disclosure will diminish and eventually, perhaps, be altogether dispensable. But not yet. For the present, the "private, raw feel" of experience cannot but be an indispensable continuant of the science of mind. *Reports of awareness, affects, images, and meanings reveal extraorganic and intraorganic events (at all times, intraorganic) and are not just verbal statements.* Hence, the heading "Behavior Is Not Enough."

A special phase of the approach is the consideration that conscious categories—i.e., their neurobehavioral correlates—typically, but by no means exclusively, control or dominate the nonconscious categories, or their correlates. The control or domination stems, naturally, from the fact that the former are higher in level of evolution and neural organization. However, there is another important determinant that has seldom been noted. For an organism to be efficient in interacting with its environment, it must be conscious not of all units of information that it receives—nor of all units of neural action that it involves—but only of integrated populations of them. That is to say, significant conscious categories are by their very nature gross and qualitative in the scope of information that they hold and in correspondence to underlying neural action—they are in tune with more massive and less detailed neural firing than those that are unconscious. And this very fact accords conscious categories special domination and control.

The Neural-Behavioral-Conscious Triad

To generalize and phrase it somewhat differently: The experimental fundamentals of mind—learning, perception, and thinking—could be studied at three levels: the neural, the behavioral, and the conscious, and their mutual interactions. The neural level admittedly is the basis of both the behavioral and the conscious levels and in theory comprehends the widest range of pertinent information. In practice, however, only a small portion of such information is so far available despite striking recent advances. Hence, so far the main burden of mind uncovery necessarily falls on behavioral and conscious analyses. Conscious analysis is handicapped not only by the limited scope of information that it possesses but also by the philosophic gap between it and its neural base. Yet recourse to some consciousness or phenomenal data is essential to any meaningful codification of the fundamentals of perception and thinking, unless one prefers simplistic contortions or total disregard of these mind categories. Moreover, while conscious categories need not—and in my view should not—be evoked in the systematization of basic mechanisms of simple conditioning, there is unmistakable evidence that in man, and presumably also in higher animals, the mechanisms of conditioning interact significantly with conscious categories when the latter are available.

In a way, one might indeed say that the present science status of mind is not unlike that of medicine in earlier periods—relying on patients' reports and behavioral changes, with only fragmentary knowledge of determining intraorganic changes. And to continue the comparison: While, with some notable exceptions, current intraorganic knowledge of disease is more advanced than intraorganic (i.e., neural) knowledge of mind, medicine has, obviously, not relinquished its earlier sources of information.

Heuristics of Awareness, Affects, Images, and Meanings

Awareness, affects, images, and meanings are, it is believed, the minimum conscious categories needed for a behavior-plus-consciousness approach to mind. Yet they should, perhaps, also be the maximum. Proliferation of such categories for "iconic" and communicative purposes is not recommended, while the view that "will and imagination" are as "operationable" as are "heat and light" surely could be contested. The four categories were most helpful to me in interpreting my own data of twenty-five years of experimentation with conditioning a variety of food-induced reactions in approximately a thousand adult human subjects to a wide gamut of sensory and verbal stimuli, complicated by designed variegations of subjects' instructions. In these experiments, most significant differences were obtained in simple Pavlov-like conditioning between subjects aware of attempts to condition them and those not aware of it, with additional indications that the subjects' degree of liking the unconditioned stimulus of food was also a conditioning differential. And when the experiments were complicated to permit (1) perceptual organization of conditioned sensory stimuli (what was called "configural conditioning") and (2) use of verbal rather than sensory conditioned stimuli, the extra relevance of subjects' imagery and meaning forced my attention. However, the evidence of my own experiments is only a very small part of the "East-West synthesis of learned behavior and cognition."

CHAPTER TWO

Learning as the Groundwork
of Mind in Evolution

In 1900, Jacques Loeb, the distinguished German and American comparative physiologist and psychologist, wrote: "Consciousness is only a metaphysical term for the phenomena which are determined by associative memory" (p. 12). At that time, there was no evidence that associative memory or learning is possible for lower animals, so the statement purported to divide the animal kingdom into two distinct levels: a lower level of unconscious or unminded (in Loeb's own terms, "tropistic") organisms, and a higher level of conscious or minded beings. Or, to put it somewhat differently, the statement meant to solve objectively, as it were, the perennial problem of where and when in evolution consciousness and mind enter life and behavior.

But as later experiments proved that lower animals, too, possess some memory and learning capacity, the Loeb categorical division was obviously no longer of specific significance. Yet the general view of learning as the core category of mind has not been thereby refuted. E. B. Holt, noted American philosopher and psychologist, stated in 1931 that "it is, indeed, the conditioned reflex which brings *mind* into being" (p. 28), and K. M. Bykov, a top Soviet physiologist, wrote, similarly, in 1949 that "formation of a conditioned reflex bears with it the formation of an elementary psychic act" (Bykov and Pshonik, 1949, p. 519). Indeed, even if one defers formally to Hebb (1958, p. 2) in restricting the possession of mind to higher animals and says with him that "when a psychologist studies learning in the ant he is not dealing with mental processes," the deference need occasion no more than rephrasing Holt's apothegm to say *"higher levels* of learning bring *mind* into being."

DEFINITION OF LEARNING

A commonsense view of learning is "profit through experience." To accept this view as a modern skeleton definition, we should replace the word "profit" by the less assuming and less evaluative "modification"—more exactly, by "modification of a reaction or reactions"—and replace "through experience" with "through reacting and interacting of reacting." And "modification" must be further enlarged to "more or less permanent central modifications," excluding therewith (1) transient changes due to fatigue and to general oscillations in organismic reactivity (known as attention, interest, and the like, in human subjects) and (2) peripheral modifications of sense organs (receptors) and muscles and glands (effectors). Russian physiologists have always considered learning a "higher nervous activity." And American psychologists' conceptions of it have also been central in essence, even if some have been labeled peripheral. It has been clearly demonstrated in recent years that full-blown conditioning may come into being through direct electrical stimulations of two brain centers when no peripheral stimuli are applied to the corresponding sense organs (Giurgea, 1953), as well as when, through curarization, no significant action of corresponding muscles or effectors is involved (Solomon and Turner, 1962).

The second part of the definition is likewise in need of specification. "Modification through reacting and interacting of reacting" puts forward the thesis that learning modifications involve two basic mechanisms: (1) "reacting," or practice, including one-trial reacting, and (2) "interacting," immanent in three kinds of associative learning: (*a*) conditioned, (*b*) configured, and (*c*) symbolic. Moreover, "reacting," together with "interacting," purports to delineate learning modifications from modifications produced through maturation, disease, drugs, and other nonlearning factors that are also more or less permanent in effect. (The tenability of the often drawn distinction between learning and performance will be considered in Chapter 7, Footnote 14.)

TYPES OF LEARNING

Learning through reacting is no doubt primarily a constituent of learning through interacting. Yet it also operates, it is believed, autochthonously without interacting, as a primitive category of nonassociative, preconditioned learning. Its two types of manifestations are (1) *habituation*—decrement and disappearance of reactions through reacting, and (2) *sensitization*—increment through reacting. Three types of simple-associative, or conditioned, learning are posited here: (1) *inhibitory conditioning*—decrement and disappearance of a reaction through an associated antagonistic reaction; (2) *classical conditioning*—evocation of a reaction by a stimulus of an associated reaction; (3) *reinforcement conditioning*—strengthening a reaction through an associated reaction, commonly called "reward learning."

Delineation of types of *configured* learning is deferred to Chapter 9, in which a large body of empirical evidence (mostly Soviet) warranting the approach will be presented; and *symbolic learning* and its types will be considered in Chapter 10. All that will be said here is that the first is held to be operative in *learning to perceive* and the second in *learning to think,* and that, although some principles and parameters of the two are continuous with those of simple conditioning, others are novel evolutionary acquisitions not reducible to them or to those of each other. Moreover, it should be noted that the term *associative* is used here as a *means of producing* learning and not as a designation of a *resulting mechanism*—and an ascending hierarchy of nine different types of such mechanisms is posited: three of conditioning, three of perceiving, and three of thinking. Put differently, the book is committed to a full analysis of both "associative conditioning" and what may be called "associative superconditioning." The combined size of Chapters 9 and 10 dealing with the latter is about equal to that of Chapters 5, 6, 7, and 8 treating the former (Chapters 3 and 4 bear upon habituation and sensitization).

CLASSES OF LEARNED REACTIONS

While the gamut of learned reactions in acquisitions of skills, language, knowledge, likes, dislikes, beliefs, attitudes, personal and abnormal quirks, etc., is almost unlimited, only those varying widely in effector, neural, and conscious levels merit being kept as separate classes for basic differential analysis. In man, behavioristic practice has long distinguished three classes of learned reactions: (1) visceral—modification of largely unconscious action of smooth muscles and glands, mediated by the evolutionarily older autonomic nervous system; (2) motor—modification of commonly conscious reactions of skeletal muscles, mediated by the evolutionarily newer central nervous system; and (3) man's extra, predominantly conscious equipment—verbal reactions under the general aegis of higher brain regions. In animals, of course, only the first two classes of reactions have managed to come into any significant being.

However, with the striking advancement of neurotechnology in recent years, a fourth distinct and portentous class of learned reactions has pushed to the forefront—neural learning and neural changing of learning. A large number of experiments in both East and West have shown unmistakably that brain wave (EEG) changes and evoked and steady neural potentials can be readily conditioned (Ádám and Meszáros, 1960; Anokhin, 1958c; Artemyev and Bezladnova, 1952; Galambos and Morgan, 1960; Jasper and Shagass, 1941; Jasper and Smirnov, 1960; John, 1961; Magoun, 1961; Morrell, 1961a; Rusinov and Rabinovich, 1958). In fact, they are commonly conditioned more readily than, and prior to, motor and visceral reactions (Iwama, 1950; Motokawa, 1949; Schastny, 1956; Voronin and

Sokolov, 1960; and others). And American experimenters were the first to demonstrate that some kinds and patterns of neural stimulations (i.e., neural reactions) act as powerful reinforcers and inhibitors of learned behavior (Delgado, Roberts, and Miller, 1954; Olds and Milner, 1954). Furthermore relatively recent Soviet experiments on interoceptive conditioning —conditioning of reactions evoked by direct stimulation of internal organs —force attention to the merit of distinguishing between the conditioning of these reactions, in commerce with animals' and man's internal environment, and the conditioning of the conventional exteroceptively-produced variety, in commerce with the external environment.

Makarov (1950a, 1950b, 1959) had a number of human subjects swallow electrodes attached to thin rubber balloons, to compare the effects of direct electrical stimulations of the interior of subjects' stomachs with the effects of like stimulation to their hands, using evoked galvanic skin reflexes and reports of conscious sensitivity as the indices of the effects. He found that whereas the subjects' GSR reactivity to the stimulation of the hand was only a little more sensitive than to stimulations of the stomach, the compass of reports of conscious sensitivity of the two kinds of stimulations was hardly comparable. Fifteen steps of increasing GSR scale deviations in response to increasing electrical stimulations were noted. Hand stimulation was reported conscious at the second step, painful at the eighth, and intensely painful at the twelfth; interior stomach stimulation became faintly conscious at the eleventh step, unpleasant at the thirteenth, and painful at the last (fifteenth) step. The normal range of interoceptive stimulation, unlike that of the exteroceptive variety, is thus widely unconscious. Or—to put it differently, in light of additional data—*while human subjects are normally conscious of exteroceptive stimuli even if the stimuli produce unconscious reactions, they are normally unconscious of interoceptive stimuli even if the stimuli produce conscious reactions.* Russian comparisons of simple interoceptive and exteroceptive conditioning in animals reveal that the former are more slowly acquired and more slowly extinguished than are the latter.

Finally, accumulated evidence on conditioning of thresholds of conscious sensitivity, qualities of sensations, affects, positive and negative afterimages, meanings, and the like suggests postulation of an additional special class of learned conscious (or cognitive) reactions. That is to say, one may discern, at present, seven different classes of learned reactions—neural, interoceptive visceral, exteroceptive visceral, interoceptive somatic, exteroceptive somatic, verbal, and conscious. But, even these widely varying classes of reactions are on the whole more alike than different in the basics of learning manifestations.

UNLEARNED LEARNING: ECOLOGY AND ETHOLOGY

Consider the following six sample findings reported relatively recently by Soviet ecologists. (1) Tiger and lion cubs react positively and secrete saliva at the first sight and smell of raw meat (Shepeleva, 1954; Uzhdavini and Shepeleva, 1966). Puppies must be conditioned to salivate at the odor of meat, but they manifest an unconditioned approach to it after about two weeks of life and unconditioned withdrawal before then (Arshavsky, 1958; Uzhdavini, 1958). Sheep and goats must be conditioned to give any reaction to the sight and odor of grass (Rakhimov, 1958). (2) Hares' unlearned respiratory reactions to the sounds of rustling leaves are of the character of primary, relatively unhabituable, unconditioned reflexes to which the sounds of buzzers, louder than the rustling sounds but relatively neutral to the animals' respiratory changes, are readily conditioned (Klimova, 1958). Dogs' reactions to the identical rustling sounds are very slight, easily habituated, and in the nature of orienting reactions. (3) Wild ducks' conditioning to their hunting decoy as well as wading birds' conditioning to the sound of splashing water are, unlike conditioning to other stimuli, effected in no more than one or several trials and are hardly subject to extinction (Slonim, 1961). A hare's running reaction to an object moving in its field of vision plus a tactile stimulus applied to its neck, was conditioned to a sound imitating the animal's lip smacking in three trials and was not extinguished, one and a half years later, in 300 nonreinforced trials; the same running reaction conditioned to a sound of a metronome was extinguished in ten trials and took hundreds of trials to be formed (Biryukov, 1960). (4) Chickens' claw-lifting is very readily conditioned through subsequent feeding, but not so the claw-lifting of pigeons, whose most common food-conditioned reaction is, as we know, neck-stretching (Biryukov, 1960). It is many times more difficult to condition a dog to lift its hindpaw than its forepaw. (5) A laboratory fox's first reaction to a mouse squeak was in the nature of an orienting reaction—that is, it disappeared after a few repetitions; but after the fox had once consumed a squeaking mouse, the reaction to the squeak persisted for years and was scarcely extinguishable (Goleva, 1955). Mouse squeaks are often the only sounds to which decorticate cats react, sometimes in very lively ways (Belenkov, 1965). (6) Desert sheep neonates salivate copiously when sand is placed into their mouth cavities, but adult specimens do not; mountain sheep possess the salivary reaction both as neonates and as adults (Fayziyev, 1957, 1963).

Three fundamentals of learning are brought to light through the six sample experiments of Russian ecologists: (1) simple identical reactions to identical stimuli may be unlearned in some species but learned in others, or they may diverge radically in biological role and stability (Samples 1 and 2); (2) learning efficacy of identical stimuli, reactions, and particular stimulus-reaction linkages may differ widely in different species, even as such efficacy may be widely different for different stimuli, reactions, and stimulus-reaction linkages in the same species (Samples 3-5); (3) simple unconditioned autonomic reflexes may disappear through learning in an untoward ecology (Sample 6). The second fundamental is attributed by

Russian scientists to a sort of species-specific phyletic readying of learning which they term *natural conditioned reflexes* and consider to be a category intermediate between laboratory conditioned reflexes and unconditioned reflexes (Ayrapet'yants, 1961; Bykov and Slonim, 1949). The first fundamental may perhaps be characterized as a species-specific phyletic equivalent of learning (or phyletic learning), while the third needs no special designation. The term *natural conditioning* is used by the Russians also to account for the quick conditioning of vertebrates, with no significant interspecies differences, when relatively natural food-securing reactions are selected—e.g., tugging at a bead for fish, pecking at a pedal for chickens, pulling a ring for rabbits, stepping on a platform for dogs, pulling down a lever for monkeys, and the like (Voronin, 1957).

Clearly, the ecology of learning and ways in which the unlearned contains and models the learned must be accorded rightful positions in any comprehensive systematization of the field. Ecology and evolution combine to challenge the adequacy of conventional egalitarianism and to search for new and further-reaching views and prospects.

The meritorious contributions of European ethologists (Lorenz, 1935, 1939, 1952, 1955; Thorpe, 1950, 1963; Tinbergen, 1951, 1960) and the cogent criticisms of their basic approach and philosophy and of their disregard of enmeshed learned substrata (Biryukov, 1960; Hebb, 1953; Lehrman, 1953; Schneirla, 1956; Slonim, 1961; and others) are well known. One obvious ethologic overreach has not, however, been sufficiently vented—extrapolation to the essence of the being and becoming of the human mind. Three interrelated theses are involved. One, the ratio of ontogenetic learning plasticity to phyletic unlearned relative fixity is a growing function of evolution and in man is very large and overriding. Two, the human import of knowledge of animal behavior is a positive function of the phyletic generality of the behavior; that is, such knowledge becomes related to what we want to know about human behavior to the extent that, we might say, the trunk rather than the far-off branches of the evolutionary tree is tracked. Three, for many thousands of years now, man's own evolution has been not biological and neural but social and cultural, and these ultimately are (one should not and can not deny) a matter of learning.

Two rather obvious implications of these theses will be noted. (1) To shed light on the basic mechanisms of the human mind, evolutionary and ecological studies of animal behavior must hinge on full-scale analyses—behavioral, neural, and chemical—of ontogenetic learning. Analyses of relatively fixed species-specific performances, such as beavers building dams, hamsters and rats hoarding, birds nesting and migrating, and even ducklings imprinting, are, to be sure, of general scientific interest, but at best of only ancillary significance to the lore of human actions. (For reasons that need not be gone into here, European ethology has been mostly concerned with the behavior of birds, which have been evolving apart for some 150,000,000 years to become not only most divergent in body structure but also, more importantly, most regressed and specialized in brain development—their cortex more primitive than that of their ancestors, the reptiles.) (2) Comparisons of special manifestations of man's mind such as aggression with like manifestations in rats, wolves, eagles, roosters, and wild turkeys have little more than literary merit. Understanding and control of human aggression rest on individual learning and social heritage—which, of course, is also individual learning, even if one assumes—as one should not—that aggression is goaded by a native horme.

A PREFATORY COMMENT ON PERCEPTION AND THINKING

A combined neurobehavioral and phenomenal definition of perception might well be that it is "an afferently configured spatiotemporal neural and basically conscious unitary reaction to a more or less complex stimulus." A simpler but less inclusive and less adequate phenomenal definition is that "perception is awareness of an object or event." As compared with just "a reaction to a stimulus" or just "awareness," perception is thus accorded *sui generis* organization arising at the organism's receiving end and, presumably, also *sui generis* stimulus isomorphism. Modern empirical evidence has demonstrated that this organization is most predominantly learned. To cite a very recent example: Monkeys reared in a vivarium lighted by short intermittent flashes, which prevent them from scanning their environs, are later as bereft of specific perception as are monkeys reared in total darkness (Ohrbach and Miller, 1969). And scanning is learning, akin in method to the successive compound-stimulus conditioning of numerous Russian studies, and in outcome to configuring or configural learning (Razran, 1961a, pp. 124-126, 1965c, 1965d; see Chapter 9 for full discussion and analysis and relation to sensory preconditioning).

The phrase that perception is "basically a conscious reaction" means that it is not exclusively so, that it may exist as "subception" when its correlative neural pattern has not yet been completed and as "postception" when the phenomenal experience has ceased. The phenomenal experience itself may well be a spatiotemporal image engendered by its present environs or complexes of stimuli (not a so-called memory image). Two other theses should be added: (1) The very view that the phenomenal does not exist by itself implies a certain revelatory and heuristic status with respect to the existence of its stimulus and neural correlates. (2) Perception is in its very essence a neurocognitive and not a neurobehavioral reaction—a historical evolvent and a continuing neural feedback of behavior *but not an effector reaction in itself.*

Thinking is "perception plus," commanding additional unique characteristics. First, it involves the formation of symbols through associative configuring of perceptions, which (1) renders the symbols in some way isomorphic with perceptions as perceptions are with stimulus complexes, and (2) imparts to them surrogate functioning when the stimulus complexes are wanting. Second, the formed symbols are actually miniature motor reactions (most predominantly verbal) equipping the individual with two sets of physical contacts with his environs—somatic and visceral macroreactions and symbolic microreactions—and thus providing him with efferent outlets for the afferent events of perception: means of communication, checks and balances, and alleviation of conflicts and tensions. Third, symbols interact through association with what they symbol and with other symbols to form a relation that might best be described as "copular" in the logical sense; that is, one connecting *subjects* and *predicates,* the basis of referential meaning. Fourth, symbols are most involved in the rise of voluntary controls or "willing." Fifth, thinking predicates complex "planning." In short, thinking is very human and, as will be argued in Chapter 10, exclusively human. Yet, it should be added that, regrettably, its parametric empirics are still in a very general, hardly more than incipient, state. Psychology may reasonably claim a relatively solid science of Conditioning, to a lesser extent also a science of Perceiving—but not really a science of Thinking.

A PREFATORY COMMENT ON EVOLUTIONARY LEVELS OF LEARNING

As already intimated, the underlying hypothesis of the present book is that learning, the groundwork of mind, is an evolved and evolving ascending hierarchical system of levels of continuity and novelty. The hypothesis rejects outright prevalent Western conceptions that all of mind's learning may be derived from one or two of its basic modes—or "processes" or "factors"—and reaches much beyond Soviet views in the scope of levels that it postulates and in the specificity of their systematic interrelations. Collated East-and-West empirical evidence in succeeding chapers will test the validity and heuristic value of the evolutionary hypothesis. However, the assumed formal properties of higher and lower learning levels need to be set forth here, beginning with the underlying postulate that levels of learning *ipso facto* predicate correlative levels of neural action mediating the learning. Five formal level properties are implicated.

(1) Higher levels of learning, arising from lower levels as antecedents, should bring into being *some* new forms and laws of learning manifestations. (2) Lower levels of learning should continue as subsystems within higher levels, so that higher-level learning is normally a resultant of higher and lower learning. (3) Higher-level learning should be more efficient in organism-environment interaction than lower-level learning, but lower-level learning should be more universal and less disruptable by outward stimuli and inward organismic states. (4) Normally, higher-level learning should control lower-level learning because of its greater efficiency; yet under certain conditions lower-level learning may predominate because of

greater universality and lesser disruptability. (5) Interaction between higher and lower levels of learning will be either synergic or antagonistic.

Wide arrays of specific questions may thus be formulated to pit the hypothesis against accumulated experimental data. The following are samples of such questions: Are there organisms and reactions which clearly manifest habituation and sensitization but not bona fide conditioning? Is inhibitory conditioning more common than classcal conditioning in the evolutionarily lowest organisms and reactions? Do habituation and sensitization operate as subsystems within classical conditioning? Does reinforcement conditioning include classical conditioning as a subsystem while classical conditioning may be in full bloom without reinforcement conditioning? Is the interaction between reinforcement and classical conditioning typically synergic or antagonistic? Does each succeeding level of the hierarchy bring into being new (i.e., supplementary) laws of learning?

Is bona fide conditioning possible for the lowest invertebrates? For human neonates? Is there evidence of configured learning in lower vertebrates? If not, and if this learning is abolished in ablations of higher brain regions which leave simple conditioning unaffected, may one not entertain the notion that this learning correlates with the action of these regions and with perception? Does configured learning normally control simple conditioning while at times it is dominated by it? Is there a like hierarchical relationship between configured and symbolic learning? Is true thinking possible without symboling? Do all levels of learning operate in some way in normal human learning? Finally, what are, or may be posited to be, the neural actions in terms of loci and patterns governing each level?

As I indicated in the Preface, the register of East-and-West experiments bearing on these questions, and on others that may be posed, runs to tens of thousands. Accordingly, I had to exercise drastic selection. My taste is, however, rather catholic, so bias was not part of my peregrination far and wide for pertinent data, old data that have been overlooked and new that have not yet been codified. The common tendency of evolutionary egalitarians to stress similarities and disregard differences was closely examined, as was that of not noting valid East-West empirical similarities because of methodologic or theoretic divergences.

LEARNING AND UKHTOMSKY'S DOMINANCE

The noted Soviet neurophysiologist A. A. Ukhtomsky (1875-1942) put forward in 1923 (1923a) a *dominance* (or *The Dominant;* in Russian, *Dominanta*) principle of neurobehavioral interaction of unconditioned reflexes based on experiments begun in 1911 that may be broadened to include the basics of learned behavior. I first argued the relevance of the principle to conditioning in 1930 and have continued the argument since. Anokhin and Strezh expressed a like view, independently, in 1934 in the

Soviet Union, where by now the neurobehavioral generality of dominance is most widely accepted (Anokhin, 1957; Fedoseyev, *Philosophical Problems of Higher Nervous Activity and Psychology,* 1963). Allport in 1924 and Sheffield, Roby, and Campbell in 1954 used similarly Sherrington's reflex concept of "prepotency," while Premack (1962, 1963, 1965) has provided wide empirical support for a dominance principle in his studies of the nature and reversibility of reinforcement. And John, familiar with the Soviet research of Ukhtomsky's students, endowed it with additional neural plausibility (1962). Ukhtomsky himself mentioned the bearing of his principle on conditioning in 1924 (which I first read after my own 1930 article had been published). Pavlov had favored Ukhtomsky's "dominance" as the mechanism of what is known in the United States as "pseudoconditioning" (*Wednesdays,* 1949, Vol. 2, pp. 20-22; original date, September 27, 1933). But while he implied its operation in conditioning in his very first publication, in 1903 (p. 19), and continued to imply it, he had not directly named it so.

In Ukhtomsky's own words, the dominance principle reads: "Sufficiently stable excitations cumulated in any neural center acquire a dominant position with respect to excitations in other centers so that stimulations directed to the other centers increase the excitation of the dominant center and decrease the excitation in their own subordinate centers" (1923a, 1923b, 1924, 1925, 1926, 1927, 1934, 1938, 1966).

In unconditioned reflex interaction—Ukhtomsky's area of direct experimentation—the behavioral manifestation of the principle has in essence been a synthetic extension of Sherrington's 1906 "reciprocal innervation" and Exner's 1882 *"Bahnung"* (facilitation) from the spinal to the cortical level. But, as will no doubt be noted, as a general principle, dominance is not unlike James's (1890) and McDougall's (1905) "drainage," which in its time was widely criticized. However, "drainage" embraced two suppositions: a hydraulics-type mechanism of neural action, in discord with modern knowledge, and a general conception of neural interdependence, in general accord with modern knowledge. Dominance rejects the former and experiments with the latter—Ukhtomsky's present-day students are testing and proving the principle through direct neural probings. A historical note would also seem to be in order. Ukhtomsky states that he borrowed the term dominance from the philosopher Avenarius, who wrote in 1890: "In the rivalry of interdependent vital series [of systems], one series must at each particular moment be regarded dominant [in German, *Dominante*], determining the general direction of the individual's behavior" (p. 277). And he declares further that the principle was distinctly implied by Kant in his *Anthropologie* in 1798.

Experimental ascertainment of the exact quantitative parameters of reactions that command "sufficiently stable [neural] excitations" to be dominant is an endeavor of vast proportions. However, six kinds of basic parameters are clearly operative. (1) *Innate character*—a species' or an individual's repertory of innate reactions constitutes a hierarchy of dominance status, with the obvious qualification that, generally, vital reactions to food, sex, pain, and the like are more dominant than reactions to lights, sounds, odors, and the like. (2) *Repetition* (practice)—the dominance of a particular reaction may be increased or decreased through repetition, the determinants of the direction of the change being presumably both the innate character of the reaction and manipulable experimental variables. (3) *Stimulus intensity*—the dominance of each particular evocation of a reaction increases as the intensity of the stimulus evoking it increases. (4) *Subsequence in time*—other things being equal and within limits of specific time intervals, a succeeding reaction is more dominant than is an anteceding reaction, both because the succeeding reaction summates the neural action of both reactions and because it is facilitated by the anteceding reaction (cf. studies of signal detection). (5) *Extrinsic parameters*—the dominance of particular reactions or groups of reactions may be increased or decreased through food deprivation or satiation, estrus cycle, disease, drugs, ablations, and other internal states or external agents. (6) *Anodal stimulation*—dominance of any reaction appears to be increased by low-current anodal polarization.

To put it more succinctly, the dominance of a reaction is a function of both its innate character and manipulable intensive, temporal, and extrinsic variables—a generalization that surely is also the crux of conditioning parameters. The determining role of innate reaction character in conditioning was stressed in an earlier discussion of natural conditioning. But its role is obviously also evident in all typical conditioning in which a reaction of greater biological significance modifies or reinforces a reaction of lesser significance. Likewise, it is just as obvious that manipulable intensive, temporal, and extrinsic factors shape the core of conditioning: its efficacy and even its very direction. Yerofeyeva (1912, 1921), Beritoff (1924, 1932), Asratyan (1961b), and others in the Soviet Union have long demonstrated reversibility in classical conditioning, and Premack (1962, 1963, 1965) in this country has done it recently in reinforcement conditioning. Morrell (1961b) and others have corroborated Rusinov's 1953 results that low-current anodal polarization engenders conditioning. Moreover, there is also reason to assume (Razran, 1968a) that the extent of the dominance differential between the interactiong pair of reactions in conditioning determines whether conditioning should be of a classical or reinforcement type.

Indeed, it may well be argued further that Ukhtomsky's principle of dominant-subordinate interdependence transforms the traditional atomism of associative interaction into a relatively holistic system—a solid stance of organization *von Unten herauf* (from below up) which *Gestalt* psychology has long stressed as *von Oben herab* (from above down).

LEARNING AND DEVELOPMENT

A preliminary statement on the relation of learning, as conceived here, to present-day concepts of development also seems in order. The views of Schneirla, Anokhin, and Lehrman need to be mentioned. Schneirla—as indicated earlier, a leading votary of evolutionism—has for years been steadfast and judicious in baring the blind-alley limitations of both American laboratory psychologists' unevolutionary and "nonnaturalistic" approaches to learning and European "little-laboratory" naturalists' doctrines of predesigned instinctual fixity. Yet his own concept of development, left unqualified, may in its own way become highly restrictive in method and information and general heuristics. Consider his most recent formulation that "the complexes denoted by the terms 'maturation' and 'experience' are not simply interrelated [in development] but constitute a *fused* system in each stage. This theory is, then, much more than 'interactionistic' " (1965, pp. 10, 11).

It is hard to get at the underlying import of the passage. Should not the laboratory try to "unfuse" what nature has fused? Are the two also *logically* inseparable? Or, to use a Pavlov expression: Must not "the laboratory learn to analyze what life has synthesized?" Moreover, there is in the formulation the unsettling tenet that "experience" must not be "incorrectly" interpreted "as synonymous with conditioning and learning" (1965, p. 10). What method other than conditioning and learning—including habituation and sensitization—is there by which to analyze adequately "experience?"

It is hoped that the present evolutionary full-spectrum view of learning —acknowledging fully both the directive role of the unlearned in learning and the exigency of combining ecologic-natural and laboratory-artificial methods—will be instrumental in rendering the Schneirla position more flexible. And it is hoped also that, as an exercise in comparative psychology, he and his followers mind the "development" concept of Anokhin (1949 and earlier), similar in general theoretical core yet quite different in specific experimental approach. The conditioned reflex is, according to Anokhin, integrally embedded in a holistic [Russian: *tselostnaya*] unconditioned-conditioned "functional system" of embryogenesis, morphogenesis, and systemogenesis, the dynamic mechanism of which is a continuous developmental interacting of structural fixation of neural pathways and functional formation of temporary connections [CRs]. . . . The unconditioned is constantly overgrown [Russian: *obrastaniye*] with the conditioned even as the conditioned is readied and shaped by the unconditioned (1949 and elsewhere). The experimental fact that human neonates commonly exhibit a sucking reflex when body parts other than the mouth region are touched is attributed by him to Ukhtomsky's *learned* dominance sensitization, while newly hatched rooks' food reactions to specific sounds, air movements, and nest shakings are viewed as instances of full-fledged prenatal conditioning.

Unlike Schneirla, Anokhin *is* "interactionistic." Development is to him a naturally fused but experimentally segregable system of the unlearned and the learned, and "experience" is but conditioning and learning. In the United States, Carmichael has long (1936) intimated the likelihood of embryonic and prenatal learning, an empirical fact which has since been replicated many times in both East and West.

To *some* extent, what has been said about the views of Schneirla applies also to those of Lehrman. There is no quarreling, to be sure, with Lehrman (1953, p. 345) that: "At any stage of development, the new features emerge from interactions within the *current* stage and between the *current* stage and the environment," or that "the organism is different at each different stage of its development." (William James said, similarly, that the "chain of consciousness is a sequence of *differents*" [1890, Vol. 1, p. 230] and Heraclitus that "you cannot step twice into the same river.") But is it not equally true that stages of an organism's development are not unique events? And that human ingenuity may well command the means to vary the interactions between the *"current* stage and the environment? Plainly, the unitariness of development to the contrary notwithstanding, the methodologic road to deciphering the "genic" and the "learning" of it not only can be but should be bifurcated, which tempts the author to cite another study by a Soviet ecologist. Promptov (1940, 1946, 1956), who noted that domesticated canaries, unlike wild finches, are almost unable to build nests, assumed the failure was due to the smooth perches of the birds' cages. Accordingly, he reared some canaries in "naturalistic" cages of swaying twigs and strewn seeds and feathers. His hypothesis was confirmed: nest building of the new generation of canaries was of high, almost faultless, caliber. Lukina (1953) replicated in part Promptov's results.

CHAPTER THREE

Habituation

DELINEATION OF THE TYPE

In 1887, Peckham and Peckham published "Some Observations on the Mental Powers of Spiders." Theirs was the first bona fide experiment in lower-animal learning. They repeatedly sounded a tuning fork 3 to 15 times a day, for 15 days, close to a spider on its web. The insect's dropping on its thread in response to the sound diminished in extent in the course of the repetitions, recovered partially on subsequent days, and eventually ceased for the duration of their study. However, whatever interest there was in animal learning at that period centered mostly on higher capacities (Lubbock, 1882; Morgan, 1891; Romanes, 1882), and the Peckhams' contribution received little notice. Moreover, while early in the twentieth century it came to be recognized as a "modification through experience" and named specifically "negative adaptation," it was not in essence accorded learning status. Only in recent years, renamed "habituation," has it gained prestige among psychologists (and physiologists)—to the extent, indeed, that some in both West and East consider habituation to be the very basis of learning (Pribram, 1969; Sokolov, 1965; Thompson and Spencer, 1966). This it is not, but a rudimentary precursor of it, it is.

Habituation is a means of producing "learning what not to do," but it is not the only means. Extinction, inhibitory conditioning, and—with respect to the *Ro*, the original reaction to the to-be-conditioned stimulus—also classical conditioning entail like effects. Yet, unlike the other three, habituation involves only *nonassociative* means and only *innate* reactions, and thus the least number of parameters with which to start an analysis. Extinction, Pavlov's term for the practice decrement and disappearance of a conditioned reaction through administering the conditioned stimulus without the unconditioned, is much more complex. Its development is governed not only by parameters of the extinction training itself, similar to those of habituation but in addition and for the most part, by the parameters of the conditioning design and the antecedent conditioning training. Moreover, the dynamics of extinction are not uncommonly affected by interoceptive and proprioceptive feedback and conditioning, by counter-conditioning, and, at higher levels, by cognition, which is nonexistent in habituation occurring in neuronal and lowest-organisms' reactions. Nor is the course of development of the two of the same dimension with identical reactions and organisms. Habituation of unconditioned reactions is, as might be expected, much slower and more difficult than is extinction of their corresponding conditioned reactions, although some habituation is fast and some extinction is slow.

In inhibitory conditioning, learning what not to do is effected when a reaction is associated with a dominant antagonistic reaction; in classical conditioning, when a reaction is replaced by an associated reaction which typically is not antagonistic. That is, in either case, the mechanisms of learning what not to do go beyond that of mere habituation and by all tokens are more effective. The extra mechanisms will be discussed in due course. What must be mentioned here, however, is that when these extra mechanisms are able to function, they *may* arise in the organism and complicate habituation even when they are not part of the experimental design or are not evident to the observer. That is to say, the uncomplicated action of habituation is fully manifest only when associative learning is not possible or not likely.[3]

HABITUATION AT BASE: SAMPLE EXPERIMENTS

Unit-Neurons

a. Vinogradova and Lindsley (1963) studied the effects of repetition on the firing reactions of unit-neurons of rabbits' unanesthetized visual cortex to several visual and auditory stimuli. Of the 147 neurons probed, 72 reacted to the stimulations and 8 showed reaction changes with repetition. The changes in the 8 "wise" neurons were, as may be seen in Figure 1, clear-cut cases of habituation, including spontaneous recovery in time and "dishabituation"—or disinhibition—when an extra stimulus, itself incapable of evoking firing, was added to the habituated stimulus.

The four lines in the left A section of Figure 1 demonstrate that a rabbit's unit-neuron ceased firing to a lighted object moving toward the

---

[3] "Reactive inhibition" and "stimulus satiation" do not involve extra parameters or concepts and thus are not considered here special forms of learning what not to do. Hull conceived "reactive inhibition" as a "more primitive principle" than "experimental extinction" (1943, p. 277), which is what habituation is; Glanzer's (1953) "stimulus satiation" is in essence only an extension of Hull's view to perception—with no concern, incidentally, for the significant modulations which perception imparts to habituation (as it does to all learning).

animal's eye on the 32nd habituatory trial. The movement is indicated by an arrow to the right; the arrow to the left refers to moving the object away from the eye, to which the neuron did not react. The two lines in the left B section disclose "dishabituation." The neuron resumed firing in response to the habituated stimulus of the moving-toward object when an airpuff was at the same time administered to the rabbit's chin. The firing could not have been due to the action of the airpuff itself, since there was none when it was combined with moving the object away from the eye. Note also, that the firing was not rehabituated in 31 combined administrations of the two stimuli.

The first two lines in the right A and B sections show habituation of a rabbit's unit-neuron firing, respectively, to a sound click on the 14th trial and to a flash of light on the 25th trial. The third line in each section reveals spontaneous recovery of the two habituated reactions, to which should be added the experimenters' statement that the habituation was specific not only to kinds of stimuli but also to their intensities. Both increases and decreases of intensities produced dishabituation.

In three later and more extensive experiments, Vinogradova (1965,

Figure 1 *Habituation, dishabituation, rehabituation, and spontaneous recovery of unit-neurons of a rabbit's visual cortex in response to visual and auditory stimuli.* In the top four lines of the left panel, the stimulus is a lighted object moving toward the animal's eye (arrow to left; arrow to right indicates movement away from the eye, to which there was no reaction). The bottom two lines disclose dishabituation with hardly any rehabituation when the habituated lighted object was combined 31 times with an airpuff to the animal's chin. In the top A section of the right panel, the stimulus is a sound click, and in the B section, a flash of light; the third line of each section demonstrates spontaneous recovery. (From Vinogradova and Lindsley, 1963)

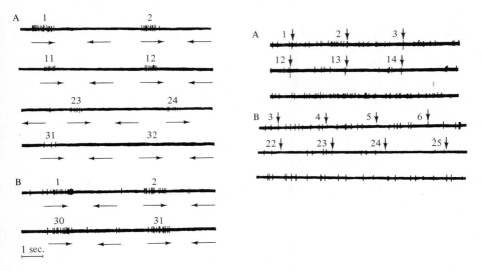

1968; Vinogradova, Konovalov, and Semyonova, 1969) investigated the habituation of rabbits' 223 reactive single neurons (tested $N = 427$) to light flashes, sound clicks, pure tones, and airpuffs to the nose in six regions of their brain: motor cortex, visual cortex, caudate nucleus, mammillary body, dorsal hippocampus, and ventral hippocampus. The modes of the neurons' specific stimuli were also ascertained—i.e., whether they were unimodal or multimodal—as was the character of their spontaneous firing, called "structured" or "specific" and "diffuse" or "unspecific." Unhabituation was assumed when no significant modification in changed spontaneous firing to the stimuli was found after 50 to 80 repetitions. The combined results are presented in Figure 2, from which it may be seen that habituation was effected in 5 per cent of the visual cortex, none in the motor

Figure 2 *Modal specificity of stimuli (top panel), character of spontaneous firing (middle panel), and habituability of changed firing (bottom panel) of 223 reactive neurons in different regions of rabbits' brains—visual and motor cortex, caudate nucleus, mammillary body, dorsal and ventral hippocampus—to light flashes, sound clicks, pure tones, and airpuffs. Numbers above columns are per cents; numbers at bottom are the numbers of reactive neurons tested in each region.* (From Vinogradova, Konovalov, and Semyonova, 1969)

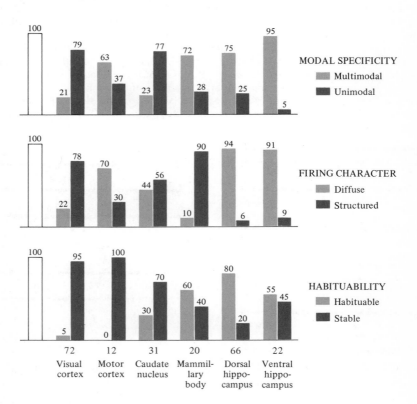

cortex (12 neurons only), 30 per cent in the caudate nucleus, 60 per cent in the mammillary body, 80 per cent in the dorsal hippocampus, and 55 per cent in the ventral hippocampus. The evidence on modal specificity of stimuli in the top panel and specificity of spontaneous firing in the middle panel of Figure 2 is self-explanatory. The correlation (ρ) between habituability and multimodality of stimuli was .6; between habituability and diffuse firing, .33.

b. Buchwald, Halas, and Schramm (1965) tracked the effect of repetition on single motoneuron firing of eighteen acute spinal cats to a 0.5-second 60-cycle shock train delivered to the peroneal nerves of the animals' hindpaws "20 or more times" at 5- to 45-second intertrial intervals. Of the 88 neurons probed, 53 decreased the firing on consecutive trials, 10 increased it, and 25 did not change. When the neurons were divided on the basis of the amplitude of their spike potentials (which ranged from 50 microvolts to 1 millivolt) into phasic with amplitudes above 250 microvolts and tonic with amplitudes below it, it was found that 39 phasic neurons showed decreased firing, 2 increased, and 12 no change; the respective figures for the tonic neurons were 14, 8, and 13. Habituation was thus observed in 74 per cent of the former and 40 per cent of the latter. Disregarding the unchanged neurons, 95 per cent of the phasic neurons and 64 per cent of the tonic were habituated. No related changes in tissue or blood pressure were noted, and the experimenters' conclusion is that the repetition changes "were most probably due to central changes within the isolated spinal reflex pathway" (p. 214).

Protozoa and Coelenterates

a. Jennings (1902) had long noted that protozoa habituate to contraction-producing mechanical stimuli repeated immediately after the animals have expanded. A *Stentor coereleus,* which for 7 trials contracted when stroked once with a fine glass rod, required 18 such strokes after 37 trials; a *Stentor roeselli,* reacting to one application for 11 repetitions, took 154 repetitions on the 27th trial; and an *Epistylis flavicans* needed 226 strokes to contract on the 23rd trial. The habituation was observed to be specific to the kind of stimulation used and inversely related to its intensity— parameters that, among others, have since become the hallmarks of habituation as central learning distinct from peripheral effector fatigue and sensory adaptation. Danisch (1921) confirmed Jennings' discovery with *Vorticella nebulifera* in an experiment in which the stimulus intensity was finely quantified. A stroke of 500 ergs effected habituation in 9 trials, one of 1,000 ergs in 15 trials one of 1,500 ergs in 40 trials, but a stroke of 2,000 ergs was not wholly effective even after 420 trials in two hours of experimentation. Jennings (1905) was also the first to study habituation in coelenterates (actinia *Aiptasia annulata*). He found that they became habituated in several trials to a contraction-producing drop of falling water and did it best with 3-minute interstimulus intervals.

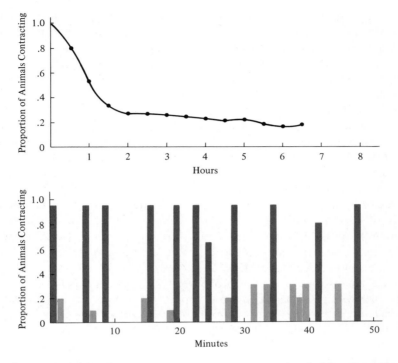

Figure 3 *Habituation, spontaneous recovery, and rehabituation of contractions of a large number of* Hydra pirardi *to a shaking stimulus of 2 seconds duration every 16 seconds.* Scores on the ordinates are the proportions of animals which contracted (initial contraction, 100 per cent). The solid columns in the lower left panel are reactions to light

b. An extensive parametric study of contractile habituation, spontaneous recovery, and rehabituation in "1,000" *Hydra pirardi Brien* was recently reported by Rushforth (1965) and his associates (Rushforth, Krohn, and Brown, 1964). In the main portion of the study, groups of animals in culture dishes, placed on rotary shakers, were shaken for 2 seconds every 16 seconds; the proportion of animals contracting in response to the shaking stimulus in consecutive trials (initial response, 100 per cent) revealed the effects of habituation or recovery. The results are presented in Figure 3. The upper left panel shows that the descending curve of habituation is exponential in form and approaches its asymptote in approximately 2 hours (450 trials). The two right-hand panels disclose the results of shaking a group of animals for 8½ hours, resting them for an hour, and comparing their rehabituation with the habituation of a control group. It may be seen here that about 80 per cent of the habituated animals resumed contracting reactions after the hour's rest, and that their rehabituation was faster than the initial habituation of the control group. The lower left panel demonstrates that the habituation was specific to the

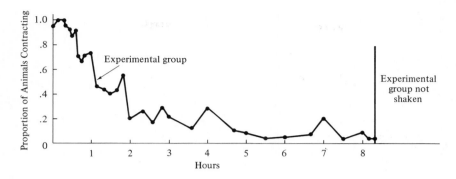

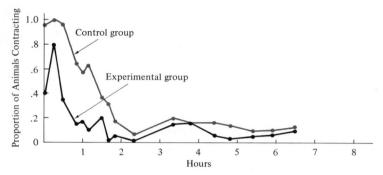

stimulation, demonstrating that the habituation was specific to the shaking stimulus; the unfilled columns represent spontaneous contractions. The experimental group in the upper right panel was permitted a rest of one hour before its habituation was compared with that of a control group (lower right panel). (From Rushforth, 1965)

shaking stimulus: light stimulations continued to evoke unabated contractions and were, interestingly, unhabituable themselves. Their "contraction rate was not reduced after 200 hours of intermittent exposure to light" (Rushforth, Krohn, and Brown, 1964, p. 761).

The slow habituation of the hydra is most likely a combined function of the high intensity of the habituatory stimulus (140 rotations per minute) and the nature of the organism itself. In an early experiment by Wagner (1905), the contractions of *Hydra viridis* to tapping their dishes was habituated only when the taps were repeated at 1-second intervals before the animals were fully expanded; that is, they were less habituable than their protozoan ancestors. Moreover, Wagner found that *Hydra grisea* and *Hydra fusca* were still less habituable—interspecies "mind" differences at the very dawn of metazoan evolution.

Spinal Animals

a. Thompson and Spencer (1966) performed the most extensive experiment in habituating the flexion reflex of "more than 100" spinal cats

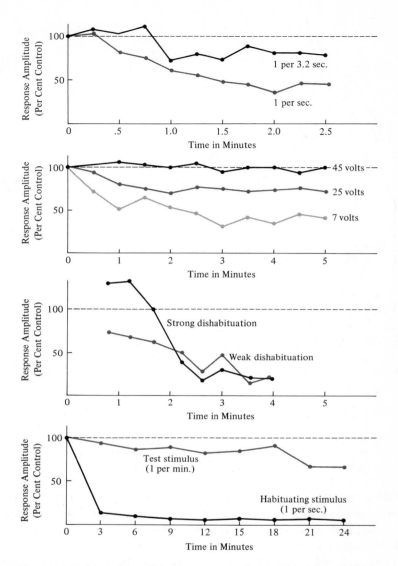

Figure 4 *Habituation, dishabituation, and rehabituation of the flexion reflex in spinal cats.* The top panel shows the effects of interstimulus intervals on the habituation; the second panel, the effects of intensities of habituatory shock stimuli. The weak dishabituation in the third panel was produced by changing the applications of the shock from one every 3.2 seconds to one every ⅓ second; in the strong dishabituation, the shocks were, in addition, increased in intensity. A certain amount of generalization of habituation from stimulating one branch of the saphenous nerve to another is disclosed in the bottom panel. (From Thompson and Spencer, 1966)

but, to date, have reported their data only in summary form. In the main portion of the experiment, the habituatory stimulus was a train of 5 electric shocks for 50 milliseconds, delivered to the skin or saphenous nerve every 10 seconds during habituation and every 3 minutes during spontaneous recovery; and the measured response was the magnitude of contraction of the hindlimb tibialis anterior muscle. Habituation was effected in a mean of 9.4 minutes (56 trials), with a range of 1.2 to 33 minutes; recovery in a mean of 25.7 minutes, with a top score of 108 minutes.

Figure 4 summarizes most of the results. The top panel shows that stimuli applied every second produced more habituation than those applied every 3.2 seconds. The second panel discloses that there was more habituation when the intensity of the stimulus was 7 volts than when it was 25 volts and practically no habituation with an intensity of 45 volts. The third and fourth panels reveal, respectively, strong and weak dishabituations and their habituations, and generalization of the habituation to a test stimulus applied to another branch of the saphenous nerve. Weak dishabituation was effected when the habituatory stimulus, which here was a single shock to the tibial nerve every 3.2 seconds, was changed to a similar shock every ⅓ second. In strong dishabituation, the habituatory shock was also increased in intensity.

Note that the strong dishabituation increased the amplitude of the flexion reflex above its 100 per cent unhabituated control level. To this we should add two significant findings that are not shown in Figure 4: habituation below zero entailed longer recovery, and rehabituation was faster than habituation—the last already evident in Rushforth's hydra studies. There is reason to contest, however, the experimenters' view that the supranormal effects of the strong dishabituation and its augmentation of unhabituated reactions prove that it is a "superimposed sensitization" and not a process of disinhibition (cf. Sharpless and Jasper, 1956). Soviet physiologists have long interpreted such phenomena, most common in extinction, as evidence of positive induction.

b. Lehner (1941) carried out a comprehensive study of habituation and habituation of dishabituation of the tail reflex in eleven spinal rats, using 21 habituation series each including from one to six consecutive habituations of dishabituation. The habituatory stimulus was a "slightly above threshold" tap delivered automatically by a metal rod for one second every 15 seconds and continued until there were three failures to respond. The dishabituatory stimulus was a pinch delivered by tweezers 15 seconds after habituation or habituation of dishabituation was effected. Lehner's results are summarized in Table 1. Note the invariant monotonic diminution of the means in the consecutive habituation cycles; from 12.7 to 2.0 for habituation trials and from 5.1 to 0.5) millimeters on a kymograph) for reflex magnitudes.

Table 1 Habituation and Habituation of Dishabituation of the Tail Reflex in Eleven Spinal Rats. (From Lehner, 1941, p. 437.*)

Consecutive Habituations	Number of Ss Used	Number of Series Used	Mean Habituation Trials	Mean Magnitude of Reflex to First Six Habituatory Stimuli					
				1	2	3	4	5	6
1	11	21	12.7	5.1	3.8	2.8	2.9	2.3	1.8
2	11	21	7.4	3.1	2.5	2.2	1.5	1.9	1.6
3	11	17	6.1	2.1	1.6	1.3	1.3	1.0	1.0
4	11	13	3.2	1.3	1.1	0.8	0.9	0.8	0.5
5	6	6	3.3						
6	6	5	2.2						
7	1	1	2.0						

*Copyright 1941 by the American Psychological Association, and reproduced by permission.

c. Nesmeyanova (1957) investigated habituation of the scratch and extensor reflexes in three spinal dogs through repetitive subthreshold stimuli. In the first part of her experiment, in which 50 to 60 trials were made in each experimental session, the scratch reflex first disappeared after approximately 1,500 habituatory trials, recovered in 5 days after 1,600 trials, ceased being evoked by stimulations in unhabituated regions (generalization of habituation) after 2,000 to 2,500 trials, and took one and a half months to recover after more prolonged habituation. The extensor reflex weakened after 5,000 to 8,000 trials but continued to be evoked after 9,500 to 10,000 habituatory trials. It disappeared in the second part of the study (in which each session consisted of 250 to 500 trials) after 8,000 additional trials in one dog and 10,000 in another. Recovery was quick, however, even after 5,500 additional trials in the first and 7,000 in the second animal. Note the difference between the two reflexes.

d. Habituation of the scratch reflex was reported also for spinal kittens (Kozak, MacFarlane, and Westerman, 1962) and for spinal frogs (Afelt, 1963), while there was habituation of the flexion reflex in the spinal dog (Sherrington, 1904), spinal cat (Prosser and Hunter, 1936; Lethlean, 1965), and spinal frog (Gos, 1932), the tail reflex in the spinal rat (Prosser and Hunter), and the toe-fanning reflex in spinal kittens (Kozak et al.).

Human Neonates

a. The pioneer experiment in this area was performed by Bronshteyn and Petrova in 1952 with 33 subjects, 2 hours to 8 days of age. They used a technique of placing a nipple pacifier, connected to a kymograph, in the neonates' mouths and tracking the habituation of cessation-of-sucking in response to auditory stimuli, mostly musical tones of 60 to 70 decibels sounded for several seconds (four individuals did not respond to the tones and were excluded). The habituation was effected, according to the experimenters' statement, in 3 trials in 15 per cent of the tests, in 4 to 5 trials in 28 per cent, in 6 to 7 trials in 42 per cent, and in more than 8 trials in 15 per cent of the subjects; corresponding scores for a group of older infants (one to five months of age) were 10, 40, 35, and 15 per cent. Moreover, while the habituation generalized to similar stimuli, it dishabituated—or disinhibited—to different tones sufficiently to provide a means of testing the subjects' discriminative auditory capacity. Fifteen per cent of the younger group discriminated between some tones of the same octave, 5 per cent between the same tones in different octaves, 25 per cent between different tones in different octaves, and 55 per cent between the tones and whistles or knocks; the older group scored on these tests 16.5, 16.5, 33, and 34 per cent, respectively.

Figure 5 presents the results of two subjects. The three panels on the left display fully the knack of 4-hour-and-25-minute-old B. (from the top down): ceasing to suck in response to tone Mi^2 ($E^2 = 660$ cycles), habituating to the tone and resuming action after 9 trials, and dishabituating or ceasing again when tone Re^1 ($D^2 = 297$ cycles) was sounded. The two right-hand panels disclose the sucking-and-ceasing performances of 7-day-old T., habituated in 7 trials.

Later, Bronshteyn and his associates (Bronshteyn, Antonova, Kamenet-

Figure 5 *Habituation of cessation-of-sucking in response to tone Mi² in two human neonates and dishabituation to tone Re¹ in one.* The left panels show the performance of B., 4½ hours of age: top, cessation of sucking; middle, habituation after 9 trials; bottom, dishabituation in response to Re¹. The right panels present data for 7-day-old T.: top, cessation of sucking; bottom, habituation after 7 trials. (From Bronshteyn and Petrova, 1952)

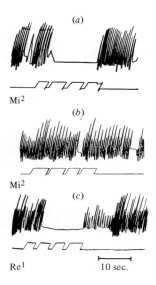

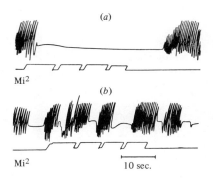

skaya, Luppova, and Sitova, 1958; Bronshteyn, Itina, Kamenetskaya, and Sitova, 1958) extended the technique[4] to study in a similar way neonatal habituation and dishabituation to a wide range of olfactory, visual, tactile, and thermal stimuli. These results are too numerous and too varied to be analyzed here, except to note that olfactory stimuli apparently were most habituable and auditory stimuli least; that hydrocephalic and traumatic neonates habituated less than normal subjects; and that another Soviet experimenter (Zonova, 1964a, 1964b) used the Bronshteyn technique successfully to ascertain neonates' color discrimination capacity. It is tempting to present Table 2 on the speed of habituation to fourteen different stimuli, even if the table and text specify neither the number nor the age of the subjects nor indeed the dimensions of the stimuli. (My guess is that the number of subjects may well have been about a hundred and the age probably less than one month and surely not more than five months.)

Table 2 *Speed of habituation of cessation of sucking to fourteen different stimuli in neonates and young infants.* Per cent of subjects habituated in specified number of trials. (From Bronshteyn, Antonova, Kamenetskaya, Luppova, and Sitova, 1958)

Stimulus	Number of Trials for Habituation						
	1	2	3	4	5	6 to 9	Over 10
Sound	11.8	22.8	21.3	16.3	10.3	12.0	5.5
Bright light	31.1	29.5	21.3	9.8	4.9	3.2	—
Pressure of shank	32.0	30.0	16.0	10.0	6.0	2.0	4.0
Touching sole with hard brush	32.6	28.2	13.0	4.3	10.8	6.8	4.3
Cooling forehead	32.7	30.8	19.2	9.6	1.9	5.7	—
Touching cheek with soft brush	34.2	45.7	14.3	—	2.9	—	2.9
Vibration	34.4	21.3	24.6	11.4	3.3	1.6	3.3
Cooling chest	40.5	21.4	16.6	9.5	7.1	—	4.8
Dim light	44.7	21.0	21.0	10.5	2.6	—	—
Cooling cheek	45.2	24.0	16.6	11.9	2.3	—	—
Anise oil	48.6	20.0	14.3	5.7	8.5	2.9	—
Iodoform	50.0	23.9	17.3	4.3	—	4.5	—
Airstream	54.1	14.6	14.6	8.3	6.2	2.0	—
Mint	58.6	24.1	6.9	3.4	—	3.4	3.6

[4] Kaye and Levin (1963) were unable to verify the technique with neonates less than 4 days of age. However, in a very extensive experiment, Bronshteyn, Petrova, Bruskina, and Kamenetskaya (1959) reported that it was effective in 86 of 109 neonates less than a day old and in 93 of 106 between 1 and 4 days of age; and in a somewhat modified way, the technique has since been replicated by Haith (1966).

Polikanina (1966) and Polikanina and Sergeyeva (1965, 1967) have experimented with habituation of bioelectric reactions in premature neonates and report that its efficacy varies inversely with extent of prematurity and is hardly manifest in subjects of 24 to 27 weeks gestation.

b. Engen and Lipsitt (1965) studied carefully habituation of respiratory changes to two mixtures of odors and subsequent reactions to the components of the mixtures in 30 neonates 27 to 77 hours of age. In the first part of the study, with 10 experimental and 20 control subjects, the mixture contained 50 per cent anise and 50 per cent asafoetida and both components were tested subsequently. In the second part, with 20 experimental and 20 control subjects, 50 per cent diethyl phthalate, 33.3 per cent amyl acetate, and 16.7 per cent heptanal were mixed and tests were made with only the last two. The mixtures were always applied for one second every minute for 10 trials, and the components—subjects divided into equal subgroups—were tried on 11th and 12th trials. The control neonates were used to test unhabituated reactions to components, while twelve graduate students rated the similarity of each tested component to its mixture on a scale from 0 to 100.

The experimenters' three figures are presented in Figure 6. To these we should add the data on the judged similarity of components to mixtures: anise, 60.8 per cent; asafoetida, 39.2 per cent; amyl acetate, 61.9 per cent; and heptanal, 73.3 per cent. Habituation to the odor mixtures was, as may be seen, fast and regular, and its generalization strikingly related to the adults' judged component-mixture similarity: generalized to anise but not to asafoetida, and to heptanal more than to amyl acetate. Respiratory habituation to olfactory stimuli was also reported earlier by Engen, Lipsitt, and Kaye (1963).

c. Keen, Chase, and Graham (1965) experimented with habituation of accelerated heart rate to a buzz of 75 decibels in 20 neonates whose mean age was 42.4 hours. The subjects were divided into two equal subgroups: one in which the stimulus was applied for 2 seconds at 90-second intervals 15 times on each of two successive days, another in which it was administered for 10 seconds the first day and for 2 seconds the second day with identical intervals and number of trials per day. The results are quite clear in showing no habituation in the 2-second group after 30 trials, but rapid manifestation of it in the 10-second group after 4 to 6 trials on the first day and retention for 24 hours on the second day. First-time responses of 20 control subjects of the same age the second day did not differ from those of the 2-second experimental group, but they differed markedly from the responses of the habituated 10-second group. Both differences were statistically significant: between the 2-second and 10-second experimental groups and between the 10-second experimental and control groups.

d. Habituation of accelerated heart rate was reported also by Bartoshuk (1962a, 1962b) and by Bridger (1961). Bartoshuk, using tones and

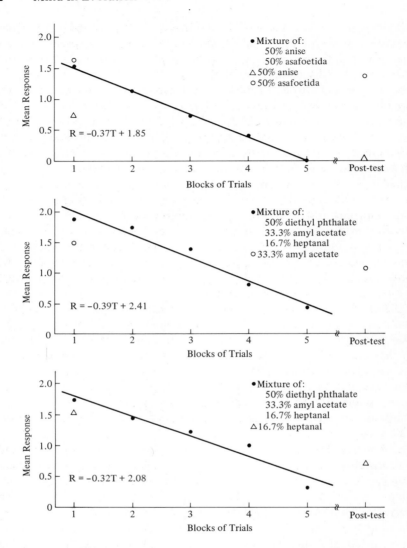

Figure 6 *Habituation and stimulus generalization and differentiation of respiratory changes to different odors in thirty human neonates 27 to 77 hours of age.* In the top panel, anise oil was judged by twelve college students to be 60.8 per cent similar to the experimental mixture, and asafoetida, 39.2 per cent similar. In the lower panels, heptanal was judged 73.3 per cent similar to the mixture, and amyl acetate 61.9 per cent similar. Unfilled circles and triangles—tests with control groups. (From Engen and Lipsitt, 1965)

clicks in 120 subjects 1 to 4 days of age, found in one part of his experiment that responses which became habituated to a tone rising monotonically from 100 to 1,000 cycles per second over a 6-second period recovered when a tone falling from 1,000 to 100 cycles over the same period of time was applied. Bridger used tones and airpuffs and, in addition to recording heart rate, rated the behavioral startle reaction of his 50 subjects, 1 to 5 days of age. He states (with no statistical presentation, just single cases) that first comes "the cessation of the marked startle" and then "the cessation of any response at all" (p. 992), and that 15 of the 50 neonates recovered their habituated reactions when the pitch was significantly changed, in one case from 200 to 250 cycles per second. And it is worth mentioning that Wertheimer (1961) observed that a 3-minute-old neonate ceased moving its eyes in response to a click after 52 trials in 7 minutes. Moreover, there is the habituation of head-turning to ipsilateral touches of the mouth region (Prechtl, 1958; Siqueland and Lipsitt, 1966), a reaction differing from the rest in being appetitive rather than aversive. But since this habituation eventually engenders contralateral responding or transformation from turning-to to turning-away, presentation of it will be deferred to a later section.

For reasons that need not be specified here, habituation in human neonates has been denied due significance in American literature. Rheingold and Stanley wrote in 1963, for instance, that ". . . any suggestion that neonatal habituation is similar to extinction, Pavlov's internal or Hull's [reactive] inhibition would be premature indeed" (p. 3). The simple question is, Why? Why has habituation of reflexes in spinal animals long been considered similar to extinction and indeed specifically named so (Prosser and Hunter, 1936; Lehner, 1941; and others)? Are spinal animals smarter than human neonates? By all tokens, it is just the reverse. And why is habituation not similar to Hull's reactive inhibition, which he conceived, as quoted earlier, as a "more primitive principle" than "experimental extinction"? And why not note that the Russians have always, since 1952, interpreted their neonatal habituation in terms of Pavlov's internal inhibition and disinhibition and, like American and Western spinal-animal experimenters, called it extinction (itself a confusing designation, as was indicated at the beginning of the chapter, but significant in pointing to common mechanisms)?

It is hoped that the adduced evidence will help raise valuations of our natal acumen and of habituation in general. Some change did indeed occur in the course of two years. In 1963 Lipsitt averred that "it is probably well to heed Rheingold and Stanley's advice," and Engen, Lipsitt, and Kaye (1963) could not quite decide whether their response decrement data disclosed *"response* habituation" or *"sensory* adaptation." Yet in 1965, Engen and Lipsitt concluded their experimental report with: "Since the present study rules out strictly sensory fatigue, the decrement and recovery must surely be classified as habituatory and, according to the

Thorpe terminology, as a learning phenomenon" (p. 316). So be it, except that Thorpe is by no means the first to have accorded habituation in-group learning status. Humphrey devoted a long and eloquent chapter to the argument in his 1933 *The Nature of Learning* and so did a number of others, including the present writer, who stated in 1930: "The impairment and final disappearance of a [reaction] pattern upon repetition is then taken as the most general fundamental phenomenon of behavior modifiability" (Razran, 1930, p. 34). Only the semantics of "fundamental" in my old statement needs, I believe, some explication in light of present evidence—namely, that the word does not mean "central" or "principal" but "primitive" and "universal."

INTERPRETIVE COMMENT

It will be noted that the sample experiments were all drawn from organisms and reactions in which habituation is either the only way of learning or the dominant way. As of today, bona fide evidence for conditioning is available for only one of the four categories of the cited experiments—that of human neonates, and presumably not as a prevalent phenomenon. Ross's (1965) recent conclusion from his extensive and well controlled experiment—that coelenterates cannot be conditioned—is convincing, as are the arguments (Forbes and Mahan, 1963; Kellogg, Deese, Pronko, and Feinberg, 1947; Shamarina and Nesmeyanova, 1953; and others) that spinal mammals may be sensitized but not truly conditioned. Moreover, even sensitization seems nonexistent in protozoa and coelenterates and is not common in spinal animals. That is to say: The data of the thirty-four cited experiments disclose the functional properties of habituation uncomplicated (or hardly complicated) by any other learning mechanism—habituation at its base.

The question whether these are veritable properties of learning is, it is hoped, readily disposed of. What else could they be? Spontaneous recovery in time, ultimately a mechanism of forgetting; stimulus generalization and differentiation, the lifeblood of all learning; disinhibition, an important determinant of many of its aspects; rehabituation, so similar in form to relearning. Yet, it is equally true that habituation cannot possibly span all or even most of learning. For one thing, it is only learning what *not* to do, and not learning what to do and how to do it better, the core of the category of learning. For another, habituation is limited in the scope of reactions that it affects and generally is less efficient in producing permanent effects. Moreover, some of its basic properties are the reverse of corresponding characteristics of associative learning or conditioning: varying inversely, for example, and not directly, with intensity of stimuli and reactions.

Plainly, collated East-and-West evidence accords neither with the exclusionist view of keeping habituation out of inner-club learning (Hilgard and Bower, 1966; McGeoch and Irion, 1952) nor with the overextended optimism that it is the master key to all learning (Thompson and Spencer, 1966). An intermediate position, which is also an evolutionary one, is ineluctable. Habituation is a prodromal stage: informing about some of learning's most significant properties, uninforming about others, and misinforming about still others—not unlike the early stage of any evolving life mechanism, including that of neural action. Or, habituation is a low—more exactly, the lowest—level of learning, functioning and prevailing in its functioning at the very dawn of life and under most drastic experimental restrictions of its neural substratum in higher animals.

What naturally comes to mind now is: What happens to habituation in evolution? In intact organisms above sessile coelenterates and natal *Homo sapiens?* Two separate questions are implicated: (1) What is the role of habituation when higher organisms and higher types of learning mechanisms come into being? (2) What are the changes, if any, in its own mechanism or basic functional properties? The first question is wide in extent and is the subject of the next section of this chapter. The answer to the second question, which might be called "The Evolution of Habituation," is, however, "None." The basic functional properties of habituation are essentially the same all along evolutionary ascent in men and animals.

Figure 7, showing three of Lehner's (1941) figures, demonstrates the close similarity, if not identity, of the developmental curves of successive rehabituations (Lehner's "successive extinctions") for (1) the tail reflex in the spinal rat, (2) the startle reflex in the intact rat, and (3) the abdominal reflex in man. And to these we could comfortably add the very similar habituation and rehabituation curves of planarians' responses to light (Westerman, 1963); worms' reactions to mechanical shock (Clark, 1960a, 1960b, 1965, in *nereis pellagica;* Horridge, 1959, in *Harmothoë imbracata* and *N. virens;* Kuenzer, 1958, in *Lumbricus*); snails' (*Limnea stagnalis*) reactions to shading (Pieron, 1910, 1913); the tail-flip response of goldfish to aquarium taps (Rodgers, Melzack, and Segal, 1963); the wiping reflex of frogs (Kuczka, 1956; Kimble and Ray, 1965); the leg-withdrawal of a musk turtle to tapping its shell (Humphrey, 1933); the "mobbing" responses of chaffinches to the sight of predators (Hinde, 1954); the galvanic skin reflex and nystagmus in mammals and man (Brown and Crampton, 1966; Davis, 1934; Dodge, 1927; Kimmel, 1964; Kimmel and Goldstein, 1967; Seward and Seward, 1934; Wickens, Nield, and Wickens, 1966; Zimny and Schwabe, 1965) and electroencephalographic changes (Galambos, Sheatz, and Vernier, 1956; Hernandez-Péon, 1960; Sharpless and Jasper, 1956; Rusinov and Smirnov, 1957; Sokolov, 1958a; Voronin and Sokolov, 1960; and others)—to name only a few of the available reports).

Mysyashchikova's (1952) study of habituation of the galvanic skin reflex in frogs (number unspecified), 4 dogs, and 4 human subjects tells the same story—with an added significant finding. Using both exteroceptive and interoceptive stimuli to evoke the reflex, the experimenter found no

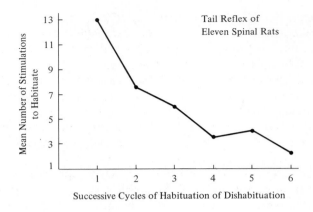

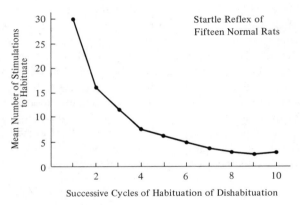

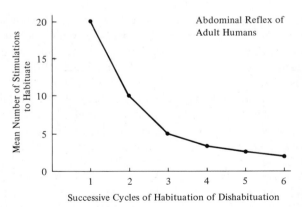

Figure 7 *Curves of cycles of habituation and habituation of dishabituation of reflexes in spinal rats, normal rats, and human adults.* Habituatory stimuli were applied at 15-second intervals in all cases. (From Lehner, 1941)

difference in the speed of its habituation among the three groups of subjects—low amphibians, higher mammals, and man—with either variety of stimuli. The exteroceptively produced reflexes (to sounds, lights, and odors) were in all cases readily habituated in 3 to 20 trials; the interoceptively produced ones (distentions of organs or mild internal electrical stimulation) were in all cases difficult or even impossible to habituate. The differences could not be attributed to differences in stimulus intensities, since it was manifested even when the exteroceptive stimuli were strong and the interoceptive were weak, while stimulus durations and interstimulus intervals were uniform throughout. (Uno's [in press] finding no such difference in college students will be considered in Chapter 9.)

The habituatory mechanism as such may thus be said to have undergone no significant evolution since earliest phylogeny and in human ontogeny. Moreover, the Mysyashchikova study seems to show that at the upper end of the evolutionary ladder not only is the general habituatory mechanism fixed but so is the habituability of different reactions: i.e., *the habituability of a reaction is determined primarily by its own character and not by the evolutionary status of the organism manifesting it.* Determinants of habituability and unhabituability will be discussed in the next section. What should be mentioned here, however, is that these evolutionary fixities are not contrary to, but rather in accord with, the doctrine of evolutionary levels of learning—a doctrine not of linear development of one learning mechanism but of a hierarchical succession of a number of mechanisms, higher arising from lower and lower coexisting with higher.

HABITUATION IN EVOLUTION

The evolutionary fixity of the habituatory mechanism to the contrary notwithstanding, the extent and role of uncomplicated habituation in evolution, from *nereids* on and very early in human ontogeny, is by all evidence constantly on the decline: generally diminished, partly superseded and subordinated, and largely specialized and transformed. Seven separate "evolutions" producing these effects need to be specified and documented.

The Spread of Unhabituation

Empirical Evidence. It will be remembered that even in the sample-experiments' organisms of prevalent habituation, some reactions were impossible or very difficult to habituate: light reactions in hydra; the extensor reflex in spinal dogs, and, in large measure, head-turning in human neonates. In addition, there is the obvious fact that in no organism do reactions to direct noxious or direct nutritive stimuli habituate in any significant sense. By all tokens, with evolutionary ascent and continued increase of organisms' reaction repertories, the realm of unhabituable reactions expands not only absolutely but relatively. Three kinds of experimental data will be cited to illustrate this assertion.

(1) Clark (1965) quotes the results of an experiment by Evans that "tactile stimulation of the posterior ends of *Nereis diversicolor* and *Plathynereis dumererelli* evokes withdrawal reflexes which habituate" but that when the prostomium is thus stimulated, the worm "attacks the object that comes in contact with it" (pp. 90, 91). And attacking, adient reactions to secure food are known to be difficult to habituate without inhibitory conditioning (Wells, 1962b, 1965; Young, 1958, 1959 and others). Moreover, while abient withdrawal reactions to stimuli that forestall noxious action—e.g., shading or lighting, taps and vibrations, sight of a predator, and the like—are generally habituable, some of these too—e.g., hares' responses to rustling of leaves, blinking, pupillary contraction, and the like—attain a high degree of unhabituability.

(2) To Mysyashchikova's finding that interoceptively produced galvanic skin reflexes resist habituation must be added the data of Davis, Buchwald, and Frankmann (1955) that so do arrays of autonomic reactions other than the GSR evoked by exteroceptive stimuli, and the experimenters' conclusion that "skeletal muscle responses, of a certain sort, have the most rapid extinction [Read: "habituation"]" (p. 22).

(3) Post-Pavlovian students of the habituation of the reaction manifold known as the orienting reflex have noted for some time that the generalized (all-analyzer) components of the reflex habituate readily while the local (specific-analyzer) components persist (Novikova and Sokolov, 1957; Sokolov, 1958a, 1959b; Vinogradova, 1961; Vinogradova and Sokolov, 1964). Sharpless and Jasper (1956), investigating habituation of the arousal reaction in sleeping cats, concluded that rapid "phasic" reactions were much more resistant to extinction than long-lasting "tonic" reactions (p. 678). Greene and Kimmel (1966) found that small-magnitude galvanic skin reflexes (GSRs) of college students do not habituate. Wickens, Nield, and Wickens (1966) noted resistance to habituation in cats' GSR and respiratory reactions to *compound* stimuli. Moreover, there is the fact that, unlike EEG changes, evoked potentials have commonly been reported relatively unhabituable (Hernandez-Peón, Scherer, and Jouvet, 1956; Gershuni et al., 1960; Marsh, McCarthy, Sheatz, and Galambos, 1961; Shaw and Thompson, 1964). Greene and Kimmel's GSR results (left), as well as those of Wickens, Nield, and Wickens comparing GSR and respiratory habituability to a compound light-tone stimulus (right), are presented in Figure 8.

Hypotheses of Unhabituability. Two broad parametric hypotheses of unhabituability are suggested by the three sets of cited data. First: Beyond the lowest three or four animal phyla, the unhabituability of reactions is positively related to their evolutionary antiquity; hence, the relative unhabituation of interoceptive versus exteroceptive and of autonomic versus skeletal reactions, the ready habituation of presumably newer orienting reactions, and the commonly accepted inverse relationship between habituation and ablation and other devolutionary agents. Evolutionary antiquity might also be a suitable account for the unhabituation of the small-magnitude GSRs of Greene and Kimmel, the reactions to compound stimuli in the study of Wickens, Nield, and Wickens, Soviet evidence on lesser habituation of localized EEG changes, and possibly also for the greater stability of evoked potentials.

The second hypothesis is an extension of the first in relating unhabituability not just to prior existence in evolution but to an accepted mechanism of it. Briefly stated, it is that *through natural selection, means-end reactions beneficent to organisms' vital functioning eventually attain a dominent share of the unhabituation of the direct reactions of that functioning.* Presumably, however, this evolving unhabituation comes to encompass the adient-approach reactions subserving appetition more than the abient-withdrawal reactions aiding defense or protection—possibly because appetition is the more primary or more immediate vital category and adient reactions are more specific and directed. And, it seems to have affected hardly at all relatively "neutral" reactions of orientation, evolution's preserve of promptest habituation in higher animals.

Putting it differently, one may well assert that the traditional dichotomy of reaction repertories into approach-withdrawal or adient-abient is wholly inadequate. Orienting reactions are neither adient nor abient yet they surely form a distinctive, ubiquitous, and basic category—indeed, a matrix category—of organismic destination. And it is equally clear that the dynamics of direct vital reactions to nutritive (or appetitive) and noxious stimuli,

Figure 8 *Left panel:* Habituation of small-magnitude (less than 1 per cent of subjects' basal skin conductance) and large-magnitude galvanic skin reflexes in 105 college students. (From Greene and Kimmel, 1966) *Right panel:* Habituation of respiratory changes and galvanic skin reflexes to a compound tone-light stimulus in six cats. (From Wickens, Nield, and Wickens, 1966)

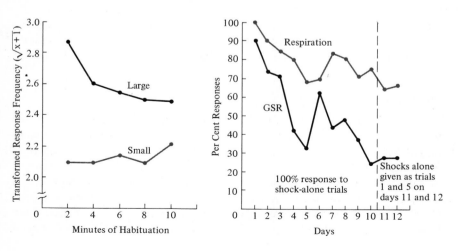

the ultimate fulcra of living and thus of learning to live, differ sufficiently from those of auxiliary adient and abient reactions, to warrant *sui generis* categorization. In fine: In higher animals, *adience and abience, or approach and withdrawal, are in essence but categories between orienting and vital functioning; the dichotomy should give way to a "pentachotomy" of nutritive (or appetitive), noxious, adient, abient, and orienting reactions.*

It is tempting to document the almost unvarying stability of the vital reactions vis-à-vis the varying plasticity of their auxiliaries. Goldfish habituate readily not to flip their tails at taps of aquarium (Rodgers, Melzack, and Segal, 1963); adult squids (Wells, 1962a; 1962b) habituate, with some difficulty, not to attack a particular prey (evolution seems to favor more the predator than the prey); and in Krasnogorsky's laboratory (Machtinger, 1933), an 11-year-old child fed only cheese for 65 days ceased to salivate at the sight of it. Yet, obviously, none of these could habituate not to accept food when very hungry or not to withdraw from shock beyond a certain intensity. The child continued to consume cheese in almost unreduced quantities, and it would seem superfluous to cite evidence on unceasing reactions to harmful stimulations. True, the child's salivation while eating was reduced, but—needless to say—unlike that at the sight of the cheese, it did not come to an end. And we might add that the finding reported in the preceding chapter—that desert sheep habituate not to salivate to sand in the mouth—is not contrary but in accord with the declared view. Sand is neither food nor significantly noxious.

The full import of the evolutionary-antiquity hypothesis of unhabituability must be qualified by the evidence from the later experiments of Vinogradova et al. (1969) that there is very little single-neuron habituation in the primary visual cortex of the rabbit as compared with that in the animal's lower brain regions. The evidence is presumably related to the relative stability of sensory limens in repeated testing. But, however, since the autonomic and skeletal effector changes accompanying the limens do disappear upon repetition, the thesis of the ready habituability of orienting reactions to sensory stimuli is not thereby negated. Moreover, as will be documented in Chapter 9, unrelated sensations (nonperceptual cognition) are of no direct significance in learning and, arguably, in behavior in general.

The Rise of Sensitization

Sensitization, that is, nonassociative increments of reactions through repeated reacting, is the topic of the chapter to follow. What needs to be mentioned here is only the obvious fact that sensitization is the antithesis of habituation and, obviously, a further important facor in stymying its role in evolution. Absent or uncommon in learning at the very dawn of life, it becomes prominent at an increasing rate from planarians and worms on (Cate-Kazejewa, 1934; Evans, 1966a, 1966b; Hullett and Homzie, 1966; Kimble and Ray, 1965; Kreps, 1925; Sergeyev, 1962, 1964a; and others).

Moreover, sensitization becomes more and more a function of kinds of re-actions than merely of intense stimulations (Hagbarth and Kugelberg, 1958; Shamarina and Nesmeyanova, 1953; Shurrager and Culler, 1940). Early evolution thus splits preassociative learning into two types of oppos-ing modifications governed by both innate qualitative and manipulable quantitative parameters—an overriding development later in evolution when learning becomes primarily a matter of coupled juxtaposition or association of reactions.

Interaction with Sensitization: Reversal and Induction

As was indicated earlier, Prechtl (1958), experimenting with habituation of head-turning to ipsilateral stimulation of the mouth regions in a large number of human neonates, found that after habituation was fully effected (17 to 38 trials) further stimulation engendered contralateral responding—turning the head away from instead of toward the source of stimulation. Buytendijk (1933) demonstrated that when 10-centimeter square white cards attached to sticks are repeatedly passed close to octopuses, the ani-mals' reactions change from "violently lowering and drawing away their heads" through "not even blinking" to "gently raising and lowering their heads and slight inclinations towards the cards" (p. 69). Both results are admittedly simple instances of reversals of reactions in the course of repeti-tive stimulation; adient to abient in the neonates and abient to adient (or orienting) in the octopuses. Presumably, when organisms come to possess reciprocal reactions to related stimulation, weakening the stronger S-R con-nection strengthens the weaker connections—or allows their expression—a view akin in a sense to Pavlov's positive induction. The concept or phe-nomenon of induction, so common in Soviet higher-nervous-activity experi-mentation and theory, has hardly been considered in the corresponding American basics of learning manifestations. Recently, however, evidence of its heuristic value has been reported by Williams (1965) and by Miller and Senf (1966).

The Advent of Inhibitory Conditioning

The evidence here is too numerous and too obvious to require mention. As early as 1911, Schaeffer noted that two "frogs" (*Rana clamata*) refused all food for 3 days after a single experience with an electric shock [while eating]" (p. 323). But let us relate specifically one modern study. Octo-puses do not habituate readily not to attack inedible objects shown to them (Wells, 1962a; Young, 1958). However, when permitted to contact the objects and take them to their mouths, they very quickly cease doing it, generalize to similar objects, and retain what they have learned for a con-siderable time (Wells, 1962b; Wells and Wells, 1956). Figure 9 demon-strates such performance very clearly in one animal. In the first 13 trials, the octopus took object S1 to the mouth four times and pulled it toward the mouth three times. But then, except for one trial after an interval of 1 hour and 40 minutes, continued to withdraw from it or reject it for 43 trials, even after an interval of 14 hours; and on the 87th trial came to reject outright similar object P3.

That inhibitory conditioning, and not habituation alone, is nature's standard way of teaching organisms what not to do hardly needs further proof, even if we accede—as we should—to philosophers, pedagogues, and circus trainers that it is not the best way.

Interaction with Classical Conditioning

It has been customary in recent years to begin experiments in classical conditioning with habituation of the *Ro*, the original reaction to the to-be-conditioned stimulus. The practice, stemming from special CR situations in which the Ro and UR (unconditioned reaction) are insufficiently different, can hardly be recommended for typical conditioning: first, because the Ro is dishabituated the moment the UR joins it (specificity of habituation documented all along); second, as long noted by Pavlov, *some Ro* is needed to effect conditioning (Anokhin, 1957; Asratyan, 1955, and others; discussion

Figure 9 *Octopus Number A129 reacting to repeated contacts with inedible objects:* S1, a smooth sealing wax cylinder, and P4, P3, R1, and R2, one smooth and three grooved Perspex cylinders. Except for the four long interludes indicated by the dashed vertical lines, the intertrial intervals were 2 minutes. In the first 57 trials only object S1 was used. (From Wells and Wells, 1956)

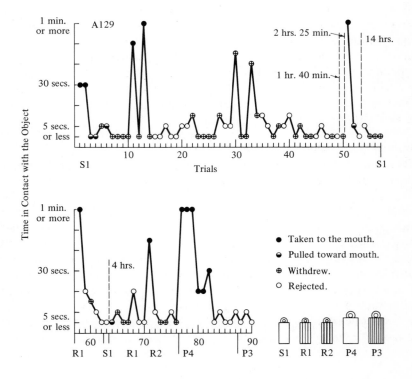

in Chapter 9). What should, however, be stressed here is that Pavlovian conditioning in itself (1) inducts a dynamic interrelationship between a habituable Ro and a sensitizable UR and thus (2) is both a habituating and a sensitizing learning mechanism. *N* combinations of an Ro and a UR engender substantially more habituation of the former and more sensitization of the latter than *N* applications of either alone (Obraztsova, 1964, among many others). Mind's two lowest levels of learning thus coexist and interact synergically with an overlying higher level which brings into being not only evolution's new and standard means of learning what to do but also the highest level of learning what *not* to do. You learn not to do something through learning to do something else instead, shifting from reaction A to reaction B—taught Pavlov, among other things, thus validating and expanding Thorndike's "associative shift" and earlier views of British associationists—and evolutionists. And you do it without the punishment sequelae of inhibitory conditioning.

Reversal by Reinforcement Conditioning

Unlike habituation and inhibitory conditioning, reinforcement—i.e., operant or instrumental conditioning (see Chapter 5 for discussion of appropriateness of the present term)—conditioning is learning what to do and, unlike classical conditioning, it is *solely* learning what to do—more exactly, how to do better what is done. And it surely is nature's most effective means of learning so far, long studied and contemplated by Thorndike and Pavlov, Konorski, Hull and Skinner, and hundreds of others. Like sensitization, reinforcement conditioning is of course an antithesis of habituation, undoing it wherever there is reinforcement—an ever more rapidly expanding realm in the course of evolution.

Habituation of Hedonic Tone

In several pages of his *Vorschule der Aesthetik,* Fechner propounded a far-reaching generalization of nonassociative hedonic learning (associative is considered by him separately)—namely, that consecutive repetition, like continuous stimulation, first quickly increase pleasantness or unpleasantness, then gradually decreases it, until finally the pleasant becomes unpleasant and the unpleasant pleasant (1876, pp. 451-457). Although plausible as common sense, the generalization has not received substantial experimental verification (Beebe-Center, 1932, pp. 237-253), not even the hedonic-decrease or habituation core endorsed by Külpe (1893, p. 269) and by Titchener (1910, p. 229). Accordingly, some years ago I put it to a large-scale test (Razran, 1938b, 1938c, 1940c) as part of a study of hedonic and perceptual conditioning of 378 college students and middle-aged laborers and housewives to 24 short, unfamiliar musical selections (45 to 60 seconds) and 24 projected slides of unfamiliar paintings. After the subjects rated the presentation of each experimental item on an affectivity scale of +2 to −2 (and also characterized it, as discussed in Chapter 9), they were divided into three equal and matched groups which were further divided into three equal and matched subgroups. To one group, the items were presented during lunch, to another two hours after the subjects had missed lunch, and to the third, two hours after lunch. All three groups rated each item on its last presentation, which in one subgroup of each group was the fourth, in another the eighth, and in the third the twelfth repetition.

Only the results of the three subgroups of the third group, in which repetitions of the items were not associated with either lunch or mild hunger, will be considered here. (See Razran, 1954, 1965c, and 1969 for some results of the other two groups.) They show no statistically significant changes ($p > .05$) in the rating of any item in the subgroup of four repetitions, but there were the following significant changes in ratings of items at the twelfth repetition: (*a*) Seven items decreased in negative affectivity: Chinese, Javanese, and Siamese dramatic songs; Copland's "Piano Variation: 8"; Helion's "Composition, 1934"; Leger's "The City, 1919"; and Miro's "Painting, 1933." (*b*) Four increased in positive affectivity: Chopin's "Mazurka No. 4, Opus 13"; Debussy's "La plus lente"; Rembrandt's "Old Woman"; and Cezanne's "Mont St. Victoire." (*c*) Five decreased in positive affectivity: a German jazz selection; a Lithuanian folksong; Rosa Bonheur's "Deer in the Forest"; Van de Veldte's "Dutch Harbor"; and W. Mount's "Long Island Farm." (*d*) The subgroup as a whole did not change significantly its positive ratings of six classical music selections, but 7 of the 42 subjects increased them and 13 decreased them. (*e*) The subgroup disclosed no significant increases in negative ratings nor any increases followed by decreases, but 9 subjects manifested the former change and 14 the latter.

While twelve repetitions may have been inadequate, and while music and painting are only two kinds of hedonic stimuli, the experiment's results do illustrate that habituation is highly complicated at the cognitive-affective level. (*a*) Negative affectivity is more subject to habituation than positive, and positive more when the stimuli are simpler (jazz, folksongs; photographic reproduction of rustic scenes). (*b*) The extreme end of negative affectivity is most easily habituated, whereas in reflexes evoked by intense stimuli it is least, if it occurs at all. (*c*) Individual differences are exceptionally wide, suggesting the operation of verbal and cognitive controls.

It will be demonstrated in Chapter 9 that at the cognitive *perceptual* level habituation is actually superseded by mechanisms of configured reorganization and differentiation.

NEUROPHYSIOLOGICAL BASIS

One of the two caveats of the present book announced in the introductory chapter is that mind as behavior should "make the most of the guidelines of its progenitor, the science of neural action" (p. 10). In habituation, however, recent affluence of separate and diverging progenitor hypotheses or models cannot, for lack of space, be done full justice here. (See Lynn, 1966, who devotes the major portion of his book to a discussion of nine such models and Thompson and Spencer [1966] for two additional accounts.) Accordingly, only several summary considerations will be weighed.

1. The models are almost exclusively concerned with the modelers' own areas of research and not with the universality of the habituation phenomenon, illustrating what I called earlier "universalization of particulars." Most of the models—all those in Lynn's book—are based on habituation of orienting reactions in higher animals and man, with total disregard for its almost identical manifestations in spinal animals, nonsynaptic and even non-neural organisms, and, we should add, the habituation of the tail-flip in goldfish (Rodgers, Melzack, and Segal, 1963), mediated apparently by just two neurons (Mauthner's cells; Retzlaff, 1957).

2. Disregard of total evidence of habituation and its properties likewise characterizes hypotheses stating that the phenomenon is merely classical conditioning of "excitatory neural structures and mechanisms to corresponding inhibitory ones"—excitatory as the *Ro* and inhibitory as the UR (Stein, 1966; and to some extent Sokolov, 1965). But, is not habituation in full bloom in organisms and under circumstances in which conditioning was *empirically* proven extremely difficult or wholly impossible? And does it not possess basic parameters contrasting with those of conditioning? And why are not the inhibitory neural structures and mechanisms the *Ros,* and the excitatory, the URs?

3. Soviet physiologists most commonly explain habituation in terms of Pavlov's "internal inhibition." Lynn's statement that this explanation "has been rejected by most of his [Pavlov's] successors" is wholly unwarranted, as is his criticism of Pavlovian inhibition as a would-be fatigue mechanism (p. 35). As Purpura (1959) rightly points out, internal inhibition is a "Wedensky Inhibition [that] . . . today can be viewed as inactivation of all-or-none spike-generating mechanism which results from sustained depolarization [and which] has been observed in the cerebellum by Granit and Phillips [1956] with intracellularly located microelectrodes" (p. 161).

4. A Wedensky-Pavlov inhibition predicates, however, a prior state of overexcitation, or accumulated excitations, tenable for the development dynamics of extinction, and conditioned delay and differentiation and so-called conditioned inhibition. But habituation of unconditioned reactions plainly lacks such an antecedent period of built-up excitations.

5. There is ample experimental evidence, established by direct extracellular and intracellular probing, that in invertebrates and the two Mauthner neurons governing the readily habituable tail-flip in goldfish neural inhibition is very prevalent and specific (Fatt, 1954; Furakawa and Furshpan, 1963; Furakawa, Fukami, and Asada, 1963; Hartline, Wagner, and Rattlif, 1956; Grundfest, 1959; Grundfest, Reuben, and Rickles, 1959;

Kuffler and Edwards, 1958; Kuffler and Katz, 1946; Tauc and Gerschenfeld, 1961; and others). Habituation in learning and inhibition in neural plasticity parallel each other in evolutionary antiquity and should be coordinated "from below up." (Also, both relate equally to the evolutionary logic that decremental or entropic mechanisms of modifying organisms' innate action should precede those which support and extend it [cf. priority of inhibitory conditioning discussed in Chapter 6].)

6. A neural account must be offered not only of the genesis of the habituatory decrement but also of its preservation or storage, which in my view means evidence of structural changes and not just of functional variations. That is, the physical basis of habituation, as of any other learning, must ultimately rest on neuroanatomy. Neurophysiology alone is inadequate and in essence only a way station in locating the engram (cf. Anokhin, 1968; Beritoff, 1969; Eccles, 1964).

SUMMARY

1. Habituation, defined as the decrement and disappearance of innate reactions through nonassociative repeated reacting, is the lowest level of learning, manifested fully in protozoa and coelenterates, human neonates, spinal animals, unit-neurons, and reactions mediated by just two neurons. Its basic mechanisms remain virtually unchanged throughout evolution; however, its extent and role diminish at an accelerating rate. Sensitization and reinforcement conditioning negate it through increasing or srengthening reactions. Inhibitory conditioning supplants it as a more efficient means of learning what not to do, and classical conditioning presses it into a mixed habituation-sensitization system. And its effects are most variable when the habituatory datum is hedonic tone.

2. Moreover, in the course of evolution the number of relatively unhabituable reactions is on the increase, embracing not only direct vital appetitive and aversive reactions but also adient and abient reactions preparatory or auxiliary to effective vital functioning. On the other hand, in higher animals there arises also a special category of readily habituable orienting reactions (presumably connatural in some way with the plasticity of general cognitivity).

3. The basic functional properties of habituation are in essence undoubtedly those of learning: retention and forgetting, stimulus generalization and differentiation, disruption by extra stimulations (disinhibition), savings in repeated training. Yet only some of the parameters of the habituation properties are analogous to those of associative learning. Others are irrelevant, and still others, such as the inverse variation of efficacy with stimulus and reaction intensity, are just the reverse of what they are in associative learning. All of this no doubt points to an evolutionary kinship of continuous and novel mechanisms in need of special systematization. Moreover, since habituation is fully operative in the low-

est organisms and the simplest reactions, it offers a closer look into the underlying neurophysiological, indeed biophysical, foundations of the learning process—into its very birth.

4. Unfortunately, however, present-day physiological accounts of habituation center largely on what it does at the upper end of the evolutionary ladder—in orienting reactions in higher animals and man—neglecting the lower end and at times telescoping the lower into the upper. A panoramic evolutionary view and hierarchical thinking are needed.

5. Habituability and unhabituability must in general be accorded high status in categorizing reactions. In simple associative learning, unhabituable reactions typically assume an unconditioned or reinforcing role, habituable reactions become the *Ro* in classical conditioning, and the less habituable adient-approach reactions are commonly the strengthened reactions of reinforcement conditioning. At any rate, adherence to a mere adience-abience or approach-withdrawal dichotomy of categories seems anachronistic. A "pentachotomy" of direct-appetitive, direct-noxious, indirect-adient, indirect-abient, and orienting reactions is surely more in keeping wih present evidence and the logic of the dynamics of mind.

CHAPTER FOUR

Sensitization

INTRODUCTORY COMMENT

In Chapter 2, sensitization as learning was delineated as "a more or less permanent increment in an innate reaction upon repeated stimulation." Another statement needed is that the phenomenon exists in two modes: (*a*) the innate reaction is increased in incidence and magnitude, shortened in latency, and lowered in threshold—traditional sensitization (Washburn, 1908); (*b*) new reactions are added to the organism's repertory—pseudoconditioning. The first mode is obviously evolution's way of reversing directly the entropic effects of habituation; the second is a primitive precursor of evolution's main learning level, simple association, or classical conditioning. Primitive precursors, also, are two parallel modes of simple-associative or *conditioned* sensitization: conditioning producing (*a*) only increases in the unconditioned reactions or (*b*) only lowered thresholds and increases of the original reactions to the to-be-conditioned stimuli—alpha conditioning. All four modes will be considered in this chapter, even if, formally, discussion of the latter two might have been deferred to the chapters on conditioning. Common functional properties suggest common mechanisms despite generic differences.

Learned sensitization has on the whole been studied—regrettably—but little, considerably less than habituation. A surface similarity that makes it appear but an unfinished prologue to other learning may well be the cause of the lag. Moreover, the most significant mode of sensitization—pseudoconditioning—has, in the United States, been studied predominantly in higher animals and man, bedeviling controls of associative factors and consequent interpretations. Badly needed are (*a*) more probings of the phenomenon in spinal animals, in which it has been clearly demonstrated (Franzisket, 1951, 1963; Shamarina and Nesmeyanova, 1953), and in such low animals as earthworms, in which it is very common (Evans, 1966a,

1966b); and (*b*) tracking and comparing its dynamics throughout the phyletic scale. Spinal mammals are by all tokens incapable of associative learning (see Forbes and Mahan, 1963, for latest evidence), hence their pseudoconditioning is uncomplicated by it, even as evolutionary tracking permits spotting such complications. Then, there is the systematic consideration that both the basic behavior and the neurophysiology of learned sensitization may hold the key to the behavior and neurophysiology of full-bodied conditioning—that learned sensitization may be, so to speak, the first crucial rung in the evolutionary ladder of *positive* learning (that is, of learning that, unlike habituation, is incremental, and not decremental, in effect; and cybernetic or "disentropic," not entropic, in essence). Yet this rung is the one that has been largely passed over.

PRIMARY EVIDENCE

Spinal Animals

a. While testing Shurrager and his associates' (Shurrager and Culler, 1938, 1940; Shurrager and Shurrager, 1941) claim of conditioning in spinal dogs and Kellogg and his associates' (Kellogg, Pronko, and Deese, 1946; Kellogg, Deese, Pronko, and Feinberg, 1947; Deese and Kellogg, 1949) disclaimer, Shamarina and Nesmeyanova (1953) demonstrated clear-cut pseudoconditioning in such animals. In one spinal dog, a tail

Figure 10 *Pseudoconditioning in a spinal dog.* After 1,200 unpaired stimulations of the animal's paws with a strong shock, the tail comes to react when the paws are stimulated. Kymograph records, from the top down: movements of the right hindpaw, movements of the left hindpaw, movements of the tail, stimulations of the tail, stimulations of the paws, time in seconds. (From Shamarina and Nesmeyanova, 1953)

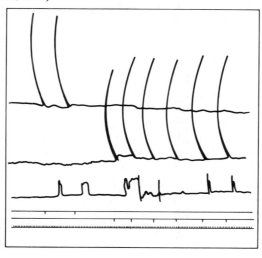

reflex came to be evoked after 1,200 unpaired stimulations of the animal's paws with a strong shock at intervals of 15 to 60 seconds; that is, the tail came to react when only the paws were stimulated. In another such dog, tail movements came to be elicited when the paws were stimulated, after 1,700 unpaired stimulations of the tail. These acquired—but not conditioned or associated—tail reflexes eventually became very stable: they were retained for months and were extremely resistant to extinction (Nesmeyanova, 1957).

Both findings of the Soviet experimenters—the kymogram of the first is presented in Figure 10—are obviously examples of pseudoconditioning. And both point to the requisite of prolonged training. Shurrager and his co-workers did not undertake this, administering no more than several unpaired repetitions of the unconditioned reaction. Neither did Forbes and Mahan (1963), who were unable to replicate the Shurrager group's results; to their statement that "even if it is possible to train the spinal cord, it is very difficult to do so" (1963, p. 40) should be added that failure to condition a spinal animal does not mean failure to pseudocondition it.

b. Franzisket (1951, 1963) experimented with the wiping reflex of spinal frogs, using a von Frey bristle No. 10 of 30 grams per square millimeter of pressure and a cross-section of .0268 square millimeter to elicit it. One hundred stimulations a day were administered to the reflexogenous zone of 8 animals for 12 days and of 4 animals for 15 days. Changes in the incidence of the reflex were studied in the first group of subjects and in its

Figure 11 *Sensitization of the wiping reflex in two spinal frogs through 100 daily stimulations of the reflexogenous zones with a No. 10 von Frey bristle of 30 grams per square millimeter pressure and a cross-section of 0.0268 square millimeter. Left panel, increase in incidence of elicited reflexes; right panel (other subject), lowering of threshold from responding to bristle No. 9 of 27 grams per square millimeter pressure to No. 3 of 9 grams per square millimeter. (From Franzisket, 1963)*

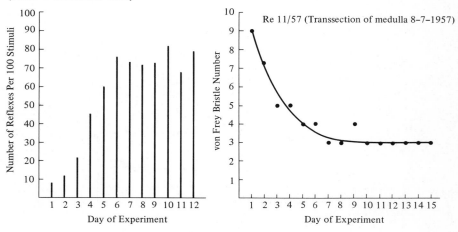

threshold in the second group. The results were—to quote the experimenter —that incidence "increased in the course of 5 to 7 days from 4 to 14 reflexes to 60-90" (1963, p. 318) and "after 5 to 7 days of training the first reflex was released by previously subliminal bristle No. 3 or 4 corresponding to a pressure of 9-12 g/mm^2" (p. 319). Moreover, the experimenter states that "in trained spinal frogs which were undisturbed for at least one day it was possible to release the wiping reflex by nonspecific stimuli such as a knock on the case in which the frogs were kept" (1963, p. 320). Detailed data for two subjects, one in each group, are presented in Figure 11.

The Franzisket experiment thus reveals specifically the concurrence of traditional incremental sensitization and pseudoconditioning. It differs from the Shamarina and Nesmeyanova study in that the repetitive stimulus was not so intense.

Planarians and Earthworms

a. Hullett and Homzie (1966) studied alpha conditioning sensitizations in 72 planarians (*Dugesia dorotocephala*) divided at random into eight equal groups. Half of the animals were kept during a pretraining period of 31 days in normal laboratory illumination and half under a constant bright light of 250 footcandles, with the following training paradigms for the four groups in each half: (a) a 2-second light increase from 6 to 250 footcandles followed by a 1-second 30-milliamp 18-volt DC shock; (b) a 2-second light decrease from 250 to 6 footcandles followed by the shock; (c) the shock followed by the light increase; and (d) the shock followed by the light decrease. In all groups, 50 light-shock or shock-light pairings were administered each day for 5 days at intertrial intervals of 50 seconds; and 32 untrained planarians, 4 in each group, served as controls in 25 post-training tests with the light alone, increased or decreased. Body contractions to the light within the first 3 seconds, rather than mere head turns, were counted as responses.

The results show that in only the two experimental groups in which light increases were followed by shock did the learned contractions to the light exceed control contractions at a statistically significant level. The effect was more pronounced for the group kept in normal laboratory illumination, and there was also evidence of a statistically insignificant increase in the contractions of the "shock—light increase" group which had had a normal light environment before training. In the five other trained groups, no differences to speak of were found between trained and control levels of responding to the light changes. Inasmuch as (a) bona fide conditioning is known to be effected with both decreases and increases in conditioned-stimulus intensities, whereas (b) alpha conditioning is logically unlikely to arise when stimuli are decreased in intensity and (c) the light changes also evoked low-level contractions in the control subjects—it would seem reasonable to attribute the learning in the two (or three) light-increase groups, with no learning in the light-decrease groups, to alpha conditioning, as the experimenter does.

b. Evans (1966a, 1966b) demonstrated in earthworms pseudoconditioned modifications, the bona fide correlates of which might well be classed as (*a*) aversive inhibitory, (*b*) aversive-classical, and (*c*) reinforcement-appetitive conditioning.

In the main part of the aversive-inhibitory study (1966a), modification of the crawling of 50 earthworms *(Nereis diversicolor)* through a 10-centimeter long black Perspex channel in 40 trials was investigated. The animals were divided into five equal groups: A, shock at exit of channel; B (control), no shock; C, shock 5 to 10 seconds after leaving the channel; D, shock 5 to 10 seconds before entering; E, 40 pretraining shocks at 1-minute intervals and shocks at exit. Modifications, described as "refusals," were evidenced when the worms reversed their crawling and left by the entrance or stayed in the channels longer than 40 seconds (pretraining crawling time, 10 to 12 seconds). The results show: (*a*) no refusal in any of the 40 trials in the No-shock B group; (*b*) means of 14.0, 14.3, and 15.5 per cent refusals in groups A, C, and D for all 40 trials (means of 75, 50, and 60 per cent refusals, respectively, for the last 5 trials); and (*c*) a mean of 77 per cent refusals for the 40 trials in Group E. No differences, to speak of, in shock-induced learned refusals were thus found among groups shocked at the channel exit, after leaving, or before entering; the refusal level of the 10 worms which received 40 unpaired pretraining shocks was very high and higher than those in the other three experimental groups ($p < .01$). The learning of the worms, the experimenter concludes, was "modified nonassociatively"—he does not use the term pseudoconditioning—and we may well agree with him.

Pseudoconditioning likewise is evident in the aversive-classical portion of Evans' series of studies (1966b). A group of 10 earthworms *(N. diversicolor),* in which a shock preceded a decrease in light by 40 seconds learned more effectively to withdraw in response to the light decrease than an equivalent group in which the shock followed and overlapped the light decrease. The mean magnitudes of withdrawal during Trials 11 to 50 was 0.79 ± 0.10 millimeters in the backward sequence (shock-light) group and 0.57 ± 0.07 in the forward sequence (light-shock) group, with 36.8 ± 10.5 per cent and 45.9 ± 10.5 per cent of the worms, respectively, withdrawing; the mean for a control group was 0.15 ± 0.06 millimeters and the percentage, 5.8 ± 4.4. Figure 12 presents the data for all 50 trials in graphic form. Recent findings, both East and West, gainsay, it is true, the older view that backward conditioning is *just* pseudoconditioning (see Chapter 5 for full discussion). But they also show that such conditioning is much less adequate than the forward variety, and, moreover, could hardly have occurred at all here as an associative process, with a backward interval as long as 40 seconds. The experimenter's view that all the

modifications were "non-associative . . . almost certainly due to the sensitization effects of the unconditioned stimulus" (p. 118)—that is, of
pseudoconditioning—is again by all tokens fully tenable.

Finally, pseudoconditioning was demonstrated by Evans (1966b) in an
experiment in which reinforcement modifications were produced through
feeding. Fifty-nine earthworms *N. diversicolor* kept in glass tubes and fed
at the end of the tube every 30 minutes six times a day for eight days, were
divided into three groups of 20, 20, and 19 subjects: (1) feeding immediately following a 2-minute increase in illumination from 1 to 9 footcandles; (2) feeding following termination of the increased illumination
by 5 minutes; and (3) a sensitization group in which the feeding preceded the change in illumination by 30 minutes. Speed of the worms'
movements toward the end of the tube in response to the light increase
was the index of the learned modification, with three unfed groups of 14,
14, and 12 animals as controls. The results do not show any difference
among the three experimental groups: the means were 82.9, 82.1, and
80.8 seconds. "Food presentation *sensitizes* worms' responses to sudden
increases in illumination" (p. 109; italics added) is the experimenter's
statement.

Figure 12 *Pseudoconditioning in earthworms*, N. diversicolor. The US was an
electric shock; the CS, a sudden decrease in illumination; and the pseudoconditioned reaction, "withdrawal" by the animal. (From Evans, 1966b)

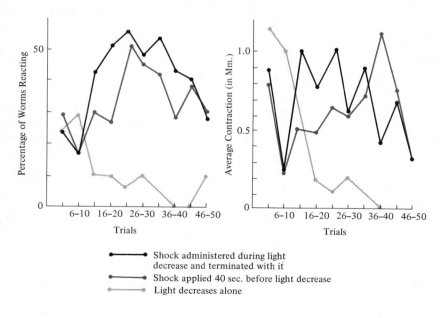

64 · *Mind in Evolution*

All of this does not mean, however, that earthworms are not capable of forming true associative or conditioned connections. They are, as will be seen in a later chapter. But, apparently, *at this thirteenth evolutionary phylum (of which there are only seventeen) pseudoconditioning—modulated appropriately by habituation—is the prevalent type of learning.*

Ascidians, Amphioxi, and Lampreys

a. Kreps' 1925 attempt to condition sessile adult ascidians is the pioneer study in what later came to be called alpha conditioning. He worked with a "considerable" number of specimens, using a drop of water falling from a calibrated height, which invariably caused the animals to contract, as the US; a flash of a 5-footcandle light, a tone of an organ pipe, or a sound of a bell as the CS; and control animals in which either the US or the CS alone was repeated. But he succeeded in conditioning only three individuals, two *Phallusia obliqua* and one *Styella rustica,* and only when the bell was the to-be-conditioned stimulus. And—the specific finding of the experiment: *While the sound of the bell evoked no detectable motor reaction in the control ascidians under normal laboratory conditions, it did, as was discovered later, produce mild contractions when the temperature of the aquarium was lowered to 8-10 degrees C.*

Kreps was not certain whether the paired training in his experiment engendered true Pavlovian conditioning to an "indifferent" stimulus or just sensitization of a reaction through "summation" (Abuladze, 1949). His conclusion was that "in primitive forms of life . . . it may be impossible to demarcate sharply acquired sensitization from conditioning [and presciently] . . . *such sensitization is, perhaps, an initial stage* (Russian: "pervichnaya stadiya") *of true conditioning"* (p. 226; cf. Pressman and Tveritskaya, 1970). The course of this conditioning itself—only its mere acquisition was studied—was conventional: effected in 11 to 15 trials, bell preceding drop by 5 seconds, CR increased in magnitude and shortened in latency and "maintained for 3 weeks." Interestingly, however, the experimenter was unable to establish it in two decerebrate *Phallusia obliqua.*

b. Sergeyev (1962, 1964a) studied extensively alpha conditioning— which he labels "temporary connections" in contrast to true-blue "signal" conditioning—in 82 amphioxi and 22 lampreys *(Lampetra fluviatilis).* The USs were flashes of strong lights, strong electric shocks, and nocuous tactile stimulations. The CSs were weak lights, mild shocks, mild tactile stimuli, sounds, and odors, and they preceded the USs by 3 to 5 seconds. The intertrial intervals lasted from 1 to 5 minutes, and the aversive motor reactions were recorded on a kymograph. Sergeyev's presentation of his results does not permit a detailed analysis of them. His stated findings are, however, most informative, beginning with the base discovery that *the animals learned to respond aversively to originally inadequate stimuli only when the stimuli were adequate at higher thresholds (lights, shock, and tactile stimuli); that is, they could only be alpha conditioned.*

Three stated findings in the Sergeyev experiment point to special characteristics of alpha conditioning: (a) When the USs and CSs were of different sense modalities, the resultant CRs continued undiminished after the URs were partially or even totally habituated through very frequent repetitions; but, when the two stimuli were of the same modality, the CRs were, thereby, diminished or abolished. (Experiment performed only with amphioxi.) (b) When the tail of an amphioxus had been repeatedly stimulated by the CS and the head by the US, and the two ends afterwards wholly separated from each other, *the tail, but not the head*, retained the acquired reaction. (c) In both amphioxi and lampreys, extinction of CRs diminished respective CRs of the same modality as well as other CRs based on the same unconditioned modality—but not, in either case, when the modalities of the tested and extinguished reactions were different. The experimenter's conclusion is that neither amphioxi nor lampreys are capable of forming "true linkages" between unconditioned and conditioned neural centers; the power of the unconditioned center here is just that of heightening or sensitizing, more or less permanently, the neural excitations of the conditioned one (1964a, p. 908).

The experiment is surely a systematic evolutionary challenge meriting high priority replication, particularly the amphioxus portion of it. That the learning capacity of prevertebrate chordates and even of primitive vertebrates should be behind that of higher invertebrates, which command a good deal of true associative learning (McConnell, 1966; Voronin, Karas', Tushmalova, and Khoncheva, 1967), need not, however, be unexpected on general grounds. Not uncommonly, bony fishes do better than frogs.

Sergeyev states further that the sensitizing modifications "were established in the amphioxi in 28 to 34 trials, retained from over 10 to over 24 hours [and] extinguished in 8 to 11 trials [but] were formed in the lampreys in 3 to 10 trials, retained for several days and often were hard to extinguish" (1962, p. 758; 1964a, p. 908). And he reports that "34 amphioxi acquired the sensitizing modifications even when their nerves were severed at pairs 7 to 8, 19 to 21, 29 to 31, or 19 to 21 and 39 to 41" (1962, p. 759). Moreover, it should be mentioned that less extensive results of earlier attempts by Soviet investigators (Baru, 1955; Fanardzhan, 1958) to condition lampreys were quite similar to those of Sergeyev—modifications were effected only to stimuli that evoked the URs at higher thresholds prior to the conditioning.

SENSITIZATION IN EVOLUTION

The foregoing data on pseudoconditioning and alpha conditioning posit a highly significant systematic generalization—that *just as at the dawn of life habituation is the most prevalent type of learned modification, sensitization is the most prevalent in subsequent early evolution.* And with this goes the plausible tenet that in later evolution and the rise of true associative learning, learned sensitization either becomes very specialized and vestigial or is but a pseudo-sensitization involving undiscerned operation of bona fide associative or "memorial-associative" mechanisms. An analysis of learned sensitization in vertebrates above cyclostomes and in man will, it is believed, bear out the tenet. The evidence comes predominantly from pseudoconditioning studies, but its core argument is readily extendable to alpha conditioning and the other two modes of this type of prelusive learning.

Pseudoconditioning

Goldfish. Sears (1934), and more extensively Harlow (1939), demonstrated pseudoconditioning in goldfish. Harlow used 49 subjects divided into three groups: forward conditioning in which a "3-second liminal shock or vibration was immediately followed by a strong shock"; backward conditioning in which the to-be-conditioned stimuli followed the shock in 20 to 30 seconds "as soon as the fish had become quiet"; and pseudoconditioning when the strong shock alone was repeated. In all cases, 10 trials were given each day at intertrial intervals of about 2 minutes. The results are clear in showing that the pseudoconditioning group readily acquired and stabilized a new reaction of struggle and flight to the originally neutral stimuli of liminal shock and audio-vibration. The mean number of trials for the first appearance of the pseudoconditioned reaction was 10; for its stabilization, 20; and it was retained for 21 days. This group was, indeed, a little more effective than the forward conditioning group; and it should be added that in both groups the reactions are reported to have been highly generalized, evoked by "any slight noise or jar" and in a "home" bowl "as dissimilar to the experimental bowl as possible." (The backward-conditioned group took longer than either of these two groups to stabilize its acquired reactions, and it apparently was not tested for specificity.)

In its time, with only a few studies extant in the area, the Harlow data may well have cast doubt on our remote aquatic ancestors' true associative ability and suggested pseudoconditioning as their prevalent mode of learning, at least in its aversive phase. Since then, however, scores of Soview experiments (Baru, 1951; Baru, Bolotina, and associates, 1959; Chernova, 1953; Karamyan, 1956; Prazdnikova, 1953a, 1953b, 1959, 1960, 1962; Tagiyev, 1958; Timofeyev, 1955; Voronin, 1954a, 1957, 1965, 1967; and others) as well as those of Bitterman (1960, 1965), Behrend and Bitterman (1961), Longo and Bitterman (1960), and Wodinsky and Bitterman (1957, 1960) have vastly expanded and radically altered our knowledge of the area. By now it is quite clear that not only the basics of *simple* conditioning and discrimination, whether classical or reinforcement, aversive or appetitive, but also its many variegations—almost all that is contained in Pavlov's and Skinner's formal books—are within the reach of these animals. Or, in other words, the older assumption must be rejected in favor of one that the pseudoconditioning of the goldfish was but a special manifestation in their learning repertory, most likely due to the high intensity of the unconditioned shock which is stated to have produced "a violent struggle or flight response" (Harlow, 1939, pp. 51-52).

Cats. A year later, Harlow and Toltzien (1940) tracked pseudoconditioning in 13 cats, 10 "mature" and 3 "immature." The US was an unavoidable electric shock of "moderate intensity" delivered to the animal's left hindfeet ten times a day for 3 days, at intertrial intervals of about 2-minutes. The pseudoconditioned stimulus was a buzzer sounded in a "neutral" room (to which the animals were transferred after the shock administration) at intervals of 5 minutes to 24 hours. The buzzer, too, was sounded ten times a day for 3 days at approximately 2-minute intervals, five in the neutral room followed immediately by five in the experimental room, to which the animals were returned. In all, each animal received 30 shocks in the experimental room followed by 30 buzzer sounds at widely varying separation intervals, half of which were in a neutral room and half in the experimental room.

No pseudoconditioning was found in the immature cats, while in the ten mature animals the mean number of pseudo-CRs with fifteen buzzer trials was 7.5 in the experimental group and 5.4 in the neutral group (one cat failing in the neutral room). In the experimental room the reactions were retained by one animal for 96 hours, by two for 72 hours, by five for 48 hours, and by two for only 24 hours. In the neutral room, the respective number of animals retaining the reaction for the respective time lapses was 0, 2, 3, 4 and with one cat failing the 24-hour test.

It is obvious that the cats exhibited much less pseudoconditioning than did the goldfish. Instead of 100 per cent acquisition and stabilization and 21 days of retention, the cats' scores ranged from 36 and 50 per cent in incidence of acquisition and from zero (one subject) to 96 hours (one subject) of retention. And there is, of course, no doubt that the cats' records would have been very much higher had buzzer and shock been combined in conventional conditioning fashion. Moreover, the evidence strongly suggests the operation of an associative factor of conditioned stimulus generalization of the spatial features of the experimental situation. The scores in the experimental room were consistently higher than those in the neutral room. And one might reasonably suppose that there were common features in the two rooms, also that there were possible similarities between the administration and even the attributes of the shock and the buzzer. One Soviet experimenter (Krauklis, 1960) wrote a significant, 317-page book on the role of background and external and internal environmental stimuli on the conditioning of rats, dogs, and man.

Harlow and Toltzien state that their "data favor an interpretation that the repetitive shock stimuli produce some generalized and long maintained *attitude of expectancy*" (p. 375). "Attitude of expectancy" is, needless to say, a concept of variegated explanatory core. But whatever it is, it would gain meaning and precision, and surely heuristic value, through analysis and control of its associative antecedence.

Rats. Wickens and Wickens (1942) did just that—they interpreted pseudoconditioning as conditioned stimulus generalization and put the interpretation to test in an experiment with 37 rats, about 90 days of age. The animals, run in a shuttle box, were divided into four groups with four conditions: (*a*) onset of both the US, a shock, and the pseudoconditioned stimulus, a light, was sudden (effected in 0.1 second); (*b*) the onset was gradual (effected in 5 seconds) for both stimuli; (*c*) the shock onset was sudden and the light onset gradual; and (*d*) gradual shock and sudden light. The first day, 10 shocks at intertrial intervals of 30 to 90 seconds were administered; the second day, 15; and the third, 10 again. Tests of pseudoconditioned reactions to the light were made at the end of the third day and on the fourth day.

Seven animals out of 9 were pseudoconditioned in the sudden-sudden group, 8 out of 10 in the gradual-gradual group, but only 1 out of 9 and 2 out of 9 in the two groups in which the onset of one stimulus was sudden and that of the other gradual. Statistically, the pseudoconditioning of the first two groups versus those of the last two yielded a significant ($p < .01$) difference: 15 out of 19 as against 3 out of 18.

Witte (1965) was unable to replicate Wickens and Wickens' experiment; he found pseudoconditioning in only 2 of 35 rats, using identical apparatus and stimuli. Yet his results obviously do not refute the associative interpretation when trained and tested situations are more similar, particularly in organisms higher than rats. And, compared with evidence presented previously, the results disclose the evolutionary demise of bona fide pseudoconditioning: very stable in spinal dogs devoid of associative learning, equal to that learning under normal conditions in earthworms, equal in goldfish with shocks of higher intensity—yet hardly operative in rats, and thus presumably its reported existence in cats is but an associative "pseudo" pseudoconditioning.

Octopuses. Young (1958, 1960), studying a large number of these animals, found that they attack moving plastic figures more readily after feeding and less readily after shock. The increases or decreases also occurred when the food or shock was administered several hours before the presentation of the figures and in the animals' "home" instead of outside it where the figures were presented. Backward conditioning thus was scarcely possible and the likelihood of associative situational commonality reduced. The effects were short-lived, however. Wells (1967) summarizes Young's data and Evans', cited earlier, as follows: "If an octopus is given electric shock or fed, and then tested soon afterwards, the probability of its responding positively toward anything that it sees or touches is found to be altered. This is an unspecific effect, affecting responses to *all* objects regardless of whether they have previously been associated with shock or food" (p. 395). But: "Sensitization phenomena are more obvious in annelids [and] sensitization is an adaptive phenomenon developed before the evolution of sequence-dependent mechanisms capable of relating actions taken with the results that follow, and the machinery of associative learning can be regarded essentially as a development from this preexisting adaptive mechanism" (pp. 392, 397).

Wells's article became known to me after the manuscript had been completed, and it is gratifying to record the evolutionary stance. However, his thesis, based on Young's experiment, that transience of effects is a general attribute of pseudoconditioning is plainly untenable. Three different accounts of Young's data are congruent with existing evidence. (1) Octopuses are more advanced than goldfish in associative capacity and thus also in demise of nonassociative pseudoconditioning. (2) They are, however, less advanced than rats in being unaffected by pseudoconditioning, and of course less advanced than cats in associating generalized situational commonalities. (3) The shocks used by Young were not of high intensity, while the effects of the food, evident only after 15 minutes, were seemingly an outcome of ongoing digestion and resultant interoceptive stimulation rather than of prior pseudoconditioning. Or, in all, octopuses are intermediate in the descending phyletic gradient of the phenomenon's efficacy.

Dogs. Pressman and Tveritskaya (1969) administered on different days airpuffs to the corneas and electric shock to the left hindlegs of five dogs, recording the "mechanograms" of both reactions and the electromyograms of the gastrocnemius. Each animal underwent four experimental sessions of 100 to 125 trials each, and all showed evidence of some pseudoconditioning: the acquired reactions first appeared after 25 to 75 trials, then throughout the experiment quickly disappeared and quickly reappeared in fluctuating waves of several trials. The mean incidence of *shock-blinking* was 51 ± .03 per cent, with a mean duration of 2.5 ± 0.15 trials. The mean incidence of *airpuff-leg action* was 22.0 ± .06 per cent, with mean durations of 1.6 to 2.6 trials.

The experiment differs from all others in that its pseudo CSs were two typical aversive USs, the reactions of which may well have become conditioned to related reaction-produced interoceptive CSs. Hence, the results, like those of Harlow and Toltzien's cats and in line with Wickens' hypothesis, may well be interpreted as a manifestation of conditioned stimulus generalization: i.e., associative "pseudo" pseudoconditioning. (Reaction-produced interoceptive conditioning is, it should be added, the logical mechanism of both short-interval temporal conditioning and saccharine conditioning of X-ray radiation [Garcia, Kimmeldorf, and Koelling, 1955] and thiamine chloride [Garcia, Ervin, Yorke, and Koelling,

1967], even as the baffling evidence that the conditioned sucrose radiation is effective at CS-US intervals of 7 hours [Revusky, 1968] could be stimulus generalization—the sucrose and the radiation giving rise to *related* conditioning of interoceptive feedbacks.)

Humans. Harris (1941), Grant (1943a, 1943b, 1945), Grant and Dittmer (1940), Grant and Hilgard (1940), Grant and Meyer (1941), Champion and Jones (1961), Martin (1962), Prokasy, Hall, and Fawcett (1962), and Prokasy and Ebel (1964) investigated pseudoconditioning, of, respectively, finger-withdrawal, eyelid, and galvanic skin reactions in adult human subjects. Elicitations of these three reactions, and others akin to them, is in these subjects substantially under verbal or cognitive control. Hence, the feasibility—although by no means inevitability—of what was termed "memorial associations" between unconditioned stimuli presented one day and neutral pseudoconditioned ones another day, particularly since in almost all pseudoconditioning studies the neutral stimulus is tested several times before the start of the experiment.

Prokasy, Hall, and Fawcett (1962) disclosed, indeed, such memorial associations with the galvanic skin reflex. They used three pseudoconditioning groups of 23 human subjects each: one in which a shock was

Figure 13 *Pseudoconditioning of the galvanic skin reflex in adult human subjects.* Left panel (from Prokasy, Hall, and Fawcett, 1962): The CS was a tone of 65 decibels and the US a shock "with intensity controlled by an AC variac." Note that the pseudoconditioning group (US 20) was much less effective than the two random groups, which were not much different from the forward-conditioning group. The number of subjects in each group was 22 or 23. Right panel (from Champion and Jones, 1961): In Group TS, a tone of 60 decibels and 0.20 millisecond duration was sounded 0.5 second before a shock of 3.2 milliamps and 600 milliseconds duration; in Group ST, the shock preceded the tone by 0.75 second; and in Group T & S, shock and tone were unpaired.

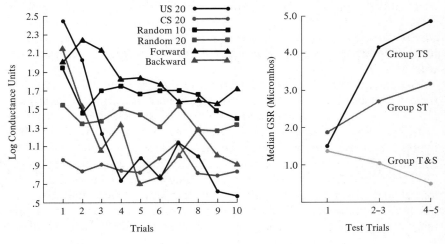

presented 20 times and a tone tested 10 times afterwards, and, two groups, called "sensitization" rather than "pseudoconditioning" groups, in which presentation of either 10 or 20 unpaired shocks was alternated randomly —but not paired—with 10 or 20 tone presentations. As may be seen in the left panel of Figure 13, there were only a few declining initial reactions to the tone in the pseudoconditioning group proper (labeled "US 20"), whereas the reactions in the two pseudoconditioned "sensitization" groups ("Random 20" and "Random 10") continued high for ten tests, indeed, as high as in the forward conditioning group. The "sensitization" groups were, obviously, offered much more opportunity to activate memorial associations than was the pseudoconditioning group proper, and presumably did so. And with this should be noted that the insignificant amount of pseudoconditioning of galvanic skin reactions found by Champion and Jones (1961)—data presented in the right panel of Figure 13—in a group which, like the "sensitization" groups of Prokasy, Hall, and Fawcett, received unpaired shocks and tones in random order (Group T & S), is in essence not at variance with the latter's results. As indicated earlier, human subjects' recourse to memorial associations in conditioning experiments is feasible but not inevitable. Or, to generalize: *In human subjects, pseudoconditioning of reactions that are largely under verbal or cognitive control may well vary—unless that control is itself in some way controlled—from zero to 100 per cent.*

Mention should be made also of Stolz's (1965) study of pseudoconditioning of vasomotor reactions in human subjects. Stolz points out that, aside from Menzies' 1937 findings, successful vasomotor conditioning was reported by only two other American experimenters—Shmavonian in 1959 and Fromer in 1963—one of whom did not control pseudoconditioning and one of whom missed the fact that vasomotor changes accompany breathing changes. Her own results, in which both factors were controlled, show no differences between pseudoconditioned and conditioned vasomotor reactions—hence, the questioning of the bona fide existence of such conditioning according to American data. However, Soviet psychophysiological literature is replete with reports of experiments of vasomotor conditioning in both man and animals which, although uncontrolled for pseudoconditioning, disclose functional properties that hardly fit pseudoconditioning: fine differentiation, specific effects of CS-US delays, differences between interoceptive and exteroceptive CSs, and the like. Moreover, Soviet experimenters are fully aware of the breathing factor and have attempted to separate it out. One such attempt is shown in Figure 14. At the far left, the subject was told to inhale. Note the deep vasomotor changes following the change in breathing. Farther to the right, the subject was told *not* to inhale when he heard the word "inhale." Note his total inhibition of the breathing but not of the vasomotor accompaniment.

Little need be said about the pseudoconditioning of two monkeys frightened ten times by a powder flash of a "snake" blow-out in Grether's

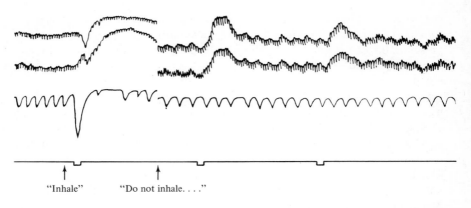

"Inhale"   "Do not inhale. . . ."

Figure 14 *Vasomotor reactions of an adult human subject as related to breathing and verbal instructions.* Top two lines, plethysmograms; third line, pneumogram. Depressions at bottom indicate E's instruction. At left, subject is told to inhale: Note substantial immediate vasomotor reaction. Then subject is instructed *not* to inhale when he hears the word "inhale": Note that the subject was able to inhibit fully his breathing but not the concomitant vasomotor reaction. (From Okhnyanskaya, 1953)

1938 experiment. Relatable, on the one hand, to the high (emotional) intensity of the US and, on the other, to monkeys' known memory capacity, it is obviously, in either case, only a special manifestation in the animals' otherwise conditioned-associative and discriminative repertory (cf. Pennypacker and Cook, 1967). On the other hand, it should be noted that Wickens and Wickens' 1940 data on pseudoconditioning in human neonates (US, shock; pseudo-CS, buzzer), which led them to conclude that "conditionability of the neonate . . . is thus not unequivocally supported" (p. 101), must be qualified by recent evidence. Bona fide classical and reinforcement conditioning have since been reported by a number of experimenters in both East and West, samples of which will be cited in Chapters 7 and 8.

Alpha Conditioning

The vestigial nature of this mode of sensitization in higher animals and man is even more evident than is that of pseudoconditioning. As indicated earlier, two kinds of manifestations are involved: (*a*) organisms and reactions become conditioned only to stimuli which evoke the UR at higher thresholds; (*b*) in *classical conditioning* the original reaction to the to-be-conditioned stimulus, the Ro, is sometimes augmented or sensitized rather than decreased or habituated. The first manifestation is abnegated naturally when organisms and reactions reach the stage of conditioning to stimuli that did not originally evoke the URs at any reasonable stimulus threshold, as is the case in higher invertebrates and in vertebrates as low as cartilaginous fish (Kogan, 1959). The second manifestation as a final product is, as Kimble rightly notes on the basis of American experiments, "not often observed" (1961, p. 477) and is, as a rule, demonstrable only in preliminary phases of Soviet studies of developmental conditioning (Razran, 1961a; Vinogradova, 1959). But what Kimble and others do not note is the phenotypic identity of alpha conditioning with reinforcement conditioning. "Augmentation by reinforcement of the original response to the conditioned stimulus" is Kimble's definition of alpha conditioning. How does this differ from reinforcement conditioning, particularly in light of Grant and Adams' (1944) data showing that alpha conditioning increased the incidence rather than the magnitude of his eyelid Ros? In other words, just as pseudoconditioning is a precursor of classical conditioning, alpha conditioning is a precursor of reinforcement conditioning. The question of why one conditioning habituates and the other augments is not within the scope of the present chapter—Chapter 5 discusses it.

Beta Conditioning

With alpha conditioning an accepted term for *associative* sensitization of the *Ro,* the original reaction to the to-be-conditioned stimulus, the term *beta* conditioning would seem appropriate for *associative* sensitization of the UR. Such sensitization was noted as early as 1905 by Yerkes (1905b) in testing hearing in frogs by what was essentially a Pavlovian technique and by Cason in 1923 in his pioneer study of the conditioned eyelid reaction, while trial-by-trial protocols of Russian experiments reveal it to be an early stage in conditioned training when the CS by itself does not as yet evoke the UR. Progressive in development and occurring also when the CS originally diminishes or has no effect on the UR, associative beta sensitization is clearly an outcome of learning and not of unlearned reflex interaction or of dynamogenesis. And its results must not be confused with those of eventual interaction between URs and fully developed CRs. The phyletic divide between beta and true conditioning has not, unfortunately, been investigated; hence, one can only speculate that it must be close to that of its alpha correlative.

Incremental Sensitization

As indicated earlier, this designation refers to long-known multiple evidence that innate reactions may increase in incidence and magnitude and decrease in latency through nonassociative repetition, that is, to the general manifestation of the phenomenon which (to distinguish it from the three special manifestations) will be termed *incremental sensitization.* Franzisket (1963), it will be remembered, showed that in the wiping reflex of spinal frogs the incidence aspect of incremental sensitization is concurrent with pseudoconditioning. However, the fact, that incremental sensitization is a more common occurrence and a much less radical change renders unlikely a view that pseudoconditioning is always engendered by it. Yet the general parameters of the two are similar and the reverse of those of habituation.

Whereas the existence and efficacy of habituation vary inversely with the intensity of the repeated stimulus, incremental sensitization and pseudo-conditioning vary directly with it. And whereas the former affects primarily biologically weak or, in Ukhtomsky's terms, nondominant reactions, the latter two come into play when reactions are biologically strong or dominant.

Kimble and Ray (1965) brought to light specific evidence on another differential sensitization-habituation parameter, long imbedded in Ukhtomsky's doctrine. The wiping reflex was repeatedly evoked in two groups of six intact frogs (*Rana pipiens*) each. In one group, the "stimulus was applied within the right half of the major dorsal reflexogenous area"; in the other group, "a precise spot within the right half . . . of the zone was determined [and stimulated] on the basis of skin markings" (p. 530). In other respects, the procedure for both groups replicated that of Franzisket: use of a No. 10 von Frey bristle for 100 trials per day. The results are presented in Figure 15, from which it may be clearly seen that sensitization came about when the locus of the repeated stimulations was variable, and habituation when it was "as far as possible" invariant. Or, in terms of dominance: *Variable stimulation brings into action subsidiary nondominant populations of neurons which enhance and, through repetition, more or less permanently sensitize the dominant populations governing directly the behavioral reaction; in invariant stimulation, participation of nondominant neuronal populations is too minimal to affect the dominant reactions, and habituation prevails.*

Figure 15 *Sensitization ["potentiation" is the experimenters' term] and habituation of the wiping reflex in twelve frogs. In the Sensitization group of six subjects, the stimulus, a No. 10 von Frey bristle, was applied 100 times a day to "various spots within the reflexogenous area of the reflex." In the Habituation group of six subjects, it was applied similarly to a "precise spot" in the zone.* (From Kimble and Ray, 1965)

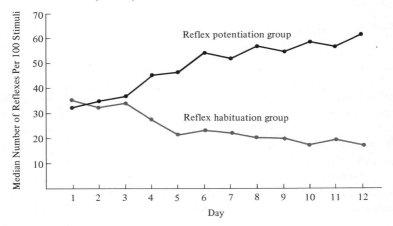

Variable populations of neuronal action are on the increase in later evolution, suggesting, on the face of it, more nonassociative sensitization. But then there is the advent of associative learning, many times more adaptive to the cybernetics of incremental learning than is mere sensitization, which thereby may well become increasingly specialized and vestigial in higher animals and man—more so indeed than uncomplicated habituation and its *sui generis* noncybernetic entropy. Still, an argument could be made for the possible existence, even at the human level, of a sensitization type of learning, named *canalization* by Janet (1925) and developed by Murphy (1947), in which a dominant innate reaction pattern is strengthened and narrowed in action through mere repetition and through dominant-nondominant interaction of neural actions, with little involvement of specific associative or conditioning mechanisms. Existence of nonassociative canalization would no doubt be difficult to prove and, if proven, would not likely be of much technologic import. Yet the problem is of theoretic interest and is not beyond experimental reach.

NEUROPHYSIOLOGICAL BASIS

That repeated stimulation of living organisms may produce more or less permanent incremental changes not only in behavioral reactions but also in underlying neural action is in 1971 not just a judicious theory. Directly observable synaptic sensitization of minutes-long duration, called "post-tetanic potentiation," has been discovered (Lloyd, 1949; Eccles and Rall, 1951; Kostyuk, 1960a, 1960b; Belekhova, 1967; and others). No longer is there the wide gulf between the time dimensions of classical neurophysiology and Pavlovian "behavioral" higher nervous activity that was stressed in 1924 by Beritoff and again as late as 1947 by Larrabee and Bronk in classing "the brief duration of the nerve impulse" vis-à-vis the "long-persistent effects of nerve impulses within the central nervous system [in] the process of learning . . . among the obscure and challenging problems of neurology." Bridging of that gulf began, in truth, with the early light of the authors' own data on "prolonged facilitation" (Larrabee and Bronk, 1938). Likewise, Ukhtomsky's "neural dominance," the leading Eastern view of the field, no longer is a mere inferable of behavioral reflex interaction. A large number of current Soviet direct neural probings of the phenomenon attest to it,[5] as do Morrell (1961b, 1963), Morrell and Naitoh (1962), John (1967),

[5] Thirty-five are listed in the References; Grechushnikova (1962), Kalinin (1963a, 1963b), Kalinin and Khan-Shen (1962), Kuznetsova (1959, 1963), Livanov (1951, 1952, 1960a, 1960b, 1965a, 1965b), Livanov, Korol'kova, and Frenkel' (1951), Livanov and Polyakov (1945), Livanov and Ryabinovskaya (1948), Naumova (1956), Novikova and Farber (1956), Novikova, Rusinov, and Semiokhina (1952), Pavlygina (1956, 1962, 1967), Pavlygina and Pozdnyakova (1960), Rusinov (1953, 1956, 1958, 1961, 1962, 1965a, 1965b, 1966), Ryabinina (1958, 1961), Sokolova (1958, 1959), Sokolova and Sek-Bu (1957).

John and Killam (1959, 1960a, 1960b), Yoshi and Hockaday (1958), and other non-Soviet experimenters. And here the long noneffector neural time course is even more marked, with the vista more encompassing—to the extent, indeed, that John made Ukhtomsky's doctrine the core concept of his *Psychophysiology of the Mind* (1962).

> The effect of the unconditioned stimulus, S_2, is to establish a dominant focus in the corresponding cortical region. Initially, the consequence of the dominant focus may be considered as essentially a sensitization of the region—such that it can be induced to massive discharge by any adequate afferent input. Repeated association of this discharge with a particular input results in the formation of a representational system which somehow stabilizes the dominant focus so that the susceptibility to that particular input persists (John, 1962, p. 93).

This statement is comparable with mine of 1930 that in conditioning,
> at first the change observed is S-O-*R*, or an increase in the magnitude of the more dominant pattern, while later a new pattern, s-O-*R*, appears, s-O-*r* [the original nondominant reaction to the conditioned stimulus] becoming subdued. . . . Let S-O-*R*, a compound pattern in which one stimulus brings about a number of responses, be repeatedly exercised, then gradually more and more of the less dominant parts of the pattern, S-O-r_1, S-O-r_2, . . . , S-O-r_n, will weaken and drop out leaving only the most dominant pattern, S-O-*R*.

(Razran, 1930, pp. 25, 26; the last sentence has particular reference to John's statement that learning is a "process of nonrandomization").

Note also the conclusion in Dykman's recent chapter, "Toward a Theory of Classical Conditioning . . . ," that

> sensitization . . . is the neuroanatomical basis of all modification (see Razran, 1930, 1957, for a similar point of view) . . . covers both the transitory "jacking up" of nervous pathways and their subsequent potentiation by use. . . . [and] implies a fundamental continuity of the simplest reflex and most complex learning (1965 p. 311).

Dykman does not mention the Ukhtomsky school.

Neither did Hughes in his "Post-tetanic Potentiation" (1958), "reviewing increased responsiveness following repetitive stimulation reported in the neurophysiological and psychophysical literature." In fact, Hughes also missed, most unfortunately, the whole manifold of behavioral "increased responsiveness following repetitive stimulation," sampled in this chapter. Nor is there any evidence, or compelling logic, for John's suggested synthesis that "the phenomena of functional transformation . . . attributed by Ukhtomski to the establishment of a dominant focus may be manifestations of locally induced postexcitatory facilitation analogous to post-tetanic potentiation, or an equivalent phenomenon" (1962, p. 86). (Kupalov is the only Soviet scientist who earlier [1956] voiced in passing the suggestion made by John, but he seems to have done it out of courtesy at an international congress; neither he nor any of his colleagues has ever mentioned it since.)

What comes to mind in perusing the full content of juxtaposed East and West research and thought is, rather, a hypothesis that learned behavioral sensitization rests on a dual neural basis: post-tetanic potentiation related to the phenomenon's direct variation with intensity of stimulation, and dominance dependent upon extent of differential action of samples of neuron populations. There is, to be sure, a far cry between stimulus intensity and frequency values in the potentiation of monosynaptic tetanization and in behavioral modifications; moreover, in the latter, sensitization effectiveness of specific stimulus intensities is very much modulated by type of reacton and organism involved. Yet in polysynaptic preparations, the peak of potentiation reportedly is reached earlier and is obtained with tetanic frequencies as low as 25 per second (Wilson, 1955), while the intensity parameter as such is an unmistakable behavioral universal in the sense that there is for each sensitizable effector reaction a stimulus intensity divide below which sensitization does not occur.[6]

Indeed, had no neural mechanism of learned behavioral sensitization other than potentiation ever been set forth, one would need to be invoked to encompass the total evidence and the logic of the field. And it would have to be one that is putatively much more central and integrative in operation, involving inter-unit more than intra-unit interactions, or variable interdependence of neuronal aggregates more than the relatively constant independence of their constituents. The mechanism of dominance, as sketched in the second chapter and used to interpret the Kimble and Ray (1965) sensitization experiment in the preceding section of this chapter (not to mention the thousands of conditioning experiments in the following four chapters), is just that. How else could we account for the finding that with equal stimulus intensities and reaction manifestations variable reflexogenous-zone simulations bring about sensitization while constant precise-spot stimulations do not? And just how may dominance be explained in terms of post-tetanic potentiation? Why not the converse? "Subliminal fringes" alongside "discharge zones" of afferent volley strengths (Lloyd, 1943) point, in fact, to a dominance-nondominance action and interaction in motoneurons' most elementary pools. Obviously, what we need are direct probings of neural events during behavioral sensitization, which, one hopes may inform us also of substrate distinctions of the four different modes.

Moreover, John's and Dykman's general position of wholly equating sen-

---

[6] Primitive organisms manifest, as is known, an intensity divide in the direction of their reactions, intense stimuli eliciting withdrawals and weak stimuli, approaches. And intense stimuli are of course the matrices of organisms' disruptive and nocuous milieus, so that increased responsiveness to them is presumably adaptive. Schneirla (1965 and earlier) has made ingenious use of the intensity divide in developing his system of "W-processes" and "A-processes" but has not linked it specifically to learned sensitization.

sitization and bona fide conditioning is unwarrantedly egalitarian and un-evolutionary; it notes similarities and continuity but not differences and novelty. Regard for total evidence and for logic tells another story—that bona fide conditioning is a distinctly higher level of learning than sensitiza-tion; that for millions of years organisms were capable of the latter but not of the former (compare ascidians and amphioxi and bony fish); and that in higher animals sensitization is at best only a subsystem of conditioning—by analogy, let us say, as the action of syncytial protoneurons is related to that of internuncial relays. Ukhtomsky himself has by no means wholly equated the dominance mechanisms of sensitization and conditioning, think-ing only of their common denominator (Ukhtomsky, 1923a, p. 31; 1927, p. 225, footnote 2); and neither have present-day Soviet followers (Anokhin, Asratyan, Ayrapet'yants—to name just "A" names). Here, again, compara-tive direct neural probings are called for.

Finally, there is the regrettable fact that as yet there is no evidence that either potentiation or dominance produces neuromorphological growths. Eccles' (1964 and elsewhere) and others' view that potentiation does it is hardly more than a theory, even as Dykman's calling sensitization the *"neuroanatomical* [my italics] basis of all modification (see Razran, 1930, 1957, for a similar view)" is obviously a misstatement.

SUMMARY

1. Sensitization, defined broadly as increased reactivity with repeated nonassociative stimulation, is manifested in two behavioral modes: (*a*) in-creases in incidence and magnitude and decreases in latency and threshold of reactions, and (*b*) pseudoconditioning, or new reactions to originally in-adequate stimuli. So far, no parametric studies of the relations between the two modes have been reported; it is assumed that the former is in some way the generic manifestation of the phenomenon.

2. There is ample evidence also for the existence of an associative sensi-tization in which Pavlovian paradigms produce no more than sensitization of (*a*) the Ro, the original reaction to the to-be-conditioned stimulus, known as alpha conditioning; or (*b*) the UR, the unconditioned reaction, for which the term beta conditioning has been coined.

3. Behavioral sensitization does not seem to be present at the dawn of organismic life, as is habituation, but there is evidence for its widespread and prevalent operation in annelids, prevertebrate chordates, and early vertebrates; and it is possible in spinal mammals in which true conditioning is not possible. In later evolution, however, *sui generis* sensitization be-comes largely vestigial, more so indeed than habituation, probably because of its greater adaptive similarity to the main course of the much more plastic learning of true conditioning. Reported evidence of pseudoconditioning in man and higher animals is by all tokens the outcome of memorial-associa-

tive or actual associative commonality of trained and tested stimulus situations.

4. Along with chemical stimulants (Kaplan and Ukhtomsky, 1923; Zalmanzon, 1929a; and others) and low-current anodal polarization (Rusinov, 1953, and others), the manipulable parameters of sensitization are, on the one hand, increases in intensity of stimulation and, on the other, increases in the variability of stimulation. It is assumed that the former relates in some way to the neural mechanism of post-tetanic potentiation and the latter to the neural dominance proposed by Ukhtomsky in the sense that variable stimulation brings into being differentials between the action of dominant and nondominant samples of neuronal populations. The two neural mechanisms are held to be distinct: one primarily a peripheral and atomistic, and relatively constant and independent intra-unit action and interaction; the other largely a central and holistic, and intrinsically variable interdependent inter-unit functioning. Interestingly, the two constitute also an East-West divide, the East half going back to the well-known research and concepts of Vvedensky (Wedensky) begun in 1886, which, his pupil Ukhtomsky concludes, prove the *"variable nature of normal nervous functioning"* (1923a, p. 31). (See Chukchev, 1956, for a theoretical interrelation of the views of Vvedensky, Ukhtomsky and Pavlov.)

5. Incremental and decremental responsiveness subsist within true conditioning. But then overriding new essences emerge: in classical conditioning, the ready evocation of reactions by originally inadequate stimuli, precursed in pseudoconditioning; and in reinforcement conditioning, the ready sensitization, in addition, of relatively nondominant reactions, presaged in alpha conditioning.

CHAPTER FIVE

A Prolegomenon to Conditioning Theory

INTRODUCTORY COMMENT

Association is man's oldest naturalistic conception of the dynamic working of human mind (Aristotle: *De Memoria et Reminiscientia,* II, 6-11), and it was a leading realm of inquiry when, more than 2,000 years later, man began to subject association to formal experimental testing (Galton, 1879-1880; Ebbinghaus, 1885; Cattell, 1886, 1887). Ever since, concern with the mind import and facts of association has proliferated into tens of thousands of published studies and discussions. Confined at first to analysis of conscious *memory,* it soon moved to the wider and essentially behavioral area of *learning,* to be finally overhauled, if not wholly engulfed, by the rapidly rising evidence of its ultimate mode of existence—*conditioning.* The underlying theory behind this latest mass of evidence is, however, so divided and unsettled that a preliminary chapter on some of its fundamentals seems advisable.

Two short statements are needed to clear the scope and intent of the preliminary chapter. First, it will deal only with appetitive conditioning and general theory and only in terms of behavior. Discussion of neural substrata and cognitive superstrata, as well as that of aversive conditioning and subsidiary theory—e.g., of extinction, generalization, schedules of reinforcement, and the like—will, except in passing, be deferred to later chapters. Second, the chapter will center on fundamentals most germane to collated East-and-West evidence and logic and will offer basic emendation and innovations. The following are involved.

THE ESSENCE OF OPERANT OR EMITTED BEHAVIOR: IS IT SUI GENERIS?

"An operant," states Skinner, "is an identifiable part of behavior of which it may be said, not that no stimulus can be found that will elicit it . . . but that no correlated stimulus can be detected upon occasions when it is observed to occur" (1938, p. 21). The formulation is admittedly that of spontaneous behavior, which—Skinner quotes Bethe (1897) as saying—"has long been used to describe behavior for which the stimuli are not known and I see no reason why the word should be stricken from a scientific vocabulary." "I do not mean," Skinner continues, "that there are no originating forces in spontaneous behavior but simply that they are not located in the environment. We are not in a position to see them and do not need to. This kind of behavior might be said to be *emitted* by the organism . . . [whereas] behavior that is correlated with specific eliciting stimuli may be called *respondent*. It is studied as an event appearing spontaneously with a given frequency" (1938, pp. 20, 21).

On first thought it might be tempting to relate the enunciated dichotomy to that of prenatal development. Nonreflexive neuromotor reactions, antedating reflexive ones, have repeatedly been uncovered in fetuses of fish, amphibia, and birds, not to mention invertebrates (Chumak, 1960; Coghill, 1929; Hamburger and Balaban, 1963; Harris and Whiting, 1954; Itina, 1958; Kuo, 1967 and earlier; Tracy, 1926; Zenkevich, 1944). But—as has long been demonstrated, by Carmichael (1934); Bridgman and Carmichael (1935); Windle, Minear, Austin, and Orr (1935); Windle (1936); Barcroft, Barron, and Windle (1936); Barcroft and Barron (1939)—this is little, if at all, true in mammals. And extensive comparative Soviet studies by Volokhov (1951, 1960, 1968), and his many collaborators, added to Western data, have led him to an all-out evolutionary generalization. "Prenatal behavior is entirely reflexive in mammals, preceded by a spontaneous neuromotor stage in birds, and by another earlier direct myogenic period in invertebrates, fish and amphibia" (Volokhov, 1960, p. 55). Interestingly, the title of Bethe's 150-page article—not given in Skinner's References—is "Das Nervensystem von *Carinus maens*. Ein anatomisch-physiologischen Versuch." That is, Bethe studied *crabs*—the "Behavior [mostly *prenatal* at that] of *Invertebrate* Organisms."

What, then, may be the "originating forces" behind spontaneous-operant behavior which "we are not in a position to see"? The following experiments are most instructive. Volokhov (1951) showed that the washing, scratching, licking, and "shaking-off" reflexes of rabbits, elicited in prenatal and early postnatal life by specific tactile stimuli and from specific reflexogenous zones, *later* (*a*) assume a spontaneous character in which the eliciting stimuli are no longer effective and (*b*) regain effectiveness by decortication or anoxia (pp. 202-249). Sedlaček (1961a, 1961b, 1962a,

1962b), observing that in rats the eliciting stage of these reflexes begins to weaken at about 14-17 days of life and the spontaneous comes in after about 20 days, brought out that in the spontaneous period the emission rate of these reflexes is readily increased (*a*) by subsequent feedings and by a light paired with the food in operant fashion but also (*b*) by neutral or eventually no-longer-eliciting stimuli that had been applied repeatedly to the animals throughout the preceding eliciting periods.

The last finding merits specification. Five experimental groups of 21 rats each were used: A, in which in the first 120 days of the animals' life the mother rats' abdomens and teats were smeared daily with a valerian tincture (odor); B, in which the tincture was similarly applied to the rats' own bodies; C, in which the animals' bedding was thus treated; D, in which, in addition, the reflexes were repeatedly elicited by appropriate reflexogenous tactile stimulations; and E, a group in which all four methods were combined. A control group with no special stimulation in the eliciting period also was employed, and tests were made during the spontaneous period—when the rats were 21 to 50 days of age. The results show quite plainly that, compared with the performance of the control group, the rate of the emitted reactions in response to the valerian odor in Groups B and C, increased by 63 and 75 per cent, to the odor plus the reflexogenous tactile stimulation in Group D by 123 per cent, and in Group E, by 185 per cent. Only the difference between Groups B and C was statistically insignificant, and only in Group A was the preceding training ineffective.

Moreover, there is the study by Franzisket (1963), who elicited the croaking reflex in six frogs by finger pressure between the animals' scapulae. He performed the experiment in the winter when "spontaneous croaking was not recorded for weeks," yet noted that after training—500 stimulations a day for three weeks—the frogs began to croak spontaneously "on an average twice a day with bursts of 4 to 7 single croaks." von Holst and von Saint Paul's (1963) finding that the head movements of a hen elicited by microelectrode brain stimulations at 15-second intervals became spontaneous in 22 repetitions is in the same vein. And so are (*a*) the highly effective temporal pupillary conditioning of 24 infants with intertrial US intervals of 20 seconds reported by Brackbill, Fitzgerald, and Lintz in 1967 and (*b*) the GSR conditioning of 12 college students with 40-second US intervals reported by Lockhart in 1966 (1966c)—not to mention (*c*) the common observation that grasping reflex, an admittedly elicited respondent in young infants, is labeled a reaching operant after some maturation and learning (cf. Schoenfeld, 1966). (Temporal conditioning is, incidentally, an unrecognized forebear of Skinner's "superstitious" behavior.)

Four far-reaching conclusions and hypotheses are immanent in the adduced evidence.

1. *Spontaneous-operant behavior is a developmental emergent of corresponding respondent manifestations.*

2. *Respondent conditioning may well be the basis of the emergence.*

3. *Highly effective "natural"[7] and "temporal" conditioning are most likely the general and particular mechanisms of this respondent conditioning.*

4. *Operant behavior, as a rule, dominates respondent behavior.* The dominance is predicated upon four propositions: (*a*) the operant behavior is developmentally more recent and neurally more complex (Volokhov, 1951); (*b*) it is evoked, or comes to be evoked, by internal stimuli which Soviet data suggest are in general more dominant than external counterparts (Razran, 1961a; partial replication by Uno, in press); (*c*) its stimuli are also characteristically variable, engendering thereby sensitization and dominance (Chapter 4, pp. 74-75); (*d*) its dominance is further enhanced by its "naturally" conditioned base.

Thus, the fixed dichotomy of operants and respondents enjoyed for several decades is hereby abnegated. What is offered instead is a dynamic view that the two are an overlapping duality—or, rather, that operants, evolving from respondents (presumably through respondent conditioning), acquire an extra essence in line with the universal principle of evolutionary continuity and novelty. It may be long past the statute of limitations to suggest replacing "operant" with "higher-level respondent." But it certainly is time—indeed, it is exigent—to temper the truncated ahistorical surface analysis and unbar the boxed-in "internal presents" and "unimmediate pasts." The cited studies presage future programs and systems, as do reports of the special and all-pervasive powers of interoceptive stimulations, of which only a token is known to American investigators.[8]

Finally, the very conceptualization of the dichotomy is replete with contradictions and puzzlements. Two will be particularized. (1) A rat escapes a shock by jumping from a charged to an uncharged portion of a simple shuttlebox. In conventional terms, the escape is an operant. Yet when the animal withdraws some part of its body or even jumps when a shock is applied to it, the reaction is presumably a respondent. And what about a lowly gastropod such as a hermit crab, which may require numerous nocuous

---

[7] Unlike Breland and Breland (1966), Soviet students of "natural conditioning"—as well as the present author—do not maintain that laboratory-rigged, non-natural conditioning may not become an integral part of an animal's acquired reaction repertory—only that the natural variety is much more efficacious. And of course, hardly anything is non-natural to human learning. Interestingly, the genetic-associative interaction seems to operate also in the behavior of the vanishing respondents: restoration of lost eliciting stimuli through decortication (Volokhov) and continuation of them through intensive application in the eliciting period (Sedlaček).

[8] Uno (in press) assumed, for instance, that a 1954 Russian reprint of Bykov's 1943 book is a "recent" summary of evidence of interceptive stimulation and conditioning, and that Russian views of the unaware nature of this stimulation are not based on direct reports of human subjects. Nor is there awareness of the reports (Ádám, 1967, pp. 117-140; Razran, 1961a, p. 93; 1965, pp. 67-68) or of my 1961a brief of "unaware ORs in interoceptive stimulations" (p. 119) in Gormezano and Moore's review (1970, pp. 175-176) which, curiously, assigns me a contrary view.

stimulations before it escapes from its shell. Is such an escape also an operant? (2) Salivation in dogs is elicited by specific stimulations, but in man and ruminants it is almost a continuous flow (Biryukov, 1935, p. 75). Is one a respondent and the other an operant, correlating with stimuli only as a pseudo-reflex or discriminated operant?

In fine, while the prevalent dichotomy has no doubt contributed greatly to knowledge of behavior in depth, it has at the same time very substantially constricted its breadth. Our horizon must be broadened and questions asked whether it is where and what it seems. Operant or emitted behavior is *specific* but in essence not *sui generis*. Compare Hinde: "There is no sharp dividing line between spontaneous and stimulus-elicited behavior" (1966, p. 226).

THE ESSENCE OF OPERANT OR R CONDITIONING: IS IT SUI GENERIS? IN WHAT SENSE?

To Skinner, operant or *R* conditioning is an *invariant* of operant behavior: "All conditioned reflexes of Type *R* are by definition operants" (1937, p. 274). Since operants are also defined as spontaneous behavior, disparity and confusion arise—as they have arisen—when nonspontaneous behavior is conditioned in operant fashion. But let us consider for the time being the definition itself: "The conditioning of an operant [*R* Type] differs from that of a respondent by involving the correlation of a reinforcing stimulus with a *response*" (Skinner, 1938, p. 21, lines 28-30) whereas the conditioning of a respondent (*S* or Pavlov type) "is defined by the operation of the simultaneous presentation of the reinforcing stimulus and another stimulus" (p. 19, lines 11-12) which elicits "no observable response" (1937, p. 273, lines 19-20). And here queries begin. Is a reaction such as pressing a lever reinforced by the *stimulus* of food or by the *reaction* of the organism to the food? Are there effective stimuli in any type of conditioning that do not produce reactions? And is it true that "*simultaneous* presentation of a reinforcing stimulus and another stimulus" results in efficacious Pavlovian conditioning?

The following seem fit replies to the questions. (1) Stimuli do not exist for an organism until they are reacted to. Reactionless stimuli are even less tenable than stimulusless reactions. (2) Over 100 years ago, Sechenov stated that "association is effected through contact of two successive reflexes [reactions]" (1863, p. 498; 1952-1956, p. 105). The pioneer of "no stimulusless reactions," he was prescient in realizing that learning is always an interaction of reactions, no matter how widely differing the stimuli which evoke them. A division of conditioning into *S* and *R* types, and not into differing *R* types, is thus, to begin with, confused and incomplete, reflecting the theorist's chosen convenience and not the organism's total action. Pavlovian conditioning is also an *R* type, correlated with "seen" and measurable Rs, the disregard of which truncates analysis even more than does disregard of operants' "originating forces." (3) *"Simultaneous"* or even "approximately simultaneous" (Skinner, 1938, p. 18, lines 33-34) presentation of stimuli, misrepresents Pavlov's bona fide paradigm, which is successive; that is, a succession of reactions not different per se from that in *R* conditioning.

As might be expected, *R* and *S* types of conditioning are juxtaposed by Skinner not only with respect to the event with which each is correlated but also with respect to the nature of its resultant modification. For the former, it is said: *"If the occurrence of an operant is followed by presentation of a reinforcing stimulus, the strength is increased"* (1938, p. 21). For the latter —that the *"presentation of two stimuli . . . may produce an increase in the strength of a third reflex composed of the response of the reinforcing reflex and the other stimulus"* (p. 8). Note that the conditioning is equated with *strengthening* in both types, unseeing the conspicuous difference that in *S* conditioning a *new S-R unit,* the "third reflex," is formed, and nolprossing Thorndike's qualified "associative shift." How does Skinner do it?

The answer is not far to seek: An interlocked revolutionary strategem: (1) supplanting "strengthening" with "reinforcement," and (2) inducting "zero strength" in *S* conditioning. The first adds subjective seduction but no objective substance, while the second is a most curious coinage. I know of no field of science in which a change from zero to "a" would not be considered different from a change of "a" to "A," with the former the more distinctive change. Moreover, the basic character of the strengthening (or reinforcement) is quite different in the two types. In *R* conditioning, *the strengthening is the learning; in S, the learned is strengthened*—one an outcome of "effect," the other of "use." And it is significant that Skinner does not compare homologous reactions to his juxtaposition. The homologue of the *existent* operant in *S* conditioning is not the "third reflex" but the *existent Ro,* the original reaction to the to-be-conditioned stimulus. *This Ro is weakened and not strengthened by conditioning* (see Chapter 3).

Add to this that as early as 1928 Miller and Konorski showed that respondents are also subject to *R* conditioning. And a host of recent studies demonstrate that so also are autonomic reactions, both deep-seated organic changes in heart rate, vasomotion, intestinal contractions, urination, and salivation and changes in such a special autonomic offshoot as the GSR. (See summaries by Kimmel, 1967; Miyata and Hamano, 1967; and Miller, 1969a, 1969b—first reported by Lisina in 1957 and by Kimmel and Hill in 1960.) And the *élan vital* of the Skinner system is encapsulated: *it strays from Sechenov's prescience that all learning is an interaction of reactions*— in his own terms, *that S is also an R type conditioning*—*while leaping the wide chasm separating the true essences of Thorndike and Pavlov learning paradigms.* A factual differential in *results* has been sacrificed on a double altar of *conditions producing the results* and the altar furthermore made to rest on a dubious base—fixity of an operant-respondent dichotomy. In historical terms, this is a mismatch of Hartley's associationism and Bain's and Spencer's algedonism.

Interestingly, while Hull's explanatory system as such is even more discordant with mine than is Skinner's, his *description* of kinds of learning is similar. "Learning," writes Hull "turns out upon analysis to be either a case of the differential strengthening of one from a number of more or less distinct reactions evoked by a situation of need, or the formation of receptor-effector connections *de novo*; the first occurs typically in simple selective learning and the second in conditioned reflex [Read: Pavlovian] learning" (1943, pp. 79-80). (Replace "simple selective learning" with "reinforcement conditioning" and delete "evoked by a situation of need.") I would add that "reinforcement conditioning"—strengthening of a reaction by an associated heterogeneous reaction—is in a sense also a *de novo* learning achievement, in fact an evolutionarily-higher level than Pavlov's basic type (see Chapter 8).

Like operant behavior, operant or *R* conditioning is thus in need of radical conceptual rethinking, despite its empirical success and far-reaching systematic advance over Thorndike's Law of Effect in freeing itself from the onus of "trial and error," in co-opting the Thorndike-spurned counterbalance of Pavlov's extinction, in discovering schedules of reinforcement, and, of course, in the ingenious invention and exploit of the Skinner box. Trapped by its own "operant" (to outdo Pavlov), the system has become doubly defective. To answer the question in the heading of the present section: (1) *The "essence of operant or R conditioning" is the strengthening of an existing reaction by a heterogeneous associated reaction à la Thorndike.* (2) *The strengthening is sui generis in that it does not occur in typical Pavlovian conditioning.* (3) *It is, however, not sui generis as an invariant or exclusive of operant behavior: the essential Thorndike-Pavlov differential is unexplained by it.*

THE CONTINGENCY-INSTRUMENTALITY CONCEPT: IS IT VALID?

A statement made by Skinner in his 1937 article reads: "For 'correlated with' we might write 'contingent upon' " (p. 272). That is, he originated also the contingency concept and consequent dichotomy of stimulus contingency and response contingency which a few years later (Hilgard and Marquis, 1940) defined the dichotomy of classical conditioning and instrumental conditioning.

On the face of it, the newer version is broader in resting the Thorndike-Pavlov difference not on the genetic natures of the to-be-conditioned reactions but on the means of getting them to interact with their respective USs (or reinforcers). Yet in essence it is even more misleading. In what true sense is classical conditioning, as is often said, not a sequence of the organism's action? (Whose action, then?) In what way do USs or reinforcers (or ultimately URs) produced by the organism, administered by the experimenter, or just occurring, actually differ from one another in resultant effects? What is the *extra interactive* correlate in so-called contingent or instrumental control? Is there such a control in Skinner's "superstitious" pigeons and none in the differing hunger states of Pavlov's dogs? And what about the statement: "Reflexes, conditioned or otherwise, are mainly concerned with internal physiology of the organism. We are most often interested, however, in behavior which has some effect upon the surrounding world" (Skinner, 1953, p. 59). Hull's 1929 "A Functional Interpretation of the Conditioned Reflex" is an all-around exposition of such effects. It was based wholly upon what Pavlov did—not a word yet about Thorndike and "reinforcement."

Put somewhat differently: Just how do an *experimenter's* two means of bringing two reactions together *ipso facto* engender in the *organism* two differing mechanisms of neural linkage? Is the concept of contingency-instrumentality not ultimately a sort of *deus ex machina,* if not altogether a doublethink: avowing a causal relation through its formulation yet leaving unspecified (even unposited) the organismic events which underlie it? Does not the concept set up in a sense a false front of causal finality, in fact, a cause-effect reversal? If reaction *A* is strengthened by reaction *B*, it might be said that a contingent or instrumental relation between *A* and *B* is thereby effected—but not the reverse, that the strengthening is the effect of contingency or instrumentality.

A 1953 Skinner statement was therefore most welcome. Discussing "superstitious' behavior," he wrote: "So far as the organism is concerned, the only property of contingency is temporal. The reinforcer simply *follows* the response. How this is brought about does not matter" (p. 85; italics in original). Quite right! *Contingency in conditioning is nothing but reinforcer or UR subsequence* (see Razran, 1939k, for a similar outlook). But, then, what about the well-established fact that such subsequence is a requisite also in *effective* classical conditioning? In it, too, the modifying unconditioned UR almost always *follows* the to-be-modified Ro, the homologue of the to-be-reinforced reaction in instrumental conditioning. True, its UR subsequence may at times fall short of the 100 per cent subsequence in the reinforcement paradigm, but this can hardly be the basis of the qualitative disparity—the opposition of reaction-strengthening and reaction-weakening, and the formation of a *new S-R unit.* And the difference may actually not exist—or it may even favor classical conditioning when instrumental reinforcement is intermittent.

Perhaps, the simplest and most clear-cut argument against the amalgamation of methods and results in the contingency-instrumentality concept is the fact that in "superstitious behavior" and "temporal conditioning" the methods are identical—even the optimum time intervals of 15 to 20 seconds for effecting each (Skinner, 1950, 1953; von Holst and von Saint

Paul, 1963; Brackbill, Fitzgerald, and Lintz, 1967)—yet the results are totally different. *In one case, an existent reaction is strengthened, in the other a reaction to some previously inadequate stimulus is formed.* The other grounds are, however, also convincing in the thesis that (*a*) neither operancy nor contingency-instrumentality is a tenable account of the Thorndike-Pavlov differential and (*b*) "strengthening *through* association" is not "strengthening *of* association." A terminological change, along with a conceptual one, is thus in order: restrict "reinforcement" to the first (Thorndike's) kind of strengthening and substitute "reinforcement conditioning" (*RC*) for "*R* or Operant or Instrumental Conditioning"—thereby denoting an actual type of modification and not an alleged causal mechanism. The *S* or Pavlov type might be termed "formation conditioning" (*FC*), except that the use of "classical conditioning" (*CC*) is not misleading. Confusion would be further reduced if "reinforcer," "reinforced," "reinforce," and "reinforcing" were used exclusively for constituent reactions, stimuli, and operations in *RC*, and unqualified "unconditioned," "conditioned," "condition," and "conditioning" for the constituents of the *CC* type. "Modifying," "modified," "modify," and "modification" are usable terms for both types. But developmental and dominance differences warrant continued distinction between Ros and *Ops* (operants), even if *RoL*s and *RoH*s (lower- and higher-level respondents) would be more accurate.

IMPORT AND STATUS OF BACKWARD CONDITIONING

While bona fide existence of such conditioning, even if only very minor, does not accord well with any American CR theory, it plainly contravenes the contingency concept. Its status is still unsettled, however, despite being on the books for over half a century (Pimenev, 1907; Krestovnikov, 1913) and commanding 87 experiments: 24 Soviet, 25 American, one Czech, and one Japanese are listed in the References.[9] Pavlov declared it "impossible" in the 1927 book (1927a, p. 33; 1927b, p. 27), and "unstable" and "inhibitory with continued training" (1927a, p. 343; 1927b, p. 393) and

[9] Anokhin, 1927; Antonova, 1955; Barlow, 1956; Beritoff, 1926, 1932; Bernstein, 1934; Bulyginsky, 1948; Cason, 1935; Champion and Jones, 1961; Coppock, 1950, 1954; Dostalek and Dostaleková, 1964; Fitzwater and Reisman, 1952; Goodson and Brownstein, 1955; Harlow, 1939; Harris, 1941; Kamin, 1963; Khodorov, 1955; Kreps, 1933; Krestovnikov, 1913, 1921; Moscovitch and LoLordo, 1968; Nagaty, 1951a, 1951b; Narbutovich, 1940; Nemtsova, 1949; Nezhdanova, 1940; Nishizawa, 1962; Pavlova, 1933; Petrova, 1933; Pimenev, 1907; Podkopayev, 1928; Porter, 1938; Pressman, 1934; Pressman and Tveritskaya, 1970; Prokasy, Hall, and Fawcett, 1962; Rite, 1928; Ryantseva, 1955; Scarborough, Whaley, and Rogers, 1964; Shnirman, 1925; Singh, 1959; Smith and Buchanan, 1954; Soloveychik, 1928b; Spooner and Kellogg, 1947; Stroganov, 1940; Switzer, 1930; Trapold, Homzie, and Rutledge, 1964; Vasileva, 1957; Vinogradov, 1933; Wolfle, 1930, 1932; Yelshina, Zimkin, and Moreva, 1955; Zeiner and Grings, 1968. The Russian list includes neither experiments of which the original publications are at present not available to me nor those involving "two-way" conditioning.

"short-lived" in 1928 (1932c, p. 405; "short-lived" is a more exact rendition of "skoroperekhodyashchiy" than "evanescent" in the English translations [1928a, p. 99; 1928b, p. 381]). Konorski's conclusions in nineteen years have been: "only a manifestation of pseudoconditioning" (1948a), "inhibitory forward cessation conditioning" (a new hypothesis, 1948b); "bona fide associated excitation" (1961, p. 112); and again "controversial" and "puzzling" (1967, p. 203).

Early American experimenters (Bernstein, 1934; Switzer, 1930; Wolfle, 1930, 1932) reported *some* positive results, and Hull in 1943 endorsed Pavlov that backward conditioning is "possible" but "weak and unstable" (p. 71). But later, with a few exceptions (Champion and Jones, 1961; Jones, 1962; Singh, 1959), America's attitude and data became almost wholly negative, even as recent Soviet counterparts—not included in my 1956 review (1956b)—are almost wholly positive. No other area of basic and long-studied learning shelters a comparable volume of evidence and interpretations that are so much at loggerheads and form such a substantial Soviet-American watershed. The watershed itself may well be attributed (if I may turn clinical) to the consideration that, unlike American theories, Soviet views of conditioning as overlapping CS- and US-initiated neural actions are sufficiently commodious to consider US-CS sequences of stimuli pessimal yet not impossible CR parameters. But this does not of course lessen the need of a comprehensive umpiring analysis of the evidence and conclusions.

Methodological Considerations: Varieties of Backward Designs

It seems essential to begin with an untried methodological division of backward conditioning into types of designs employed which comprehend almost all possible designs. For didactic reasons, CSs and USs will be used instead of Ros and URs but, while Ops (operants) will be continued as separate terms, S^Ds will not be severed from CSs. There are three main types: (1) The CS is administered or the Op introduced x time units after the US, continued for y units, and terminated simultaneously with US or after it. (2) The CS or Op is terminated z time units before the termination of the US. (3) The CS is administered or the Op introduced x units *after* US termination, zero being one of the magnitudes of x. Moreover, because of the wide basic difference between appetitive and aversive conditioning, each of the types needs to be split into two subtypes, while the Op-CS distinction makes for an extra subdivision of the third type. (The durations of ys of Ops are neither readily controllable nor sufficiently disparate to warrant such a subdivision in the first two designs.)

Differences Between Possible Mechanisms of the Designs

Each design permits its own action to be modified radically and differently by the coaction of different other mechanisms. In the first design, for instance, one may posit most tenably the coexistence of two mechanisms:

(*a*) excitatory forward conditioning to the *US-in-action* summating with the backward counterpart, and (*b*) counteracting forward conditioning of *US-cessation* inhibiting it. Forward *in-action* conditioning is not, however, likely to be determinative and certainly is not a sole explanation of positive backward results. Consider that similar results also obtain in the third design, in which forward conditioning is hardly feasible, unless *x*s are very short and latencies and aftereffects of URs very long—not to mention the general consideration that *initiated* rather than *in-action* USs are CRs' wonted framework. On the other hand, forward US-cessation CRs do command initial US action and, more importantly, have specifically been proven effective for appetitive conditioning (Zbrożyna, 1957, 1958a, 1958b, 1959) and aversive conditioning (Galeano, Roig, Segundo, and Sommer-Smith, 1959; Rowland, 1957; Segundo, Galeano, Sommer-Smith, and Roig, 1961). And here it should be stressed that the cessation of intensive aversion is a much more potent US than the cessation of appetition. The experiment of Segundo et al. demonstrates definitively that a tone repeatedly anteceding the cessation of a shock in cats not only came to inhibit completely the evoked potentials of the shock but also reversed radically the cats' general aversive behavior and facial expressions from writhing in seeming pain to total re-

Figure 16 *Sample record of an aversive cessation CR of evoked potentials in the contralateral sensory cortex of a cat.* Dashes—applications of an intense subcutaneous shock to animal's foreleg; solid lines—presentation of a tone. Top panel—presentation of a previously unused tone; middle—of a habituated tone; bottom—of a tone paired 200 times with the cessation of the shock. Note the complete inhibition of the evoked potentials in the lower panel. (From Segundo, Galeano, Sommer-Smith, and Roig, 1961; changes in facial expression are not shown because of poor reproductive quality of the experimenters' figure.)

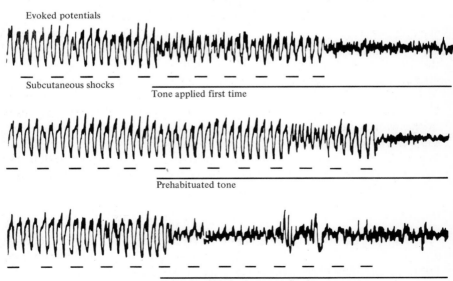

Evoked potentials

Subcutaneous shocks

Tone applied first time

Prehabituated tone

Tone after 200 shock-tone applications

laxation (Figure 16). It is highly unlikely that appetitive cessation conditioning would produce such basic changes. Zbroźyna's reports note only that her dogs ceased eating in response to the pre-cessation CS. In Mowrer's system, "relief" is more biotic than "disappointment." More historically and also more specifically, ending pleasure is not as algetic as ending pain is hedonic, even if we do not concur with Schopenhauer that pain as such is life's stronger "spirit."

An extra CR mechanism may well be assumed to be operative in the second design—namely, counteracting forward *CS-cessation conditioning* (Zeliony, 1908). But this, too, could not be decisive—otherwise forward "trace" conditioning, permitting equally such counterconditioning would be *much less* effective than CS-US overlapping and not merely *less* effective. In other words, in the first two designs, the *main* scuffle is between backward excitatory US *activation* and forward inhibitory US *cessation*. Konorski's considering only forward inhibitory cessation is untenable because (*a*) there is no forward cessation in the third design and (*b*) in the first two, it must be preceded by some initial excitation. *The CR must first be formed to be later inhibitory.*

As already indicated, there normally cannot be much *forward* inhibitory cessation in third backward design. However, there is a like *backward* mechanism which, to distinguish it from the forward compeer (and because of an actual intrinsic distinction), will be named a *termination CR:* the backward conditioning of a CS or *Op* to the termination and not the initiation of the preceding US, a temporally closer connection. When USs are intensely aversive, termination CRs are dominant, to begin with, producing either (*a*) conditioned classical inhibition, as in the two groups of 8 dogs each in the experiment of Moscovitch and LoLordo (1968; the experimenters' interpretation of the results of another group, BIR, is, I posit, in error—see discussion below) or (*b*) termination reinforcements, as in several rat studies (Barlow, 1956; Coppock, 1950, 1954; Goodson and Brownstein, 1955; Smith and Buchanan, 1954). When, however, the USs are appetitive or only mildly aversive, Soviet data suggest that the inhibitory US-termination CRs gain the upper hand only after their excitatory antagonists weaken in the course of training—presumably because of *some* overconditioning (which Hovland years ago—1936—called "inhibition of reinforcement").

The operation of initially dominant backward-connected termination CRs is not readily evident, which may well account for a substantial number of negative findings reported by American investigators of such conditioning with aversive USs (appetitive not used—but not, it is hoped, because of a quale of our culture). Consider Kamin's (1963) failure to note backward aversive effects on the CERs (conditioned emotional responses) of 8 rats. He would not find it, if the tone was conditioned to the termination and not the initiation of the shock. Moreover, the backward conditioning of cognitively or verbally controlled reactions in human subjects may well involve additional mechanisms (Razran, 1956b, p. 67), as demonstrated recently

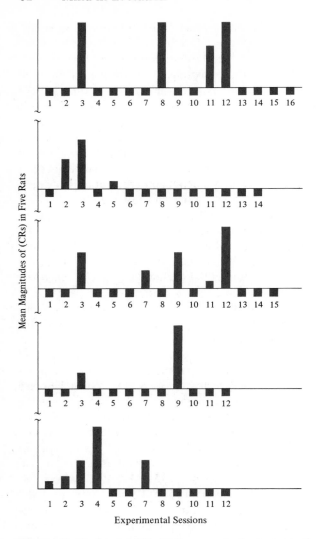

Mean Magnitudes of (CRs) in Five Rats

Experimental Sessions

Figure 17 *Backward CRs to the sound of a buzzer administered 3 seconds after feeding five white rats in a Kotlyarevsky apparatus.* The animals in small chambers facing food-pellet trays beyond glass doors first obtained the food by pushing the door and then were conditioned to push it only in response to the buzzer. The heights of the columns above the horizontal lines indicate force of push; below the lines, failures. (From Ryantseva, 1955)

by Zeiner and Grings (1968), using twenty college students, GSRs, US-CS intervals of 750 milliseconds, and seven training and four testing trials.

Specific Analysis of Four Sample Experiments

Two of the experiments are Soviet and two American. The USs in the Soviet ones are appetitive, and the experimenters attest to bona fide backward conditioning. Those in the American experiments are aversive, and the experimenters reject the existence of backward conditioning. The Soviet samples were chosen from the same issue of a journal. One of the American studies was singled out for being the most frequently cited, the other is the most recent.

a. Ryantseva (1955) experimented with five white rats placed in small chambers restricting extra movements and fronted by glass doors and food-pellet trays. The animals were trained to push the door to obtain the food, and three seconds after the pushing-and-eating a buzzer was sounded. Eleven to 16 test trials—each after 10 training trials—of the animals' reactions to the buzzer were made. The results are presented in Figure 17. The columns above the horizontal lines in the figure indicate positive reactions of pushing the door, those below the line denote failures; the heights of the upward columns mark the force with which the door was pushed. Note that all animals became conditioned to the buzzer after 10 to 20 training trials but the conditioning was quite unstable, appearing only in 2 to 5 of the test trials and disappearing after 30 to 120 training trials. The rats did not learn to react to stimuli other than the buzzer.

The experiment, obviously of the third design, differs from the conventional Soviet manifold in connecting an Op and an S^D instead of a US and a CS and, perhaps because of it, yielding scantier, below-normal positive results. Yet these could in no sense be attributed to pseudoconditioning or to forward conditioning to long-lasting aftereffects of noxious stimuli, as Cautela (1965) hypothesized. The answer to his statement: "Before either the sensitization [pseudoconditioning] or the duration-of-pain hypothesis can be ruled out, backward conditioning will have to be obtained without the use of a noxious stimulus" (p. 143), is obvious: *It has been obtained.*

b. Antonova (1955) performed with three dogs the most extensive study of classical salivary conditioning: 1,006 to 1,258 training trials and 76 to 118 test trials. The sounds of bubbling water (40 decibels), a "knocker" (63 decibels), and a bell (73 decibels) were administered at different times for 20 seconds, 3 to 5 seconds after the animals began eating which lasted approximately 40 seconds. Intertrial intervals ranged from 3 to 6 minutes, and CR effects were tested after 6 to 25 training trials. The results, averaged by me from the experimenter's trial-by-trial protocols, are presented in Figure 18 as total drops of saliva in blocks of ten tests of 20 seconds of CS action. They were, as may be seen, considerably more positive than those of the preceding study—in fact, as supernormal as those were subnormal. But compared with typical forward Pavlovian conditioning, the CRs are only about one-third in magnitude and their stabilization is very irregular and in large measure incomplete: All dogs are said to have manifested eventually neurotic symptoms. Of course here, too, the salivation could not possibly have been anything but an outcome of *particular* associations. This was, the experimenter states, the dogs' first experimental experience.

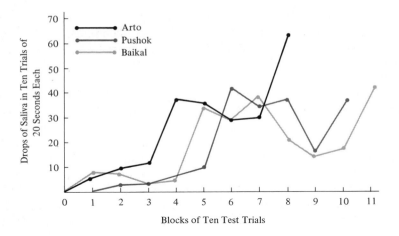

Figure 18 *Development of backward salivary conditioning with US-CS intervals of 3 to 5 seconds in three dogs.* Entries are total drops of saliva in blocks of ten successive 20-second periods of CS action. The range of training trials for the animals was 1006 to 1258; of test trials, 76 to 118. (Drawn from data of Antonova, 1955)

Three further statements germane to the two experiments are in order: (*a*) Since conditioned dogs consume their USs in less than a minute, there is ample opportunity for the forward cessation conditioning to be operative in either the first or the second design, and there is, unfortunately, no good way of ruling it out to isolate its effects. (*b*) Two experimenters (Bulyginsky, 1948, and Nezhdanova, 1940), using the first design, reported salivary backward conditioning in no sense different from its forward counterpart: undiminished after 430 and 435 training trials, regular course of development, and of general animal behavior. Other results do not, however, show this design to be superior per se. (*c*) Nor is there, on the other hand, convincing evidence that the third design is optimal. Indications of it (Beritoff, 1926, 1932; Moscovitch and LoLordo, 1968; Narbutovich, 1940) may well be due to different quantitative parameters within each design: the nature of the interacting reactions, and their temporal and intensive magnitudes.

c. Spooner and Kellogg (1947) experimented with 60 female college students "naive with respect to a knowledge . . . of the nature of conditioning." The CS was a 55-decibel 0.2-second buzzer and the US a make-break 0.2-second shock adjusted to produce a "withdrawal movement for each *S* . . . about 6 in. in extent." The subjects, not permitted to escape the shock, were divided into six equal groups: three with CS-US intervals of 0.5, 1.0, or 1.5 seconds; two with US-CS intervals of 0.25 or 0.5 seconds; and one of simultaneous administration. The results are presented in the upper two panels of Figure 19. As may be seen in the left panel, backward conditioning was effected (the data of the simultaneous and the backward groups are reported to have been little different), but it diminished with continued training, fitting, exactly Pavlov's characterization twenty years earlier. The experimenters' empirical generalization reads that "the treatment of our results forces [!] us to the conclusion that backward conditioning exists and that it must [!] be accepted as an established fact" (p. 328), to which should be added the other fact that the results differ from accumulated Soviet evidence since Pavlov only in that their positiveness is, in my estimate, at about the 40th percentile of its total. (Changes in the first 20 trials were, unfortunately, not presented.) Note, however, the interpretation that *"backward conditioning is apparently an entirely different phenomenon from forward conditioning"* (p. 328; italics in original) and "it is possible

Figure 19   *Upper panels—the Spooner and Kellogg (1947) comparative data of backward, simultaneous, and forward conditioning in 60 college students with tone as the CS and electric shock as the US. Lower panels—the Moscovitch and LoLordo (1968) study of the effects of CSs, in varying backward (shock-tone) sequences, on Sidman avoidance conditioning in 38 dogs. B1—8 animals with tone administered 1 second after shock termination; C—8 with tone onset 1 second before the shock termination; R—6 controls with unpaired administration of the stimuli (Rescorla, 1966); B15—8 with shock-tone intervals of 15 seconds; B1R—8 dogs with a shock-tone interval of 1 second and random, 0 to 15 minute, intertrial intervals. Note the absence of effects in Groups R and B1R.*

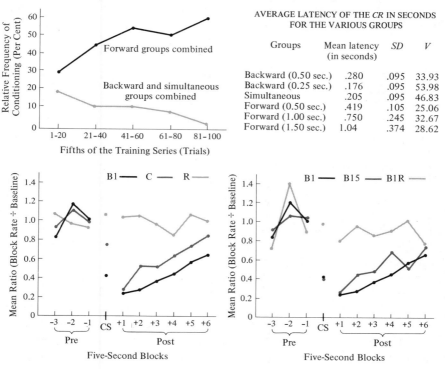

AVERAGE LATENCY OF THE *CR* IN SECONDS
FOR THE VARIOUS GROUPS

Groups	Mean latency (in seconds)	SD	V
Backward (0.50 sec.)	.280	.095	33.93
Backward (0.25 sec.)	.176	.095	53.98
Simultaneous	.205	.095	46.83
Forward (0.50 sec.)	.419	.105	25.06
Forward (1.00 sec.)	.750	.245	32.67
Forward (1.50 sec.)	1.04	.374	28.62

that backward conditioning is a special case of pseudoconditioning" (p. 330).

The grounds of the experimenters' straying interpretation are not difficult to uncover. First, they were not concerned with the core of the problem —in Pavlov's terms, not with backward CRs as *having lived* but as *short-lived*. Second, they mistook the nature of the indigenous attributes and ultimate causal mechanisms of reported manifestations of pseudoconditioning. As set forth in Chapter 4, a number of experimenters in both East and West found this "conditioning" to be relatively stable and of considerable magnitude (Evans, 1966a, 1966b; Grant, 1943a; Harlow, 1939; LeLord, 1966; Nesmeyanova, 1957; Prokasy, Hall, and Fawcett, 1962—their two "random" groups; Shamarina and Nesmeyanova, 1953). And its causal mechanisms are by all tokens of two main varieties: (1) *nonassociative,* as (*a*) operative in spinal and lower animals, and (*b*) produced by very intense aversive stimuli; and (2) *associative* in the wake of (*a*) CS commonality between trained and tested situations, (*b*) "memorial" association of unpaired USs and pseudo-CSs (primarily in human subjects), and (*c*) activation of temporal conditioning. The pseudo-CRs of the *nonassociative* variety differ little from forward counterparts. But not so those of the *associative*. Since in its first subvariety the common elements are likely to be few, in the second the remote associations weak and not always exercised, and in the third the necessary conditions for temporal activation commonly unmet— resultant conditioning is typically, although by no means exclusively, minimal. *To maintain then, that US-paired backward conditioning is nonassociative because its manifestation resembles poorly associated, and in essence misnamed, pseudoconditioning is scarcely cogent.*

Spooner and Kellogg are not alone in this kind of ensconced interpretation. Also invoking it was Nagaty, experimenting with 40 white rats, two groups of which showed statistically significant increases ($p < 0.2$ and $p < 0.05$) in an avoidance CR to a buzzer when a shock repeatedly preceded it by 1 or 20 seconds. His conclusion was that "the presence of the shock . . . had a general facilitating effect on this response analogous to that of pseudoconditioning" (1951a, p. 245). And, as indicated earlier, the facile use of pseudoconditioning as an explanatory catch-all is quite popular —not long scuttled, as it should have been. Moreover, neither Nagaty nor Spooner and Kellogg used a pseudoconditioning group. Fitzwater and Reisman, who did, found that it excelled the performance of a matched backward group in both CR frequencies and magnitudes (1952; shock as the US and 10 college students in each group).

Third, as might be expected, Spooner and Kellogg did not relate the special status of backward conditioning to US-termination CRs and effects of cognitive attitudes. Nor, finally, do the obtained shorter latencies of their backward CRs, shown in the table in Figure 19, warrant the dictum that *"forward and backward conditioning are fundamentally distinct processes"* (1947, p. 334; italics in original). Differences in time of effective interaction of the CS- and US-initiated neural actions may well be presumed to be the differential causes—not to mention that, as may be seen in the table, the latency difference between US-CS and CS-US intervals of 0.5 second was less than that between the CS-US of 0.5 second and CS-US of 1.0 second. In fine, the *Spooner and Kellogg study, cited commonly as a "classic" disproof of bona fide existence of backward conditioning, actually proves it.*

d. Moscovitch and LoLordo (1968) used 32 dogs divided into four equal groups to test the effects of first- and third-design backward sequences on Sidman avoidance conditioning. In Group C, the first second of a 5-second tone overlapped with the last second of a shock of 4, 5, or 6 seconds duration. In Groups B1 and B15, the tone was sounded, respectively, 1 and 15 seconds after the termination of the shock, while Group B1R differed from B1 in that the interstimulus intervals between US-CS pairs were programmed by random numbers to range from zero to 15 minutes. Sidman avoidance was trained on odd days of a consecutive 13-day training period, backward classical conditioning on even days, and the avoidance was tested afterwards: 15 seconds before the presentation of the tone, 5 during its action, and 30 following it. Each CR training session consisted of 24 pairings at interstimulus intervals of 2.0, 2.5, and 3 minutes in the first three groups and a mean of 2.5 minutes in the B1R group. The results—with those of a control Group R of 4 dogs in which the US and CS were administered separately (Rescorla, 1966)—are presented in the lower panels of Figure 19.

As may be seen in the two graphs, avoidance reactions in response to the CS decreased substantially in three of the four experimental groups. On the face of it, there is clear evidence of the formation of US-termination inhibitory CRs through backward classical connections of CSs to the termination of aversive USs, comparable to backward acquisition of reinforcement by CSs following aversive terminations in four American experiments mentioned earlier. However, the negative results of the Group B1R lead the experimenters to an altogether different conclusion—namely, that all their results are "not due to a backward associational process, but to the fact that, when CS follows US [aversive] and the ITI [interstimulus interval] is long, the CS signals safety" (p. 673). Besides the mystique of a neural correlate of "a signalling long ITI" and the arbitrariness of the "long" parameter, two other simple and tenable hypotheses for the negative turn of the B1R Group are at hand. (*a*) The likelihood that a counteracting forward shock initiation CR is formed in trials in which the intervals between a US of a succeeding pair and a CS preceding it are not too long. (There need be only a few such trials.) (*b*) While several variable ITIs do not interfere with conditioning, a kaleidoscopic scramble of them may very well do it. Soviet studies of "dynamic stereotypes" clearly disclose that ITIs are to an extent integrals of *all* conditioning, and, as far as I know, there is no evidence that a CR has ever been formed with such total ITI randomization. Add to this the considerable number of Soviet third-design backward initiation CRs and the four American termination CRs, and it is surely "safer" to conclude that the *experimenters have not disproved what they did prove.*

Supplementary Systematic Evidence and Views

a. *Appetitive USs or Reinforcers Preceding Ops.* Nagaty (1951b) found no associative effects when a pellet of food was repeatedly administered to 22 rats, trained in a Skinner box, 1 or 20 seconds prior to the insertion of the bar. The animals' bar-pressing performance equaled that of an extinction group. No data on initial backward sequences of food-bar pressing are available, however.

b. *In-Action Forward Excitatory CRs in Long-Latency URs.* The comparisons of backward conditioning in GSRs, eye-blinks, and finger-withdrawals of 20 college students by Trapold, Homzie, and Rutledge (1964) suggest strongly that such a mechanism is operative in reported GSR evidence; this need not, however, negate concomitant idiopathic backward associations.

c. *Optimum Intensity of USs.* Pavlov and Beritoff asserted that weak solutions of HC1 and shocks that are not too intense, respectively, are conducive to backward conditioning. My 1956 review of the area, dealing only with classical conditioning of US-initiation—and, incidentally, only with Soviet experiments before 1941—supported the assertions. But they obviously do not hold for backward US-termination. The rationale given for the assertions was that "the US must not be excessively dominant over the CS" and "the organism must not be so much preoccupied with the US as to fail to attend in some degree to the CS" (Razran, 1956b, p. 67)—or in strict Pavlovian terminology, that "very intense USs produce an unfavorable excessive amount of negative induction."

d. *Optimum CS Intensity.* In line with the above rationale, I stated also that a "favorable condition for the formation of backward CRs . . . is a CS that is not weak" (p. 67). Neither should it be too strong, particularly since its very subsequence augments its dominance.

e. *Cognitive Factors.* In the light of the presented evidence, the data of Zeiner and Grings (mentioned earlier) that "backward conditioning was found only with those Ss attributing significance to the CS" (1968, p. 232) could hardly be generalized to experiments with dogs and rats. The experimenters' report ends: "Further research is needed to answer the question of . . . . Is backward conditioning in humans no more than the development of an expectancy or is it something that can develop at several levels as suggested by Razran (1955[a])?"

f. *Backward and Reverse CRs.* Soviet investigators commonly equate backward with reverse CRs, in which the succeeding US in a forward sequence comes to invoke the preceding Ro. It is clear, however, that this evocation is not only a backward connection but also a reversal of modifying and modified reactions.

Final Statement

My 1956 view that "backward conditioning is a genuine CR-associative manifestation" (1956b, p. 67) is, I maintain, much more tenable now than it was fourteen years ago. The present account goes far beyond the review in augmented positive evidence and even more in new interpretations, not thought of then (cf. Smith, 1965).

TWO-WAY CONDITIONING AND TYPES OF CONDITIONING

The doctrine of "two-way conditioning," little known in the West, was first proposed by Beritoff in 1924. Briefly, the doctrine contends that classical conditioning brings about not only the evocation of the UR by the stimulus of the CR, but also, in some degree, the evocation of the original reaction to the conditioned stimulus (the Ro) by the stimulus of the UR. Put in neural terms, which Beritoff prefers: Conditioning sets up not only *direct* connections between the neural centers of the *Ro* and UR but also, in some degree, *reverse* connections between the latter and former centers. The neural excitability or plasticity is enhanced in both centers (Beritoff, 1924, 1927, 1932, 1947, 1956a, 1959, 1960, 1961, 1969). The Beritoff doctrine has of late received substantial empirical support in a number of Soviet experiments bearing on both its behavioral and its neural tenets. Space permits brief mention of the findings of only several of these.

Lyan-Chi-an (1959, 1962a, 1962b, 1962c; part of data reported by Asratyan in 1961b) experimented with six dogs. In four dogs, administration of a relatively mild electric shock—10 to 20 per cent above threshold —to the animals' foreleg preceded feeding; in the other two, the feeding preceded the shock. Stable direct classical conditioning was found in both versions of the experiment (cf. early studies by Petrova, 1914, Savich, 1913, Yerofeyeva, 1912, 1921, and a summary of recent ones by Asratyan, 1969) —but there was also clear evidence of unstable reverse modifications in both. Antecedent shocks readily evoked salivation and masticatory movements, and antecedent eating just as readily produced foreleg withdrawal. But subsequent shocks occasionally produced eating reactions and subsequent feeding occasionally caused foreleg withdrawal. The reverse conditioning was strengthened when the stimuli of the antecedent reactions were increased—the shock in intensity, the feeding through increased portions or increased hunger—also, to some extent, when the stimuli of the subsequent reactions were decreased.

Dzhavrishvili (1956) studied reverse conditioning in two dogs in a Konorski Type II paradigm. Passive pulley lifting of the foreleg of one dog was followed by feeding; that of the other animal, by ringing of a bell and then feeding. Dzhavrishvili's results are clear in demonstrating not only that the dogs learned to lift their forelegs without the aid of the pulley in reinforcement fashion and to salivate and masticate while doing it, in the manner of conventional classical conditioning, but also that the feeding as well as ringing the bell came to elicit foreleg lifting: reverse conditioning. Finally, there is the experiment by Shvets (1965) lending support to Beritoff's conviction that conditioning enhances action in the neural centers of both the UR and the Ro. When DC shifts—changes in steady potentials—in a rabbit's cortex were studied while the animal was forming a conventional conditioned defense reaction to a flash of light followed by an electric shock to the foreleg, the shifts were noted first in the visual cortex, then in the parietal-motor area, and after sufficient training were evoked in both areas by either the light or the shock.

The two-way doctrine admittedly calls for some emendation of the dominance view of conditioning posited in Chapter 2—namely, that while, in the main, dominant reactions *modify* nondominant ones, they also become, in some degree, *modified* by them. The view itself that dominance determines which reactions are modifying and which modified—although conceived ultimately in terms of parameters of extent of neural action—is the correlate of Premack's (1962, 1965) concept that probability of occurrence resolves which reactions are reinforcing and which reinforcible. Yet, despite surface similarity, there is a basic difference between Beritoff's direct and reverse conditioning and Premack's "reversibility of the reinforcement relation." Premack does not profess that a less probable reaction may in some degree reinforce a more probable one, only that the relation may be reversed, whereas Beritoff maintains the existence of two relations, an extra reverse relation.

Beritoff's systematic account of the difference between reinforcement and classical conditioning—or in his terms, using Konorski's designation, between Type II and Type I conditioning—is of recent vintage (1956a; 1960). (One must remember that theoretical concern with the difference has long lain fallow in the Soviet Union and even now is hardly a central problem there.) "In Type II, unlike in Type I, conditioning," Beritoff asserts, "reverse and not direct conditioning connections predominate—from the strong [dominant] neural center of the modifying subsequent reaction to the weak [nondominant] neural center of the modified antecedent reaction, and not from the weak, modified, and antecedent one to the strong, modifying, and subsequent neural center" (1960, p. 66). There is, on the face of it, a disparity in the formulation in that the reverse connections are assumed to generate not only reinforcement conditioning but also some reverse classical conditioning—that is, not only reinforcement of the modified reaction by the modifying one but also some classical replacement of the latter by the former. The disparity is resolvable, however, by the view that the *two* behavioral modifications are the outcome of *one* general type of neural modification—*conditioned enhancement of the neural center of the modified reaction*—and the two thus differ only phenotypically and not genotypically.

Nor is it difficult to fit two-way conditioning to the existence of backward conditioning, in which reinforcement conditioning presumably would be mediated by direct (forward) connections and classical by reverse (backward) ones. The essence of the doctrine is not that a different *temporal* direction engenders each type of conditioning but that a different *type* of direction does it—from weak and modified to strong and modifying neural center in one case (classical type) and from strong and modifying to weak and modified in the other (reinforcement type). The temporal relation is significant only in that subsequence adds conditioning strength to a reaction and antecedence reduces such strength, so that conditioning is best when the dominant modifying reaction is also the subsequent one. Or, to put it somewhat differently: *In classical conditioning the enhanced neural center of the modifying reaction—typically the subsequent and dominant one—draws the modified reaction—typically the antecedent and nondominant one—into its orbit, whereas in reinforcement conditioning the enhanced center of the modified reaction draws that orbit to itself.*

The Beritoff view of the classical-reinforcement differential is no doubt of high theoretical and empirical merit [10] as far as it goes. Unfortunately, it does not go far enough—saying nothing about what determines the differential, the direction of the modification. Why should two types of modified reactions ensue with an identical modifying reaction such as administration of food? A tentative causal hypothesis will be attempted in the next section.

RELATIVE UNHABITUABILITY OF THE MODIFIED REACTION AS A DETERMINANT OF REINFORCEMENT CONDITIONING

When the antecedent modified reactions in Pavlov-type and Skinner-type conditioning paradigms are compared, it is quite evident that the two differ in ease of habituability. The former, *typically* orienting reactions to sensory stimuli, are readily habituated; the latter, *typically* adient reactions auxiliary to securing food, are not. Empirical evidence on parameters of

---

[10] Interestingly, Pavlov, too, intimated a similar conception of reinforcement conditioning in two sentences of his "The Reply of a Physiologist to Psychologists" (1932b, p. 124): "When food is given on raising the paw, a stimulus undoubtedly runs from the kinesthetic centre to the feeding centre. But when the connexion is established and the dog, under the urge of food, gives the paw himself, obviously *stimulation runs in the opposite direction*" (italics added; see also, 1936a, pp. 115-116; *Wednesdays*, 1949, Vol. 1, pp. 225-226; 1955, pp. 307-308). It should be noted that the interpretations of reverse conditioning by Pakovich (1963) and by Varga and Pressman (1966) overlook the complexity of evoked reactions in backward sequences as discussed in the preceding section.

unhabituability is sparse. Yet what is known permits basing the greater persistence of the adient reactions on three factors: (1) a more direct means-end relation to vital functioning, (2) much more variable stimulation, and (3) much wider scope of neurobehavioral involvement. That variability of stimulation will hamper habituation is a matter of simple logic as well as an experimental fact (Kimble and Ray, 1965). An inverse relationship between habituation and scope of neurobehavioral action of different reactions follows from the established existence of such a relationship with the intensity of stimulation of the same reaction (Chapter 3). And one might well expect selective evolution to impart unhabituation to reactions closely related to vital functioning.

Italicization of "typically" orienting and "typically" adient reactions is meant to convey the thought that non-orienting reactions may also be classically conditioned and non-adient may also be reinforced. The determiner of reinforcement conditioning is the relative unhabituability of the reinforced reaction and not its general classification. Moreover, it should be made clear that reinforcement conditioning does not extrude the classical mechanism but only dominates it. Feeding reinforces paw-lifting and lever-pressing but also evokes conditioned salivation (Kintsch and Witte, 1962; Konorski and Miller, 1936; Shapiro, 1962; Shapiro and Miller, 1965). Only classical CRs incompatible with the reinforced reaction are eliminated or not manifest at all—e.g., turning the head toward the food instead of lifting the paw, or biting or licking the lever instead of pressing it. Typical classical conditioning does not, however, involve a reinforcement mechanism.

Putting it differently, reinforcement conditioning differs from classical conditioning in two respects: (1) the reaction it modifies is more stable and thus relatively less nondominant, (2) the modification produced includes the classical type and is more effective. The first difference is the hypothesis for the existence of the second; the second, evidence that reinforcement conditioning is a more recent evolutionary acquisition. The differences are expanded in a later section of this chapter and in Chapter 8, but three general propositions are worth mentioning here. (1) It is obvious that one type of conditioning is concerned with forming new connections and the other with preserving the already formed (cf. Ivanov-Smolensky's view that reinforcement is a conditioned conditioning.) (2) There is evolutionary adaptive logic in the evidence that the former is realized earlier. (3) Whereas in nonassociative learning, sensitization evolves as an antithesis of habituation, in associative learning, the relation of reinforcement to classical conditioning is that of a synthesis.

A DYNAMIC INTERRELATIONSHIP AND AN EMENDATION OF "DOMINANCE"

The offered hypothesis espouses further a dynamic and relative conception of what Pavlov and Konorski-Skinner have brought to light, in lieu of a dichotomic and absolute one. Hinde (1966), discussing what he calls "decremental and incremental" practice effects in unlearned behavior—that is, habituation and sensitization—points out that at times the two coexist and interact with each other. And Prechtl (1958), and Siqueland and Lipsitt (1966) demonstrated that in human neonates habituation of head-turning to ipsilateral touches of the mouth region gave rise to contralateral responding—transformation from turning-to to turning-away. Related dynamisms in conditioning may be found in more than a score of Soviet experiments, three of which will be cited:

1. When a slow rhythmic tactile stimulus applied to a dog's foreleg was followed by an electric shock to his hindleg, the animal learned, as might be expected, to flex the latter in response to the stimulation of the former. But when the tactile rhythm was faster, the conditioned flexion transferred to the touched foreleg. The *type* of the conditioned reaction continued to be classical while its *locus* attested to the development of an enhanced *reinforced* rather than *reinforcing* neural—or reaction—center (Bykov and Speransky, 1924). The ambiguous reinforcement may well have been due to the lesser habituability of the faster tactile rhythm.

2. When interoceptively produced vasodilation or vasoconstriction was followed by opposite but equal-magnitude exteroceptively produced vasomotion, the common result was reinforcement of the preceding interoceptive reaction. Yet when a similar exteroceptively produced reaction was similarly followed by an opposite interoceptively evoked one, the former was generally replaced by the latter in classical fashion (Pshonik, 1952). The difference, however, is not an absolute categorization, since both exteroceptively and interoceptively produced changes have long been known to be capable of either type of conditioning. Likewise, while Sheffield in 1965 set forth a proprioceptive view of reinforcement conditioning, Konorski abandoned in 1967 his 1964 position that "the connections involved in instrumental conditioning lead only (or in most part) from the centres of the proprioceptive analyzer to the centres of the motor responses" (p. 171). And there is no doubt that recent evidence of deafferentation and reinforcement conditioning of autonomic reactions, including the GSR, preclude considering proprioception a *sine qua non* for such conditioning. Yet this evidence does by no means counter the present avowal that motor and interoceptive reactions are subject more readily to reinforcement than to classical conditioning and are so because of their relative unhabituability.

3. Vinogradova (1959) paired the sound of a metronome with unavoidable shock in human subjects and tracked the vasomotor reactions to each stimulus—the metronome preceding shock by 10 to 20 seconds —throughout the conditioning. The vasodilative orienting reaction to the metronome was habituated prior to the experiment; yet, with one exception, it recovered at the first conditioning trial and as a rule continued unabated and was even strengthened for a number of trials. In the experimenter's words, "a struggle between the orienting and defense reflexes set

in [in which, however] sooner or later the defense one came out the winner" (p. 121)—that is, the metronome acquired a vasoconstrictive defense reaction. Thus, a reinforcement stage of conditioning preceded a classical one, again suggesting that in the "struggle," the orienting reflex has not been sufficiently habituated. To be sure, another hypothesis lurks here: The orienting reflex being not uncommonly equated with cognitivity, and the subjects college students, the first stage may have been a conditioning of "expectancy." But it obviously was not viable in a psychologic Tolmanite sense, since the biologic shock came out the winner. Likewise, a dynamic interrelationship of the two types of conditioning is in a somewhat different way evident also in the reinforceability of autonomic reactions, which also fits the unhabituability hypothesis.

Viewed differently, the present hypothesis of conditioning accepts Beritoff's doctrine that classical conditioning is mediated by direct connections and enhanced neural action of the modifying reaction, and reinforcement conditioning by reverse connections and enhanced neural action of the modified reaction. My hypothesis, however, sets forth the condition or cause of the reversal—a modified reaction that is relatively unhabituable. And it thereby calls for a significant emendation of Ukhtomsky's concept of dominance: Namely, *not only does the coaction of the dominant and nondominant neural centers enhance the dominant centers, but under certain circumstances, when reinforcement conditioning is effected, it also enhances the nondominant one.* Recent evidence has demonstrated directly the existence of such "corticofugal" dominance and conditioning (see Meshchersky, 1965, 1966, for a summary). Morover, the hypothesis maintains that reverse connections of reinforcement conditioning dominate the direct connections of classical conditioning—that they are, that is, a higher neurobehavioral level. (Limbic reinforcement, and punishment, are discussed in Chapter 8.)

A SCHEMATIC SUMMARY

The main features of what might be called a "new look" at the comparative designs and outcomes of classical and reinforcement conditioning are summarized in Figure 20. Six basic propositions are attested. (1) The modified antecedents in both designs—backward sequences need not be considered here—are complete stimulus-reaction units (s_1-r_1). That is, the antecedent stimulus in the classical design evokes some measurable reaction, even as the antecedent reaction in the reinforcement design is evoked by some existent stimulus. (2) As indicated by larger letters and heavier connecting lines, the modified s_1-R_1 unit in the reinforcement design is less habituable or less nondominant than its classical counterpart. (The dominant unit is of course in both designs the subsequent and modifying S_2-R_2.) (3) A classical s_1-R_2 CR (CR1) is formed in both designs (designated s_1-R_2 in the reinforcement design). (4) An R_1-strength-

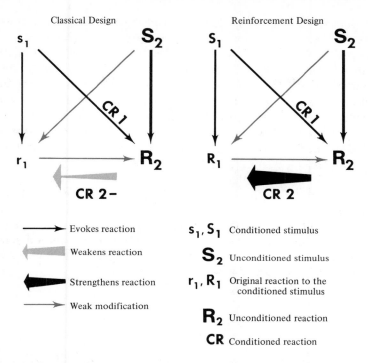

Figure 20 *Collation of classical and reinforcement conditioning.* (Additional explanation in text)

ening reinforcement CR (CR2), which dominates the classical CR when the two are in rivalry, is formed in the reinforcement design. (5) An r_1-weakening CR, best designated CR2–, is formed in the classical design. (6) The S_2-R_2 unit is to some extent itself modified by the s_1-r_1 (or s_1-R_1) unit through: (*a*) the formation of a classical S_2-r_1 (or S_2-R_1) CR and (*b*) the strengthening or weakening of R_2, typically strengthening in the classical and weakening in the reinforcement design.

There is adequate empirical evidence for the existence of all five modifications and even for their synergic, antagonistic, and hierarchic interactions, present enshrinement of one or two of them to the contrary notwithstanding. And note that no attempt has been made here to equate reinforcement conditioning with the genesis of voluntary action, as was done by Kimble in 1966, invoking explanatory concepts of Sechenov and James. One demurrer is that since 1951 more than a score of East and West experiments have proven brainless fish to be full masters of such putative "will" conditioning—which would no doubt have dismayed Sechenov and James and surely Schopenhauer. Early-evolutionary existence of reinforcement conditioning strains also the force of Konorski's (1964) "drive centre" as a *sine qua non* for it. In truth, I have never been too impressed by the neurobehavioral heuristics of the drive concept in general. Hinde's recent statement, "As physiological analysis proceeds, drive constructs cease to be relevant" (1966, p. 147), is a thoughtful prevision. And I am tempted to cite a conclusion which I reached in a 1957 review of 618 Russian experiments on salivary conditioning of dogs: "What correlates with variations in CR-efficacy are [among other things] variations in UR-magnitude, and *it seems to matter little whether these magnitude variations are produced by differences in US-magnitudes, differences in the duration of food deprivation, administration of drugs, bodily injuries, or mere individual differences between animals, or something else*" (Razran, 1957, p. 5; cf. Miller, 1959, pp. 276-280).

Finally, two other germane propositions are in order. (*a*) Skinner's "rate of 'emission' " as the sole gauge of the strength of the reinforcement of R_1 is a methodological shortcoming (Hodos and Valenstein, 1960; Notterman, 1959; Notterman and Mintz, 1965). (*b*) As already indicated, there is now substantial evidence (Premack, 1962, 1963, 1965) for a dominance, R_2/R_1-strength view of reinforcement conditioning which I have advocated for the classical type since 1930.

CHAPTER SIX

Aversive Inhibitory Conditioning (Punishment)—Incomplete Associative Manifestation

BASIC THEORY AND RELEVANT SOVIET DATA

Inhibitory conditioning is considered here a learned yet incomplete type of conditioning. It was defined in Chapter 2 as a "decrement and disappearance of a reaction through an associated antagonistic reaction"—that is, *progressive decrements of a reaction through association with a reaction that inhibits it without formation of another reaction.* In theory, the antagonistic inhibiting reaction might, presumably, be not only aversive but also appetitive—and, indeed, not merely in theory. Protocols of more than a score of Soviet experiments bear out Yerofeyeva's 1912 conclusion that in classical shock-food conditioning "the food reactions inhibit fully the shock reactions *before* conditioning them" (p. 143) even as shock reactions inhibit thus food reactions when the sequence is reversed (neither to be confused with the habituation of orienting reactions in like paradigms occurring *in the course* of conditioning).

These inhibitory-plus-classical-conditioning experiments are, however, relatively few. Experimental evidence on inhibitory conditioning by itself —and there is a substantial mass of it, from headless insects to intact college students—is available only when the inhibiting reaction is aversive. [11]

---

[11] Inhibitory appetitive conditioning is, however, in essence the rationale of Wolpe's (1958) "therapy by reciprocal inhibition." And it interprets well Konorski and Miller's finding that in shock-flexion-food reinforcement conditioning "the So [shock] plays only a subsidiary role" (1937, p. 267)—namely, that the reactions to the shock become inhibited by the *antagonistic* reactions to the food and the basically *nonantagonistic* stimulations of getting into the harness become the effective Sos.

That is, when this conditioning is in essence the equivalent of what is known as "punishment learning" or—with lower animals as subjects—"conditioned inhibition" (Hovey, 1929; McConnell, 1966; Ross, 1965). (Curiously, neither group of experimenters seems to see the identity of their concepts and data.) "Conditioned inhibition," already used in one different sense by Pavlov and in still another by Hull, is a rather infelicitous term. But, despite its evaluative connotation, "punishment" will be used henceforth synonymously with "aversive inhibitory conditioning."

American experimenters and theorists of operant behavior define aversive reactions (or stimuli) in terms of their learning consequences—strengthening antecedent operants through termination, and weakening them through activation. Soviet scientists have, however, also explored the physiological properties of such reactions. Only electric shocks of considerable intensity and reactions conditioned to them have, for instance, been shown to produce in subjects "defensive-type" (i.e., "aversive-type") vasomotor changes, low-intensity shocks entailing "orienting" vasomotion (Sokolov, 1958a; Vinogradova, 1959, 1961). Moreover, Soviet data suggest some modulation of our views that the direct relation between intensity of aversive stimuli and extent of their decremental effects is wholly monotonic (Azrin and Holz, 1966; Solomon, 1964). Fedotov (1954) found that electric shocks of long duration and high intensity brought about increases as well as decreases in the conditioned salivation of three dogs—sixteen instances of the former, seventeen of the latter. And he earlier demonstrated (1950a, 1950b, 1951) like results with identical "punishment" of the patellar reflexes of three other dogs. Such high-value shocks, the Russians maintain, may not only inhibit the neural center of the "punished" reaction but may, through irradiation, raise its excitability.

Another systematic Soviet finding is that shocks of moderate intensity inhibit much more the motor components (licking, turning toward, etc.) and even the salivation of food conditioning than they do comparable components (spitting, turning-away, etc.) and salivation of acid-based conditioning, which in turn are inhibited to an extent by food conditioning (Konradi, 1932; Marukhanyan, 1954; Mikhelson and Yurman, 1929). That is to say: *Inhibitory conditioning is a function of not only the autochthonous characteristics of the inhibiting and inhibited reac-*

Skinner's statement that this "case comes under Type R only when the correlation with *So* is broken up" and that the "strong respondent (shock-flexion) . . . brings out at the same time the operant (*s*-R), which sums with it" (1937, p. 276) leaves unanswered questions. *Why* is the correlation with *So* broken up? Just how does an "unseen" *s* of an operant sum with a "strong" *S* of a respondent? And why must Type R wait for a total demise of Type S? The appetitive-inhibition account applies obviously to only a very special case of reinforcement conditioning; but it is, in general, in line with the unhabituability hypothesis. There is need to replicate in American laboratories the shock-food (and food-shock) CR experiments of both Yerofeyeva's classical and Konorski's reinforcement types—above all, to determine the differential parameters of the types.

tions but also of the specific degree of their neurobehavioral antagonism— not just aversion versus appetition or negative versus positive affect. And we might also heed Sereysky's 1946 assessment that "shock stimulation affects primarily the diencephalon and not the cortex" (p. 240) in light of data that it decreases innate reactions more consistently than learned behavior (cf. Solomon's quandary, 1964, p. 241).

Aversive inhibitory conditioning may be demarcated further by comparing it to aversive (defense) classical conditioning, reinforcement conditioning, and habituation. Like habituation, it produces decremental changes in organisms' reaction repertories through practice, including of course one-trial practice. Its effects are, however, much faster and much more universal, and—contrary to some assertions—may well be more permanent. An earlier statement that "aversive inhibitory conditioning is nature's way par excellence of teaching [organisms] . . . what not to do" is well warranted in light of present-day total evidence. Compare Azrin and Holz: "Indeed, punishment appears to be potentially more effective than other procedures for weakening a response" (1966, p. 436). Aversive inhibitory conditioning differs, on the other hand, from aversive classical conditioning, first, in being limited to an interaction of antagonistic reactions, and, second, in effecting, as it were, only a prodromal stage of the classical variety: the modified reaction is decreased but not replaced by the modifying one.

A modicum of historical perspective is needed to set the relation of inhibitory to reinforcement conditioning. In Herbert Spencer's and Alexander Bain's nineteenth-century pain-pleasure psychology of learning and in Thorndike's 1913 to 1931 conception of "satisfiers" *and* "annoyers," "punishment" was firmly held to be an equal, or symmetrical, opposite of "reward." But, then, in 1931, Thorndike halved his "law of effect" to avow that "annoyance" or punishment is not true learning. Skinner in 1938 and Estes in 1944 reavowed this. As late as 1953, Skinner's thesis was that punishment is but "a temporary suppression of behavior . . . in agreement with Freud's discovery of the surviving activity of what he called repressed wishes" (p. 184). *Yet present-day American students of the field think quite differently.* Solomon's 1964 statement reads: "The popularized Skinnerian position concerning the inadequacy of punishment in suppressing *instrumental* behavior is, if correct at all, only conditionally correct" (p. 252). And the Azrin and Holz 1966 review of the operant area in the field *contravenes altogether the nonlearning punishment credos of the later-Thorndike and Skinner and Estes*—and restores to it, in fact, its traditional and early-Thorndike status as an "equal opposite" of reward.

ESSENTIALS RESTATED

The present view of punishment as aversive inhibitory conditioning does not of course deny that it is bona fide learning. But neither does it accord it the role of an *equal* opposite of reinforcement or reward learning. As already indicated, such conditioning or punishment learning is posited here as an incomplete type of associative learning, produced by association but not in essence producing any new association. That is, it is a type of learning that has not reached the full associative level of classical conditioning, whereas typical reinforcement conditioning is considered to have gone beyond it, subsuming and dominating classical conditioning.

The empirical argument (evidence is given in a later section) for the evolutionary antiquity of inhibitory conditioning is immanent in (1) its ready manifestation in lowest animals in which classical conditioning is difficult or even impossible to obtain and (2) its coming into being before the latter in special experiments in higher animals. A pure ratiocinative thesis might also be invoked, however. The weakening of the modified reaction in inhibitory conditioning is an *inevitable* outcome of the neurobehavioral antagonism of its interacting reactions. But there is no such inevitability in the reaction-interactions of the learnings, each in its own way, of classical and reinforcement conditioning. A postulate that the associative learning of inhibitory conditioning is the simplest of the three types of conditioning in underlying mechanism, the oldest in evolutionary advent, and nonetheless the most variable in specific effects, packs a lot of logic.

Nor does this view, as already indicated, stake the effects of punishment on *general* aversion, catechized as what-it-does and not what-it-is and hence hardly more basic than traditional "annoyance" and "negative affect" or "pain." What is offered, instead, is: *Punishment is a specific and complex neurobehavioral interaction of antagonistic inhibiting and inhibited reactions akin to traditional neurophysiological inhibition not just in resultant decremental effects but in underlying mechanisms.* Yet punishment is, obviously, a *special* development of that inhibition. Whereas the inhibition of Sherrington, Vvedensky, Sechenov, and Weber, is *nonlearning* or terminal, that of punishment clearly possesses a *learning* character. And the learning, unlike that in Pavlov's "external inhibition," is primarily *cumulative and not habituatory,* the difference involving both quantitative stimulus-intensity parameters and qualitative parameters varying with the innate natures of the interacting reactions. A very loud noise is as a rule a cumulative "punisher," a less loud one, a habituatory "external inhibitor." An electric shock at *low* intensities is an "inhibitor," not a "punisher." And in either case the outcome is also a function of the nature of the "punished" or "externally inhibited" reaction (cf. the simpler divide between habituation and sensitization in Chapter 4).

A hypothetical account of the distinction between waxing punishment and waning external inhibition will also be ventured. In "punishment," either the inhibiting reaction is relatively unhabituable or its habituation is less than the inhibition which it produces. Accordingly, its inhibitory effects increase with subsequent trials. In "external inhibition," the reverse is true. The extent of the habituation of the inhibiting reaction may exceed the inhibition of the inhibited one and its effect be thereby decreased. The hypothess, in line with simple logic, is, of course, readily testable. And, viewing punishment as an outright integral of inhibition as such adds to the operational similarity of the two the advantage of letting the former make the most of the basic neurophysiology of the latter and pursue like analysis of its own operation (cf. Hoyle, 1965).

A word should be said also about incremental or facilitatory effects of punishment. Such "exceptions" become manifest under three different circumstances: (1) when there is much overlapping between the innate reactions to the stimuli of the punishing and punished reactions; (2) when the punishing reaction is nondominant either because of the low intensity of its effective stimulus or because it antecedes the punished reaction; (3) when the punishment decrements in one trial are followed by increments in the succeeding trial, known in the United States as "contrast" (Azrin and Holz, 1966; Brethower and Reynolds, 1962; Rachlin, 1966) but readily subsumed under Pavlov's old staple of "positive induction" (see above). The last two manifestations need no enlargement here in light of related prior discussions, except to mention the historical fact that as early as 1864 Schiff noted that mild pains increased human heart action while severe ones decreased it, which Asp in 1867 replicated with nociceptive stimulation of animals. The first disclosure calls, however, for a specific illustration.

Russian experiments have for years shown that electric shocks elicit unconditioned salivation in men and animals (Stol'nikov, 1875-1876; Pavlov, 1877; Ostrogorsky, 1894; Frolov, 1951; Florovsky, 1917; Serebrinnikov, 1939a; and others). And two of them (Florovsky, 1917; Serebrinnikov, 1939a) further found, as might be expected, that such shocks increase unconditioned salivation—in contrast to their effects when the salivation is conditioned. There are, to be sure, other reactions elicited by both aversive and nonaversive stimuli producing such increments through punishment. But these are, obviously, summations of like reactions and not facilitations by heterogeneous ones. Interestingly, except for evacuation, other digestive reactions—gastric, intestinal, pancreatic, and biliary secretions, and peristaltic movements—are readily "inhibited" by shock and other aversive stimulations and thus are punishable in conventional manner (Abuladze, 1924; Gayet and Guillaummie, 1933; Serebrinnikov, 1932a, 1932b, 1939b, 1939c—to mention but a few of the large number of available references).

In other words, none of the three types of incremental effects of punishment contravenes the present view. The first two, indeed, corroborate it, stressing the requisites, respectively: (1) neurobehavioral antagonism between the punishing and punished reactions, and (2) dominance of the punishing reaction over the one punished. And the third, disclosing increments subsequent to decrements—reported for over a half a century by Pavlovians and recently in a number of Western studies (Lipsitt and Kaye,

1964; Miller and Senf, 1966; Prechtl, 1958, 1965)—is, obviously, a general behavioral alteration wider than any specific conception of punishment.

VARIETIES OF PUNISHED INNATE REACTIONS

To get at the basis of the punishment phenomenon, it is necessary to begin the analysis with its effects on innate reactions, particularly in lower animals. In punishment of learned and even innate reactions in higher animals, manifestations of idiopathic aversive inhibitory conditioning is complicated by (1) ready formation of classical aversive conditioning and by (2) rising manifolds of alternate or competing reactions, either of which obscures its core mechanism. An almost complete evolutionary range of experiments on innate punished reactions has long been available and the number is increasing.

Leg Position in Headless Locusts and Cockroaches

This pioneer experiment was reported by Horridge (1962a, 1962b, 1965), who used 200 insects in pairs of experimental and control sub-

Figure 21 *Inhibitory conditioning of two headless locusts.* In the upper panel, the experimental animal to the left (P) was shocked whenever its leg extended below the surface of a saline solution, while the control animal (R), connected in series to the stimulator, was shocked at random. Note that only the experimental animal learned to keep its leg above the set point. In the lower panel, both animals, connected in parallel to the stimulator, were rendered experimental and both were shocked whenever their legs extended beyond the set point. Note that here both learned to keep their legs above the set position. (From Horridge, 1962b)

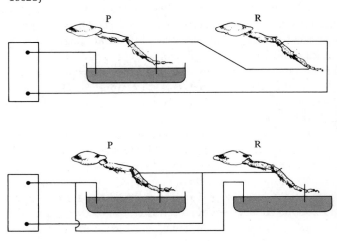

jects. The experimental insects, suspended over an electrifiable saline solution, received by means of a silver wire an electric shock to the tarsus of
one leg for several milliseconds every one to two minutes whenever the leg
was extended beyond a set point; the control insects, connected in series
to the stimulator, were shocked irrespective of leg position. After 30 to
45 minutes of training, the animals were connected in parallel, and each
member of the pair was shocked whenever its leg extended beyond the set
position.

The results for one pair are presented in Figure 21, from which it may
be seen that in the first part of the experiment only the experimental insect—designated P (*positional*) in the diagram—learned to keep its
shocked leg above the set point, but that in the second part both did
(the control insect is marked R, *random*). The differences between numbers of shocks received—i.e., errors made—by the animals in all the pairs
in the second part of the experiment are stated to have been significant
at p <.01. "Of 200 animals tested in groups of 20, about 70 per cent
behave in this way, 10-20 per cent hold up their leg for a period of up to
5 min. after receiving one or two shocks, and 15-25 per cent behave un-
satisfactorily and may never change their behavior" (1962b, p. 697). And
in a later report, the experimenter adds that "after training, the animals can
be left without stimulation for several hours and when retested they still
perform better than naive animals" (1965, p. 165).

Figure 22 *Inhibitory conditioning of six headless cockroaches with only
one prothoracic leg in which the appropriate ganglia were wholly isolated
from the insects' central nervous systems. The left-hand graph shows the
progressive decrease of shocks—i.e., errors the trained animals made
whenever they extended their legs beyond the set point. The right-hand
graph demonstrates the difference between the negligible number of
shocks or errors made by the previously trained group—called the "positional" group—and that made by a "random" group of six animals with
no prior training. (From Eisenstein and Cohen, 1965)*

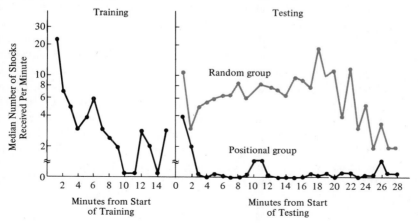

Eisenstein and Cohen (1965) replicated Horridge's findings with the left prothoracic legs of 6 experimental and 6 control headless cockroaches in which the appropriate ganglia were wholly isolated from the insects' central nervous systems. Clear-cut data on progressive punishment learning in the experimental group and wide subsequent differences between it (the "positional" group) and the control ("random") group are presented in Figure 22. Eisenstein and Cohen also found that when in "an additional group of animals the prothoracic ganglion was removed [with only] the effects of the shock on the peripheral neuromuscular apparatus itself. . . . The response was stereotyped [and] no P-R [experimental-control] difference was obtained" (p. 108). Finally, there is Hoyle's (1965) electrophysiological analysis of Horridge's experiments in three headless locusts and his identification of the punishment learning with three- to fourfold increases in the background action-potential frequencies of the insects' coxal adductor muscles, which "pull the rear, inner rim of the coxa towards the body and slightly upwards [and] the concerted action of these muscles raises the whole leg" (p. 205).

Body Extension in Hydra

Zubkov and Polikarpov (1951) placed a number of *Hydra vulgaris Pall* in partially filled concave watchglasses 5 millimeters from the water's edge, thus inhibiting in part the animals' usual circumferential body extensions. After the animals had been in such a position for 2 hours and 34 minutes and had changed radically the pattern of their extensions in number, duration, and length, water was added and a normal environment restored. But it took the hydra 3 to 4 hours to resume their normal extensions. The aversive inhibition persisted. The results are presented in Figure 23.

Intake of Inedibles

In 1907, Fleure and Walton observed the following. When pieces of filter paper were placed every 24 hours on one of the tentacles of *Actiniae* or *Tealia,* they were "carried to the animals' mouths, very often swallowed, to be ejected after a longer or shorter period. . . After 2 to 5 days, the fragment is no longer swallowed and, in about another two days, the tentacles will no longer take hold of it" (p. 215). Ross (1965) was unable to repeat the finding: his *Actiniae,* to begin with, would "not accept filter paper at all" (p. 45). But there can be no doubt, of course, that the rejection of inedibles is a most prevalent manifestation of aversive inhibitory conditioning in the animal kingdom (Buytendijk, 1918a, 1918b, Cott, 1936, in toads; Haecker, 1912, in axolotls; Schaeffer, 1911, in frogs; Wells, 1965, and Wells and Wells, 1956, in octopuses [Figure 9]; and others).

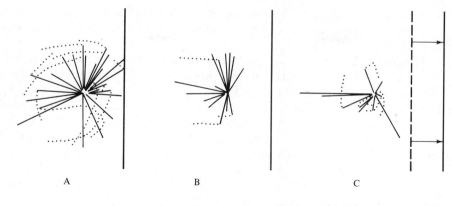

Figure 23 *Sample of inhibitory conditioning of circumferential body extensions of hydra* (vulgaris Pall), *placed in partially-filled concave watchglasses 5 millimeters from the water's edge.* A—forced inhibitions of extensions upon reaching the edge, in the first 67 minutes; B—evidence of conditioning in inhibitions occurring before the edge is reached, in the next 97 minutes; C—persistence of inhibitions during 77 minutes after the water level is raised and a normal circumferential environment restored. Vertical line in each case represents the water's edge. Dotted lines—hydra's extensions changed direction. At left —schematic diagram of hydra in water in watchglass, looking down. (After Zubkov and Polikarpov, 1951)

Swimming of Coelenterates (Stomphia Coccinea) Toward Starfish (Dermasterias Imbricata)

Ross (1965) discovered that these particular coelenterates possess a species-specific response of leaving their substratum and swimming toward this particular starfish, while mechanical prodding of their base causes them to contract down onto their substratum. The swimming could be readily evoked, it had been found earlier (Ross and Sutton, 1964), by touching one of the coelenterates' tentacles with a pipe cleaner that had been rubbed on the aboral surfaces of the starfish. Ross had thus applied the starfish materials to the *Stomphiae's* tentacles 2 seconds before prodding their bases with appropriate discs and found that after 5 days of experimentation and 13 to 32 paired trials, the swimming was aversively inhibited in all 8 animals when the starfish materials alone were administered. One animal continued to manifest the aversive inhibition for 13 trials over a period of 108 hours, the range of the 7 remaining animals being 2 to 12 trials, with a median of 7, and a high correlation between the numbers of training and successful testing trials. Two control coelenterates

—one receiving in the 5 experimental days 35 applications of the starfish material and the other 28 mechanical prods—showed no significant reaction changes.

Moreover—and this is of particular importance—*none of the eight Stomphiae could be conditioned to swim by repeated applications to its tentacles of a pipe cleaner with an extract of starfish Pecten or the starfish Henricea prior to administration of the adequate unconditioned Dermasterias stimulus.* The *Stomphiae* responded to the to-be-conditioned stimuli by holding them with their tentacles but failed to effect thereby a classical-conditioning association. Other attempts by Ross to condition coelenterates *classically* likewise failed. *And he thus proved specifically that classical conditioning is a higher-evolutionary level of learning than is aversive inhibitory conditioning, i.e., punishment.*

Photokinesis in Marine Flatworms and Negative Phototropisms in Cockroaches

Hovey (1929) experimented with aversive inhibitory conditioning of photokinetic reactions of 17 polyclad flatworms *(Leptoplana)* exposed to a strong light 25 times for 5 minutes, at intervals of 25 minutes. The moment the worms, kept quiescent in a darkened finger bowl, began to move in response to the light, they were stopped by contact with a rounded matchstick. A mean of 100 contacts were needed to keep the animals still in the first 5 minutes, whereas in the last exposures "some individuals would lie still without being once touched for one or more exposures in succession; others remained quiet as a result of contact stimulation only once or twice during an exposure" (pp. 325-326). On the 26th exposure, 10 hours later, the acquired aversive inhibition persisted to the extent of requiring only 20 contacts to be effected, while in the 27th through 30th exposures the number required was less than 10. A control group of 12 animals stimulated only with the strong light showed no habituation to speak of, and another group of 10 animals whose snout tips were cut off performed as well as the experimental group, proving that snout injury was not a factor in the performance. When the cephalic ganglia of 6 of the worms were removed, the animals took fewer match contacts to aversively inhibit their movements to the strong light, but there was absolutely no evidence of learned reduction in successive 5-minute exposures. The results of the main experimental group are presented in Figure 24.

Szymanski (1912) used the "punishment method" of an electric shock to inhibit the innate reactions of 10 cockroaches (male larvae of *Peliplaneta orientalis L.*) to move to the dark part of their vivarium box. The insects were placed in the light part of the box and shocked whenever they entered the dark part. Ten successive turnings back from the dark portion without the shock administration served as the criterion of learning, and the number of shocks to attain it ranged from 16 to 118. Five of the 10

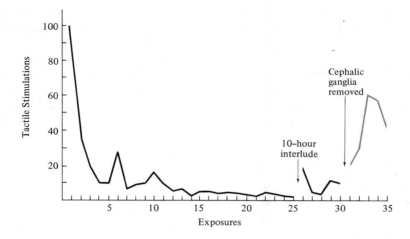

Figure 24 *Inhibitory conditioning of photokinesis in six polyclad flatworms* (Leptoplana) *exposed to a strong light for 5 minutes at intervals of 25 minutes.* The animals were touched and stopped by a rounded matchstick when they began to move in response to the light. In the first 5-minute exposure, a mean of 100 contacts were needed to keep the animals still, while in the last exposures they remained quiet in response to the light either "with no contacts at all or with only one or two." A control group of 12 animals stimulated only with the strong light showed no habituation; another group of 10 animals, whose snout tips were cut off, performed as well as the experimental group, proving that snout injury was not a factor. Curves to the right—no learned inhibitory conditioning in 6 worms whose cephalic ganglia were removed. (From Hovey, 1929)

animals were tested for retention of their learning by the "savings method," 1 to 9 days after their last experimental session. The results, comparing relearning and original learning in terms of the stated criterion, for different animals were: 17 vs. 118 after 1 day, 12 vs. 37 after 2, 4 vs. 23 after 3, 5 vs. 16 after 6, and 7 vs. 37 shocks after 9 days—surely a high degree of retention. And it should be noted that, while turning back might be interpreted as an aversive *classical* CR, it seems more logical to consider it a natural consequent of the learned inhibition. (Compare with neonates' contralateral head-turning after ipsilateral habituation.)

Gill Membrane Extension in Fish

Adler and Hogan (1963) investigated the effects of electric-shock punishment on gill membrane extensions in four male Siamese fighting fish *(Betta splendens).* The extensions, produced by presenting for a maximum of 120 seconds mirror images of live fish, were followed by strong 0.5-second shocks at 10-minute intervals until the fish failed to respond in three consecutive 120-second trials. Each fish had a matched control that was exposed to the extension stimulus the same number of times and for the same duration and received the same number of identical *random* shocks. All fish decreased their extension responses. But while all control fish recovered within 6 hours or less, no experimental fish recovered in less than 12 hours. Interestingly, the experimenters succeeded also in conditioning classically the extension response to a mild electric shock in 5 fish after 10 to 50 trials, *but were unable to strengthen it through reinforcement.*

Eating in Frogs, Dogs, Cats, and Monkeys

In 1911, Schaeffer reported that two *"Rana clamata* refused all food for three days after a single experience with an electric shock [while eating]" (p. 323) and that "earthworms [one was paired with electric shock] were not eaten for seven days" (p. 334). It remained, however, for Masserman (1964), Gantt (1944), Lichtenstein (1950), and Masserman and Prechtl (1953)—following earlier leads in Pavlov's laboratory—to prove the drastic effects of electric shocks on the eating behavior of cats, dogs, and spider monkeys. Space permits summarizing only the Lichtenstein experiment. But it should be mentioned that one of Masserman's cats "was subjected to only two grid-shocks at feeding, yet for sixteen days thereafter refused to feed from the open food box" (p. 68) and that a large number of his cats and two dogs developed "neurotic" behavior of differing degrees, including food refusal, through administering "grid-shocks and air-blasts at the moment of feeding" (p. 66); that in one of Gantt's neurotic dogs, Nick, "the nervous symptoms [including food refusal] have continued for 10 years without the original conflict [with] spread to the urinary and sexual systems . . . several years after the conflict" (p. 51); and that Masserman and Prechtl obtained related results with presentations of a toy snake to seven spider monkeys.

The 13 dogs in Lichtenstein's experiment—trained first to eat in a conditioning stock—were fed 20 pellets each experimental session, at intervals of 20 to 60 seconds. A shock of 85 volts was delivered for 2 seconds to the right forepaws of 10 dogs while they were eating and to the other 3 dogs before they ate. Refusal to eat in the conditioning stock during three consecutive sessions following the last in which the shock was applied (sessions on alternate days) was the criterion for the aversive inhibitory conditioning. It was attained after 1 to 3 shocks in the animals which were shocked while eating, and after 23 to 29 shocks in those shocked before eating. Moreover, one dog refused to eat pellets even in its own cage, and two refused for a number of weeks meat placed in the food box of the conditioning stock.

Copulation in Male Rats and Monkeys

Beach and his associates (1956) experimented with the effect of electric-shock punishment on the copulation of 19 rats previously tested for sexual vigor with receptive females. The shock was delivered at the moment the male clasped the female with his forelimbs; the animals were divided into two groups—10 rats in one group which received a "high" shock of 380 volts and 9 in another were first shocked with 100 volts ("low") and were later shifted to the high shock. The low shock had little effect on the animals' sex behavior, but the high shock produced in all animals "sexual inhibition"—no attempt to mount a receptive female in two successive tests—after a mean of 52.2 shocks in one group and 56.3 in the other. A majority of the rats recovered their normal sex capacity in 12 to 30 days. Six who did not recover spontaneously were, interestingly, restored to normal sex action after the application of 12 electroconvulsive shocks. Throughout the experiment records were kept not only of mountings but also of extent of copulations (intromission and ejaculation). These results are presented in Figure 25. And we should add the copulation inhibition of Gantt's dog, Nick, mentioned earlier.

Entering a Darkened Hole by Mice

Essman and Alperin (1964) divided 75 mice into an experimental group of 35 and a control group of 27. In both groups, each mouse was

Figure 25 *Inhibitory conditioning of copulation in 19 male rats with receptive females after a "low shock" of 100 volts and a "high shock" of 380 volts were delivered repeatedly the moment the male clasped the female with his forelimbs. N—normal pre-experimental behavior; 1 and 3—results of first and third experimental tests; L—last test in which mounting occurred. Inhibition was considered complete when the male made no attempt to mount a receptive female in two successive tests. (From Beach, Conovitz, Steinberg, and Goldstein, 1956; additional information in text.)*

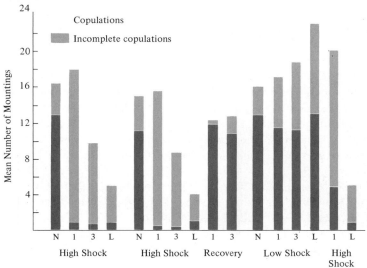

placed on an enclosed lighted platform with a darkened 4-centimeter hole in the front panel; both groups took a median of 1 to 2 seconds to enter the hole in the single training trial. However, the experimental animals received a 2-milliamp 0.5-second shock immediately after entering. And now, when the two groups were retested after 24 hours in their home cages, 24 of the experimental animals stayed on the platform for 20 seconds—at which time they were removed—and the latencies of another 8 were considerably longer than the median latency of the control group, which remained unchanged. The statistical difference between the latencies of the two groups was significant at $p < .001$.

Patellar, Plantar, and Pancreatic Reflexes in Dogs

It was mentioned earlier that Fedotov (1950a, 1950b, 1951) noted that strong and lasting (30-second) electric shocks brought about both decrements and increments in the patellar reflexes of three dogs—specifically, decrements followed by increments, which the Russians call "phasic changes." Bobrova's (1959) data on the effects of 67 exteroceptive and 56 interoceptive shock stimulations on the plantar reflexes of four dogs were largely similar, except that in her study the exteroceptive shocks produced more decrements and the interoceptive more increments. The effect differences between the two loci of stimulations—hip in one case, interior of gastrum in the other—might, on the face of it, be attributed to differences in shock thresholds. But in view of the experimenter's report that the animals' recorded general behavior disturbances in response to the shocks were alike, what comes to mind is the consideration that interoceptive stimulation involves more generalized body reactions than does exteroceptive (Razran, 1965b).

Serebrinnikov's (1932a) results, with electric-shock influences on the pancreatic secretions of a dog evoked by feeding it 80 cubic centimeters of sunflower-seed oil, were likewise deviant. While for 5 minutes after its application the shock did completely inhibit the secretion, and its total for 3 hours in the first test was no more than 45 per cent of the norm, later tests showed its effect to be habituatory and even incremental rather than cumulatively decremental. Russian experiments on inhibitory influences of shock and related aversive stimulation on other digestive secretions (except salivation, discussed earlier) follow in the main the course of Serebrinnikov's study. The Russians have, however, for years continued to induce experimental neuroses and food refusal in dogs through shock and other aversive stimulation during normal functioning and eating (Borukayev, 1961; L. N. Fedorov, 1927; V. K. Fedorov, 1933; Fedorov and Yakovleva, 1949; Gakel, 1960; Grigoryan, 1954; Guseva, 1956; Kaminsky, 1939; Kryazhev, 1945; Kupalov, 1941, 1960; Lekishvili, 1954; Petrova, 1914, 1926, 1939; Suvorov, 1962a, 1962b; Yerofeyeva, 1921; Zakharzhevsky, 1960; Zalmanzon, 1929b; and others). And Pavlov's statement that the 1924 Leningrad flood, from which his dogs were saved only with difficulty, "resulted in that one dog refused to take food offered in customary manner [and he was] by no means an exception" is, I assume, well known (1926b, p. 1016; 1928b, pp. 364, 366; also 1927a, pp. 272-273; 1927b, pp. 313-314; and Speransky, 1927).

PUNISHED INNATE REACTIONS: GENERALIZATIONS OF RESULTS

The cited samples of experiments have brought to light, it is felt, the essence of the mechanism of aversive inhibitory conditioning or punishment at its very base. Enumeration of its leading characteristics is in order.

1. Punishment is effective through almost the entire animal kingdom, from coelenterates to monkeys and, of course, men. (Its existence in protozoa, unlike that of habituation, is controversial, and the argument will not be considered here.)

2. Its effectiveness may be very fast and in vertebrates apparently independent of the evolutionary position of the organism involved. One or two administrations of electrical shock while eating led in some cases to self-starvation in frogs, cats, dogs, and monkeys alike.

3. However, at the lower end of the evolutionary scale—coelenterates, flatworms, and cockroaches—and in such particular preparations as headless insects and isolated ganglia, and with special reactions such as breaking up tropisms in cockroaches, the punishment generally takes a considerable number of trials to be well effected, yielding typical acquisition learning curves.

4. Patellar and plantar reflexes and digestive secretions in dogs do not, according to Soviet results, follow the regular course of shock-induced punishment; instead, increments alternate with or follow decrements, and effects are habituatory rather than cumulative.

5. Yet, with only the last exception, there is no doubt that the punishment phenomenon is long-lasting in ascending degrees: from marine flatworms to spider monkeys and from cockroaches to cats. Even Horridge's headless locusts retained their punishment for "several hours."

6. The intensity of the punishing reaction and its subsequence to the punished one appear to be the two leading quantitative parameters of the efficacy of the phenomenon. Shock intensity of 100 volts produced practically no decrements in rats' sex behavior, whereas a shock of 380 volts inhibited it completely for 12 to 30 days. Dogs shocked *while eating* refused food after 1 to 3 trials; those shocked *before* eating required 23 to 29 trials.

7. The nature of the punished or inhibited reaction is apparently also a significant determinant of the progression of the punishment. Copulation in rats took means of 52.2 and 56.3 shocks of 380 volts to be inhibited, whereas Lichtenstein inhibited eating in his dogs with only 85 volts in several trials.

SYSTEMATIC IMPORT

The evidence of innate punishment of innate reactions is by itself almost sufficient to offer a full systematic account of the core operation of the phenomenon. It bears out the theoretical views of the first two sections of the chapter and is not at variance with basic present-day knowledge in the much larger area of the effects of innate and learned punishment on learned behavior. Indeed, since this smaller-area evidence is least (if at all) complicated by coaction of other learning mechanisms, it guards against recourse to them when none is needed.

It is clear that the evidence as a whole supports the view that punishment learning: (*a*) is the most universal and basically also the most effective type of conditioning, operative in ascending degrees throughout the metazoic kingdom and asymptotic early in the vertebrate subphylum, and (*b*) is *sui generis,* an associative mechanism of learning what not to do that is evolutionarily and functionally prior to classical and reinforcement conditioning. And the evidence attests to the regrettable fact that American systematic students of punishment have failed—no doubt because of conceptual engrossment in the two conventional CR types—to consider its manifestation at the lowest, even the lower, end of the evolutionary scale (no such citations in Solomon, 1964, and Azrin and Holz, 1966).

More specifically, it is maintained here that punishment learning is a learned inhibition and not a learned avoidance or "passive avoidance." Avoidance in general is not a term of objective substance but of subjective appeal, and with respect to punishment it lacks even that. When the gill membranes of fighting fish stop expanding, do they avoid shock or inhibit movement? Likewise, are flatworms *avoiding* a light when they merely cease responding to it? And is "avoidance" really applicable to learned changes of leg position in headless cockroaches in which "the appropriate ganglia were wholly isolated from the insects' central nervous system"? Another example of concepts reflecting theorists' thoughts rather than organisms' actions, and failure to consider learning in lower animals! Note, however, that Hovey wrote of his flatworms' "acquirement of conditioned inhibition to photokinesis" (1929, p. 325), and that the title of Lichtenstein's experiment is "The Production of Feeding Inhibition in Dogs," and that of Beach et al. (1956), "Experimental Inhibition . . . of Mating Behavior."

PUNISHMENT OF LEARNED BEHAVIOR:
PRIMARY PARAMETERS

Most Soviet evidence in the area is concerned with the much-studied "experimental neurosis," which, since it is more general and ramified in scope, might better be considered in the next chapter. American studies, however, are primarily concerned with the specific role of punishment in variegated yet normal action of reinforced behavior and thus are directly relevant. Yet their number is too large to permit consideration of more than six leading empirical generalizations, to which a seventh derived from Soviet data will be added.

Intensity of the Punishing Reaction

A large number of studies (Appel, 1963; Appel and Peterson, 1965; Azrin, 1958, 1959, 1960a, 1960b); Filby and Appel, 1966; Hake and Azrin, 1963; Karsh, 1962; Solomon and Wynne, 1954; and others) has brought home the readily understood direct variation of the effects of punishment with the intensity of the punishing reaction. Using rates of bar-pressing in rats and monkeys and of pecking in pigeons and milliamp variations of shock intensity, Appel and Peterson have indeed fitted their data to the exponential equation of $R_I = R_o e^{-5.16I}$ where R_I is the emission rate of the punished reaction at specific milliamp intensity and R_o, the prior unpunished rate. There is, however, no American evidence to match Soviet data showing that high-shock intensities may in some cases *increase* punished reactions through "irradiation" and that such increases may occur when a nonaversive reaction, for instance, *unconditioned salivation,* is to some extent also evoked by shock. On the other hand, mild intensities of shock have been found to *strengthen* punished reactions (Karsh, 1962; Kovach and Hess, 1963; and others). Moreover, there is a substantial body of American findings (Azrin, Holz, and Hake, 1963); Brethower and Reynolds, 1962; Hake and Azrin, 1963; Masserman, 1964; Miller, 1960; and others) showing that *gradual* increases of shock intensity reduces punishment value and *sudden* increases enhance it; this the Russians have not investigated, but it could be well ascribed to, respectively, shock habituation and the special power of sudden stimuli—both intrinsic Soviet concerns.

Subsequence of the Punishing Reaction

This parameter, evident in Lichtenstein's study of punished innate reactions and differences between classical conditioning data when shock precedes food and when the sequence is reversed in a number of Soviet experiments, has been fully borne out in punishment of a variety of learned behaviors—it is, indeed, the very technique of punishing *operant* learning. A significant, although complex enterprise would be a comprehensive quantitative collation and interrelation of the potencies of the reaction-intensity and reaction-subsequence parameters by holding one constant and varying the other, which so far the Russians have attempted in only a most general way (Varga, 1955; Lyan-Chi-an, 1959, 1962a, 1962b, 1962c; Asratyan, 1961b, 1969). It should be noted, however, that subsequence of the punishing reaction does not invariably yield punishment.

When Masserman's cat fully enjoyed her food, a mild shock presented during the eating became not a punisher but a CS to the eating. And Kovach and Hess (1963) conclude that "the performance of following [in chicks] is approximately an inverted U [function] of the neural activity associated with the administration of the painful stimulaton" (p. 461). Similar Soviet data could be cited.

Immediacy of Punishment

Here available data seem to segregate punishment from other kinds of learned modifications in suggesting that it may be effective even when delivered considerably after the punished reaction (Estes, 1944; Hunt and Brady, 1955). Azrin (1956) has, however, found that when the delivery was immediate the punished "responses were reduced indefinitely and often completely whereas non-immediate delivery entailed quick recovery." But he, too, found little difference among deliveries during the first hour, which is surprising. The evidence is very sparse, and control of punishing-punished interaction in the prepunished period is difficult and complex. Much more experimentation is needed to settle the operation of this parameter, including the use of lower animals. *And of course there is the possibility of a pseudoconditioning mechanism.*

Retention and Forgetting of Effects

Recent evidence, contrary to earlier findings, has demonstrated that the retention may be very long-lasting and that its duration varies directly with the intensity of the punishing reaction (Appel, 1961; Azrin, 1960b; Filby and Appel, 1966; Masserman, 1964; Storms, Boroczi, and Broen, 1962; and others). But of course the punished reaction recovers in time—that is, the effects, like those of any other learning, are forgotten.

Generalization and Discrimination

Several experimenters (Azrin, 1956; Dinsmoor, 1952; Honig and Slivka, 1964) have disclosed that the generalization of the decrement of a punished reaction to related nonpunished ones is quite temporary and commonly followed by an incremental change in the "safe period." More recently, however, a generalization that "endured for ten days" was reported (Azrin and Holz, 1966), which by itself does not negate the consideration that the underlying mechanism of the generalization of punishment may be different from that of classical and reinforcement conditioning. On the other hand, it is quite clear that whenever an organism reduces or ceases responding through punishment to some stimulus, it learns *ipso facto* to discriminate between stimuli. "Orderly discrimination gradients . . . during recovery from punishment" were thus reported by Honig (1966b) in pigeons, and Ayllon and Azrin (1966) demonstrated "punishment as a discriminative stimulus and conditioned reinforcer in human patients."

Schedules of Punishment

Azrin, Holz, and Hake (1963) found that with fixed ratios the frequency of punished reactions was a direct function of the ratios, and that continuous punishment produced the greatest effect, even as DeArmond (1966) concluded that "continuous punishment suppressed the fixed ratio performance more than did punishment of the first response" (p. 327). Dardano and Sauerbrunn (1964) brought out the significance of the location of the punishment in the ratios: "punishment of the 25th response in a 1:50 ratio disrupted responding in the first half of the ratio with little effect on the last half" (p. 255). And Storms and Boroczi (1966) report that in "only the shorter shock duration was partial reinforcement less effective than punishment for every response" (p. 447).

With interval ratios, Azrin (1956) noted a temporal patterning of responses analogous to that under FI food reinforcement, to which might be added the existence of "similar patterning of 'dynamic stereotypes' in Soviet classical-conditioning studies" discussed by me elsewhere (Razran, 1965d) and expanded in chapters to come. Superimposing variable-interval punishment during variable-interval reinforcement, Filby and Appel (1966) found little effect with mild shocks but "at 0.6 ma, complete suppression occurred almost uniformly" (p. 52). And Snapper, Schoenfeld, and Locke (1966) uncovered a "marked drop of responding at the highest shock probabilities" (p. 65). In general, however, "schedules of punishment," unlike "schedules of reinforcement," are still in a very preliminary state of knowledge. (See, however, Camp, Raymond, and Church, 1966, and Storms and Boroczi, 1966.)

Degree of Antagonism Between Punishing and Punished Reactions

As noted earlier, Soviet investigators disclosed that shocks of moderate intensity inhibit (punish) the motor components (licking, turning-toward, etc.) and even salivations of food-based conditioning more than they do comparable components (spitting, turning-away, etc.) and even salivation of the acid-based conditioning. This relation of learning to the antagonism of interacting reactions sets punishment learning against any other kind. Moreover, Russian reports show also that acid-based CSs inhibit food-based CRs, and vice versa.

A FINAL SYSTEMATIC STATEMENT

The cited characteristics of punished reinforced behavior, studied extensively in American operant laboratories, corroborate the tenet, based on punished innate action and correlative Soviet evidence, that punishment is a highly efficacious type of learning and that its paramount parameters are the intensity and subsequence of the punishing reaction. And the characteristics certainly do not contravene the tenet that learning through punishment is autochthonous and unanchored to any other kind—"a primary process" in the words of Azrin and Holz (1966, p. 382); thus there need be no recourse to "avoidance" stemming from aversive classical conditioning. However, the very nature of the operant data precludes their relevance to my view that punishment is the most primitive type of associative learning, as does the absence of lower animals as subjects. And, of course, operant psychologists' conception of punishment as merely a reduction in the probability of a response through a stimulus which reduces it (Azrin and Holz, 1966, pp. 381, 441) is to me a short-circuiting of causal analysis. It ignores the intrinsic and interactive attributes of the punishing and punished reactions—the autonomic aversive reactions of the first, the dominance of each, and the dominance and antagonism of one to the other—not to mention the search for the neurophysiology underlying the process and outcome (Hoyle, 1965).

Aside from its existence in lowest animals, the evolutionary antiquity and idiopathic status of punishment learning are best attested to by Soviet findings that its efficacy is positively related to the degree of antagonism between the punishing and punished reactions. This sets punishment against all other types of associative learning in which interactive antagonism is a deterrent to and not a facilitator of effects. Dominance in punishment is a pre-Ukhtomsky operation, related to Sherrington's studies of final common path and antagonism of spinal reflexes (1898a, 1898b, 1906). The nondominant reaction is inhibited by the dominant not because of interdependence of the organism's total repertoire of reactions but because of specific antagonisms of two reactions. And there may very well be here no *Bahnung* or strengthening of the dominant reaction, which is the core of the Ukhtomsky doctrine. *Punishment is not an equal symmetrical opposite of reinforcement but a different and primitive contrary of all learning.*

NEUROPHYSIOLOGICAL BASIS

Hoyle's (1965) electrophysiological analysis of the punishment learning of three headless locusts in Horridge's experiment, quoted earlier and discussed by Horridge (1965), is the only one in the field. That the oldest, simplest, most universal, and most effective level of associative learning should have thus been neglected is probably related to its confused conceptual status. (Limbic punishment is considered in Chapter 8.)

GENERAL SUMMARY

1. When two antagonistic reactions, one inhibiting the other, are repeatedly coactivated, the inhibition may decrease or increase. When it is an increase and the inhibiting reaction is aversive, it is *aversive inhibitory conditioning or punishment learning.*

2. In typical punishment, the punished reaction does not acquire any

characteristics of the punishing reaction. Nor is there reason to assume that the latter is strengthened by the action of the former. Put differently, aversive *inhibitory* conditioning is not an aversive *classical* conditioning, and a concept of "avoidance" based on prior classical action is inapplicable to its typical existence.

3. The chief positive parameters of punishment learning are the absolute and relative intensity of the punishing reaction, its subsequence to the punished one, and the degree of their interactive antagonism. The first two parameters are in line with the dominance principle of all conditioning. The third is unique to punishment.

4. Punishment learning is highly effective throughout the metazoic kingdom. The effectiveness increases in early evolution but reaches its asymptote relatively early. A plausible corollary is that punishment is an associative learning least affected by concomitant cognition.

5. Either the punishing or the punished reaction or both may be either innate or previously conditioned. However, since punishment is the most primitive type of conditioning, its basic study in lower animals should center on the interaction of innate reactions—best in animals that are not readily, or not at all, subject to the other types of conditioning.

6. Most of the above statements, related to uncomplicated base operations of punishment, militate against the view that punishment is an equal and symmetrical opposite of reinforcement. In fact, even studies in higher animals with undoubted coaction of classical conditioning bring out sufficient basic differences between the two—e.g., in generalization and scheduling—to cast grave doubt on their symmetry.

7. The decrements of punishment, like those of habituation, recover in time, which means only that its effects, like those of all learning, are eventually forgotten. This forgetting may, however, be very slow—under certain circumstances, indeed, the slowest known.

8. The neurophysiology of punishment in lowest animals may well be the simplest of all associative learning.

9. While the sequelae of punishment may be malevalent to the organism, its indigenous incidence in the animal kingdom hardly needs stressing—nor, for that matter, does its near inevitability, in one form or another, in human interrelations.

CHAPTER SEVEN

Classical Conditioning—The Core of the Associative Process

INTRODUCTORY COMMENT

In Chapter 2, classical conditioning was denoted as "the evocation of a reaction by a stimulus of an associated reaction." That is to say, it is a type of learning in which a stimulus inadequate for some reaction becomes adequate by being associated one or more times with a stimulus adequate for that reaction. More exactly, the stimulus becomes adequate through associative linkage of its own reaction with the reaction of the adequate stimulus. And most typically, the inadequacy is originally absolute, although some instructive results have been secured also when the inadequate stimulus initially evoked a minor form of the adequate reaction.

The story of classical conditioning is traced, rightly, to Pavlov's earlier research in the reflex mechanisms of digestion in general, for which he was awarded the Nobel prize in 1904. A lengthy article in the eleventh volume of the *International Encyclopedia of Social Sciences* (Razran, 1968b) details this evolvement and its rationale, and only three short statements about it need to be cited here. (1) In the '90's Pavlov used freely the term "psychic secretion," contrasting it sharply (in his own words) with "reflex secretion" and speaking of the "digestive effects of his dogs' thoughts, desires, and feelings" (Pavlov, 1897). (2) In 1898, however, he deleted from the manuscript of his pupil, S. G. Vulfson's doctoral dissertation, "The Work of the Salivary Glands," the sentences, "The role of the psyche in salivary secretion is of course undeniable," and "The psyche determines the work of the salivary glands, choosing between acceptable and rejectable substances" (reproduced in photocopy by Anokhin, 1949c; pp. 55 and 61 of the dissertation). (3) And in the Preface to his first book on the topic (1923), Pavlov relates that in 1901, another of his pupils (A. T. Snarsky: "An Analysis of Normal Conditions of the Work of the

Salivary Glands in Dogs") "clung to subjective interpretations of data" but that he [Pavlov] "came to realize the scientific barrenness of the approach and after persistent thought and taxing mental conflict, finally decided to remain a pure physiologist and deal exclusively with external phenomena and their relations" (1923, p. 7; English edition, 1928b, p. 38). And to this should be added that Pavlov first used the term "conditioned reflex" in 1903 [12] and that the first four dissertations from his laboratory on acquired salivation (Babkin, 1904; Snarsky, 1901; Vulfson, 1898; Zelgeym, 1904) were "natural" experiments—animals tested for their reactions to sights and smells of foods and objects and stimuli naturally associated with them. Boldyrev, in 1905, was the first to demonstrate that "artificial," laboratory-rigged auditory, visual, and olfactory stimuli could be conditioned.

Classical conditioning is held here to be the core of the associative process on several grounds. First, it gave the field, in a comparatively short period, its most basic modern empirical generalizations—the indispensables of extinction, generalization-differentiation, inhibition-disinhibition, spontaneous recovery, higher-order and compound-stimulus conditioning, associative conditioning (termed "sensory preconditioning" in the United States), and others, each with several varieties and subvarieties. In the glossary of America's standard textbook on conditioning and learning (Kimble, 1961), we note thirty-four terms attributed to Pavlov and twenty-five to all other psychologists and physiologists combined. Second, the essence of classical conditioning is truly a continuation of traditional British associationism. The 1923 and 1927 books on Conditioning by Ivan Pavlov are quite like the 1746 and 1749 treatises on Association by David Hartley, about whom Joseph Priestley wrote in 1787: "Compared with Dr. Hartley, I consider Mr. Hume [that is, his association views] as not even a child" (Vol. I, p. 126). Both authors are concerned *not with rewards and the strengthening of existing events but with evoking new ones,* and both are thoroughly committed to the neural substratum—"vibrations" of its "infinitessimal particles" in Hartley's primal lore. "One may expect,"

[12] In 1912, I. F. Tolochinov, a former pupil of Pavlov who in 1902 reported on the "study of the physiology and *psychology* of the salivary glands" at the Northern Congress of Physiologists and Physicians in Helsingfors, intimated in a special pamphlet (1912a) and an article in *Russky Vrach* (1912b) that his data suggested the term "conditioned" reflex to Pavlov. And, incidentally, while "conditional" is the accurate translation of Russian "uslovny," the verb derivative "conditioned" denotes more appropriately the dynamic attributes of the phenomenon. The Russians themselves have in recent years "verbalized" and thereby expanded the term, using in addition to "uslovny": "obuslovit' " and "obuslovlenny'," "obuslovlivaniye," "obuslovlennost' " for "to condition," "conditioned," "conditioning," and "conditionability." Thus, Gantt's titling the current periodical which he edits "Conditional Reflex," after his own long practice of "conditioned" in the three Russian books that he translated —two by Pavlov (1928b, 1941) and one by Bykov (1957)—may well be hardly warranted and a Sisyphian task.

stated Hartley in the first paragraph of *Observations on man* . . . , "that *Vibrations* should infer *Associations* as their effect, and *Association* point to *Vibrations* as its cause" (1749, p. 6; italics in original). A sentence in Pavlov's last (1936) formal article reads: "The temporary nervous connection [the conditioned reflex] is the most universal physiological phenomenon both in the animal world and in ourselves . . . which psychologists call association" (1936b, p. 434; English edition, 1941, p. 171). How comparable!

Third, only for classical conditioning is "double stimulation" (Meyer, 1925) a *sine qua non*. It alone rests on a dual neurobehavioral topography. Reinforcement conditioning may be effected through actions of single central-neural or intraorganic topographies. A curious paradox! Operant conditioning, involving neither brain nor the organism's interior, is, much like innate action, increasingly coming under direct neural and intraorganic control. Whereas the classical type, begotten by a "pure" physiologist, cannot leave the old philosopher's-and-psychologist's path of *genuine* paired association, even when the members of the pair are but neural— Aristotle's and Hartley's hold (through Pavlov) on modern neuro- and chemotechnology.

Finally, we must heed the vast expanse of data on classical conditioning: over 7,000 experiments published in twenty-nine different languages (as far as I could ascertain). Needless to say, this expanse calls for a change in treatment to be feasible in one chapter. Our main concern must be with leading general empirical and theoretical codifications, and presentation of individual experiments kept to a minimum. Still, to highlight the wide operative range of this type of learning, it seems desirable to present at the outset several sample experiments in early ontogeny and phylogeny, and at the level of complex human action.

CLASSICAL CONDITIONING IN EARLY ONTOGENY AND PHYLOGENY

1. Blinkova (1961) inserted electrodes in a large number (not specified) of incubating hens' eggs to study cardiac and motor conditioning in the developing chick embryos. The US was an electric shock of "3.5 to 6.0 volts," which evoked a characteristic motor reaction, and the CS was a sound imitating the peep of a chick. The experimenter reports evidence of unstable conditioned movements in response to the "peep" on the 13th day of incubation and stable conditioning on the 16th day. Conditioned cardiac changes were evident only occasionally. However, in a later experiment (Blinkova and Bogdanov, 1963), in which 150 embryos were used, cardiac conditioning was clearly evident in two-thirds of the experimental specimens. These results are presented in Figure 26. The light gray columns in the figure represent conditioned motor changes and the dark gray columns, conditioned cardiac action. The motor conditioning appeared

first on the 14th day of incubation and attained a high frequency on the 15th day; the cardiac conditioning first appeared, with considerable frequency, on the 17th day. In a still later study (Blinkova, 1966) with 52 embryos, the conditioned motor reactions were preserved after decerebration in a number of specimens removed from the shell. Motor conditioning of chick embryos has also been reported by Gos (1933) and Hunt (1949) as well as by Sedláček (1962a, 1962b).

2. Stanley, Cornwell, Poggiani, and Trattner (1963) discovered both appetitive and aversive conditioning in 26 puppies, 3 days old at the start of the conditioning and 10 days at the end. Eight animals were used in the appetitive experiment and 9 in the aversive, and 9 served as controls. In both experimental groups, the CS was the insertion in the puppies' mouths of a manometer nipple for 5 seconds; this was followed, in the appetitive group, after a 5-second interval, by nipple-dropper feeding of milk for 15 seconds, and, in the aversive groups, by similar "feeding" of 0.5 cubic centimeters of a quinine hydrochloric solution. In the control group, the manometer nipple was reinserted for the same period. The results, presented in Figure 27, clearly indicate both conditioned sucking and conditioned struggling. (Note the mixed classical-reinforcement type of conditioning; the method was classical, however.)

Golubeva (1939) reported successful conditioning, and extinction, in 76 of 85 guinea pig neonates less than 11 days old. The CS was a 2400-

Figure 26 *Motor and cardiac conditioning in 150 chick embryos.* The US was an electric shock administered through inserted electrodes, the CS a sound. Light gray columns indicate motor conditioning; dark gray columns, conditioned changes of cardiac action. (From Blinkova and Bogdanov, 1963)

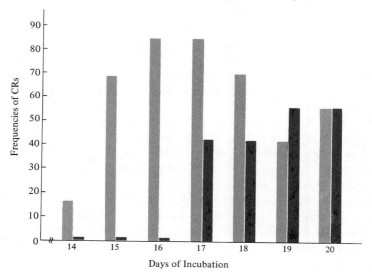

Days of Incubation

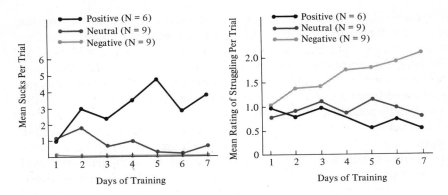

Figure 27 *Conditioned sucking (left panel) and conditioned struggling (right panel) in 17 puppies, 3 to 10 days of age.* The CS was insertion in the animals' mouths of a manometer nipple for 5 seconds; in the "positive" group this was followed by nipple-dropper feeding of milk for 15 seconds, and in the negative group by nipple-dropper "feeding" of a quinine solution for the same time. In the "neutral" or control group, the manometer nipple was reinserted. (From Stanley, Cornwell, Poggiani, and Trattner, 1963)

cycle sound, the US an unavoidable electric shock, and the CR (jumping) first appeared after 3 to 25 paired trials. Some animals were also conditioned not to react to the sound of bubbling water, to which the CR originally generalized (differential conditioning by method of contrasts).

3. Bystroletova (1954) disclosed conditioned prefeeding sucking and head reactions in twelve human neonates after two to six days. Figure 28 is a graphic record of one on a 4-hour feeding schedule. Upper panel, the third day; lower, the fifth day. In each panel the top line is a record of sucking and head reactions, and the lower lines show feeding periods and time in 5-second units. Note the clear-cut appearance of sucking and head reactions about 20 seconds before the 18:00 (6:00 p.m.) feeding on the third day, and the increased and persistent manifestations of them about 5.4 minutes before the feeding on the fifth day. Voronin (1948a) discovered such reactions in monkey neonates, kept on a 2-hour feeding schedule, only after 2 weeks of life.

The study is an example of temporal conditioning to internal—presumably interoceptive—stimuli, as is Krachkovskaya's (1959) report of the occurrence of prefeeding digestion leucocytosis in 42 neonates on the 6th to 10th days. Other kinds of classical conditioning of human neonates less than 10 days of age reported recently are: the Babkin reflex with arm flexion as the CS (Kaye, 1965), sucking with a CS of a 23-cycle 90 decibel tone (Lipsitt and Kaye, 1964), sucking with an electric bell as the CS (Dashkovskaya, 1953), head-turning with an electric bell as the CS (Papoušek, 1960b, 1967a; Papoušek and Bernstein, 1967), and blinking with auditory CSs (Dashkovskaya, 1953; Kasatkin, 1952). Papoušek

(1960a) disclosed further that prefeeding sucking is largely extinguished in later infancy, and Janos, Papoušek, and Dittrichová (1963) that appetitive conditioning appears earlier than aversive.

Highly effective temporal pupillary conditioning in 24 infants, 26 to 86 days of age, by Brackbill, Fitzgerald, and Lintz (1967) and temporal GSR conditioning by Lockhart (1966c) in 12 college students were noted in Chapter 5. Of the 24 infants, 8 were reliably conditioned—4 to constriction, 4 to dilation—when the US (onset or offset of a light for 4 seconds) was administered 32 times at fixed intertrial intervals of 20 seconds, 8 when a "complex sound of 23 cycles and 65 db" was added to the fixed-interval US and the sound tested alone, but none of the remaining 8

Figure 28 *Prefeeding sucking and head reactions of neonate K. on the third and fifth days of life. Four-hour feeding schedule. Upper panel—reactions on the third day, lower—on the fifth day. Upper line in each panel—sucking and head reactions; marks in middle lines of upper segments of each panel—beginning and end of feeding; lower line—time in 5-second units. Note the clear-cut appearance of sucking and head reactions about 20 seconds before the 18:00 (6:00 p.m.) feeding on the third day and increased and persistent manifestations of them about 5.4 minutes before the feeding on the fifth day. (From Bystroletova, 1954)*

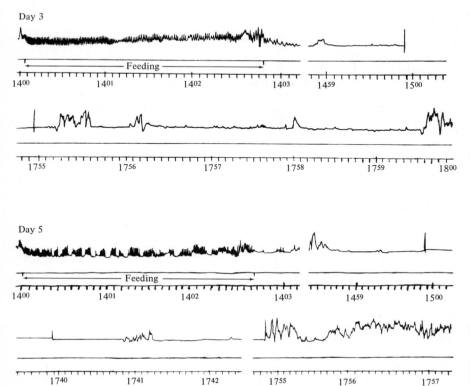

when the sound was paired with the US at *varying* intertrial intervals. In addition to the 6 experimental groups of 4 subjects each there were 4 pseudoconditioning groups of equal size. Acquisition was rapid, with no significant age differences, and extinction was "complete" in 9 trials. Interestingly, only 2 of 8 college students manifested this temporal conditoning, and their CRs did not extinguish in 35 trials. Yet, all 12 students in Lockhart's GSR experiment were successfully conditioned with shock at intertrial intervals of 40 seconds, although their CRs also persisted—no changes in 10 trials. Temporal conditioning is patently very special.

4. Ratner and Miller (1959) experimented with 32 earthworms (*L. terrestris*) kept in circular tubes. The US was a bright light which "evoked rearing and withdrawal of the anterior segments of the animal's body." The CS was the vibration of a doorbell buzzer with the bell removed. The worms were divided into four equal groups: an experimental group (E) of 100 conditioning and 30 extinction trials; a vibration control group (V) of 100 trials; a light-sensitization (pseudoconditioning) control group (L) of 100 light and 35 vibration trials; and a random-response control group (R) of 100 trials. The results, presented in Figure 29, reveal clear evidence of both true conditioning and extinction.

5. V. A. Sokolov (1959) used 9 *Physa acuta* snails kept in a water-filled glass tube connected at the top with another, similar tube. The US

Figure 29 *Conditioned withdrawal reactions in earthworms with a bright light as the US and a vibration as the CS. Group E—experimental group; Group V—vibration-control group; Group R—random-control group; Group L—light-sensitization (pseudoconditioning) control group. Each group included 8 animals. (From Ratner and Miller, 1959)*

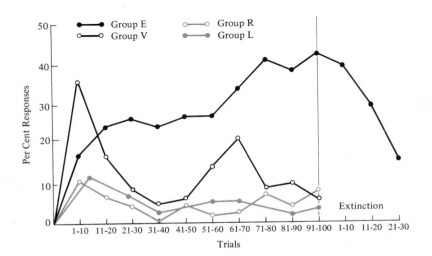

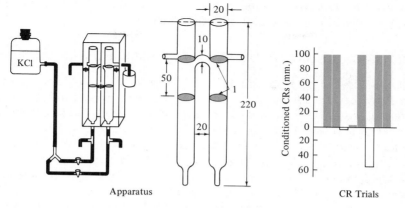

Figure 30 *Simple and differential classical motor conditioning in 9* Physa acuta *snails.* The US was a methyl blue solution of KCl, the CS a change in illumination, and the differential CS a flickering light. The KCl solution, delivered through the bottom of a water-filled glass tube in which the snails were kept, invariably caused the animals to move upward and as a rule to enter the connecting tube. The apparatus is shown in the left panel; the gray ellipses are nets between which the animals were placed, and numbers indicate distances in millimeters. The conditioning results are presented in the right panel; the positive conditioning in the gray columns, and the negative differentiation in the unfilled column. Note that the differential stimulus caused the snail to move downward. (From V. A. Sokolov, 1959)

was a 0.2 per cent methyl blue solution of potassium chloride delivered from below, which invariably caused the animals to move up and as a rule to enter the other tube. The CS was an increase in the illumination of the tube by a two 6-volt light; an attempt was made to train the animals to differentiate this from a flickering light of the same intensity. The experimenter reports that the CR of moving up the tube in response to the increase in illumination was formed in all animals, appearing first in 3 to 6 trials and becoming stabilized in 8 to 29 trials. The differentiation which as a rule caused the snails to move downward was, however, often unstable. Figure 30 presents data for one animal over 8 trials and a diagram of the apparatus. The gray columns represent upward movements in response to the positive CS, and the unfilled column, downward movement to the differential stimulus. Light sensitization tests were not made, but the existence of the differentiation suggests that the conditioning was bona fide.

Space prevents citing additional experiments in the area; however, none disproves the view that classical conditioning is a higher evolutionary level of learning than is aversive inhibitory conditioning and, of course, sensitization and habituation. It should be remembered from the preceding chapter that (*a*) Ross (1965) demonstrated failure of classical conditioning in coelenterates, which readily manifested aversive inhibitory conditioning, and that (*b*) earthworms, though they can be conditioned, are much more easily habituated and sensitized (Chapters 3 and 4).

CLASSICAL CONDITIONING IN COMPLEX HUMAN ACTION

1. Volkova (1953) conditioned a 13-year-old boy to salivate when the Russian word *khorosho* (well, good) was pronounced and to differentiate it from the word *plokho* (poorly, badly, bad). The boy was then presented, at intervals of 2 to 8 minutes, with 16 sentences which did not contain either word, but 9 of which the experimenter expected would evoke attitudes of approval (*khorosho*), 6, disapproval or condemnation (*plokho*), and one, an intermediate attitude. Examples of sentences expected to win approval were: "The Soviet army was victorious," "The pioneer helps his comrade," "The fishermen caught many fish." Examples of sentences expected to elicit disapproval were: "The Fascists destroyed many cities," "My friend is seriously ill," "The brother offends his sister." The results demonstrated definitive conditioning differences between the two types of sentences: those assumed approved evoked in 30 seconds 14 to 24 drops of saliva, those disapproved, 0 to 2 drops. Thus, presumably an objective and finely quantified technique of assessing human attitudes was demonstrated. Results of Acker and Edwards (1964) on conditioned vasoconstriction to the words "good" and "bad" in the main support the Volkova findings.

2. Razran (1954) presented short unfamiliar musical selections, color slides of unfamiliar paintings and of college girls, and short verbal statements to a group of 10 college students while they were consuming lunch. A control group of 10 students was exposed to the same experimental items without the luncheon. After six sessions, all subjects underwent three tests. They were asked to: (*a*) verbalize freely on "what the experimental items remind you of and make you feel like doing"; (*b*) find rhymes to 16 words such as "beat," "boast," "born," and the like, which could be food-related or neutral; and (*c*) unscramble 8 food-related words such as "bhurrmaeg," "digdpun," "ledmat," and the like. The results are presented in Table 3, from which it may be seen that the pairing of the experimental items with the six luncheons increased the number of food-related words in free verbalization and of food-related rhymes, and decreased the time of unscrambling food-related words. Twelve of the fifteen mean differences between the experimental and control groups were significant at the 1 per cent level.

3. Staats and Staats (1957) presented 86 pairs of nonsense syllables with meaningful words to 86 college students. The subjects were divided into three groups: one of 32 subjects in which the meaningful words were "evaluative" according to the Osgood semantic differential system, another of 24 subjects with "activity" meanings, and a third group of 30 subjects with "potency" meanings. Each nonsense syllable was presented

Table 3 *Conditioned Evocation of Food Attitudes in Ten Adult Ss.* Evocation of food-related verbal responses and facilitation of solutions of food-related verbal problems by stimuli that had been combined with six luncheons. (From Razran, 1954)†

| | Indices of Conditioning | | | | | |
| *Conditioned Stimuli* | *Mean % of Food-Related Material in Free Verbalizations* | | *Mean % of Food-Related Rhymes* | | *Mean Speed (Min.) of Unscrambling Food-Related Words* | |
	Control Ss	*Exp. Ss*	*Control Ss*	*Exp. Ss*	*Control Ss*	*Exp. Ss*
5 musical selections	4	12*	34	43	2.9	1.8*
5 Paintings	3	9*	33	48	3.0	1.4*
6 Photographs	3	7	28	46*	2.6	1.4*
6 Verbal statements	2	10*	22	41*	2.7	1.3*
Overall means	3.0	9.4*	29.3	44.8*	2.8	1.5*

* Difference between experimental and control groups significant at the 1% level. Percentages were used as scores in the first four columns, and *t* values were used to determine *p*'s in all columns.
† Copyright 1954 by the American Psychological Association, and reproduced by permission.

18 times, each time with a different meaningful word but one of the same semantic category. The data of 9 subjects who at the end of the experiment "indicated awareness of a relationship between certain words and syllables [nonsense]" (p. 77)—as well as those of 3 other subjects—were discarded. In the remaining 74 subjects, the nonsense syllables still acquired respectively, "evaluative," "activity," and "potency" semantic factors. The acquisition was statistically significant at, respectively, the .001, .05, and .06 levels.

4. Landis and Solley (1965) report successful salivary conditioning in three subjects to a negative afterimage. Subjects were pretested for ability to see such images and only those who reported them at two divergent parts of the spectrum were used. An analysis of variance differentiated between this conditioning and conditioning to the original stimulus or the pattern of light-dark changes—and the experimenter's conclusion is that "a percept may be used as the conditioned stimulus in a classical conditioning situation" (p. 553). Razran's "cotton absorbent" technique was used to measure salivation, and the US was mint candy.

PRIMARY PARAMETERS OF ACQUISITION OF CLASSICAL CONDITIONING

In general, these parameters are of three categories: (1) *reactional-organismic*—conditionability differences among different reactions (both URs and Ros) in the same organisms and among the same reactions in different organisms; (2) *perceptual-attitudinal*—evident and argued in my 1935 monograph on the conditioning of salivation in human subjects, and by now well recognized in the analysis of America's leading classically-conditioned response—the human eye-blink (Kimble, 1967b; Spence, 1963); (3) *intensive-temporal*—conditionability related to variations in the intrinsic stimulational Pavlovian design: intensity and duration of the CS and US; magnitude and duration of the Ro and UR; duration of CS-US delay and CS-US coaction; duration of "trace" in "trace" conditioning, and of US-deprivation when food is the US. Of these twelve parameters, *US-intensity* (or magnitude), *CS-intensity, CS-US delay,* and *US-food deprivation* have been most frequently studied, and several correlate highly with each other. It will be convenient to consider each of the three parameter categories.

Reactional-Organismic

The parameters of this category, involving approximately 400 widely different reactions and organisms, are inherent in the interrelated triad of ecology, evolution, and extent of perceptual-attitudinal involvement. The ecology of conditioning was discussed in Chapter 2, while the evolutionary phase—which at one time I attempted to explore fully in simple conditioning (Razran, 1933b, pp. 261-324; 1935, pp. 109-124)—has since proven to be best reflected in its complex manifestations, the subject of Chapters 9 and 10. And it is my intention to bring to light a separate monograph on interoceptive conditioning, where reactional differences due to perceptions and attitudes are minimal.

Still, four generalizations are of overriding systematic significance. (*a*) While salivary conditioning in dogs has yielded most of the generalizations in the field, it is not its most efficient example—it is relatively slowly formed and very readily extinguished. (*b*) In animals, the most efficient example is classical aversive conditioning with stimuli of relatively high intensity—quick formation, slow extincton (cf. punishment). (*c*) In accordance with the evolutionary status of reactions and organisms, perceptual-attitudinal factors affect classical conditioning in different degrees, or not at all, but seldom nullify its effects completely. The tendency to ignore either the factors or the conditioning is perhaps the most glaring theory-bound shortcoming of modern American psychology; yet the task of unraveling the interaction of the two is most complex and difficult. (*d*) Interoceptive conditioning appears to differ from comparable exteroceptive varieties in being slower in formation but more resistant to extinction.

Perceptual-Attitudinal

My initial exploration of salivary conditioning involved 37 adult human subjects and a total of approximately 16,000 trials using sensory and verbal CSs and cryst-o-mints or small pretzels (which the subjects ate, observed others eating, or thought of eating) as the US. It led me to a "tri-attitudinal 'psychological' and bi-factorial 'physiological' theory" of my data (Razran, 1935). Based on modes of distributions of magnitudes of CRs as well as on subjects' verbal reports at the end of the experiment, the theory held out two theses. (*a*) Subjects assume toward conditioning experiments positive, indifferent, or negative "psychological" attitudes, which—when the reactions are cognitively or verbally controllable—produce, irrespective of amount of training, positive, zero, or negative (below-control salivation) CRs. (*b*) The magnitudes of the reactions are, on the other hand, "physiologically" determined in the sense that they depend considerably upon the nature and interrelation of the US and the CS and extent of training. Humphreys (1943), experimenting with conditioned eyelid reactions in human subjects and using factor analysis, found similarly an incidence-magnitude distinction "quite comparable to the attitudinal and physiological factors of Razran" (p. 110). As revealed in their verbal reports, the subjects' three types of attitudes were described in 1935 as: "I should do '*b*' when I see or hear '*a*' . . . I mustn't do anythink that I'm not asked to [and] He can't fool me into doing '*b*' when I just hear or see '*a*' " (p. 42). Later analysis suggested dividing the attitudes into "(1) what might presumably be called . . . *perceiving,* or catching on to the purpose of the experiment and thus becoming influenced by the nature of the experimental setting and the personality of the experimenter, or the like; as well as (2) the presence of such *judgmental* or symbolic-semantic content as 'He will not fool me' or 'If I don't cooperate, he will not use me again,' and the like" (Razran, 1965c, p. 238; italics added).

The initial experiment attempted also to control the subjects' attitudes through instructions of "positive and negative volition," such as: "Please connect in your mind ZAG DIH [the CS] with saliva so that when you see or think of ZAG DIH you will also think of saliva" and "Please do not connect in your mind . . ." (Razran, 1935, p. 74). The instructions produced the desired differences in 87.5 per cent of the trials. Figure 31 juxtaposes my 1935 data with 1964 results of human eyelid conditioning by Nicholls and Kimble (lower left). Note that the upper right panel represents a subject in my experiment who was largely uninfluenced by the given instructions. Control of conditioning attitudes by the experimenter and even by the subject himself is not always successful. Use of naive subjects misinformed about the purpose of the experiment, and thus unaware of what is "expected" of them, has proven most workable in my conditioning studies since 1939. [13]

[13] Feather (1967), repeating the "no instruction" portion of my initial experiment with 22 college students and using saliometers, confirmed my main data that amount of training is an insignificant factor in the acquisition of the reaction, but, unlike me, he found that the salivary CRs extinguished in a few trials (p. 142). He reports, however, wide intersubject variability, which may conceivably account for the discrepancy between our results. There is a large number of untranslated Russian reports of human experiments in the area, and Feather's review of it is, unfortunately, very fractional—indeed, quite incomplete also with regard to available material in English, German, and French.

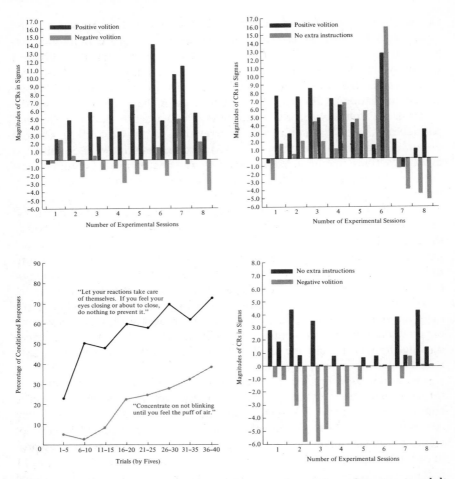

Figure 31 *Effects of instructions on salivary and eyelid conditioning in adult human subjects.* Note that one subject in Razran's experiment, upper right panel, was little influenced by the instructions. (From Razran, 1935, and Nicholls and Kimble, 1964)

Intensive-Temporal

Analysis of Russian Data. For a number of years, I have used a Wherry-Doolittle correlational technique to ascertain the proportion of variance in each of two indices of conditioning efficacy accounted for by each of two parameters in Russian and Soviet studies of salivary conditioning in dogs. Out of 618 such studies (listed in References, Razran, 1957), I chose 161 employing 100 different dogs plus 100 animals used in two experiments but showing no generalization from one to the other—a total of 300 individual experiments (Russian experimenters typically report the experimental vitae of their conditioned animals, and the dogs have different names; Pavlov records the names of 141 dogs in *Wednesdays* [1949, Vol. 3, 422-425].) The indices of CR-efficacy chosen were: (*a*) *CR-speed*—speed of CR formation as means of ordinal trial "stabilization," as the Russians call it, and (*b*) *CR-magnitude*—the amount of conditioned salivation in 30 seconds. The parameters were: (*a*) *UR-magnitude*—mean amount of *unconditioned salivation* in 30 seconds prior to the formation of the conditioned reflex, and (*b*) *CS-intensity*—the intensity of the conditioned stimuli when variations in CS-US delays and duration of food-deprivation were insignificant. Of the 600 zero-order correlations of CR-magnitude and CR-speed with UR-magnitude, 527 were linear and positive. Those with CS-intensity presented more of a problem. For one thing, there were eight different dimensions of CS-intensity (decibels, foot-candles, thermal variations, taps per minute, and the like), suggesting the need to compute separate correlations for each dimension and average them by means of z-transformations. For another, with two exceptions, at the upper end of the CS-intensity scale, 89 zero-order correlations with CR-efficacy were negative (means of $-.41$ with CR-speed and $-.49$ with CR-magnitude).

The results of the analysis were highly instructive. *UR-magnitude accounted for 31.2 per cent of the variance in speed of CR-formation and for 36.5 per cent of that in CR-magnitude, and CS-intensity—when high-score values were excluded—for 21.4 per cent and 24.7 per cent, respectively.* Moreover, while the zero-order correlations of CR-efficacy with US-magnitude (food or HCl) and with duration of food deprivation in 90 additional animals were also substantial, they were partialled out in the total analysis by the higher UR-magnitude correlations with which they themselves were rather highly correlated. Three systematic parameters of salivary conditioning in dogs appeared to be warranted within the limits of the technique: (1) *UR-magnitude is the best single predictor of CR-efficacy in terms of speed of CR-formation and CR-magnitude.* (2) *US-magnitude and duration of food deprivation (Hull's w and C_D) are predictive only when UR-magnitude is not considered.* (3) *Except for high values, CS-intensity, like UR-magnitude, is a significant predictor of both CR-magnitude and speed of CR-formation.*

Analysis of My Own Studies. A Wherry-Doolittle analysis was applied also to the acquisition of salivary conditioning in adult human subjects in ten of my studies in which attitudes were controlled by misinforming the subjects about the purpose of the experiment (list in Razran, 1957). Results from 150 subjects were available, but only CR-magnitude was used as an index of CR-efficacy. Moreover, CS-complexity—number of simultaneous flashes of small light bulbs or words—replaced variations in CS-intensity, and two "central" parameters were added: (*a*) *CS-attensity*—subjects' attention to the conditioned stimuli evidenced by their knowledge, at the end of the experiment, of the number of presented stimuli (they were not told that they would be tested for memory), and (*b*) *UR-affectivity*—subjects' ratings of their liking of the consumed USs on a 5-point scale. Zero-order correlations of CR-magnitude with UR-magnitude and UR-affectivity were, again, overridingly linear and positive, but those with high values of CS-attensity and CS-complexity—22 in the first instance, 16 in the second—were negative. Still, when the negative correlations were excluded, the computed regression beta weights were: CR-magnitude = .37 CS-attensity + .31 CS-complexity + .31 UR-affectivity + .37 UR-magnitude; these, multiplied by respective zero-order correlations with CR-magnitude, accounted for variances in CR-magnitude of 19 + 15 + 17 + 21 per cents.

The Dominance-Contiguity Theory. This theory (Razran, 1957) added three tenets to the correlational analysis: (1) Changes in CS-intensity, CS-complexity, and CS-attensity parallel changes in the potency of CS-initiated neural action, even as changes in UR-magnitude and UR-affectivity parallel the potency of the US-initiated neural action. (2) Classical conditioning is effected only when US-initiated neural potency exceeds significantly CS-initiated potency. (3) Increases in effective US-initiated/CS-initiated neural potency ratios at first increase but then decrease CR-efficacy—or, to put it differently, CR-efficacy varies not only with the absolute values of US- and CS-initiated neural actions but also with the optimal ratios between them. The theory involved no extra statistical probing. The basis of the first tenet is obviously logical, the second is related to qualitative evidence that very intense sensory and shock stimuli cannot become food CSs, while the third and most comprehensive tenet is an "inductive jump," taking off from the mere observation that the negative correlations between CS-intensity and CS-attensity and CR-efficacy were three times as common when UR-magnitudes and UR-affectivities were low. More exact empirical anchoring would require variations of CSs and USs, matched groups, and factorial analyses beyond the design scope of either the Russians' or my experiments. Still, it is felt that both the correlations and the theory add a valid behavioral approach to the direct neural probing of the Ukhtomsky doctrine in conditioning. And it bears repeating that dominance must be considered not as an omnibus principle but as an evolving mechanism of continuity and novelty; its operation in classical conditioning transcends that in sensitization, and is in turn transcended in reinforcement conditioning (Chapter 5).

Collation with Other Evidence. It seems best to center the collation on American studies of the role of CS-intensity. Russian unequivocal positive correlations between UR-magnitude prior to conditioning and CR-efficacy are fully paralleled by our findings of the positive parametric value of US-intensity (Spence and Platt, 1966), while there is no evidence on the effects of CS-complexity, CS-attensity, and UR-affectivity,

and it would take us far afield to consider the problem of whether knowl
edge of US-deprivation is needed when UR scores are available. On the
other hand, Soviet-American divergence with respect to CS-intensity is
most glaring. To the Russians, the Law of Strength—long promulgated by
Pavlov—is a most universal empirical generalization holding throughout
the phyletic scale, for CRs no less than for URs. Yet American data on its
CR power are by no means uniform (Gray, 1965). Experiments using
resistance to extinction as an index of conditioning negate the power
completely, while those employing indices of acquisition are by no means
wholly supportive. Two theories have been advanced for the divided acquisition data: one by Perkins (1953) and Logan (1954) stemming from
Spence's conception of discrimination learning, the other by Grice and
Hunter (1964) involving Helson's "adaptation level."

A footnote in my 1957 article read: "Grant and Schneider's (1948,
1949) finding that resistance to extinction did not vary with CS-intensity
in human eyelid [and GSR] conditioning bears but little upon the parameter under discussion, both because the parameters and mechanisms of
CR extinction differ from those of CR acquisition (Razran, 1939f; 1956a)
and because, as Grant and Schneider would no doubt admit themselves,
of the possibility of attitudinal modification" (p. 3, Footnote 1). The first
part of this statement should be enlarged. It means that Hull's juxtaposition of n (number of unreinforced reactions to produce extinction) with
A and s^tR and P (amplitude, latency, and probability of evocation) as
CR measures to the contrary notwithstanding, extinction is not conditioning, any more than forgetting is learning. Invariant between-subject positive correlations between CR acquisition and resistance to extinction are
not only contraindicated by Pavlovian typology and Soviet empirical findings but also by our own data and even our theory (Razran, 1939f).
Hunter concluded long ago, for instance, that "rats that condition quickly
may have either quick or slow extinction but rats which condition slowly
have their responses extinguished quickly" ["or slowly," the Russians
would add; cf. the evidence of quick or slow learners vis-à-vis quick or
slow forgetters] (1935, pp. 147-148). And, irrespective of Pavlov, it
seems logical to assume that individual differences in CR excitatory and
CR inhibitory actions, the dialectics of behavior theory, are to a considerable extent independent continua. Nor is there reason to disregard
the likelihood of discrete parametric variations of the two actions in the
same subjects.

The Perkins-Logan and Grice-and-Hunter theories command solid specific evidence but do not reach beyond that evidence. The former, positing
that CSs (or S^Ds) of higher intensity entail less generalized inhibition of
the nonreinforcement of what Perkins calls the "situation *minus* the CS,"
fails to note the qualitative distinction between reinforcement and classical
differential conditioning. Whereas reinforced reactions are typically differentiated from their background almost automatically and early in train-

ing, classical CRs long continue to include the background—to be reactions to the "situation *and* the CS." Significant classical differentiation is as a rule effected only by the specific Pavlovian method of *contrasting* US-paired and US-unpaired trials, and only some differentiation follows *prolonged* uncontrasted classical training. The functional statuses of the two twosomes, CS+ and CS−, and S^D and $S^\triangle$, are related but not identical. To use a perceptual simile, typical sensory-orienting classical conditioning does not segregate "figure" from "ground" the way the typical manipulatory reinforcement type does. And, of course, a differential-conditioning hypothesis immolates the operation of the Law of Strength in lower and decorticate animals, for which CR differentiation may be very difficult or wholly impossible.

Still more limited is the level-of-adaptation view of Grice and Hunter, predicating the efficacy of CS intensity on within-subject adaptive contrast, and thus running smack up against hundreds of Russian studies, my statistical analysis, and such a between-subjects experiment as that of Kamin and Schaub (1963), who conclude that their "data very clearly indicate that the rate of acquisition of the CR is . . . a positive monotonic function of CS intensity . . . the intensity of the CS has an overwhelming effect on acquisition of a true CER" (pp. 504, 506). Neither theory discloses more than supplementary mechanisms—which, it is hoped, are not just cognitive.

So it is that I venture the dominance-and-optimal-ratio theory and contend that while in unconditioned-reflex action on the one hand and reaction time on the other the Law of Strength rests on only one S-R set, in conditioning two interacting sets must be brought into the equation; that is, *higher intensities of CSs engender greater efficacy of CR acquisition only when US-CS ratios are optimal.*[14] Kimmel, Hill, and Morrow (1962), Kimmel (1959, Lockhart (1966a), and Walker (1960) brought to light the experimental reality of the interaction, and Lockhart stated: "The results . . . were interpreted as providing partial support for a 'dominance'

[14] The distinction between the effects of stimulus intensity on one reaction and on two interacting reactions is offered in lieu of the common divide between learning and performance. The latter is in general alien to the higher-nervous-activity tradition of learning as a change in neural action or in a state of neural action, and, consequently, if the change is not manifest or altered, what is implied is coaction of some other "correcting" neural factor rather than the existence of a separate category of performance. And the divide is, I assume, irrelevant to the systems of either Skinner or Guthrie. Moreover, it is, specifically, inapplicable to nonassociative learning: the well-established variations of habituation and sensitization with stimulus intensity. On the other hand, it seems reasonable to think that while in nonassociative learning and reaction time the Law of Strength relates to only one S-R, in conditioning it involves two, both intrinsic integrals of learning. The learning-performance divide is thus held to be, first, unheuristic with respect to all effects of CS-intensity and, second, in general devoid of objective substance—based on subjective appeal and consonance with everyday language rather than on total evidence and universal logic.

theory of classical conditioning in which conditioning is thought to be a function of the intensive relation between CS-initiated and US-initiated neural events" (p. 317B). To be sure, these are the only relevant American experiments, and it is regrettable that I myself failed to provide a wide and direct evidential basis for the doctrine—I first advocated dominance in 1930 and its behavioral ratio extension thirteen years ago. Perhaps now, at the end of my professional career, others will redress my shortcoming. To trace the waxing and waning effects of the ratios is a task of vast complexity. But it can be done. I trust also that the subjects will be not only human.

Finally, mention should be made of some prevalent CS-intensity designs of Soviet experiments. Kamin writes: "Typically the animal [in Soviet laboratories] is trained with a standard CS and then, after the CR is well established, is presented with stronger or weaker CSs on occasional tests [in which] generalization decrements may be expected to cloud the picture" (1965, p. 128). This has not been true for many years. Here is a 1940 report of a within-subject design in the dog Pincher (Dolin, 1940). After several years of training to a sequence of 9 trials of 5 different CSs separated by 4.5 minutes, the animal's salivary CRs during 30-second periods were in April, 1933: bell, 125 scale divisions; light, 84; bubbling of water, 119; metronome of 120 beats, 112; metronome of 60 beats (differential), 10; metronome of 120, 110; bubbling, 120; light, 78; bell, 122. Nine months later, during which the dog was further conditioned to a compound CS (the sight of a whirligig and the sound of a rattle), the scores were: bell, 115; compound, 83; positive metronome, 95; negative metronome, 8; positive metronome, 96; compound, 82; bell, 108.

To be sure, this is a somewhat unusual record. Yet I have long been struck by the not uncommon regularity and stability of dogs' salivary CRs to CSs differing in intensity and quality in Soviet experiments which I not only read in reports but in recent years have observed directly in their laboratories. The only possible account reconciling the discrepancies between their reports and ours was intimated to me at the 1963 Symposium on Classical Conditioning (Prokasy, 1965)—namely, that students of salivary conditioning of dogs in laboratories of American universities (Emory, Indiana, Pennsylvania, and Yale) were by far more concordant with one another in their results than investigators using other classical CRs or other organisms.

LONG CS-US INTERVALS

Recently, American experimenters using CS-US intervals longer than the latencies of corresponding unconditioned autonomic reactions (Fehr and Stern, 1965; Fromer, 1963; Grings and Lockhart, 1963; Grings, Lockhart, and Dameron, 1962; Kugelmas, Hakerem, and Mantgiaris, 1969; Lockhart and Grings, 1963, 1964; Prokasy and Ebel, 1967; Smith and Stebbins,

1965; and several others) have noted two or three temporally separated acquired reactions: one, shortly after the onset of the CS; another, prior to the onset of the US; and a third, after the latency of the US-UR in test trials. And in some of the experiments it came to light that the post-US acquired reaction is larger in magnitude, faster in discrimination, less subject to perceptual-attitudinal control, and more extensive in scope than the other two. This discovery confirms Sechenov's old dictum that "association is effected through contact of successive reflexes" and is of high systematic significance in (*a*) shifting the emphasis of classical conditioning from an anticipatory-preparatory to a neural-overlapping event, and (*b*) putting it differently, presumably providing a serviceable means of separating cognitive from noncognitive phases of the phenomenon. Highly provocative results have been reported by the Grings laboratory comparing pre-US and post-US CRs in normal and severely retarded subjects and in subjects aware and unaware of interoceptive CSs (Lockhart and Grings, 1964; Uno, in press). Additional research, evolutionary tracking, and concomitant electrophysiological probing are surely in order.

EXTINCTION, SPONTANEOUS RECOVERY, AND DISINHIBITION

Extinction

Extinction is probably the most distinctive single contribution of classical conditioning to present-day fundamentals of associative learning. Earlier students of such learning had not noted it, and Thorndike negated its significance as late as 1931 (p. 110), in sharp contrast to the wide use made of the phenomenon by the emerging systems of Hull and Skinner. Pavlov described extinction in his first address on conditioning in 1903, and the available classical-conditioning experiments involving it run into thousands. Yet its underlying theory continues to be highly divergent both in the Soviet Union and outside it: "internal inhibition" (Pavlov), "reverse conditioning" (Beritoff), "acceptor action" (Anokhin), "reactive inhibition" (Hull), "cessation conditioning" (Konorski, 1948b), "just the antagonist of excitation" (Konorski, 1967, p. 312), and views of "counterconditioning-and-interference." Also unsettled are a number of primary parameters of extinction, not to mention the glaring rift that on the one hand typical verbal associations scarcely manifest it at all, and on the other, some of its basic characteristics operate also in nonassociative habituation (Chapter 3).

I have dealt in detail with extinction as such—facts and theory—in two earlier publications (Razran, 1939j, 1956a). The first publication contained 31 factual generalizations plus a discussion of eight theories which cannot readily be reproduced here. The second, however, set forth a relatively new theory, and it will be briefly restated. The theory comprises four main propositions: (*a*) *Automatic deconditioning*—Extinction comes into being through the loss of interoceptive and proprioceptive CSs of the UR "which in the original conditioning were an integral part of the CR situation and which when the unconditioned stimulus is withheld . . . cease to exist" (p. 45).[15] (*b*) *Autochthonous counterconditioning*—Extinction is maintained through transformation of the conditioning datum from an increase to a decrease of a response, which thus becomes "a sort of self-propelling mechanism, the reduced CR reducing the CS components and the reduced components reducing further the CR" (p. 46). (*c*) *"Heterochthonous" counterconditioning*—The weakened CR is more readily interfered with in some situations by reactions "other than the UR which during conditioning [were] held in abeyance by the UR [greater effect of competing reactions]" (p. 49). (*d*) *Counterperception*—Extinction is accelerated when in some CR situations ". . . subjects perceive the changed significance of the CS when the US is withheld" (p. 49).

The evolutionary import of the theory is in accord with commonly reported Soviet evidence that extinction of well-established CRs is much slower in lower than in higher vertebrates (Barkhydaryan, 1967; Voronin, 1957, 1962, 1965, 1967; and others) and is also slow in interoceptive conditioning (Ayrapet'yants, 1952; Bykov, 1943; Moiseyeva, 1952); in either of these, response-produced conditioning (proposition *a*), interfering reactions (proposition *c*), and counterperception (proposition *d*) presumably are less. Yet, extinction is commonly fast in early ontogeny of vertebrates (Chinka, 1952; Polivannaya, 1965; Polivannaya and Kharchenko, 1965), suggesting a special primitive manifestation of the phenomenon associated with inadequate conditioning.

Spontaneous Recovery and Disinhibition

In terms of the offered theory of extinction, spontaneous recovery of extinguished CRs occurs primarily because the newer counterconditioning of their CSs is forgotten faster than the older original conditioning (Jost's [1897] Law?). Likewise, one must consider that when an extra stimulus disinhibits—or "inhibits the inhibition of"—an extinguishing reaction it also at the same time inhibits the original conditioning, but less effectively. In other words, here too, the outcome rests on a differenial in potency of

---

[15] In 1961, G. A. Kimble suggested a "generalization-decrement" theory of extinction that in essence is identical with my automatic-deconditioning proposition. "All extinction procedures involve changes in the experimental situation in that the proprioceptive [and interoceptive, in my view] consequence of reinforcement, and eventually responding, are eliminated . . . extinction should be hastened to a degree which depends upon the magnitude of these differences in stimulation between conditioning and extinction. The generalization-decrement hypothesis stresses this interpretation" (p. 293). However, he does not consider the three other significant supplementary propositions in my formulation, not to mention that "generalization" conveys the similarity rather than the difference between conditioned and extinction stimulation and is here in essence a special Thorndike variety of "identical elements"—what I call *residual components* (see below)—and not the usual Pavlov-Hull-Skinner type.

two opposing processes. Empirical evidence for such a view is presented elsewhere (Razran, 1939f, 1939g).

CLASSICALLY CONDITIONED PUNISHMENT

The most common technique was introduced by Estes and Skinner in 1941 under the name "conditioned emotional responses (CER)" and studied particularly by Kamin (1963, 1965), Kamin and Brimer (1963), and Kamin and Schaub (1963). Rats pretrained to press a bar in a Skinner box are repeatedly presented with a stimulus followed by an electric shock and the decrement in bar-pressing in response to the CS is the dependent variable. The technique is highly successful, and, as noted earlier, resembles Pavlovian conditioning in that acquisition varies directly with CS intensity. So far, its results (Kamin, 1965) do not, however, confirm Pavlovian findings that CS intensities of high values are less conditionable. Possibly the discrepancy is due to the greater complexity of the CER, which not only evokes a conditioned reaction but punishes another reaction therewith and is in a sense an interaction of two kinds of learning.

THE CONUNDRUM OF AVOIDANCE CONDITIONING

In 1927, and more definitely in 1934, Petropavlovsky discovered that dogs learn more readily to flex their paws in response to CSs paired with an electric shock when, after an initial pairing period, the shock is delivered only when the animals fail to react to the US than when it is administered irrespective of their reactions. This was a belated discovery (Gambaryan, 1962). For years the Russians seem to have been unaware that aversive conditioning, unlike the appetitive variety, comprises by its very nature a drastically negative phase of learning. The paw-flexion in response to the CS is punished by the shock which brings it into being. Moreover, they failed to note that unless the shock is of weak intensity, its conditioning is much more resistant to extinction and much more subject to the negative effects of overconditioning than is food conditioning. And, accordingly, its efficacy rests on an optimal balance between conditioning and punishing and between conditioning and overconditioning, and not on unceasing CS-US sequences. Bekhterev's aversive associations were not symmetrical opposites of Pavlov's appetitive ones. When their USs were relatively intense, the conditions of their efficacy resembled Thorndike's more than Pavlov's appetitive paradigm—more exactly, what Skinner discovered Thorndike's to be: *programmed scheduling.*

However, this Bekhterev-Thorndike parity is but a subsidiary functional similarity. *The essential mechanism of aversive conditioning is Pavlovian, not Thorndikian.* It is "a strengthening *of* an association" and not "a strengthening *through* association." And it is sustained by only classical associations—of the original classical UR, its occasional renewal, and classical second-order CRs—and not by any Thorndike "reward" reinforcements. Specifically, *after initial CS-US pairings, the effect of omitted shock stems not from what it does but what it misses—punishment and overconditioning—and the effect of the delivered shock relates not to contingency on what the organism does but to reconditioning an extinguished (or weakened) classical CR.* America's thirty-year attempt to bestow behavioral status on "avoidance learning" is scarcely more than an unacknowledged exercise in "crypto-phenomenology." *The concept's rightful realm is cognition and not behavior.*

Putting it differently, it is my view that with one notable exception all aversive conditioning is classical in both genesis and continued existence. The exception is the offset or termination of an aversive reaction (or stimulus), no less a bit of real behavior than its onset or initiation, to which Skinner rightly accorded the role of a Thorndikian reward reinforcer.

VARIETIES OF CONDITIONED STIMULUS GENERALIZATION

The Pavlov system posits the existence of two kinds of such generalizations: that of the first-signal system common to animals and man, and that of a second-signal system unique to man. The former is assumed to be an outcome of neural irradiation of the excitatory or inhibitory phases of the conditioning process, which putatively produce a smooth and regular declining gradient as the tested generalization stimuli become less similar to the formed or extinguished CS. The generalizations and the gradients are achievements of conditioning or extinction and not merely unconditioned or psychophysical failures to differentiate between the stimuli. What spreads is a special type of conditioned neural energy which at times operates cross-modally and at all times may involve discriminable stimuli.

Generalization of Pavlov's second-signal system is putatively related to three characteristics: (*a*) Words are, to begin with, generalized categories of nonverbal events. (*b*) In the course of use and development, they acquire generalized meanings. (*c*) Words acquire additional semantic significance in becoming parts of sentences or propositions (Krasnogorsky, 1954, 1958; Kol'tsova, 1958, 1967; Pavlov, 1927a, 1932a; Shvarts, 1954, 1960).

In 1949 (1949e), reviewing the then available experimental classical-conditioning literature of stimulus generalization, I challenged the existence of smooth generalization gradients as well as Pavlov's doctrine of neural irradiation and concurred with Lashley and Wade (1946) that reported results may be due to "failure of association" or prior "relational learning." I named "failure of association" "pseudogeneralization" because it was not what the Russians meant generalization to be. However, I added a hypothesis that conditioned stimulus generalization of *absolute* stimuli exists and is mediated by a crude categorization of generalization stimuli on a similarity-dissimilarity scale, and contended that generalization develops not during original conditioning but during subsequent testing of generalization stimuli.

A large volume of experimentation since 1949 has, however, substantially modified my position. For one thing, some evidence for a neural hypothesis of stimulus generalization has been forthcoming (Anokhin, 1968; Kogan, 1965; Rabinovich, 1967; Thompson, 1965), rendering tenable the existence of smooth declining gradients during formation of conditioning of the first-signal system. For another, reported regular declining gradients for stimuli in interoceptive conditioning (Ayrapet'yants and Pyshina, 1941; Sovetov and Chernigovsky, 1959) can hardly be accounted for by the perceptual categorization doctrine which I proposed. Third, smooth gradients have been successfully attained in reinforcement conditioning (Guttman and Kalish, 1956; and others).

On the other hand, Soviet data on classical compound-stimulus conditioning point to crude gradients of generalization when one or more aspects of the stimulus are omitted (cf. Fink and Patton's [1953] similar results with pigeons in reinforcement conditioning). And one may argue that all stimuli are compounded in some way (although, to be sure, not in the sense of actual compound-stimulus conditioning). When the pitch of a CS is changed, the relatively unchanged loudness and unchanged duration may well be the *residual* carriers of the conditioned generalization. Indeed, in man, such *residual-component generalization* is evident even when elements of the original compound are implicit. Thus, in my own experiments, when a subject is conditioned to the sound of a metronome out of sight, he generalizes with a decrement his reaction to the sight of the metronome without the sounding, and vice versa. Finally, the experiments of Asratyan (1938) and Petrov (1941) demonstrate that in the course of conditioning internal stimuli tend to take over the role of the original external stimuli and thus become an extra medium of generalization in recoding and compressing information of external CSs.

Likewise, there is no doubt that generalization of the second-signal system operates quite differently. Maltzman (1968), for instance, presented an extensive argument for the need of a special mechanism of semantic generalization even in pure S-R theory. And there is reason to favor Soviet conceptions that the second-signal system is a composite of mere-verbal, semantic, and sentence-proposition modes of operation, and that only it brings into being similarity-dissimilarity categorizations.

In short, a collated summary of East-and-West evidence suggests the operation of not one or two types of conditioned stimulus generalization but a family of eight: (1) total failure to discriminate between the stimuli, (2) generalization of otherwise discriminable stimuli, (3) residual-component generalization, not unlike the "identical elements" of Thorndike and Guthrie, (4) generalization mediated by internal or internalized stimuli,

(5) generalization of prior relational learning, and (6) mere-verbal, (7) semantic, and (8) sentence-proposition generalizations in the second-signal system. For the time being, it would seem more heuristic to design experiments for separate delineation of each of the eight than to look for common elements among them. Moreover, we may well be justified in asserting that in man all eight are present and interact with each other, but that in fish only the first or the first and second are operative. This is the story of evolution.

DIFFERENTIAL AND DELAYED CONDITIONING

Numerous experiments on these two types of conditioning have been reported since publication of Pavlov's 1923 and 1927 books, but its basic theory has changed little. The prevalent Soviet view continues to be that such conditioning is a manifestation of "internal inhibition," which, as stated earlier, Purpura (1959) equated with " 'Wedensky inhibition' [that] . . . today can be viewed as inactivation of all-or-none spike-generating mechanism which results from sustained depolarization [and which] has been observed in the cerebellum by Granit and Phillips (1956) with intracellularly located microelectrodes" (p. 161). Roytbak in Beritoff's laboratory reported that internal inhibition is accompanied by a sharp lowering of electroencephalographic activity (1958, p. 142), while John, Leiman, and Sachs (1961) noted that "cortical slow waves are associated" with differential conditioning of avoidance reactions (p. 118). The problem is by no means settled, however, not even the locus of such inhibition, which Pavlov himself placed in the region of the CR, Anokhin (1958a, 1968) in that of the UR and Asratyan (1955, 1961a) in the internuncial neurons connecting the two reactions.

Yet the history of conditioning demonstrates that the field simply cannot operate without invoking a concept of a special kind of central inhibition, the neural basis of which is quite obscure. Present neural evidence is insufficient to mediate between the behaviorally deduced versions of Pavlov, Beritoff, Anokhin, Konorski, and Hull. More data of the type of Roytbak, (1956, 1958), Szentágothai (1965), Granit and Phillips (1956), and Kogan (1960, 1965), and others are needed.

Irrespective of divergence in theory, Soviet experimenters have produced some very striking examples of differential conditioning, of which one by Moiseyeva (1952) will be presented. The dog Tomik possessed two intestinal fistulas, one adjacent to the ileal side of its ileocecal valve, the other next to the cecal side of the valve. A rubber balloon was inserted into the cecal (large intestine) fistula, and an electric shock was applied to the animal's foreleg whenever the cecum was inflated with air at 30 millimeters Hg of pressure. After a stable interoceptive reflex was established—the dog lifting its leg regularly at the appropriate inflation—like pressure was

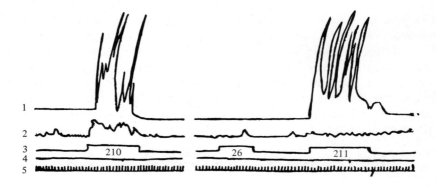

Figure 32 *Sample ileocecal differential conditioning in one of two dogs.*
The US was an electric shock applied to the dog's foreleg. The positive
CS was distention of the animal's cecum (large intestine) at 30 millimeters Hg of pressure next to the ileocecal valve and the differential CS
an identical distention of the ileum on the other side of the valve. Trials
210 and 211 represent stimulations of the cecum, trial 26, stimulation of
the ileum. Lines, from above: 1—paw-withdrawal; 2—respiration; 3—CS;
4—US; 5—time in seconds. Note that the differentiation was absolute.
(From Moiseyeva, 1952)

applied to the animal by the same means through the ileal fistula without
subsequent shock administration. Figure 32 presents the kymographic record of results. Conditioned cecal applications 210 and 211 produced unmistakable foreleg-lifting of high amplitude; the differentiated ileal application
26 did not. The differentiation was absolute. Compare DiCara and Miller's
(1968) differential *reinforcement* conditioning of vasomotion in the two ears,
and note that human subjects are unaware of such pressure and vasomotion
(Mysyashchikova, 1952; Lisina, 1957, 1960).

The relatively recent extensive experiment by Kharchenko (1960) on
delayed conditioned reflexes is also of interest. Unlike earlier Pavlovian investigators, who started with short CS-US delays of 3 to 10 seconds and
lengthened them gradually, Kharchenko began by delaying the feeding for 3
minutes. The task was too difficult for 2 of his 7 dogs, which required
gradual lengthening to form stable conditioning. However, the 5 which mastered the 3-minute delay at the start exhibited the characteristics of lengthened delay conditioning long reported in the Pavlov laboratory: ready inhibition, extinction, disinhibition, and spontaneous recovery. Soviet data
(Polivannaya, 1965; Polivannaya and Kharchenko, 1965) suggest that the
maximum CS-US delay which an organism can master is a positive function of evolutionary ascent.

American experimenters with differential and delayed conditioning (Kimmel, 1965; Rodnick, 1937; Spence and Beechcroft, 1954; and others) have
in the main confirmed Pavlov's behavioral generalization, including the inhibition phases. But, unlike the Russians, they have, except for John and
his associates, wholly ignored any electrophysiological analyses of the phe-

nomenon. To some extent, this situation is probably due to the fact that American classical conditioning is largely confined to the eyelid and galvanic skin reflexes of human subjects. Yet there is also of course the positivistic tradition.

HOW SIMILAR IS THE CR TO THE UR?

Konorski's text (1967, pp. 268-270) offers specific answers to the query. Three sentences merit direct quotation:

> In two groups of dogs the alimentary CRs were established by reinforcing a CS, by either presenting the bowl with diluted milk (or water), or introducing this fluid directly into the mouth through a hole made in the cheek. It was found that whereas in the first instance the conditioned response consisted mainly of the posture of expectation, in the second instance the vigorous mouthing movements and even swallowing movements (!) were observed in response to the CS. As a matter of fact, the conditioned response was so similar to the unconditioned response that by observation of the behavior of the animal it was not possible to tell at which moment the fluid was introduced into the mouth. (Footnote, p. 270)[16]

On the other hand, it is surprising to find Konorski interpreting all conditioning in perceptual terms. How can he extend such a view to the conditioning of headless insects (Horridge, 1962a, 1962b, 1965); chick embryos (Blinkova, 1961, 1966; Blinkova and Bogdanov, 1963; Gos, 1933; Hunt, 1949; Sedlaček, 1962c, 1962d); neonate guinea pigs (Klyavina, 1961), rats (Caldwell and Werboff, 1962), rabbits (Golubeva, 1939; Malakhovskaya, 1961), dogs (Stanley, Cornwell, Poggiani, and Trattner, 1963); goats (Moore, 1958); monkeys (Green, 1962); spinal frogs (Franzisket, 1963); cats with midpontine pretrigeminal transection (Affani, Marchiafava, and Zernicki, 1962); and conditioned gamma radiation (Garcia, Kimmeldorf, and Koelling [1955])—not to mention unconscious interoceptive conditioning and the fact that the basics of classical conditioning are about the same in nonverbal idiots as in college students (Grings, Lockhart, and Dameron, 1962). Perception surely has a role in conditioning but only at its proper level.

EXPERIMENTAL NEUROSES

The first evidence (Petrova, 1924, 1925, 1926; Razenkov, 1925; Speransky, 1927) of what later came to be known as "experimental neurosis" was noted by Yerofeyeva in 1912 in her use of electric shocks as conditioned

---

[16] CR-UR similarity—indeed, identity—in chemical nature and composition of secreted saliva in dogs has long been established in Pavlov's laboratory (Vulfson, 1898; Zellgeym, 1904; Boldyrev, 1905). Based on food, conditioned saliva is viscid and rich in mucin and enzymes, while it is almost wholly watery when HCl is used. This is not to argue that such similarity is present in (*a*) other organisms and reactions, (*b*) when CS training and testing conditions are radically different, or (*c*) when significant cognition is available.

food stimuli in seven dogs. The conditioning itself was successful. But when an attempt was made to test for generalization in three dogs by applying the shock to parts of the body other than the conditioned spot (left hip), the animals became highly excited and, instead of salivating, reacted violently to all electrical stimuli, including those of very weak intensity. It took three months to restore the CR in one dog, while in the remaining two it was never re-established (cf. Petrova, 1914). A more common manifestation of the phenomenon was revealed by Shenger-Krestovnikova in 1921. A dog learned to differentiate, after considerable training, between a circle and an ellipse of equal area when the axes of the latter were gradually changed from 2:1 to 3:2, 4:3, and 5:4. But when the ratio became 9:8, the animal broke down completely: he lost all his previous CRs, became alternately lethargic and violent, and could no longer be used in the laboratory.

Razenkov followed Shenger-Krestovnikova in producing "neurosis" through difficult appetitive differentiation. His dog managed to form a differential CR between a metronome of 120 and 60 beats per minute but failed when the task was a differentiation between a rhythmic "toucher" of 24 and 12 contacts per minute applied to the same spot on the skin. A "severe collision between excitatory and inhibitory processes ensued," and the animal not only lost his old CRs but gradually began to manifest special successive "neurotic" phases. After the inhibitory phase of several days, a "paradoxical" phase set in. The dog responded now with reactions of high magnitude to weak stimuli and of small magnitude to strong stimuli. Then came an "egalitarian" phase in which the animal no longer distinguished between strengths of stimuli, followed by an "ultraparadoxical" one in which inhibitory stimuli produced positive reactions and excitatory stimuli negative ones. The phase doctrine was fully approved by Pavlov, who suggested that it "may parallel Wedensky's discovery of such phases in peripheral neural action" (1924, p. 50; 1928b, p. 334; cf. Chukchev, 1956).

At the same time, Petrova found a third way of producing neuroses—by delaying unduly the application of the unconditioned food stimulus. Moreover, she discovered (1925) that the trained neuroses could be ameliorated and even cured by the administration of bromide salts and that their specific manifestations—excessive excitation or inhibition—are a function of the animals' type of nervous system, which also was integrated in the Pavlov system.

Since then, "experimental neuroses" have become a dominant aspect of Soviet classical conditioning experimentation, and methods of producing them have multiplied greatly. The following is a sample of such methods: (*a*) overtraining excitatory processes by formation of an excessive number of positive CRs (Soloveychik, 1928a); (*b*) excessive use of external inhibition (Rikman, 1928a); (*c*) overstraining inhibitory processes by excessive use of differentiation and conditioned inhibition (Mayorov, 1938); (*d*) differentiation between sequences of presentation of components of successive compound stimuli (Ivanov-Smolensky, 1927a); (*e*) changing components of such sequences (Guseva, 1956); (*f*) differentiation of symmetrically located stimuli (Kasyanov, 1967); (*g*) differentiation of simultaneously presented positive and negative stimuli (Dolin, 1962); (*h*) excessive use of backward conditioning (Petrova, 1933); (*i*) shocking the animals during acquisition of appetitive conditioning (Kryazhev, 1945); (*j*) general collision of alimentary and defensive reflexes (Zakharzhevsky, 1960); and others.

Space prevents discussion of the specifics of these experiments. We should note, however, that there are hundreds of them, and that the Russians attach much more significance to the phenomenon than do the relatively few American experimenters in the area (Anderson and Liddell, 1935; Brady, 1958; Gantt, 1942, 1944; Liddell, 1938; Masserman, 1964, 1946; and several others). As disclosed in such extended texts as Bykov and Kurtsin's *Corticovisceral Pathology* (1960), Davidenkov's *Neuroses, Epilepsy and Narcolepsy* (1960), Dolin's *Pathology of Higher Nervous Activity* (1962), and Ivanov-Smolensky's *Interaction of Experimental and Clinical Cerebral Pathophysiology* (1965), experimental neurosis, interrelated on the one hand with the older Russian view of *nervism*—that the nervous system affects in some way all behavior—and on the other with the role of interoception and interoceptive conditioning and with interaction of the first- and second-signal systems, renders a specific distinctness not only to the basics of Soviet psychiatry but also to a dominant portion of its medicine.

NEURAL BASIS: SUMMARY STATEMENTS

1. As indicated earlier (Chapter 4), neurophysiological findings are only way stations in locating the engram of any learning. The relative stability and permanence of the chief attribute of mind just do not fit the notion of reverberating circuits, which themselves may well operate significantly only through generated changes in neuromorphology. Indeed, even the very existence of a distinctive reverberatory category of short-term learning should be questioned in light of the high efficacy of one-trial aversive inhibitory conditioning in vertebrates (cf. Spevack and Suboski, 1969).

2. The numerous reports that conditioning is accompanied by parallel electrophysiological changes have so far not established empirically that the latter is the basis of the former. Several experimenters (Beck, Doty, and Kooi, 1958; Key and Bradley, 1959, 1960; Milstein and Stevens, 1961) obtained behavioral conditioning without concomitant EEG desynchronization, and there is likewise no adequate replication of claims, mostly Soviet (Beritoff, 1960, 1969; Kogan, 1960, 1965; Livanov, 1960a, 1960b; Makarov, 1960; Oniani, Naneyshvili, Koridze, and Abzianidze, 1969; Roytbak, 1958, 1960a, 1960b; Sakhiulina, 1960; Sakhiulina and Lyubchinsky, 1968; Shvets, 1965; and others), that conditioning *invariably* engenders changes in evoked and steady potentials—fast EEG waves when it is

formed and generalized, slow when it is extinguished, when it is differentiated, and during CS-US delays.

3. Rusinov's 1953 discovery that following (and during) low-current (1- to 10-microamp) anodal polarization of neuromotor areas controlling specific motor reactions the reactions may be evoked by tactile, visual, and auditory stimuli is now an established fact, confirmed and expanded in a number of later studies. Figure 33 (from Podsosennaya, 1956) illustrates one such finding: leg flexion in response to a buzzer. Moreover, the Rusinov mechanism is not just pseudoconditioned sensitization. Kalinin (1963a) showed that when the lateral geniculate body was polarized along with the motor cortex, reactions to visual stimuli were enhanced, while identical supplementary polarization of the medial body enhanced reactions to auditory stimuli. And Morrell (1961b) demonstrated that 20 minutes after the cessation of polarization, a tone that was repeatedly paired with it evoked a motor reaction, but a light that was not thus presented did not—a finding replicated recently by Rabinovich and Kopytova (1969). There is further the general consideration that during its action the polarizing current produces no observable behavioral or electrophysiological change other than conditioning.

4. No less significant is the evidence that conditioning is accompanied by *assimilation* of the rhythm of the CS in frequency-specific potentials. First observed by Livanov and Polyakov in 1945, the evidence has since been

Figure 33 *Sample rhythmic flexions of the right forelegs of rabbits to the sound of a buzzer 10 to 20 minutes after anodal polarization of the motor area of the limb 3 to 12 times per minute. Lines, from the top: 1—reaction of left foreleg; 2—right foreleg; 3—application of buzzer; 4—stimulation of right foreleg (none); 5—time in seconds. (From Podsosennaya, 1956)*

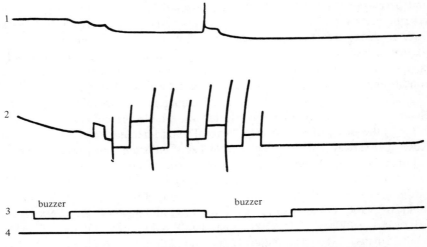

corroborated by a number of experimenters, notably by John and Killam (1959, 1960a, 1960b; John, 1967), who have reported that the acquired rhythm (*a*) disappears when the CR is extinguished, (*b*) appears in response to generalized stimuli, (*c*) may be differentiated from other rhythms, and (*d*) may be evident also in the harmonics of the rhythm. The two Soviet leads, both by students of Ukhtomsky's "dominance," are surely of suggestive import, yet they hardly tell the whole or even the main story of what the brain does when the mind learns. The effects of anodal polarization in the absence of observable electrophysiology point up the insufficiency of our brain-probing technique—even as much more and different probing by our present technique is needed.

5. At about the time that experimenters outside the Soviet Union (Eckert, 1963; Hagiwara and Morita, 1962; Tauc, 1959; Wanatabe and Bullock, 1960; and several others) discovered nonsynaptic electrotonic neural transmission in leeches, lobsters, and mollusks, Belenkov and Chirkov (1961, 1964, 1965, 1969) found it in the cortex of cats. Extra- and intracellular probings of hundreds of unit-neurons in cortical "islets" severed neurally from their subcortex and adjacent cortex disclosed potentials and potential changes of two different latencies when the nearby cortical areas were stimulated by strychnine or shocks of high intensity. The first, of 1 to 2 milliseconds, was by all tokens an electrotonic manifestation, and the second, of more than 8 milliseconds, synaptic (cf. Li and Chou, 1962); and of course the cortex-"islet" transmission was electrotonic.

Belenkov and Chirkov did not, however, show that electrotonic neural action is more than ancillary and supplementary to synaptic action; thus it could hardly be the main basis of learning as postulated by Köhler, particularly in light of the experimental disproof by Lashley, Chow, and Semmes (1951). Still, such action must have a specific role for which, in anticipation of empirical evidence, the following hypothesis is advanced: *Electrotonic neural action is the underlying mechanism of long-lasting effects of the inhibitory conditioning of punishment on the one hand, and of short-term learning on the other.* The apparent antinomy between the two parts of the hypothesis is not real, since both punishment and short-term learning are incomplete associations and may not need the extra synaptic mechanisms. Moreover, punishment, like electrotonic action, is distinctively effective only with stimuli of high intensity, while bona fide short-term learning is apparently only a few seconds in duration (Chorover and Schiller, 1965). And it is of course clear that the core of normal learning is unlike either.

6. Earlier views (Tanzi, 1893; Ramón y Cajal, 1897; Kappers, 1907) that the enduring effects of learning predicate junctional neural growth are in good standing among contemporary students of the field in both East and West (Anokhin, 1968; Beritoff, 1969; Eccles, 1964; Hebb, 1966; Konorski, 1967; Young, 1951). However, empirical evidence is sparse and not specific to results of conditioning. All that seems to be definitive is that

stimulation, involving learning, on the one hand increases growth in cortical mass (Bennett, Diamond, Krech, and Rosenzweig, 1964; Krech, 1966; and others) and on the other increases the ratio of specific cortical and sub-cortical cells (Altman, Das, and Anderson, 1968) and of cortical dendritic spines (Schapiro and Yukovich, 1970). The neuroanatomy of learning is in an even more incipient stage than is its neurophysiology: without tech-nological breakthroughs, it is not likely to demonstrate its own compelling theory.

7. Neurochemical concomitants of learning (Hydén, 1965, 1969) are in essence not the basis of it but the basis of its basis: the mechanisms dis-cussed in the preceding six statements (cf. Barondes, 1965).

8. Ukhtomsky's "dominance" applies to both the neural and the behav-ioral phases of learning, operating at each level of both as an evolutionary mechanism of continuity and novelty. (A simple behavioral manifestation is evident in Franzisket's [1963] experiment on conditioning the arm-wip-ing and foot-wiping reflexes to each other in four spinal frogs [which, un-like spinal mammals, *can* be conditioned]. The evidence is presented in Figure 34 and Table 4. The reflexogenous zone of each reflex is quite dis-tinct, and both are readily evoked concomitantly through stimulations with von Frey bristles. However, when a weak but adequate stimulation in one zone is paired with a strong one in the other, only the reflex to the stronger stimulus is elicited [top two panels in the Figure 34], even as after 500 to 700 pairings the weak stimulus alone comes to evoke the reflex to the strong stimulus [middle two panels]. Moreover, when the leg of another spinal frog was sewed down to its body, 300 stimulations of its reflexo-genous zone came to evoke an arm-wiping reflex [bottom panel], while re-moval of the stitches—after 1,000 additional stimulations in 10 successive days—reactivated the foot-wiping reflex [Table 4].)

SUMMARY

1. Classical or Pavlovian conditioning is the most typical objective man-ifestation of simple associative learning. A stimulus originally inadequate to evoke some reaction (the CS) becomes adequate by being paired one or more times with the adequate stimulus (the US) of the reaction. Evidence and logic suggest that the paired stimuli produce conditioning through asso-ciative linkage of their respective reactions (URs and Ros).

2. Classical conditioning has been studied most frequently—approxi-mately 1,100 experiments—in dogs with salivation as the UR and a sensory-orienting reaction as Ro. Other kinds of classically-conditioned reactions are, however, imposing in number and range—approximately 400 kinds of reactions, from changing movements in chick embryos and spinal frogs to producing salivation in response to afterimages, changing meanings of words and attitudes, and facilitating solutions of food-related scrambled words. Still, as documented in earlier chapters, classical conditioning is not

Figure 34 *Dominance and conditioning of arm-wiping and foot-wiping reflexes in a spinal frog.* Top left panel—arm-wiping reflex when the stimulus of the foot-wiping reflex is weaker than that of the arm-wiping reflex; top right panel —foot-wiping when the stimulus of the arm-wiping reflex is weak; middle left panel—arm-wiping reflex conditioned to weak stimulus of foot-wiping; middle right panel—foot-wiping reflex conditioned to weak arm-wiping stimulus; bottom panel—arm-wiping reflex evoked by foot-wiping stimulus when one foot is sewn down to the animal's body. (From Franzisket, 1963)

Table 4 *Reflexes of a Spinal Frog with Leg Sewn Down to Its Body When the Reflexogenous Zone of the Foot-Wiping Reflex Is Stimulated.* (From Franzisket, 1963)

2/57	Transsection of Medulla	16. 5. 1957	
	Test Series with the Untrained Spinal Frog		
9. 8. 57	100 stimuli cause	0 arm-wipings	13 foot-wipings
	Training Series with Fixed (Stitched) Leg		
10. 8. 57	100 stimuli cause	0 arm-wipings	
11. 8. 57	100 stimuli cause	0 arm-wipings	
12. 8. 57	100 stimuli cause	0 arm-wipings	
13. 8. 57	100 stimuli cause	4 arm-wipings	
14. 8. 57	100 stimuli cause	2 arm-wipings	
15. 8. 57	100 stimuli cause	8 arm-wipings	
16. 8. 57	100 stimuli cause	7 arm-wipings	No wiping re-
17. 8. 57	100 stimuli cause	4 arm-wipings	flexes with the
18. 8. 57	100 stimuli cause	11 arm-wipings	fixed leg
19. 8. 57	100 stimuli cause	17 arm-wipings	
20. 8. 57	100 stimuli cause	12 arm-wipings	
21. 8. 57	100 stimuli cause	7 arm-wipings	
22. 8. 57	100 stimuli cause	11 arm-wipings	
23. 8. 57	Stitches removed		
	Test Series with the Trained Spinal Frog		
23. 8. 57	100 stimuli cause	11 arm-wipings and 19 foot-wipings	

readily effected at the lowest end of the evolutionary scale and, indeed, is considered here the fourth evolutionary level of learning—after habituation, sensitization, and inhibitory conditioning.

3. Classical conditioning of salivary reactions in dogs of Russian and Soviet laboratories has provided most of the objective empirical generalizations and theoretical suppositions about simple associative learning. This conditioning is not, however, as stable in terms of extinction as are aversive or defensive classical conditioning and comparable appetitive reinforcement conditioning.

4. Unconditioned aversive reactions exercise a double and contradictory role in classical conditioning—*they produce the CR and punish it when it is produced*. Because of this and relative resistance to extinction and susceptibility to overconditioning, aversive conditioning is more efficient when it is a so-called avoidance than when it is a nonavoidance variety—that is, when the US is administered only when the CR is weakened or absent.

5. "Avoidance conditioning" involves no mechanisms other than classical aversive conditioning: its likeness to reinforcement conditioning is

based only on its mooring to scheduling designs, and its essence is extra only in terms of cognition and not behavior.

6. The Estes-Skinner-Kamin "conditioned emotional response (CER)" is an effective technique of classically-conditioned punishment. As such, however, it departs from the simple classical paradigm and is in essence an outcome of two kinds of aversive conditioning: classical and inhibitory (Chapter 6).

7. A Wherry-Doolittle correlational analysis of the data of 251 Soviet salivary conditioning experiments in dogs and 1290 zero-order correlations reveals two leading parameters of its efficacy in terms of the magnitude of the CR and the speed of its formation. The two are: (*a*) the magnitude of the UR and (*b*) the intensity of the CS. Duration of food deprivation is significant only as a determinant of the UR magnitude, and it is not the only determinant.

8. The "dominance" theory adds to the correlational analysis the thesis that CR efficacy is a function of not only the absolute values of CS intensity and UR magnitude but also their interaction. More exactly, it posits that for classical conditioning to be effected, the potency of the US-initiated neural action must exceed that of its CS-initiated counterpart and that an increase in the ratio of this potency at first increases and then decreases the effectiveness.

9. Soviet findings that CR efficacy varies directly with UR magnitude prior to conditioning are in accord with American findings that it varies similarly with US intensity. American experiments negate, however, the relation of the efficacy to CS intensity when resistance to extinction is used as a CR measure and do not support it fully with direct indices (magnitude, latency, incidence) of CR acquisition.

10. The negative extinction data are accounted for by the consideration that extinction is *sui generis*—no more an intrinsic integral of conditioning than forgetting is of learning—and that the correlation between resistance to extinction and CR acquisition is by no means always positive, nor always significant when it is. Failure of the CS-intensity relation with direct indices of CR acquisition is attributed to unpropitious US-CS ratios. Two other theories—differential conditioning and level of adaptation—disclose, it is maintained, supplementary mechanisms but not the basis of the phenomenon.

11. In human subjects, there is agreement on the significant effects of perception and attitudes on salivary, eyelid and galvanic skin reflex conditioning (systematic discussion in Chapter 9). And there exists additional evidence that in human salivary conditioning the subjects' attention to the conditioned stimuli and their liking of the food are positive conditioning factors.

12. When conditioning involves CS-US intervals longer than the latencies of corresponding unconditioned autonomic reactions, those acquired reactions appearing after the unconditioned latencies manifest a higher efficacy of conditioning than those occurring earlier. The discovery is signifi-

cant in shifting the emphasis of classical conditioning from an anticipatory-preparatory to a neural-overlapping event.

13. The entire field of conditioning and associative learning can hardly operate without a concept of a special kind of central inhibition, the neurophysiological basis of which is still very obscure. More direct neural evidence of the type brought forth by Roytbak (1956, 1958), Granit and Phillips (1956), Szentágothai (1965), and Kogan (1965) is needed to settle among the Pavlov, Beritoff, Anokhin, Hull, Konorski, and other behaviorally inferred versions of the concept.

14. Collated East-and-West evidence suggests the existence of eight different mechanisms of conditioned stimulus generalization—five operative in primary or first-signal system conditioning and three additional ones in the verbal or second-signal system. Both smooth and crude gradients may be the outcome of more than one mechanism.

15. Soviet work in experimental neuroses is extensive, and claims of its significance are very far-reaching not only in psychiatry but also in a large portion of its medicine.

16. Soviet physiologists commonly posit that interoception and interoceptive conditioning are to a large extent the basis of unconscious action and change of action (Ayrapet'yants and Bykov, 1945; Bykov and Kurtsin, 1960; and others [Razran, 1961a]). Watson's assigning this role to visceral *reactions* must surely be expanded to stress visceral *stimulations*.

17. Neural basis: See the preceding section (pp. 155-158).

CHAPTER EIGHT

Reinforcement Conditioning— Strengthening of Reactions Through "Reward" Associations

INTRODUCTORY AND HISTORICAL NOTE

In Chapter 2, reinforcement conditioning was denoted as the "strengthening of reaction by an associated reaction, commonly called 'reward learning.'" And in Chapter 5, it was stated that such strengthening is not confined to operant or even skeletal reactions but that a primary condition is the relative unhabituability of the reaction to be strengthened. Moreover, it was posited that reinforcement conditioning is a higher evolutionary level of learning than is classical conditioning, the former typically subsuming the latter. And, again, reinforcement was not considered an associative essence of classical conditioning, the strengthening of which is but a matter of practice.

Reinforcement conditioning is admittedly a continuant of Thorndike's law-of-effect learning. However, its two current common techniques, the straight runway and the Skinner box, have specific Russian antecedents. In 1913, Zeliony (1913b) covered a pathway with smoked paper and conditioned rats to run on it to a feeding tray in response to a sound of F_2 on a tuning pipe. He measured the speed and course of the animals' running and the size of their steps and reported a generalization gradient—slower speed and shorter steps—with similar sounds, and an absolute differentiation of not running at all when tone E_2 was repeatedly sounded without feeding (see also Zeliony, 1910b, 1913a, 1918). In 1927, Ivanov-Smolensky introduced his bulb-pressing method, which has since been used very extensively in the Soviet Union to study reinforcement conditioning in children and mental patients (1927b, 1927c, 1928a, 1928b, 1929, 1930, 1933, 1934, 1935a, 1935b, 1952, 1965; Ivanov-Smolensky and Shurpe, 1934). Figure

35 is a diagram of the original apparatus, the upper panel showing its arrangement when food—typically a piece of chocolate visible under a glass plate at point V—is the reinforcement, and the lower panel, when the reinforcement is sensory-orienting—exposure of changing pictures or objects. The subject is first shown that pressing the bulb enables him to get the food or see the pictures (experimenter doing it with subject's hand) and then is conditioned to press or not to press in response to a variety of anteceding stimuli.

Both Zeliony in 1913 and Ivanov-Smolensky in 1927 had thus studied, using current American methods, what is generally known as shaping of responses and formation of discriminated operants, without so naming them, and, more importantly, without acknowledging their extra significance as a manifestation of a special and overriding *R* type of conditioning. Zeliony's special term "heterodynamic conditioning" (Zeliony et al., 1937;

Figure 35 *Ivanov-Smolensky's method of studying food (upper panel) and sensory-orienting (lower panel) reinforcement conditioning in children and mental patients.* In the upper panel: A—tube shutter in experimenter's room; B—bell and its recording; C—recording of subject's pressing the bulb; D—recording of experimenter's opening and closing the tube; L—sloping shelf; NN₁—sloping metal tube; V—glass window; R—experimenter's rubber bulb; R₁—subject's rubber bulb. In the lower panel: L—lamp; M—manometer; P—shutter; T—tachistoscope; W—wall. (From Ivanov-Smolensky, 1927b)

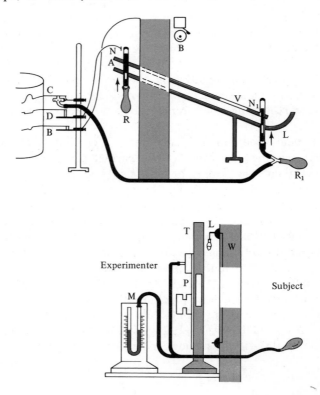

cf. Hilgard, 1937) and Ivanov-Smolensky's "conditioned conditioning" were in no sense intended to transcend Pavlovian formulations—only to broaden their application. And, as may be seen, Ivanov-Smolensky experimented also with sensory reinforcements, of comparatively recent vintage in the United States. Again, it might be added that in 1911 Krasnogorsky demonstrated that repeated passive flexion of dogs' paws followed by feeding readily evoked conditioned salivation, a technique that soon became the Konorski and Miller Type II conditioning in Pavlov's laboratory. (Krasnogorsky argued that the conditioned flexion stimuli were wholly proprioceptive since their conditioned reactions were preserved upon ablation of the animals' ectosylvian and coronary gyri, whereas tactile CRs were thereby abolished.)

Soviet experimenters have continued to study various kinds of reinforcement conditioning, including verbal reinforcement (Fadeyeva, 1960; Ivanov-Smolensky, 1927 and later), running to feeding places (Beritoff, 1934 and later; Skipin, 1951; Kupalov, 1964, with a special method;[17] and

[17] A very large experimental room, 7.5 x 5 meters, with its floor marked off in 70 numbered squares, is equipped with two tables on which food trays are automatically placed, and a large variety of movable auditory and visual stimulators on the walls and floor of the room. The dogs' approach to the food trays is shaped by a "meat path": small pieces of meat are placed in a direct line from the entrance to either table, the distances between meat pieces are lengthened in consecutive trials, and, finally, the baiting is altogether eliminated. Following this, the dogs are, as a rule, trained to respond: (1) only to the sound of the moving trays, (2) to that sound plus some visual or auditory stimulus and, finally, (3) when the animals are occupying particular squares on the floors, irrespective of kind of accompanying stimuli. Sometimes the first step is omitted and the second and third are reversed in sequence. Approach to the trays is usually effected in one experimental session, but the complete cycle takes about two weeks to be stabilized. When it is completed, the animals not only walk to the designated squares before running to be fed but return to them to wait for the next feeding. Moreover, the conditioning to designated squares is facilitated by placing small rugs on them. The animals' entire behavior is recorded automatically and photographed by motion picture cameras, the experimenter observing them from an adjacent room.

The Kupalov method is not only one of a "free operant" in the fullest sense of the word, but it also discloses the dynamics of the interaction of reinforcement and classical conditioning as no other method does. Figure 36 shows, for instance, how in initial training, a dog reacts to the classical stimulators on the floor (upper panel) and on the wall (lower panel) before it learns to go directly to the food-tray table and finally to lie down first in a particular square and wait for the feeding signal. The two most significant empirical disclosures of the method are: (*a*) that conditioned reinforcement action dominates and eliminates incompatible and superfluous classical action, and (*b*) that "waiting to be fed" is as much an "operant" as "pressing a lever" or "pecking at a key." And it goes without saying that the method utilizes such typical Pavlovian designs as: going to different food trays when different stimuli are administered, and differentiation of squares and of the stimuli themselves, as well as the effects of drugs, ablation, ionic radiation, and the like (Denisenko, 1960; Khananshvili, 1956, 1960; Kupalov, 1964; Popova, 1960; Syrensky, 1960, 1962a, 1962b; Volkova, 1961; Volkova and Kudryavtseva, 1962; Voyevodina, 1960; and a number of others). Kupalov (1964) reported that "more than 100 dogs" had undergone such positional, or what he calls *situational,* conditioning in his laboratory since 1942.

Figure 36 *Kupalov's laboratory of conditioned situational [positional] reflexes combining classical and reinforcement conditioning.* The experimental room, 7.5 x 5 meters, is divided into 70 numbered squares and provided with (1) two tables onto the tops of which food trays are automatically moved, and (2) a large variety of movable auditory and visual stimulators on the walls and floor of the room. The animals' approach to the food trays is "shaped by a meat-path" and conditioned first to the auditory and visual stimuli and then to lying in a particular square on which a small rug is usually placed. The drawings show the first stage of conditioning: upper panel—dog contacting a stimulator on the floor; lower—one on a wall. (From Kupalov, 1960; additional explanation in Footnote 17, p. 165)

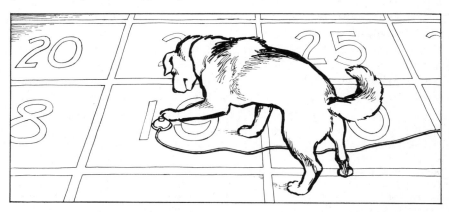

others), and variations of bar-pressing from fish to apes (for summary, see Razran, 1961b; Voronin, 1965). But Soviet theory has not accorded this conditioning due distinctness. Nor have American theorists, in my view, adequately exposed its singularity—not only those who fused Pavlov and Thorndike (Hull, Guthrie, Tolman, Miller) but also those who severed the two (Skinner) and even those for whom the two interact with each other (Sheffield; Rescorla and Solomon). Preoccupation with procedural differences and with types of modified *reactions* rather than with types of resultant *modifications,* the alluring fiction of contingency, and general unevolutionary thinking may be offered as reasons for this. Yet there is ample empirical evidence to warrant the view that the *"laws" of reinforcement conditioning are not just those of classical conditioning but are of a higher evolutionary level, manifesting novelty as well as continuity.* Elsewhere (Razran, 1955e, 1961a, 1965c) I have called attention to one such distinctness, and it will be my task here to codify others. Kimble's statement that "most of the usual conditioning variables seem to influence classical and instrumental conditioning in the same ways" (1961, p. 103) will be qualified.

PARAMETRIC DISTINCTNESS OF REINFORCEMENT CONDITIONING

The Conditioning-Extinction Ratio and Intermittent Reinforcement

Skinner's statement that "operant extinction takes place much more slowly than operant conditioning" (1953, p. 69) is undoubtedly true. He reported one conditioning-extinction ratio of 1:50 with a single reinforcement for bar-pressing in rats (1938, p. 87) and stated that with "some schedules of intermittent reinforcement as many as 10,000 responses may appear in the [pecking] behavior of a pigeon before extinction is substantially complete" (1953, p. 70). Nothing even remotely like this holds for *appetitive* classical conditioning. Examining at one time extinction data in 100 reports of exteroceptive conditioning from Pavlov's laboratory, I found the median conditioning-extinction ratio to be 36:1 and a median yield of 9 reactions in the first extinction session. Even "natural" conditioned salivation at the sight of meat powder was extinguished in the very first session by Babkin (1904) at intertrial intervals of 2 to 16 minutes.

The difference between the ratios and the numbers of extinction reactions of the two types is too vast to be accounted for by such likely contributing factors as differences in quality of reaction and the fact that the Russians typically begin extinction tests after a large number of conditioning trials. The conclusion is wholly warranted that reinforcement conditioning is *by its nature* a much more irreversible and thus a more efficient and a higher-level type of learning than classical conditioning. Much less dependent upon the agent which brings it into being, this conditioning is a step toward the almost total unextinction of verbal associations which, among other things, prompted Pavlov to consider human language a special system (*Wednesdays,* 1949, Vol. 1, p. 240; original date, November 2, 1932). Or, to put it somewhat differently: While in classical *appetitive* conditioning one must generally count the number of conditioning trials producing one extinction reaction, in reinforcement conditioning one counts the number of extinction reactions per reinforcement, and in verbal association, the number of associations mastered in one trial. "Appetitive" is italicized above, since, as noted in the preceding chapter, classical aversive conditioning is considerably more resistant to extinction and, with USs of high intensity, may approach or even exceed the resistance of reinforcement conditioning.

The higher-level distinctness of reinforcement conditioning is equally unmistakable when reinforcement is intermittent. Skinner (1938) reports rapid bar-pressing in rats when a pellet of food was administered in a ratio of 1:192. Podkopayev and Vyrzhikovsky were unable, according to Pavlov (1927a, p. 334; 1927b, p. 384), to form a salivary CR in a dog dog fed every fourth application after 240 feedings. Usiyevich (1938) found such a CR extremely difficult to form, only about 50 per cent effective, and accompanied by neurotic manifestations. And Brogden (1939a), among others, showed that a transition from 100 to 20 per cent feeding produced considerable decrements in conditioned salivation. The rapid extinction of classical appetitive conditioning and ineffectiveness of significant US intermittency are no doubt the prime factors in limiting radically the extent of feasible classical "schedules," so wide and varied in reinforcement conditioning (Ferster and Skinner, 1957). Yet other scheduling factors also operate to produce the distinction. The decremental effects of overconditioning, first pointed out by Pavlov, appear in classical conditioning only after considerable training (Stroganov, 1929; and others) but affect reinforcement conditioning early (Ison, 1962; North and Stimmel, 1960; and others) or even initially (Skinner, 1938). Likewise, reinforcement conditioning—at least in comparison with salivary conditioning—commands much more feedback to permit the chaining and patterning of schedules. Bar-pressing itself is of course a chained reaction; Skinner (1938, p. 54) decomposed it into four reflexes, and Keller and Schoenfeld (1950) into six units.

The Inhibition of Classical Extinction and the Punishment of Nonreinforcement

Whatever the exact mechanisms of the inhibition of extinction may be, there is the fact that in typical Pavlovian experiments the extinction sessions are rather passive behavioral events. Experimenters' protocols describe the dogs as quiet, sometimes drowsy, but seldom agitated or aggressive. Extinction by itself is not one of the many methods which the Russians use to produce, through frustration, experimental neuroses. In Pavlovian theory, it is the most normal manifestation of inhibition (Frolov, 1926), rarely overstrained or clashing with excitation per se. Its decremental effects on other reactions do not accumulate, as in punishment learning, but dissipate in consecutive trials.

On the other hand, reinforcement conditioning had for some time disclosed the aversive role of nonreinforcement. Kapustnik and Fadeyeva, working in Ivanov-Smolensky's laboratory with children five to twelve years old, noted in 1930 that when pressing the bulb failed to yield chocolate "some children cried loudly and others ran out of the room" (p. 37). Miller and Stevenson reported in 1936 "agitated behavior of rats during experimental extinction [of reinforcement]" (p. 205). The early evidence— the Russian study was most likely unknown in the West—had, however, little impact on the prevailing theory that nonreinforcement is just a passive unwinding of reinforcement. But in time, probably due to thoughts about "expectancy" and "anticipation," views changed. The common-sense and clinical term "frustration" was brought in. Rohrer (1949) considered extinction a "frustration drive," and Amsel (1951, 1962) added a formal new concept to Hull's system: r_f, "fractional anticipatory frustration." Spence (1960) sanctioned the concept as paralleling r_e, "the hypothetical emotional response . . . resulting from a noxious stimulus" in his own system (p. 98). Significant empirical data were provided by Ferster (1958) on the decremental effects of nonreinforcement of "time out" from a positive reinforcer in pigeons and chimpanzees, and by Wagner (1963, 1966) on the aversive effects of stimuli paired with nonreinforced trials— conditioned nonreinforcement—in rats.

Three qualifying propositions are in order, however. (1) The nonreinforcement aversion may not be universal—it may not hold, for instance, when the onset of a light rather than food is the reinforcer, or when a galvanic skin reflex is the reinforced reaction, or when fish are the subjects. (2) The aversion is a learned reaction and *ipso facto* does not possess the full properties of an innate noxious stimulus in inhibiting for long periods, for instance, copulation or eating—in fact, it may not be a true punishing reaction at all in the modern sense of producing more or less permanent learning changes (Chapter 6). (3) When the subjects are children, classical conditioning extinction not uncommonly also gives rise to aversive reactions (Krasnogorsky, 1907, 1913, 1929, 1931, 1934, 1954, 1958; Mateer, 1918). These qualifications need not mean that this aversion is a function of affective or cognitive action, but only that it is an outcome of adaptive evolution.

Secondary Reinforcement

On the face of it, the term suggests a parallel of second-order classical conditioning, as indeed it did, to Hull (1943, Chapter 6, Frolov's experiment) and originally also to Skinner (1938, pp. 81-82; 244-245). However, the parallel is faulty, since secondary reinforcers derive their strength from unconditioned reinforcers and not from previously conditioned reactions. And Skinner later (1953, p. 76) uses correctly the term "conditioned reinforcers" in juxtaposing "the acquisition of the power to *elicit* . . . with the power to reinforce." That is, both are considered first-order conditioned modifications. An "empty dish will [after prior pairing with food] elicit salivation [and] will also reinforce an operant," he states, and he goes on to discuss the "natural contingencies" of conditioned reinforcers the way Soviet theorists do "natural" classical conditioning.

Skinner is not concerned with interaction between reinforcement and classical conditioning. Secondary or conditioned reinforcement is, however, a telling illustration of it and of the higher-level manifestation it engenders in reinforcement conditioning. By all accounts (Bersh, 1951; Bugelski, 1938; Cowles, 1937; and others), this kind of reinforcement, too, is more resistant to extinction than is classical appetitive conditioning. Still, one may well doubt Skinner's tenet that "generalized" secondary reinforcers become independent of the primary reinforcers which brought them into being— which, incidentally, is also implied in Mowrer's "secondary" quaternion of fear, hope, relief, and disappointment. The Soviet view that such independence or permanent "unextinction" is unique to man and his second-signal system is ostensibly more in accord with total East-and-West evidence and logic. Note that Mowrer's human—one is tempted to say "humane"—concepts go Skinner one better in unevolutionary systematization. Not only is the behavior of man fishlike, but the cognition of fish is manlike—egalitarianism folded over.

Stimulus Control in Classical and Reinforcement Conditioning

In classical conditioning, stimulus control of reactions is rather limited. Stimulus generalization is wide, and, except for configuring in higher animals (Chapter 9), precise differentiation is effected only through contrasting US-paired and US-unpaired trials. In reinforcement conditioning, however, the stimulus control of S^D-$S^\triangle$ is commonly a natural accompaniment of the development of simple reinforcement. Yet, as in secondary reinforcement, this higher efficacy is an outcome of the interaction of classical CSs (better, Ros) with reinforced and reinforcing reactions, not of a *sui generis* S^D operation. On the other hand, the present account disputes common Soviet views that reinforcement conditioning as such is only a special manifestation of classical conditioning. Skinner's tenet (and Thorndike's) that reinforcement is an independent learning mechanism is fully upheld, with the single proviso that this mechanism does not in itself abrogate concomitant and subsistent operation of classical conditioning. A reinforcer not only strengthens a reaction but conditions it classically to itself, which is quite different from saying that reinforcement is a direct outcome of this conditioning or, conversely, that it is a basically unrelated supersedure of it. In fine, compressed into one sentence, the import of the four kinds of conditioning-reinforcement distinctness is: *While Pavlov disclosed the basic attributes of conditioning, Skinner has demonstrated their higher and more complex level of existence.* Pavlov himself presaged the distinction in stating: "In our experiments . . . the connections are quite temporary. . . . In Thorndike's studies the connections are of a more permanent nature" (*Wednesdays,* 1949, Vol. 2, p. 581; original date, December 5, 1934 [English edition, 1955, pp. 583-584]).

Significantly, recent evidence of Miller and his associates (Miller, 1969a, 1969b) shows that reinforcement of visceral reactions is likewise more stable and precise than their typical classical modifications. On the other hand, while two recent American experiments (Schuster and Brady, 1964; Slucki, Ádám, and Porter, 1965) also disclose that interoceptive or visceral stimulation may become effective S^Ds and $S^\triangle$s of reinforcement, Soviet evidence and the consideration that classical URs are more universal than reinforcers impels the view that these built-in and almost ever-present stimuli are primarily classical CS^+s, CS^-s, and USs. That is to say, the Miller breakthrough is in the main a complement of those of Bykov, Alekseyev-Berkman, Ivanova, and Ivanov in 1928 and Ayrapet'-yants and Balakshina in 1935. Note, for instance, Miller's statement, "The experiments have deep implications . . . for the cause and cure of abnormal psychosomatic symptoms" (1969a, p. 434), and Ayrapet'yants and Bykov's that "The relation and place of interoceptive conditioned [classical] connections explain important aspects of the subconscious, giving the phenomenon a vigorous scientific foundation" 1945, p. 592). What puzzles me, however, is Miller's belief that the reinforceability of visceral reactions *disproves* views that reinforcement is a higher level of conditioning than the classical type, whereas actually his data *demonstrate* that to a considerable extent it is higher even when the reinforced reactions are of a lower neural level.

REINFORCEMENT CONDITIONING IN LOWER ANIMALS, HUMAN NEONATES, AND DECORTICATE CATS

1. Prazdnikova (1953a, 1953b) was the first to experiment with simple and differential reinforcement conditioning in fish (goldfish). Her method consisted of providing the fish with food through a funnel in one corner of the aquarium whenever they tugged at a suspended bead in another corner. The tugging was a "natural" reaction, but it took the animals 20 to 30 trials to tug and swim immediately to the feeding place. The experimenter's task, however, was to train the fish to tug-and-swim in response to a 5-second flash of a green light, at intervals of 1 to 3 minutes, through reinforcement administered only when the light was on. The results for one fish are presented in Figure 37, from which it may be seen that (*a*) the fish mastered the task at the end of the first experimental session; (*b*) while frequent tuggings in intertrial intervals recurred in the first part of the second session, they were extinguished more quickly; and (*c*) in the seventh session (94th trial), correct responding to the light occurred at the very beginning of the session.

In the same experiment, Prazdnikova established in two fish "conditioned inhibition" (no responding when another stimulus was repeatedly

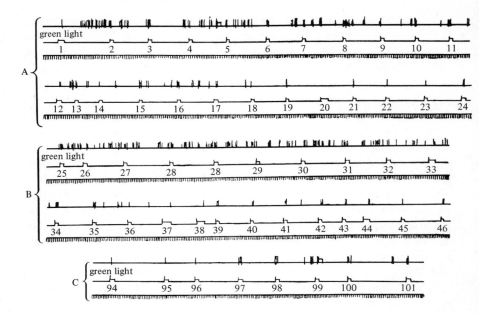

Figure 37 *Fish tugging at a bead to obtain food in response to a flash of a green light.* Panel A—data of the first experimental session; B—second session, the following day; C—seventh session. Lines in each panel, from the top: tuggings, flash of green light, time in seconds. Note the gradual elimination of interstimulus tugs in the first session, reappearance and faster elimination in the second, and almost total absence in the seventh when the fish tugged only when the green light was flashed. (From Prazdnikova, 1953b)

added to the positive stimulus without feeding); a second-order CR in a third fish; and alternation of conditioned inhibition with second-order CRs in a fourth. And in a later study (Prazdnikova, 1962), she was able to form in a fish a similar CR with an S^D-reinforcer delay of 3 minutes, lengthening the delays gradually.

2. Dewes (1959) trained three octopuses to pull a ¼-inch brass lever which lit a lamp which in turn was followed by delivery of a small piece of fish on a nylon line with a glass sinker. The animals' reactions were first modified by feeding them for six days in the presence of the light, while approach to the lever, introduced on the seventh day, was facilitated by covering its lower end with rubber tubing and attaching to it a small swaying cross. All three octopuses learned after a few days of experimentation to pull the lever, having been at first reinforced upon mere approach to it. The learning was, however, rather unstable. Extinction was rapid, and an attempt to use a 1:3 fixed ratio of reinforcement with one animal met with little success. Moreover, one octopus developed a tendency to pull the lamp rather than the lever and to spray jets of water at the experimenter, which terminated further training.

3. Chesnokova (1959) experimented with seven marked honeybees and the discrimination of a pattern of cues to enter the arm of a T-maze in which a bit of syrup was placed. The pattern consisted of a chain of three light filters of different colors at the bottom of the maze, from which the insects were required to discriminate (*a*) like chains of different colors, (*b*) one or two components of the positive chain, and (*c*) the positive chain in reverse sequence. Moreover, there were two kinds of discriminations: one in which the positive and negative chains were in the arms of the maze, and another in which they were in its stem, signaling in which arm the syrup was present. The simplest learning of positive versus negative chains of different colors in the arms of the maze took the insects 5 to 29 trials to master. The most complex, discriminating in the stem which arm to enter when the chains differed only in sequence, required 67 to 158 trials. The last performance is said by the experimenter to indicate that the bees' learning ability is higher than that of rodents and about equal to that of carnivores (!). (Lopatin and Chesnokova [1965] reached the same conclusion.)

4. Siqueland and Lipsitt (1966) performed three successful experiments with reinforcement of head-turning in 46 human neonates less than 4 days old. The stimulus eliciting the head-turning was an ipsilateral touch of the subject's cheek, and the reinforcer was a dextrose solution. In the first experiment, only one cheek was stimulated, and the tactile stimulus was preceded by the sound of a buzzer. In the second, both cheeks were touched alternately, a buzzer preceding the touch of one and a tone the other; in the third experiment, with one cheek, reinforcements of touch plus one auditory stimulus were alternated with nonreinforcements of touch plus the other. Moreover, in the second part of the third experiment, the reinforced and nonreinforced stimulations were reversed, and in the first two experiments 12 to 30 extinction trials were administered. There were 18 experimental subjects in the first experiment, 20 in the second, and 8 in the third, with an equal number of controls in each case.

The results are presented in Figure 38—the top, middle, and bottom panels referring, respectively, to the first, second, and third experiments. The figure demonstrates that the neonates mastered well both simple and discriminative reinforcement conditioning, as well as reversal of the latter. They also showed evidence of typical extinction.

5. Belenkov (1950b, 1965) formed stable discriminative reinforcement conditioning of moving toward a feeding box in four bilaterally decorticate cats (removal of neocortex only). The S^{D}s were a metronome of 120 beats per minute for two animals, a bell for the third, and a 100-watt light for the fourth. The discriminative CR to the bell, and to the metronome in one animal, first appeared after 25 trials, to the metronome in the other animal after 45, and to the light in the fourth cat after 65 trials. (Only a few trials were made each day.) When the CRs were well estab-

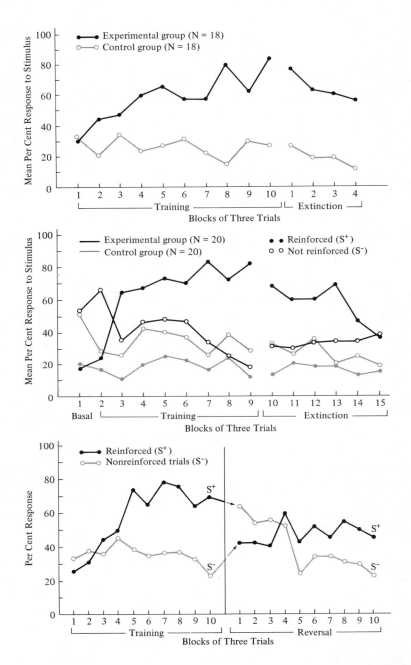

Figure 38 *Simple, differential, and reversal reinforcement conditioning and extinction in 46 human neonates less than 4 days old.* Head-turning, elicited by ipsilateral touch of the subjects' cheeks, was the reinforced reaction and a dextrose solution the reinforcer. Only one cheek was stimulated in the groups of the top and bottom panels; both cheeks alternatively in the group of the middle panel. The number of experimental and control subjects in the group of the bottom panel was 8. (From Siqueland and Lipsitt, 1966)

lished, light S^Ds replaced the metronome, and the metronome replaced the light and the bell. The results show that the CR to the light required 30 additional trials in one animal and 40 in the other, to the metronome replacing the light 25, and to the metronome replacing the bell 10. The S^Ds thus were wholly specific, with no evidence of cross-modal generalization, and only possible facilitatory effects from bell to metronome. Moreover, when the cat with the bell and metronome S^Ds was trained to a light S^D, the CR required 120 additional trials. On first appearance, the latencies of the CRs were as long as 8 seconds, and the time to reach the feeding box was approximately 30 seconds; after the CRs were well established, the respective figures were 1-2 and 4 seconds.[18]

Interpretive Comment

It is often implied (Kimble, 1961, p. 72; McConnell, 1966; and others) that reinforcement conditioning may be effected in organisms of very low phylogeny. Perusal of available evidence reveals, however, that it comprises either punishment (a number of examples of which were presented in Chapter 6) or classical aversive conditioning in T or Y mazes or it is unverified, e.g., Gelber's (1952) study of paramecia (see Katz and Deterline, 1958). Evans' (1966b) recent well-controlled investigation of 59 earthworms in what was essentially a straight 10-centimeter long runway with food as the sole modifier shows the food to be a general energizer rather than a specific reinforcer. His conclusion is that "food presentation sensitizes worms' responses to sudden increases in illumination" irrespective of the temporal relations [contingencies?] of the two, and the title of his experiment is "Non-associative Behavioral Modifications in the Polychaeta *Nereis diversicolor*" (cf. Young, 1958, 1960; Wells, 1967, with octopuses). The position is warranted that full-fledged reinforcement-reward conditioning is significantly operative only in the learning of higher invertebrates, and vertebrates, from bony fish on. Compare a similar view by Wells (1965).

On the other hand, the Siqueland-Lipsitt study (1966) and the studies by Papoušek (the pioneer in head-turning CRs: 1959, 1960b, 1961, 1965, 1967a, 1967b, 1967c, 1969; Papoušek and Bernstein, 1967) leave no doubt that such conditioning is fully developed in human neonates. Note that head-turning in human neonates is a relatively unhabituable reaction and at times appears spontaneously (Prechtl, 1958).

---

[18] In an earlier experiment, Belenkov (1950a, 1965), formed classical CRs in four decorticate cats with unavoidable shock to a paw as the US and metronomes and lights as the CSs, using a similar design of first stabilizing the conditioning to one CS and then beginning to train it to another. The CRs appeared after 32 to 241 trials (20 to 25 trials per day), and here, too, there was absolutely no evidence of cross-modal generalization and the latencies were shortened manyfold upon CR stabilization.

AMERICAN EXPERIMENTS ON VERBAL REINFORCEMENT

Soviet second-signal system theory equates classical verbal conditioning with verbal reinforcement and, moreover, relates both exclusively to the operation of "higher mental processes" in man (Kol'tsova, 1958, 1967; Krasnogorsky, 1954, 1958; Povorinsky, 1954; Pratusevich, 1960, 1964; Shvarts, 1954, 1960; and others)—and will, therefore, be discussed in Chapter 10, on Thinking. However, a number of American experimenters recently have reported suggestive results with verbal reinforcements (or punishments) considered no different from other [infrahuman] reinforcers (or punishers), in line with Skinner's view of "verbal behavior as [but] behavior reinforced through the mediation of other persons" (Skinner, 1957, p. 2) and as a continuation of Thorndike's early studies with the word "right" as a "satisfier" and "wrong" as an "annoyer." Three of these experiments will be presented.

1. Greenspoon (1955) used the sound "Mmm-hmm" as a reinforcer and "Huh-uh" as a punisher of two classes of words in the free verbalizations of discrete words by seventy-five college students. The students were divided into a control group which received no reinforcement or punishment and four experimental groups: I—plural words reinforced and "Mmm-hmm" as the reinforcer; II—plurals punished by "Huh-uh"; III—nonplurals reinforced by "Mmm-hmm"; and IV—nonplurals punished by "Huh-uh." The experimental sessions lasted 50 minutes, of which only the first 25 were reinforced or punished. The data of ten subjects who indicated at the end of the experiments that they had caught on to the experimenter's intent were discarded.

The results of all groups are presented in Table 5, which is a summary of Greenspoon's Tables II and III, while those of Group I are given also in Figure 39. The entries in Table 5 are mean numbers of words spoken in 5 minutes in the first and second 25-minute periods. As may be seen, only in Group I and partly in Group II were the reinforcers or punishers effective, the respective means for the two groups in the two halves of the experiments being 21.99 and 11.88, and 5.99 and 5.44, as against 11.32 and 8.45 in the control group. That is to say, "Mmm-hmm" as a reinforcer increased the plurals, which later decreased during nonreinforcement, while "Huh-uh" as a punisher decreased them a little more than in subsequent nonpunishment. Greenspoon's conclusion that "both [reinforcers and punishers] tended to increase the frequency of 'non-plural responses' " (p. 416) is, however, unwarranted, since the means of experimental groups III and IV differed little from those of the control group. But we may well agree with him that the nature of the reinforced response is "a determinant of the reinforcing character" of the reinforcer. In the control group, nonplurals were approximately seven times as frequent as plurals.

2. Verplanck (1955) modified the opinions of 24 adult human subjects, mostly college students, through reinforcement and extinction in

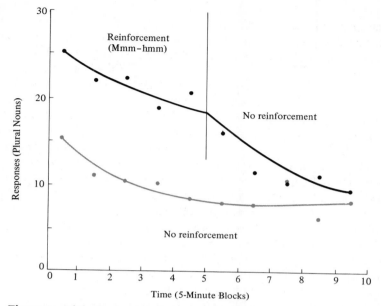

Figure 39 *The effects of verbal reinforcement "Mmm-hmm" on response frequencies of plural nouns in college students (N = 13).* (Figure from Holz and Azrin, 1966; drawn from data of Greenspoon, 1955.)

casual conversations with 17 experimenters. The subjects were not aware of the intent of the experimenters, who used with different groups of subjects two different methods for each type of modification: *A*—agreement

Table 5 *Effects of "Mmm-hmm" or "Huh-uh" on Verbalizations of Discrete Words by Sixty-Five College Students.* Mean number of words uttered in five minutes. (From Greenspoon, 1955)

Group	Reinforced or Punished Words	Reinforcer or Punisher	Mean Number of Words in 5-Minute Periods of Reinforcement or Punishment (First 23 Minutes)	Mean Number of Words in 5-Minute Periods of Nonreinforcement or Nonpunishment (Second 25 Minutes)
I	Plurals of Nouns	Mmm-hmm	21.99	11.88
II	Plurals of Nouns	Huh-uh	5.99	5.44
Control	Plurals of Nouns	None	11.32	8.45
III	Nonplurals	Mmm-hmm	84.10	73.08
IV	Nonplurals	Huh-uh	88.95	74.49
Control	Nonplurals	None	80.47	70.09

(" 'You're right.' 'I agree,' 'That's so,' nodding the head, or smiling"); *P*—paraphrasing the subject's opinions; *E*—extinction or withholding comment; and *D*—disagreement [strictly, punishment rather than extinction]. The conversations lasted for 30 minutes; the first 10 were spent in ascertaining the "operant level" of opinion and non-opinion statements, the second 10 in reinforcing the opinions, and the last 10 in extinguishing or disagreeing with them. Moreover, to control for changes due to passage of time, the sequence in one group of 7 subjects was: agreement, extinction, and agreement again. An opinion was considered a sentence beginning with " 'I think . . . ,' 'I believe,' 'It seems to me,' 'I feel,' and the like."

Verplanck evaluated his data in two types of frequency ratios: (*a*) opinion/non-opinion statements, and (*b*) reinforcement/operant-and-extinction and extinction/reinforcement of opinion statements. Combining both methods of reinforcement and of extinction, he found the opinion/-non-opinion ratios in the main groups to be: .32 in the initial-operant level, .558 in the reinforcement period, and .333 in the extinction period, with respective ratios of .574, .302, and .603 in the group with the sequence reinforcement, extinction, and reinforcement again. The mean ratio of opinion in the reinforcement periods to that in operant-and-extinction periods was 2.91 for all 24 subjects, and the extinction/reinforcement ratio was .67. The differences between the ratios were mostly significant at the .05 level or better. The experimenter's own conclusion was: "Every *S* increased in his rate of speaking opinions with reinforcement by paraphrase or agreement. Twenty-one *S*s decreased in rate with nonreinforcement" (p. 676). Figure 40 presents his results graphically.

3. Salzinger and Pisoni (1958) studied reinforcement and extinction of "affect" responses in 20 schizophrenics in the course of two routine 30-minute interviews on consecutive days by two interviewers, a week after the patients' admission to the hospital. The first 10 minutes of each interview were given to ascertaining the "operant level" of the responses, the second to reinforcing them, and the last 10 to extinguishing them. "Affect" responses were statements such as: "I am satisfied. . . . We enjoyed it. . . . 'I'm very close to him. . . . I was mad at him. . . . We hated her. . . . I am a lonely person. . . . I always suffer. . . . Etc." (p. 84). Reinforcers were: " 'Mmm-hmm,' 'I see,' 'Yea,' etc." Extinction consisted of withholding reinforcement and continuing to ask questions. A control group of 16 schizophrenics with neither reinforcement nor extinction and one 30-minute interview also was used.

Table 6 summarizes the experimenters' results in terms of number of "affect" responses (sum of ranks) in the three 10-minute periods in each of the interviews of the experimental group, and in the one 30-minute interview of the control group. The differences among the periods of the experimental group were statistically significant by Wilcoxon's nonparametric analysis in the first interview (*p* <.01), but not quite so in the sec-

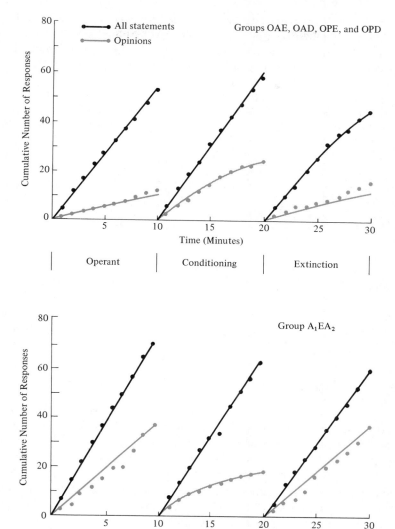

Figure 40 *The effects of verbal reinforcement and their extinction on frequencies of opinion statements in arranged casual conversations between 24 adult human subjects and 17 experimenters.* The letters used to designate the groups are: O—operant level, A—reinforcement by agreement, P—reinforcement by paraphrasing, E—extinction by withholding comment, D—"extinction" by disagreement. Upper panel—combined means of four groups of 17 subjects, with 2 to 6 in each. Lower panel—data of a special control group of 7 subjects in which agreement was followed by extinction and then agreement again. (From Verplanck, 1955)

ond ($p = .2$). The experimenters attribute the high extinction scores in the second interview to the positive effect of reconditioning. They also state that the two interviewers agreed fairly well in their scorings of the three periods in the experimental group: ρ's of .79, .54, and .52.

Table 6 *Effects of Reinforcement and Its Extinction on "Affect" Responses of 20 Schizophrenics in Two 30-Minute Routine Interviews on Consecutive Days by Different Interviewers. Scores are numbers of "affect" responses (sum of ranks) in initial-operant, reinforcement, and extinction periods of 10 minutes each. (From Salzinger and Pisoni, 1958)**

Type of Period	Number of "Affect" Responses (Sum of Ranks) in Consecutive 10-Minute Periods		Control Group	Rank-Order Correlation (ρ)
	Experimental Groups First Interview	Second Interview		
Initial	39.5	33.5	32.0	Reinforcement vs. initial period, .46
Reinforce-ment	51.0	45.0	34.0	Extinction vs. initial period, .41
Extinction	29.5	41.5	36.0	Reinforcement vs. extinction, .73

Interpretive Comment

The three experiments are a small sample—but one hopes a representative one—of the technology of reinforcement conditioning expanded to modifications of normal and abnormal human behavior. In the abnormal area, this expansion has been particularly rapid (Krasner and Ullmann, 1965; Ullmann and Krasner, 1965). As a learning theory search for the basics of psychotherapy, the approach is most welcome. Yet it has often moved in the simplistic direction of untenable rat-man egalitarianism in learning and total excision of the symbolic and predicative uniqueness of language. Mandler and Kaplan noted, for instance, that "Mmm-hmm" increased "plurals of nouns" in some subjects but decreased them in others, depending upon whether the sound "meant" to a subject "doing all right" or "giving the wrong kinds of words" (1956, p. 582). More such findings could be cited. But we might just mention that Thorndike's (1935) series of studies, in which it was assumed that the word "wrong" was an "annoyer" (or punisher) *par excellence* to subjects, had for several decades stymied our understanding of the true nature of punishment learning.

One might dwell on the thesis that cognition no doubt pervades reinforcement much more than classical conditioning. Yet it is classical conditioning which in so many ways put to test and acknowledged, in both East and West, the role of cognitive factors in its operation (Avakyan,

1960; Hilgard, 1938; Kimble, 1967b; J. Miller, 1939; Pratusevich, 1960, 1964; Razran, 1935; Spence, 1963; and many others) and which with some success even managed to distill the semantic from the phonetic in its verbal stimuli (see Razran, 1952, 1961a, and Maltzman, 1968, for summaries). American reinforcement conditioning in the main continues to remain aloof (or, shall we say, beneath?)! May we hope that empirical limitations will eventually impel it to change its course—or pray for a general *Zeitgeist* evolution—or revolution?

All of this is not, to be sure, intended to undervalue the general efficacy of reinforcement technology: its utility in the rehabilitation of autistic children (Ferster and DeMyer, 1961), severe retardates (Kerr, Myerson, and Michael, 1965), and psychotics (Isaacs, Thomas, and Goldiamond, 1960). Yet technology cannot afford to contract unduly its scientific base —to fail to fit the evolutionary level of the *learner* to the evolutionary level of *learning*. And one thinks, further, that reinforcement has, after all, operated on man and even God since time immemorial. Genesis 1:4 reads: "And God saw the light and it was good: and He divided the light from the darkness."

LIMBIC REINFORCEMENT AND PUNISHMENT: LIMITS AND ESSENCE

The discovery (Delgado, Roberts, and Miller, 1954; Miller, Roberts and Delgado, 1953; Olds and Milner, 1954) that electrical stimulations of certain areas of the limbic system of the brain are highly effective reinforcers and/or punishers of higher-animal behavior is no doubt a milestone in bringing together the neurology and psychology of learning. The limits and essence of the discovery have not, however, been adequately codified. First, limbic learning does not apply to lower animals. Second, direct limbic learning obviously is not the natural way of learning in higher animals. Third, it does not actually offer a neural account of learning—only a correspondence between the behavioral effects of certain neural stimulations and of certain behavioral S-R interactions. And that correspondence may, in fact, be very rough: substantial parametric differences between limbic and conventional reinforcement have been reported with respect to extinction, overreinforcement (satiation), massed trials, retention, CER sequels, and the like (Brady, 1957, 1961; Mogenson, 1965; Seward, Uyeda, and Olds, 1959, 1960; and others).[19] Then, there are the further considerations that limbic stimulations also evoke or inhibit specific primary drives (hunger, sex, rage, fear), and that, while conventional punishment is by all tokens more universal in the animal kingdom than is

---

[19] In the same vein, my hypothesis that the relative unhabituability of the modified reaction is a determinant of the occurrence of reinforcement conditioning may well not hold for limbic reinforcement.

conventional reinforcement, the limbic loci of the latter are approximately five times as numerous as those of the former.

The vast literature on the topic warrants, to my mind, six systematic propositions:

1. Limbic reinforcement and punishment are later evolutionary acquisitions and not the underlying general mechanisms of the two types of modifications.

2. Their later emergence, combined with reports of human subjects, strongly suggests that limbic stimulation engenders conscious experience.

3. The experience is, however, a primordial affection and not an organized relational perception, which the coming chapter posits is operative in sensory preconditioning and configuring and is abolished only upon ablation of higher cortical regions.

4. The positive and negative affects of limbic loci are not sequels of evoked or inhibited specific drives but are overall *sui generis* evolvements —the primordial Affectional Mind of philosophic, commonsense, and clinical renown, which the limbic discovery bids fair to embody through controlled experimentation.

5. Affects alter noncognized learning differently than do relational perceptions. Whereas the latter become in essence new and higher levels of learning, the former are only variations of the old levels.

6. The neural engrams of reinforcement and punishment are, in the main, like those of classical conditioning discussed in the preceding chapter. That is, the engrams may reside in any neural locales which join reinforced or punished and reinforcing or punishing reactions, and they must involve correlative growth of junctional tissue and specific *sine qua non* neurophysiological action, even if the neural changes are putatively distinct in each of the three types of conditioning (see Hearst, Beer, Galambos, and Sheatz, 1960, for an inkling of an electrophysiological difference between classical and reinforcement conditioning).

THEORETIC RESUMÉ OF ALL OF SIMPLE CONDITIONING

It seems advisable to end this chapter with a summary not just of reinforcement conditioning but of all simple conditioning considered in the last four chapters. Nineteen basic propositions are called for:

1. All conditioning involves the interaction of two reactions and the modification of one by the other (Doctrine of Modifying and Modified Reactions).

2. The modification is mediated by an overlapping of the neural correlates of the two reactions and, it is assumed, by the greater potency of the correlate of the modifying reaction (Doctrine of Neurobehavioral Dominance).

3. Three distinct kinds of modifications or *types of conditioning* are evident: (*a*) *inhibitory*—the modified reaction is progressively decreased,

(*b*) *classical*—the modified reaction acquires characteristics of the modifying reaction, (*c*) *reinforcement*—the modified reaction is progressively strengthened (Doctrine of Three Types).

4. *Aversive inhibitory conditioning* typifies "punishment learning"; *classical conditioning*, formation of "simple associations"; and *reinforcement conditioning*, formation of "reward associations."

5. The primary conditions for the three types of conditioning, are respectively: *neurobehavioral antagonism of interacting reactions, habituability of the modified reaction, and relative unhabituability of the modified reaction.* It is assumed that the neural engrams of the three types have both common and separate mechanisms.

6. Inhibitory conditioning is pre-classical in the sense that (*a*) in its typical form the inhibited (punished) reaction does not acquire the characteristics of the inhibiting (punishing) reaction, and (*b*) it may be effected in organisms in which classical conditioning is not possible (e.g., coelenterates—Ross, 1965).

7. Reinforcement conditioning is post-classical in the sense that (*a*) it typically includes classical-conditioning operations; (*b*) it may be impossible when classical conditioning is possible (lower invertebrates; gill extension in fish—Adler and Hogan, 1963); and (*c*) within it, the functional laws of classical conditioning attain a level of substantially higher efficiency and qualitative novelty.

8. Classical conditioning comprises two distinct basic varieties, (*a*) *appetitive,* which is readily extinguishable, and (*b*) *aversive,* which is relatively stable, that stability being an accelerated direct function of the intensity of the unconditioned aversive reaction. (Mildly aversive and "neutral" classical conditioning behave, however, as appetitive conditioning.)

9. Reinforcement conditioning typically is effected through a modifying reaction that is either (*a*) the activation of an appetitive reaction or (*b*) the termination of an aversive reaction. "Appetitive" and "aversive" are to be construed in a broad operational—and eventually physiological—sense and not as involving *ipso facto* "positive" and "negative" affects and drives.

10. Skinner's use of "reinforcement" as synonymous only with "strengthening" or commonsense "reward" is endorsed. However, his term "negative reinforcement" is often wrongly confused with "punishment," hence "aversive reinforcement" is suggested instead. Aversive reinforcement does not, however, differ basically from appetitive reinforcement in the same way that aversive classical conditioning does from appetitive classical conditioning. Both aversive and appetitive reinforcements are "rewards."

11. Reinforcement conditioning includes classical conditioning, not in the sense that the latter (*a*) becomes operative in some segment of a reinforced reaction as a "fractional anticipatory r_g, r_e, or r_f" (Spence, 1960) or (*b*) "mediates it by a common central state" (Rescorla and Solomon,

1967) or (c) antedates its functioning (Mowrer, 1960a) or (d) is its guiding mechanism (Konorski, 1967), but in the sense that the two types coexist or, more exactly, that one, the classical, subsists within the other.[20]

12. Classical conditioning does not, however, include reinforcement conditioning, since no "strengthening of the existing modified reactions" may be disclosed in its typical paradigm. Statements that classical conditioning does include reinforcement conditioning stem from theoretical analogies and not empirical evidence.

13. Propositions 5 through 12 support the view that the three types of conditioning are in essence three ascending evolutionary levels of learning.

14. Effective classical conditioning of interoceptive or visceral stimulations and reinforcement conditioning of visceral reactions predicate the existence of a wide *autonomic substructure* of noncognitive learning in human somatic and verbal behavior, long intimated by Watson and considered by non-Freudian students of psychosomatics in both East and West ("corticovisceral pathology," in Russian terms). Yet, there is also ample evidence that a large portion of our behavior is greatly affected by a learned *cognitive superstructure* which may be assumed to be most operative in reinforcement conditioning, least in the inhibitory conditioning, with classical conditioning in an intermediate position.

15. Changes in drives or "motivation" are but secondary parameters of conditioning in the sense that they modify its separate interacting reactions but not the interaction itself, and they are thus not indispensable for its existence. Indeed, there is no known drive-mediating mechanism in organisms of lower phylogeny in which inhibitory and classical conditioning are readily effected and some reinforcement conditioning is also possible. And one may well argue that the wholesale mixing of drives and "motivation" with conditioning, begun by Hull and recently revived somewhat differently by Konorski, may delay discovery of the idiopathic neurobehavioral essence of the conditioning mechanism as such.[21]

16. Avoidance conditioning," as the term is used in the United States and as used by Konorski in his Type II conditioning with an "unattractive

---

[20] This does not mean that the two types of conditioning may not be separated experimentally (Ellison and Konorski, 1965, 1966), but it does mean that dominant reinforcement conditioning thrusts out incompatible or superfluous subordinate classical conditioning, as in the positional experiments of Kupalov considered at the beginning of the chapter.

[21] Compare Hinde: "There are no clear criteria for distinguishing changes in behaviour which are to be ascribed to motivational factors from those which are not. . . . Drive concepts . . . can be valuable when a positive correlation between the possible dependent variables is of primary interest but are misleading when the extent to which such correlations are not perfect becomes important [and] can be dangerous if used to explain diverse characteristics of behaviour which could result from quite different aspects of underlying mechanisms; if they lead to oversimple implications about the manner in which independent variables affect behaviour" (1966, p. 147).

US," is ultimately held here to be a classical aversive conditioning and not reinforcement conditioning.

17. Past analyses of types of conditioned modifications have erred in (*a*) confusing the essences of the modification with the methods of producing it and the reactions involved in it and (*b*) overlooking the totality of available evidence. Particularly diversionary are (*a*) the pre-Humean view of *contingency* and the resultant distinction between "stimulus-contingent" and "response-contingent" conditioning and (*b*) the penchant for anthropomorphic "passive" and "active" *avoidance* when objective evidence for a difference between aversive *inhibitory* and aversive *classical* conditioning is at hand.

18. There is as yet no directly proven neuromorphology of conditioning —only clues that stimulation increases junctional growth. And so far no neurophysiological mechanism has been demonstrated as more than a frequent correlate of conditioning—not a *sine qua non*. Nonetheless, neural evidence is shaping more and more our main thinking in the area, and conditioning systems which ignore it are arguably on the wrong track and not likely to be productive for long.

19. Limbic stimulation engenders conscious positive or negative affects when it reinforces or punishes behavior. It cannot, however, be the neural basis of these modifications, if for no other reason than that these are fully evident in lower organisms without limbic systems. Nor does limbic stimulation apparently involve full-fledged perception, which the coming chapter posits is operative in sensory preconditioning and configuring and is abolished only upon ablation of higher cortical region. The most tenable assumption for the system is that, among other things, it is the neural locale of the Nonperceptual Affectional Mind, inducting variations in correlative prelimbic associative mechanisms of rewards and punishments.

CHAPTER NINE

Sensory Preconditioning and Configuring—The Learning of Perceptions

SENSORY PRECONDITIONING

Sample Soviet Experiments

"Sensory preconditioning" was first noted by Panferov in 1926 in salivary conditioning of children and by Narbutovich and Podkopayev in 1936 in salivary and shock conditionings of dogs. It was named the "formation of an association" or "associative temporary connections." Three dogs were used in the Narbutovich and Podkopayev study. In two animals, a noise was sounded for 5 seconds and joined for another 5 by the sight of a whirligig; the whirligig was later paired with an electric shock to the animal's left hindleg. In the third, with identical time relations, a tuning fork preceded the flash of an electric lamp and the US was the administration of food. The number of preconditioned pairings ranged from 21 to 30. Sensory preconditioning is shown by the presented data to have developed in all cases. *The noise paired with the whirligig but not the shock evoked leg flexion, and the lamp paired with the tuning fork but not the food came to evoke salivation.* Indeed, in the third dog, the preconditioning was, as may be noted, a "backward sequence," the preceding and not the succeeding stimulus having been conditioned to the food. The effects of generalization are said to be ruled out by the fact that the associated stimuli were of sense modalities different from those of the conditioned stimuli, yet they evoked substantially larger reactions than the tested generalization stimuli of the conditioned modalities. The experimenters also report, significantly, the formation of conditioned orientation in later preconditioned pairings— that is, dogs turning to the source of one stimulus upon administration of the other.

It will be convenient to cite samples of further Soviet studies in order of ascending phylogeny and to add to them a number of generalizations culled from a recent summary of the topic in a special book by Sergeyev (1967). And it seems advisable also to present specifically only three of his nine earlier experimental reports, including the remaining six (Sergeyev, 1960, 1961a, 1963, 1964a, 1965a, 1965b) among the generalizations.

Birds. Sergeyev (1961b) experimented with eight titmice (*Parus major L.* and *Parus ater L.*). The US was an automatic movement of a 10-centi- · meter disk which caused the birds to react defensively in three ascending degrees of intensity: (*a*) jumping from perch to perch in an outer cage; (*b*) flying to and hiding temporarily in an inner cage; (*c*) prolonged stay in the inner cage. The two preconditioned stimuli were lights and sounds which at no time evoked defensive reactions. They were paired 30 to 50 times at intervals of 3 to 5 seconds, and there was a series of "comparable control stimuli to test for generalization." The data show that only one bird failed to be preconditioned. The mean reaction to the associated stimulus in the other seven birds was 65 per cent of that to the CS—specifically, 2 vs. 20 high-intensity reactions, 11 vs. 15 of medium intensity, 13 vs. 5 of low intensity, and 8 vs. zero of no reaction. The preconditioning was more effective when the associated stimulus preceded the to-be-conditioned stimulus. The control stimuli are stated to have evoked no reactions in any test.

Guinea Pigs and Rabbits. Oreshuk (1950) investigated sensory preconditioning in two guinea pigs and three rabbits. The US was an electric shock applied to one of the animal's legs, and evoked respiratory changes were the primary CRs. The associated stimulus was the flash of a light and the to-be-conditioned stimulus was the sound of an electric bell, neither of which produced changes in respiration. Both guinea pigs, but none of the rabbits, were preconditioned. The upper panel of Figure 41 shows the response to the conditioned bell and the associated light. The experimenter does not state the number of preconditioned pairings.

Malinovsky (1953) did succeed in preconditioning four of six rabbits, using a food-obtaining reinforcement technique (pulling a ring). The associated stimuli were lights, and the to-be-conditioned stimuli were a tone for two animals and an electric bell for two others. The number of pairings ranged from 24 to 32. The lower panel of Figure 41 presents the data for one rabbit: clear-cut pulling in response to the associated light (5th entry in the upper segment and 4th in the lower) and none to the control stimulus, the sight of a whirligig (3rd entry in the upper segment and 7th in the lower).

Dogs. Rokotova (1952) worked with three dogs using classical salivary conditioning and a somewhat modified method of preconditioning. In one

Figure 41 *Sample sensory preconditioning in 1 of 2 guinea pigs (upper panel) and in 1 of 4 rabbits (lower panel).* In the guinea pigs, classical conditioning was used. The to-be-conditioned stimulus was the sound of a bell, the associated stimulus a flash of a light, and the US a shock producing changes in respiration, which neither the bell nor the light originally did. The records, from the top, are: respiration, administration of the conditioned and the associated stimuli, administration of shock (none), and time in seconds. Note the clear-cut reaction to the light. (From Oreshuk, 1950) In the rabbits, preconditioned discriminative stimuli in reinforcement food conditioning were used—animals pulling a ring to obtain food. The to-be-conditioned stimulus was a tone, the associated stimulus a light, and the control stimulus the sight of a whirligig. Note that the light evoked a very pronounced reaction, while the control whirligig had no effect whatsoever. (From Malinovsky, 1953)

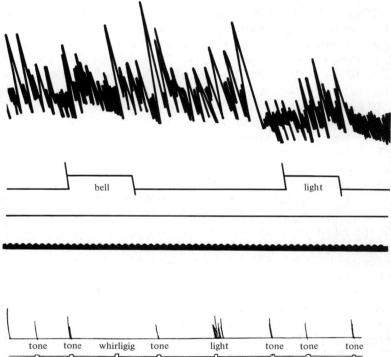

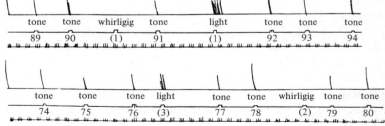

dog, two associated stimuli, a whistle and a dark circle on an illuminated screen, were paired with a to-be-conditioned tone stimulus, each stimulus applied for 10 seconds with 10-second intervals between them. The control stimulus was an electric bell. With the second dog, four experiments were performed at different times. In the first, the associated and the to-be-conditioned stimuli were, respectively, the sight of a circle and the sound of bubbling water, with an interstimulus interval of 15 seconds and a noise as a control stimulus. In the second, they were: a light, a tone, an interval of 20 seconds, and, again, a noise as a control. In the third, a noise, a whistle, a 30-second interval, and an electric bell as a control; and in the fourth, a bell, a rhythmic "toucher" applied to the hip, an interval of 60 seconds, and a rhythmic "toucher" applied to the shoulder as a control. In the third dog, the associated stimulus was the bubbling of water, the to-be-conditioned stimulus a rhythmic "toucher," and the interstimulus interval 10 seconds. The number of preconditioned pairings ranged from 24 to 84.

The experimenter presents the data of the first five experiments in protocols of five experimental sessions in each of which the nonconditioned associated stimuli produced substantial salivation and the control stimuli *none* whatsoever. It will be noted that in four of the five experiments, the associated and conditioned stimuli were of different sense modalities, whereas the control stimuli were of the same modality as the CS. The difference between the reactions to the associated and control stimuli, moreover, was absolute—all-or-none—which the Russians hold to be unqualified proof that they were an outcome of preconditioning and not generalization. Indeed, this absoluteness is considered fully convincing in the third experiment with the second dog, when "noise" produced almost as much saliva as the conditioned "whistle" while the "electric bell" was wholly ineffective. (The results with the third dog are not specified but are merely described as being "as successful as those of the first two.")

In a later study (1954), Rokotova used classical and reinforcement food conditioning with one dog, and classical food and shock conditioning with two others. In the reinforcement conditioning, the flash of a light preceded the sound of a metronome 72 times in three experimental sessions. And, as seen in Figure 42, when the metronome was made an S^D (discriminative stimulus) for bar-pressing for food, the flash of a light became equally adequate (2nd entry), while an illuminated circle, the control stimulus, was wholly ineffective (5th entry). In the classical food conditioning of the same dog, sensory preconditioning failed when the sound of a siren of high intensity preceded a to-be-conditioned flash of a weak light, presumably because—the experimenter states—*high intensity stimuli interfere with the formation or maintenance of orienting reflexes which mediate the phenomenon* (cf. Thornton, 1956). In the other two dogs, preconditioning was fully successful with a combination of a "toucher" applied to the hip and the sound of a metronome later made a CS to food condition-

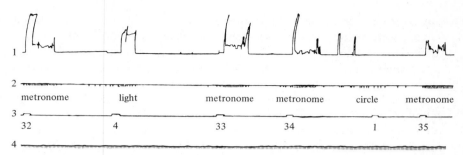

metronome	light	metronome	metronome	circle	metronome
32	4	33	34	1	35

Figure 42 *Sensory preconditioning of S^Ds in a dog's bar-pressing for food.* The S^D was the sound of a metronome, the associated stimulus was the flash of a light bulb, and the control stimulus the sight of an illuminated circle. Note that the light was very markedly effective and the circle not at all. (From Rokotova, 1954)

ing. Moreover, *the associated food reaction to the "toucher" became automatically a shock reaction when the CR to the metronome was transformed through pairings with a shock stimulus,* a finding that contrasts with earlier outcomes in second-order conditioning in which similar transformations of first-order CRs did not affect the nature of the second-order CRs (*Wednesdays,* 1949, Vol. 1, p. 240; original date, November 2, 1932).

Rokotova's significant transformation finding was not fully replicated by Sergeyev (1967) in his experiment with nine dogs and three consecutive series of transformations. In the first series, transforming food into shock conditioning caused the associated stimulus to evoke automatically a shock reaction in only three animals. In four others, the associated reactions retained their food character, while in the remaining two they were mixed: either food in some trials and shock in others, or some combination of the two in the same trials. In the second series, retransforming the shock into food conditioning in the three animals in which the associated reaction had been transformed resulted in the associated stimulus evoking food reactions in one dog and mixed reactions in two. Finally, in the last series of food-shock transformation, in which the two animals with mixed reactions in the first series were not used, the associated-stimulus results were identical with those of the first series: shock reactions in three dogs and food reactions in four—the same dogs in each case.

Data of an earlier experiment with one dog should be added (Sergeyev, 1955). Here, the associated stimulus was a decrease in illumination; the to-be-conditioned stimulus, the sound of a whistle; the US, food; the control stimulus, onset of darkness; and the number of preconditioning trials, 30. After the reaction to the associated stimulus was observed to be substantial—50 scale divisions of saliva in 20 seconds versus a mean of 70 for the conditioned whistle and none for the control stimulus—the animal underwent bilateral ablation of its temporal cortex, which eliminated its

CR for three weeks. Yet 6 and 10 days after the operation, the decrease in illumination evoked 40 and 25 scale divisions of saliva, with none for the control or CS.

Sergeyev's results disclose that the acquired reaction to an associated stimulus *may* become independent of the conditioned reaction but this does not always happen. Obviously, the evidence of three of his dogs and of the two of Rokotova's which did show such dependence must also be considered. Similarly, relatively recent evidence shows that when a reaction to a first-order CS is transformed from a food reaction to a shock reaction, its second-order stimulus either acquires the shock reaction (Drozdenko, 1950; Voronin, 1957) or retains the food reaction (Khekht, 1957; Malinovsky, 1952; Skipin, 1952). That is to say, both kinds of results have been obtained in both sensory preconditioning and second-order conditioning, and in both the differences relate apparently to uninvestigated parameters rather than to methodological discrepancies. Still, it is quite obvious that the two kinds of higher-than-simple conditioning are in essence different. Second-order conditioning is not afferent-afferent learning, since there is always an efferent reaction in its activation. It does not require orienting-reflex mediation and is fully operative in low-level interoceptive stimulation (Pauperova, 1952; Vasilevskaya, 1948, 1950) and in lower animals (Razran, 1955c). An assumption that it is an evolutionary precursor of sensory preconditioning may be warranted.

In another experiment (1956), Sergeyev investigated two types of *inhibitory* sensory preconditioning in classical food conditioning of four dogs. In one type, the to-be-conditioned stimulus was made a conditioned inhibitor by being applied a number of times with a CS without a US, and the associated stimulus was tested for similar inhibition; in the other, the experimenter presumed that the associated stimulus would acquire inhibitory properties through excessive pairing with the to-be-conditioned stimulus. In the first type, used with only one dog, the experiment consisted of two parts. In one part, the associated stimulus was the flash of a flickering light, the to-be-conditioned inhibitor the noise of a motor, and the number of pairings 129. In the other part, begun when all effects of the first part were gone, the associated stimulus was the sound of bubbling water, the to-be-conditioned inhibitor the sight of a moving disk, and the number of pairings 50. The control stimuli were the sound of bubbling water in the first part and a hissing sound in the second, while the previously conditioned and later inhibited stimulus was the sound of a flute in both parts of the experiment. The results were clear. The associated stimuli became automatically conditioned inhibitors—the one of 129 paired preconditionings halted completely the conditioned salivation to the sound of the flute, and the other of 50 trials halted it partly—whereas the control stimuli themselves evoked a certain amount of conditioned salivation, presumably because of their modality relation to the flute.

Four dogs were used in the second type of preconditioned inhibition.

With a to-be-conditioned tactile stimulus in all cases, for one dog the sound of bubbling water preceded it 120 times, for another the same sound preceded it 50 times, while for the remaining two animals a tone of 120 cycles preceded it 100 times. The results bore out the experimenter's hypothesis. *The associated stimuli inhibited the conditioned salivation to the tactile CS, and the extent of the inhibition was a direct function of the number of preconditioned pairings.* Moreover, this associated inhibition manifested a gradient of generalization. When, in the last two dogs, tactile stimuli were applied at distances of 9, 18, and 27 centimeters from the conditioned spot in the preconditioning experiment and the stimuli were made CSs for food reactions, the associated stimulus inhibited the conditioned salivation to the nonpreconditioned spots in inverse proportion to their distance from the paired spot.

Cats. In his 1955 experiment, Sergeyev also studied the dependence of the associated reaction upon the conditioned reaction in two cats by means of a special technique. The skulls of both animals were trephined symmetrically above their occipital lobes, and the openings were covered with skin, which permitted applying mild pressure to the lobes; this pressure halted for approximately one minute the manifestation of any CR to a visual stimulus (a common Soviet technique, effected more precisely through implantation of tiny metallic devices). In one animal, the associated stimulus was the sound of an electric bell, the to-be-conditioned stimulus was the flash of a 60-watt lamp, and the occipital lobe was pressed in the post-conditioning tests of the associated stimulus. In the other, the roles of the two stimuli were reversed and the lobe was pressed during the subsequent conditioning. In each case, 30 preconditioning pairings were used and food was the US; the occipital pressure was repeated many times singly between conditioning trials to prevent its becoming a CS.

The top two panels in Figure 43 demonstrate the general efficacy of the technique in a cat not used in the preconditioning experiment—pressing the occipital lobe (heavy bars along the bottom in some blocks) (*a*) reduces greatly, during the pressure, CRs to visual stimuli (4th and 6th entries in top panel and 5th in the second panel) but not to an auditory stimulus (2nd entry in the top panel), and (*b*) affects neither reaction after the pressure is stopped (all other entries). The bottom three panels compare the sensory preconditioning of the two experimental cats. In the first animal, the associated bell acquired an adequate food-motor reaction (5th entry in the third panel) which was also at full strength when the occipital lobe was pressed (5th entry in the fourth panel), thus showing the eventual independence of the associated reaction. Yet in the second cat, the associated light failed to evoke any post-conditioning reaction, even when the occipital lobe was not pressed (4th entry in the bottom

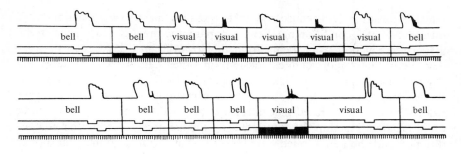

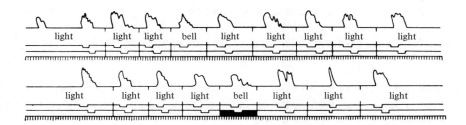

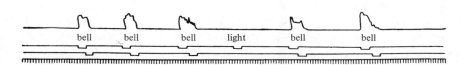

Figure 43 *Sensory audiovisual food reinforcement preconditioning in two cats whose occipital lobes were pressed to prevent the manifestation of conditioned visual reactions during the pressure, approximately one minute.* The first two panels demonstrate the technique in general with a cat of another experiment. Note that the pressure (heavy bar along bottom) halted visual CRs (4th and 6th entries in top panel and 5th in the second one) but did not affect the CR to a bell (2nd entry in first panel) when it was on, nor the visual CRs when it was off (3rd, 5th, and 7th entries in first panel and 6th entry in the second). The preconditioning procedures for the two experimental animals differed. In one (third and fourth panels), the to-be-conditioned stimulus was a flash of a light and the associated stimulus the sound of a bell, and occipital pressure was exerted *after* the conditioning had been effected. Note that the associated food-motor reaction to the bell (5th entry in fourth panel) was in full force during occipital pressure, disclosing the *eventual* independence of the associated from the conditioned reaction. In the other cat (bottom panel), the to-be-conditioned stimulus was the bell, the associated stimulus a light and the occipital lobe was pressed *during the conditioning.* Here no preconditioning was effected; the associated light (4th entry) failed to evoke it in post-conditioning trials of no pressure— presumably, because the bell did not elicit *any* light reaction during the conditioning. (From Sergeyev, 1955)

panel), presumably because the lobe pressure halted *any* reaction to it during the bell conditioning; hence, apparently the CS must elicit *some* associated reaction while being trained. However, in a later report Sergeyev states that "with identical designs in other cats as well as dogs the associated reaction to the light did appear" (1967, p. 155). And he continues with the conclusion that "transformation, ablation and pressure studies have demonstrated that in sensory preconditioning the neural center of associated reaction is connected to the centers of both the unconditioned and the conditioned reactions but that the first connection mostly comes to dominate the second" (p. 156). Put differently and more basically, this means that while during preconditioning the connection is obviously between the to-be-conditioned and the associative neural centers, during conditioning the UR may either transfer directly to the associated stimulus or be evoked only through the mediation of the conditioned center. The problem is surely of high theoretical import.

Baboons. Rokotova (1954) probed backward sensory preconditioning in two animals and what might be called a "natural" manifestation of it in two others, with bar-pressing for food as the reinforced reaction in all cases. In one of the first two animals, the associated stimulus, the sight of an illuminated circle, *followed* the sound of a metronome which later was made an S^D for bar-pressing. The two stimuli were paired 48 times in two experimental sessions; the control stimuli were a crackling noise and the sound of a street organ. The results, presented in Figure 44, show that neither control stimulus produced bar-pressing (3rd entry in upper panel and 2nd in lower panel), whereas the sight of the associated circle did (5th entry in lower panel). Moreover, the baboon "continued to press the bar in response to the circle for a year in the course of hundreds of nonreinforced trials" (p. 520). The performance of the other baboon, for whom the sound of bubbling water followed the flash of a green light and the light was made an S^D, is stated to have been similar, except that this animal retained the reaction to the associated stimulus "for only several months" (p. 520).

In the preconditioning of the last two baboons, a toy cuckoo saying "cuckoo" was presented a "number of times" over a period of three days. After that, the sound alone was made an S^D for bar-pressing, and the sight alone of the toy, the associated stimulus, thereby became effective. The same results were obtained also with the second of the first two baboons, in which an interesting difference between its two kinds of preconditioning was disclosed. When the associated reaction to the sight of the cuckoo was extinguished, the reinforced reaction to the sound "cuckoo" disappeared and was restored only upon food reinforcement, which also activated the associated reaction. But, when the associated reaction to the bubbling of water was extinguished, the reinforced reaction to the green light was unaffected and, indeed, restored the associated

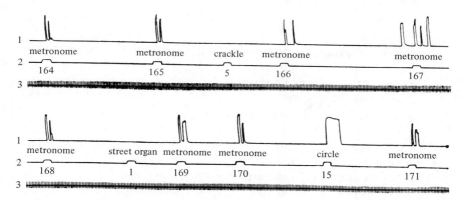

Figure 44 *Sensory preconditioning in bar-pressing for food in a baboon.* The to-be-conditioned S^D was the sound of a metronome and the associated stimulus an illuminated circle, and the controls were a noise and the sound of a street organ. Note that the control stimuli (3rd entry in upper panel and 2nd in lower) produced no reaction, whereas the associated circle (5th entry in the lower panel) did. (From Rokotova, 1954)

reaction through one pairing, in the manner of second-order conditioning. Here we have another variation in the interrelation between associated and conditioned reactions, probably due to the baboon's different reactions to the different interrelations of the stimuli of the associated and conditioned reactions: "natural" in the sound and sight of the toy cuckoo, and "laboratory" in combining a green light with the bubbling water.

Man. Shichko (1959, 1969) experimented with nine adult human subjects. He used combinations of two to four sensory or verbal preconditioned stimuli, one of which was later paired with salivation, swallowing, hand withdrawal, eye-blink, respiratory change, or vasoconstrictive URs, produced, respectively, by the administration of sugared beets, an avoidable electric shock, airpuffs to the cornea of the right eye (Korotkin's method of scoring), and a special instrument preventing breathing for 30 seconds. The preconditioned combinations were: a tactile stimulus plus the sound of bubbling water; the words "bell" and "press" or "toucher" and "red light"; a tone of 200 cycles, a flash of a blue light, a tactile stimulus, and the sound of a simple melody; and the words "tone," "toucher," "metronome," and "red light." The stimuli were presented mostly in forward sequences at interstimulus intervals of a few seconds, except for a backward sequence in one subject in a two-stimulus combination. The orienting reflexes to all stimuli had previously been habituated in 80 to 125 trials, while the number of preconditioning pairings ranged from 25 to 35. All reactions were recorded objectively, but at the end of the experiment the subjects were questioned about their experiences and tests were made with control stimuli.

The results, presented in part in Figure 45, show that stable reactions to the associated stimuli, unaffected by the extinction of reactions to the CSs were formed in all subjects except one who manifested only little evidence of salivary and eyelid conditioning to a verbal stimulus. Specifically, when the preconditioned combination was a tactile stimulus and the sound of bubbling water, and the latter was paired with breath-withholding, the tactile stimulus and "I am going to touch you" and "Bubbling water is coming" evoked automatically clear-cut vasoconstriction of the radial pulse in eighteen tests and in eleven of the eighteen changes in respiration also (top panel of Figure 45; three subjects used). Other results were quite similar. When the bubbling of water in the tactile-bubbling water combination became a CS to eyelid conditioning, vasoconstriction and frequent blinking were evoked by the words "I am going to touch you" (same three subjects). When the preconditioned combination consisted of the words "bell" and "press" and the latter was made a CS for eyelid and vasoconstrictive conditioning, the sound of the bell evoked only vasoconstriction but mild pressure on the shoulder and the word "bell" evoked both kinds of reactions (middle panel of Figure 45; two other subjects). However, when the combination comprised the words "toucher" and "red light" and a flash of a red light was made a CS for vasoconstriction and changes in respiration, not only the words "toucher" and the "red light" but also the tactile stimulus itself were fully effective (bottom panel; one subject). Still, when with the same combination and subject the word "red light" was made a CS for salivary and swallowing conditioning (saliometers and automatic delivery of 5 cubic centimeters of sugared beets used), the word "toucher" and the flash of a red light—but not actual touching—evoked adequate CRs.

Finally, when in the four-stimulus combination the flash of the light was paired with an electric shock to a subject's finger, the associated stimuli—tactile, simple melody, and a 128-cycle tone—as well as the word "tone," produced hand withdrawal (one subject). When eyelid conditioning to a tone of 200 cycles was for some reason unstable, the associated reactions in a four-stimulus combination of the words "tone," "toucher," "metronome," and "red light" were not too pronounced and were evident at all only in response to the words "metronome" and "toucher" and the actual flash of a red light (another subject). Shichko states that successful results were obtained also with preconditioned combinations of three stimuli in three subjects, but he presents no details. Moreover, the experimenter notes that the two-stimulus backward sequence in one subject was as good as the forward sequences in two others.

The verbal reports of Shichko's subjects revealed their unawareness of

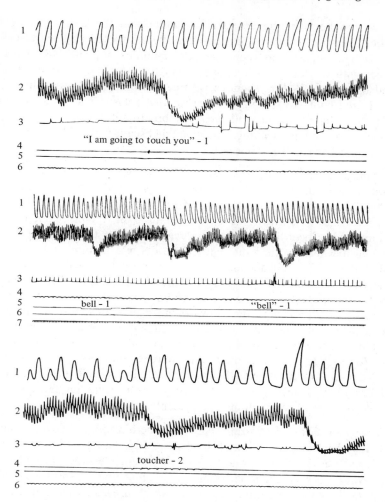

Figure 45 *Sample sensory preconditioning of radial-pulse vasoconstriction and its sensory-verbal and verbal-sensory generalizations in three of nine adult human subjects.* The top panel discloses the reaction to the words "I am going to touch you" when a tactile stimulus was associated with the sound of bubbling water and the sound later combined with withholding air by a special instrument. The middle panel is the record of a reaction to the sound of a bell (1st entry) and the word "bell" (2nd entry) when the latter was associated with the word "press" as a to-be-conditioned stimulus. The bottom panel records the reaction to a tactile stimulus when the associated stimulus was the word "toucher" and the to-be-conditioned stimulus the word "bell." (From Shichko, 1959)

the relation between the associated stimulus and the UR, but they were of course aware of the relation between the associated and the to-be-conditioned stimuli, and between the latter stimulus and the UR. Thus, the subject with a "toucher"-"red light" word combination and the flash of a red light as a CS for reactions to breath-withholding stated that he expected "red light" to follow "toucher" and the flash of a red light and the word "red light" to be followed by breath-withholding but not that "toucher" or actual touching would entail breath-withholding. His report was identical when the US was food.

Infants. Kasatkin, Mirozyants, and Khokhitva (1953) established conditioned orientation, a variety of sensory preconditioning, in ten infants 46 to 222 days of age at the start of the experiment. A flickering 6-volt light 90 degrees to the right of the infant lying on his back in a crib equipped with recording instruments was the US of the orienting reaction (turning the head toward the light). The CS was a sound 40 centimeters behind the subject's head, and it in no case evoked head-turning. (In 8 subjects, the sound was an 810-cycle tone of 40 to 50 decibels; in the 9th, a bell, and in the 10th, the sound of an organ pipe.) All infants were eventually conditioned to turn toward the light in response to the sound. The two youngest infants—46 and 58 days old at the start of the conditioning—first showed evidence of conditioning on the 74th day. The two oldest—215 and 222 days old—were conditioned on the first day. A 93-day-old infant whose CS was the sound of a bell managed to form a differential no-turning CR to a tone of 510 cycles on the 147th day. Sample records of four infants are presented in Figure 46.

Sergeyev's Generalizations. All the generalizations below, except the first and the last two are derived from experiments with dogs (the very last is not Sergeyev's but mine). And all except the first two and the last three will be best understood when one assumes that sensory preconditioning is mediated by orienting reactions, which are as a rule quickly extinguished and are inhibited by stimuli of high intensity and long duration. The generalizations are but little documented, partly because of lack of space, partly because Sergeyev reports in his 1967 book new experiments which understandably are rather general in presentation, and partly because some of the original experiments on which the generalizations are based are not available to me at this time.

(1) Sensory preconditioning has been formed to some extent in turtles (the data of the original experiment [Karamyan, Sergeyev, and Sollertinskaya, 1964] are not too convincing), in canaries *(Serinus canarius),* starlings *(Sturnus vulgaris),* white mice, hedgehogs *(Erinaceus europeans),* bats *(Plecotus auritus* and *Myotis mystacinus),* polecats, and chimpanzees (pp. 190-218), but it could not be formed in bony fish, frogs *(Bufo bufo),* salamanders *(Triturus vulgaris),* axolotls *(Siredon pisciformis),* amblystoma

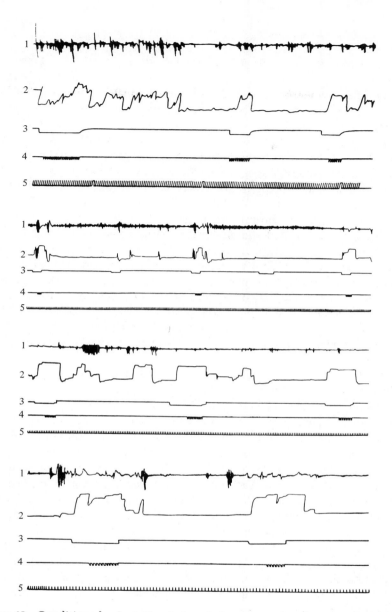

Figure 46 *Conditioned orientation in four infants, 74 to 223 days of age.* Sample records of head-turning toward a flickering light (the US) at 90 degrees to the right when a 40-decibel tone of 810 cycles (the CS) was sounded. Top panel— training begun at 58 days, tested at 74; second panel—training at 93, tests at 147; third panel—training at 137, tests at 214; bottom panel—training at 222, tested at 223 days. In all panels, numbers 1 through 5 denote, respectively: record of general activity, head-turning, application of the CS, application of the US, and time in seconds. In the second panel, the CS of the infant was the sound of a bell which was differentiated from a tone of 510 cycles (4th entry in line 3). (From Kasatkin, Mirozyants, and Khokhitva, 1953)

(Amblystoma tigrinum), or in puppies less than six months of age (pp. 169-190.

(2) Maximum retention of the reaction to the associated stimulus in the different animals was found to be: 14 days for birds, 15 for rodents, 19 for insectivores, 29 for bats, and several months for carnivores (p. 220); and it should be added that one baboon retained it for one year (Rokotova, 1954; not mentioned in Sergeyev's book). Maximum retention of the preconditioning—that is, the effective interval between preconditioning and conditioning—was observed to be less: 3 days for birds, rodents, and insectivores, 6 for bats, and 12 for carnivores (p. 220).

(3) In dogs, maximum preconditioning efficiency is attained in 15 pairings when the associated stimulus precedes the to-be-conditioned stimulus by a few seconds and is terminated when the latter begins, and it may be quite effective even after 4 to 6 pairings. When the two stimuli are presented simultaneously, the maximum is reached after 20 pairings, while with interstimulus intervals of 30 seconds it is reached at 30 trials (p. 99; evidence derived from comparison of three groups of 17, 12, and 10 dogs). More than 30 trials impair efficacy, and after 50 the associated stimulus acquires inhibitory properties (Sergeyev's 1956 experiment, cited earlier).

(4) In preconditioning, simultaneous and backward designs do not reduce efficacy as much as they do in simple classical and reinforcement conditioning (pp. 99, 105).

(5) Prior habituation of the orienting reaction to the associated stimulus affects but little the development of sensory preconditioning, whereas prior habituation to the to-be-conditioned stimulus makes the preconditioning difficult or wholly impossible (pp. 113-114). In other words, to be effective, the associated stimulus must acquire the mediating orienting reaction of the to-be-conditioned stimulus, an observation which is in accord with the finding (not mentioned by Sergeyev) that sensory preconditioning is much more readily effected when the intensity (dominance) of the to-be-conditioned stimulus is higher than that of the associated stimulus (Voznaya, 1966). That sensory preconditioning is possible at all with the habituation of the to-be-conditioned stimulus is probably due to the partial restoration of the latter's reaction when the two stimuli are combined (cf. Parks, 1963, 1968).

(6) Associated stimuli of high intensity or long duration, interfering with evocation and maintenance of the orienting reaction, interfere with or nullify completely the formation of sensory preconditioning (Rokotova, 1954; Sergeyev, 1967, p. 105).

(7) In dogs ($N = 10$) only the ablation of the association cortex abolishes and prevents the manifestation of sensory preconditioning. *Otherwise, with cortical-sensory and subcortical ablations, it is preserved and new varieties are formed when participating stimuli continue to evoke indi-*

vidual reactions (pp. 130-150). This is a very important finding, and it will be discussed in a later section.

(8) In school children, when the second of five sequential stimuli is made a CS for a food reaction and the third a CS for a shock reaction, or vice versa, the first stimulus acquires the reaction of the second stimulus while the fourth and the fifth stimuli acquire the reaction of the third stimulus. However, when either food or shock conditioning is more developed, it imparts its reaction to all three associated stimuli.

(9) Fragmentary evidence suggests that sensory preconditioning has evolved from birds and rodents to carnivores, primates, and man, not only in the longer retention of its effects (2nd generalization) but also in such factors as: smaller number of preconditioning trials needed; greater efficacy of simultaneous, backward, and longer interstimulus-intervals; more independence of the associated from the conditioned reaction; less overt manifestations of orienting reactions; and greater number of stimuli feasible in preconditioned combinations. In man and baboons, backward sequences are fully effective; in dogs, their effectiveness is much reduced. In man, extinction of the conditioned reaction to the CS does not affect the associated reaction; in baboons and dogs, it does. In man, sensory preconditioning is possible even when the orienting reaction to the to-be-conditioned stimulus is fully habituated; in dogs, it is impossible. In adult dogs, 15 preconditionings insure as a rule maximum preconditioning efficacy; in six-month-old puppies, 50 trials are required.

American Experiments Compared

Five specific features of these experiments stand out. (1) Not one of them has ever mentioned Soviet counterparts, approximately four times as many and seven times as varied in types of problems investigated. (2) American methodological controls are superior to those used by the Russians. (3) Nonetheless, in comparable inquiries, American findings are strikingly similar to the Russians', reported as a rule a number of years earlier. (4) There is, furthermore, a basic American-Soviet convergence, although a formal divergence, in interpreting the phenomenon. (5) In the American enterprise, the ratio of human to animal experiments is much higher, the CRs are more complex, and interest in evolutionary progression is scarcely more than marginal. The second, third, and fourth of these specifics will be enlarged in coming paragraphs. However, because space is limited and because most American experiments have been reviewed by Seidel in 1959 and also by Kimble in his 1961 standard text, only three of them will be detailed here: one which for some reason has been overlooked by reviewers, and two that have been published since 1961.

Sample of Unreviewed Studies. Thornton (1956) experimented with 48 rats divided into two experimental and four control groups. In one experimental group, the associated stimulus was a 10-watt light and the to-be-conditioned stimulus a very weak buzzer; in the other group the two stimuli were, respectively, a 200-watt lamp and a loud 6-volt buzzer. In both groups, light and buzzer were presented *simultaneously* 24 times, and the US was a strong electric shock in a runway. Thornton obtained reliable preconditioning only in the group in which the associated and the to-be-conditioned stimuli were of weak intensity. He is puzzled at his results and suggests that the strong buzzer might have been a "punisher." It will be remembered that Rokotova in 1954 failed to secure preconditioning with a siren of high intensity as the associated stimulus, and her interpretation was that "high-intensity stimuli interfere with the formation and maintenance of orienting reflexes that mediate the phenomenon" (see above). I assume that Thornton would accept this, and would consider also that a *simultaneous* pairing design does not help (see above, 3rd generalization). Wokoon (1959) reported similarly an inverse relation between efficacy of preconditioning and stimulus intensity.

Parks (1963, 1968) divided 54 rats into six equal groups: (*a*) two standard Preconditioning Groups, for which on the first experimental day a tone of an intensity that "caused the subjects to prick up their ears and sniff" but "did not produce a startle response" preceded for 200 trials a buzzer which "did produce a noticeable startle"; (*b*) a "Pseudoconditioning" Group with 200 applications of the tone alone; (*c*) a Prehabituation Group, for which 300 administrations of tone alone preceded the preconditioning; (*d*) a Chlorpromazine Group, with 3-milligram/kilogram injections preceding preconditioning; and (*e*) a Physiological-Saline Group of identical dosage and order. All groups rested on the second day, and on the third all were (*a*) trained to form a shuttlebox avoidance CR to the buzzer by combining it with an electric shock, and (*b*) immediately tested with the preconditioned tone. The results show that the tone was effective with 6 out of 9 rats in each of three groups—the Physiological-Saline, the Prehabituation, and with one standard Preconditioning Group—and with 5 of 9 animals in the other Preconditioning Group, but with only 1 out of 9 in the Pseudoconditioning Group and 2 out of 9 in the Chlorpromazine Group. The reaction-to-tone differences between the Pseudoconditioning Group and all others except the Chlorpromazine Group are statistically significant at $p < .05$; the difference between the Chlorpromazine Group and the three groups with 6-out-of-9 positive scores was significant at $p = .07$. Parks' finding that chlorpromazine injection, known to suppress the manifestation of orienting reactions (Anokhin, 1958b; Gliedman and Gantt, 1956; Kaada and Bruland, 1960; Key and Bradley, 1960; and others), interferes with sensory preconditioning is new, and he should be congratulated. On the other hand, the finding which surprises him—that prehabituation of the *associated* stimulus has no effect—is in line with prior Soviet data (above, 5th generalization).

Thompson and Kramer (1965) used six groups of five cats; three unoperated, two in which "all association response areas" were removed, and one with ablation of the sensory somatic cortex. The associated stimulus was a two 100-watt lamp, the to-be-conditioned stimulus a 1000-cycle 60-decibel tone, and the US a one-second pulse of a constant current in a Brogden-Culler apparatus. There were two control groups for the un-operated animals: one with no preconditioning training and another with random pretraining on each stimulus; one randomly pretrained control group for the animals with association areas removed; and none for the one with the sensory somatic cortex ablated. The results are quite clear. The mean light response for both control groups of unoperated cats was 0.6 and that in the experimental groups, 11.4. The means for the experimental and control groups with association areas removed were, respectively, 1.6 and 0.2, and the mean for the sensory-cortex-ablated group was 11.0, firmly establishing the specific role of the association areas in forming preconditioning. *This most significant finding is identical with that reported by Sergeyev in ablation of ten dogs (above, 7th generalization).*

Comparative Methodology. Brogden (1939b), the first American to discover sensory preconditioning and to name it so in 1939, used a non-preconditioned control group to test for stimulus generalization. And since the criticism of Reid (1952; see also Brogden, 1942, 1947), control groups of subjects exposed to each preconditioned stimulus separately (to rule out "differential stimulus familiarity") have commonly been added. Yet the Russian results with control stimuli certainly must not be undervalued. As already indicated, in more than 90 per cent of the Russian experiments, the associated stimuli were of different modalities from the conditioned stimuli, whereas the control stimuli were of the same modalities. Cross-modal generalization does of course exist, but certainly not to the extent that a cross-modal stimulus would evoke a substantial CR and a unimodal *none* whatsoever. The "no reaction" to the control stimulus and "substantial reaction" to the associated one, invariably documented in Russian tables and graphs in the area, is more than suggestive in ruling out stimulus generalization, even when both stimuli are of the same modality as the CS. Nor is the posited effect of "differential stimulus familiarity" empirically significant. Silver and Meyer (1954) found no preconditioning differences among three control groups—one exposed to the associated stimulus, another to the to-be-conditioned stimulus, and a third to neither—while a number of other American experimenters (Coppock, 1958; Seidel, 1958; and others) failed to discover any effects of un-paired preconditionings, which "makes the heavy investment of animals and time [in such controls] unnecessary," state Hoffeld, Kendall, Thompson, and Brogden in 1960.

This is not a formal adjuration for loosening methodological controls and statistical inferences—only a pragmatic assertion that some very valid and far-reaching results may be obtained with lesser exercise of them.

204 · Mind in Evolution

The advanced stage of Soviet knowledge of sensory preconditioning is a case in point and the Hoffeld et al. 1960 statement an admission that the tail has somehow been wagging the dog. It is tempting to note that not one of Pavlov's experimental reports of conditioning meets American methodological and statistical standards for publication in, say, the *Journal of Experimental Psychology*. Fortunately, Pavlov had access to other media.

Comparative Findings. Two hundred simultaneous preconditioned presentations of a buzzer and a light were made in the pioneer American experiment by Brogden in 1939. In the first Soviet animal experiment by Narbutovich and Podkopayev in 1936, the number of pairings of a noise and the sight of a whirligig ranged from 21 to 30, with interstimulus intervals of 5 seconds. Dogs were the subjects in both experiments. In 1958, Hoffeld, Thompson, and Brogden, working with cats, found that 4-second interstimulus intervals produced the best results, and, in 1960, Hoffeld, Kendall, Thompson, and Brogden reported that 4 preconditioning trials were optimal (the same number used by Davis and Thompson, 1968). Both findings are congruent not only with present-day Soviet knowledge (3rd generalization) but also with the design of its first experimenters, and they are at variance with that of Brogden's own pioneering first. In 1936, Narbutovich and Podkopayev disclosed also that backward preconditioning sequences may be effective. Such sequences were first used in the United States in 1954 with rats by Silver and Meyer, who found them effective but inferior to the forward counterparts—again wholly in accord with Soviet data (see above, 4th generalization and text) except for baboons and humans, in which the evidence of equal effectiveness of the two sequences is fragmentary but intimates that the sequence differences become less pronounced with evolutionary ascent (see above, 9th generalization).

The striking important likenesses of the outcomes of the ablation experiments of Thompson and Kramer and of Sergeyev were noted earlier, as were those of Thornton, Wokoon, and of Rokotova on negative effects of high-intensity stimuli. Manifestations of overt orienting reactions to preconditioned stimuli, observed in the first experiment in the Soviet Union and since replicated there, have been described by Parks (1963); he has not, however, noted the intersensory classical conditioning of the reactions, which the Russians frequently report.

There are, regrettably, no further significant comparisons, not just because of the limited number of American experiments but chiefly because of their predominant concern with the role of preconditioning as umpire between S-R and S-S theories of learning rather than with its parameters.

Comparative Interpretations. The empirics of sensory preconditioning was certainly—no one should be surprised—a boost to S-S theorists in the

American arena. But, needless to say, the S-R rivals were not so easily floored. Hull's R_G and S_G, the intervening fractional anticipatory do-alls and sense-alls, were unsheathed and emplaced in the wide interstitial catch-all of mediation to bolster and hold the stance (Osgood, 1953). However, the S-R-niks do not seem to have gotten the better of S-S-niks. Kimble, three quarters one and one quarter the other, writes, for instance, that "this [R_G-S_G] explanation of the sensory preconditioning phenomenon leads the S-R theorist into a position which is somewhat out of character [to] posit the existence of covert, difficult to recognize, responses. In this shifting of ground, the S-R theorist moves, in effect, a step closer to expectancy theory" (1961, p. 217). And Seidel avers: "In the most conservative sense . . . SPC [sensory preconditioning] studies have given results different from those previously gotten in conditioning or those implied by any S-R mediational learning hypothesis" (1959, p. 71).

Soviet evidence in the area can, however—if one so wills—get S-R theory off the hook. Overt conditioned orientation in sensory preconditioning periods was noted as early as 1936, and, as multiply documented, a wide variety of correlations between the two phenomena have been obtained repeatedly. The inferable "coverts" of mediation thus become observable "overts"—that is, sensory preconditioning *intermediated* (preferred to *mediated*) by observable classical conditioning of the associated stimulus (more exactly, "of the orienting reaction of the stimulus") to the observable orienting reaction to the to-be-conditioned stimulus. And it is of course also true that in modern times reactions and their conditionings are observable, even if in the lingering Watson litany of effector worship they continue to be labeled "covert." Varga and Pressman (1958), experimenting with five dogs, found clear-cut electromyographic conditioning when a tone of 1000 cycles was paired with passive flexion of the animal's left hindpaw with no concomitant paw-lifting—and no "reinforcement" (Figure 47). Then, there is the host of both American and Soviet experiments of successful sensory-sensory conditioning of electroencephalographic reactions that customarily are considered components of orientation. Modern evidence of feedback does not limit it to proprioception. Moreover, there is the possible hypothesis of sensory preconditioning as an "associative transfer from linked centers of neural reactions in the manner of response generalization."

Yet, the orienting interpretation is by no means incompatible with that of S-S or cognition (e.g., that of Hebb, 1966, pp. 114-115, to cite a recent espousal). Elsewhere (Razran, 1961a), I have meditated on the connaturalness of orienting reactions and cognitivity with respect to: relatively recent phyletic emergence (presumed for cognitivity), rapid evolution of the scope of manifestation (significant differences among fish, pigeons, rabbits, polecats, dogs, monkeys, apes, and children of different ages [e.g., Vedayev and Karmanova, 1958; Dolin, Zborovskaya, and Zamakhover, 1958; Karlova, 1959]), functional lability and modifiability,

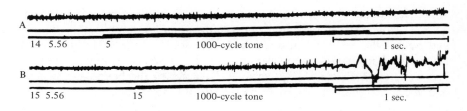

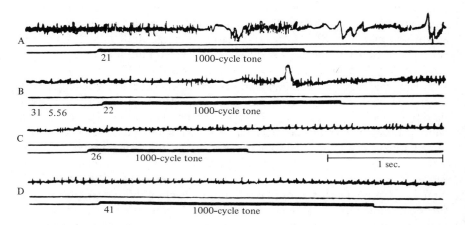

Figure 47 *Sample record of electromyographic evidence of the classical conditioning of the flexion of a dog's paw to a tone of 1000 cycles, with no food reinforcement or shock as a US.* The upper panel shows the conditioning when the tone preceded passive flexion (forward sequence); the lower, when the tone followed the flexion (backward sequence). In each segment of the panels, the records are, from the top: dropping out of electromyogram spikes, "mechanograms," and onset of tones. The numbers preceding tone onset are trials. Note that in the forward sequence, the conditioning appeared on the 15th training trial (bottom right) and continued, according to the experimenter, for 60 to 70 pairings; while in the backward sequence it appeared on the 21st trial (top right) and was no longer evident on the 26th trial. Data were essentially similar for five other dogs. (From Varga and Pressman, 1958)

and preparatory-mobilizing role in action. I noted there also that temporary orienting conditioning in typical shock conditioning appears to be similar to conditioned "expectancy" and that Soviet investigators have reported many times that the orienting lowers sensory thresholds and correlates with subjects' verbal reports of awareness. I did not suggest that orienting reflex (so called) is predicated on cognition (since it exists also in noncognitive interoceptive stimulation [Makarov, 1959; Mysyashchikova, 1952], in patients whose exteroceptive cognitive sensitivity has been impaired [Gershuni, 1947; and elsewhere], and in some limited phases of noncognitive exteroception [Bykov and Pshonik, 1949])—only that the converse may hold: cognition predicated on orienting. And to this evidence of the higher nature of the putative mechanism of sensory preconditioning must be added its own evolutionarily-higher behavioral status: the established fact that (*a*) *it is feasible only in higher animals and abolished only when higher regions of the cortex are ablated (concurrence of East and West data),* and (*b*) *its basic parameters are in large measure different from, and even contrasting with, those of simple conditioning.* More about its essence and import in coming sections.

CONFIGURING

Russian Experiments: Basic Statement

In 1906, Palladin in Pavlov's laboratory noted two far-reaching conditioning manifestations. A thermal stimulus which when paired with an unconditioned acid stimulus readily evoked conditioned salivation in three dogs failed to do so alone when trained in another dog for 156 trials together with a tactile stimulus and the acid. Yet when the conditioned reflex to the active tactile stimulus was completely extinguished, salivation continued to be elicited by the tactile-thermal compound. That is to say: (*a*) *the CR efficacy of a CS was affected by simultaneous activation of another CS, and* (*b*) *simultaneous activation of two CSs was effective when separate administration of each was not.* A patterning or configuring principle in learned afferent-afferent interaction was indicated, and conditioning as an objective behavioral method of studying it was put forth.

Palladin's findings were replicated, in the main, in the following five years in seven extensive studies (Babkin, 1910; El'yasson, 1908; Kasherininova, 1908; Nikolaeff, 1911; Pereltsvayg, 1907; Zeliony, 1907, 1910a) using combinations of two, three, or four component stimuli of the same or different sense modalities. And it was soon discovered that only components of weak intensity lost CR efficacy in compound-stimulus training, that of strong components remaining unchanged or at first even increasing. Moreover, in 1910, Zeliony (1910a) modified Palladin's method by continuing to alternate the pairing of the compound CS and US with not pairing, or extinguishing, its components, a procedure Babkin used in the same year to train dogs to differentiate different sequences of identical CSs. In one of Zeliony's experiments, in which the compound CS was an A_1 tone plus three adjacent 16-candlepower lights, the lights alone were wholly ineffective while the sound alone was highly effective, extinguishing completely only after 399 trials with 135 intermittent compound-food pairings. But, then, as the two inactive stimuli—one extinguished, the other at no time overtly effective—were applied together, conditioned salivation occurred, undiminished and regularly evoked. "Togetherness" begot something very special.

Since then, Soviet laboratories have yielded approximately 750 experiments on compound-stimulus conditioning containing significant data

208 · *Mind in Evolution*

on configuring. Three varieties of compounds have been used: (*a*) simultaneous (called "complexes" by the Russians), in which the CSs, typically two to four, are presented at the same time; (*b*) successive (called "chains"), in which two to four CSs are applied at intervals of several seconds; and (*c*) "dynamic stereotypes"—special successive compounds of four to eight CSs, of which, as a rule, all but one are paired separately with the US and the one is left unpaired. And two methods have been used to produce configural—or compound-without-component—conditioning: (*a*) differential contrasting, involving extinction of the components, and (*b*) mere prolonged CR training of the compounds without contrasting. On the face of it, the extinction method may mask the genuineness of the resultant configuring. But, as will be demonstrated later, mere differential conditioning cannot generate by itself exclusive compound conditioning. Something must be formed in the compound that is not in the components. Long ago, Beritoff stated that "such integrated compound conditioning could not arise without concomitant emergence, in the course of training, of a supplementary neural CS center connecting independently with the neural center of the US" (1932, p. 430). Recent studies showing that brain ablations affect differentially configured and component conditioning (Batuyev, 1964, 1965, 1966a, 1966b; Lagutina and Batuyev, 1966; Sovetov, 1967; Voronin, 1948a) bolster Beritoff's position.

Data of Soviet experiments are definitive in disclosing that configuring is not pre-existent in the compound CS but *develops* in the course of its conditioning. Three consecutive stages are discerned in the training: an initial one, when the components tested alone are not yet affected by being in the compound; an intermediate one, when the weaker components lose effectiveness; and a final stage, in which only the compound CS is effective (Beritoff, 1932; Voronin, 1957; Sergeyev, 1967; and others). In the initial stage, extinction of all component CSs diminishes almost completely the CR to the compound; in the intermediate stage, the diminution is only partial; and in the final stage it is almost wholly absent. Table 7

Table 7 *A Schema of Developmental Dynamics of the Configuring of a Three-Component Simultaneous CS Compound:* (*a+b+c*). Plus sign after letters indicates increase in CR efficacy; "0" denotes inactivation of the CR.

Developmental Stage	Effective Stimuli						
I	a	b	c	(a+b)	(a+c)	(b+c)	(a+b+c)
II	0	b+	c+	(a+b)+	(a+c)+	(b+c)+	(a+b+c)+
III	0	0	c+	(a+b)+	(a+c)+	(b+c)+	(a+b+c)+
IV	0	0	0	(a+b)+	(a+c)+	(b+c)+	(a+b+c)+
V	0	0	0	0	(a+c)+	(b+c)+	(a+b+c)+
VI	0	0	0	0	0	(b+c)+	(a+b+c)+
VII	0	0	0	0	0	0	(a+b+c)+

is a schema of Soviet results on the developmental dynamics of configuring to a simultaneous compound CS: (a+b+c).

Soviet Experiments: Configuring as a Higher Level of Learning

Phylogeny. Soviet data reveal that configuring (typically called "inter- or "intra-analyzer synthesis") is not only an achievement of conditioning but, in full-fledged form, a most distinctive divide between the learning of higher and lower vertebrates. Two summary tables will serve as illustrations. Table 8 compares configuring of a three-component *successive* compound in fish, turtles, birds, rabbits, dogs, and baboons. The compound consisted of a succession of a sound, a light, and a different sound as an S^D in food-obtaining reinforcement conditioning. (The fish tugged

Table 8 *Successive Configuring in Several Classes and Orders of Vertebrates.* Total inactivation of changed sequences and constituent components of a three-component compound. [After Baru, Malinovsky, Ovchinnikova, Prazdnikova, and Chernomordikov, 1959]

Kind of Animal	Number of Subjects	Number of Successful Subjects	Compound Trials for Inactivation of Changed Sequences	Compound Trials for Inactivation of Constituent Components*
Goldfish	6	2	not studied	780,[a] 1282[a]
Turtles	5	3	not studied	600-800[b]
Birds	15	12	247-453	334-410
Rabbits	8	2	420, 650	678, 1200[c]
Dogs	2	2	264, 270	399, 410
Baboons	2	2	30-60	30, 60

*There is an error in this entry reported elsewhere (Razran, 1965d): in place of "sequences," read "components."
[a] Required, respectively, 63 and 144 nonreinforcements of components.
[b] Only partly successful.
[c] Four others successful with the aid of nonreinforcements of components.

at beads, the turtles and rabbits pulled rings, the birds pecked at pedals, and the dogs and baboons pressed bars; see Razran, 1961a, 1961b.) Table 9 juxtaposes the results of *simultaneous* configuring in fish, frogs, turtles, birds, guinea pigs, hedgehogs, bats, and dogs. Both classical and reinforcement conditioning were used in these experiments.

All animals learned readily to respond to the compound stimuli as such with few phyletic differences. But, as may be seen in Table 8, only 2 of the 6 fish managed to configure the *successive* compound, and they required 780 and 1282 reinforced compound trials and 63 and 144 nonreinforced trials to effect it, even as 3 of the 5 turtles learned configuring only in part after 600 to 800 compound trials. Yet 12 of the 15 birds mastered it without differential conditioning in 247 to 543 trials for sequences and 334 to 410 for components; 2 of the 8 rabbits in 420 and 650 trials for sequences, and 678 and 1200 trials for components (4 others did so with the aid of differential conditioning); 1 dog in 264 and 399 and another in 270 and 410 trials; and the 2 baboons in only 30 and 60 trials for both sequences and components. And Table 9 shows the complete failure in fish, frogs, and turtles of *simultaneous* configuring without component extinction, which birds and subprimate mammals attained in 56 to 220 trials.

Table 9 *Simultaneous Configuring in Several Classes and Orders of Vertebrates.* Total inactivation of components without differential conditioning in three-component compounds. [After Sergeyev, 1967]

Kind of Animal	Number of Animals	Number of Compound Trials Producing a Configure Through Overtraining
Fish, frogs, and turtles	"Large number"	"Failure after 700 to 1,000 trials"
Titmice	5	95-220
Starlings	4	76-92
Guinea pigs	4	89-126
Hedgehogs	6	78-104
Bats	3	65-90
Dogs	5	56-80

The phylogeny of configuring thus seems to have been set; It is *within the capacity of birds and mammals but not of fish and turtles.* True, the phyletic rule is not so invariant as to submerge individual differences entirely. Two of the eight fish mastered successive configuring with the aid of component extinction, and Sergeyev reports that a "negligible number" of piscine geniuses manifested the simultaneous variety on "occasional trials" even without such extinction (1967, p. 45). But this is to be expected. Another basic generalization evident in Tables 8 and 9 is that simultaneous configuring is easier to obtain than successive configuring, a finding curiously reminiscent of Wundt's 1896 introspection that "creative synthesis" is favored by "simultaneity rather than succession of psychic processes." A third finding, indicated in Table 8, is the existence of a primate-subprimate divide, corroborated by the studies of Shirkova (1951) and Voronin (1952, 1954a, 1957, 1965). And a fourth hints that changed sequences are more easily inactivated than are constituent components.

There is merit in presenting in some detail Sergeyev's (1967) attempt to form simultaneous configuring in a single wrasse *(Cranilubrus tinca)* and a single land turtle, the fish conditioned to tug at a bead in response to a red light plus a bell and metronome, the turtle to pull a ring in response to a flickering light plus a rhythmic "toucher" and a vibration. In the first 280 training trials with the fish, there were few differences between test-trial reactions to the components and to the compound. But the latency of the reaction to the weakest component, the metronome, increased, and after 500 compound training trials a test-trial disclosed that it was no longer effective alone. The reaction to the bell disappeared after 760 trials, but the light continued to evoke tugging and swimming-to-feeding-place throughout the long experiment. The data for the turtle were: disappearance of reaction to the flickering light after 350 trials, disappearance of reaction to the vibration after 820, but continued evocation of the reaction by the rhythmic "toucher." Both subjects reached what will be called a stage of *preconfiguring,* comparable in a sense to the *leveling* and *sharpening* of Gestalt psychology, but not true configuring (cf. Kasherininova, 1908; Kupalov and Gantt, 1928; Rikman, 1928b [Razran, 1961a, 1965c, 1965d]; and others).

Two other closely related individual experiments are those of Toporkova (1961) and Vedayev (1956). Toporkova used the same components in simultaneous and successive compound classical respiratory conditioning of four cats. They were a bell, a light, and a rattle, with the US an intranasal instillation of a 15 per cent solution of ammonia. In the simultaneous compound, used with two animals, individual components and two-component combinations became ineffective, each at a different rate, in "100 compound trials." The light and rattle were inactivated first, next the bell, then light plus rattle, and finally bell plus light or rattle. In the successive compound—bell, light, rattle—with the remaining two cats, no total component inactivation, or true configuring, was noted during 100 compound trials. In one animal, the bell and light became ineffective after 80 trials, but the rattle continued to be active; in the other, the light and rattle failed when tested after the thirteenth compound trial while the bell retained effectiveness. The data are in accord with other evidence that: (1) successive configuring is formed less readily than simultaneous configuring; (2) two inactive components may become active when applied together; (3) in simultaneous compounds, the effectiveness of a component is a positive function of its general CR strength ("Law of Strength"; the bell here is operationally the strongest); and (4) in successive compounds, the effectiveness of a component is, in addition, directly related to the temporal closeness of a component to the US, which commonly, as in the performance of the third cat, outweighs the "strength" factor.

Vedayev (1956) compared simultaneous and successive configuring in classical shock and reinforcement food conditioning of "a number" of rabbits and pigeons (number not given, but protocols show that there were at least nine rabbits and four pigeons). He used throughout the experiment the same light and tone compounds and a component-extinction method instead of just testing. The rabbits attained stable simultaneous configuring in 117 to 149 compound trials, but in the pigeons it was relatively unstable even after 200 to 250 trials, and for all subjects successive configuring was much more difficult. *Thus, component extinction is apparently not a basic factor in the simultaneous-successive differential of configuring in the data of Toporkova vis-à-vis those in Tables 8 and 9. Nor is it presumably an overriding factor in the very formation of simultaneous configuring when the results of Vedayev are compared with those summarized in Table 9.* On the other hand, the surface discrepancy between performances of rabbits and pigeons in the experiment and the rabbits and birds in Table 8 may be accounted for by the fact that the "birds" included crows, which are tops in avian learning ability and striatal mass and cytoarchitecture (Coburn and Yerkes, 1915; vs. Bingham, 1913; Krushinsky, 1960; Svetukhina, 1961).

In another germane individual experiment, Beritoff and Bregadze (1929a, 1929b, 1931) disclosed a quantitative configuring difference between dogs and rabbits. Two dogs learned in 22 days to run to their feeding places in response to a simultaneous auditory compound of two tones of 340 and 755 cycles plus two bells differing in timbre and intensity, and not to run when any component or combination of components was sounded; two rabbits took 91 days to master this. Moreover, a dog was readily trained in a reverse task of running in response to any component and not to the compound; this task was effected in a rabbit only partly and after many more trials. And Bregadze and Tarugov (1937) reported how a rabbit learned to go to a feeding box at the right when either the compound or one of the tones plus one of the bells was sounded and to a feeding box at the left in response to the other tone and bell, a task which four dogs mastered even when the compounds were successive (Bregadze, 1937). Firsov (1955) found configuring considerably less developed in four-year-old chimpanzees than in mature specimens, and Voznaya (1963) was unable to obtain it in puppies 21 to 30 days of age. Chesnokova (1959) and Lopatin and Chesnokova (1965) discovered successful simultaneous configuring in seven bees, the only invertebrates so gifted as far as we know.

Finally, some consideration should be given to the pioneer experiment of configuring in human subjects from Bekhterev's laboratory. In 1912, Platonov conditioned the plantar reflexes of four adult subjects (see Bekhterev, 1913 and 1933, for specific technique) using an avoidable electric shock as the US and a simultaneous compound of a bell and a 20-candlepower light as the CS. When after 140 to 1220 training trials the CR was well established, the compound, the bell, and the light were each tested approximately 40 times a day without the shock. In the course of seven days, the CR-evocation frequency of the compound *increased* in two subjects from 77 and 65 to 100 and 92 per cent, while that of the bell *decreased,* respectively, from 66 and 58 to 0 and 25 per cent, and that of the light from 35 and 6 to 0 per cent. In the third subject, the compound was fully effective—100 per cent—through the seven days, but the bell and light decreased from 100 to 37 and 17 per cent effectiveness. In the fourth, the compound increased in three days from 95 to 100 per cent as the bell and light decreased from 20 and 17 to 0 per cent incidence. The protocols of the experiment show further that after the sixth testing day in one subject and the seventh in another, even the CR to the compound began to decrease in frequency and eventually was completely extinguished. (No such tests were made with the remaining two subjects.) Platonov's results could, of course, be interpreted in terms of attitudinal or verbal controls. Yet they strikingly presaged basic generalizations in later infrahuman studies.

Ablation of Cortical Areas. Batuyev (1964) performed bilateral ablations of areas 3, 4, and 6 (motor) of the cortex in five cats and found that two animals lost permanently their appetitive reinforcement CRs to a simultaneous two-component audiovisual configure and that the remaining three, without such prior training, could not attain it. Yet, in the first two, the components quickly gained individual CR efficacy, and the latter three had no difficulty forming component conditioning. In three later abstracts (1965, 1966a, 1966b), the experimenter reports that ablation of area 7 (parietal) in cats prevented the formation of a simultaneous audiovisual configure for only one and a half months, while ablation of area 8 (frontal) had no effect. But, in monkeys, he states, as does an abstract by Lagutina and Batuyev (1966), ablation of frontal areas affects configured and not component conditioning (original reports of experiments not seen). Similar differential effects were obtained by Voronin (1948a) with moderate occipital, temporal, and occipital-temporal-parietal lesions in 8 dogs, and by Sovetov (1967) upon bilateral ablation of cortical areas, 2, 5, 7, and 21 in 3 dogs. Curiously, when experimental gastritis or ulcers are inflicted upon dogs, the relation is reversed: impairment of component conditioning but not of configuring (Raytses, 1963).

Adrianov (1961) formed in three dogs a simultaneous two-component configure to a tactile and a visual stimulus, using a Kupalov design of combined classical and reinforcement food conditioning. After the CRs were fully stabilized, deep bilateral two-stage incisions reaching the lateral ventricles were made between the animals' occipital and parietal lobes and in one of them also a prefrontal lobotomy, 4 weeks after the second incision. Post-operative tests showed that in all cases the animals eventually reinstated the configures and that the prefrontal dog, prior to the lobotomy, was able to form a new visuotactile configure—a black circle replacing the white and the tactile stimulus applied to a different part of the body. The dogs were then sacrificed and their brains studied histologically. The configuring was retained, it was thought, because large portions of the association cortex were unaffected.

The number of cortical-ablation experiments in the area is small, just beginning to grow. Yet the evidence indicates consistently and definitely that configuring, like sensory preconditioning, is mediated by higher cortical regions, whereas simple and simple differential conditioning may, as is well known and as was documented earlier, be effected and retained even after decortication. More empirical data are thus added to uphold the stance that configuring is not just simple differential conditioning. Beritoff's

1932 view of "an emergent neural-CS center" was most perspicacious—it was paralleled recently by Konorski and Lawicka's statement that "the cortical representation of the compound of conditioned stimuli cannot be simply considered as composed from the particular centers representing each element of the compound . . . the compound stimulus must be considered as a stimulus different from its component stimuli" (1959, pp. 195-196).

Soviet Experiments: Configuring in Human Ontogeny

Configuring was first observed in 1925 by Shastin, who put blindfolds on three young children (one 4-year-old and two 6-year-olds) a few seconds before presenting conventional auditory stimuli followed by feeding to form salivary CRs, and found that the children salivated in response to the blindfold plus the auditory stimulus but not to either alone. Two significant recent experiments come from Kol'tsova's laboratory: one by Zaklyakova (1963) with twenty children, 4 to 5 years old; another by Degtyar (1965) with twelve children 29 to 42 months old. (There are some minor discrepancies between some details in the original report of the first experiment and its presentation in a book by the Head of the Laboratory [Kol'tsova, 1967, pp. 48-51]; the later version will be used; see also Degtyar, 1965, 1966, and Zaklyakova, 1965.)

Zaklyakova presented four auditory stimuli—a buzzer, an electric bell, a metronome, and a whistle—to three groups of five subjects each for eight days. In the first group, the stimuli were given in random order; in the second, in the order mentioned above, and in the third, in reverse order. Subsequently, the eye-blinks (airpuff to the eye as the US) of all groups were conditioned to the buzzer-bell-metronome-whistle sequence. A control group with no prior presentation of sensory stimuli was also used. The results show unmistakably that the second group, in which the conditioned and prior sensory sequences were identical, formed a conditioned configure much faster than the other three groups.

Degtyar brought out the dominant role of sensory-sensory vis-à-vis sensory-motor connections in children. The eye-blinks of his twelve 29- to 42-month-old subjects were first conditioned to an auditory sequence of a metronome of 160 beats, a street organ, an electric bell, a metronome of 60 beats, and a whistle. Then, the subjects were divided into two equal and matched groups: one in which the eyelid conditioning was transformed into food conditioning, and another in which, with continued airpuff pairings, the order of presenting the CSs was reversed. Both groups effected the change, but the first group attained it in a mean of 4 experimental days and the second in a mean of 9, thus indicating that, in contrast to dogs, children's sensory-sensory interactions prevail in some way over their sensory-motor ones.

Soviet Experiments: The Role of Differential Conditioning

Consider the following proposition. Obviously, differential conditioning can be effected only with two *different* stimuli—differing neural events. Hence, there arises the simple question: *Wherein is a compound a different stimulus?* It could not be the compound's greater stimulus value, since configuring is uninfluenced by increasing the intensity of the components, and this reasoning is obviously invalid when the compound is successive and the difference is between a trained and a tested sequence. An answer that the difference is innate is no doubt true for limited instances, such as musical intervals, to which both dogs and college students condition outright and transfer the conditioning irrespective of the absolute values of component tones (Kleshchov, 1933; Razran, 1938a; and others; also Humphrey's 1928 datum that a CR to an isolated musical note disappears when the note is "part of an arpeggio or melody"). But even the most committed Gestaltist would demur at positing as an innate configure a sequence of a metronome of 120 beats per minute + a "toucher" of 24 contacts per half minute + a flash of a lamp of 50 candlepower. Such compounds clearly must become different stimuli in the course of their CR training.[22]

Now, consider the basic differences between the empirical attributes of differential conditioning and configuring. (1) Differential classical conditioning is fully evident in some lower invertebrates (V. A. Sokolov, 1959), differential reinforcement conditioning in human neonates (Siqueland and Lipsitt, 1966), and both varieties are surely wholly effective in fish. Yet, with the possible exception of bees, configuring, in any significant degree, is attainable only in birds and mammals. (2) Configuring in higher mammals is abolished only by the ablation of higher cortical regions and retained despite the severing of the projection areas of their constituent components, whereas differential conditioning is possible even in decorticate animals (Belenkov, 1950a, 1950b, 1965). (3) Configuring takes very much more training than differential conditioning. (4) The dif-

[22] Vatsuro (1949, 1952, 1961, 1967) found that dogs configure olfactory and visual stimuli more readily than olfactory and auditory ones. That is to say, there is evidence of "natural" configuring in addition to "natural" conditioning (Chapter 2) and "natural" sensory preconditioning (preceding section)—a most systematic discovery in need of further research and parametric analysis. Baker's 1968 review, entitled "Properties of Compound Conditioned Stimuli and Their Components" and characterized as "An attempt to integrate Russian and American literature" (p. 611), notes only one (1961) of Vatsuro's publications. His review is, unfortunately, very limited: only nine experiments—five from the 1961 issue of the translation of *Pavlov's Journal of Higher Nervous Activity*—are of later dates than those in my 1939 review (1939a) which, although it was more detailed than my 1965 review (1965d) and in essence contained all of the principles mentioned in the later one, is not mentioned.

ference between the number of trials needed to form configuring through differential conditioning and through overtraining, in which several widely spaced test trials constitute the only differential conditioning or extinction of components, is relatively small. (5) Overtrained configuring is most common in reinforcement food conditioning, which is highly resistant to extinction, so several extinction trials could hardly effect any actual difference.

Plainly, both the logic and the empirics of the scores of Soviet experiments on compound-without-component conditioning impel the view that *the learning of differential conditioning is but ancillary to the learning of afferent-afferent stimulus configuring* and, in fact, is not a *sine qua non* to its coming into being. Pavlov was on the right track when he avowed, in the later years of his life, that "associations form *Gestalten* and not *Gestalten* associations" (*Wednesdays,* 1949, Vol. 3, p. 46; original date, December 5, 1934), as was Beritoff, who even earlier (1932) posited that "integrated [configured] compound conditioning" could not arise without the activation of "a supplementary neural CS center" (p. 43). Compare Tolman in 1959: "Although I became convinced that the whole in some way governs its parts, these wholes, I felt, were acquired by learning and were not autochthonously given. That is, I talked about sign-gestalten rather than about innately ready pure perceptual gestalten" (p. 95). There is, of course, no reason to assume that Tolman was at all familiar with his predecessors' theses, and in other respects his system is, of course, quite different from theirs, particularly from that of Pavlov.[23]

American Experiments

Configuring through learning, first called "configural conditioning" (Razran, 1938a), has long lain fallow in American psychology. Not only my own seven studies (1938a, 1939a-1939e, 1940a) but, more importantly, my review (1939a) of thirty-five original reports of Soviet experiments was left unturned. (Seventeen with dogs from Pavlov's laboratory, eight with dogs and rabbits from Beritoff's, eight with children from the laboratories of Krasnogorsky and Ivanov-Smolensky, and two with adult humans from the laboratory of Bekhterev.) Hull's two chapters ("Some Dynamics of Compound Conditioned Stimuli" and "The Patterning of

[23] My own cognate view of "Gestalt learning," advocated since 1938, was not, however, instigated by Pavlov. His *Wednesdays* was published in 1949, and his 1927 book, in which compound stimuli were discussed in only seven pages, was by no means explicit about the special systematic import of their conditioning. What influenced me first was Beritoff's 75-page chapter in his 1932 book (*Individually-Acquired Activity of the Central Nervous System*) setting forth the concept of the supplementary neural CS centers on the basis of germane experiments from his own and others' laboratories. A few years later, the commitment was consolidated by interrelating an analysis of the original reports of thirty-five Soviet CR experiments with the *Gestalt-qualität* writings of von Ehrenfels—and of course by my own "configural" studies (Razran, 1938a, 1939a-1939e, 1940a).

Stimulus Compounds") in his 1943 *Principles* were based on two American studies—one with humans and one with dogs (Hull, 1940; Woodbury, 1943)—and a quotation from Pavlov's 1927 book (1927b) with no quantitative data. His statement that my finding that "configurational generalization was considerably wider than was simple stimulus generalization," should be "explained" by my use of "verbally sophisticated subjects" (1943, p. 176) could hardly have been made, had he read in the review that *Zeliony* [working with dogs in 1910] found that *the generalization of a combination of stimuli does not follow the generalization of its components and is much wider in scope"* (Razran, 1939a, p. 312; italics in the original).

Likewise, while since 1956 Grings and his associates (Grings and O'Donnell, 1956; Grings and Kimmel, 1959; Grings and Shmelev, 1959; and Grings, Uno, and Feibiger, 1965) and since 1955 Wickens and his associates (Wickens and Snide, 1955; Wickens, 1959; Wickens, Cross, and Morgan, 1959; Wickens, Gehman, and Sullivan, 1959; Wickens, Born, and Wickens, 1963; and Wickens, 1965) and also Kimmel, Hill, and Fowler (1962) have carefully probed the interrelation of compound and component conditioning with the GSR in college students, and with cats in one case, no one has stepped into the "beyond" of configuring. The significant findings of these probings, among others, were ably and comprehensively reviewed by Grings in 1969. However, four recent (1967-1969) American CR experiments are wholly concerned with configuring proper and will be summarized here.

Guth (1967) trained a group of 84 rats to press a bar in response to a simultaneous compound S^D of a 1000-90-decibel tone plus a 140-millilumen light, and an equal control group to respond to either stimulus separately. He then divided each group into three equal subgroups—in one the light, in the second the tone, and in the third the compound stimulus was extinguished. Now, dividing the six extinction subgroups (experimental and control) into fourteen testing subgroups and using a factorial 2 x 2 analysis of variance, he found that in the trained compound-stimulus groups, but not in the control groups, the response strength of CRs to the compound stimulus (one component of which was extinguished) was significantly greater than that of CRs to any nonextinguished component. The experimenter's conclusion is that the results suggest that "even in a situation when no compound vs. component discrimination is given, a compound stimulus cannot be considered merely a mixture of its physical components, but rather must be endued with its own specific characteristics which we prefer to ascribe to patterning effects" (p. 480). Interestingly, this finding is comparable with Palladin's 1906 pioneer data that conditioned salivation was evoked when an extinguished component was combined with one that did not gain separate CR strength in the compound training. "Togetherness begot something very special," was my comment on Palladin's experiment at the beginning of this section.

Thomas, Berman, Serednesky, and Lyons (1968) studied configuring

218 · *Mind in Evolution*

in conditioned reinforcement of a sequence of two lights in 30 pigeons trained to peck at a white illuminated key for food. Their study consisted of three separate experiments with an equal number of subjects in each, and an $S_1 \rightarrow S_2$ sequence—reversed in equal subgroups in three experiments —which was a one-second green light followed immediately by a one-second vertical white line in the first two experiments and 90-degree and 60-degree white lines of equal duration in the third. The first experiment showed that after 30 conditioned reinforcements S_2 was a significantly stronger reinforcer than S_1 but that after 180, S_1 was significantly stronger. ("Reinforcement strength was defined by the rate of responding maintained in extinction by response-contingent presentations of different test stimuli"—p. 181.) The results of the second experiment, in which tests were made after 50, 650, 1250, and 2050 conditioned reinforcements and included the sequential compound, corroborated the results of the first: with longer training (650 and 1250 reinforcements) S_1 became more effective than S_2. But they add the important evidence that when the CR training was still longer (2050 reinforcements), the compound clearly gained the upper hand, even as the strengths of the components were reduced and equalized. Finally, in Experiment III, in which tests were administered only after 2145 food reinforcements, the *compound was significantly more effective than either component, a reversed sequence, and a sequence with an untrained S_2* (a blank; main results in the upper panels of Figure 48).

Thomas et al. conclude that their results "demonstrated unequivocally the phenomenon of stimulus configuring within the conditioned reinforcement paradigm" (p. 188). They are particularly impressed—as they should be—with the outcome of Experiment III, in which the configuring was effected "without the repeated testing (and the resulting differential reinforcement of compound and components)" (p. 188). And they note the similarity of their finding a shift in reinforcement efficacy from S_2 to S_1 to that of Beritoff in 1932 (as reported in English—Razran, 1965d), which he interpreted as a preliminary stage of configuring. Moreover, they suggest that the data of Egger and Miller (1962) on "information value and reliability of stimuli in secondary [conditioned] reinforcement" could be interpreted in this way.

Booth and Hammond (1969) used with 30 rats classical-punishment conditioning—the "CER (conditioned emotional response)" of Skinner and Estes—which, as is known, is very quickly formed and most uniform in increasing effects. After bar-pressing for water has been established, the animals, divided into three equal groups, were presented four times each day with a simultaneous light-tone compound followed by a shock: ten, 4 times; ten, 12 times; ten, 40 times. At the end of the CER training, each group was tested in random order 6 times: twice each with compound, light, and tone. The ratios of suppression of bar-pressing were the indices of the conditioning, with supplementary extinction tests for each

Figure 48 Upper panels: Configuring of conditioned reinforcement of a successive $S_1 + S_2$ compound of two different lights in two groups of 10 pigeons each keypecking for food. Group A—the compound became a much stronger reinforcer than either component after 2050 compound trials, but not after 50, 650, or 1250 trials. Group B—the compound was much stronger than either component, a reversed $S_2 + S_1$ compound and a compound with a different S_2 when tested for the first time after 2145 compound trials. (From Thomas, Berman, Serednesky, and Lyons, 1968) Lower panels: Configuring of a simultaneous light-tone compound in CERs (conditioned emotional responses) of three groups of 10 rats each bar-pressing for water and differing in number of compound-shock pairings. Note the wide suppression ratio difference in the 40-trial group between the compound and the light in the first test and between the compound and both the light and the tone in the second test. All three differences were significant at $p < .01$, even as in a follow-up study with a 60-trial group (personal communication) the difference between the compound and the tone was significant also in the first test. (From Booth and Hammond, 1969)

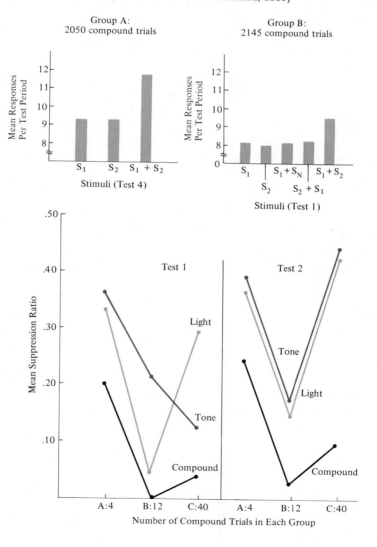

CS and pre-experimental verification of original CS ineffectiveness. The main results (lower panels, Figure 48), from which it may be seen that *while the compound was in all groups more effective than either component, the difference was clearly a positive function of the number of compound trials.* In the 40-trial group, the compound-component difference was statistically significant at the 1 per cent level in the second trial but only at 5 per cent in the first trial, with the light as the component. However, a follow-up with a 60-trial group (personal communication) demonstrated a 1 per cent significance level for both trials and either component.

Booth and Hammond state that "the results strongly confirm the major assumption of Razran that overtraining alone is sufficient for the formation of a configure" (p. 4). The experiment is special in its: (*a*) between-subjects design, not used by the Russians, (*b*) quick results, no doubt a function of the high efficacy of the CER, and (*c*) rate of acquisition as an index of conditioning, uncommon in American experiments.

Baker (1969) used both between-subjects and within-subject designs in the avoidance conditioning of 67 rabbits to a 2-second simultaneous compound of a light and a tone. In the between-subjects design, 60 animals were first divided into four equal groups which received 50, 150, 450, or 1350 acquisition trials. Then, each group was divided into three equal subgroups: one undergoing 150 extinction-of-the-compound trials; another, 50 extinction-of-the-light trials followed by 50 of the tone and 50 of the compound, and a third in which the sequence was 50 tone-, 50 light-, and 50 compound-extinction trials. In the within-subject design with 7 subjects, 50 acquisition trials on Day 1 were followed by a total of 1300 on Days 2 through 14, 100 each day, and 3 test trials of the effectiveness of the compound and either component were made on each day. The results show that *while in the within-subject design increases in compound efficacy paralleled fully decreases in the efficacy of either component, no such parallels were evident in comparing the four groups in the between-subjects design—only differences in rate of improvement with training.*

Baker's data with a between-subjects design are thus in direct opposition to those of Booth and Hammond, and one might only guess that the discrepancy is an outcome of the difference in (*a*) species, (*b*) type of conditioning, and (*c*) index of its strength. (Think also of Guth's positive between-subjects results.) What is amazing, however, is Baker's statement that within-subject data of compound versus component conditioning are just matters of generalization decrements and that: "At present, support for the occurrence of stimulus configurations appears lacking" (p. 352). He cavalierly dismisses the mass of Soviet evidence on its phyletic and ontogenetic evolution, the specific effects of cortical ablations, and *the plain fact that their overtraining experiments disclose a total failure and not just a decrement of component CR action.* Moreover, as intimated earlier, there is the simple logic that a generalization decrement cannot occur without a differential datum between the trained and the generaliza-tion stimulus. What is the datum, then, if not stimulus configuring, in Ex-periment III of Thomas et al.—in which pigeons responded on the first test much more effectively to the trained $S_1 \rightarrow S_2$ sequence than to either component *and* to the reversed sequence $S_2 \rightarrow S_1$, thus *nullifying possible differences in both quantity and primacy of stimulation?*

Nor should we disregard the likelihood of methodological "contamina-tion" in the between-subjects design. Different subjects may well require different degrees of overtraining to begin configuring, which group means of training trials may well not reflect—and which, without in the least con-doning Soviet confinement to one design, suggests the merit of using both. The Russians have been remiss in general, of course, in not using thorough methodological controls. Yet, as multiply documented, their main findings and generalizations are nonetheless well founded. Consider their advanced contribution to the essence of sensory preconditioning. And, in contrast (if I may so so), our scruples about possible generalization decrements have for years stymied our accepting Pavlov's 65-year-old Law of Strength, that CS intensity is an important parameter of CR efficacy (Chapter 7). Of first priority is the need to replicate Soviet ablation experiments in con-figuring. In the related field of sensory preconditioning, Thompson and Kramer's (1965) definitive demonstration that it is abolished only when association areas, and not sensory projection areas, of the cortex are ablated is a milestone of systematic disclosure.

Finally, it is gratifying to note that mathematical-model learning theo-rists of stimulus sampling have recently moved from "component" to "pattern" and "mixed" matrices (compare Burke and Estes, 1957, with Estes, 1959, and Atkinson and Estes, 1963; also with Friedman and Gelfand, 1964, and Friedman, 1966)—and to record the Estes and Hop-kins 1961 statement that their data on "acquisition and transfer in pat-tern-vs.-component discrimination learning [are] quite compatible with the pattern hypothesis" (p. 32).

In limbo here for almost three decades, learned configuring is happy to enter the American paradise of experimentation and theory.

SENSORY PRECONDITIONING AND CONFIGURING COMPARED

It must be clear by now that the two phenomena of "superconditioning" have a great deal in common. First, both become manifest to any sig-nificant extent only in higher animals—birds and mammals. Second, both are governed by brain centers higher in evolution than those of simple conditioning—logically related but empirically based on different types of studies. Third, they both represent afferent-afferent or sensory-sensory learning, involving the activation of sensory-orienting reactions. The simple operation of these reactions in sensory preconditioning has been experimentally delineated to a considerable degree. Their more complex role in configuring is still predominantly only a compelling hypothesis—although, as noted, some experimental verification of its existence and direct analysis of its effects in young children, 29 to 60 months, has already been reported (Zaklyakova, 1963; Degtyar, 1965).

Beyond this, however, there is a methodologic and ontologic divergence between the two. Sensory preconditioning comprises only the learning of sensory-sensory interactions, whereas configuring experiments have involved, in addition, interactions with biological USs or reinforcers. Leading Soviet animal experimenters in the area (Beritoff, 1932; Sergeyev, 1967; Voronin, 1965) agree that the biological sensory-motor conditioning of component sensory reactions in a compound precedes—and probably dominates—the intercomponent sensory-sensory interactions. Moreover, the experimenters concur that the latter comprises two consecutive stages: *preconfiguring,* in which only strengthening of strong and weakening of weak components are produced, something like the "leveling and sharpening" of Gestalt psychology, and *configuring proper,* with categorical no-reactions to components. All of this, together with the fact that Soviet experimenters have used "naturally" unrelated components and the logical consideration that configuring as such is more complex than is sensory preconditioning, are no doubt the reasons that, without differential contrasting, the former is formed much more slowly than the latter. Still, baboons have attained spontaneous configuring in 30 to 60 trials, and three-year-old children have proven that learned CS sequences are more stable—less readily transformed—than the types of CRs which they evoke.

That intermediating orienting reactions should continue throughout prolonged training of configuring may be accounted for by the following three considerations: (a) Sergeyev's finding that such training does not inactivate associated stimuli but renders them inhibitory, which is integral to the formation of configures; (b) the quick recovery of extinguished orienting reflexes with slight internal or external "signaling" changes, found by a number of Soviet experimenters, and the Hoffeld, Thompson, and Brogden (1958) finding of a second peak of sensory preconditioning efficacy at 200 trials; and (c) the likelihood—already indicated—that the orienting commences its intermediation early in compound-stimulus training but that its effects are suppressed by dominant biological conditioning. Empirical data to replicate the first two findings and confirm the third theoretical position are surely in order as are configuring experiments without concomitant biological conditioning—that is, in which *orienting reactions* were evoked through learning by configures but not components. And there is high merit in probing, through conventional configuring-conditioning techniques, whether the loss of reactions to components is only behavioral or also neural. None of the several hundred Soviet studies in the area offers any information on it.

The ontologic divergences of preconditioning and configuring are even more definitive. A moment's thought will convince one that the former is not a new kind of learning but a higher form of effecting an old kind—association. True, the means are putatively new, but obviously the end results are not. Yet configuring is just that—the bringing into being of new end results, neurobehavioral (a+b+c)s that are different from a's, b's, and c's and learned independently of them. That is to say, learned *emergence* or *inference,* both behavioral and neural, is directly immanent in configuring but not in sensory conditioning, the novelty of which is, to reconstrue a term from philosophy, a new "explanans" for an *old existent* and not a new "explanandum"—a *new existent* and its "explanans." Note, however, that the emergence or inference considered here is neurobehavioral, and not philosophical. Beritoff's view (1932) that learned configuring brings into play unutilized neural matrices does by no means imply physically unattached "creative evolution" (Bergson, 1907) or "emergent evolution" (Alexander, 1920). Nor, for that matter, does unlearned configuring need to involve it.

Moreover, to pass from ontology to pragmatics, there is the fact that while sensory preconditioning enhances substantially organisms' acquired reaction repertories, the effect is rather limited. Not so with configuring; enhancement through it is immense. Organisms that do not configure can respond to N stimuli in only N different ways. Those that do configure may learn to do it in $N!$ ways. And they are able, furthermore, to respond unitarily to larger portions of their environment, a very significant gain of adaptive economy in organism-environment interrelations.

Still, the distinctions between the two phenomena must not obscure their commonality. They both are, it will be contended later, ascending levels of cognitive-perceptual learning—sensory preconditioning a "sign," and configuring a "Gestalt" learning, to split Tolman's combination. Moreover, although what is learned in sensory preconditioning does not differ from that in simple conditioning, the means of learning it could be subsumed under configuring—namely, the acquisition of a cognitive relation characterized long ago by Selz (1913) as *Sachsverhältnis;* unified knowledge of a thing-in-relation to another and not of either the thing by itself or the relation by itself.

Finally, we must pause at an overriding parametric puzzle: Just when does combining sensory-orienting reactions lead to the conditioning of one reaction *to* another and when to integrating one *with* another? A view that the former is favored when only two reactions, one following another, are combined and the latter when more than two are presented simultaneously (cf. Bregadze, 1956; also Wundt, 1896) is hardly more than a general guideline, since both results have been obtained with both conditions. Specific research is sorely needed.

224 · Mind in Evolution

PERCEPTION, HUMAN LEARNING WITHOUT AWARENESS, AND KINDS OF PERCEPTUAL LEARNING

Perception as Such: Inferred and Phenomenal

To say that animals perceive should mean that they possess phenomenal experiences similar to ours. But since this is obviously but an inference from relative similarity of behavior (including neurobehavior and underlying structure), it cannot be proven, and radical behaviorists must not be pushed outside the pale when they say, for instance, that perception is but the ability to respond to the environment with "stimulus control," "discriminated reactions," or something like it. Still, there is not only evolutionary, philosophic, and aesthetic merit in granting the inference but, with respect to higher animals, methodologic merit as well. Experimental evidence of the capacities and learning ways of these animals can be juxtaposed and integrated with those of humans in such areas as perception and thinking, in which experiential rather than behavioral reports are at hand: e.g., leveling and sharpening vis-à-vis preconfiguring, differential limens obtained through psychophysical methods and through differential conditioning; the possibility of effecting the latter in paradoxical cold (or warmth), correlations between orienting reactions and cognitivity; and the like. To be sure, radical behaviorists may rebut that these reports are nothing but behavioral verbal reactions. Renouncing experience in human beings, however, is not worth the arguing or the space for doing so.

Early in the century, leading subjective biologists and animal psychologists (Jennings, 1905; Lukas, 1904; Washburn, 1908; Wheeler, 1910; Yerkes, 1905a, 1911) assumed that experience exists throughout the animal kingdom and that its nature varies in accordance with general phyletic differences in structure and function. Yerkes' "psycho-phylogenetic tree" ranged from "Group I" of "unicellular organisms" and the "dawn of consciousness" to "Group VI" of "monkeys and apes" and the "dawn of reason." (A general basis of inference, "associative memory," was used also by Loeb, the objectivist, in his unsuccessful attempt to restrict consciousness to vertebrates, the fourth subphylum of the highest—seventeenth —phylum.) The early subjectivist view minus its evolutionary distinctions may well persevere in some form among radical present-day cognitionists. However, the position of three leading modern students of neurobehavior is quite different. Beritoff limits "image-directed behavior" to "higher vertebrates," Hebb states that "when a psychologist studies learning in the ant he is not dealing with mental processes" (1958, p. 2), and Konorski relates perception and imagery to cortical action. Moreover, all three employ, as they should, specific bases of inference, which merit brief mention—and criticism.

Beritoff's bases of inference are, first, what might be called one-trial learning and, second, higher-level developmental and functional characteristics of short-axon stellate cells in cortical layers III and IV. Dogs shown meat in one place and bread in another may later run to the meat location after one showing, and dogs or cats may retrace triangular and quadrilateral routes to feeding places after single blindfolded transportations in baskets. And in their turn, the stellate cells, located at the end of the afferent brain and posited to be the *producers* of imagery, "have multiplied most rapidly in vertebrate evolution, with marked intumescence of dendrites unencumbered by small collaterals and very profuse intercalation with internuncial and small pyramidal association neurones, but no connections with efferent neurones" (Beritoff, 1960 and elsewhere; see also Filiminov, 1959, 1960; O'Leary, 1941; Polyakov, 1953, 1956, 1965; Polyakov and Sarkisov, 1949; Sarkisov, 1948; Sarkisov and Bogolepov, 1967; Shkol'nik-Yarros, 1954, 1958, 1959; and others). My criticism is that one-trial learning may still be unimaged and that more germane evidence is needed before we can consider the stellate cells the *organs* of imaging. Hebb's specific basis is even more open to question. He states that "higher behavior [perception and thinking equated with the "mediation process"] arises when there is a delay [of several seconds] between a stimulus and a response" which only "Lorenté de Nó's [1922, 1933, 1934] closed cortical pathways" may handle (1966, pp. 79, 90). But here one may well ask, what about the minutes-long persistence of post-tetanic potentiation (Lloyd, 1949; and others) and of conditioning through anodal polarization (Morrell, 1961b; Rusinov, 1953; Podsosennaya, 1956; and others) in the simplest neural structures? Finally, there is Konorski, "extrapolating" the basic neurophysiological mechanisms of perception from Hubel and Wiesel's classic studies (1959, 1961, 1962, 1963, and elsewhere) of the increasing differential qualitative complexity of single-neuron reactions in the ascending hierarchy of the visual cortex—specifically, his view is that "perceptions experienced in humans' and animals' lives, are represented not by the *assemblies* of units but by *single* units in the highest levels of particular analyzers . . . *gnostic units*" (Konorski, 1967, p. 755; italics in original). Recent discoveries that comparable specialized unit-neurons of complex and directional sensitivity may also be found in the ganglion cells of the retina of the cat (Rodieck, 1967; Rodieck and Stone, 1963; Stone and Fabian, 1966; and several other reports) certainly strain the extrapolation. Is the bare eyeball also a mind?

The image as the phenomenal core of perception is, of course, a tradition. "Perception is image," wrote K. Buhler in 1907, improving on Aristotle's "thought is image." But clearly, in modern times, neither the image nor any of the experiential marginalia accrued to it is all there is to perception. Sound philosophy of psychology impels the position that its neural correlate pre-exists, post-exists, and controls it. That is, there must be neural perception-like action before the pattern is ripe for phenomenal manifestation as well as when such manifestation is no longer evident. The first phase has been labeled in American psychology "subception" (Lazarus and McCleary, 1951); the second, in light of Beritoff's long-standing avowal of "automatization of imagery" (1947 on), may well be designated "postception." In other words, perception is in all a neurophenomenal—or better—a neurocognitive category of mind. And it comprises, it may well be said, two dimensions: a *horizontal* one that deals with essences or ontology, which psychology shares with philosophy and the controversies of which are basically metaexperimental; and a *vertical* one that is wholly psychological and experimental and centers on how perception is changed and formed—perceptual learning. Before discussing this learning, however, it might be best to consider briefly a relatively recent American doctrine that "learning without awareness in human Ss is not adequately proven" (Eriksen, 1960, p. 898; see also Adams, 1957; Farber, 1963; and others).

Human Learning Without Awareness: Proof

Basically, the doctrine is a reformulation of Tolman's all-cognitive view of learning of the preceding generation, with the difference that it concerns itself with men and not rats, and tenders a new mixture of radical behaviorism, orthodox Freudianism, and either panpsychism or Cartesianism. The flavor of the first ingredient of the mixture comes through as the reformulation tends toward an operational identification of awareness with verbal reports and thus becomes a "no human learning without verbalization," *conceivably* reconcilable with behavioristic philosophy. The second may be scented through the hidden thesis that the perceptual ego, and not the conative id, learns, while the fact that hydra and earthworms learn must obviously mean either that they are aware, or that while they can do it unaware, we cannot. A host of philosophic, evolutionary, logical, and plain commonsense arguments could be leveled against this position. These will, however, be passed over in favor of opposing empirical evidence, which the adherents of the reformulation are either unfamiliar with or for some reason ignore.

Interoceptive Conditioning. Soviet experimenters have for years reported successful experiments with interoceptive conditioning in man and animals, together with the unawareness, in man, of most interoceptive stimulation (Ayrapet'yants, 1949, 1952; Ayrapet'yants and Balakshina, 1935; Bykov, 1943; Bykov, Alekseyev-Berkman, Ivanova, and Ivanov, 1928; Makarov, 1950a, 1950b, 1959; Mysyashchikova, 1952; Pshonik, 1952; Razran, 1961a [partial summary]). Their results with animals have of late been fully replicated in the United States (Cook, Davidson, Davis, and Kelleher, 1960; Schuster and Brady, 1964; Slucki, Ádám, and Porter, 1965), and little needs to be said about the validity of their carefully probed interoceptive awareness data (normal subjects swallowing balloons with fluoroscopically positioned electrodes, and experimenters inserting them in fistulated patients). Boring's 1915 conclusions from his less technical study, "Sensations of the Alimentary Canal," are mainly in accord, while Titchener's 1909 statement that "the intestinal track from stomach to rectum is usually free from sensations, with the exceptions of occasional colic pains" (p. 189) must be corrected. High-intensity stimuli do evoke specific sensory content, prior to pain (Makarov, 1959). Mysyashchikova (1952) noted galvanic skin reflexes to intestinal pressure of 10 millimeters Hg, awareness of the pressure at 40, and awareness of pain at 45 millimeters. And it will be remembered (Chapter 2) that similar results were obtained with interoceptive electric shocks of the stomach by Makarov (1959), who found further definitive EEG changes to stomach tubes with water below 37 degrees C and above 40 degrees C, but *awareness of cold* only below 10 degrees C, and of warmth at 41 degrees C only after prolonged stimulations. (Double tubes, a thin inner one and a thick outer one, were used—the outer tubes removed after the water had reached the subjects' stomach to rule out the effects of oral, pharyngeal, and esophageal stimulations.) Yet these unaware stimuli are fully conditionable.[24] Moreover, there is clear-cut evidence of unaware interoceptive conditioning of another kind. Figure 49 shows the apparatus used and Figure 50 the results of conditioning a patient with a urinary-bladder fistula to readings of a manometer associated with inflating a tube within the bladder. As may be seen, the conditioning was evident first in a GSR reaction, then in a change of respiration, followed by contraction of bladder muscle *M. detrusor urinae*—all prior to the subjects' conditioned awareness.

Nor is there lack of evidence for unaware interoceptive *discrimination*. Ádám (1967) studied habituation of unaware frontal-occipital alpha blocking in 14 subjects who swallowed triple-walled duodenal tubes with two inflatable balloons 15-20 centimeters apart. Eight subjects reacted in full to the inflation of one balloon when their blocking reaction to the other had been completely habituated (pp. 127-128, Figures 86, 87).

[24] Uno's (in press) careful study of interoceptive stimulation and conditioning in 48 college students is to a considerable extent not comparable with Soviet counterparts. First, the stimulation was applied to the esophagus, which 55 years ago Boring found substantially more sensitive than the gastrointestinal tract studied and conditioned in typical Russian experiments. (Note that the Titchener "free of sensation" statement refers only to the "track from stomach to rectum" and that Makarov controlled esophagus effects.) Second, the specific stimuli used, balloons with water at 50 or 0 degrees C., were much above exteroceptive thresholds, and it is no wonder that only 14 subjects were unaware of them (cf. Boring and Makarov). Nonetheless, Uno's data replicate significantly the two main Soviet generalizations of interoceptive conditioning: (1) *its slower formation* and (2) *its existence without awareness*. The fact that the first generalization was disclosed only with presumably cognitive "pre-US" (FIR) conditioned GSRs and the second only with presumably noncognitive "post-US" kinds does not negate the essence of the replication. Moreover, Uno confirmed in part also the Soviet conclusion that interoceptive CRs are more potent than exteroceptive (Razran, 1961a). Only the finding of no significant differences in interoceptive-exteroceptive habituation is divergent, and it could also be attributed to the awareness of the interoceptive stimulus in 71 per cent of Uno's subjects.

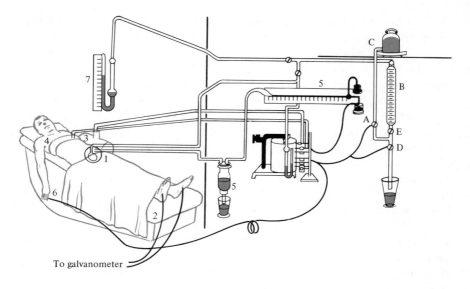

Figure 49 *Apparatus for interoceptive conditioning of human subjects with urinary bladder fistulas.* 1—bladder fistula; 2—GSR electrodes; 3—plethysmograph; 4—respiratory cuff; 5—registration of urination; 6—subject's report of urge to urinate (press button); 7—manometer; B—graduated cylinder; C—water vessel regulating pressure; A, D, and E—valves. (From Ayrapet'yants, Lobanova, and Cherkasova, 1952)

Subliminal Exteroceptive Conditioning. Here, a considerable amount of the evidence is, in truth, controversial. However, there can be no doubt about the validity of the data of Gershuni (1946, 1947, 1950, 1955, 1957) and his associates (Gershuni and Korotkin, 1947; Gershuni et al., 1948; Chistovich, 1949; Kozhevnikov and Maruseva, 1949; Korotkin, 1947)—Gershuni is the Soviets' and perhaps the world's most outstanding audiometrist—on conditioned galvanic skin reflexes and electroencephalographic changes to "subsensory" auditory stimuli 5 to 12 decibels below the awareness thresholds of dozens of subjects. (The USs were shocks or lights, and pseudoconditioning was ruled out by controls.) Some of the data are presented in Figures 51 and 52. Figure 51 shows GSR conditioning of one of ten subjects conditioned to a sound 10 decibels below awareness. Note that the CRs were first evoked by supraliminal stimuli and only later by the subliminal ones, and that the latter produced no reaction in the three days of prehabituation—true also of five other subjects, with the remaining four yielding one reaction each (Chistovich, 1949). The top four panels of Figure 52 demonstrate EEG conditioning in one of fifteen subjects conditioned to a sound 6 decibels below awareness: first, no reaction prior to experiment; second and third, clear-cut alpha blocking (parietal-occipital and parietal-temporal) after 3 and 20 combinations with a light; fourth, control—21st trial with no stimulus (Kozhevnikov

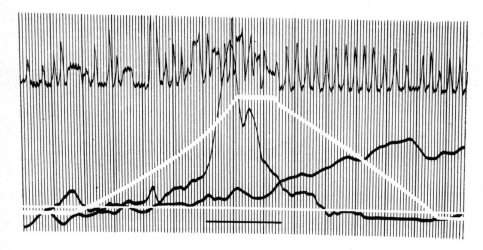

Figure 50 *Sample of interoceptive conditioning of patients with urinary bladder fistulas.* The US was the distention of the bladder with calibrated inflows of a physiological solution through an inserted tube, registered on a manometer with a large dial. The dial readings, watched by the patient, became CSs when, unknown to him, the experimenter activated the manometer without distention. Black lines, from top, are records of conditioned respiration, GSR, contraction of urinary muscle (*M. detrusor urinae*), and subject's report of urge to urinate (button pressed). White pyramid-shaped line is the record of the administration of the CS—the experimenter moving up the readings, keeping them at peak, and then lowering them. The lower white line denotes the US, distention, which was not administered. Note the sequences of the appearance and disappearance of the four conditioned changes: the subjective urge as well as the peripheral contraction appearing last and disappearing first. (From Ayrapet'yants, 1952, and Ayrapet'yants, Lobanova, and Cherkasova, 1952)

and Maruseva, 1949). Here, too, pre-experimental reactions to the sounds were rare—even with lights between trials (pseudoconditioning) in no case more than 30 per cent and thus little above "spontaneous" frequencies. The bottom panel is a record of EEG (occipital-parietal) and GSR conditioning of one of six subjects conditioned to a sound 6 decibels below awareness after 20 combinations with a shock (Gershuni, 1955).[25]

Nor is there reason to question the authenticity of the subliminal GSR conditioning of six subjects to lights 20 to 80 per cent of the intensity of

---

[25] Dawson and Satterfield's (1969) recent results that GSR conditioning did not occur significantly in a group of human subjects misinformed about the pertinent CS-US relations, but did occur in a comparable informed group, scarcely warrant the sweeping conclusion that "relational learning is a necessary condition for the establishment of human autonomic classical conditioning" (p. 70). The plausible interpretation of the difference is that the general CR conditions were not optimal (shock was liminal, etc.) for the misinformed group, and that in the informed group "cognitive relational learning"—easy for normal adults and practically free of the optimal-pessimal onus—produced the effects. There is only one interpretation for the subliminal conditioning of Gershuni et al.

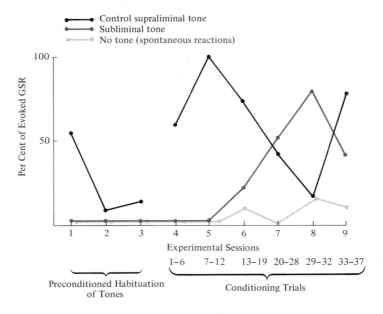

Figure 51 *Sample GSR conditioning to a tone 10 decibels below liminal consciousness, with electric shock as the US, in Gershuni's laboratory.* Lines in Figure: black—reactions to a control supraliminal tone; dark gray—to the subliminal tone; light gray—spontaneous reactions. Note that the subliminal tone evoked no preconditioning reaction (needed no habituation), and that the subliminal conditioning, appearing after 12 CR training trials and reaching its peak at 30, was first manifested in response to the supraliminal control tone. (From Chistovich, 1949)

liminal awareness in an experiment by Samsonova (1953) or the subliminal reinforcement conditioning of micromovements by Hefferline, Keenan, and Hartford (1959), not mentioned in Eriksen's survey.

Conditioning Human Neonates and Aments. As documented in preceding chapters, more than a dozen American and Soviet experimenters have disclosed fully reliable simple and differential conditioning—not to mention habituation and sensitization—in human neonates, a few days old. And Kecen (1966) reports clear evidence of conditioning and extinction in two autosomal trisomy-18 infants, one 2 years and 8 months old and another 4 years and 11 months old, with "estimated IQs of 10." But since these were nonverbal and thus arguably not truly human, the trump experiment in the area should be brought forth. Grings, Lockhart, and Dameron (1962) found no differences in simple and discriminatory GSR conditioning between two groups of 14- to 15-year-old subjects, twenty in each: one with an IQ range of 20 to 45 and a median of 33; the other, a range of 55 to 78 and a median of 62. Surely, the awareness, verbalization, and perception of the two groups differed most substantially. More-

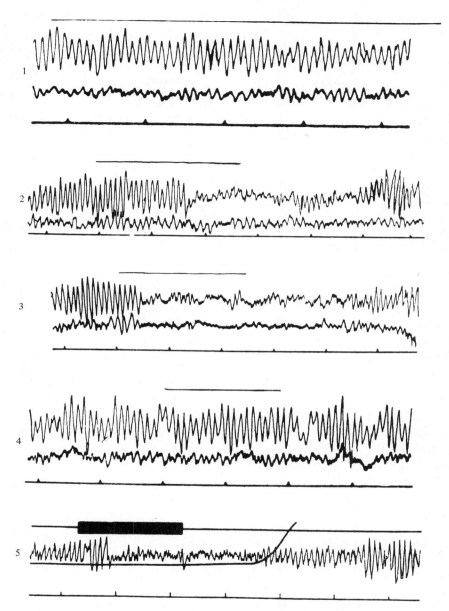

Figure 52 *Sample conditioning of parietal-occipital and parietal-temporal alpha blocking (top four panels) and of GSR and parietal-occipital blocking (bottom panel) to a tone of 6 decibels below liminal consciousness, in Gershuni's laboratory.* The US was a light in the first experiment, an electric shock in the second. The upper line in the first three panels mark the administration of the tone; in the fourth panel (control), time parallel to tone administration. The administration of the tone is denoted in the bottom panel by the bar and in the other four panels by the line at the top, while in all panels the bottom line indicates time in seconds. Panel 1—reaction to tone before conditioning; Panel 2—after 3, and Panel 3, after 20 conditioning trials, respectively; Panel 4—control; Panel 5 (second experiment)—conditioning after 20 trials. (From Kozhevnikov and Maruseva, 1949; and Gershuni, 1955)

over, the experimenters' data show that all subjects conditioned more readily and more regularly than college students.

Instructions and Self-Instructions in Classical Conditioning. The findings of the Grings laboratory are in line with those of Razran: (*a*) data that subjects who are aware or are made aware through instructions of the conditioning relations of consciously or verbally controlled reactions do not condition regularly, and that instructions to condition or not to condition greatly affect obtained results (1935); (*b*) survey evidence that classical conditioning "manifests itself best only [in] young children and subnormal adults; [and in states of] fatigue, hypnosis, emotional stress, and absorption in some other task" (1936, p. 335); (*c*) disclosure that subjects who are misinformed about the purpose of a conditioning experiment, and thus are unaware of involved relations, condition much more regularly than aware subjects (1939 on). Scores of American, Soviet, and western European experiments are by now available in the area, with scarcely any divergence in outcomes: awareness is not a *sine qua non* of human classical conditioning. Nothing more will be said about it here, except—with an apology for singling out my own experiment—that some of my subjects (not college students) could not be made aware of some conditioning relations, even though the attempt was explained to them after the experiment. Rating and characterizing musical selections and paintings during lunch and after it (Razran, 1938b, 1962, 1969), all they would believe was that "the mind may work differently during a meal," or that it may "change after you've heard [or seen] something before," but not that it can change because I heard [or saw] it during a meal." "Not me. What will professors think of next?"

Instructions and Self-Instructions in Reinforcement Conditioning. The argument goes back to Thorndike's view that a satisfying aftereffect does not act "by any mystical or logical potency [but] is as natural in its action as a falling stone, a ray of light, a line of force, a stream of water, or as a hormone in the blood" (1933, p. 435) and "could strengthen the connection which it followed and to which it belonged in cases where the learner did not know what the connection was" (Thorndike and Rock, 1934, p. 1). No doubt, a good deal of Thorndike's empirical evidence is unconvincing, and, unknowingly, he seems to endow the "Law of Effect" with an absolutism that is neither logical nor natural. Yet on the whole he steered in the right direction. The literature here is considerable, and it seems advisable to defer to Postman and Sassenrath's 1961 review. Their conclusion that *"the verbalization of a principle [through the "law of effect" or "reinforcement conditioning"—G.R.] may be considered at the same time a result of past improvement and a condition of further improvement"* (p. 124; italics in original) is in essence only a somewhat different and longer way of saying that "awareness is not a *sine qua non* of classical conditioning." A recent report of an experiment with school children ends: ". . . demonstrable conditioning [reinforcement] occurred prior to awareness [yet] an increase in rate followed awareness [and] the results support Postman's interpretation" (Vogler, 1968, p. 125). It should be noted, however, that while awareness of a reward may be expected always to increase learning, awareness of classical conditioning, may, and often does, do the reverse.

While some portions of the adduced empirical evidence may conceivably be contested, the weight of it all is overwhelming in negating the assertion that "learning without awareness in human Ss is not adequately proven" (Eriksen, 1960, p. 298). Put differently, it means that the underlying mechanisms of the five types of learning discussed in the preceding chapters are *basically* noncognitive—*neurobehavioral* and not *neurocognitive*. This chapter is, however, devoted to the first of the two types of posited neurocognitive learning, learning related to perception, which upon analysis turns out to be of four kinds.

Four Kinds of Perceptual Learning

The First Two Kinds: Modificatory. The first two kinds of perceptual learning are manifest in a substantial number of experiments in which percepts are modified by punishment, classical, or reinforcement conditioning: e.g., McNamara, Solley, and Long (1958), Smith and Hochberg (1954), Solley and Murphy (1960), Staats and Staats (1957, 1958; verbal learning, but directly pertinent here), my own (Razran, 1938c, 1940b, 1954, 1969), and others. When the subjects are unaware of or do not perceive (used synonymously here; distinction discussed in a later section) the conditioning relations, it is the first kind, which may be designated broadly as *conditioning of perception*. When they do perceive the relations, it is the second kind, for which *conditioning through perception* would seem the most fitting term. The significant determinant is the *perception of the relations* and not perception of the *interacting reactions*. When these relations are *unperceived,* there is little difference between the conditioning of perceptual and nonperceptual reactions (Razran, 1955a, and elsewhere)[26]—inclining S-S theorists to honor only the second kind and S-R devotees only the first.

The S-R—S-S irresolution is complicated by the fact that most experimenters working with humans do not separate relation-unperceived and relation-perceived subjects, and in animals there is of course no way of knowing the difference. It is hoped, however, that distinctive functional separation of the two will eventually be forthcoming. Already, there are: (*a*) the broad thrust of the solid evidence showing basic parametric differences between preconditioning and simple conditioning; (*b*) the penetrat-

---

[26] But, to be sure, there can be no perception of relations when one of the interacting reactions (or stimuli) is itself unperceived.

ing goad of the Grings laboratory's comparisons of conditioning in normal human subjects and in severe retardates; and (*c*) the hopeful prospect of questionnaires to pinpoint "attitudinal factors" (Kimble, 1967b).

In 1955, I called the second type "relational learning" (Razran, 1955a). The term, since used by Grings and his associates, is, however, too broad —it embraces four separate varieties. (1) Learning to respond to relations that by all tokens have, to begin with, innate unitary existences as stimuli— such as being conditioned to sound ratios as CSs, reported by a number of Soviet experimenters with animals and by me with humans (Dolin, 1937; Kleshchov, 1933, 1944; Korotkin, 1938; A. Novikova, 1938; Razran, 1938a; and others)—and, in another area, segregating "figure" from "ground" (Hebb, 1949). (2) The much discussed learning to respond to "more than" or "less than" stimuli, which, while progressive in acquisition, may still inhere in corresponding patterns of innate unitary responding in line with Lashley and Wade's assertion that "the *basic* nervous mechanism of integration is one of reactions to ratios of excitation" (1946, p. 86; italics added). (3) Learning to perceive obvious and existing, yet in essence arbitrary, temporal and spatial relations—e.g., that a specific reaction (or stimulus) follows another reaction (or stimulus) in simple-conditioning designs, or equally, that food, or a predator, is to the right or left of some location.[27] (4) Learning to perceive novel and unobvious relevant relations, e.g., that a stick can rake in a banana. Hence, my present view that only the third variety represents *basic* perceptual learning designated above as *conditioning through perception*. The first two are not considered perceptual and the fourth is a higher level of it. Two distinctions are thus drawn—on the one hand, between *reacting* (or learning to react) to a relation and *cognizing* it, and on the other, between *cognizing* and *producing* it. The first distinction is in line with Pavlov's "there is nothing special in an organism [i.e., any organism] responding to ratios or relations" (*Wednesdays,* 1949, Vol. 3, p. 153); the second, with my according higher evolutionary status to productive learning.

Moreover, since without relational awareness conditioning *of* perception does not differ from simple conditioning, conditioning *through* perception is obviously the only modificatory perceptual learning—an evolvent, it is held, of modificatory simple conditioning and an antecedent of the productive level. A later section will equate this basic perceptual learning with the underlying mechanism of sensory preconditioning, possible only in birds and mammals. Add to this that while conditioning through perception is faster and more permanent than conditioning without it, perception itself is slow in coming and as such is often confronted by some pre-perceived conditioning.

[27] Compare Lashley that the "rats' visual system functions most efficiently in spacial orientation—the recognition of relative distance—and that the recognition of objects, though possible, is secondary to a system of space coordinates" (1938, pp. 187-188).

Thus, there is substantial evidence for the bona fide existence of both S-R and S-S mechanisms of modificatory learning: S-R coeval with the very genesis of the phenomenon; S-S, a later evolutionary acquisition. Exclusionist views will, it is assumed, decline and eventually disappear as the two divide peacefully their psychologic territory and "in the end of days lie down together . . . not hurt nor destroy."

The Last Two Kinds: Productive. The first of these two kinds is best illustrated by the "learning sets" of Harlow (1949, 1959), on the one hand, and by Köhler's "insights" (1917, 1925), on the other—both notably in primates. Learning and perception here come pretty close to each other. But note that for essentially similar behavior Harlow abnegates the latter and Köhler the former. "If such phenomena [insight and hypothesis] appear independently of a gradual learning history, we have not found them in the primate order," states Harlow (1949, p. 65), even as the unlearned nature of the "Aha!" of insight is avowed in all the writings of Köhler and other psychologists of Gestalt or cognition. Total East and West evidence and logic in the area point, however, to two generalizations which in large measure reconcile the Köhler-Harlow data. (*a*) Insight, or the perception of new and unobvious relevant relationships, is most commonly a function of past learning. (*b*) The possibility that it may also emerge without learning depends upon one's definition of learning. Support for the first generalization is ample in the works of Harlow, Pavlov (1949—original dates, 1932-1936), Birch (1945), Rensch and Döhl (1968), Ruger (1910), and a number of other American and Soviet experimenters, and is, in fact, evident in Köhler's own protocols.

The quandary of the second generalization is well highlighted in the "extrapolative reflexes" studied by the Soviet biologist Krushinsky and his associates (Krushinsky, 1958a, 1958b, 1958c, 1959, 1960, 1961; Flyoss, Krushinsky, Molodkina, and Ochinskaya, 1963; Krushinsky, Flyoss, Molodkina, Ochinskaya, and Popova, 1965; Krushinsky, Flyoss, Molodkina, Popova, and Ochinskaya, 1964; Krushinsky, Molodkina, and Popova, 1963; and Molodkina, 1966), who experimented mainly with stupid and wise birds—pigeons, ducks, and chickens; and crows and magpies —but also with rabbits, and with dogs and cats. In the main technique, the animals were permitted to feed themselves from the top of a box moving on a track at a speed of 8 to 10 centimeters per second for a distance of one and a half meters and then disappearing in a three-meter tunnel of two equal sections before coming out in the open again. The sections were either joined or separated by an opening of 3 to 5 centimeters.

Krushinsky's objective was (*a*) to study the birds' behavior in response to the disappearance of the feeding box [the tunnel entrance closed the moment the box was inside] and (*b*) to see if they moved along the tunnel and to record their behavior if they moved sufficiently to reach the mid-tunnel opening as the feeding box came through. The latter behavior was nonexistent for the pigeons, ducks, and chickens and rabbits; when the box disappeared, they, respectively, almost immediately turned backwards or sideways, stood still for 7 to 22 seconds before turning away, moved along the tunnel for a maximum of half a meter (chickens and rabbits behaving equally). Not so the crows and magpies—or the cats and dogs. When the tunnel sections were joined, they zigzagged along almost its entire length but did not get to the exit. With a mid-tunnel opening, however, they zigzagged a little around it and then rushed to the exit to wait for the feeding box. Possible effects of the noise of the movement of the box were ruled out by control groups and trials. (I believe Krushinsky told me also that most of the birds were hatched in the laboratory and their prior behavior controlled.) Figure 53 presents the results of a pigeon, a chicken, a crow, and a magpie.

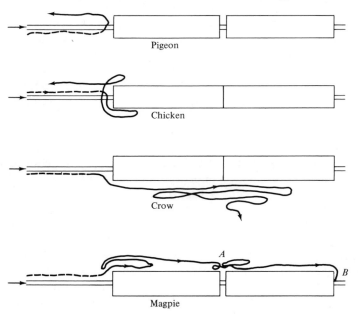

Figure 53 *Krushinsky's extrapolative experiments with stupid and wise birds: pigeons and chickens vs. crows and magpies.* A feeding box, moving for 1.5 meters at a speed of 8 to 10 centimeters per second (left portion), disappeared in a tunnel 3 meters long (right portion), and then reappeared (far right). The birds fed themselves from the top of the moving box. The tunnel consisted of two equal parts either joined or separated by an opening of 3 to 5 centimeters. Note that the pigeon turned around immediately after the box disappeared. The chicken walked along the tunnel for approximately 0.5 meters, then turned away. The crow progressed all along the tunnel (no opening in it), zigzagging but not getting to the final exit to get the food. The magpie moved along the tunnel, noticed the mid-tunnel opening of the box, zigzagged around it (trial and error), and then rushed to the final exit in wait of food. (From Krushinsky, 1960)

The "extrapolative" experiments are surely of systematic significance in disclosing through a uniform technique a wide *qualitative* difference in capacity among subprimate orders of mammals and birds, which sensory preconditioning and configuring differentiate only *quantitatively*. And it is worth noting that Kukuyev (1953) and Shkol'nik-Yarros (1959) found the cortex of dogs to be much more evolved in mass and cytoarchitecture than that of rodents; so did Svetukhina (1961), comparing the *striatum* of *corvidae* with that of pigeons, chickens, and ducks (Birds' cortices are poorly developed, and interorder differences are both small and scarcely reflected in behavior.) Yet Krushinsky's view that he demonstrated in *corvidae*, dogs, and cats unlearned "rudiments of reason" may well be contested. After all, these subjects reacted to the feeding box both when it entered and when it reappeared between tunnel segments, from which its further direction could have been educed through learning. The effects of one-trial learning must not be misprized. They are at times full-blown in simplest conditioning, and there is no reason to think that this is not true—indeed it is truer—when learning is of a higher level. To be sure, the divide between learning and innate perception (or "reasoning" in Krushinsky's words) becomes thereby quite thin; yet learning has the advantage not only of parsimony but of providing a common behaviorally testable frame of reference. In Soviet terms, "extrapolative reflexes" may well be classed as "conditioned extrapolative reflexes."

It would take us far afield to relate the work and views of Krushinsky (an English translation of his 1960 book is available) to those of Köhler, Pavlov Harlow, and Ladygina-Kohts (1923, 1929, 1935, 1958, 1959). Ladygina-Kots' 232-page *Psychic Development in the Evolution of Organisms* (1958) and most particularly her 398-page *Constructive and Tool-Using Activities in Higher Primates (Chimpanzees)* (1959), regrettably, remain untranslated. (Her 1935 volume has a long English summary of her data.) Originally, I had planned a chapter on tool-using and reaction-chaining (Russian: effector chains). However, the consideration that the essence of this phase of learning is more pragmatic than systematic —Mandler's (1962) "analogic structures" to the contrary notwithstanding —made its omission, for lack of space and time, expedient. Nor do I intend here to discuss to any extent Maier's "reasoning in rats and human beings" (1929, 1930, 1931, 1932a, 1932b, 1933, 1936, 1937). His evidence of "the production of new combinations of old experiences" and view of "a process of integration of a higher order" (Maier, 1937, pp. 370, 383) can be accommodated within my "higher levels of productive-integrative learning."

What nonplusses me, however, is Maier's finding that in "reasoning" tests, "nursery children . . . below five years of age . . . were surpassed by adult rats" (1937, p. 367). As documented earlier and in the next chapter ("Thinking"), Soviet data demonstrate unmistakably that even 18- to 20-month-old infants are much superior in integrative capacity to anything that any *Rattus norvegicus* could dream of. And Soviet students of evolutionary cytoarchitectonics would no doubt be dumbfounded by the reported signal smartness of our favorite laboratory minion. Kukuyev (1953), after extensive probing of the brains of twenty-one species in six orders of mammals, concludes that the rodent cortex is more primitive than that of primitive kangaroos and anteaters and substantially inferior to that of ungulates, not to mention that of carnivores. But let me expiate my seeming unpatriotism. Hungry rats are extremely "mobile" ("highly motivated" in some vocabularies), and this may mask the veritable quality of their exploits vis-à-vis those of not-so-mobile, and generally fed, nursery children—mobility, an esteemed road to payoffs in the American ethos.

Finding a suitable term for this learning—embracing the special empirics and systematics of Köhler, Ladygina-Kots, Harlow, Krushinsky, and Maier—should also be considered. *Perception through learning* or *through conditioning* has the disadvantage of not excluding the emergence of pure awareness nor the simple relations of conditioning through perception (second kind), while *inferential learning* is a too-obvious amalgam and, more importantly, a somewhat misleading denotation of Krushinky's data. *Eductive learning* is suggested.

The last kind of perceptual learning, *configuring proper,* goes to the very heart of the novelty of perception, as "a unitary reaction to a multiplicity of stimuli"—an integration of the discrete and a production of wholeness which have long been central to the thoughts of leading philosophers, not just of psychologists in the area. More concretely, this kind of learning is that of organisms' perception of objects and complex events involving not only new relations but new relata, commonly unquestioned but systematically and genetically most intricate and challenging. There is nowadays not much divergence from the view that most perception, by far, is formed through learning. Yet, the mechanisms of this learning have, unfortunately, hardly been studied by objective lowest-common-denominator methods outside the Soviet Union. Hebb's concept of the "superordination" of the "phase sequence" in the formation of perception is, for instance, clearly related to hundreds of Soviet experiments on configuring. But there is no inkling that he is familiar with any of them.

CONFIGURING AND PERCEPTION: BASIC RELATION AND POSITED NEUROPHYSIOLOGY

Relation

Configuring bears not only on the vertical, learning dimension of perception. It also is the most plausible specific basis for inferring perception in animals. Consider the following propositions. (1) Configuring becomes manifest in phylogeny just when the higher regions of the brain are beginning to develop, rises rapidly in efficacy with continuing phylogeny, and, unlike simple conditioning, is impossible to form upon ablation of higher cortical areas. (2) The functional essence of configuring, like that of perception, is the ingathering and integration of discrete incoming information into unified and organized wholes, the information being most likely radically transformed through the interaction of orienting reactions in both cases (see below). (3) The scope of information in configuring, like that in the neurocognitive perceptual image, is selective, compressed, and global, lacking behavioral and experiential reactivity to components. (4) The globalness of the information in configures and perceptual images bears a high degree of adaptive economy in relation to the environment. Higher organisms which reacted behaviorally or experientially to every detail would not function efficiently. The usual statement that experiential data are but "raw and private and may even be misleading" is valid *with respect to the scientific objective of unraveling all of mind's information but not with respect to the pragmatic task of relevance to its "private" commerce with the world that surrounds it.*

Withal, the most salient feature of configuring is its close similarity to the learned formation of perception—a most objective slow-motion means of studying the essentially subjective manifestations of the latter. The parallel of "preconfiguring" to "leveling-and-sharpening" and of configuring to Hebb's "superordination" has already been noted. The *Actualgenese* and microgenetic approach to perception of Undeutsch (1942) is related, and, as will become evident, so are a number of other tenets in the two areas, including the Werner and Wapner (1952 and elsewhere) sensory-tonic view. However, presumably because Soviet investigators of configuring have been physiologists and not psychologists, there has been no attempt to gear it toward perceptual parameters and essence. Even an in-passing mention of the relation of configuring to perception is extremely rare and then is made only by psychologists (e.g., Kovalev, Stepanov, and Shabalin, 1966, p. 132; Smirnov et al., 1956, pp. 146-148). Pavlov's term "synthesis" of higher nervous activity is used without ever referring to, say, Wundt's (1896) "creative synthesis" or Ehrenfels' (1890) *"Gestaltqualität,"* to which it is close. And his "associations form *Gestalten"* has never been extended to "association-formed *Gestaltung* or configuring is the learning core of perception." Still, while detailed parametric collations of these objective and subjective parallels of mind's action must await future research, the general formula of their relationship can hardly be contested. *Configuring is to perception as conditioning is to association, and (1) configures, (2) percepts, (3) Gestalten, and (4) perceptual images are basically equal.*

Posited Neurophysiology

It seems in order to consider now a possible common neurophysiological basis for the three faces of mind's higher category of configuring-perceiving. The offered basis differs from those postulated by Beritoff, Hebb, and Konorski for perception in being predicated not on *assembled activation of neurons of a special kind*—different in each postulation—but on a *special kind of assembled activation,* the specific participating neurons of which cannot as yet be discussed with comfort. The activation rests, it is assumed, on (*a*) the presence of sensory-orienting reactions, (*b*) their *integration,* and (*c*) their *proprioception.* *"Sensory"* emphasizes that "subsensory" or below-awareness orienting reactions are inadequate; *"integration"*—that there must be an interacting assemblage of adequate reactions; and *"proprioception"*—that it is the proprioceptive consequences of the sensory-orienting reactions which are integrated and not the reactions themselves. *Proprioception* is the key determinant; to wit, more generally and basically the thesis is: *At its higher level, mind is a recode of the direct code of information that it receives—a recode in terms of organisms' proprioception.*

It needs to be noted that *"proprioception" is used here in a wider scope than usual—to include "interoception," or all "effector reaction" feedback.* While Sherrington (1906) was most perspicacious in separating exteroceptors from interoceptors and proprioceptors, the last two are insufficiently antithetic to constitute a dichotomy. Thus, independently, Bykov in 1941 and Fulton in 1943 suggested subsuming proprioception under interoception. Yet clearly proprioception is etymologically the express term for feedback, and, as revealed in modern, particularly Soviet, research, it operates fully in scores of effectors that are not skeletal muscles, its traditional locale. Chernigovsky's 1953 statement, "we are confident that there is not an organ or tissue in the body that has no receptors of its own" (p. 359), rested on well validated evidence that in the main has since gained further support. And, of course, *sensory-orienting reactions are as often nonskeletal as skeletal, if not more so.*

On the other hand, a distinction should be drawn between "effector" and "central-neural" feedback, and consideration should be given to the probably higher-level status of the former. The distinction is implied in Anokhin's concepts of "acceptor action" predicating antecedent effector reactions and "return afferentation" of feasible pre-effector manifestation, and follows from his finding that deafferentation impeded "reintegrative" compensations of impaired functions (1935b; 1966, p. 73), whereas its effects in "connective" reinforcement conditioning are not too significant (Gorská and Jankovká, 1961; Gorská, Jankovká, and Kozak, 1961; Knapp, Taub, and Berman, 1958). Specific knowledge of levels of feedback is lacking, however, as is any knowledge of its evolution, including the challenge of its relation to the origin of innate orienting and preparatory abient and adient reactions. Such "antedating" prevital reactions—whether they be a rabbit's pricking up its ears at the rustling of leaves, a stickleback attacking another whose belly is red, a nestling thrush gaping at the sight of a parent's head, or a tiger cub salivating at the odor of meat—are absent in lower animals and strongly suggest a feedback genesis. And since, to boot, simple *feedback conditioning* is the plainest putative mechanism of the genesis, there arises inevitably the pertinacious evolutionary puzzle: How do ontogenetically acquired CSs parallel phyletically bequeathed USs?

Traditional Precursors

Brentano's "act psychology" (1874; see Carmichael, 1926), Dunlap's "motor theory of consciousness" (1912, 1914; see Max, 1934, 1935, 1937), Washburn's "movements and mental imagery" (1916), and others are, each in its own way, representative of the proclivity of Western subjective psychology toward a view that "the mental follows the motor." Act psychology was both popular and authoritative in Europe (Austrian school), as was the later American "motor theory of consciousness," aiding indirectly classical behaviorism and directly reflected in some neobehaviorism: e.g., Guthrie's tenet that "movement-produced stimuli" are a *sine qua non* to learning; it is contended here that they are not a *sine qua non* to learning but are to perceiving. In pre-Soviet Russia, as early as 1888, N. Lange (Professor of Psychology in the University of Odessa) put forward a "motor theory of attention and mind in general" (p. 413) which William James characterized as "ably advocated" (1890, Vol. 1, p. 444) but which he criticized: "But it is one thing," wrote James, "to point out the presence of muscular contraction as constant concomitants of our thoughts, and another thing to say, with Herr Lange [his early publications were in German] that thought is *made possible* by muscular contractions alone. . . . In the chapter on the Will we shall learn that movements themselves are results of images" (p. 445; italics in original). Yet, as noted, the approach of Lange and not that of James came to dominate twentieth-century American psychology. Not, of course, because Lange's numerous publications, including his 1914 textbook, were known. Like the psychological treatises of Sechenov, they were all in Russian and were never mentioned in another language; the writings of both illustrate a historical thesis that the radical ideology of a segment of Russia's nineteenth-century intelligentsia conduced to their radical psychology.

It would take me far afield to bring in the related views of modern American philosophers, such as Perry (1926; James' biographer) and Sellars (1932). It should be mentioned, however, that the present-day Soviet definition of the psyche or mind as "a function of brain action reflecting external objective reality" is directed against philosophies that either gainsay reality (idealism) or divorce it from psychic action (dualism) but not against a proprioceptive or kinesthetic recoding of it. Both Sechenov and Pavlov accorded a leading role to kinesthesis, the former pioneering for its recognition and the latter avowing that the motor area of the brain is its primary afferent analyzer. And proprioceptive recoding is not at variance with Soviet textbooks' "psychic reflection is both formed and verified through practice" or with Rubinshteyn's "the psyche is both a conditioned and a conditioning event" (1959, p. 19). Moreover, when proprioception includes autonomic reactions, it, obviously, does not preclude consciousness in curarized subjects.

BARE (LIMINAL) CONSCIOUSNESS AND THE ORIENTING REFLEX

Earlier motor theorists of mind knew nothing of proprioception and later ones nothing of the orienting reflex. Pavlov himself, who first identified the reflex [reaction], had not realized its reach in collating micromotor behavior and experience, as disclosed, for instance, in the data of the experiments in Gershuni's laboratory (Gershuni, 1945, 1946, 1949a, 1949b, 1955, 1957, 1966; Gershuni et al., 1945, 1964) and in Pshonik's (Pshonik, 1946, 1948a, 1948b, 1949a, 1952; Bykov and Pshonik, 1949). The Gershuni laboratory brought out three systematic findings: (*a*) the human orienting-reflex threshold of pupillary dilation, GSR, and alpha blocking to auditory stimuli normally almost always parallels the verbally reported threshold of their awareness, and may, therefore, be viewed as a more objective as well as a more consistent index of experience than verbalization; (*b*) yet when subjects' hearing is functionally impaired, the orienting reflexes continue to be evoked and, interestingly, are of larger magnitude (Figure 54); (*c*) thresholds of awareness are, however, changed but little when concomitant orienting reflexes are habituated. The first of the three findings was corroborated on a smaller scale with visual stimuli by Samsonova, while the second points to an intriguing interaction between orienting and experiencing, as if the former compensates for the absence of the latter or the latter detracts from the former. The third finding is self-explanatory.

Pshonik probed a different yet related dimension of the orienting-awareness dyad: the effects of awareness on the quality of the orienting reaction and of conditioning on the subject's becoming aware. When mustard of mild concentration was applied to the backs of subjects' right wrists, they showed: no evidence of algesis or change in vasomotion during a latent period of a few minutes; clear-cut *vasodilation* of the stimulated wrist, but no awareness, for another several minutes; and finally, verbal reports of mild burning sensations and *vasoconstriction* of *both hands* (top panel of Figure 55). Then, when a supraliminal blue light was repeatedly flashed when the mustard evoked vasodilation without awareness, its CR was at first also vasodilative, and unaware (middle panel), but in the course of two months became *spontaneously algesic and vasoconstrictive* (bottom panel). The first finding discloses an unaware orienting reaction in an exteroceptive modality and in normal subjects but, more significantly, a reversal of its microbehavior from vasodilation to vasoconstriction, when through longer stimulus duration (equivalent to higher intensity) the orienting reaction becomes aware. The second shows that when the unaware

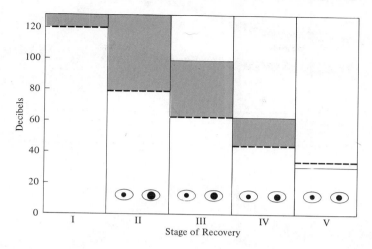

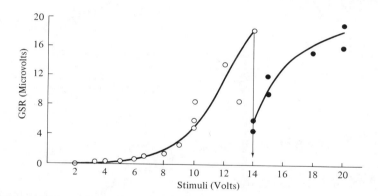

Figure 54 *Sample studies of the interrelation of consciousness and orienting reactions in Gershuni's laboratory.* Top panel—pupil dilations to auditory stimuli in a subject whose hearing was temporarily impaired by a brain contusion. The dashed horizontal lines indicate the limens of dilation; the solid lines above, those of consciousness. Note that (*a*) the dilation limens were below the consciousness limens during the impairment but the two became identical upon recovery, and that (*b*) the dilations to unconscious stimuli (right-hand eye drawings in each column; left-hand eye drawings—no stimulation were larger than those to conscious ones (eyes, last column)—also consistently shorter in latency. Bottom panel—GSRs of a brain-damaged subject whose cutaneous sensitivity to electrical stimulation was permanently impaired. The open circles represent GSR magnitudes to stimuli below liminal consciousness; the solid circles, to those above it. Note that here, too, the magnitudes of the GSRs declined as the subject became conscious of the stimulation. (From Gershuni, 1947; Gershuni et al., 1945)

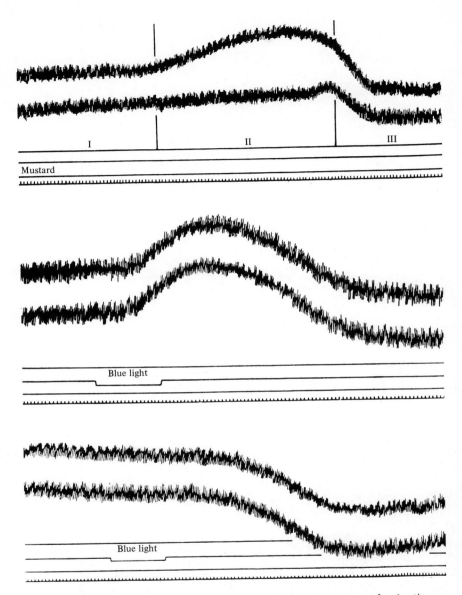

Figure 55 *Sample study of the interrelation of consciousness and orienting reactions in Pshonik's laboratory.* Top panel—three stages of a subject's reactions to an application of a mild mustard stimulus: first—several minutes of no vasomotor reaction and no consciousness; second—another several minutes of vasodilation but still no consciousness of stimulation; third—consciousness of mild burning and transformation of vasodilation into vasoconstriction. Middle panel —an unconscious vasodilative CR to a supraliminal blue light paired repeatedly with the second unconscious vasodilative stage of the US. Bottom panel—the unconscious vasodilative CR to the light becomes in time, spontaneously, conscious and vasoconstrictive. (From Pshonik, 1946, 1948a, 1948b. 1952; Bykov and Pshonik, 1949)

reaction is conditioned, the unaware CR in time becomes spontaneously aware (conditioned to an algesic US?) Pshonik's way of attaining "awareness through conditioning" is novel. Other experimenters have done it through specific combining of unaware CSs with aware USs (Ádám, 1967; Alekseyenko and Blinkov, 1955; Hilgard and Marquis, 1940; Poznanskaya, 1938; Sears and Cohen, 1939; and others).

Ádám's results with interoceptive CSs and verbal instructions as USs merit special mention. Eight subjects, who swallowed double-walled duodenal or intestinal tubes with inflatable balloons, came to lower very substantially the thresholds of their awareness of the inflations in 10 to 30 trials in which the experimenter informed them each time of the nature and occurrence of the stimulations. The data of two subjects are given in detail. One whose duodenal pressure threshold for alpha blocking was 40 millimeters Hg and for awareness of the pressure 80 millimeters, lowered the awareness to 50 millimeters in 22 informed trials (no further lowering in 32 additional attempts, however). Another subject lowered in 23 trials his threshold of awareness of intestinal pressure from *70 to 30 millimeters Hg, the equal of his alpha blocking threshold.* (See above [p. 227] for evidence of the eight subjects' unaware interoceptive discrimination.) Compare the views of Kovalgin (1959), Leont'yev (1959), Luria (1963), and Orlov (1966).

PERCEPTION AND SENSATION — RESYSTEMIZING AN OLD PROBLEM

Basic Argument

The evidence on liminal awareness raises the problem of whether it is perceptual or, more generally, the old problem of whether consciousness is two-phased, (*a*) perceptual and (*b*) sensory or nonperceptual, or better, preperceptual. Traditional structural psychology has, as is known, considered sensation the essence and perception merely a complex cumulation of it, whereas Gestalt psychology recognizes only perception and has ruled sensations out of existence. My present position accords full status to both, but grants hierarchical regnancy to perception. It agrees with Gibson that "Thomas Reid's assertion in 1785 is just as true as it ever was, that 'the external senses have a double province; to make us feel and to make us perceive [to] furnish us with a variety of sensations [and to] give us a conception of external objects' " (1966, p. 319). Yet it disputes Gibson's: "Sensations are not . . . the basis of perception," as it does William James's: "Perception always involves sensation as a portion of itself" (1890, Vol. 2, p. 1). The thesis here is that perception is *functionally but not genetically autonomous of sensation*—evolving from it phyletically and ontogenetically. And while in accord with Gestalt psychology on the paramount role of organization in perception, the position is that the very "laws" of organization evolve and, at least in human subjects, are much affected by sets or attitude—and are not just compelling functions of contemporaneous stimulations.

More basically, it is assumed here that the entire reach of *consciousness* —or awareness or cognitivity, the three used synonymously—*inheres in the proprioceptive sequelae, or kinestheses, of sensory-orienting reactions: liminal consciousness, or sensation, in those of unintegrated or even individual reactions, and organized consciousness, or perception, in the integrate transforms of the reactions.* There surely is a wide ontologic and genetic chasm between the liminal consciousness of 15 decibels of sound or 15 quanta of light and the apprehension of a triangle—visually or tactually— or of a melody. And the chasm is by no means just of vast differences in amount of activated energy. The qualitative perception-sensation gap is just as impressive if not more so. Consider that the liminal consciousness of a sensation is anchored to a particular modality or quality, whereas perception is largely inter- or rather super-modality and quality, in line with the Gestalt thesis of its transposability and a mass of recent Soviet evidence on vicarious interanalyzer action (Ayrapet'yants and Batuyev, 1969). And consider also—perhaps more importantly—the fact that while a limen of a sensation may be lowered somewhat by associative or conditioned pairings, even by mere practice (Milleryan and Tkachenko, 1961), its modality or quality is unchanged. You do not learn new sensory qualities nor alter them substantially any more than you do innate reflexes—an intriguing recapitulation or parallel of evolutionary manifestations separated presumably by many eons. Yet learning renders the manifolds of perception almost kaleidoscopic: parts variously integrated, patterns variously differentiated, and both parts and patterns variously modified by punishment and classical and reinforcement conditioning, let alone practice as such.

Moreover, the kinesthesis of largely innate sensation is admittedly sustained by *existing* natal, and maturing early postnatal, brain loci and patterns. But learned perception presumably develops *new* loci and patterns, which, although by all tokens much more complex, are readily understandable in the light of increasing evidence of learned brain burgeoning. And, then, there is the plausible assumption that in sensation, proprioception is but a *feedback* interaction with primary stimulus information, whereas in perception it is a recoded *feed-elsewhere* integrator—in a true sense, a second signal system, Pavlov's second being a third.[28]

───────

[28] Following Krasnogorsky's evidence in 1911 that classical conditioning of dogs' passive flexion of the talocrural or metatarsal joint of their paws is abolished upon ablation of their sigmoid and not ectosylvian and coronary gyri, Pavlov concluded

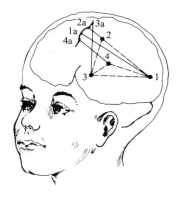

Figure 56 *Kol'tsova's diagram of cortical-analyzer integration of the formation of an image of an object [configure].* Dots 1 to 5—loci in sensory projection areas; bars 1a to 4a—loci in motor analyzer. Solid lines—connections between sensory and motor cortical analyzers. Dashed lines—potential sensory inter-analyzer connections between components of images (or configures). (From Kol'tsova, 1967)

However, all this hardly negates the logic and some empirical evidence that perception is a phyletic and ontogenetic evolvement of sensation. Space prevents discussing Gibson's severing the two, except to say that while I concur with his: "Proprioception or self-sensitivity is . . . an overall function, common to all systems, not a special sense [and] orienting . . . extracts the external [and internal—G.R.] information from the stimulus flux while registering the change as subjective feeling" (1966, p. 320—I would not quibble about replacing "self-sensitivity," which is a bit too mentalistic for me, with "reaction sensitivity"), our systems are substantially dissimilar. Compare, for instance, the differing italicized words with respect to a specific clinical implication: "Just as there are patients who sense but do not perceive, there should be *as many* [in his system] and *some* [in mine] who perceive without sensing."

Figure 56 represents Kol'tsova's motor-analyzer view of proprioception, which has since been developed by Ayrapet'yants and Batuyev (1969). Two germane Soviet experiments—one relating to proprioceptive inter-

---

that motor areas are primarily afferent proprioceptive analyzers, a view expressed in part by Luciani and Sippelli as early as 1885 and in related fashion by Penfield and Jasper in 1954. The conclusion has been bolstered by demonstrations of Soviet evolutionary neurologists that in mammals the motor cortex evolves very substantially (1) from order to order, (2) within ungulates from horses to swine (Kukuyev, 1953), and (3) within carnivores in the sequence of families *Felidae, Canidae, Mustelidae,* and *Ursidae* (Svetukhina, 1959), and (4) within the suborder *Anthropoidae* in the sequence of *Callitrichidae, Cebidae, Cercopitheadae, Hylobatidae, Pongidae,* and of course *Hominidae* (Kukuyev, 1953). In birds, the neurologists continue, there is a similar evolution of the *striatum* from pigeons to *Corvidae* (Svetukhina, 1961); and in human ontogeny, a rapid prenatal and early postnatal development of both cortical and subcortical motor regions, not yet fully matured at the age of 7 years (Kukuyev, 1961). Hrbek (1960) argues, however, that the "powerful" proprioceptive analyzer is cortically projected in the parietal lobe—Broadman areas 5, 7, 39, and 40—while Batuyev (1966b; Ayrapet'yants and Batuyev, 1969) maintains that the integration of the parietal analyzer precedes the final integration of the motor one. The problem, while in itself highly interesting, is too complex and also too marginal for the chief intent of the present book, to be considered further here.

nalization in dogs, the other to the evolution of perception from sensation in human subjects—will be cited.

Two Experiments

a. Petrov (1941) trained a dog with a "dynamic stereotype" of seven different CSs: metronome of 150 beats per minute, noise, crackling sound, metronome of 75 beats (differential), a light, a bell, and bubbling of water. Each CS was applied for 15 seconds prior to feeding with intervals of 5 minutes between CSs. After 17 months of training, the mean magnitudes of the CRs to the respective CSs, for the last 9 sessions (presented in the

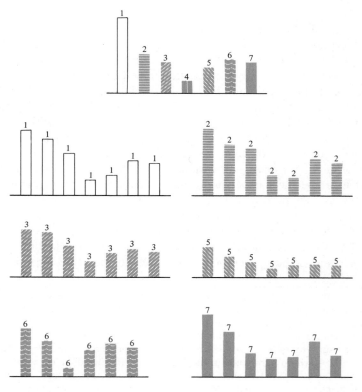

Figure 57 *Dynamic stereotypes in the salivary conditioning of a dog to one negative and six positive CSs.* Column heights denote CR magnitudes. Top panel—results of 17 months of a trained sequential pattern to different CSs. Other panels show the pattern of magnitudes when only one CS was used throughout. 1—a metronome of 150 beats per minute [Razran's (1965d) statement that it was 60 beats is incorrect]; 2—a noise; 3—a crackling sound; 4—differentiated metronome of 75 beats; 5—light; 6—electric bell; 7—bubbling water. (From Petrov, 1941)

top panel of Figure 57), were 70, 42, 37, 16, 23, 34, and 32 scale divisions in 15-second pre-US trials. Next, the objective of the experiment was put to test. Six sessions followed in which 6 of the 7 CSs, excluding the differential metronome, were applied singly with the same interstimulus interval. The results are given in the six lower panels of Figure 57; as may be seen, not only the general pattern of the "stereotype" but also the specific CR magnitude of each *unapplied* CS was basically preserved in all six sessions. Evidently, a number of *specific* proprioceptive stimuli take over the roles of specific exteroceptive CSs that are not there, a phenomenon corresponding to "internalization" in experiential psychology—here, more exactly, "differential internalization." Attention should be turned, however, to the fact that this feat is attained only after prolonged training. In earlier stages, even once omitting one CS or replacing it with another stimulus or interchanging the positions of the CSs disrupts the conditioning, while prolonged or summed omissions and substitutions often produce general behavioral disturbances—an "experimental neurosis." Indeed, this is currently a common means of producing it.

"Dynamic stereotypes" are of course a special kind of configuring. Their developmental stages and even basic attributes differ, however, from those of the conventional kind. Preconfiguring in the sense of strengthening strong CS reactions through weakening weak ones is poorly developed, presumably because the CSs are individually reinforced and separated from one another by long intervals. On the other hand, proprioception is much more overtly manifest in the dynamics of stereotypes, and US-unpaired sequences and components disrupt their integration more frequently than they succumb to it, so to speak, and become inactive, as in simple configuring. Then, there is the aspect of information: configuring continues to lose it, and "dynamic stereotypy" eventually recoups what is lost and even augments its operational scope. All of this suggests a plausible theoretic that "dynamic stereotypes" parallel not only perceiving but also chaining—although, obviously, not that of *different CRs,* since only one is involved.

Pavlov considered the formation of "dynamic stereotypes" the top achievement of the dog's brain and, except for the second-signal system, no doubt of the brain in general. He did not, however, offer a *sui generis* detailed analysis of it and neither have the post-Pavlovians. No attempt will be made here to seek out specific parameters of its possible distinctness —only to stress that Petrov's wholly objective data, of which there are a number of current replications and even some antecedents, not only bring home the potency of internalization in rendering higher animals relatively autonomous of their surrounding but also *intimate the evolutionary mechanism transforming neurobehavior into neurocognition.*

b. Bzhalava (1958, 1965) paired a 300-cycle tone with the sight of an illuminated red circle or triangle in a number of dark-adapted subjects,[29] trained in image and afterimage observations, 300 times, 10 a day. The tone was sounded for 30 seconds, after which the figure was illuminated for 2 seconds and the sound continued until the subject reported, by pressing a key, that he no longer experienced any afterimage; the mean duration of this in initial trials, was 20.16 seconds. Evidence of fully formed direct conditioning—the sound clearly evoking the light percept —was reported by all subjects; and there were also indirect indications of it in that the duration of the visual afterimage doubled after 18 trials and increased ninefold in the 300 trials. Bzhalava's data are particularly pertinent in that his subjects apprised him of five evolving levels of conditioning, the tone evoking consecutively: (*a*) fleeting amorphous light sensations "resembling moving clouds," which the experimenter labels "retinal," (*b*) relatively stable sensations of an "amorphously illuminated gray field," (*c*) "square outlines of the field" (perception), (*d*) "varying outlines of a number of geometrical figures," and (*e*) clear perception of "the illuminated circle or triangle"—the US.

Bzhalava's successful experiment of sensory-perceptual conditioning raises the question of why repeated sensory-sensory pairings have not been fortunate in yielding a CS-UR type of CR (Ellson, 1941; and others). An answer will be attempted in a later section.

EIGHT SENSATION-PERCEPTION POSTULATES, AND A SEVEN-RUNG EVOLUTIONARY LADDER OF REACTIONS

1. Unconscious (subsensory) orienting reactions lack *adequate* proprioception, which they gain when they are paired with reactions of adequate proprioception—that is, they become conscious reactions through a conditioned supplementation of their proprioception. Gain of proprioception is equally the basis of rendering conscious orienting reactions through increasing the intensities of their stimuli. Orienting reactions altogether wanting in proprioception, such as the pupillary reflex, can never become conscious, even as the conscious status of vital and adient and abient reactions (Chapter 3) is aided by the extra proprioception of their specific actions.

2. Conscious reactions must be consciously related to form any kind of cognitive learning. Unrelated consciousness is of no direct significance to it. Or, put differently, learning is affected *by perceptions and not bare*

---

[29] Number of subjects, unfortunately, not known to me. I copied it four years ago but cannot identify it now and the publication is not available in the United States. Bzhalava's 1965 book describing the study does not give the number, either. Bzhalava is a noted Georgian psychologist, familiar with both Pavlovian and experiential set-psychology techniques, and is the author of two noted books: *Set and Perception* (1965) and *The Psychology of Set and Cybernetics* (1966).

sensations, which, to extend the thesis, may well mean that bare sensations are in general events of genetic and not immediate pragmatic efficacy.

3. Reactions gain affective consciousness when in addition to adequate proprioception they are in some way *adequately* connected to the "affective" brain or limbic system. Affection is thus assumed to be a later evolutionary acquisition than irreducible sensation, a *special* consciousness significant as a phenomenal correlate of higher stages of reinforcement conditioning. *"Affectional learning" and even "affectional mind" are thus warranted concepts.*

4. The doctrine of *adequacy* in Postulates 1 and 2 is not beyond the reach of direct experimental verification—i.e., it is not just an "intervening" theoretical construct.

5. While the full-scale equivalence of behavioral configuring and experiential perceiving makes it logical to infer that only higher vertebrates, who configure, perceive, evolutionary considerations suggest that sensations may well be present in earlier phylogeny. There is, however, no specific basis for inferring sensations, since while initial tests with normal human subjects disclose that consciousness is almost invariably accompanied by some orienting reaction, the reactions may be evident without consciousness in non-intense interoceptive stimulations and in traumatized subjects.

6. Like sensation, affection is assumed to antecede perception in evolution.

7. The possibility that in some instances, particularly in human ontogeny, perception may precede discernment of sensory-affectional qualities by no means negates the basic evolutionary sensation-to-perception relation, any more than—to put it grossly—the precedence of a neocortical to an archipaleocortical reaction means that the latter evolved from the former.

8. Inference of experience in animals based on functional equivalence in human subjects must be qualified by a principle which, for lack of a better name, will be termed "encognization," comparable to "encephalization": namely, that the general evolutionary tendency to telescope functions to more recent brain formation may also hold for cognition. A specific reaction, conscious at the human level, may still be unconscious in higher animals, with a similar relation of higher to lower animals. Encephalization is, however, a relative and correcting rather than an absolute and superseding phenomenon, which should be true also for "encognization."

Figure 58 is a diagram of an evolutionary ladder of seven varieties of reactions: consummatory adient-abient, preparatory adient-abient, subsensory orienting, conditioned subsensory orienting, sensory orienting, integrates of sensory orienting or percepts, and replicates of percepts or symbols. The assumed nature of the first six should be familiar by now, while the seventh will be discussed in the following chapter.

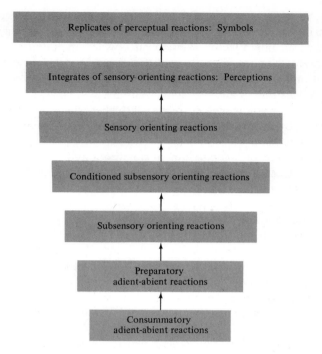

Figure 58 *Evolutionary ladder of reactions.*

REANALYSIS OF SENSORY PRECONDITIONING AND ANALYSIS OF EDUCTIVE LEARNING

Sensory Preconditioning

Cumulated evidence and logic impel a basic deepening and widening of the interpretation of sensory preconditioning given at the beginning of the chapter. First, it was demonstrated that while orienting reactions may function without consciousness—either because they have never been within it, as in most interoception, or because they have been deprived of it through organic or functional traumas—even liminal consciousness is almost always attended by *some* orienting reactions.[30] Second, it was realized that analysis of sensory preconditioning must consider not only its orienting-intermediating character but probe all its manifestations and mechanisms and probe them in their own rights. Third, it was reasoned that sensory preconditioning is fully operative also in conventional classical and reinforcement conditioning commanding sensory outlets, and is thereby enlarged immensely in operational scope. Fourth, with a plausible

---

[30] The exception, evident only when orienting reactions are persistently habituated, is of little significance both because such habituation is rare in life situations and because it is so readily reversible by any slight change in the environment.

division of perceptual learning into four kinds, it was thought that sensory preconditioning bears a specific relation to one of the four, namely, the second.

In other words, the reanalysis deployed a double strategy: (*a*) an empirical codification of the facts, varieties, and distinctness of sensory preconditioning, and (*b*) a theoretic "inductive leap" to emplace it within the hierarchical framework of the systematics of learning. The codification revealed that repeated pairing of two sensory reactions engenders, in addition to preconditioning, four other varieties of learned modifications: (*a*) *conditioned orientation*—the stimulus of one orienting reaction acquires some characteristics (overt-skeletal or autonomic) of the other; (*b*) *neural*—one stimulus evokes the neural changes of the other; (*c*) *liminal facilitation*—the conscious limen of one reaction becomes lowered by the stimulus of the other reaction; and (*d*) *conditioned consciousness,* or *sensory* conditioning—a stimulus of one sensory modality or quality is augmented by that of another (human subjects in the last two varieties). *Liminal facilitation* (Bogoslovsky, 1936a, 1936b; Brogden, 1950; Dobryakov, 1948; Kekcheyev, 1948; and others) is surely not distinct. Chapter 4 identified this sensitization of a UR by a CS as "beta conditioning," extant throughout the realm of learning: from increased US salivation to prolonged visual afterimages, and as a general observation first noted, in fact, in Yerkes' attempt to expand the scope of stimuli for hearing in frogs. On the other hand, the wide gap between the ready CR efficacy of *conditioned orientation* in higher animals and infants and the difficulty of obtaining *conditioned consciousness* in adult human subjects (Bogoslovsky, 1936a, 1936b; Ellson, 1941) is puzzling. Yet a combination of Gershuni's data and Ukhtomsky's "dominance" offers a plausible tentative account for the discrepancy. Consciousness, evolving from orienting, is nonetheless a *sui generis* supersedure whose qualitative compartmentalization among sensory continua overshadows the quantitative "dominance" differences within continua requisite for CR efficacy. Accordingly, if one is to condition consciousness, the US must be rendered more complex and not just more intense, that is, it must be rendered perceptual, the secret of Bzhalava's success. Some years ago (Razran, 1957), I found that in human salivary conditioning the parametric strength of CS complexity is very considerable, about 84 per cent of that of UR magnitude. But I have not compared it with CS intensity. Stimulus intensities have not been varied sufficiently in the several studies of "conditioned consciousness" nor have USs been particularly intense.

The core thesis of the reanalysis is, however, the depth judgment that *what is learned in sensory preconditioning is more perceptual than sensory —a perception of simple and obvious temporal sequences and spatial contiguities.* It is learning not only without "insight" but also without its traditional rival, "trial and error" (Pavlov's "transforming chaotic into signalling reactions," Woodworth's "trial-and-checks," Hilgard's "provisional tries," and the like). Its aim is *uncovery* rather than *discovery,* "lessons" rather than "problems"—to use Woodworth and Schlosberg's apt wording. Yet it is indubitably a perceptual learning, although low in the package: specifically, *conditioning through perception,* an analogue of *perception of conditioning.* (As was noted earlier, the lowest conditioning *of* perception, does not involve any perceptual surplus—and is thus *but* conditioning.) Tolman's "sign learning" of "expectancy" or "anticipation" is, needless to say, an equivalent formulation, as is the concept *"Und-Verbindungen"* ("and-connections"), used perjoratively by Gestalt psychology to characterize anteceding non-Gestalt German associative-cognitive psychology.

Gestaltists have certainly rendered a singular service to psychological thought in stressing that mind's qualia are much more than the attributes of *Und-Verbindungen.* But they have been deleterious in derogating and even entirely negating the cognitive integral import of these *Und-verbundene* mechanisms in mind's evolution and action. Learning to perceive that a dark cloud is followed by rain or that food or a predator—or prey—is in a particular location is as nodal a phyletic acquisition as learning that a stick may rake in food (when the organism is equipped to do it); that a disappearing food box may reappear; or that a correct pathway to food may be a combine of the learning of two prior pathways. And, of course, cultural human acquisitions—certainly in early ontogeny—are substantially, if not predominantly, outcomes of kith-and-kin's "lessons" and not just self-initiated discoveries of problems and solutions. Indeed, it may well be argued that no matter what the ultimate nature of *necessary causation* be from Hume to Nagel, the pith of the simple "because" of causal perception of "If A, then B" is rooted in learned *Und-Verbindungen.*

Three further propositions will bear repeating. (1) The pragmatic outcome of sensory preconditioning or *conditioning through perception* differs from that of *simple conditioning* only quantitatively—it is more plastic in acquisition and disruption, so that relating "cloud" and "rain" may be also effected, contrary to Gestalt psychology, in the "antechamber of consciousness," to use Galton's words of almost 100 years ago. (2) Empirical evidence refutes the existence of sensory-sensory learning in lower organisms. (3) Ablation data and general cortical status suggest that this learning could gain effective potency only in the highest mammals, probably only in primates, and prepotency in *Homo sapiens* only.

All of this is at variance with not only the Gestalt system of phenomenal perception but also against Tolman's inferred perception (1936, 1948, and elsewhere). His philosophy that the cognitive map of a rat at a choice point in a maze holds the basic information of all of our wisdom and woes is clearly unevolutionarily egalitarian, as is his failure to discern modificatory "sign" and productive "Gestalt" learning. Add to this Tolman's rat-ministered inference of the unconscious (1955) and the ploy of Freudian terms and concepts—and his graciously-verbalized be-kind-to-all system looms in all its glory. America's most "perceptive" psychologist was also its most global "joiner" theoretician: high in "excitatory" generalizations but hardly in "inhibitory" differentiations.

Eductive Learning

Analysis here is somewhat complicated by the divergences of the Köhler, Maier, and Krushinsky enterprises. Future research will, it is hoped, provide evidence to demarcate adequately the differences, but it will no doubt also demonstrate the basic commonalities of this learning. It plainly is not a family of the lower suborder of modificatory perceptual learning but of the higher productive suborder. An educed relation is a new cognitive configure, not just cognition of an obvious spatial or temporal relation. It is presymbolic cognitive reasoning or problem-solving through learning—not just cognitive learning in general. (Curiously, Russian does not use *learning* as a fundamental concept the way English does, while Semitic languages often use it in the sense of reasoning.)

GESTALT "LAWS" AND THE ROLE OF ATTITUDES

Gestalt Laws

In three separate experiments (Razran, 1939a, 1939c, 1940a) it was demonstrated that the magnitudes of salivary CRs in adult human subjects (total $N = 36$) were substantially greater when the CSs (one-second simultaneous or successive flashes of miniature lights at 0.5 or 1.0 inch from each other) were of different colors. And in one (1939c) it was shown that this was true also when in the simultaneous flashings the different color lights were at distances of 2 inches or were of different intensities (2 and 10 candlepower) although not when the distances were 4 inches or when the combination consisted of the light and the sound of a small bell. Largely similar results were evident when the CSs were twelve different musical intervals (Razran, 1938a). While the lowest conditioning —4.5 ± 1.9 and 7.5 ± 1.3 centigrams of conditioned saliva per minute— was obtained with the minor second and major seventh of vibration ratios 16:15 and 15:8, the CR was also very low—9.5 ± 1.3 for the simplest 2:1 ratio of the octave, and the highest—23.3 ± 2.2 and 19.8 ± 2.1—for the fourth and the minor third of 4:3 and 6:5 ratios. Moreover, the conditioned complex intervals were strikingly more resistant to extinction. After 20 CR training trials, the least amount of extinction (18 and 26 per cent) was recorded for the major second and minor sixth of ratios 9:8 and 8:5, and the most (64 and 50 per cent) for the simplest intervals: the octave and the 3:2 ratio of the fifth. The subjects were invariably misinformed about the purpose of the experiment by being told that it was "an investigation of the effects of eye-fatigue [or of listening to music] on digestion," but they obviously perceived their CSs. That is to say, the conditioning was a means of disclosing the perceptual nature of the CSs, but it was not itself perceptual since the subjects were presumably unaware of the requisite CS-US relation. (The US was eating small pretzels or sucking cryst-o-mints for 2 or 3 minutes.)

The results were at variance with both Pavlovian data on salivary conditioning of dogs, in which close and similar visual stimuli and simple sound ratios are most conditionable, and with human Gestalt "laws." The *"gute Gestalt"* was not always *"gut,"* and it was *"besser"* for dogs than for college students. An experiment was thus devised (Razran, 1939d, $N = 8$) to condition subjects to simultaneous flashes of miniature red and green lights in arrangements identical to the dot patterns used by Schumann (1900), Wertheimer (1923), and Schroff (1928), and to test subpatterns of the flashes at different stages of CR training. (Human salivary conditioning is rather rapid in acquisition, a finding corroborated recently by, among others, Feather, 1967). The trained patterns and tested subpatterns are presented in the upper panel of Figure 59, and the conditioning results in the lower panel and in Figure 60. As may be seen in the figures, all sixteen tests disclose what may be called "steeplechase" effects: the simple *gut-gestaltete* patterns condition best in early training stages while later they subside and the more complex or *schlim-gestaltete* gain ascendancy.

My 1938 and 1939 conclusions read: "There are no definite, specific, *static,* final laws of pattern organization. . . . The only more or less defined principle . . . is the simple-complex trend of individuals to respond, upon repeated exposure, more and more readily to complex stimuli arrangements and to disregard more and more frequently the simple patterns" (1939d, pp. 11-12). "The basic determinants of the direction of CR patternization, of 'good' and 'poor' patterns, are psychological, acquired, and changing rather than physical, preformed and fixed" (1938a, p. 470). And: "A true dynamic psychology seeks and finds its dynamics in functions and their changes, action and its antecedents, learning and its varieties, or in short in ever-evolving man transforming and being transformed by an ever-evolving environment" (1939d, p. 14; cf. similar factor-analysis results and interpretations by Roff, 1952, and Thurstone, 1944).

The Role of Attitudes

In a preliminary study (Razran, 1936), I found that the magnitudes of the salivary CRs of four college students to flashes of miniature green and red lights, which served as right and wrong reactions in the subjects' solving a bolthead maze (top panel of Figure 61), while eating, were different for each light at different stages of CR training. At the beginning, the conditioning to the correct green lights was higher, but later the conditioning to the wrong red lights gained the upper hand (upper graph in Figure 61); the verbal reports stated that "the positive feeling tone towards the green lights continually declined and tended to the neuter, as the negative tone to the red flashes assumed a positive quality and changed from an 'annoyer' to a guide for 'what not to do.'" In my main experiment, directly pertinent to the present discussion (Razran, 1939b), twelve

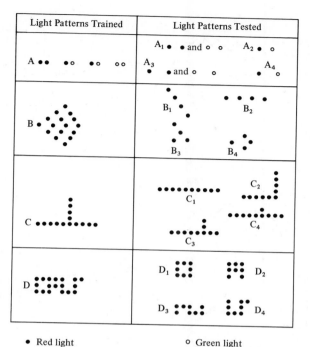

Light Patterns Trained	Light Patterns Tested
A ●● ●○ ●○ ○○	A_1 ● and ○ ○ A_2 ● ○ A_3 ● ●and○ ○ A_4 ● ○
B	B_1 B_2 B_3 B_4
C	C_1 C_2 C_3 C_4
D	D_1 D_2 D_3 D_4

● Red light   ○ Green light

--- Like lights at 0.5 inch   —— Like lights at 2.0 inches
—— Unlike lights at 0.5 inch   – – Unlike lights at 2.0 inches

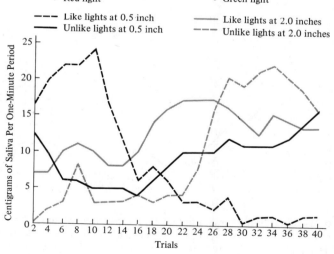

Figure 59 *Similarity and proximity in configuring-perceiving of eight college students divided into groups of two.* Upper panel—subjects watched patterns of simultaneous flashes of miniature red and green lights (similar to the dot arrangement in the perception studies of Schumann, Wertheimer, and Schroff) while they were consuming small pretzels or tea sandwiches or sucked cryst-o-mints; later they were tested for conditioned salivation to portions of the patterns. Lower panel—results of CR tests with portions of the first of the four patterns. Note that while in earlier training trials conditioning was greatest to like lights at the closest distance of 0.5 inches, it latter shifted to unlike lights at the same distance, like lights at 2.0 inches from each other, and unlike lights at 2.0 inches, with like lights at 0.5 inches losing their original effectiveness. (From Razran, 1939c)

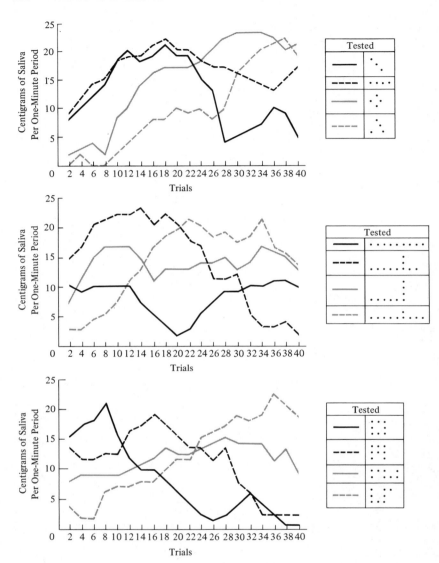

Figure 60 *Gestalt "laws" and configuring-perceiving.* Magnitudes of salivary CRs of college students to varying subpatterns of simultaneous flashes of miniature lights identical with the dot arrangements of the perception studies of Schumann, Wertheimer, and Schroff (upper panel of Figure 59). Note the invariant "steeplechase" effect: subjects conditioned at first to the simple *gut-gestaltete* subpatterns and later to the complex and *schlimm-gestaltete* ones. Patterns of 14, 16, and 18 light flashes were used in the CR training, and subpatterns of 4, 8, and 10 flashes in testing. (From Razran, 1939d)

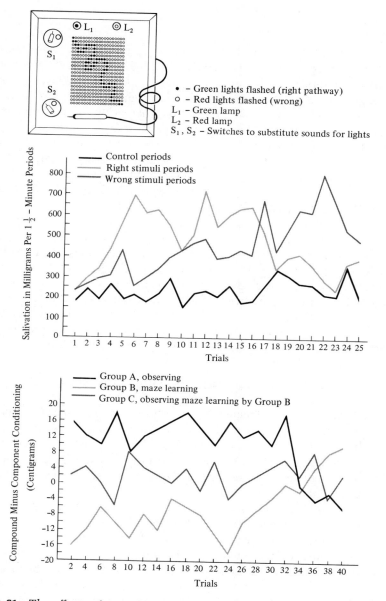

• – Green lights flashed (right pathway)
o – Red lights flashed (wrong)
L₁ – Green lamp
L₂ – Red lamp
S₁, S₂ – Switches to substitute sounds for lights

Figure 61 *The effects of attitudes on conditioning and configuring of 17 college students (5 in the conditioning experiment, 12 in the configuring). Top panel—bolthead maze of a sequence of flashes of green lights, with red flashes as wrong cues, solved by subjects during 2-minute eating periods. Middle panel—correct ["right"] green lights evoked more conditioning in the first part of the experiment, incorrect ["wrong"] red lights, more in the second part. Bottom panel—Group A, observing random successions of like and unlike lights, conditioned more to unlike successions ("compound" in ordinate); Group B, solving the maze while eating, more to like successions ("component" in ordinate); Group C, eating while observing Group B, about equally to either succession. Groups B and C acquired segregating attitudes toward the differing lights which, respectively, reversed or nullified the normal perceptual integration of unlike lights manifested by Group A. (From Razran, 1936, 1939c)*

college students were divided into three equal groups: A, one observing red + red, green + green, and red + green lights in various locations on the board of the maze; B, one attempting to solve the difficult maze by touching the bolts with a stylus (green lights–right, red–wrong; 56 per cent improvement in 40 trials), and C, a group observing the performance of Group B. In the course of five experimental sessions, forty training periods of eating plus solving the maze of red and green lights, or eating plus observing the lights, were made with each subject and followed by testing periods. The results (lower graph) reveal quite clearly that Group A was much more conditioned to the unlike lights, Group B to the like, with Group C zigzagging between them. Only the results of subjects in Groups B and C call for special comment—namely, that for them the two lights acquired, respectively, differential action and thought import, including thereby *varying segregating* attitudes and consequent nullification (Group C) or reversal (Group B) of the integrating mission of normal perception. (Compare the pioneer experiment of Carmichael, Hogan, and Walter [1932] on the determinant role of induced attitudes in the related area of reproducing perceived figures.) Again, I will let stand my 1939 statement: "Attach any interest to a dot or a figure pattern, and what is pleasing or 'good' or efficacious shifts and changes" (1939d, p. 13).

PERCEPTION AND NONASSOCIATIVE PRACTICE

It was documented in Chapter 3 that, by and large, typical human reflexes habituate in the same manner as animal and even spinal-animal counterparts, and that to a considerable, although variable extent so do hedonic tones of musical selections and paintings. The effects of nonassociative repetition upon *perception,* however, was demonstrated to be different in the main phase of the music-and-painting experiment. There, the 378 college students and middle-aged laborers and housewives characterized the 48 experimental items by checking adjectives on a modified Kate Hevner octagon of 80 adjectives (shown in Figure 62), and the change in the correspondence of their characterizations to those of five professional musicians and five professional painters was the measured effect. Correspondence was scored simply as per cent overlap between subjects' and experts' adjectives, and this was considered an *index of aesthetic veridicality*.

The results for two musical items, 45- and 52-second extracts of Shostakovich's "Age of Gold (Russian Dance)" and Copland's "Piano Variation: 18," are presented in Figure 63 (see results of twenty-two others, Razran, 1969). As in the hedonic phase of the experiments, the presentation of each item was repeated 4, 8, and 12 times under three conditions: "2 hours after lunch" (repetition proper), "during lunch" (repetition plus

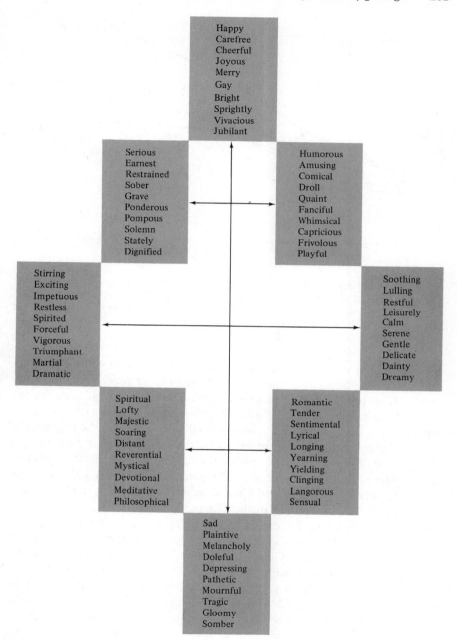

Figure 62 *A modified Kate Hevner octagon of 80 adjectives used by 378 adult subjects to characterize 24 short musical selections. (From Razran, 1968a)*

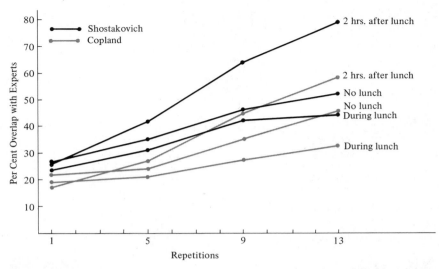

Figure 63 *Changes in mean per cent overlap between adjectival characterizations (Figure 62) of two short musical selections by 378 musically unsophisticated subjects and 5 expert musicians when the selections were presented to 9 equal and matched groups 5, 9, and 13 times during lunch, two hours after lunch, and when lunch was missed. (From Razran, 1969)*

food association), and "no lunch" (repetition plus mild hunger). Equal and matched groups were used for each number of repetitions and each condition of presentations, with all subjects characterizing all items on the first and last presentation. All three groups increased their per cents of overlapping, or aesthetic veridicality, with $p < .02$ to $p < .05$. But the increases in the Repetition Groups were higher than those in the other two groups, with $p < .01$ to $p < .001$, and, unlike the results of the other two groups, were evident also in special results of the remaining 22 musical selections (in 8, the increases in the Food Groups were not significant, and in 9 they were significantly lower than in the Hunger Groups).

With due allowance for the ontologic difference between aesthetic and physical perception, the experiment's results do weight the conclusion toward the Gibson and Gibson view that repeated perception means "greater correspondence with stimulation . . . richer in differential responses . . . responding to variables of physical stimulation not previously responded to" (1955, p. 34). And, we may add, they are in line with Sechenov's 1892 statement: "The more frequent the repetitions of the influences of objects, the clearer and firmer in memory are their more permanent and more striking attributes" (Russian edition, p. 204; English edition, 1952, p. 451). Postman's "association theory," staking "perceptual learning" on the "elaboration of new qualities" (1955, p. 444), was reflected in the study only in that, compared with mere repetition, food association raised the subjects' positive hedonic tone toward the experimental items and increased the repertory of checked adjectives. But these are in essence negative bestowals obfuscating perception's very *metier* and lessening its veridicality. Still, Gibson and Gibson, in rejecting association, and Postman, in embracing it, share a blind spot. Both are thinking in terms of traditional *extrinsic* associative connections and not modern *intrinsic* integrations and differentiations. The bone of contention they picked is cartilage, not hard to chew away.

It is instructive to contrast the beneficence of practice on perception with its bearing on bare liminal consciousness. As noted earlier, conscious limens can be modified—lowered—through conditioning, or even mere practice, which no doubt involves such conditioning. Admittedly, however, the modifications are not basic nor readily realized, so that on the whole, discounting nonlearning oscillations, one's conscious limens are as stable as his vital reflexes, say, reactions to food when hungry or to dire injury. And both are paradigms of innateness and maturation. You learn neither. Yet both surely are the raw material for all learning. But note that vital reflexes set forth the connective and summative phase, limens the integrative and supra-summative phase of it. Lest I be impeached for dualism, let me add one more word. The plain fact is that the two—reflexes and limens—are most distinctive otherwise: in higher animals, one is the relatively narrow efferent neck of mind's funnel, the other, the wide afferent one.

SUMMARY

1. When two sensory stimuli, such as a light and a sound, are paired and repeatedly presented to higher animals, three kinds of learning ensue: (*a*) *neural*—one stimulus comes to evoke neural changes characteristic of the other, (*b*) *orienting*—one stimulus causes the animal to orient to the other, and (*c*) *preconditioning*—when one becomes a CS for some CR, the other does also. Because the last-mentioned learning is most overt and definitive, the American term for the phenomenon has been *sensory preconditioning* (Brogden, 1939 on). Soviet experimenters, discovering this learning as early as 1926, have, however, termed it "associative," a more comprehensive sensory-sensory denotation.

2. In human subjects, two additional types of learning are observed following repeated sensory-sensory pairing: (*a*) *liminal*—one stimulus lowering the limen of the other, (*b*) *sensory conditioning proper*—one stimulus acquiring the sensory experience of the other (occasionally manifested). Preconditioning is possible in dogs also with a combination of three sensory stimuli and in school children with five.

3. Soviet experimenters report ready formation of sensory preconditioning in birds and a wide variety of mammals, but not in fish or amphibians or early higher-animal ontogeny. Reported evidence of its existence in turtles is inconclusive, but it is unmistakable in infants 74 to 223 days old.

4. *Sensory preconditioning in dogs and cats is abolished upon ablation of their associative areas but not with ablation of sensory-projective cortex* (East and West concur).

5. Basic parameters of sensory preconditioning are different from—indeed, even contrast with—those of simple classical conditioning: within limits, greater efficacy with fewer training trials, longer interstimulus intervals, and low-intensity stimuli; and disruption by injection of chlorpromazine. Known properties of the nature and the conditioning of orienting reactions are wholly in accord with its parametric specificity.

6. Moreover, the parameters correlate, positively with continuing ascent in phylogeny and ontogeny: faster formation, longer retention, more stimuli possible in preconditioned combinations, greater efficacy of simultaneous, backward, and longer inter-stimulus intervals, and lesser negative effects of prehabituation.

7. There are two basic varieties of compound-stimulus conditioning: (*a*)*simultaneous*—when the CSs are administered at the same time (Russian term: "stimulus complexes"), and (*b*)*successive*—the CSs given in succession and the last paired with the US (Russian term: "stimulus chains"). A "dynamic stereotype" is a variety of successive compound in which each CS is paired with the US, with intervals of several minutes between successive CS-US pairings, and as a rule an unpaired or differential CS in an intermediate position.

8. Compound-without-component conditioning, and in successive compounds also without the conditioning of changed sequences, was first termed *configural conditioning* (Razran, 1938a) and then simply *configuring* (Russian equivalent: "intra- or "inter-analyzer synthesis"). Two methods have been used to attain configuring: (*a*) contrasting the pairing of the compound with the US with unpaired applications of the components or changed sequences, and (*b*) continued CS-US pairings of the compound and only occasional testing of the components and/or changed sequences.

9. It is clear that the first method involves conventional differential conditioning and the second *some* of it. Since, however: (*a*) efficacy of the first method is only somewhat greater than that of the second, (*b*) evidence of partial configuring is at hand also in between-subjects designs with no differential conditioning, and (*c*) lower animals, fully at home with differential conditioning, are unable to configure—it is safe to conclude that configuring is *primarily* an outcome of the *training* of its compounds and not of the *untraining* of its components or changed sequences.

10. Compound-stimulus training engenders—it is posited—a special CS-integrate best designated as a *configure* that is scarcely innate since (*a*) its components are mostly unrelated (e.g., metronome of 120 beats + 24 rhythmic touches of the hip + a light flash of 75 watts), and (*b*) its formation takes many trials. Yet related components are more readily con-

figured, and some very simple compounds require no special training: e.g., musical intervals, to which both dogs and college students condition as such, with transfer a function of the relatedness of intervals and not of the specificity of component notes.

11. In cats, bilateral ablation of areas 3, 4, and 6 (motor) abolishes audiovisual simultaneous configuring and prevents its further formation but leaves component conditioning intact. Similar ablation of area 7 (parietal) disrupts this configuring less, while ablation of area 8 (frontal) has hardly any effect. In macaques, however, ablation of the frontal lobes is most disruptive of audiovisual configuring, both simultaneous and successive. In dogs, visuotactile configures eventually reappear after severance of the occipital and parietal lobes. Experimental ulcers and gastritis in dogs yield a reverse relation: component conditioning is much impaired and configuring is left undiminished.

12. In children as young as 4 to 5 years, configured conditioning is much facilitated by repeated prior presentations of the compound stimulus without the US. And even in younger children, 29 to 40 months old, it is easier to transform configured aversive into configured appetitive conditioning than to retain the aversive CR and reverse the sequential-component order of the configure. In dogs, however, the formation of sensory-motor conditioning precedes—and probably dominates—sensory-sensory interaction.

13. Configuring is cognate to sensory preconditioning in that both are afferent-afferent learning involving sensory-orienting reactions—significantly manifest only in birds and mammals—and are abolished only by ablation of higher regions of the cortex. The two differ, however, in that sensory preconditioning is only a higher form of *old-type* associative learning and thus *modificatory* in essence, whereas configuring brings into being *new* neurobehavioral *existents* and is distinctly *productive*. The parametric divide between the two phenomena—conditioning sensory-orienting reactions *to* one another versus integrating them *with* one another—has not been ascertained. Most likely it inheres largely in the time and intensity relations of the interacting reactions.

14. Configuring is assumed to be integrated by the proprioceptive (subsuming here interoceptive) sequences, or kinesthesis, of its constituent sensory-orienting reactions. There is evidence that in carnivores the first cortical relay of proprioceptive integration is the parietal area and the second, the motor area.

15. Motor-proprioceptive views of mind and perception have been current and authoritative in both Western and Eastern thought for many generations.

16. The proprioceptive integration of configuring transforms primary stimulus information, it is maintained, not just because integration as such is comparative and supra-summative, but also because proprioception is

an overall transformative modality. The essence of resultant configures rests, therefore, not only on relations among constituents but also on relations among proprioceptive transforms of the *relata* of the constituents: the number, duration, intensity, recruitment, ratio, sequence, and other characteristics of *both incoming stimulations and subsequent reactions—a true recode and, in a sense, a second-signal system, Pavlov's second being a third.*

17. Behavioral configuring is held to be a very close parallel of phenomenal perceiving. Both ingather and integrate discrete stimulus information, organize it into unitary reactions to variegated multiples of stimuli, and lose stimulus information yet gain adaptive economy in commerce with the environment (higher organisms could not function efficiently if they reacted to every detail), and both fit the postulate of an underlying proprioceptive mechanism; there is also the established fact that only higher animals configure. Animals' capacity to configure thus seems a most logical basis for inferring that they perceive, with the attendant corollary of a *basic ontologic and genetic equivalence of configures, percepts, images, and Gestalten.*

18. Evidence (Gershuni and others) that even bare liminal consciousness is accompanied by some orienting reactions suggests that just as configured sensory-orienting reactions parallel organized perception, mere manifestation of *adequate* orienting is the compeer of bare liminal consciousness (sensations; see below). Thus, liminal consciousness is held to be an evolutionary antecedent of perception, and perception a *recoded* integrate which is functionally but not genetically autonomous—even if *some* perceptual mechanisms are ready at birth.

19. The evolutionary view of "liminal consciousness-to-perception" gains support from a conditioning experiment in which the evocation of an illuminated geometrical figure by a sound manifested in the course of prolonged CR training a progressive and transformational "liminal consciousness-to-perception" sequence: "fleeting light sensations," "an amorphously illuminated gray field," "square outline of field," "outline of differing geometrical figures," and, finally, "clear apprehension of the particular figure"—the US. And there is, of course, the fact that there is a vast difference between the physical energy requisite for the elicitation of liminal consciousness and that necessary for the perception of an object or event.

20. The proposition that liminal consciousness is predicated on *adequate* orienting reactions stems from evidence that these reactions exist also without such consciousness—notably, in not-too-intensive interoceptive stimulation, in exteroceptive stimulation of hysterical and traumatized subjects, and in normal exteroception when the intensity of the stimulus is so low that consciousness arises only after a number of minutes. It is assumed that orienting adequacy means sufficient propioceptive sequelae and that

experiments demonstrating that unconscious reactions become conscious by repeated pairings with conscious reactions are interpreted as outcomes of conditioned supplementation of proprioception. The proposition is, it is posited, within the reach of experimental testability—i.e., it is not an "intervening" theoretical construct.

21. Formally, granting liminal consciousness *sui generis* status redomiciles traditional "sensation." But there is the crucial difference that both ontologically and pragmatically perception is held to be the overriding category and bare sensations (unrelated consciousness) events of genetic and not immediate pragmatic efficacy.

22. A further assumption is that affection is a later evolutionary acquisition than sensation but antecedes perception. (The limen of awareness is lower than that of pain in experiments in which intense interoceptive stimulation is aversive.)

23. There is ample proof for "human learning without awareness" in experiments of (*a*) interoceptive conditioning, (*b*) exteroceptive conditioning to stimuli 10 to 12 decibels below the limen of auditory awareness (Gershuni and others), (*c*) conditioning neonates and 2- to 4-year-old trisomy-18 infants with "estimated IQs of 10, (*d*) basic equivalence of simple conditioning in children with median IQs of 33 and 62 (Grings and associates), and (*e*) manipulated awareness through instructions (scores of American and Soviet studies).

24. It is reasonable to assume that a reaction which is unconscious at the human level is also unconscious in animals. The converse, however, may not be *wholly* true. A principle of "encognization" comparable to that of "encephalization" may conceivably be one of evolution's specialties. That is to say, just as it is generally maintained that evolution telescopes functions to more recent neural acquisitions, to the extent that comparable functions are in higher animals governed by more recent formations while in lower animals they continue under older aegis even upon acquisition of the formations—it may similarly be contended that neurobehaviorally equivalent reactions and their learning manifestations may be conscious in man yet unconscious in animals, with an analogous relation of higher to lower animals. Still, encephalization is relative and supplemental, not an absolute and superseding principle, and basic neurobehavioral correspondence is thereby corrected rather than negated. "Encognization" may well be similar in status.

25. Four kinds of perceptual learning are distinguished: (*a*) *Conditioning of perception,* in which existing innate or acquired perceptions are modified through punishment, or classical or reinforcement conditioning, without the subject's awareness of the conditioning relation. (*b*) *Conditioning through perception,* when simple and obvious associative relations between CSs and USs or between reinforced reactions and reinforcers are *perceived.* (*c*) *Eductive learning,* when the perceptual relations are *new*

and unobvious, as in the "insight" experiments of Köhler, the "reasoning" of Maier, and the "extrapolation" of Krushinsky. (*d*) *Configural learning,* or simply *configuring,* the very mechanism of the formation of the perception of objects and events, the objective analysis of which has long been neglected but which configuring bids fair to decode—to do for perception what conditioning has done for association.

26. No special mechanism, over and above simple conditioning, is believed involved in the *conditioning of perception.* East and West evidence is convincing that when subjects are unaware of the relations between CSs and USs or between reinforcers and reinforced reactions, parameters of the modification of perceptual and nonperceptual reactions are basically similar. Not so *conditioning through perception.* This is considered here a cognitive *sui generis* S-S learning of "expecting" or "anticipating," the basis of which is posited to be the learning manifest in sensory preconditioning —namely, *the formation, through repeated juxtapositions, of a simple perceptual relation between two sensory reactions, including that between the sensory sequelae of motor and visceral reactions.* Since, however, lower animals cannot master sensory preconditioning, and higher animals and to some extent even man may have difficulty maintaining it vis-à-vis inveterate simple conditioning, no omnipotence of this S-S learning is implied— only an acknowledgment of the coexistence and rivalry between newer and older evolutionary weaponry.

27. Eductive learning is, however, not just a cognition of an existing relation but a production of a new one: "reasoning" (or problem solving) and not just conditioning through perception. Thus, it is a higher level of configuring. Levels in cognitive learning are even more warranted than in simple conditioning.

28. Configured-conditioning experiments with college students using Gestalt-type patterns of flashes of miniature lights (similar to the dot arrangements of Schumann, Wertheimer, and Schroff) and twelve different musical intervals as CSs disclose (*a*) that Gestalt "laws" of perceptual organization are valid only initially, but not after repeated exposures, when subjects tend, within limits, to react less and less frequently to simpler *gestalten* and more frequently to complex ones, and (*b*) that the subjects' attitudes and specific task-objectives affect greatly whether they react to configures or components.

29. Unassociated practice of the perception of a complex stimulus, unlike that of simple reactions, results not in habituation or sensitization but in better—more veridical—integration and differentiation of its constituents. Sechenov's 1892 statement: "The more frequent the repetitions of the influences of objects, the clearer and firmer are their more permanent and striking attributes" (Russian edition, p. 204; English edition, 1952, p. 451), is upheld, as is in a sense Gibson and Gibson's related view. The associative mechanism, however, is not that of traditional extrinsic connections but of intrinsic configuring and reconfiguring. On the

other hand, discounting nonlearning oscillations, the limens of bare consciousness (RLs) are, like vital reflexes, basically stable and only little affected by practice. Yet, limens, like vital reflexes, are the raw material of all learning: limens of the integrative, and vital reflexes of the connective dimension.

CHAPTER TEN

Symboling—The Learning of Thinking, Planning, and Willing

SYMBOLING VERSUS PERCEIVING AND "CONCEIVING"

General Statement

The preceding chapter set forth the view that the learning of perception is a triadic hierarchy of: (*a*) *uncovery* of existing and obvious relations, (*b*) *discovery* of new and unobvious ones, and (*c*) *apprehension* of objects and complex events. Configuring and sensory preconditioning evident in numerous Soviet experiments with higher animals were taken to be the behavioral schemata of the triad: configuring of its last two manifestations, and sensory preconditioning of the first. Perception was consequently inferred to be an integral of the mind armamentarium of higher animals, although it was contended that it likely attains significant potency, vis-à-vis simple conditioning, only in primates and prepotency only in man. Moreover, it was posited that configuring (including sensory preconditioning) is in essence a learned integrative transformation of the proprioceptive and interoceptive sequences of interacting sensory-orienting reactions—a recode of primary stimulus information. And it was maintained that both configuring and perceiving are functionally, but not genetically, autonomous from and dominant over their evolutionary and temporal antecedents: constituent orienting reactions and primordial sensing. The connaturalness of orienting and sensing was noted, also that configuring-perceiving is in a way a second-signal system, Pavlov's second being really a third.

Perceiving is not, however, mind's highest integrative capacity, not the highest even in the minds of animals. Above it is "conceiving" or concept formation, the capacity to integrate aspects of different portions of the environment and not just of one particular portion. Concern with concepts is the oldest approach in mental analysis, and it was reflected early in modern animal experimentation. In 1913, Bingham, using a discrimination box, found that while a chick could learn to react differently to a circle and a triangle equal in area and brightness, it failed when the triangle was inverted, suggesting a distinction between "shape" and "form" (Bingham, 1914) cognate to that between "percept" and "concept" in the present treatment. In the same year, Coburn (1914) reported that a crow similarly trained did respond correctly on the first test to such an inversion. But Coburn obviously has not proven thereby that the bird learned the concept of triangularity, which would require training and testing a multitude of shape, size, and brightness variations, and ruling out in each test the possibility that the reaction to the triangle was a result of its not being a circle. In 1933, Gellerman showed, although not altogether convincingly, that two chimpanzees did learn the concept in approximately 1,000 trials. Moreover, he definitely proved that 2-year-old children surpassed the chimpanzees, a finding contrasting sharply with the data of Maier (1937; see Chapter 9) that rats' "reasoning" is on a par with that of 5-year-olds.

The experimental laboriousness of fully ascertaining in animals the distinction between "perceiving shapes" and "conceiving forms" is no doubt the reason that research in the area in the last 50 years has been concerned with shape (although called form). Reports are available, for instance, that: oppossums learn to discriminate between a black ball and a cube of equal area but not between a white square and an equilateral rectangle (James and McFarlane, 1966); rats trained to discriminate between an upright and an inverted triangle fail when the inverted triangle is rotated more than 50 degrees (Fields, 1931, p. 353); dogs discriminate between a circle and an ellipse of an axis ratio of 5:4 but become neurotic when the ratio is 9:8 (Shenger-Krestovnikova, 1921); capuchin monkeys reverse learned brightness or position discriminations much more readily than they do those of shape (Gossette and Brown, 1967); and children less than four years old react more readily to color than to "form" (Kol'tsova, 1967; Suchman and Trabasso, 1966). The relation of this evidence about "form" (i.e., "shape") to "conceiving" is rather indirect: e.g., that shape differences are more difficult for higher animals to master than is position, brightness, or size, and in children also more difficult than color; and that, apparently, it is much easier to learn to react *differentially* than *equivalently* to substantially different shapes of the *same* form, which, perhaps, is reflected in the fact that young children respond more correctly to "In what way are things different?" than to "In what way are they alike?"

Still, animal psychologists have not, by and large, relinquished conceptual learning in their subjects—they have just bypassed the Bingham-Coburn road of study in favor of less toilsome approaches. Weigel's "oddity problem," in which the task is to single out not only a particular unlike object among three but also anything odd in any threesome, has, perhaps, been the most productive. Begun with monkeys in the Wisconsin University laboratory (Robinson, 1933; Young and Harlow, 1943), it has since spread to other institutions and extended to other animals. Significantly, while conceptual oddity has to some extent been mastered by some subprimates (Warren, 1960; Warren and Baron, 1956; Warren and Kimball, 1959: cats), it remains primarily a distinctive primate capacity, yielding a third qualitative phyletic divide of learning above simple conditioning, in addition to (1) configuring and sensory preconditioning, commencing in birds and mammals and (2) Krushinsky's eductive extrapolation confined to higher birds and higher subprimate mammals.

(Maier's "reasoning," well manifest in rats, is apparently no more differentiating than is configuring, while Hobhouse's and Köhler's box-stacking and raking-in-food are not comparable when appropriate prehensibility is lacking. And it should be added that, as noted, the phyletic divides are not altogether absolute: crows surpass rabbits, swine equal dogs, some fish do better than frogs and turtles, even as earthworms and chick embryos condition more readily than ascidians and amphioxi. In mammals and birds, behavioral superiority of families within an order and orders within a class is paralleled, as was noted earlier, by like differences in cortical and subcortical masses and cytoarchitectures.)

The underlying mechanism of conceptual learning in animals is surely still a *terra incognita*. In man, conceptualization is mediated by symbols or language—defined in the next section—which in human ontogeny may possibly be developmentally prior to conceptualization. But while Gardner and Gardner (1969) recently succeeded in teaching a chimpanzee a modicum of symbolic gesturing, this obviously is not an integral of Pongidae's natural evolutionary acquisitions. (Earlier prolonged and painstaking efforts with vocal symbolizing have yielded negligible or wholly negative results: Furness, 1916; Garner, 1900; Hayes, 1951; Kellogg, 1968; Kellogg and Kellogg, 1933; Ladygina-Kots, 1923, 1958; Yerkes and Learned, 1925.) And it equally seems untenable to "deduce" abstraction in concepts from Pavlov's CR generalization, as he himself refused to do. Some years ago (Razran, 1940a), evidence was adduced that even transfer of simplest configural conditioning does not follow this type of generalization in that it expands rather than shrinks with training. Ten years later, a view was expressed (Razran, 1949a) that higher-level generalization may operate as a similarity-dissimilarity categorization of the relation of generalization to conditioned stimuli. But this, too, hardly fits conceptualization, the essence of which is not the acquisition of a particular reaction but the integration and abstraction of an array of them. Conceptual abstraction and conditioned generalization, separated by hundreds of millions of years of evolution, are remotely related but hardly homologous or analogous.

Animal "conceiving" might, however, be considered a qualitative outgrowth of perceiving and configuring—a concept as a configure of configures, a percept of percepts or, phenomenally, an image of images, known traditionally as a "generic image." Or, putting it differently, we might say that a continuum of relational proprioceptive information bridges the apprehension of a particular triangle and *a* triangle, a particular and *any* odd object, and the like. There is need, however, to juxtapose generic imagery with generic neurobehavior. Learning to separate "toys" from "non-toys," Kol'tsova's two- to three-year-old children almost always asked "What kind?" when requested to "Draw a toy," which they did not do with similar training and requests involving a "doll" cr a "book." Presumably, the scope of neurobehavioral integrations is wider than that of any image. However, the problem may not exist in animals whose conceptualization is not likely to be so inclusive.

Conceiving Without Symboling: Do Higher Animals Think?

The question, old and common, and not devoid of systematic significance, might be rephrased as: Do highest animals' acquired neurocognitive concepts *in foro interno* thereby guide their behavior *in foro externo?* Philosophers long preoccupied with Aristotle's *universalia in rebus* and the lofty status of conceptual ideas may well answer "yes," as laymen no doubt will. Yet simple logic and some available experimental evidence appear to negate such a tenet. Consider the following propositions. (1) Concepts obviously cannot be communicated without the aid of behavioral symbols. (2) While higher animals communicate in some way with each other, the communication can hardly be expected to include concepts which they learn only with difficulty. (Animal experimenters would surely be sore-stymied if their cats, monkeys, or chimpanzees passed on their solutions of oddity problems—and "learning sets"—to kith and kin.) (3) Animal thinking in images as symbols is not likely because of its tenuity—even human exclusive nonverbal sensory thinking is not, contrary to Freudian vocabulary, established—nor is it significant, because of its obvious abortiveness: lodged in the individual and dying with him, with no group interaction or "social heritage."

Figure 64 illustrates the "no-true-thinking" of a very sophisticated and conceptually-trained chimpanzee in Pavlov's laboratory. Raphael learned, among other things, to push a stick into a box to obtain an empty cup, fill the cup with water by turning the spigot of a jug in another part of the laboratory, and then go and put out a flame barring a banana in a food dispenser. Yet when spending considerable time one summer on a raft on Lake Ladoga, the chimp quickly learned to scoop water to cool himself, and then was confronted with the food dispenser and burning flame on his raft and the jug on another raft 3 meters away, he was quite frustrated until he managed to join two banana poles, cross over them with the cup, pour water from the jug, recross, and put out the flame to get the food. *No attempt was made to use the water around his own raft, which he had so often scooped with the same cup.* Describing Raphael's exploits, Vatsuro

Figure 64 *Raphael's "idealess" behavior.* In the laboratory, Raphael was taught to extinguish a flame, which was barring a visible fruit in a fruit dispenser, by inserting a stick in a hole of a box to obtain a cup, filling the cup with water by turning on a faucet in a water jug, and pouring the water on the flame. At first, the jug was on a platform above the flame, but later it was placed at some distance on a separate stand. On hot summer days, Raphael was taken to Lake Ladoga, where he stayed on a float 5 meters away from another float. He quickly learned to cool himself by pouring over his body water which he obtained from the surrounding lake by means of the cup in the box. Now, the fruit dispenser was brought to the lake and placed on the float on which Raphael was staying,

while the water jug was put on the other float. The flame barring the fruit was lit, and two bamboo poles were made available. As may be seen in the Figure, Raphael finally solved the problem of securing the fruit in a very laborious and "idealess" way. He obtained the cup, joined the poles, threw them to the other float, crossed over, filled the cup with water from the jug, recrossed, and extinguished the flame. Because of the lack of a second-signal system, the water-in-the-cup-obtained-from-the-lake-to-cool was not "ideated"—combined or abstracted—with the water-in-the-cup-obtained-from-the-jug-to-extinguish-the-flame. (From Vatsuro, 1948)

states that since it did not possess a second-signal system—i.e., language or symboling—the chimp was essentially "idealess," which might be anyone's conclusion. In contrast, there is the striking case of "Peeta," a microcephalic girl of 8 to 10 years of age, studied most intensively from 1933 to 1935 in the Tbilisi Institute of Physiology by Beritoff and a team of associates (Beritoff and Dzidzishvili, 1934; Natashvili et al., 1936). Postmortem examination (she died after two years and three months of study) showed that Peeta's cerebral hemispheres had weighed 17 per cent less than those of the average newborn child and that the surface area of her cortex had been 23 per cent less. Her performance on detour tests never attained the level of dogs and 15-month-old infants, and her use of tubes to rake in food was much inferior to that of apes. Yet, in the course of one year, Peeta learned more words than any chimpanzee in many years of assiduous training, and spontaneously began to sing with a definite melody and dance with a specific rhythm.

All of this surely strengthens Pavlov's view that with the advent of language "a new principle of neural action is introduced" (1933, p. 1154), in contrast with Nissen's, that "language does not seem to introduce any really new psychological process [only] enormously increases the speed and efficiency of processes already present to some extent in nonverbalizing animals" (1958, p. 197). Still, a categorical Cartesian man-brute dichotomy of mind in the manner of Pavlov on the one hand (language "allowing neither qualitative nor quantitative comparison with any conditioned stimuli in animals" [1927a, p. 357; 1927b, p. 407]) and, interestingly, Chomsky (1959, 1966) on the other is hardly warranted—except, perhaps, that in a large sense the evolutionary transition from ape to man is wider than that from hydra to earthworm, earthworm to fish, fish to dog, and dog to ape. The dictum of evolutionary continuity and novelty—novelty in varying degrees—is not challenged but affirmed by the total evidence and logic in the area. Moreover, the fact that apes do eventually master a negligible modicum of true language militates against absolutistic Cartesianism.

SYMBOLING: DEFINITION AND EXPERIMENTAL DISTINCTION OF SYMBOLS AND SEMEMES

Basic Statement

Symboling will be defined as *"associative formation of communicable referential replicates of concepts and percepts."* "Communicable" means of course that the replicates or symbols must be behavioral effector reactions, "efferenting" the intraorganismic neurocognitive afferent actions of the concepts and percepts which underlie them. Yet to neither communicants nor communicatees are symbols just interpersonal behavioral reactions "reinforced through mediation of other persons," *à la* Skinner. Both communicants and communicatees cognize the communication, and there is normally the former's cognition of immediately anteceding percepts or concepts and the latter's recall of them. To be sure, a communicant may convey a symbolic message without cognizing it, and a communicatee may respond appropriately to symbols yet be devoid of them. But then the status of the two is, respectively, (*a*) that of a phonograph record or a myna bird, and (*b*) the correct reaction of a dog or monkey to a vocal or gestural stimulus—and not that of true language (cf. Shustin, 1949).

The "referential" character of symbols is another distinctive determinant of their special status. It stems from the transformation of the mere linkage of symbols to what they symbol into a contextual *reference relation* long regarded as a crux of *meaning*. Indeed, another level of transformation is effected when different symbols come to bear identical and similar reference relations. A number of American and Soviet experiments have demonstrated that college students, as well as older normal children, when conditioned—salivary, GSR, vasomotor—to some word, transfer (generalize) the conditioning much more to synonyms than to homophones and in general much more to semantically than to phonetically related words. Specifically—to cite one instance of each type of experiment—they transfer much more from *surf* to *wave* than to *serf* (Razran, 1939i; Riess, 1940), from *doktor* to *vrach* [physician] than to *diktor* [announcer] (Shvarts, 1954, 1960), from *dog* to *terrier* than from *flower* to *glower* (Razran, 1949c), from *skripka* [violin] to *arfa* [harp] than to *skrepka* [paper clip] (Vinogradova and Eysler, 1959), and from *koshka* [cat] to *zhivotnoye* [animal] than to *kroshka* [crumb] (Luria and Vinogradova, 1959). Yet three of these experiments and two others (Riess, 1946; Peastral, 1961) show also that younger children, aments, and schizophrenics, as well as normal adolescents and adults in states of fatigue and intoxication, transfer their conditioning more—or only—along phonetic and not semantic dimensions.

The combined results point, accordingly, to a two-level existence of symboling: (*a*) a lower, concrete level in which specific symbols are units of both intraorganismic neurocognitive meaning and extraorganismic linguistic communication, and (*b*) a higher, abstract level in which the neurocognitive meaning phases of specific symbols become transformed into higher and essentially independent configures and the linguistic communication phases continue as discrete subserving reactions. The higher configures of meaning, which might be named *sememes* [linguistics' *semanteme* is too general for present denotation], imply the emergence of a new realm of symbolic neurocognition and concomitant existence of two ascending levels of symbolic thinking. Paucity of experimental evidence, unfortunately, does not permit ascertaining the exact modern-human ontogenetic divide between the two levels, except to say that it has no doubt been paralleled in phyletic anthropogeny—*thought and meaning becoming more and more configured and abstract in quality, and language able to catch up only through increases in quantity*. It would take me too far afield to attempt to relate the present formulation to the ontogenetic thinking stages of Piaget (1923, 1951), Goldstein's (1948) clinical distinction between concrete and abstract thinking, and the views of Penfield (1966, 1969), Penfield and Perot (1963), and Penfield and Roberts (1959).

BASIC ORGANIZATION OF SEMEMES

Neurocognitive sememes, the ultimate units of *sui generis* meaning, interact among themselves to form higher unitary configures of meaning otherwise known as propositions, each of which presides over a number of corresponding sentences in language. An experiment will serve as an illustration (Razran, 1949a). Four college students were conditioned to produce 189 to 531 milligrams of conditioned saliva (above control level) in one minute at the sight of the sentence "Poverty is degrading" projected on a screen. When the subjects were subsequently presented with the sentences "Wealth is uplifting," "Poverty is not degrading," and "Poverty is uplifting," the respective generalizations (transfer) of the conditioning were 59 per cent, 37 per cent, and 33 per cent. "Poverty is degrading" was propositionally more similar and generalized more to "Wealth is uplifting" than to "Poverty is not degrading" or "Poverty is uplifting," even though it was obviously less similar sententially.

The differences between the first and the last two sentences were statistically significant, consistent for three of the four subjects, and, as seen in Table 10, generally true for similar variations of two other propositions: "Socialism is desirable" and "Roosevelt will be elected." Shakespeare's "A rose by any other name . . ." presumably pertains not just to the meaning of single words but also to that of complete sentences. Arrays of sentences

Table 10 *Mean Generalization of Salivation in Four College Students Conditioned to Sentences: "Poverty is degrading," "Roosevelt will be elected," and "Socialism is desirable."* (From Razran, 1949a)

Generalization Sentences	Logical Formula	Per Cent of Generalization	Mean Per Cent
We⟶ Ul; De⟶ Df; Ca⟶ Ud	S'C'P' ✓	59; 53; 63	58
We⟼ Dg; De⟼ El; Ca⟼ Ds	S'C'P ✓	49; 50; 58	52
Po⟼ Ul; Ro⟼ Df; So⟼ Ud	SC'P' ✓	44; 41; 51	45
We⟶ Dg; De⟶ El; Ca⟶ Ds	S'CP x	38; 31; 39	36
Po⟼ Dg; Ro⟼ El; So⟼ Ds	SC'P x	37; 28; 34	33
Po⟶ Ul; Ro⟶ Df; So⟶ Ud	SCP' x	33; 36; 30	33
We⟼ Ul; De⟼ Df; Ca⟼ Ud	S'C'P' x	19; 28; 27	25

*Each entry in the third column is a mean of 64 measurements, 16 for each of the four subjects in the experiment.

Abbreviations and symbols: We—wealth; Ul—uplifting; De—Dewey; Df—defeated; Ca—capitalism: Ud—undesirable; Dg—degrading; El—Elected; Ds—desirable; Po—poverty; Ro—Roosevelt; So—socialism; S—subject; C—copula; P—predicate; S', C', P'—reversed subjects, copulae, and predicates; →, is or will be; ⟼, is not or will not be; ✓, proposition affirmed; X, proposition negated.

come to subserve identical or nearly identical semantic or logical propositions organized as *sui generis* neurocognitive wholes that might be termed
logicemes. Symboling thus actually gives rise to three ascending levels of
thinking: (1) a *specific-symbolic* level, in which neurocognitive meanings
are not yet separated from effector units of language and for which the
term *symbosemic* will be coined, (2) a *sememic* level, when ultimate units
of identical as well as related meaning are served by different linguistic
units, and (3) a *logicemic* level, with general logical propositions dominating particular language. It should be noted, however, that logicemic thinking is to some extent affected by the forms of its individual terms—what
Woodworth and Sells (1935) called the "atmosphere effect" and what is
likewise deducible from the data in Table 10—as is sememic thinking by
symbosemic factors. Nor is it warranted to conclude that the dominance
of thought over language indicates which came first. It may well be that
language was first and thought took over. As indicated in an earlier section, the developmental dynamics of thought are largely qualitative, those
of language primarily quantitative.

BASIC ORGANIZATION OF LANGUAGE

Experimental Analysis and Sample Clinical Evidence

Language may well have been historically the behavioral predecessor
and substratum of meaning. Now, however, it is its immediate subsequent
behavioral expression. And then and now it is, obviously, an *efferent* system that cannot parallel the *afferent* configuring of meaning's neurocognition. Yet the organization of language is manifestly the most accessible
means of analyzing the component structure of the latter and is of paramount significance in its own right. This organization is unique and complex and scarcely interpretable in terms of simple modificatory conditioning, the gallant attempts of Mowrer (1954), Skinner (1957), and Osgood (1963)—each in his own way—to the contrary notwithstanding
(cf. Lashley, 1951). But it is encompassable within productive learning
and specifically comparable to the referential relations of single symbols,
or words, to what they symbol, the precursors of sentences. Moreover,
while simple conditioning does not account for the genesis of the organization, it can be utilized as a *technique* to disclose significant aspects of its
nature beyond the reach of linguistics proper.

Consider the following two experiments. El'kin (1955), in the Soviet
Union, conditioning thirty university students to withdraw their fingers
at the sight of a sentence *Student vyderzhal ekzamen* [The student passed
the examination] by pairing the sentence with the administration of an
electric shock, found 87 per cent transfer to *passed,* 50 per cent to *examination,* and only 10 per cent to *student.* Razran (1952) conditioned
four college students to salivate in response to the sentence *Ya dal yemy
novy myach* [I gave him a new ball] and noted 35 per cent transfer to the

verb, 27 per cent to the *direct object,* 18 per cent to the *indirect object,* 11 per cent to the *adjectives qualifying the direct object,* and 9 per cent to the *subject* of the sentence. (The subjects knew the meaning of the sentence but were misinformed about the purpose of the experiment.) As seen in Table 11, Razran's results were quite similar when he used the sentences

Table 11 *Mean Per Cent Transfer of Conditioned Salivation in Four College Students from Three Five-Word Russian Sentences to the Individual Words (Grammatical Parts) of the Sentences.* Subjects were told the meanings of the sentences and words but misinformed about the purpose of the experiment. (From Razran, 1952)

Sentences	Mean Per Cent Transfer to:					
	Qualifier of Subject	Subject	Predicative Verb	Indirect Object	Qualifier of Direct Object	Direct Object
Ya dal Yemu novy myach [I gave him a new ball.]		Ya [I] 9%	Dal [gave] 35%	Yemu [him] 18%	Novy [new] 11%	Myach [ball] 27%
Belokuraya devochka nashla zolotoye pero [The blond girl found a golden pen.]	Belokuraya [The blond] 13%	Devochka [girl] 18%	Nashla [found] 30%		Zolotoye [golden] 13%	Pero [pen] 26%
Ona khochet kupit' sery koshelyok [She wants to buy a gray purse.]		Ona [she] 14%	Khochet kupit' [wants to buy] 46%		Sery [gray] 12%	Koshelyok [purse] 28%

Belokuraya devochka nashla zolotoye pero [The blond girl found a gold pen] and *Ona khochet kupit' sery koshelyok* [She wants to buy a gray purse]. However, El'kin's data show 100 per cent transfer to each of the two words in the sentence *Vklyuchayu tok* [I am turning on/the shock] and none to each separately in the sentence *Rukopis' prochitana* [The manuscript/was read].

El'kin's last two sentences are special: one describing the accompanying experimental operation, the other showing no transfer, and both consisting of only two words. But his first is quite comparable to the sentences used by Razran in structure as well as in results of transfer. The consistency of Razran's results for each of his three five-word sentences merits specification. The per cents of transfer to the *subjects* of the sentences were 9, 14, and 18; to the *predicative verbs,* 30, 35, and 46 (combining the auxiliary verb and infinitive complement in the third sentence); to the *direct objects,* 26, 27, and 28; and to the *adjectives qualifying the direct objects,* 11, 12, and 13 (15 per cent to the *indirect object* in the first sentence and 13 to the *adjective qualifying the subject in the second*). The transfer differences between *predicative verbs* plus *direct objects,* and *subjects* plus *adjectives qualifying direct objects* were statistically reliable (*p* <.01) and, as evidenced in a control study, not due to differences in the conditioning efficacy of individual words. To be sure, these results need to be tested with words of wider lexical range (emotion-laden words might, for instance, draw more transfer), and the technique is difficult to apply to languages of much affixation: e.g., Hebrew *Pegashtihah* [I met her], Turkish *Sevisdirilememek* [not to be able to cause to be loved by each other; *sevmek*—to love, *is*—each other, *dir*—to cause, *il*—passive tense; *eme*—not to be able], not to mention the polysynthesis of Paiute—quoted by Sapir (1921)—Wii-to-kuchum-punku-rügani-yugwi-va-ntu-m (ü) [they who are going to sit and cut up with a knife a black cow (*or* bull)]. Still, the significance of the presented pilot data to a basic understanding of the underlying mechanisms and dynamics of grammatical structure is beyond doubt.

Two systematic propositions are involved. (*a*) Grammatical organization differs from preconfiguring in compound-stimulus conditioning in that the potency which certain components gain at the expense of others is solely a function of the compounding and not of the original inequality of the components. (*b*) The organization inheres in the interaction of generalized sememes and not specific words or phonemes. That is to say, "generative grammar" is in essence "generative neurocognition of grammar"—evidenced in a way also (*a*) in that a four-word sentence is as quickly perceived as two similar unconnected words (even as a familiar eighteen-letter word is a tachistoscopic equal of four unconnected letters), and, more relatedly, (*b*) in various speech pathologies.

A case of a 50-year-old Polish artist left aphasic as a result of an epileptic fit, reported by Konorski at Pavlov's Wednesday colloquia in 1934, will be cited. The artist, who retained fully his drawing ability and intelligence, understood well and responded correctly to requests: "Draw a lady feeding a child," "Draw an artist painting a portrait," and the like. Yet he would draw only one of two objects when the requests were: "Draw a man and a dog," "Draw a man and a candle," and even "Draw a black and a yellow line." Somewhat similarly, while he could repeat after the examiner only one of two nouns or pronouns, even if they were very short, such as *"Pyos i koni"* [dog and horses] and *"Ya-Ya"* [I-I], he had no difficulty reproducing a pronoun plus a verb such as *"Ya sizhu* [I sit], failing only when the task was *"Ya sizhu na stule"* [I sit on the chair]. In simple sentences, his understanding span was apparently "subject-verb-direct object," his reproduction span "subject-verb," whereas in either case two words of identical parts of speech were beyond his competence. The patient communicated his needs through drawings: man in tub—"wants a bath"; medicine bottle—"wants medicine"; heated oven—"is cold"; and the like (*Wednesdays,* 1949, Vol. 2, pp. 468-475; original date, October 3, 1934).

Linguistic Approaches

Only one of these approaches will be mentioned—that of "language universals," the view that *Homo sapiens* everywhere organizes the basics of his language in identical or at least similar patterns. Yet Smith and Miller's particular view that these universals represent "innate linguistic competence" (1966b, p. 6) surely needs to be qualified, as does Lenneberg's related Cartesian treatise, *The Biological Foundations of Language* (1967). For one thing, human language has been on this planet too short a time to have evolved a significant *sui generis* genetics. For another, the modicum of true language taught to a chimpanzee (see p. 272) is prima facie evidence that this putative genetics may not be severed from corresponding prehuman antecedents. And, most importantly, consider the thesis of Chapter 2 that "the ratio of learning plasticity to unlearned relative fixity is a growing function of evolution and in man is very large and overriding," and that "the organization of language inheres in its neurocognition and not behavior." Hence, the traditional assertion that the universality of this organization is an outcome of commonality of environment and learned "social heritage" can hardly, without definitive contraries, be set aside. Or, in all, the man-brute dichotomy of mind and language is, as stated earlier, very special but not absolute and not at variance with the general principle of evolutionary continuity and novelty. To repeat a quote of a noted Soviet evolutionist, "the second-signal system did not just drop from heaven" (p. 6).

It will bear citing a few common examples of the vagaries of similarities and differences among languages. (1) Modern English is organizationally much more closely related to Chinese, Siamese, and Malay, than to Latin, Old Germanic, and modern Slavic languages in its minimal inflection and relatively fixed word-order. (2) Several Far-Eastern languages use differences in pitch as differential determinants of meaning; Russian does the same with stress. (3) The English kinship word "brother-in-law" is rendered in Russian by four different words of distinct meaning and sounds: *dever*—husband's brother, *shurin*—wife's brother, *svoyak*—husband of wife's sister, and *zyat'*—sister's husband (*zyat'* means also, interestingly, daughter's husband). Yet there is no such sharp specific distinction between English and eighty Indian languages (Gifford, 1922). (4) While some languages modify words only through suffixes (Turkish, Hottentot, Eskimo), others primarily through prefixes (Cambodian, Hupa, Navaho) and still others (most common European languages) use both, the Semitic languages employ, in addition, internal vocalic and to some extent also consonantal changes. (5) Polish and Czech are very similar to each other, yet in the former the stress is always on the penultimate syllable and in the latter always on the first. (6) English, and to a lesser extent all

Germanic and Romance languages as well as Bengali, have continued to lose inflection in modern times, while agglutinated Finnish is becoming more and more inflected.

THE DOMINANCE OF SYMBOLS

The neurocognition of man's symboling, reflected in meaning and thought, normally dominates not only its own linguistic behavior but also the neurocognition of perception, which in turn normally dominates the behavior of conditioning. The last relation was noted in Chapters 7, 8, and 9 and need not be enlarged. Anyone experimenting with human conditioning knows full well that when the subjects perceive what is wanted of them, conditioning of controllable reactions changes radically, and, ignoring contorted explanations, the changes are the outcome of nothing but the perceiving. Pavlov, who did not accord perception qualitative distinction, nonetheless affirmed: "Thoughts [of adult human subjects in conditioning experiments] about 'what is done to them and why' inhibit the formation of conditioned reflexes" (*Wednesdays,* 1949, Vol. 1, p. 244; original date, November 9, 1932; cf. Luria, 1932, 1961). But the posited dominant relation of symboling to perceiving must be explicated. Percepts obviously are the primary sources of information about the world around us, whereas the concepts of symbols are superstructural derivatives. However, perceptual veridicality and stability are much offset by (*a*) the inconstancy of the environment which bears the information, (*b*) the variance in sense-organ actions which receive and transmit it, and (*c*) the extrinsic effects of positive and negative affects and associations—punishment, reinforcement, and classical conditioning—which modify it. But, concepts are fairly stable and veridical, both because they are less dependent upon environmental and sensory variations and because in combining percepts they correct and "average out" the latter's variations. Indeed, they may be stable and veridical even if their constituent percepts are not, in somewhat the same sense that conclusions in logic are valid even when their premises are incorrect.

Nonetheless, the basic postulate of symbol-over-percept dominance must be qualified. First, the outcome must be presumed to be a correction rather than a distortion of percepts and the ratio of correction to distortion a growing positive function of anthropogeny, which, fortunately, is by and large the evolutionary story of *Homo sapiens.* Second, percepts must forestall the autochthony of symbols, holding them to their task of checking and balancing the reality information of their constituent percepts which, too, appears to be spurred by evolution. Human progress and individual adjustment break down otherwise. Nor are the effects of neurocognition in general, symbolic and perceptual, unbounded in scope and chronology. Soviet experiments on interoception and interoceptive and autonomic conditioning (Razran, 1955a, 1961a, 1965a, 1965d) have not only confirmed the long-maintained view of the vast realms of noncognitive reactivity beyond the reach of cognition but also demonstrated that this reactivity can be brought under noncognitive conditioned control. One moves his fingers or foot at will, can secrete saliva by invoking special thoughts or symbols, and even may be able thus to constrict or dilate his blood vessels—but would hardly be expected to move, say, his spleen. Yet splenic movements have been conditioned several times in dogs (Bykov and Gorshkov, 1932; Kel'man, 1935, 1937; Polosukhin, 1938), and this could no doubt be replicated in human subjects. Symbolic instructions are sufficient to teach an adult or older child to step on the brakes in response to a red light without recourse to paired conditioning, but few would suggest deferring toilet training until perceiving and symboling are *fully* developed. And, of course, the effects of the lower five levels of learning become ingrained before the upper six come of age and thus command temporal advantage. Fortunately, this temporal advantage is mainly temporary and seldom complete, Freud's orthodox doctrine notwithstanding.

Probably, the overriding thesis here is the fact that man's symboling is (*a*) admittedly mediated by the most recent and thus most efficient cortical structures and (*b*) accelerated to the extent that his symbolic reactions exceed his primary perceptions early in ontogeny and exceed them many times early in maturity. Symboling without perceiving becomes more and more common, even as perceiving without symboling becomes rarer and rarer. Time-bound biography rather than space-bound contemporaneity is the domicile of man's mind. It is tempting to quote a Sechenov statement of 79 years ago: "Man juxaposes not only his experience of childhood, adolescence, and old age, not only what he saw, say, in America, and here, in Moscow, but also the life of today with that of antiquity . . . he becomes a part, so to speak, of the life of the universe without leaving the narrow limits of his terrestrial existence" (1892, p. 201).

THINKING

Basic Statement

A specific definition of human thinking has not yet been offered, only a delineation as "an outcome of acquired symboling involving the neuro-cognition of meaning." The essence of "acquired symboling" has been considered, although it will bear repeating that it predicates associative genesis of ontologic novelty and enlargement and validation of the reality of perceiving. Also meriting restatement is my earlier contention that "meaning," like perception, is organized in configured or *gestaltet* fashion. The neuro-cognition of thinking as such, however, calls for further explication, as does the allegation of its special "directedness," not mentioned earlier. Neuro-cognition includes *cognition* and *neural* action, but not Watson's *effector* action: thinking as but "implicit language activity and other activity substitutable for language activity" (1925, p. 157). It is by no means denied that man's thinking has evolved out of his behavior, nor that its neural base is to the present day much affected by feedback from behavior. What is asserted is that the neurocognition of thinking has long been emancipated from and, at least in normal adults, generally dominates and controls its evolutionary antecedent. Sechenov's view that *"human thought is the first two-thirds of a psychical reflex"* (1863, p. 503; italics in original), that is, of receptor and adjustor (central-neural) but not effector action, is more in line with modern evidence than is Watson's, particularly when Sechenov adds that effector action is inhibited [or suppressed] in human ontogeny in two stages: first gross motor, then verbal (1863). Just why, one may ask, should not speech behavior be reduced beneath subvocal proportions to become neurobehavior and the basis of thinking?

Traditional Analyses and Controversies: Relation to Imagery

Introspective search for the quale of thinking produced a sharp division among experimental, i.e., introspective, psychologists at the turn of the century. The Würzburg school (Mayer and Orth, 1901; Marbe, 1901; Külpe, 1904, 1912; Ach, 1905; Watt, 1905; Messer, 1906; Buhler, 1907), joined by Binet (1903) and Woodworth (1906), broke with Aristotle to bring forth the rather radical view that it is *imageless,* whereas Titchener at Cornell (1909) and his pupils insisted that it was invariably *imaged.* The imagelessness of thinking was designated by the Würzburgers first as a *Bewusstseinslage* (conscious state or attitude) and then as a *Bewusstheit* (knowing that . . .) interacting with an *Aufgabe* (task) or *Determinierende Tendenz* (determining tendency)—all representing a higher level of cognition in direct apprehension of meaning (see below). On the other hand, Titchener and his students, from Clarke in 1911 to Comstock and Crossland in 1921, continued to report thinking in terms of not only imagery but also kinesthetic and organic sensations and affections, all vague, to be sure. Several examples will be cited from Clarke (1911, p. 215): *doubt*—"failure of an incipient movement to go to its usual terminus"; *newness*—"impresses as a cutting, as a bit of knife blade"; *pride*—"slight tendency to straighten up my neck and smile"; *security*—"long, easy breathing, straight position of body"; *waiting*—"sensation of *heat,* stamping of feet, and extreme unpleasantness"; and the like. And one of Titchener's own earlier statements was: "I was not at all astonished to observe that the recognition of a gray might consist of a quiver of the stomach" (1909, p. 179).

Adjudication of controversial introspection is not exactly within my competence. But there is no doubt that the predominant body of Western psychology favors the Würzburg stance. Woodworth's statement: "Imageless thoughts are simply the subject's meanings" (1938, p. 788) and Moore's subjects' "reporting meanings, much sooner than images" (1910) are quite representative. And Soviet physiology and psychology are in accord. That perception and the first-signal system reflect the concrete, and thought and the second-signal system the abstract, was the view not only of Pavlov but also of Lenin. Buhler's 1907 statement: "Perception is image; the other self-sufficient object-consciousness is the consciousness of a rule *(Regelbewusstsein)* . . . a very frequent experience in scientific thinking" (p. 340), might well have been taken from a recent Soviet text. Moreover, the Usnadze (Georgian) wing of "Set Psychology" (Bzhalava, 1965, 1966; Khodzhava, 1960; Natadze, 1958; Norakidze, 1958, 1959; Prangishvili, 1967; Prangishvili and Khodzhava, 1958, 1963; Usnadze, 1950) in the Soviet Union is in large measure a wide modern expansion of the Würzburg school.

It seems reasonable, in light of modern evidence, to attribute the reported kinesthetic and organic sensations in thinking to muscular tension and action, general or linguistic, which often—although by no means always—accompanies thinking (Bills, 1927; Davis, 1937, 1939; Jacobson, 1930, 1932; Lorens and Darrow, 1962; Max, 1935, 1937; L. Novikova, 1957; and others) but which few would consider integral constituents of it. Likewise, it is tenable to assume that, because imagery is known to diminish in the course of practice, the much practiced and indirect generic variety in thinking is lessened and lost much sooner and more irreversibly than the less practiced and direct specific kind in perceiving. Woodworth presented in 1938 a thoughtful and convincing "Final Comment on Imageless Thought":

> It is curious what different semi-emotional reactions are made by different persons to the notion of imageless thought. To some it seems entirely natural and acceptable, while others shrink from it as a strange, mystical theory and insist that there simply must be some image or sensation to 'carry the meaning'. . . . The present writer would like, however, once more to record his own view that imageless thought is no more mysterious than the everyday perception of facts. Let us suppose that while you are reading in your room a sudden noise tells you that your neighbor has gone out of the adjoining room and slammed the door. The fact of which you thus become aware is very different from the mere occurrence of a sudden noise. . . . A little later you recall the fact . . . your neighbor has gone out—perhaps with a revival of your previous visual or verbal image, perhaps without. Under cross-examination you might not be sure of the precise sensations, images and motor reactions occurring in the original experience, but you are sure of what the experience meant to you, that is, the fact of your neighbor's going out. Mysterious? (pp. 788-789).

I concur fully. Meaning is man's most advanced and most effective level of functioning.

Three Pertinent Modern Experiments, Physiological Meaning, and Unconscious Cerebration

The Experiments. Razran (1949c) conditioned nine college students to salivate at the sight of the word *dog,* then divided them into three equal groups each of which practiced different types of associative word-word relations before being tested for CR transfer to the words *terrier, animal,* and *cat.* Group A wrote down *coordinates* of a list of twenty-five words; Group B, *coordinates* of one list and *supraordinates* of another; Group C— *coordinates* and *subordinates* (no names of animals or animal-related words in the lists). The mean per cents of transfer to the three words in the three groups were, respectively: *terrier,* 38, 60, and 26; *animal,* 28, 45, and 15; *cat,* 43, 43, and 47. The *terrier-dog* CR relation during the transfer tests was thus very significantly facilitated by prior practice of *supraordinate* associations and inhibited by the practice of *subordinate* associations, even as the *animal-dog* relation was conversely inhibited by the former and facilitated by the latter ($p < .01$ in all cases). Moreover, without the practice of *coordinates,* the mean per cent of CR transfer from *dog* to *cat* was 38 in eight other subjects (Razran, 1949b). A questionnaire at the end of the experiment revealed subjects' "vague feelings" of "directed thought" but no "specific imagery" of the "induced relations"—in other words, a putative operation of highly effective imageless *Bewusstseinslagen, Regelbewusstsein,* or plainly, in Woodworth's sense, *imageless meanings.* Indeed, there is reason to assume that the results of the experiment (Razran, 1954) reported in Chapter 7—in which music, art and verbal selections presented during several luncheons came to facilitate college students' unscrambling food-related words and in which *food imagery was reported after and not before the unscrambling*—were in essence *conditioned Bewusstseinslagen.* (Compare Külpe's introspection that "the supraordinate idea of 'vermin' was present as a *Bsl.* [*Bewusstseinslage*]" when his free-association response to "horse-fly" was "dragonfly" [Messer, 1906].)[31]

Physiological Meaning. The thesis stems from Titchener's either-or commitment that when thinking is not sensory-imaginal, meaning is " 'carried' in purely physiological terms" (1909, p. 179), raising thereby the more general question of what happens to meaning and thinking when their sensory underpinnings are gone. Do they plummet to a low niveau of subliminal reactions? Or rise to a higher phenomenal level of pure

[31] The reports of my 1949 experiments set forth fully the argument for the operation of implicit supraordinate categories within a context of a general theory that "CR generalization develops not during the original training to the conditioned stimuli, but during the subsequent testing for the generalization stimuli" (Razran, 1949b, pp. 650-651). The reports did not include, however, the introspective data and interpretations which then, since I was not particularly interested in Thinking and in the Würzburg school, I considered of little significance and believed the editor would have a similar opinion. I now have relinquished my "subsequent testing" hypothesis with respect to animal conditioning and human conditioning in which verbal-cognitive control is not too extensive (cf. Maltzman, 1968)—but I do feel, on the other hand, that my omitted data are valuable. Volkova (1954) in the Soviet Union found, similarly, that semantic generalization of salivary conditioning is most pronounced in school children when the generalization words were subordinates of the conditioned words, but she used no introspective and free-associative tests.

knowledge? Within limits, the cited experiments offer a positive answer to the second question and a negative to the first, and suggest that combining Würzburg views and modern objective indicators—preferably electroencephalography added to conditioning—is within experimental reach and will, it is hoped, be undertaken.

Unconscious Cerebration. This term was used by Carpenter in his 1877 *Mental Physiology* to denote high-level unconscious thinking, since attested to by a large number of scientists, artists, inventors, and poets (see summaries by Hadamand, 1945; Humphrey, 1948; Meinecke, 1934; Patrick, 1935, 1937; Platt and Baker, 1931; Rossman, 1931; and others), but which modern psychology can hardly accept. The attestations may be much more readily construed as outcomes of recovery from fatigue or disengagement from what Dunker (1935) called "functional fixity" than as "creative unconsciousness," "illumination" in the wake of "incubation," and the like. On the other hand, there is, as is known, substantial bona fide evidence that thinking is (*a*) facilitated by unconscious factors, and (*b*) rendered less conscious through improvement with practice. Examples of the first type of effect are: Usnadze's (1931, 1950) reports of size-weight illusions in psychophysics when subjects are hypnotized and forget their prior judgments, Maier's (1931) induction of unconscious "direction" in thinking, and Razran's (1949d) finding that pre-experimental practice of associative categories facilitates greatly their semantic generalization even when what has been practiced is no longer recalled. The examples are admittedly in line with the hardly-disputed general view of the emergence of conscious from unconscious events, which as such calls for no further comment (cf. Köhler, 1923).

The conscious-becoming-unconscious phase of thinking is, however, in need of several systematic statements. For one thing, there is no reason to assume that portions of thinking which become unconscious through practice are still manifestations of thinking (Beritoff, 1961). For another, there is reason to maintain that the thinking act as a whole does not thereby become unconscious (Puni, 1955). The effects of practice appear to reside, rather, in a redistribution of consciousness, whereby it is broadened and centered in key launching and consummating phases while nonconscious and made-unconscious processes are utilized as subserving mechanisms. Moreover, it must be remembered that just as specific symbolic reactions and interactions lose consciousness through practice, they also are brought *into* consciousness through the directedness of thinking. The process is by no means irreversible.

Phenomenological and Neo-behavioristic Approaches

Selz (1913, 1922) was the first to extend Meinong's (1906) phenomenology to the psychology of thinking, replacing Marbe's *Bewusstseinslage* and Ach's *Bewusstheit* by *Wissen* (knowledge) and introducing *Sam-*

taufgabe (total task) and *Sachverhältnis* (relational fact), to the effect that thinking is unified knowledge of a thing-in-relation-to-another and not of either the thing by itself or the relation by itself. Thinking in controlled association was his experimental mainstay. Later, the Gestalt psychologists (Dunker, 1935; Koffka, 1927, 1935; Köhler, 1917, 1925; Wertheimer, 1920, 1925, 1945) radically transformed the approach, placing emphasis upon: novelty; contemporaneity; insight; organized wholes; *internal* stresses, strains, and structures; isomorphism; recentering; and the like— and almost total banishment of association, *Aufgaben,* and past events as such.

Little needs to be added to explicate the relation of the present position to *Gestalttheorie.* There is a kinship but also a very wide gulf between the two. As noted, the position offered here maintains that novelty and organization are primarily evolving learning achievements of higher organisms and not compelling functions of a priori stimulational attributes. More specifically, the integrative and meaningful emerge from the connective and meaningless, and the emergents continue to interact with the antecedents, dominating them normally but by no means invariably. Association and novelty, meaning and no meaning, and for that matter trial-and-error and insight and the like, are reconcilable and interpenetrable, not antagonistic and mutually exclusive. All of this is quite foreign and contrary to the Gestaltist philosophy. Nor may one overlook the vagueness of specific Gestalt hypotheses—unanchored or unanchorable to substantial objective data; e.g., respectively, (*a*) Köhler's organized electrocerebral fields, refuted by Lashley, Chow, and Semmes (1951), and (*b*) thinking "directed by internal structural stresses and strains," unrelated to any verifiable bodily reactions. Most valuable as an *antithesis* of earlier psychology, *Gestalttheorie* failed to comprehend and accord due status to the *thesis* which it contested, and thus it remained largely an extremism, which in my book is not a virtue.

Likewise, while I fully share the neo-behaviorist guidepost that psychology must be built *von Unten herauf* (from below up), I am not content to let it dwell only in *Unten.* Neo-behaviorists' total neglect of the emergent evolutionary novelty of patterned and symbolic learning, and their exclusive concern with the laws of modificatory conditioning well developed in fish and octopuses, have long been stumbling blocks to my joining the club. It is hoped, however, that what has been said will induce some of its Thinking theorists (Cofer, 1951; Maltzman, 1955, 1968) to modify their tenets somehow. For the time being, mere recognition that man is not a fish would be a salutary advance—but would it also, perhaps, be some acknowledgment that man is in possession of a neurobehavioral hierarchy of true (not just deduced concepts of) meanings? Note that one theorist, Maltzman, abandoned in 1968 the do-all staple of "mediated generalization," which, as he states, "I have never embraced" (p. 335). And note a most definitive Pavlov statement: "After it is learned, human speech, unlike second-order conditioning, remains constant [relatively unextinguished]. *That is, our words are not conditioned reflexes—the process here is different"* (*Wednesdays,* 1949, Vol. 1, p. 240; original date, November 2, 1932; italics added). Moreover, there are sufficient indications that Pavlov, like Sechenov, did not wholly equate thoughts with words.

PLANNING AND WILLING

Planning

"Planning" is presumably a phase of thinking while "willing" will be considered so. The experimental pivot of planning may be said to go back to Kries's 1895 *Einstellung* and Watt's 1905 *Aufgabe,* nowadays rendered usually as "set" in English (Duncan, 1967) and *ustanovka* (set or attitude) in Russian (Prangishvili and Khodzhava, 1958, 1963). However, since planning comprises both pushing sets and pulling goals, Maier's single term "direction" (1930) may be more appropriate, even though it is more general. No distinction will be made here between the essences of sets and goals: they both are learned, in large measure *outside* the intrinsics of thinking, and both, particularly set, tend to become less phenomenal than thinking—perhaps they are so to begin with. Moreover, it should be made clear that, at least for the present, planning is much more a life-situation act than an experimental problem and that its posited species-genus relation to thinking is debatable. One might, for instance, juxtapose planning with problem solving, which is wider than thinking in operating also without symboling, and, on the other hand, contend that all thinking is in some way directed. Still, planning without symboling is palpably unreal, distinctions between undirected and directed thinking have been current since the days of Hobbes, and there is of course no doubt that such directedness varies along a continuum. Setting up and perusing common-sense planning as a special category of directed thinking seems heuristic, theoretically and experimentally.

Planning has of late been the subject of a stimulating essay by Miller, Galanter, and Pribram (1960). The present view of thinking certainly has no quarrel with the authors' general definition: *"A plan is any hierarchical process in the organism that can control the order in which a sequence of operations is to be performed"* (p. 16; italics in original). Hierarchical control and organization have, most evidently, been the keynote of this entire book. My view diverges from theirs, however, in maintaining that the psychology and underlying neurophysiology of the human organism is composed of several hierarchical processes, *is indeed a hierarchy of hierarchies.* While man is not a dog, a pigeon, or a fish—still dog, pigeon, fish, and even sponge mechanisms are within us. And there is of course no doubt that recent research has brought to light the vast effects of feedback (see Granit, 1966, for one summary), calling for substantial emendation of reflex lore. In the Soviet Union, Anokhin, on the basis of surgical studies of anastomosis and compensation (1935b), has for years (1955, 1957, 1963, 1965, 1968) strongly stressed the power of "reverse afferentation" and the merit of a four-link reflex, similar to the TOTE (Text-Operate-Test-Exit), while Bernshteyn (1947, 1957, 1961, 1963) suggested replacing the term "reflex arc" with "reflex loop" (*reflektornoye kol'tso*) as early as 1935. Emendation should not, however, mean outright rejection, and the understanding that consequents move and correct antecedents should not cause a post-Humean jettisoning of the antecedent-consequent progressions of living and thinking. Interestingly, while many American psychologists relish narrowing and even abandoning the reflex concept despite their old penchants for a "motor theory of consciousness," Sechenov, the most committed reflexologist, included within it a two-link receptor-adjustor unit of no motor action. Nor, as multiply documented, did Pavlov's engrossment in reflexes keep him from viewing human language as a unique attainment (almost, but not quite, as does Chomsky).

The Miller, Galanter, and Pribram essay is open to some objections also for equating (*a*) Plan with Image, (*b*) Image with Knowledge, and (*c*) Plan with Knowledge. "Changes in the Plans can be effected only by information drawn from the Images" (p. 18). "The Image is all the accumulated, organized knowledge that the organism has about itself and its world" (p. 17). True, it is further stated that the "Image consists of a great deal more than imagery, of course" (p. 17). Yet the term is historically and didactically unfortunate. Since the days of Galton (1880) it has been known that imagery fades with time and knowledge, scholars and scientists reporting it least. And even earlier, Fechner (1860) found extreme individual differences and the momentary glimpse of an image giving way to *ein blösses Gedankending* (bare object thought). Binet's 1903 view was that "experience is much better rendered by reports of 'thoughts' than by that of 'images' " while Bühler's "perception is image and [imageless] consciousness of a rule . . . a very frequent experience in scientific thinking" was quoted earlier, as was, at greater length, Woodworth's careful conclusion of the much greater stability of imageless thought of meanings and facts than of any imagery involved in them. Personally, I am able to bring up visual images only of individual objects and simple functions—I cannot combine them. Repeated trials fail to invoke in me an image of "a man writing 8 on a blackboard," although I readily image—sensorially or verbally—"man," "hand" or "chalk," "8," and "blackboard." If imagery alone were the vehicle of thinking, I could not manage it.

A more substantial objection is raised by the essay's equating Plan with Knowledge. The tenor of this chapter has been that normally the neuro-cognitive dominates the noncognitive. But this is quite different from ignoring the latent force of the latter: its genetic primacy, common everyday priority, and ingrained readied organization. Part of the argument, from Würzburger *unbewusste Aufgaben* to conditioned toilet training, has been

292 · *Mind in Evolution*

presented in earlier sections. Man is not one kind of computer, and he requires more than one kind of program to plan efficiently. And the bases of his plans—even the plans themselves—are by no means exclusively cognitive. And here I offer a general statement. The essay is entirely in accord with the prevalent American either-or philosophy of psychology: overkill of the antithesis and "functional fixity" toward any synthesis. Indeed, it is even tempting to attribute this polarization to the American ethos. American universities are unsurpassed in domiciled coexistence of *antithetical psychologists* but are hardly implicated in fostering confluence and synthesis of *antithetical views*. Such "planning" obviously cannot be programmed outside but must be arrived at inside. It is time it was.

Willing

"Will" is the second largest chapter in William James' 28-chapter *Principles* (1890)—106 pages. No such chapter will be found—the topic is hardly even mentioned—in American textbooks of psychology in the last twenty-five years, although Soviet textbooks continue to feature it. Pavlov originally related the "physiology" of voluntary action to reinforcement conditioning and to Krasnogorsky's (1911) passive-movement classical conditioning (*Wednesdays,* 1949, Vol. 1, pp. 225-226; original date, May 24, 1932) but later stated specifically: "Involuntary action can become voluntary only with the aid of the second-signal system" (Vol. 1, p. 337; original date, May 24, 1933). Pavlov was very much impressed with the Hunter and Hudgins 1934 report of conditioning pupillary contractions to words and thoughts (ibid.), extolling it at length when I visited him in 1934. As is known, the experiment has not been replicated, and it is, at any rate, an incomplete paradigm of a voluntary act. Since the contractions were elicited only by specific words and thoughts and not by a mere desire or "will" to contract, they are comparable to subjects' invoking salivation by thinking of food rather than to the regular willing of motor action. However, an extensive, six-series study by Lisina (1957, 1958, 1960) in Zaporozhets' Moscow University laboratory with vasomotor conditioning and cognition in 43 subjects and "more than 1000" experimental sessions, each including approximately 10 trials, provides such a paradigm—and data that by all tokens are reliable.

Four series of the study will be considered: one in which delivery of a moderately painful electric shock to two of the subjects' fingers produced vasoconstriction, but occasionally, after a while, vasodilation, which was then and there rewarded by removal of the shock (Skinner's negative reinforcement); another in which, in addition, an illuminated indicator of the vasomotion permitted the subjects to see when the shock was terminated (reinforcement plus knowledge of results); a third in which vasoconstriction to a light plus a sound increasing in intensity was punished by a shock but with the shock omitted when the same light and a decreasing sound produced vasodilation (differential and no doubt cognized punishment); and a fourth in which the subjects first (*a*) were trained to become aware of and discriminate between the two kinds of vasomotion by applying both vasoconstrictive and vasodilating stimuli and correcting their verbal designation, and then (*b*) were asked to constrict or dilate their vessels at the experimenter's request or the subjects' thought (cognition and instruction as means of volition). All vasomotor reactions were digital and were recorded photoplethysmographically.

The results were clear-cut. No subject in the first series learned to dilate his blood vessels in response to the shock. All subjects in the second series learned it to the extent that dilation became substantially more frequent than constriction. All in the third series increased the frequency of vasodilation in response to the light and decreasing sound. And all in the fourth series were able to constrict or dilate vessels at will. Figures 65 and 66 present the data of one subject in each series. It should be added that the subjects' verbal reports were quite similar to those reported in Ach's *"analyses of will reactions"* (1905, 1935): no special phenomenal content, but clear recognition of when "willing" occurs. The phenomenal recognition of willing suggests the merit of searching for possible specific electrophysiological correlates of "will", which is exactly what Gilden, Vaughan, and Costa (1966) found. Their data, presented in Figure 67, show marked summated EEGs one second prior to EMG manifestations of fist contraction and foot dorsiflexion in seven subjects (records of two others were said to be similar). The potentials begin as slow negative shifts, followed by abrupt negative and then positive shifts. Thus, here is another area of definitive research in the subjective-neural niveau. The results are *to an extent* similar to those of Walter et al. (1964, 1965), in which subjects were asked to respond with a motor reaction to the second of two associated stimuli.

Lisina's positive data that knowledge of results may bring about learned control of vasomotion do not (by themselves) validate her negative finding that without such knowledge reinforcement conditioning is ineffective. Rather, in light of recent evidence (pp. 85, 104, 171), her experiment suggests (*a*) the existence of two levels of control, cognitive mediated by symbols and noncognitive attained through simple conditioning, and (*b*) the consequent thesis that only the symbolic control is voluntary in being (1) independent of the activation of particular stimuli, (2) unaffected by extinction, and (3) phenomenally, and apparently also neurally, distinct. And, of course, noncognitive control is an outcome of not only reinforcement but also classical conditioning, as demonstrated by Pshonik specifically with respect to vasomotion, and by other, notably Soviet experimenters in a wide variety of noncognitive reactions (p. 115 and elsewhere), and as is no doubt true for common toilet control in man and higher animals.

The first experiment in acquiring voluntary control was, in fact, performed in an American laboratory—Bair (1901) trained twelve students of the University of Michigan to wiggle their ears. All twelve attained control in 1 to 4 sessions, each consisting of four consecutive parts: (1) in-

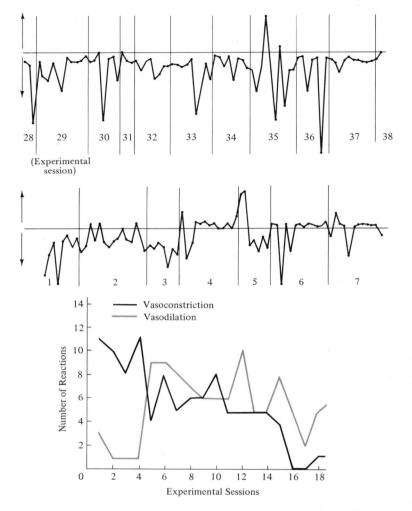

Figure 65 *Sample records of the development of voluntary control of vaso-motor reaction to an electric shock or a light in three groups of adult subjects, 5 to 8 each.* Top panel, upper segment—record of a subject in a group in which a shock was terminated when the reaction to it was vasodilative (Skinner's negative reinforcement); lower segment—subject informed, in addition, by an illuminated pointer which of the two reactions is followed by shock termination (reinforcement plus knowledge of results). Bottom panel—shock following vasoconstriction to a light-plus-a-tone-*increasing*-in-vibration but omitted when the reaction to the light-plus-a-*decreasing*-tone is dilative (differential punish-ment presumably cognized). In the top panel, records below the horizontal line disclose vasoconstriction, and above it, vasodilation. Bottom panel: vasocon-striction is represented by the black line and vasodilation by the gray line. No subject in the first group evidenced increases in vasodilation, but all subjects in the second and third groups did: in the second in response to shock, and in the third when a light was accompanied by a *decreasing* tone. (From Lisina, 1957, 1958)

voluntary evocation of the reaction through an attached electrode, (2) subject's voluntary effort to augment this evocation, (3) his effort to resist it, and, finally, (4) a test of his voluntary wiggling. Tests were also made of the effects of training one ear on the reactions of the other, and of the subjects' ability to wiggle only one at a time. Illustrative kymographic records are presented in Figure 68, in which may be seen the gradual development of voluntary control, its automatic transfer from ear to ear, and the extra training needed to wiggle only one ear. It should also be added that the data from one subject who underwent 29 complete trials after first learning voluntary control demonstrate that the mean magnitudes of the wiggle in evoked, evoked-against-resistance, and voluntary periods hardly differed—only the mean of involuntary + voluntary facilitation was somewhat higher. The respective scores were: 3.0, 2.8, 2.9, and 3.6 millimeters.

Even more patently, recent American tendencies to equate voluntary ac-

Figure 66 *Subject trained to effect at will vasodilation (upper panel) and vasoconstriction (lower panel) through cognized discrimination and self-instruction —the subject was asked to identify the nature of his vasomotion in response to randomly presented vasodilative and vasoconstricted stimuli, and his errors were corrected by the experimenter. Voluntary control follows quickly correct discrimination, vasodilation requiring considerably more training than vasoconstriction.* (From Lisina, 1960)

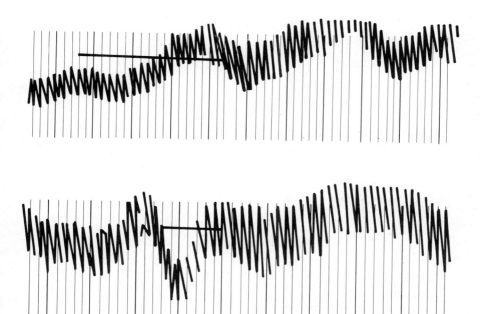

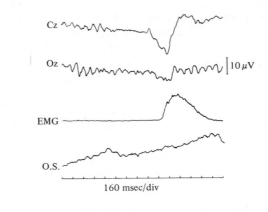

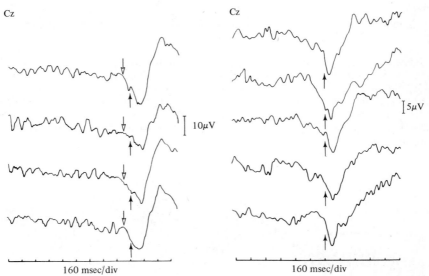

Figure 67 *Summated EEGs prior to EMGs in the voluntary contractions of the extremities of seven subjects.* All traces are based on 100 samples. Upper panel —dorsiflexion of the left foot of one subject (Cz and Oz—locations of electrodes; O.S.—potential below the left eye). Lower left—fist contraction in another subject; Cz—location of electrode. Lower right—same contraction in five other subjects. Unfilled arrows—beginning of abrupt negative deflection; black arrows— onset of EMG. (From Gilden, Vaughan, and Costa, 1966)

tion with operant or emitted behavior are, in the present view, counterproductive. Setting up voluntary action as a nativistic category of phyletic antiquity and not as a learned achievement of man extends a back-door welcome to nineteenth-century mentalism and earlier voluntarism, no matter how newly sliced and defined.

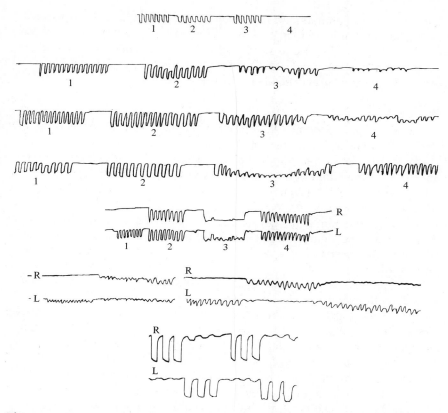

Figure 68 *Sample records of twelve college students learning to wiggle their ears.* In first five panels: 1—involuntary evocation of the reaction through attached electrode; 2—subjects' voluntary efforts to augment the evocation; 3—their resistance to it; 4—voluntary wiggling. Panel 5—automatic transfer of training from left to right ear. Panels 6, 7, and 8—gradual successful learning to wiggle only one ear at a time. (From Bair, 1901)

THE ONTOGENY OF SYMBOLING: SAMPLE EXPERIMENTS

Regrettably, space prevents citation of any substantial number of experiments on symboling and thinking beyond those already presented. Available American and Soviet literature is vast,[32] and relating a representative group to the author's position would take a volume by itself. Still, to main-

[32] See Anderson and Ausubel, 1965; Dixon and Horton, 1968; Duncan, 1967; Harper et al., 1964; Jacobovitz and Miron, 1967; McGuigan, 1966; and Voss, 1969, for portions of the former—and Gvozdev, 1961; Kopnin and Vilnitsky, 1964; Landa, 1966; Leont'yev, 1959; Luria, 1956, 1958; Ponomarev, 1960; Rayevsky, 1958; Rubinshteyn, 1958; Shemyakin, 1960; Shorokhova, 1966; Slobin, 1966; and Vygotsky, 1934, 1954, 1960, for segments of the latter.

tain the book's commitment, two additional series of sample experiments on human symboling-thinking will be presented: one Soviet and one American, both with children and both empirically representative of the evolutionary dynamics of mind's capstone—yet theoretically distinctive in their respective Pavlovian and neo-behavioristic approaches.

Kol'tsova's Series

Kol'tsova, the head of a laboratory of Higher Nervous Activity of the Pavlov Institute of Physiology of the USSR Academy of Sciences (Leningrad), has studied primarily the "higher operations" of the higher nervous activity of infants and young children (1949, 1958, 1960, 1961a, 1961b, 1961c, 1961d, 1962, 1963, 1965a, 1965b, 1967). The theoretical framework of Kol'tsova's laboratory is germanely related to Sechenov's general views of the relation of thought to speech and to Pavlov's specific precept that "words, the signals of signals of speech, are in essence abstractions of reality and means of generalization [involving] a new principle of neural action" (1933, p. 293).

The eyeblinks of ten 240- to 250-day-old nursery infants were conditioned to the sound of the word *kisa* ("kitty") plus the sight and, as a rule, also the touch of a plush toy kitten (airpuff to the eye as the US; see Brackbill, 1960, and Yevdokimov and Zaklyakova, 1962, for descriptions of apparatus and technique). In one group of five subjects, the toy kitten was placed in front of the subjects seated at a table and the experimenter pronounced *kisa,* always with the same intonation. In another group, the presentation of the toy varied in four ways—on the table, within ready sight above the table, within sight and touch on the floor, and among other toys on the floor with the infant alongside—and the word was pronounced alternately by the experimenter and the medical nurse and with varying intonations. Except when the toy was held high, the infants invariably touched it.

The results show that the first group became conditioned to the combined stimulus in fewer trials—7 to 15 versus 30 to 45 trials—*but the word became an independent CS very much faster in the second group*—in several weeks versus several months—disclosing the requisite of a varied S-R milieu for word potency. Interspersed tests demonstrated that at first the separate CR efficacy of the word was very insignificant compared to that of sight-and-touch of the toy but that in the course of training it gained strength to the extent that it alone evoked the CR. Moreover, *when the blink CR to the "kisa" was extinguished, the inactivated sensory CSs of sight-and-touch recovered their strength and evoked it, and when "kisa" was restored by airpuff pairings, sight-and-touch failed again.* (Presumably, this sensory-verbal rivalry is characteristic of only the initial stage of language acquisition, even if both Pavlov and Freud postulated some relatively permanent either-or relation between the two realms.)

In two other experiments, Kol'tsova investigated the generalization and differentiation of the second-signal-system, in essence comparing these in conditioning and thinking, a glaring void in American experimental psychology. In the first experiments, she taught ten 14- to 15-month-old nursery infants, in 1500 trials during two months, to select dolls of different sizes, shapes, colors, and material from a number of other related toys in response to the words "Give me a doll." The infants, who had had no experience with dolls, were divided into two equal groups. In one, the doll was accompanied 500 times each by the statements "Here is a doll," "Take the doll," and "Give me the doll" and the infants' corresponding motor reactions. In the other, 30 different statement-reaction units of 50 trials each were used: the first three plus "Lift the doll," "Cover the doll," "Rock the doll," "Seat the doll," "Look for the doll," and the like. In the test trials, the second group was clearly superior in selecting a variety of dolls from among a variety of related toys—a performance contrasting with simple conditioning, in which it would be expected that conditioning 3 reactions in 500 trials each would be more efficient than conditioning of 30 reactions in 50 trials each, particularly with such young subjects and no biological reinforcement.

Kol'tsova's second experiment in the area corroborated the findings of the first, with significant augmentations. The subjects were 18 to 20 months old, the test object was a book with which the children had had no experience, and the total number of trials was only 20. Nine subjects were divided into three groups: one in which only one book was shown and touched; another with 20 different books and the same treatment; and a third with one book and 20 different motor reactions of the type used in the first experiment. In the post-experimental tests of selecting a variety of books from among a variety of related objects, the third group was most successful, the second only partly so, and the first a total failure. The special significance of these data is that (*a*) word-integrates may attain full adequacy in so few trials and (*b*) variability of kinesthesis is much more efficacious than that of vision. And here the data surely do not follow the laws of simple conditioning. For the most successful group, one stimulus was associated once with 20 different reactions of no special biological potency.

Finally, although they are only tangentially related to symboling, it is tempting to cite also two highly instructive experiments on the production and conditioning of rudimentary speech sounds in 52 two- to eight-month-old infants from the same laboratory (Lyakh, 1968a, 1968b). In the first part of the first experiment with 18 subjects, the experimenter, facing the infant lying on a padded table, articulated, somewhat exaggeratedly, the vowels "a" and "oo" (Russian "y") without actually saying the sounds for 2 seconds, at 5-second intervals, 6 to 10 trials a day. The infants began to imitate the articulation—opening the mouth or rounding it—in a mean of 8.9 trials (range 1 to 25) and to *spontaneously* voice the vowels in a mean of 17.7 trials (range 5 to 49). Most interestingly, the two- to four-month-olds did better than the four- to eight-month-olds (equal number in each group): respective means of 5.7 versus 12.2 for the articulation and 11.9 versus 23.3 for voicing the sounds. A period in which the experimenter stabilized the infants' performance through articulation plus vowel utterances followed. Then came a period of testing the effects of excluding the visible articulation: for one group of infants, the experimenter's face was covered with a gauze mask while she was uttering the sounds; for another, her face was in full view but immobile and the vowels were produced by a phonograph. The learned reaction was *extinguished* in both groups at different rates: means of 5.5 and 7.4 trials for the sound and articulation in the Gauze Mask Group and 9.25 and 13.4 trials in the Phonograph Group. The intensity of the sound was regulated to 40 decibels, and the intonation was even throughout. The differences between the group means were statistically significant at $p < .05$.

Simple and differential eyelid conditioning were studied in the remaining 34 infants, divided into three groups. The positive stimulus was in all groups "a" and the differential "oo"; but in the first group they were articulated without sound, in the second, sounded without visible articulation, and in the third, visibly articulated and sounded. The respective results for the three groups show: (*a*) well-developed simple conditioning in 13 to 65, 50 to 134, and 4 to 32 trials; (*b*) differential conditioning after 24 to 42 applications of the differential stimulus in the first group and 10 to 36 in the third, with no differentiation in the second group after 104 applications of the differential stimulus. The differences among the three groups in speed of acquisition of simple conditioning were statistically significant at $p < .05$, as was the difference between the differential conditioning of the first and third groups, and of course that between either group and the second with no differentiation.

Four significant conclusions are conspicuous in the data of the two experiments. (*a*) Infants' acquisition of the rudiments of speech sounds are very much affected by imitative training and need not be left to mere "natural" reinforcement of "spontaneous" vocalization. (*b*) The training is effective as early as 2 to 4 months of life, indeed more effective than during the 4- to 8-months period. (*c*) Seeing the articulation of a sound, and not hearing it, is paramount for the infants' imitative reproduction, and, at least in that period, the sight is a more efficient CS for eliciting another reaction. (*d*) The *motor* reproduction of articulation plays a leading role in the learning of speech almost at its very origin—fully in accord with the prime significance of kinesthesis in its later generalization and differentiation and the entire dynamics of symboling and thinking. Needless to say, the mechanisms of spontaneous vocalization and S^D discrimination are not denied—but they are, as noted in Chapter 5, later evolvements.

See Figure 69 for results with two infants: photographs—3-month-old's imitating articulation of "a" and "oo" ("y" in Russian); lower panel—

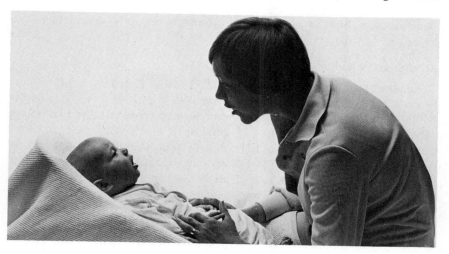

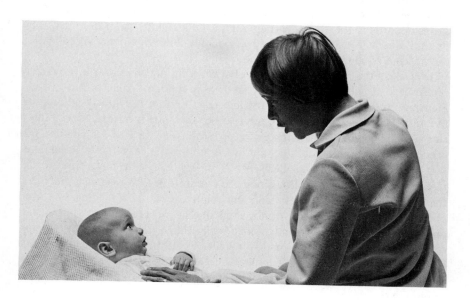

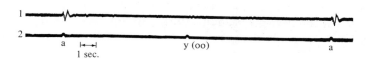

Figure 69 *Sample record of 2- to 4-month-old infants learning (a) to produce vowels "a" and "oo" [Russian "y"] through imitating experimenter's nonvoiced articulation, and (b) to blink to "a" but not to "oo."* Photographs—imitative articulation and vowel production of a 3-month-old. Lower panel—blinking to "a" and not to "oo" of a 4-month-old. (Photos from Lyakh, 1968a; graph, adapted from Lyakh, 1968b)

4-month-old's blinking in response to experimenter's articulation (no sound) of "a" and not at all to "oo."

Kendler and Kendler's Series

Kendler and Kendler (1959, 1962, 1966), Kendler, Kendler, and Learned (1962), Kendler, Kendler, and Wells (1960), and T. Kendler (1964) compared the mastery of and preference for reversal versus nonreversal discrimination shifts in 736 children 3 to 10 years of age. In reversal shifts, the subjects, presented with four stimuli, two differing in size and two differing in brightness, are first trained, for example, to react to the larger stimulus regardless of brightness, and then to reverse and react to the smaller (or shift from smaller to larger, brighter to duller, or duller to brighter). In nonreversal shifts, the change is from one dimension to the other, say, from the larger regardless of brightness to the brighter regardless of size. In some experiments, the stimuli were inverted cups; lifting one of the cups uncovered the reinforcement (a marble), and only one kind of shift was reinforced. In others, with squares mounted on a pasteboard as the to-be-learned relata, either shift was reinforced, and the children had a choice. The effects of the children's overt verbalization on the kind of shift were also studied.

It is clear that reversal shifts involve reacting negatively to a previously reinforced stimulus and positively to a nonreinforced one within one dimension, and nonreversal shifts involve reacting to a previously ignored dimension and difference. In common sense, the former means "reversing a rule" and the latter "changing its basis," and, needless to say, if the children were first told that "the marble is under the larger cup" and later that "it is under the smaller" or "the brighter," the outcome would scarcely warrant inquiry. But since the children had to discover the rules, the course of their discovery and the relative ease of replacing one kind of rule by another are no doubt constituents of problem-solving mechanisms. And, more importantly, since with related designs rats master nonreversal shifts much more readily (Kelleher, 1956) and college students reversal ones (Buss, 1956; Kendler and D'Amato, 1955; and others), the Kendler and Kendler data bear significantly on the evolution of symboling in human ontogeny.

Heretofore, sample experiments have been scrutinized individually. However, the Kendlers have summarized their main experiments themselves in a theoretical publication (1962), so, for lack of space, what will be presented here is a summary of their summary and a scrutiny of their views. Figure 70 brings together five of their figures. The top left panel is a diagram of their main design in studying the two kinds of shifts, while the top right panel shows a special design used to study the effects of verbalization on the reversal of a "larger than" discrimination. Both designs are self-explanatory: *plus* signs mean correct stimuli and reinforced reactions, and *minus* signs incorrect and nonreinforced ones. The left mid-

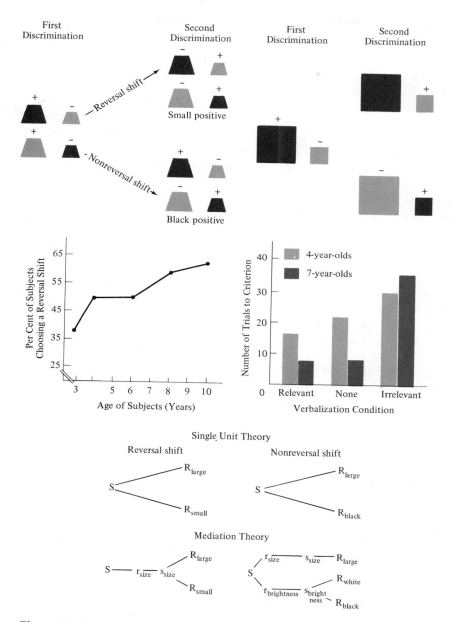

Figure 70 *Reversal vs. nonreversal shifts of size and brightness discrimination in 3- to 10-year-old children.* Top left panel—main design in studying the two kinds of shifts; top right panel—special design used in the study of the effects of verbalization on the choice of shifts of "larger than" discrimination. *Plus* signs denote correct stimuli and reinforced reactions; *minus* signs, incorrect ones. Middle left panel—increase in the percentage of children choosing reversal shifts from 3 to 10 years of age. Middle right panel—comparing the effects of verbalization on reversal shifts of size discrimination in 4- and 7-year-old children. Bottom panel—mediated generalization interpretation of increases in reversal shifts. (From Kendler and Kendler, 1962; additional explanation in text.)

dle panel shows the steady increase in the percentage of children choosing reversal shifts from 3 to 10 years of age—specifically, from 37.5 to 62.5 per cent. The right middle panel, comparing the effects of verbalization in reversal shifts of size discrimination in 4- and 7-year-old children, calls for a bit of explanation. Each group was divided into three subgroups: one was required in the original discrimination to name the *relevant* dimension of the correct stimulus—"large" or "small"; another, to name the *irrelevant* dimension—"black" or "white"; and a third, not required to say anything. As may be seen, relevant verbalization increased reversal shifts (fewer trials to criterion) only in the 4-year-olds, with no effect in the 7-year-olds—presumably because they effected the appropriate verbalization themselves—while irrelevant verbalization interfered considerably with reversals in both groups. (The Kendlers did not administer any verbalization questionnaire.)

The bottom panel in Figure 70 presents the Kendlers' interpretation of the evolutionary trend toward easier reversal and harder nonreversal shifts in terms of " 'single unit [S-R] theory' which accurately represents the behavior of rats" and " 'mediation [S-R] theory' . . . required for the concept learning of articulate humans" (1962, p. 8). In organisms that do not command mediating responses "the difference between . . . the incorrect habit and the to-be-correct habit is much greater for the reversal, as compared with the nonreversal shifts" (p. 7). But in those that do command mediation: "A reversal shift enables the subject to utilize the same mediated response. Only the overt response has changed. A nonreversal shift, on the other hand, required [requires] the acquisition of a *new* mediated response, the cues of which have to be attached to a *new* overt response" (p. 8; italics in original).

So far so good. But, unfortunately, the Kendlers' concept of mediation teems with parochial systematic commitments. Three neo-Hullian articles of faith are asseverated. First—a caveat that it "would be unwise, and strategically short-sighted, to *identify* mediational events with introspective reports or language behavior or other observable events. The 'validity' of the mediational mechanism does not depend on being coordinated with observable events but depends instead on being utilized in a successful explanatory system" (p. 6). Leave off, that is, observations, and plug loopholes with "logicals," which by now is not only dubious psychology but questionable philosophy as well. Just why should language-behavior mediation in "articulate humans" not be coordinated with its observable attributes and kind of learning? Chapter 9 demonstrated how interpreting sensory preconditioning in observable properties of conditioned orienting reflexes, instead of in inferable R_Gs and S_Gs, was paramount in predicting the specific parameters of the phenomenon. And while I cannot cite direct experimental data that observable attributes of symboling—which the Kendlers acknowledge is the matrix of human mediation—favor reversal versus nonreversal shifts in discrimination, there certainly is a lot of related general evidence in the area. Consider the fact that similarity and contrast have for centuries been classed as one continuum, that opposites are the most frequent responses in free association tests and the fastest in controlled association, that semantic generalization may be as high to antonyms as to synonyms. And, with apologies for a personal example, I can recall that at the age of 4 my daughter's most frequent questions to my telling her that "Something is . . ." or "Something does . . ." were "What is not. . .?" or "What does not do . . .?" Such "dialectics" seem integral to what was called earlier "logicemic" or judgmental thinking.

Second comes the avowal that "the implicit stimulus and response events [in mediation] obey the same principles that operate in observable S-R relationships" (p. 6). This is of course the egalitarian approach to learning, at variance with Pavlov's main doctrine of two qualitatively different signal systems, the findings of Kol'tsova quoted in the preceding section, the entire tenor of evolutionary levels in the present book, and the views of many other Western psychologists and philosophers. Just how does this egalitarian approach accord with the Kendlers' approved quotation of Luria that speech "organizes [the child's] own experience and regulates his actions" (p. 9)? Organization and regulation bear with them specific and more efficacious qualia. The cortex could not regulate properly the subcortex if the cytoarchitectures of the two were identical! (Incidentally, the Kendlers' use of *"vertical* and *horizontal* processes" is a *"reversal"* of that of the late McGeoch, who in his presidential address to the American Psychological Association in 1936—"The Vertical Dimensions of the Mind"— meant by *vertical* time-accrued or learning changes and not, as the Kendlers do, simultaneous concurrence of different reactions to the same stimulus.)

Third, there is the Kendlers' bypassing the possible role of nonverbal perceptual mechanisms. It might be that not only smart kindergarten children but also apes, monkeys, and even dogs and pigs may tend to easier mastery of reversal shifts than do rats. A noted Soviet neuroanatomist reports that the cytoarchitecture of rats and rabbits is the most primitive among mammals, less differentiated even than that of kangaroos, anteaters, and hedgehogs (Kukuyev, 1953). Again, I must refer to Chapter 9 and the coexistence and interaction of conditioning and perception. And I am also tempted to parallel Chapter 9 that "in the end of days, S-R and S-S theories will lie down together . . . not hurt nor destroy" with an excerpt from St. Matthew and St. Luke: "Render unto Caesar the things which be Caesar's and unto God the things which be God's."

SUMMARY

1. Symboling is best defined as an *associative formation of communicable referential replicates of concepts and percepts.* "Communicable" implies that symbols are *behavioral effector reactions* and "referential" that they involve *neurocognitive meaning,* while the "replicates of percepts and

concepts" predicate another neurocognitive dimension—*abstraction.* Concepts differ from percepts in being integrated reactions to different portions of the environment and not just to one particular portion.

2. Symboling is almost exclusively an evolutionary fulfillment of man. Only a modicum of it has recently been taught to a chimpanzee after prolonged training. Yet human language and its organization represent the behavioral and not the neurocognitive phase of symboling and may well be altogether unsymbolic in early ontogeny and obviously also in many utterances of mature individuals.

3. Experiments in semantic and phonetic conditioning suggest that originally particular words, or phonemes, comprised both the meaning *and* the behavior of symbols but that later a *sui generis* higher semantic level, presumably mediated by higher-level neural action and linked to the action of arrays of lower phonetic levels, came into being.

4. The experiments and related logic also indicate that the neurocognitive meaning and behavioral language differ in the developmental dynamics of their learned organization. Meaning, an afferent system, becomes more and more configured and abstract in quality; language, an efferent one, increases mainly in quantity.

5. Two levels of semantic organization may be discerned: (*a*) related meanings of different words are integrated into unitary configures or *sememes* subserved by these words; (*b*) *sememes* interact with each other to form *logicemes,* the unitary meanings of logical propositions expressed equivalently by a number of linguistic sentences.

6. Pilot experimental analysis of two modern European languages, English and Russian, by a conditioning technique discloses that *predicative verbs* and *direct objects* command much more import in sentences than *subjects* and *qualifying adjectives.* The unequal imports are by all tokens an outcome of learned sememic interactions and not behavioral specifics of *sui generis* genetics—contravened more generally, by (*a*) the recency of this planet's evolution of language and (*b*) the fact that a modicum of it was taught to a chimpanzee.

7. Learned meanings and concepts are the units of thinking, and learned behavioral symbols are the means of communicating it. Thinking also involves, however, direction by learned sets and goals which become, or may be at the start, nonsymbolic or even noncognized.

8. Experimental introspection has long "proven" that the phenomenal core of thinking, unlike that of perceiving, is not imagery but direct apprehension. Evolutionary considerations suggest that such apprehension is a higher level of phenomenal experience which a modicum of objective evidence of conditioned semantic generalization supports.

9. Numerous allegations of the existence of high-level "unconscious thinking" are much more readily construed as outcomes of recovery from fatigue or disengagement from "functional fixity" than as "creative unconsciousness" and "illumination" in the wake of "incubation." And it seems

true also that practice reduces and nullifies consciousness in only portions and not whole acts of thinking. More exactly, practice alters and enhances the economy of consciousness, broadening it and centering it in key launching and consummating phases while utilizing made-unconscious processes as subserving mechanisms. Yet all this by no means negates the vast *ancillary* effects of unconscious neural action on thinking.

10. Planning is an aspect of thinking in which directedness is most prominent. "Willing" is a process through which symbols gain control over somatic and visceral reactions, and which, unlike the control through conditioning, is neither dependent on the activation of particular stimuli nor subject to extinction. There is evidence of EEG changes during the experience of "willing" prior to any motor manifestations of its effects.

11. While primates, and to a much lesser extent some subprimates, may learn to react differentially to concepts and thus are evidencing abstractive capacity, a view that they are thereby able to think is hardly warranted. Since they lack replicative behavioral symbols, they obviously cannot communicate what they learn, and since thereby they *ipso facto* lack their meanings, they may well be devoid also of the intraorganismic units of thinking. To say that higher animals think in images, which they presumably possess, is equally contraindicated, if for no other reason than that even in man the existence of such exclusive thinking has not been demonstrated and is not readily demonstrable.

12. Soviet experiments (Kol'tsova, 1967 and earlier) show that two- to four-month-old infants learn to produce simple vowels through imitating the experimenter's nonvoiced articulation and that the learning is gradually extinguished when the vowels are then voiced but not articulated. Other experiments done in the same laboratory have proven that in one- to two-year-old infants second-signal (i.e., verbal or symbolic) abstracting does not follow the laws of simple conditioning and generalization. The number of ways in which a stimulus object is handled, and not repetitions of particular S-Rs, is the critical parameter. Nor is reinforcement or pairing with primary biological USs needed.

13. Normally, symboling greatly affects perceiving just as perceiving does conditioning. American experiments (Kendler and Kendler, 1962, and elsewhere) have revealed what may well be called a "dialectic" in the developmental dynamics of symboling in children 3 to 10 years of age. The older the children were, the more they were able to reverse the rules of their learned discrimination, in contrast to what the laws of simple conditioning would predict, and in line with the dominant and productive role of symboling. The experimenters' own neo-Hullian interpretation of their data is disputed.

CHAPTER ELEVEN

Epilogue

INTRODUCTORY COMMENT

Final chapters of books synthesizing experimental disciplines vary in their contents. Some strive primarily to epitomize what has already been said —to consolidate enunciated theses. Others suggest programs for new experiments and approaches to test the theses. Still others discuss their import to life situations—here, the educational, social, and clinical problems of understanding and managing man's mind. Finally, some explain why phases of the treated theme have not been considered.

This epilogue will involve briefly all four practices. Let it be said at the outset, however, that the present synthesis of the learning mind is unlike any other in drawing fully on the reasearch and thought of the differing traditions of East and West. Pavlovian and Thorndikian experiments and the postulates of Gestalt and semantics have been set within a Darwinian frame of continuity and novelty, free of language barriers and divisive methodological niceties. Pavlov's role is major—separating the lowest common denominator of traditional associationism in the connective behavior of animals from its unique integrative role in the language of man, and, to an extent, also from the special connectionism of Thorndike. Yet Pavlov did not cultivate Thorndike's distinctness (even as neo-behaviorists unduly inflated it), and he failed to note the systematic relevance of stimulus configuring to perceiving, orienting to sensing, and *sui generis* meanings to his second-signal system. To be sure, the predominant body of empirics underpinning these Darwinian considerations have come to light since his day.

REVIEW OF LEADING THESES

Learning and Mind

The title of Chapter 2, "Learning as the Groundwork of Mind in Evolution," is not meant to deny organized phenomenal experience—only to affirm that this experience is a neurocognitive evolvement of the organized neurobehavior of learning. Six propositions have been educed in later chapters to weigh the view.

(*a*) Lower types of simple-conditioning, or connective, learning, fully evident in lower animals and decorticate higher animals, may be effected in man without concomitant experience.

(*b*) Higher types of integrative learning, such as stimulus configuring, possible only in birds and mammals and abolished by higher-cortical ablations, closely parallel phenomenal configuring in human perception and imagery. Hence, an inference that perception and imagery are constituents of the minds of these higher animals.

(*c*) The higher integrative types do not seem, however, to influence too significantly the potency of lower connective learning in subprimates and may not be prepotent even in subhuman primates. The neural structures mediating higher integrative learning are in animals presumably less massive and less ingrained than those mediating the lower connective antecedents, although their relative role is obviously a positive function of evolutionary ascent.

(*d*) Human thinking rests on associative learning of behavioral symbols to communicate what is thought and on referential symbolic meanings as content, and commonly also on directional sets to guide it (planning). Even the highest primates do not naturally acquire behavioral symbols, vocal or gestural, to communicate what they learn, and they are thereby putatively unequipped with the referential meaning of symbols. Thus, they cannot be assumed to think in human fashion. The man-ape divide is very special.

(*e*) The evidence of the relation of connective to integrative learning in human ontogeny is meager and is complicated by the early advent of language in the human infant and his total immersion in a man-made language environment. Scientists have indeed missed by hundreds of thousands of years the opportunity for unqualified experimental studies and observations of the genesis of symbols and meanings. In animal ontogeny, integrative learning is evident much later than connective learning.

(*f*) Conditioned chainings of different reactions in man and higher animals are effector concatenations and not receptor configuring, and thus are not in essence correlates of learning to perceive.

The evolutionary view that organized phenomenal experience arises from learned behavior is open to two arguments: (*a*) Some simple perceiving and configuring is apparently innate; perceiving figure and ground and configuring sound ratios. (*b*) Human liminal consciousness is presumably also innate. The rebuttal must be indirect—related to current Soviet concepts of "natural conditioning" and "unconditioned signalization" as accounts of wide species-specific differences in simple conditionability of stimuli and reactions and the fact that reactions innate in some organisms need to be learned in others (Chapter 2). Liminal consciousness (irreducible sensations) will serve as an example. At one time, it may be supposed, organisms' reactions to their environment were not just consummatory but also what might be called consumptive: the organisms consumed parts of the environment or portions of them were consumed by it. In time, however, anticipatory sensory-orienting and preparatory-motor reactions were added, presumably through micromutational genic changes, yet formally similar to the juxtaposed pairing in conditioning. And these innate, relatively unorganized manifestations of the sensory-orienting reactions somehow became the correlates of liminal consciousness (empirical evidence in Gershuni et al.; see Chapter 9), and the antecedents of evolved configured organization of the reactions became the correlates of organized phenomenal experience in perception, whose occasional innateness may similarly be allied to what was called earlier (Chapter 9) "natural" configuring and "natural" sensory preconditioning. No attempt will be made, however, to collate in any way the genic and conditioning parallels—that reactions formed in remote ontogeny somehow become phyletic bequests—except to repeat that by far most of the neurocognition of perception and all of semantics are admittedly learned in ontogeny and thus unencumbered by the perennial puzzlement.

Learning and Evolution: Levels and Superlevels

A noted American psychologist remarked once that evolution may relate to the basic mechanism of learning no more than it does to mitosis, which produces the "obvious differences between the bodies of Rita Hayworth and an artichoke" (Miller, 1951, p. 376). The present book takes a diametrically opposite view. It invariably adheres to the basic learning model of neural interaction and transformation culminating in the brain, nature's most evolved and continually—indeed, acceleratedly—evolving integral. (Miss Hayworth is not only bigger than an artichoke; she is better.) Nor is the disparity just theoretic. A vast body of empirical data from both East and West attest to an evolving multiformity of the basics of learning—specifically to an ascending hierarchy of no less than eleven delineated levels: two nonassociative or preconditioned (habituation and sensitization), three of conditioning (inhibitory [punishing], classical, and reinforcing), three of perceiving (sensory-sensory learning [sensory preconditioning], configuring, and eductive learning), and three of thinking (symbosemic, sememic, and logicemic).

All levels share some characteristics, but each ascending level is novel in essence and in parameters is not reducible to or deducible from those preceding it, and there are clear phyletic and reactional divides between the levels. Coelenterates are readily habituated but cannot be conditioned. Prevertebrate chordates, such as amphioxi and ascidians, and spinal mammals habituate, become sensitized, but likewise are not conditionable (spinal frogs are). Gill extension in fighting fish is modified by inhibitory (punishing) and classical conditioning but not by reinforcement (reward) conditioning. Otherwise, however, lower vertebrates, including fish, manifest fully both classical and reinforcement conditioning, while most invertebrates (earthworms on) master classical conditioning and higher invertebrates the reinforcement type. On the other hand, sensory preconditioning and learned stimulus configuring is possible only in birds and mammals; eductive learning (Krushinsky's technique) in crows, magpies, dogs, and cats, but not in pigeons, chickens, ducks, and rabbits. And oddity learning and "learning sets" in general are largely primate exploits, and symboling an exclusive human achievement.

Inherent in the view is the tenet that lower evolutionary levels of learning coexist with and interact with higher ones; that while the higher, mediated by more recent neural acquisitions, are more efficient, the lower are more universal and less disruptable by untoward influences; and that the interaction is paralleled by that of the evolution of the brain. Moreover, for didactic convenience, the eleven learning levels might be compressed into four superlevels: *reactive,* comprising the two nonassociative levels; *connective*—the three of conditioning; *integrative*—the three of perceiving; and *symboling*—the three of thinking. The quaternary compression highlights the chief qualitative transformation of the process in its hundreds of millions of years of existence—namely, that connective conditioning, needing no encephalon and no cognition, is but one realm of learning, that the integrative learning of cognized and primarily cortical perceiving is another, and the capstone of learned symbolic thinking a third, with nonassociative or preconditioned mechanisms in the role of ultimate rudiments.

The Neural Substratum

While thousands of careful neurophysiological and neuromorphological experiments of the last decades have not yet pinpointed empirically the engram of even the simplest association of the learning mind, they certainly have provided direction to its theory. The very discovery of electroencephalographic conditioning casts grave doubt on the theoretics of Hull's "drive-stimulus reduction" and Guthrie's "movement-produced stimuli," even as its frequent occurrence prior to behavioral conditioning accords it a significant correlative and predictive (although not causative) status. Nor can there be any doubt that post-tetanic potentiation, anodal polarization, and rhythm assimilation relate to some mechanism of learning, even if their exact roles are still to be determined. Moreover, contemporary neurophysiology is sufficiently variegated to offer plausible mechanisms for the continuity and novelty of ascending levels of learning—the similarities and differences between habituation and inhibitory conditioning, sensitization and true conditioning, types of conditioning, configuring, and in the future, one hopes, also symboling. The counterproductiveness of "denervated" learning systems is becoming more and more glaring, notwithstanding the consideration that the field is as yet without a specific empirical neuromorphology.

312 · Mind in Evolution

Interoception

A significant portion of American neo-behaviorism has for some time been not only "denervated" but "eviscerated." Not Watson, of course. The viscera and glands were to him the wellsprings not only of emotions but also of unverbalized implicit habits—the core of the "myth of unconscious." In his day and for some time afterwards, he was surely on the right track and it is highly regrettable that neo-behaviorists have not followed—notably, that the "verbal conditioning" of their most prestigious spokesman led him to avow that "visceral conditioning" is but "internal physiology" of little "effect upon the surrounding world" (Skinner, 1953, p. 59). Compare Watson: *"We may earn our bread with the striped muscles but we win our happiness or lose it by the kind of behavior our unstriped muscles or guts lead us into"* (1928, p. 349).

By now, however, Watson's correct thesis should be emended. Unconscious action parallels much more closely visceral stimulation—i.e., interoception—than visceral reaction. Careful Soviet experiments of comparative liminal interoceptive and exteroceptive consciousness, in which human subjects swallowed rubber tubes with attached electrodes and pipettes while confronted with visual and auditory apparatus, have plainly demonstrated that *while the main exteroceptive continuum of stimuli is consciously supraliminal even if produced reactions are unconscious, that of interoception is unconscious even if the reactions produced are conscious.* Yet over one hundred experiments have shown that these unconscious events are fully conditionable—the intestine and uterus as "wise" as the eye and the ear (wisdom without knowledge, that is). And there is another paramount phase of the interoceptive-exteroceptive divide: the interoceptive stimuli are more limited in scope but patently more recurring in time and thus more constant in effect. Add to this (*a*) the fact that the interoceptive stimuli are obviously direct sequels of vital functioning—organismic *par excellence*—and (*b*) the evidence that even when coaction of interoceptive and exteroceptive conditioning is synergically directed, the outcome is more conflict than cooperation (cf. Uno, in press).

Ukhtomsky's Dominance

The principle is more universal than that of learning yet surely an overriding guideline to the latter's mechanisms and functioning. Neurally, it has yielded the two most significant leads to the basis of simple conditioning, and behaviorally, it is hard to avoid when total evidence is contemplated. It has surfaced only occasionally in the West, but it is rapidly gaining wide support in the Soviet Union. Consider that the very distinction between *modifying* and *modified* reactions is a commitment to a view that mind, unlike matter, develops through the interaction of unlike forces. Chemical interactions hardly involve such a distinction—yet theories of perception and thinking, personality and social behavior, and even economics and history often imply and even express it. This book has; however, dealt not with general implications but with specific operations of the leading attribute of mind in evolution. It is hoped that the demonstration was valid.

BROADENED RESEARCH AND AN ALTERED APPROACH

This section is directed primarily to the American learning enterprise—the continual decline of its earlier major systems despite the rapid growth of its store of new empirical information. The causes of the decline are evident: basic "laws" derived from a restricted area of subjects and methods, top-heavy and wide-open logical deductions or descriptive extrapolations, stress on similarities and disregard of differences, institutionalized reification of verbal definitions, etc. There has come to pass, in fact, a crisis in the chief systematics of current American psychology: a replicate, in a sense, of the aftermath of Titchener's engrossment in a "generalized mind" and several institutionalized ultimates—aggravated by a loss of a once unbounded faith in logical positivism. Or, in all, the sequelae of egalitarianism in a discipline in which hierarchical evolutionary dynamics of continuity and novelty are most distinctive, more so than in any other discipline.

It is clear, however, that while the book's evolutionary approach to the learning mind is anchored to a considerable body of solid experimental findings, much more is needed to fasten and enlarge the anchor. The climate in the past has not been conducive, and it should be altered by design. Several suggestions for the future follow.[33]

Empirical Diversity and Theoretic Hierarchization: Phyletic, Ecological, Ontogenetic, and Methodological

The constricted range of species used in the predominant majority of American experiments of animal learning scarcely needs documentation. Moreover, when species are diverse, learning tasks are not as a rule of comparable increasing difficulty to permit tracking increasing mastery in evolutionary ascent. The common Soviet practice of making phyletic com-

---

[33] In part, the section is relevant also to Soviet codifications of the field—inadequate particularization and systematization of general evolutionary views, gaping lacunae between Pavlov's two signal systems, and uneven distribution of experimental concern. Moreover, there is the special patent shortcoming in use of statistical inference so incongruous with the advanced level of Soviet mathematics and most impressive Russian contributions to the theory of probability (Chebyshev, Markov, Kolmogorov, Gnedenko). The not uncommon poorly organized and incomplete reportage is likewise not in keeping with the traditional tenor of Russian writing. There is evidence that both deficiencies are to an extent being redressed—but not enough to dispel irksome qualms about the conclusiveness of a number of reported findings. Note, however, the discussion of Soviet methodology of sensory preconditioning and configuring in Chapter 9 and of conditioning in general elsewhere (Razran, 1965d).

parisons of sensory preconditioning, stimulus configuring, and "extrapolation" (Krushinsky) should be paralleled, and Bitterman's evolutionary excursions and the use of Harlow's higher-level "learning sets" fully expanded and collated with Soviet approaches. Likewise, the wide species-specific differences in *simple* conditionability of particular stimuli and reactions discussed in Chapter 2 must become integrals of America's psychology of learning. The ecologists' tenet that the unlearned models the learned does not warrant the ethologists' "release-mechanism" dictum that learning effects are minimal. As noted earlier, "the ratio of ontogenetic learning plasticity to phyletic unlearned fixity is a growing function of evolution" (p. 21).

Recent American, Soviet, and Czech experimenters have established that human neonates master the basic aspects of conventional classical and reinforcement conditioning. Their further mind evolution may thus be expected to involve higher levels of sensory-sensory integrative learning. The data of Kasatkin, Mirozyants, and Khokhitva (1953) on conditioned orientation in two-and-a-half-month-old infants, possible only in relatively mature specimens of higher animals, and Lyakh's spectacular addition that infants of this age learn by observation to imitate successfully the articulation and production of simple vowels, are clear empirical proof of the logical supposition. *The superior specificities of the human mind must be studied systematically while it is still subverbal (or subsymbolic)—uncomplicated by the second surrogate tier of behavioral evolution.*

Then, when the verbal or symbolic realm begins to gain ascendancy, the systematic exigency is for a hierarchy of experiments to separate the dynamics of the semantic and phonetic aspects, the empirical feasibility of which has, again, already been demonstrated on a small scale in both Soviet and American laboratories. Kol'tsova's and her many associates' probes of the uniqueness of the child's associative linguistic acquisitions and generalization, and the many American analyses of "learning sets" in children are rootless otherwise. The essence of the oneness as well as the discreteness of language and thought—surrogate behavior and meaning—must not be left to philosophy and ingenious hypotheses. Experimental psychology possesses the tools to aid in unraveling the two and should start when they are still in their initial stages. And, incidentally, there is merit also in tracing evolutionary progression from simple conditioning to integrative sensory learning in infrahuman ontogeny, only the beginnings of which have so far been reported by several Soviet experimenters.

Finally, there is the intricacy of the basic objective attributes of configuring, the posited underlying mechanism of both perceiving and thinking. In large measure, the numerous Soviet experimenters have only posed the problem. Wholly uninvestigated systematic queries are: (*a*) Is component inactivation a temporary inhibition or a permanent disruption? (*b*) Is the inactivation neural or only behavioral? (*c*) What are the characteristics of learned configuring of sensory-orienting reactions in animals when it is unaccompanied by conventional conditioning? (Its mechanism in human subjects is obscured by verbal integration.) (*d*) When do repeated juxtapositions of sensory-orienting reactions result in sensory-sensory learning and when do they produce new configures? An overriding question.

And, above all, there are the two vast tasks of integrating the empirics of learned objective configuring with experiential *Gestaltung* and of integrating phonetic versus semantic conditioning with rote versus meaningful learning (Underwood and Schulz, 1960, among others). And needless to say, my two main hypotheses call for valid experimental demonstration: (*a*) that configuring and perceiving are organized proprioceptive transforms of sensory information, and (*b*) that meaning is a configured hierarch of *sui generis* neurocognitive existents. Both are testable and, I posit, not alien to the main trend of contemporary thought. Then, there is the need to (*a*) replicate and extend Soviet experiments on the connaturalness of orienting and sensing and the conversion of subsensory- into sensory-orienting, and to (*b*) verify my third hypothesis that unorganized liminal consciousness and its behavioral base of mere orienting are the evolutionary antecedents of the organized consciousness of perception and objective configuring. Each curve of the expanding evolutionary spiral of the systematics of learning is cogent, and each fits a particular position.

Resolution of the Classical-Instrumental (Type I-Type II) Conditioning Dichotomy

Begun by Miller and Konorski and fixed somewhat differently by Skinner, the absolutistic dichotomy has by all counts stimulated a multitude of solid research efforts. Yet it is also a classic example of the confining effects of a theory (and a theory it is!)—of theory-bound research. Consider, for instance, the fact that for several decades experimentalists failed to question the dictum, noted by Miller and Konorski in 1928 and formalized even more by Skinner in 1938 and by Mowrer in the same year, that autonomic reactions are not subject to instrumental conditioning. Only very recently have some plucky spirits tried it and come up with sufficient incontrovertible evidence to have Konorski state in 1969 that the dictum "seems now to be seriously undermined by . . . most important research" (p. 189). The theorists' human need to be different was thereby served but not the scope of the research. Moreover, dichotomic absolutism provokes a reverse human tendency—to disregard relative differences and convert the dichotomy into an absolute oneness. Witness Hilgard's and Kendom Smith's denial of classical conditioning, even as Mowrer, and Rescorla and Solomon, and Sheffield attribute to it all the basics of the instrumental type. Long ago Pavlov acknowledged that Thorndike's technique yields more permanent associative connections than his own, an admission which, bolstered by the large body of empirical evidence documented in Chapter 8, led me for some time to consider instrumental or reinforcement conditioning a higher evolutionary level than its classical antecedent—specifically to conclude in Chapter 8: *"While Pavlov disclosed the basic attributes of conditioning, Skinner has demonstrated their higher and more complex level of evistence"* (p. 170).

Skinner's absolutistic dichotomy of unconditioned emitted and elicited behavior is likewise open to grave questions. Chapter 5 brought out (*a*) the extensive evidence of Volokhov and Sedláček that the emitted is a later developmental stage than the elicited and (*b*) the experiments of Sedláček, Franzisket, von Holst and von Saint Paul, Brackbill, Fitzgerald, and Lintz, and Lockhart, showing that it may be produced by repeated stimulations or classical temporal conditioning. (Skinner's own evidence of the acquisition of "superstitious" behavior is, in fact, a case in point—and it merits mentioning that the results of von Holst and von Saint Paul were obtained by direct brain stimulations.) Hinde's statement that "there is no sharp dividing line between spontaneous [emitted] and stimulus-elicited activities" (1966, p. 226) is well said, with the telling addition that the former may be either a "natural" evolvement or a learned outcome of the latter. To be sure, more searching may be needed to establish the position fully, yet the available data are convincing.

Concomitant Neural and Interoceptive Action

American S-R psychology begun by Thorndike and continued by Watson has since been bifurcated. (*a*) Tolman elevated the O in Woodworth's commonsense S-O-R expansion to the status of intervening variables, which Hull and Spence, unencumbered by cognition and more dedicated, developed to the nth degree as an S-L-R system (L = logical constructs). (*b*) Skinner inverted the original formula, putting R before S and thereby extruding the O or rather emptying it of variables anteceding the R. On the other hand, the S-N-R (N = neural governance) of Sechenov and Pavlov changed only in adding to the N a subsidiary I: interoceptive correction of S-R relations. Note that the N correlate of Woodworth's O is a hypothetical and not a logical construct—an ad hoc and not an everlasting inferable—and the I, a correcting, and not a governing or mediating one. And consider that this oldest approach is also most modern. The following specific suggestions for future research are offered:

(*a*) Probe the neural concomitants of behavioral conditioning, a common practice in Soviet but not American laboratories.

(*b*) Expand the studies of rhythm assimilation and anodal polarization in conditioning, and attempt to find the neural changes during the latter's action (finer instruments).

(*c*) Compare the neural concomitants of classical and reinforcement conditioning and probe that of sensory preconditioning and configuring. Test Beritoff's hypothesis that a supplementary neural center is activated when configuring emerges.

(*d*) Track the evolutionary progression of electrotonic neural action and determine at each level its role vis-à-vis the synaptic kind.

(*e*) Continue the long search for the neuromorphology of any kind of learning.

(*f*) Replicate and expand Soviet studies of interoceptive conditioning (only four American studies so far)[34] and compare its attributes with those of the exteroceptive dimension; *relate interoceptive classical conditioning to visceral reinforcement conditioning.*

(*g*) Replicate and expand Soviet comparative studies of human interoceptive and exteroceptive continua of reactivity and liminal consciousness.

(*h*) Replicate and expand Soviet studies of the effects of unconditioned and conditioned interoception on unconditioned and conditioned action, keeping in mind Chernigovsky's 1953 statement that "we may confidently assert that no organ or tissue in the body is without interoceptors." (A review of the field six years ago disclosed Soviet reports of the existence of interoceptors in the following: adventitia, bile duct, cisterna chyli, endocardium, epicardium, gall bladder, kidneys, liver, lung, mammary glands, mesentery, ovaries, pancreas, salivary glands, spleen, suprarenals, testes, thyroid gland, urinary bladder, and uterus—not to mention the main portions of the vascular and digestive systems, such as the abdominal aorta, aortic arch, caecum, duodenum, ileum, esophagus, pulmonary artery, rectum, vena cava.)

Dominance

Four avenues of research are within reach:

Basic Neural Mechanism.   Replicate and expand the studies of Ukhtomsky's present-day students of the area—notably, Rusinov and Livanov and their many collaborators and followers. Make use, in addition, of Leǎo's technique of spreading depression (Leǎo, 1944; Bureš and Burešova, 1960a, 1960b, 1965; Fifkova, 1968; Ochs, 1962; Zachar and Zacharová, 1961, 1963; and several others). And probe the likely contribution of electrotonic neural transmission to synaptic neural interdependence.

Parameters of Behavioral Manifestation.   Replicate and extend the gamut of studies ranging from conditioned wiping reflexes in spinal frogs to shock-food and food-shock combinations in dogs, and GSRs and eyeblinks in college students. No American animal laboratory has experi-

---

[34] The American lag in interoceptive conditioning may be in part professional—in the United States over 90 per cent of conditioning experiments are performed by psychologists and in the Soviet Union by Pavlovian physiologists, long adept in visceral and particularly fistular surgery. And the difference may also be societal: Soviet scientists find it easier to recruit as subjects fistulated patients and normal individuals ready to swallow rubber tubes.

mented with the CR combinations of shock and food—and for that matter none has tried with animals the successful dominance design of Grings and his associates (Kimmel, Lockhart—also Walker), let alone my broader formulation of its desiderata (Razran, 1957).

Varied Stimulation. Kimble and Ray's finding that varied stimulation engenders sensitization of frogs' wiping reflex and stereotyped stimulation its habituation is far-reaching both as a parametric divide of nonassociative learning and as a unique contribution to the dominance doctrine. More than that, there is every reason to assume that the finding pertains also to the divide between classical and reinforcement conditioning, the stimuli of the modified reaction of the latter being certainly more variable than those of the former and the reaction thus sensitizable instead of habituable (Figure 20). The experiment cries out for replication and extension.

Conceptual and Empirical Integration. The shortcoming is most glaring. Neither Franzisket nor Kimble and Ray, nor Sheffield using Sherrington's "prepotence," nor Premack and his "reversibility of reinforcement," nor Dykman and his engrossment in "sensitization," evinces awareness of Ukhtomsky's doctrine, which relates basically to the research and thought of each and all. Only John and Morrell, concerned with the neural rudiments of conditioning, are seemingly familiar with it. Western students of behavioral conditioning with evidence of dominance have in fact not even interrelated to any extent their own behavioral results and interpretations; Premack is the only one to note that his "reinforcement theory" is akin to "versions of dominance theory . . . by Razran (1957) and Grings (1960)" (1965, p. 175). Conceptual and empirical integration and broadened future research are long overdue.[35]

[35] Ukhtomsky's prestigious status in the Soviet Union is attested to by the "Resolutions of the 1962 Moscow All-Union Conference on the Philosophical Problems of the Physiology of Higher Nervous Activity and Psychology," which states that "the theoretical foundations of Soviet physiology and psychology were formulated by I. M. Sechenov and then elaborated by I. P. Pavlov, N. E. Vvedensky and A. A. Ukhtomsky and their many students" (*Zhurnal Vysshey Nervnoy Deyatel'nosti imeni I. P. Pavlova*, 1962, p. 981; *Voprosy Psikhologii*, 1962, 8, No. 4, p. 4; Fedoseyev, 1963, p. 756). "These foundations," the Resolutions continues, "must be strengthened through intensive use of cellular and subcellular electrophysiology and fruitful interrelation with the accordant approach of cybernetics." No other such Conference has been held since.

And here it should be noted that Cole and Maltzman are patently mistaken in their view that "the use of Pavlovian principles will continue to decline in the established areas of Soviet psychology and higher nervous activity" (Editors' Introduction, *A Handbook of Contemporary Soviet Psychology*, 1968, p. 11), and are truly amazing in their allegation: "In 1965 the competition of 'cybernetic' and Pavlovian psychophysiology and prevalence of the former was symbolized by Anokhin's election to full membership in the Academy of Sciences" (Editors' Introduction, p. 441). Consider the following facts: (*a*) Kolmogorov, the distinguished student of Probability, wrote in 1963 that "cybernetics is after all only a step in Pavlov's program of analysis of higher nervous activity" (p. 17). (*b*) Voronin, the Director of the Department of Higher Nervous Activity of the University of Moscow, avowed in 1969 that the "TOTE does not differ in *principle* from the dynamic stereotypes of conditioned reflexes" (p. 915; italics added). (*c*) Anokhin's long-awaited 1968 systematic text is named *The Biology and Neurophysiology of the Conditioned Reflex*. (*d*) The two chapters following the introductory chapter of the 1966 *The Study of Thinking in Soviet Psychology*, published by the Institute of Philosophy of the USSR Academy of Sciences, are titled: "Sechenov's Reflex Theory and Thinking" and "Pavlov's Higher Nervous Activity and the Psychology of Thinking."

The continued predominance of Pavlov's "principles" is in fact fully evident in almost all of the thirty translated articles of the Cole and Maltzman *Handbook*: Ladygina-Kots and Dembovski state that in the "psychology of primates" the "conditioned reflex is . . . the expression of the brain's synthesizing activity acting as a single unit" (p. 55); Bozhovich concludes that "the major approach to the study of personality of the child in Soviet psychology . . . is in essence . . . the Pavlovian approach of the study of the complete organism" (p. 244); Galperin relates the "development of mental acts" to Pavlov's "dynamic stereotypes" (p. 264); Luria declares "Vygotski's theoretical position [is] a view close to Pavlov's basic idea of the interaction of the two signal systems" (p. 283); and Slonim's interrelates ethology and higher nervous activity—not to mention the full-fledged Pavlovianism of articles involving direct conditioning research (those of Asratyan, Kasatkin, Kupalov, Skipin et al., Teplov and Nebilytsin, and Vinogradova) and Anokhin's assertion that his cybernetic tenet—"afferent synthesis is the most crucial aspect of brain activity"—is like that which "Pavlov long ago expressed . . . when he said that the afferent aspect of the central nervous system is the 'creative' one, whereas he ascribed a merely 'technical' role to efferent functions" (p. 834; cf. my characterizing the former as the "wide funnel of the mind" and the latter as "but its narrow neck" (p. 263).

Only Beritoff (Beritashvili) and Bernshteyn may be considered outside the Pavlov stream. As an old votary of Beritoff, I have long deplored the insufficient attention accorded his outstanding research and thought and surely welcome his present increasing influence—indeed, I feel that his name should be added to the Sechenov-Pavlov-Vvedensky-Ukhtomsky foursome of the Russo-Soviet brain-mind revolution. In all, however, Beritoff is an innovator and not an adversary of the system and by now seems closer to Pavlov than ever. Bernshteyn's stimulating feedback and related views are not, on the other hand, of the same caliber, having been championed and tested more fully by Anokhin (starting with his 1935 surgical studies of anastomosis and compensation).

Cole and Maltzman's source of error stems from their *failure to realize that Pavlov modified his position to accord a role to psychology and cognition,* declaring as early as 1924: "Certainly psychology, in so far as it concerns the subjective state of man, has a natural right to existence; for our subjective world is the first reality with which we are confronted" (p. 43; Gantt's translation, 1928b, p. 329). The error is glaring on page 4 of the *Handbook,* where the editors assign "1927" to Pavlov's statement that "psychological reasoning is indeterminate [and] explanations are fantastic and without basis" which *actually was made in 1911* (p. 187; Gantt's translation, 1928b, p. 164). Incidentally, I discussed at length the "inferable conscious in Soviet psychophysiology" in a 1961 article (1961a) in which the expression was part of the title. And may I add that I *personally* know that the editors' interpretation of Anokhin's election to the academy is wrong.

(For that matter, the editors seem to be not at all aware of the recent reburgeoning of Pavlovian principles in *American* psychology, the evidence of which is unmistakable. Witness Hilgard and Bower adding a special chapter, "Pavlov and the Con-

The Empirics of Cognition: Method, Role, and Mechanism

Contemporary American psychologists vary widely in their views on cognition. Three main groups are involved: phenomenologists, cognitive behaviorists, and peripheral behaviorists. To phenomenologists, the source of the power and structure of cognition is direct human experience. Its mind role is exclusive to the extent of synonymity. Animals' minds are by analogy also wholly cognitive, and little concern is shown for evolutionary status and specific bases of the analogy. Likewise, there is almost no attempt to correlate posited cognitive concepts—tension, force, balance, etc.—with underlying physical events. Phenomenology's recent recourse to information theory, while highly significant, hardly provides a substitute. By itself, the mathematics might even postpone finding the ultimate empirical.

Cognitive behaviorists—Hebb and Tolman as somewhat differing representatives—concur with the phenomenologists in considering cognition the essence of mind in man and higher animals. But they derive it and its characteristics from external behavior. The knowledge of direct experience is either wholly immolated or denied specific psychologic status. Hebb's statement is: "For modern objective psychology introspection does not exist . . . mind is not able to observe itself . . . we know mind, and study it, as the chemist knows and studies the properties of the atom" (1966, p. 11,

---

ditioned Reflex," to their 1966 edition of *Theories of Learning,* absent from the 1948 and 1954 editions by Hilgard. And, most significantly, read Seward's 1970 "Mechanisms of Conditioning" chapter in Marx's *Learning: Theories,* in which he concludes that classical conditioning is the very basis of the "current" learning positions of Miller, Mowrer, Sheffield, and Spence—also of Konorski, and Razran [pp. 93-107; add Rescorla and Solomon].)

In a Preface to the *Handbook,* Leont'yev, Luria, and Smirnov state, among other things: "Soviet psychology has never accepted the limits imposed by the limits of positivist descriptions of mental phenomena, aiming instead to fathom their *physiological mechanisms*" (p. vi; italics in original). I wonder, however, whether these leading psychologists noted the editors' statement about Pavlov's decline. Or, were they thinking of textual adherence to his writings (prevalent in the early 'fifties but read out of court at the 1962 Conference) and not of his system as a whole, which of course they know has for years been one of behavior *and* cognition?

Curiously, Cole and Maltzman base their assertions also on a *presumed* change in the attitude of the Communist Party—that "the 23d Congress of the Communist Party in the Soviet Union, which met in 1964 [made] no reference to Pavlovian principles" (pp. 11-12). I have before me the two volumes of the complete stenographic report of that Congress (which, incidentally, met not in 1964 but in 1966—March 29-April 8). *Pavlov is not there, but neither is psychology or physiology.* The only pertinent theoretic turn in Soviet ideology at the Congress is the commitment to a study of Sociology, and thus by extension also Social Psychology, ignored for some thirty years. The specific sentence reads: "A most important task for Soviet scientists is the study of economics, philosophy, sociology, history and law in their close relation to the practice of building communism" (*Pravda,* April 9, 1966, p. 4; Stenographic reports, Vol. 2, p. 812). (The sentence is reproduced in the 1966 issue of *Voprosy Psikhologii* which—not the protocols themselves—is a reference item in the Editors' Introduction.)

287), while Tolman long avowed that introspection provides only "raw feels" and more recently specified "immediate phenomenologies as merely the initial experiential matrices out of which all sciences, physical as well as psychological, develop [offering no] scientifically useful constructs" (1955, p. 34). Their views on *where to look for cognition* are identical—Hebb's: "the focal problem of psychology is found in the mental processes of the higher animal" (1966, p. 8) and Tolman's: "Everything important in psychology . . . can be investigated in essence through the continued experimental and theoretical analysis of the determiner of rat behavior at a choice point in a maze" (1938, p. 34). Neither accords singularity to the cognition of man's mind nor distinctive significance to its evolutionary progression in animals, the consideration that one is a neurobehaviorist and the other a molar behaviorist notwithstanding.

A section of America's peripheral behaviorists excludes the consideration of cognition, staking all their formulations on observable behavior, including the verbal kind. An increasing portion admits it, however, as a mediating variable: "cognition" following "mediation" in parentheses, and vice versa, are becoming common twosomes in recent literature. Yet the admission is only in a limited technological sense a sign of the dovetailing of the two wings of American behaviorism. The systematic divergence is unaffected. To peripheralists, cognition (*a*) is not an overriding mind category but only another variable bridging peripheral behavior and *operating according to the same laws* and (*b*) in human experiments, moreover, is commonly identified with peripheral linguistic process. If inferences are the putative mechanism and not just theorists' exercises, surely the ontology and genesis of cognitive maps must be miles apart from those of R_GS and S_GS. Posited synchronous action of the mechanisms of both behavioristic wings is the road to ultimate synthesis—to a system in which in the minds of man and higher animals the two coexist and coact in degrees differing with the evolutionary ascent of organisms and reactions. But even then, there is the bypassed problem of the specificity of the human mind and the discreteness as well as the oneness of language and thought within it.

It is clear that the cognition view of the present book differs from those discussed, first, in being generally not an either-or position, and, second, in including several extras. Systematic and heuristic theses render the view distinct. The systematic theses have been laid down in earlier sections and call here only for a consolidation statement—namely: (*a*) that organized cognition in the form of perception is a neurocognitive evolvement of neurobehavior which inferentially is held to appear first in relatively mature birds and mammals and empirically is mediated by the higher regions of the animals' respective striata and cortices; (*b*) that its further progression in animals manifests evolutionary novelty, along with evolutionary continuity, as ascending higher levels of cognition correlate with the evolution of brain mass and cytoarchitecture and with the status of the reactions involving them; (*c*) that cognitive and noncognitive neurobehavior coexist and continually interact, and the relative role of the former is a positive function of phyletic and neural evolution—i.e., a significant distinction must be drawn between the existence and potency of cognition; (*d*) that *man's cognition, commanding true thought and learned symbolic communication, is a very special novel acquisition* which, too, evinces several ascending levels in accordance with his ontogeny and presumably with anthropogeny; and (*e*) that evolutionary and logical and some plausible empirical considerations suggest that relatively unorganized liminal consciousness (sensations) and affects are phyletic antecedents of organized perception.

The heuristic theses refer to the methodologic means of studying cognition and will be somewhat explicated. Five current means will be considered:

Direct Human Experience. As noted in Chapter 1, the book is based on the view that observing one's experience is not just a verbal exercise and is more significant to psychology than to physics or biology. What is deplored is its use as an exclusive source of information and above all the failure to apprehend that experience, as only the highest small bit of evolving nature, does not hold within itself the natural laws of the mechanisms underlying its own existence and control. Or more plainly, experiential data and their posited cognitive parameters must be validated objectively—they are not privileged autochthonies.

Animal and Preverbal-Infant Behavior: Inference. Inference of cognition in animals should be based on close parallels of their learned behavior to experiential learning in human subjects (e.g., stimulus configuring vis-à-vis perceiving). Posited neuroanatomical and neurophysiological bases are unconvincing, while logical constructs beg the essence of the question in ignoring the specific experiential correlates and higher evolutionary status of cognition. Behavioral-experiential parallels warrant also inferring in the evolution of higher animals ascending cognitive (perceptual) levels of qualitative distinctions, not to mention quantitative variations within each level ("extrapolation" mastered by dogs and cats but not rabbits, and by crows but not pigeons and chickens, and "learning sets" largely a primate exploit). And several experiments suggest strongly the merits of inferring cognition in preverbal infants, whose mind capacity has heretofore been so grossly misprized.

Verbal Subjects: Meaning and Thought. This capstone of cognition is best tapped by semantic conditioning. The method is laborious but fundamental, and uniquely systematic in comparative studies of the objective bounds and structure of meaning in ascending ontogeny, varying intellectual capacity, disruptive pathology, and temporary effects of drugs and related physiological and psychological states. Veritable wellsprings of theory, these studies' empirical base is as yet deplorably very narrow. Needless to add, meanings are considered here the essential constituents of the neuro-cognition of thinking.

Verbal Subjects: Perception and Its Effects on Conditioning. The view that learned stimulus configuring is the objective correlate of animals' cognitive perceiving also applies of course to verbal humans and calls for the repetition of my own configural studies and some Soviet counterparts. Likewise, the study of the effects of perception on human conditioning, positive results of which others and I have long obtained, must be greatly enlarged. And here, too, the most heuristic methods are comparative: mainly subjects differing in age and intelligence, and instructions varying in kind and amount of transmitted information. In a broad sense, this is the experimenter's special province of probing the interaction of the cognitive and noncognitive.

IMPORTS: EDUCATIONAL, SOCIAL, AND CLINICAL

Educational

Two interrelated propositions are most germane: (*a*) man's learning mind is much more distinct and educable than was formerly thought, and (*b*) learning is multiform, a hierarchy of ascending levels. The first proposition is based on such current East-and-West evidence as the following: (1) the sucking reactions of human neonates are conditioned to temporal intervals on the third day of life while monkeys attain this only after approximately two weeks; (2) human neonates less than 4 days of age readily master simple and differential reinforcement conditioning and its extinction and *reversal*; (3) 3-month-old infants are fully capable of sensory-sensory learning, evident only in relatively mature specimens of higher animals; (4) infants of the same age learn by *observation* to imitate the articulation and production of simple vowels, and above all, (5) the basic associative mechanism of linguistic acquisition and generalization in one- to two-year-old children is distinct from that of simple conditioning. Space prevents citing additional data. What has been said should suffice, however, to conclude that the "laws" of animal learning—"learning by doing," "by conditioning and chaining"—extend only in part to the human education and, moreover, that language is not just an emitted operant.

The second proposition, that learning is an evolutionary multilevel hierarchy complete in man's normal mind, brings home even more the wide scope of his educational capacity. However, it also prompts the need for new means to convert potential capacity into actual ability—a change in pedagogy, principles, and methods. Current American either-or theories of learning cannot but be divisive, each predicating its own pedagogical system. True, the teacher and professional trainer, unlike the learning theorist, are no doubt less "single-minded" and more eclectic. But, first, the expediency is *untoward* in divorcing practice from theory, and, second

324 · Mind in Evolution

—and most important—the system offered here is not culled eclectics but a hierarchical synthesis. The pedagogue must be familiar with both the attributes and efficacies of each level and their specific and changing "group status." Not only do learning through conditioning, perceiving, and thinking—to name only the main categories—coexist and interact, but the mechanism and relative role of each is a function of the whole learning task and the whole of the learner. Moreover, there are the extras: (*a*) the levels interact both synergically and antagonistically, and pedagogy's objective is, obviously, synergy, and (*b*) the view of the unique quality of man's language and thought not found in any existing *American* system of *learning*.

Social

Two areas should be singled out: (*a*) cultural anthropology, and (*b*) social psychology. The key import of the present system to both areas is that mind's two dimensions are learned neurobehavior and learned neurocognition, the latter an evolvement from and normally dominant over the former. However, while social psychology relates to the entire system, cultural anthropology, concerned with "highest common factors" (Kroeber and Kluckhohn, 1952), is involved mainly in the top symbolic levels of cognition. Yet Kroeber and Kluckhohn's statement that "culture systems may, on the one hand, be considered as products of action, on the other as conditioning elements of further action" (1952, p. 181) is an exact counterpart of Rubinshteyn's "the psyche is both a conditioned and conditioning event" (1959, p. 19), cited approvingly earlier. Equally congruous with my system is the authors' emphasis on the *patterning* of culture and vesting its transmission in *symbols*. The only discordant note is their attempt to sever present-day culture from behavior as if the behavior-cognition interrelation is no longer reversible. Would not a contemporary society forced to change its behavior eventually also alter its culture? Moreover, the culture of early anthropogeny may well have been *symbosemic,* in which the symbol was a synchronous behavioral and cognitive unit, as discussed in Chapter 10.

Social psychology may well be said to rest on the operation of both "highest-common-factors" and "lowest-common-denominator" mechanisms. Experimental changes of attitudes will serve as illustrations. Some years ago (Razran, 1938c, 1940b, 1940c), I reported changes in ratings of sociopolitical slogans and controversial literary statements on a +3 to −3 scale for Personal Approval, Truth, Literary Value, and Propaganda Value by 120 adult subjects, as an outcome of pairing the showing of the slogans and statements with consuming one to eight free luncheons or with unpleasant odors. The subjects were misinformed about the purpose of the experiment. The results, presented in part at several meetings of the American Psychological Association and recorded by Sound Seminars (Razran, 1962), were never published in full. However, most of the differences were statistically significant, and the conditioning technique itself was replicated by Janis, Kaye, and Kirschner (1965) and Daabs and Janis (1965) and with a different US by Staats and Staats (1958). Yet the conditioned changes as a rule attained little permanence (long retention, resistance to extinction) unless the subjects were asked subsequently to explain their ratings, even as the changes were commonly insignificant when the subjects were told the purpose of the experiment or "caught on" to it. The efficacious strategem was to begin with conditioning in which the "conditioner" was fully cognizant of the wanted change and the "conditionee" wholly unaware of it, and then have the "conditionee's" cognition take over and consolidate what the "conditioner" had initiated. Effective means of altering man's acquired nature hinge apparently upon paralleling the ontogenetic sequence of its dominant levels by reaching the conditioned-affective level prior to the cognitive-symbolic level—no easy matter in adult life situations.

Clinical

Six underlying tenets will be ventured. (*a*) Both the formation (etiology) and the alleviation (therapeusis) of mind abnormalities are actions of subtle learning mechanisms embedded in total life situations, difficult to discern and consequently either unacknowledged or very divergently conceived. (*b*) The learned formation of abnormalities is primarily an outcome not of the confrontation of the innate and the learned but disparities between different levels of learning and the collision of learned contradictory reactions within the same levels. (*c*) Between-level disparities are most prominent in (1) unconscious versus conscious learning, (2) affectional versus perceptual, and (3) perceptual versus symbolic—all activated synchronously. (*d*) Within-level collisions result from learned anchoring of incompatible reactions to identical or closely related situations: doing versus inhibiting, liking versus disliking, perceiving *A* versus *B*, and symboling *A* versus *B*. (*e*) Because lower levels of learning are more universal and ontogenetically earlier integrals of man's mind, their incurred abnormalities are particularly basic and transferable to higher levels. (*f*) A multilevel conception of mind bears the merit of multilevel means of alleviating its abnormalities: a therapy of unlearning and relearning commensurate with the level of the origination and prevalent manifestations of what has been learned.

Put differently, the offered system maintains that the Unconscious Mind proper is devoid of affection (and of course conation), not an Eros and Thanatos but solely a behaviorally conditioned Robot of potent, difficult to cope with vagaries and derangements. Studies of interoception and interoceptive conditioning are of major relevance to the position but by no means its exclusive basis. Yet the system suggests also the existence of a high-powered *Nonperceptual* and only primordially cognitive Affectional Mind, wreaking upon us its brimful irrationalities. Eros would seem a fit name for it: in deference to tradition and, even more, because sex-linked affection seems most representative of the ontology and pragmatics of the category. Thirdly, the system bisects the cognitive mind, which it would like to name *Minerva,* into *perceptual contemporaneity* and *symbolic historicity.* And it accords the latter the chief guardianship of veridicality and rationality, not just because symbols check percepts but also because they are much less subject to the irrationality of Eros and the unaware vicissitudes of the Robot. And now a statement on practice: Behavioral, affectional, and rational therapies are each rightful within bounds but monopolistic and wrongful when they invade the entire area.

OMISSIONS

The size of the book was limited by design, and drastic selection was thus inevitable. Still, four glaring omissions need to be explained. First comes the entire area of *emotions.* It was not included because of the view that it is an additive to, but not an intrinsic of, learning—modifying learning, buoying or masking its stimuli, evoking or suppressing its participatory reactions, but not constituting the essence of its mechanism. *The basics of the learning mind would not be different, according to the view, in a hypothetical Martian wholly devoid of emotions.* Learning is, to be sure, replete with them. Think of appetitive and aversive conditioning and the fact that one noted theorist and experimentalist (Mowrer, 1960a) posits that all that one learns are expansions of four emotions: fear, hope, relief, and disappointment (cf. Descartes' six passions: joy, sadness, hate, love, wonder, and desire). But this does not alter the thesis that emotions are a *sine qua non* in a system of all of behavior but not in one of learned behavior and cognition.

Another omitted field is the *chaining of motor reactions* and the using of tools. An explanation was intimated earlier. Both are of overriding importance to the technology of learning but are not, in essence, a new mind mechanism. Nor, for that matter, is the vast realm of conventional verbal learning more than a proving ground of the mind novelty of language and meaning and thus is likewise too technologic (also too vast) to have been included here.

The third is the prestigious area of the heuristics of mathematical models and information theory, omitted partly because its singular quantitative concern is not abreast of mind's manifold of qualitative novelties and hierarchical organization, and partly because an East-West synthesis of the area is a task of vast proportion, better left to specialists in the field.

Finally, the recent revival of Müeller and Pilzecker's 1900 theory of memory consolidation in studies of short-term learning as a *sui generis* category was bypassed for two reasons: (*a*) Its nature, dimensions, and very existence are still highly controversial (Adams and Peacock, 1965; Chorover and Schiller, 1965; Lewis and Adams, 1963; Spevack and Suboski, 1967, 1969; Suboski et al., 1969; and others). (*b*) Its investigators are unaware of the evidential and conceptual distinctions between reaction-decreasing aversive inhibitory and reaction-increasing aversive classical conditioning, let alone of the plausible role of electrotonic factors in both memory and punishment.

FINAL STATEMENT

A somewhat philosophical evolutionary attribute of all learning is its general beneficence—that despite reversals it tends on the whole to be self-correcting and to improve in the life of the individual and the history of the race. Rousseau's avowal of the *immanent* goodness of man's nature is true only in the sense of the *eventual* goodness of his learning and culture. Current evidence tells us that even man's individual mind abnormalities are much ameliorated by his own further undirected learning, and, contrary to pessimists, the human race is advancing not only technologically but also in welfare and morality. Man is not moving to degeneration and perdition—at least not as an outcome of his learning.

References*

Abuladze, K. S. Reflex inhibition of gastric secretion. *Russky Fiziologichesky Zhurnal*, 1924, *7*, 281-287.

Abuladze, K. S. The summation reflex. *Trudy Fiziologicheskikh Laboratorii imeni I. P. Pavlova*, 1949, *15*, 5-16.

Ach, N. *Uber die Willenstätigkeit und das Denken*. Göttingen: Vanderhoeck and Ruprecht, 1905.

Ach, N. *Analyse des Willens*. Berlin and Wien: Urban and Schwartzenberg, 1935.

Acker, L. E., and Edwards, A. E. Transfer of vasoconstriction over a bipolar dimension. *Journal of Experimental Psychology*, 1964, *67*, 1-16.

Adám, G. *Interoception and behavior*. Budapest: Akadémiai Kiadó, 1967.

Adám, G., and Meszáros, I. Conditioned and unconditioned cerebral cortical activation to renal pelvic stimulation. *Acta Physiologica Academiae Scientiarium Hungaricae*, 1960, *18*, 137-141.

Adams, D. K. Behavior without awareness. *Psychological Bulletin*, 1957, *54*, 383-405.

Adams, H. E., and Peacock, L. J. Retrograde amnesia from electro-convulsive shock: Consolidation, disruption or interference? *Psychonomic Science*, 1965, *3*, 37-38.

Adler, N., and Hogan, J. A. Classical conditioning and punishment of an instinctive response in *Betta splendens*. *Animal Behaviour*, 1963, *11*, 351-354.

Adrianov, O. S. The structure of conditioned reflexes to complex simultaneous stimuli. *Zhurnal Vysshey Nervnoy Deyatel'nosti imeni I. P. Pavlova*, 1961, 1019-1025.

Afelt, Z. Variability of reflexes in chronic spinal frogs. In E. Gutmann and P. Hnick (Eds.), *Proceedings of the conference on central and peripheral mechanisms of motor functions*. Prague: Czechoslovak Academy of Sciences, 1963. Pp. 37-41.

Affani, J., Marchiafava, D. L., and Zernicki, B. Higher nervous activity in cats with midpontine trigeminal transections. *Science*, 1962, *137*, 126-127.

Alekseyenko, N. Yu., and Blinkov, S. M. Conditioned reactions to tactile stimuli in unilateral injury of the parietal lobe. *Trudy Instituta Vysshey Nervnoy Deyatel'nosti imeni I. P. Pavlova, Seriya Fiziologicheskaya*, 1955, *1*, 235-246.

Alexander, S. *Space, time and deity*. London: Macmillan, 1920.

Allport, F. H. *Social psychology*. Boston: Houghton Mifflin, 1924.

---

* Titles of Russian periodicals are transliterated; titles of articles and books are translated. The periodical citations permit ready location of the articles without transliteration. With a few appropriately designated exceptions, cited books published in Soviet cities are all Russian. German, French, Italian, Spanish, and Romanian references are reproduced as is; titles of Czech, Polish, and Hungarian articles and books are translated. My system of transliteration (Razran, in *Science*, 1959) differs only slightly from that of the *U.S. Government Printing Office Manual*.

Altman, J., Das, C. O., and Anderson, W. Effects of infantile stimulation on morphological development of the rat brain: An exploratory study. *Developmental Psychobiology*, 1968, *1*, 10-20.

Amsel, A. A three factor theory of inhibition: An addition to Hull's two factor theory. *American Psychologist*, 1951, *6*, 387.

Amsel, A. Frustrative nonreward in partial reinforcement and discrimination learning. *Psychological Review*, 1962, *69*, 306-328.

Anderson, O. D., and Liddell, H. S. Observations on experimental neuroses in sheep. *Archives of Neurology and Psychiatry*, New York, 1935, *34*, 330-354.

Anderson, R. C., and Ausubel, D. P. (Eds.) *Readings in the psychology of cognition.* New York: Holt, 1965.

Anokhin, P. K. The interaction of the neural centers of the conditioned and unconditioned stimuli during the action of the latter. *Trudy Fiziologicheskikh Laboratorii I. P. Pavlova*, 1927, *2*(1), 107-115.

Anokhin, P. K. (Ed.) *Problems of center and periphery in contemporary physiology of nervous activity.* Gorky: GIZ, 1935a.

Anokhin, P. K. Problems of center and periphery in contemporary physiology of nervous activity. In P. K. Anokhin (Ed.), *Problems of center and periphery in contemporary physiology of nervous activity.* Gorky: GIZ, 1935b. Pp. 9-70.

Anokhin, P. K. (Ed.) *Problems of higher nervous activity.* Moscow: Medgiz, 1949a.

Anokhin, P. K. Key Problems in study of higher nervous activity. In P. K. Anokhin (Ed.), *Problems of higher nervous activity.* Moscow: Medgiz, 1949b. Pp. 9-128.

Anokhin, P. K. *Ivan Petrovich Pavlov. Life, activity and scientific school.* Moscow: Akademiya Nauk SSSR, 1949c.

Anokhin, P. K. The reflex and the functional system as factors of physiological integration. *Fiziologichesky Zhurnal SSSR imeni I. M. Sechenova*, 1949d, *35*, 491-503.

Anokhin, P. K. Characteristics of the afferent appartus of the conditioned reflex and their significance to psychology. *Voprosy Psikhologii*, 1955, *1*(6), 16-38.

Anokhin, P. K. The physiological nature of vegetative components of the conditioned reaction. *Zhurnal Vysshey Nervnoy Deyatel'nosti imeni I. P. Pavlova*, 1956, *16*, 32-43.

Anokhin, P. K. New data on the characteristics of the afferent system of the conditioned reflex. In B. G. Anan'yev, A. N. Leont'yev, A. R. Luria, N. A. Menchinskaya, S. L. Rubinshteyn, A. A. Smirnov, and B. M. Teplov (Eds.), *Materials for the conference of psychology.* Moscow: Akademiya Pedagogicheskikh Nauk RSFSR, 1957. Pp. 104-124.

Anokhin, P. K. *Internal inhibition as a problem in physiology.* Moscow: Medgiz, 1958a.

Anokhin, P. K. The role of orienting-investigatory reactions in the formation of the conditioned reflex. In L. G. Voronin, A. N. Leont'yev, A. R. Luria, E. N. Sokolov, and O. S. Vinogradova (Eds.), *The orienting reflex and orienting-investigatory activity.* Moscow: Akademiya Pedagogichiskikh Nauk RSFSR, 1958b. Pp. 9-20.

Anokhin, P. K. *Electroencephalographic analysis of the conditioned reflex.* Moscow: Medgiz. 1958c.

Anokhin, P. K. New conceptions of the physiological architecture of the conditioned reflex. In L. F. Delafreshaye (Ed.), *Brain mechanisms and learning.* Springfield, Ill.: Charles C Thomas, 1961. Pp. 188-224.

Anokhin, P. K. A methodological analysis of key problems of the conditioned reflexes. In P. N. Fedoseyev (Ed.), *Philosophical problems of the physiology of higher nervous activity and psychology.* Moscow: Akademiya Nauk SSSR, 1963. Pp. 156-214.

Anokhin, P. K. Key mechanisms of the "functional system" as a self-regulatory system. In E. A. Asratyan (Ed.), *Reflexes of the brain.* Moscow: Nauka, 1965. Pp. 297-315.

Anokhin, P. K. Special features of the afferent apparatus of the conditioned reflex and their importance to psychology. In A. N. Leont'yev, A. R. Luria, and A. A. Smirnov (Eds.), *Psychological research in the USSR.* Vol. I. Moscow: Prosveshcheniye, 1966. Pp. 67-98.

Anokhin, P. K. *The biology and neurophysiology of the conditioned reflex.* Moscow: Meditsina, 1968.

Anokhin, P. K., and Strezh, E. Dynamics of higher nervous activity. VI. Characteristics of the receptive functions of the cortex when an unconditioned stimulus is in action. *Fiziologichesky Zhurnal SSSR imeni I. M. Sechenova,* 1934, *17,* 1225.

Antonova, A. A. Formation of conditioned reflexes in a backward sequence to stimuli of different physical intensities. *Trudy Instituta Vysshey Nervnoy Deyatel'nosti imeni I. P. Pavlova, Seriya Fiziologicheskaya,* 1955, *1,* 46-54.

Appel, J. B. Punishment in the squirrel monkey *Saimiri Scuirea. Science,* 1961, *133,* 36.

Appel, J. B. Punishment and shock intensity. *Science,* 1963, *141,* 528-529.

Appel, J. B., and Peterson, J. B. Punishment effects of shock intensity on response suppression. *Psychological Reports,* 1965, *3,* 721-730.

Aristotle. *Collected Works: De memoria et reminiscientia.* Paris: Firmin-Didot, 1878.

Arshavsky, I. A. Instincts and ontogenetic periodicity. In D. A. Biryukov (Ed.), *The evolution of functions of the nervous system.* Leningrad: Medgiz, 1958. Pp. 190-200.

Artemyev, V. V., and Bezladnova, N. I. Electrical reaction of the auditory area of the cortex of the cerebral hemispheres during formation of a conditioned defense reflex. *Trudy Instituta Fiziologii imeni I. P. Pavlova,* 1952, *1,* 228-236.

Asp, Dr. Beobachteungen über Gefassnerven. *Bericht über die Verdhanlingen der Sächsische Akademie der Wissenschaften. Mathematische-Physische Klasse,* Leipzig, 1867,*19,* 135-189.

Asratyan, E. A. Systematicity in the work of the cerebral cortex. *Trudy Fiziologicheskikh Laboratorii imeni I. P. Pavlova,* 1938, *8,* 1-15.

Asratyan, E. A. *Physiology of the central nervous system.* Moscow: Akademiya Meditsinskikh Nauk, 1953.

Asratyan, E. A. New views of unconditioned and conditioned reflexes. *Zhurnal Vysshey Nervnoy Deyatel'nosti imeni I. P. Pavlova,* 1955, *4,* 480-491.

Asratyan, E. A. The initiation and localization of cortical inhibition in the conditioned reflex arc. Pavlovian Conference on Higher Nervous Activity. *Annals of the New York Academy of Science,* 1961a, *92,* 1141-1159. (Russian: *In Higher Nervous Activity, Joint USA-USSR Pavlovian Conference.* Moscow: Medgiz, 1963. Pp. 289-333.)

Asratyan, E. A. Some aspects of the elaboration of conditioned connections and formation of their properties. In J. F. Delafreshaye (Ed.), *Brain mechanisms and learning.* Springfield, Ill.: Charles C Thomas, 1961b. Pp. 95-113.

Asratyan, E. A. The conditioned reflex and related phenomena. In P. N. Fedoseyev (Ed.), *Philosophical problems of the physiology of higher nervous activity and psychology.* Moscow: Akademiya Nauk SSSR, 1963. Pp. 323-357.

Asratyan, E. A. (Ed.) *Reflexes of the brain. International conference dedicated to the 100th anniversary of the appearance of I. M. Sechenov's work of the same name.* Moscow: Nauka, 1965a.

Asratyan, E. A. Characteristics of formation, functioning, and inhibition of two-way conditioned reflexes. In E. A. Asratyan (Ed.), *Reflexes of the brain.* Moscow: Nauka, 1965b. Pp. 114-126.

Asratyan, E. A. Functional architecture of instrumental conditioned reflexes. *Symposium 4: Classical and instrumental conditioning, XVIII International Congress of Psychology,* Moscow, 1966. Pp. 16-54.

Asratyan, E. A. The mechanism of conditioned reflex formation. *Zhurnal Vysshey Nervnoy Deyatel'nosti imeni I. P. Pavlova,* 1969, *19*, 741-751.

Atkinson, R. C., and Estes, W. K. Stimulus sampling theory. In R. Luce, R. Bush, and E. Galanter (Eds.), *Handbook of mathematical psychology.* Vol. 2. New York: Wiley, 1963. Pp. 121-268.

Avakyan, R. V. Studies of auditory analyzer through conditioned eyelid reflexes. *Zhurnal Vysshey Nervnoy Deyatel'nosti imeni I. P. Pavlova,* 1960, *10*, 23-31.

Avenarius, R. *Kritik der reines Erfahurung.* Leipzig: Fuess, 1888-1890.

Ayllon, T., and Azrin, N. H. Punishment as a discriminative stimulus and conditioned reinforcer with humans. *Journal of the Experimental Analysis of Behavior,* 1966, *9*, 411-419.

Ayrapet'yants, E. Sh. The formation of conditioned interoceptive motor connections. *Byulleten' Eksperimental'noy Biologii i Meditsiny,* 1937, *4*, 396-406.

Ayrapet'yants, E. Sh. The interoceptive conditioned reflex. *Trudy Voyenno-Morskoy Meditsinskoy Akademii,* 1949, *17*, 19-62.

Ayrapet'yants, E. Sh. *Higher nervous function and the receptors of internal organs.* Moscow: Akademiya Nauk SSSR, 1952.

Ayrapet'yants, E. Sh. (Ed.) *Problems of the comparative physiology of analyzers.* Leningrad: Leningrad University, 1960a.

Ayrapet'yants, E. Sh. A comparative study of the principle of vicariousness in interanalyzer integration. In E. Sh. Ayrapet'yants (Ed.), *Problems of the comparative physiology of analyzers.* Leningrad: Leningrad University, 1960b. Pp. 9-40.

Ayrapet'yants, E. Sh. Some problems of the comparative physiology of the conditioned reflex. *Trudy Leningradskogo Obshchestva Yestestvoispytateley,* 1961, 72, 3-9.

Ayrapet'yants, E. Sh., and Balakshina V. L. Interoceptive connections. *Trudy Leningradskogo Obshchestva Yestestvoispytateley,* 1935, 429-443.

Ayrapet'yants, E. Sh., and Batuyev, A. S. *The principle of convergence of analyzer systems.* Leningrad: Nauka, 1969.

Ayrapet'yants, E. Sh., and Bykov, K. M. Physiological experiments and the psychology of the subconscious. *Philosophy and Phenomenological Research,* 1945, *5*, 577-593.

Ayrapet'yants, E. Sh., Lobanova, L. V., and Cherkasova, L. S. Materials on the physiology of the internal anlayzer in man. *Trudy Instituta Fiziologii imeni I. P. Pavlova,* 1952, *1*, 3-20.

Ayrapet'yants, E. Sh., and Pyshina, S. P. Interoceptive conditioned connections. Dynamics of process of inhibition in the cortex of the cerebral hemispheres elicited by interoceptive impulses. *Doklady Akademii Nauk SSSR,* 1941, *30*, 538-541.

Azrin, N. H. Effects of two intermittent schedules of immediate and nonimmediate punishment. *Journal of Psychology,* 1956, *42*, 3-21.

Azrin, N. H. Some effects of noise on human behavior. *Journal of the Experimental Analysis of Behavior,* 1958, *1*, 183-200.

Azrin, N. H. Punishment and recovery during fixed-ratio performance. *Journal of the Experimental Analysis of Behavior,* 1959, *2,* 301-305.

Azrin, N. H. Sequential effects of punishment. *Science,* 1960a, *131,* 605-606.

Azrin, N. H. Effects of punishment intensity during variable interval reinforcement. *Journal of the Experimental Analysis of Behavior,* 1960b, *3,* 123-142.

Azrin, N. H., and Holz, W. C. Punishment. In W. K. Honig (Ed.), *Operant behavior: Areas of research and application.* New York: Appleton-Century-Crofts, 1966. Pp. 380-447.

Azrin, N. H., Holz, W. C., and Hake, D. F. Fixed-ratio punishment. *Journal of the Experimental Analysis of Behavior,* 1963, *6,* 141-148.

Babkin, B. P. *Systematic study of complex-nervous (psychic) phenomena in dogs.* St. Petersburg: Military Medical Academy, 1904. (Thesis)

Babkin, B. P. The characteristics of the auditory analyzer in dogs. *Trudy Obshchestva Russkikh Vrachey v St. Peterburge,* 1910, *77,* 197-232.

Bain, A. *The emotions and the will.* London: Parker, 1859.

Bair, J. Development of voluntary control. *Psychological Review,* 1901, *8,* 474-510.

Baker, T. W. Properties of compound conditioned stimuli and other components. *Psychological Bulletin,* 1968, *70,* 611-625.

Baker, T. W. Component strength in a compound CS as a function of number of acquisition trials. *Journal of Experimental Psychology,* 1969, *79,* 347-352.

Barcroft, J., and Barron, D. H. The development of behavior in fetal sheep. *Journal of Comparative Neurology,* 1939, *70,* 477-502.

Barcroft, J., Barron, D. H. Windle, W. F. Some observations on genesis of somatic movements in sheep embryos. *Journal of Physiology* (London), 1936, *87,* 73-79.

Barkhydaryan, S. S. Evolution of extinctive inhibition. *Zhurnal Vysshey Nervnoy Deyatel'nosti imeni,* I. P. Pavlova, 1967, *17,* 998-1003.

Barlow, J. A. Secondary motivation through classical conditioning: A reconsideration of the nature of backward conditioning. *Psychological Review,* 1956, *63,* 406-408.

Barondes, S. H. Relationship of biological regulatory mechanisms to learning and memory. *Nature* (London), 1965, *205,* 19-21.

Bartoshuk, A. K. Response decrement with repeated elicitation of human neonatal cardiac acceleration to sound. *Journal of Comparative and Physiological Psychology,* 1962a, *55,* 9-13.

Bartoshuk, A. K. Human neonatal cardiac acceleration to sound: Habituation and dishabituation. *Perceptual and Motor Skills,* 1962b, *15,* 15-27.

Baru, A. V. *Comparative physiology of conditioned reflexes.* Leningrad, 1951. (Thesis)

Baru, A. V. Temporary connections in cyclostomes and fish. In D. A. Biryukov (Ed.), *Problems of comparative physiology and pathology of higher nervous activity.* Leningrad: Medgiz, 1955. Pp. 92-101.

Baru, A. V., Bolotina, O. P., Krasuskaya, N. A., Lukina, E. V., Pavlov, B. V., Prazdnikova, N. V., Saf'yants, V. I., and Chebykin, D. A. Dynamics of conditioned-reflex activity in representative classes of vertebrates. *Trudy Instituta Fiziologii imeni I. P. Pavlova,* 1959, *8,* 99-106.

Baru, A. V., Malinovsky, O. V., Ovchinnikova, N. P., Prazdnikova, N. V., and Chernomordikov, V. V. Conditioned motor food reflexes to chains of stimuli in some vertbrates. *Trudy Instituta Fiziologii imeni I. P. Pavlova,* 1959, *8,* 107-113.

Batuyev, A. S. The mechanism of interaction of the visual and auditory analyzers. *Zhurnal Vysshey Nervnoy Deyatel'nosti imeni I. P. Pavlova,* 1964, *14,* 834-846.

Batuyev, A. S. Central mechanisms of integration of analyzèrs in rodents, carnivores, and primates. In *Theses, 4th Scientific Conference on Evolutionary Physiology in Memory of Academician L. A. Orbeli.* Leningrad: 1965. Pp. 27-28.

Batuyev, A. S. Central mechanisms of interanalyzer synthesis. In M. M. Khananshvili (Ed.), *Structural and functional bases of conditioned reflexes.* Leningrad: Akademiya Nauk SSSR, 1966a. Pp. 11-14.

Batuyev, A. S. Structure of central apparatus in integration of analyzers. In *Theses, 21st Conference on Problems of Higher Nervous Activity.* Moscow-Leningrad: Nauka, 1966b. P. 29.

Bayandurov, B. I. The physiology of conditioned inhibition in birds. *Zhurnal Eksperimental'noy Biologii i Meditsiny,* 1926, *6,* 210-221.

Beach, F. A. The snark was a boojum. *American Psychologist,* 1950, *5,* 115-124.

Beach, F. A., Conovitz, M. W., Steinberg, F., and Goldstein, A. C. Experimental inhibition and restoration of mating behavior in male rats. *Journal of Genetic Psychology,* 1956, *89,* 165-181.

Beck, C. E., Doty, R. W., and Kooi, K. A. Electrocortical reactions associated with conditioned flexion reflexes. *Electroencephalography and clinical Neurophysiology,* 1958, *10,* 279-289.

Beebe-Center, J. G. *The psychology of pleasantness and unpleasantness.* New York: Van Nostrand, 1932. Pp. 237-253.

Behrend, E. R., and Bitterman, M. E. Probability matching in fish. *American Journal of Psychology,* 1961, *74,* 542-551.

Bekhterev (Bechterew, Bekhtereff), V. M. *Objektive Psychologie oder Psychoreflexologie, Die Lehre von den Assoziations-reflexen.* Leipzig and Berlin: Teubner, 1913. (Russian edition, 1907; French, 1913)

Bekhterev, V. M. *General principles of human reflexology.* London: Jarrolds, 1933.

Belekhova, M. G. Post-tetanic potentiation and recruitment in the cortex of turtles. *Zhurnal Vysshey Nervnoy Deyatel'nosti imeni I. P. Pavlova,* 1967, *17,* 513-520.

Belenkov, N. Yu. Conditioned reflexes in decorticated cats. I. Conditioned defensive reflexes. *Byulleten' Eksperimental'noy Biologii i Meditsiny,* 1950a, *29*(2), 100-103.

Belenkov, N. Yu. Conditioned reflexes in decorticated cats. II. Conditioned food-motor reflexes. *Byulleten' Eksperimental'noy Biologii i Meditsiny,* 1950b, *29*(3), 182-185.

Belenkov, N. Yu. *The conditioned reflex and subcortical brain formation.* Moscow: Meditsina, 1965.

Belenkov, N. Yu., and Chirkov, V. D. Irradiation of strychnine stimulation of the cortex. *Zhurnal Vysshey Nervnoy Deyatel'nosti imeni I. P. Pavlova,* 1961, *11,* 512-521.

Belenkov, N. Yu., and Chirkov, V. D. Origin of generalized convulsive discharges in the cerebral cortex. *Zhurnal Vysshey Nervnoy Deyatel'nosti imeni I. P. Pavlova,* 1964, *14,* 68-76.

Belenkov, N. Yu., and Chirkov, V. D. The mechanism of synchronization of neuronal activity. *Zhurnal Vysshey Nervnoy Deyatel'nosti imeni I. P. Pavlova,* 1965, *15,* 128-139.

Belenkov, N. Yu., and Chirkov, V. D. Nonsynaptic (ephatic) factors in the function of cortical neurons. *Zhurnal Vysshey Nervnoy Deyatel'nosti imeni I. P. Pavlova,* 1969, *19,* 1033-1043.

Bennett, E. L., Diamond, M. C., Krech, D., and Rosenzweig, M. R. Chemical and anatomical plasticity of the brain. *Science,* 1964, *146,* 610-619.

Bergson, H. *L'evolution créatrice.* Paris: Alcan, 1907.

Beritoff (Beritashvili, Beritov), J. S. On the fundamental nervous processes of the cortex of the cerebral hemispheres. *Brain,* 1924, *47,* 109-148; 358-376.

Beritoff, J. S., Über die Individuell-erworbene Tätigkeit des Zentralnervensystems bei Tauben. *Pflügers Archiv für die Gesamte Physiologie des Menschen und der Tiere,* 1926, *213,* 370-406.

Beritoff, J. S. Über die Individuell-erworbene Tätigkeit des Zentralnervensystems. *Journal für Psychologie und Neurologie,* 1927, *33,* 113-335.

Beritoff, J. S. *Individually acquired activity of the central nervous system.* Tbilisi: GIZ, 1932.

Beritoff, J. S. Studies of individual behavior of dogs. *Fiziologichesky Zhurnal SSSR imeni I. M. Sechenova,* 1934, *17,* 176-183; 699-705; 1187-1196.

Beritoff, J. S. Studies of individual behavior of dogs. *Fiziologichesky Zhurnal SSSR imeni I. M. Sechenova,* 1935, *19,* 496-507.

Beritoff, J. S. Comments on the experiments of Bregadze and Tarugov on rabbits' individual reactions to complex auditory stimuli. *Trudy Instituta Fiziologii imeni I. S. Beritashvili,* 1937, *3,* 449-462.

Beritoff, J. S. The structure of the cortex and its relation to individually-acquired reflex action. *Soobshcheniya Gruzinskogo Filiala AN SSSR,* 1940, *1*(2), 149-156.

Beritoff, J. S. *Basic forms of nervous and psychonervous activity.* Moscow: Akademiya Nauk SSSR, 1947.

Beritoff, J. S. Morphological and physiological fundamentals of temporary connections in the cerebral cortex. *Trudy Instituta Fiziologii GSSR Akademii Nauk,* 1956a, *10,* 3-70.

Beritoff, J. S. The mechanism of external and internal inhibition. *Gagrskiye Besedy,* 1956b, *2,* 201-266.

Beritoff, J. S. *Neural mechanisms of spatial orientation of higher vertebrates.* Tbilisi: Akademiya Nauk GSSR, 1959.

Beritoff, J. S. Morphological and physiological bases of the mechanism of temporary connections. *Gagrskiye Besedy,* 1960, *3,* 43-81.

Beritoff, J. S. *Neural mechanisms of the behavior of higher vertebrates.* Moscow: Akademiya Nauk SSSR, 1961. (English translation by W. T. Liberson, Boston: Little, Brown, 1965.)

Beritoff, J. S. *Memory in vertebrates: Characteristics and genesis.* Tbilisi: Metsniyerba, 1968a.

Beritoff, J. S. (Ed.) *Current problems of the activity and structure of the central nervous system.* Tbilisi: Metsniyereba, 1968b.

Beritoff, J. S. *Structure and function of the cerebral cortex.* Moscow: Nauka, 1969.

Beritoff, J. S., and Bregadze, A. N. Physiology of behavior to complex stimuli: II. Individual reflex reactions of animals to complex sound stimuli. *Mediko-Biologichesky Zhurnal,* 1929a, *3,* 131-150.

Beritoff, J. S., and Bregadze, A. N. Physiology of behavior to complex stimuli: III. Role of special experimental settings and conditions. *Mediko-Biologichesky Zhurnal,* 1929b, *4,* 83-100.

Beritoff, J. S., and Bregadze, A. N. Physiology of behavior to complex stimuli. *Trudy Obshchestva Russkikh Fiziologov,* 1931, *5,* 45-46.

Beritoff, J. S., and Dzidzishvili, N. N. Study of the behavior of a microcephalic. *Trudy Biologicheskoy Sektsii Gruzinskogo Otdela Akademii Nauk SSSR,* 1934, *1,* 75-104.

Berlyne, D. E. *Conflict, arousal and curiosity.* New York: McGraw-Hill, 1960.

Bernshteyn, N. A. *General principles of work.* Moscow: Biomedgiz, 1935.

Bernshteyn, N. A. *The structure of movements.* Moscow: Medgiz, 1947.

Bernshteyn, N. A. Some timely problems of the regulation of motor acts. *Voprosy Psikhologii,* 1957, *7*(6), 70-90.

Bernshteyn, N. A. Approaches and problems of the physiology of action. *Voprosy Filosofii,* 1961, No. 6, 77-92.

Bernshteyn, N. A. New lines of development in physiology and their relation to cybernetics. In P. N. Fedoseyev (Ed.), *Philosophical problems of the physiology of higher nervous activity and psychology.* Moscow: Akademiya Nauk SSSR, 1963. Pp. 299-322.

Bernstein, A. L. Temporal factors in the formation of conditioned eyelid reaction in human subjects. *Journal of General Psychology,* 1934, *10*, 173-179.

Bersh, P. J. The influence of two variables upon the establishment of a secondary reinforcer for operant responses. *Journal of Experimental Psychology,* 1951, *41*, 62-73.

Bethe, A. Das Nervensystems von *Carinus maens.* Ein anatomisch-physiologischer Versuch. *Archiv für Mikroskopische Anatomie und Entwicklungs-mechanik,* 1897, *50*, 460-546.

Bills, A. G. The influence of muscular tension of the efficiency of mental work. *American Journal of Psychology,* 1927, *38*, 227-251.

Binet, L. *L'étude expérimentale de l'intelligence.* Paris: Alcan, 1903.

Bingham, H. C. Size and form perception in *Gallus domesticus. Journal of Animal Behavior,* 1913, *3*, 65-113.

Bingham, H. C. A definition of form. *Journal of Animal Behavior,* 1914, *4*, 136-141.

Birch, H. G. The relation of previous experience to insightful problem-solving. *Journal of Comparative Psychology,* 1945, *38*, 367-383.

Biryukov, D. A. *Unconditioned salivary reflexes in man.* Rostov-on-Don: Azova, 1935.

Biryukov, D. A. (Ed.) *The evolution of the functions of the nervous system.* Moscow: Medgiz, 1958a.

Biryukov, D. A. The nature of orienting reactions. In L. G. Voronin, A. N. Leont'yev, A. R. Luria, E. N. Sokolov, and O. S. Vinogradova (Eds.), *The orienting reflex and orienting-investigatory activity.* Moscow: Akademiya Pedagogicheskikh Nauk RSFSR, 1958b. Pp. 20-25.

Biryukov, D. A. (Ed.) *Studies of the evolution of nervous activity.* Leningrad: VIEM, 1959.

Biryukov, D. A. *Ecological physiology of higher nervous activity.* Leningrad: Medgiz, 1960.

Biryukov, D. A. Basic philosophical problems of the evolutionary physiology of higher nervous activity. In P. N. Fedoseyev (Ed.), *Philosophical problems of higher nervous activity and psychology.* Moscow: Akademiya Nauk SSSR, 1963. Pp. 358-392.

Bitterman, M. E. Toward a comparative psychology of learning. *American Psychologist,* 1960, *15*, 709-712.

Bitterman, M. E. Phyletic differences in learning. *American Psychologist,* 1965, *20*, 396-410.

Blinkova, T. P. Characteristics of unconditioned- and conditioned-reflex reactions in chick embryos. In *Theses, 3rd Scientific Conference on Evolutionary Physiology in Memory of Academician L. A. Orbeli.* Leningrad: 1961. Pp. 30-31.

Blinkova, T. P. Intercentral interrelationships in the embryogenesis of chicks. *Fiziologichesky Zhurnal SSSR imeni I. M. Sechenova,* 1966, *52*, 8-13.

Blinkova, T. P., and Bogdanov, O. V. Development of vegetative reactions in chick embryogenesis. *Byulleten' Eksperimental'noy Biologii i Meditsiny,* 1963, *56*(12), 32-35.

Bobrova, M. V. Action of interoceptive and exteroceptive painful stimulation on spinal reflexes. *Fiziologichesky Zhurnal SSSR imeni I. M. Sechenova,* 1959, *45,* 423-431.

Bogoslovsky, A. I. Forming conditioned sensory reflexes in man. *Fiziologichesky Zhurnal SSSR imeni I. M. Sechenova,* 1936a, *20,* 1017-1029.

Bogoslovsky, A. I. Conditioned-reflex changes of critical flicker frequency in central and peripheral vision. *Sovetsky Vestnik Oftamologii,* 1936b, *8,* 795-803.

Boldyrev, V. N. Formation of artificial conditional (psychic) reflexes and their characteristics. *Trudy Obshchestva Russkikh Vrachey v St. Peterburge,* 1905, *72,* 321-347.

Booth, J. H. and Hammond, L. J. Differential fear to a compound stimulus and its elements. Paper read 40th Meeting of the Eastern Psychological Association, 1969, Philadelphia, Pa.

Boring, E. G. The sensations of the alimentary canal. *American Journal of Psychology,* 1915, *26,* 2-57.

Borukayev, P. K. Interrelation of transwitched conditioned reflexes upon changes of the functional state of the cerebral cortex in dogs. *Trudy Instituta Vysshey Nervnoy Deyatel'nosti, Seriya Patofiziologicheskaya,* 1961, *9,* 63-72.

Brackbill, I. Experimental research with children in the Soviet Union: Report of a visit. *American Psychologist,* 1960, *15,* 226-233.

Brackbill, I., Fitzgerald, H. E., and Lintz, L. M. A developmental study of classical conditioning. *Monographs of the Society for Research in Child Development,* 1967, *32* (8, Whole No. 116).

Brady, J. V. A comparative approach to the experimental analysis of emotional behavior. In P. H. Hoch and J. Zubin (Eds.), *Experimental psychopathology.* New York: Grune and Stratton, 1957. Pp. 20-33.

Brady, J. V. Ulcers in "executive" monkeys. *Scientific American,* 1958, *199*(4), 95-100.

Brady, J. V. Motivational-emotional factors and intracranial self-stimulation. In D. E. Sheer (Ed.), *Electrical stimulation of the brain.* Austin: University of Texas Press, 1961. Pp. 413-430.

Bregadze, A. The formation of individual reactions to a complex of musical tones in dogs. *Trudy Instituta Fiziologii imeni I. S. Beritashvili,* 1937, *3,* 415-430.

Bregadze, A. Physiology of differentiation of successive tonal complexes. In *Theses, 5th All-Union Congress of Physiologists, Biochemists and Pharmacologists.* Moscow: Medgiz, 1943. P. 74.

Bregadze, A. N. The formation of temporary connections between indifferent stimuli in dogs. In *Contemporary problems of the physiology of the nervous and muscular systems. Volume honoring the 70th birthday of I. S. Beritoff.* Tbilisi: Akademiya Nauk GSSR, 1956. Pp. 279-283.

Bregadze, A. N., and Tarugov, S. Individual reactions of rabbits to complex sound stimuli. *Trudy Instituta Fiziologii imeni I. S. Beritashvili,* 1937, *3,* 431-447.

Breland, K., and Breland, M. *Animal behavior.* New York: Macmillan, 1966.

Brentano, F. *Psychologie vom empirischen Standpunkt.* Leipzig: Duncker and Humboldt, 1874.

Brethower, D. M., and Reynolds, G. S. A facilitative effect of punishment on unpunished behavior. *Journal of the Experimental Analysis of Behavior,* 1962, *5,* 191-199.

Bridger, W. H. Sensory habituation and discrimination in the human neonate. *American Journal of Psychiatry*, 1961, *117*, 991-996.

Bridgman, C. S., and Carmichael, L. An experimental study of the onset of behavior in the fetal guinea pig. *Journal of Genetic Psychology*, 1935, *47*, 247-267.

Brogden, W. J. The effect of frequency of reinforcement upon the level of conditioning. *Journal of Experimental Psychology*, 1939a, *24*, 419-431.

Brogden, W. J. Sensory preconditioning. *Journal of Experimental Psychology*, 1939b, *25*, 323-332.

Brogden, W. J. Test of sensory pre-conditioning. *Journal of Experimental Psychology*, 1942, *31*, 505-517.

Brogden, W. J. Sensory preconditioning by the facilitation of auditory acuity. *Journal of Experimental Psychology*, 1950, *40*, 512-519.

Bronshteyn, A. I., Antonova, T. G., Kamenetskaya, A. G., Luppova, N. N., and Sitova, V. A. Development of analyzer functions in early ontogenesis of infants and some animals. In A. G. Ginetsinsky (Ed.), *Problems of evolution of physiological functions.* Moscow: Akademiya Nauk SSSR, 1958. Pp. 149-165.

Bronshteyn, A. I., Itina, N. A., Kamenetskaya, A. G., and Sitova, V. A. Orienting reactions of human neonates. In L. G. Voronin, A. N. Leont'yev, A. R. Luria, E. N. Sokolov, and O. S. Vinogradova (Eds.), *The orienting reflex and orienting-investigatory activity.* Moscow: Akademiya Pedagogicheskikh Nauk RSFSR, 1958. Pp. 237-241.

Bronshteyn, A. I., and Petrova, E. P. Study of the auditory analyzer in neonates and young infants. *Zhurnal Vysshey Nervnoy Deyatel'nosti imeni I. P. Pavlova*, 1952, *2*, 333-343.

Bronshteyn, A. I., Petrova, E. P., Bruskina, A. M., and Kamenetskaya, A. G. Studies of the audition of neonates and very young infants. *Problemy Fiziologicheskoy Akustiki*, 1959, *4*, 114-122.

Brown, J. H., and Crampton, G. H. Concomitant visual stimulation does not alter habituation of nystagmic, occulogyrae or psychophysical responses to angular acceleration. *Acta Oto-Laryngologica*, 1966, *61*, 80-91.

Brunswick, E. Scope and aspects of the cognitive problem. In *Contemporary approaches to cognition.* Cambridge: Harvard University Press, 1957. Pg. 5-31.

Buchwald, J. S., Halas, E. S., and Schramm, S. Progressive changes in efferent unit responses in repeated cutaneous stimulation in spinal cats. *Journal of Neurophysiology*, 1965, *28*, 200-215.

Bugelski, R. Extinction with and without sub-goal reinforcement. *Journal of Comparative Psychology*, 1938, *26*, 121-134.

Bühler, K. Tatsachen und Probleme zu einer Psychologie der Denkvorgange. I. Über gedanken. *Achiv. für die Gesamte Psychologie*, 1907, *9*, 297-365; 339-340.

Bulygin, I. A. *A study of the mechanism of interoceptive reflexes.* Minsk: Akademiya Nauk BSSR, 1959.

Bulygin, I. A. *Afferent pathways of interoceptive reflexes.* Minsk: Akademiya Nauk BSSR, 1966.

Bulyginsky, G. N. Formation of conditioned reflexes when the unconditioned stimulus precedes the conditioned one. In *Theses, 13th Conference on Problems of Physiology.* Moscow, 1948. Pp. 21-22.

Bureš, J., and Burešová, O. The use of Leão spreading depression in research on conditioned reflexes. In H. H. Jasper and G. D. Smirnov (Eds.), The Moscow Colloquium on Encephalography of Higher Nervous Activity. *Electroencephalography and Clinical Neurophysiology*, 1960a, Supplement 13, 359-376.

Bureš, Y., and Burešová, O. The use of spreading depression in the study of conditioned reflexes. *Gagrskiye Besedy,* 1960b, *3,* 269-297.

Bureš, Y., and Burešová, O. The use of Leão spreading depression in the study of interhemispheric transfer of memory traces. *Journal of Comparative and Physiological Psychology,* 1960c, *53,* 558-563.

Bureš, J., and Burešová, O. Spreading depression and cortical-subcortical interrelations in the mechanism of conditioned reflexes. In E. A. Asratyan (Ed.), *Reflexes of the Brain.* Moscow: Nauka, 1965. Pg. 55-63.

Burke, C. J., and Estes, W. K. A component model for stimulus variables in discriminative learning. *Psychometrika,* 1957, *22,* 133-145.

Bush, R., and Estes, W. (Eds.) *Studies in mathematical learning theory.* Stanford: Stanford University Press, 1959.

Buss, A. H. Reversal and nonreversal shifts in concept formation with partial reinforcement eliminated. *Journal of Experimental Psychology,* 1956, *52,* 162-166.

Buytendijk, F. J. J. Instinct de la recherche du nid et expérience chez les crapauds (*Bufo vulgaris et Bufo calamata*). *Archives Néerlandaise de Physiologie de l'Homme et des Animaux,* 1918a, *2,* 1-50.

Buytendijk, F. J. J. L'instinct d'alimentation et l'expérience chez les crapauds. *Archives Néerlandaise de Physiologie de l'Homme et des Animaux,* 1918b, *2,* 217-228.

Buytendijk, F. J. J. Das Verhalten von *Octopus* nach teilweiser Zerstorung des "Gehirns." *Archives Néerlandaise de Physiologie de l'Homme et des Animaux,* 1933, *18,* 24-70.

Bykov, K. M. The functional connection of the cortex with internal organs. *Vestnik Khirurgii i Pogranichnikh Oblastey,* 1932, *27,* 12-27.

Bykov, K. M. Interoceptors. *Arkhiv Biologicheskikh Nauk,* 1941, *61*(1), 56-75.

Bykov, K. M. *The cerebral cortex and the internal organs.* Moscow: VMMA, 1943. (English translation, New York: Academic Press, 1957.)

Bykov, K. M. (Ed.) *Problems of the physiology of interoception.* Moscow: Akademiya Nauk SSSR, 1952.

Bykov, K. M., Alekseyev-Berkman, I., Ivanova, E. S., and Ivanov, E. P. The formation of conditioned reflexes to automatic and interoceptive stimuli. *Trudy III-go S'yezda Fiziologov,* Leningrad, 1928, 263-264.

Bykov, K. M., and Gorshkov, M. A. Formation of conditioned splenic movements. *Vestnik Khirurgii i Pogranichnykh Oblastey,* 1932, *27,* 46-50.

Bykov, K. M., and Kurtsin, I. T. *Corticovisceral pathology.* Leningrad: Medgiz, 1960.

Bykov, K. M., and Pshonik, A. T. The nature of the conditioned reflex. *Fiziologichesky Zhurnal SSSR imeni I. M. Sechenova,* 1949, *35,* 509-524.

Bykov, K. M., and Slonim, A. D. Habitat and physiological functions in mammals. *Vestnik Akademii Nauk SSSR,* 1949, *9,* 3-10.

Bykov, K. M., and Speransky, A. D. A dog with a transected *corpus callosum. Trudy Fiziologicheskikh Laboratorii I. P. Pavlova,* 1924, *1*(1), 47-59.

Bystroletova, G. N. Formation of conditioned reflexes to time intervals in neonates during periodic feeding. *Zhurnal Vysshey Nervnoy Deyatel'nosti imeni I. P. Pavlova,* 1954, *4,* 601-609.

Bzhalava, I. T. *Natural-science foundations of psychological action.* Tbilisi: Metsniyerba, 1958.

Bzhalava, I. T. *Perception and set.* Tbilisi: Metsniyerba, 1965.

Bzhalava, I. T. *The psychology of set and cybernetics.* Moscow: Nauka, 1966.

Caldwell, D. F., and Werboff, J. Classical conditioning in newborn rats. *Science,* 1962, *136*, 1118-1119.

Camp, D. S., Raymond, G. A., and Church, R. M. Response suppression as a function of the schedule of punishment. *Psychonomic Science,* 1966, *5*, 23-24.

Carmichael, L. What is empirical psychology? *American Journal of Psychology,* 1926, *37*, 521-527.

Carmichael, L. An experimental study in the prenatal guinea-pig of the origin and development of reflexes and patterns of behavior in relation to the stimulation of specific receptor areas during the period of active fetal life. *Genetic Psychology Monographs,* 1934, *16*, 337-491.

Carmichael, L. A re-evaluation of the concepts of maturation and learning as applied to the early development of behavior. *Psychological Review,* 1936, *93*, 456-470.

Carmichael, L., Hogan, H. P., and Walter, A. A. An experimental study of the effect of language on the reproduction of visually perceived form. *Journal of Experimental Psychology,* 1932, *15*, 73-86.

Carpenter, W. B. *Principles of mental physiology.* London: King, 1877.

Cason, H. The conditioned eyelid reaction. *Journal of Experimental Psychology,* 1923, *5*, 153-196.

Cason, H. Backward conditioning of eyelid reactions. *Journal of Experimental Psychology,* 1935, *18*, 599-611.

Cate-Kazejewa, B. Ten. Quelques observations sur les Bernards l'ermit (*Pagurus arrosar*). *Archives Néerlandaise de Physiologie de l'homme et des Animaux,* 1934, *19*, 502-508.

Cattell, J. M. The time taken up by cerebral association. *Mind,* 1886, *11*, 220-242, 377-392, 524-528.

Cattell, J. M. Experiments on association of ideas. *Mind,* 1887, *12*, 68-74.

Cautela, J. R. The problem of backward conditioning. *Journal of Psychology,* 1965, *60*, 135-144.

Champion, R. A., and Jones, J. E. Forward, backward, and pseudoconditioning of the GSR. *Journal of Experimental Psychology,* 1961, *62*, 58-61.

Chebyshev, P. L. *Theory of approximations.* St. Petersburg: Obshchestvannaya Pol'za, 1879 (2nd edition; Thesis, 1849).

Chernigovsky, V. N. Current problems in the physiology of interception. In *The teachings of I. P. Pavlov and theoretical and practical medicine.* Vol. 2. Moscow: Ministerstvo Zdravokhraneniya, 1953. Pp. 357-382.

Chernigovsky, V. N. *Interoceptors.* Moscow: Medgiz, 1960. (Translated into English [and edited by D. B. Lindsley.]: American Psychological Association, 1967.)

Chernigovsky, V. N. (Ed.) *Problems of the physiology of interoception.* Vol. 2. Moscow-Leningrad: Nauka, 1965.

Chernova, N. A: Conditioned respiratory reflexes in fish. *Trudy Instituta Fiziologii imeni I. P. Pavlova,* 1953, *2*, 364-369.

Chesnokova, E. G. Conditioned reflexes in bees to chains of visual stimuli. *Trudy Instituta Fiziologii imeni I. P. Pavlova,* 1959, *8*, 214-220.

Chinka, I. I. Development of cortical internal inhibition in ontogeny of dogs. *Trudy Instituta Fiziologii imeni I. P. Pavlova,* 1952, *2*, 86-107.

Chistovich, L. A. Formation of galvanic skin reflexes to unaware auditory stimuli. *Izvestiya Akademii Nauk SSSR, Seriya Biologicheskaya,* 1949, *5*, 570-583.

Chomsky, N. Review of *Verbal Behavior* by B. F. Skinner. *Language,* 1959, *35*, 26-58.

Chomsky, N. *Cartesian linguistics.* New York: Harper and Row, 1966.

Chorover, S. L., and Schiller, P. H. Short-term retrograde amnesia in rats. *Journal of Comparative and Physiological Psychology*, 1965, *59*, 73-79.

Chukchev, I. P. *Commonality of the theoretical position of I. P. Pavlov, N. E. Vvedensky, and A. A. Ukhtomsky.* Moscow: Sovetskaya Nauka, 1956.

Chumak, V. I. The dynamics of active "spontaneous" and reflexive motor reactions of chick embryos. In A. G. Ginetsinsky (Ed.), *The evolution of physiological functions.* Moscow: Akademiya Nauk SSSR, 1960. Pp. 77-82.

Clark, R. B. Habituation of the polychaete *Nereis* to sudden stimuli. I. General properties of the habituation process. *Animal Behaviour*, 1960a, *8*, 82-91.

Clark, R. B. Habituation of the polychaete *Nereis* to sudden stimuli. II. Biological significance of habituation. *Animal Behaviour*, 1960b, *8*, 92-103.

Clark, R. B. The learning abilities of *nereid polychaetes* and the role of the supra-oesophageal ganglion. *Animal Behaviour*, 1965 (Supplement 1), 89-100.

Clarke, H. M. Conscious attitudes. *American Journal of Psychology*, 1911, *22*, 214-219.

Coburn, C. A. The behavior of the crow, *Corvus Americanus Aud. Journal of Animal Behavior*, 1914, *4*, 185-201.

Coburn, C. A., and Yerkes, R. M. A study of the behavior of the crow, *Corvus Americanus Aud.*, by the multiple choice method. *Journal of Animal Behavior*, 1915, *5*, 75-114.

Cofer, C. N. Verbal behavior in relation to reasoning and values. In H. Guetzkow (Ed.), *Groups, leadership and men.* Pittsburgh: Carnegie Press, 1951. Pp. 206-217.

Goghill, G. E., *Anatomy and problems of behavior.* Cambridge: Harvard University Press, 1929.

Cole, M., and Maltzman, I. *A handbook of contemporary Soviet psychology.* New York. Basic Books, 1969.

Comstock, C. Relevance of imagery to the processes of thought. *American Journal of Psychology*, 1921, *32*, 196-230.

Cook, L., Davidson, A., Davis, D. J., and Kelleher, R. T. Epinephrine, norepinephrine, and acetylcholine as conditioned stimuli for avoidance behavior. *Science*, 1960, *131*, 990-991.

Coppock, H. W. An investigation of secondary reinforcing effect of a visual stimulus as a function of its temporal relation to shock termination. Unpublished doctoral dissertation, Indiana University, 1950.

Coppock, H. W. Stimuli preceding electric shock can acquire positive reinforcing properties. *Journal of Comparative and Physiological Psychology*, 1954, *47*, 109-113.

Coppock, H. W. Pre-extinction in sensory preconditioning. *Journal of Experimental Psychology*, 1958, *55*, 213-219.

Cott, H. B. The effectiveness of protective adaptations in the hive bee illustrated by experiments on the feeding reactions, habit formation and memory of the common toad *(Bufo bufo bufo). Proceedings of the Zoological Society*, London, 1936, 111-113.

Cowles, J. T. Food-tokens as incentives for learning by chimpanzees. *Comparative Psychology Monographs*, 1937, *14*, No. 71.

Crossland, H. R. A qualitative analysis of the process of forgetting. *Psychological Monographs*, 1921, *29*, Whole No. 130.

Daabs, J. M., and Janis, I. L. Why does eating while reading facilitate opinion change? *Journal of Experimental Social Psychology*, 1965, *1*, 133-144.

Danisch, F. Über Reizbiologie und Reizempfindlichkeit von *Vorticella nebullifera*. *Zeitschrift für Allgemeine Physiologie*, 1921, *19*, 133-190.

Dardano, J. F., and Sauerbrunn, D. Selective punishment of fixed ratio performance. *Journal of the Experimental Analysis of Behavior*, 1964, *7*, 255-260.

Darwin, C. H. *The origin of the species by means of natural selection*. London: Murray, 1859.

Darwin, C. H. *The variations of animals and plants by domestication*. London: Murray, 1868.

Darwin, C. H. *The descent of man in relation to sex*. London: Murray, 1871.

Dashkovskaya, V. S. First conditioned reflexes in human newborn in normal and some pathological states. *Zhurnal Vysshey Nervnoy Deyatel'nosti imeni I. P. Pavlova*, 1953, *3*, 247-259.

Davidenkov, S. N. (Ed.) *Neuroses, elipepsy and narcolepsy*. Moscow: Medgiz, 1960.

Davis, J. L., and Thompson, R. F. Sensory preconditioning of cats in a shuttle box avoidance situation. *Psychonomic Science*, 1968, *13*, 37-38.

Davis, R. C. Modification of the galvanic skin reflex by daily repetition of a stimulus. *Journal of Experimental Psychology*, 1934, *17*, 504-535.

Davis, R. C. The relation of certain muscle action potentials to "mental work." *Indiana University Publications, Science Series*, 1937, No. 5.

Davis, R. C. Patterns of muscular activity during "mental work" and their constancy. *Journal of Experimental Psychology*, 1939, *24*, 451-465.

Davis, R. C., Buchwald, A. M., and Frankmann, R. W: Autonomic and muscular responses, and their relation to simple stimuli. *Psychological Monographs*, 1955, *69* (20, Whole No. 405).

Dawson, M. E., and Grings, W. W. Comparison of classical conditioning and relational learning. *Journal of Experimental Psychology*, 1968, *76*, 227-331.

Dawson, M. E., and Satterfield, G. H. Can human GSR conditioning occur without relational learning? *Proceedings of the 77th Annual Convention of the American Psychological Association*, 1969. Pp. 69-70.

DeArmond, D. Multiple punishment schedule. *Journal of the Experimental Analysis of Behavior*, 1966, *9*, 327-334.

Deese, J., and Kellogg, W. N. Some new data on the nature of spinal conditioning. *Journal of Comparative and Physiological Psychology*, 1949, *42*, 157-160.

Degtyar, E. N. The interrelation of different temporary connections in the formation of stereotypes in children. *Zhurnal Vysshey Nervnoy Deyatel'nosti imeni I. P. Pavlova*, 1961, *11*, 640-644.

Degtyar, E. N. Functional and sequential transformation of a stereotype in preschool children. In V. N. Chernigovsky (Ed.), *The physiology and pathology of higher nervous activity*. Moscow-Leningrad: Akademiya Nauk SSSR, 1965. Pp. 33-35.

Degtyar, E. N. The role of the motor analyzer in formation of systematicity in children. In *Theses, 21st Conference on Problems of Higher Nervous Activity*. Moscow-Leningrad: Nauka, 1966. P. 110.

Delafreshaye, J. F. (Ed.) *Brain mechanisms and learning*. Springfield, Ill.: Charles C Thomas, 1961.

Delgado, J. M. R., Roberts, W. W., and Miller, N. E. Learning motivated by electrical stimulations of the brain. *American Journal of Physiology*, 1954, *179*, 587-593.

Denisenko, P. P. The effects of cholinolytics on the conditioned-reflex activity of rabbits. *Zhurnal Vysshey Nervnoy Deyatel'nosti imeni I. P. Pavlova*, 1960, *11*, 730-737.

Dewes, P. B. Some observations on an operant in the octopus. *Journal of the Experimental Analysis of Behavior*, 1959, *2*, 57-64.

DiCara, L. V., and Miller, N. E. Instrumental learning of vasomotor responses by rats: Learning to respond differentially in the two ears. *Science*, 1968, *159*, 1485-1486.

Dinsmoor, J. A. A discrimination based on punishment. *Quarterly Journal of Experimental Psychology*, 1952, *4*, 27-45.

Dixon, T. R., and Horton, P. L. (Eds.) *Verbal behavior and general behavior theory*. Englewood Cliffs, N. J.: Prentice-Hall, 1968.

Dobryakov, O. A. Conditioned-reflex changes of visual sensitivity. *Problemy Fiziologichiskoy Optiki*, 1948, *6*, 308-313.

Dodge, R. *Elementary conditions of human variability*. New York: Columbia University Press, 1927.

Dolin, A. O. The law of relations in cortical-analyzer activity. *Proceedings of VI Congress on Physiology, Biochemistry, and Pharmacology*. Tbilisi: 1937, 740-747.

Dolin, A. O. The synthetic reflex and physiological interrelations of its components. *Trudy Fiziologicheskikh Laboratorii I. P. Pavlova*, 1940, *9*, 23-36.

Dolin, A. O. *Pathology of higher nervous activity*. Moscow: Vysshaya Shkola, 1962.

Dolin, A. O., Zborovskaya, I. I., and Zamakhover, S. M. The role of the orienting-investigatory reflex in conditioned-reflex action. In L. G. Voronin, A. N. Leont'yev, A. R. Luria, E. N. Sokolov, and O. S. Vinogradova (Eds.), *The orienting reflex and orienting-investigatory activity*. Moscow: Akademiya Pedagogicheskikh Nauk RSFSR, 1958. Pp. 47-60.

Dostálek, C. Zpătné podmineni—soucăst ucéni (Backward conditioning—an integral of learning). *Céskoslovenská Psychologie*, 1968, *12*, 111-118.

Dostálek, C., and Dostáleková, J. To the associative character of backward conditioning. *Activitas Nervosa Superior*, 1964, *6*, 69-70.

Drozdenko, N. P. The effector pathway of conditioned reflexes of the second order. *Fiziologichesky Zhurnal SSSR imeni I. M. Sechenova*, 1950, *36*, 519-523.

Duncan, C. P. (Ed.) *Thinking: Current experimental studies*. Philadelphia: J. B. Lippincott, 1967.

Dunker, K. *Zur Psychologie des produktiven Denkens*. Berlin: Springer, 1935. (English translation by L. S. Lees, *Psychological Monographs*, 1945, *58*, Whole No. 270.)

Dunlap, K. *A system of psychology*. New York: C. B. Scribner's, 1912.

Dunlap, K. *An outline of psychology*. Baltimore: Johns Hopkins Press, 1914.

Durup, G., and Fessard, A. L'électroencéphalogramme de l'homme. *Année Psychologique*, 1935, *36*, 1-32.

Dykman, R. A. Toward a theory of classical conditioning: Cognitive, emotional, and motor components of the conditioned reflex. In B. A. Maher (Ed.), *Progress in experimental personality research*. Vol. 2. New York: Academic Press, 1965. Pp. 229-318.

Dzhavrishvili, T. D. The problem of two-way temporary connections. *Trudy Instituta Fiziologii imeni I. S. Beritashvili*, 1956, *10*, 163-187.

Ebbinghaus, H. *Über das Gedächtniss. Untersuchungen zur experimentellen Psychologie*. Leipzig: Duncker and Humboldt, 1885.

Eccles, J. C. *The neurophysiological basis of mind. The principles of neurophysiology*. Oxford: Clarendon Press, 1953.

Eccles, J. C. *The physiology of synapses*. Berlin: Springer, 1964.

Eccles, R. M., and Rall, W. Effects induced in a monosynaptic reflex path by its activation. *Journal of Neurophysiology,* 1951, *14,* 353-376.

Eckert, R. Electrical interaction of paired ganglion cells in the leech. *Journal of General Physiology,* 1963, *46,* 573-587.

Egger, M. D., and Miller, N. E. Secondary reinforcement as a function of information value and reliability of the stimulus. *Journal of Experimental Psychology,* 1962, *64,* 97-104.

Ehrenfels, C. F. von. Über Gestalqualitäten. *Vierteljahrschrift für Wissenchaftliche Philosophie und Soziologie,* 1890, *14,* 249-292.

Eisenstein, E. M., and Cohen, M. J. Learning in isolated prothoracic ganglia. *Animal Behaviour,* 1965, *13,* 104-108.

El'kin, D. G. The characteristics of conditioned reflexes to a complex verbal stimulus. *Voprosy Psikhologii,* 1955, *1*(4), 79-89.

Ellison, G. D., and Konorski, J. An investigation of the relations between salivary and motor responses during instrumental performance. *Acta Biologiae Experimentalis,* 1965, *25*(4), 297-315.

Ellison, G. D., and Konorski, J. Salivation and instrumental responding to an instrumental CS pretrained using the classical conditioning paradigm. *Acta Biologiae Experimentalis,* 1966, *26*(4), 159-165.

Ellson, D. G. Hallucinations produced by sensory conditioning. *Journal of Experimental Psychology,* 1941, *28,* 1-20.

El'yasson, M. I. *The study of the auditory capacity of dogs, normal and with partial bilateral ablation of the temporal lobes.* St. Petersburg: VMA, 1908. (Thesis)

Engen, T., and Lipsitt, L. P. Decrement and recovery of responses to olfactory stimuli in the human neonate. *Journal of Comparative and Physiological Psychology,* 1965, *59,* 312-316.

Engen, T., Lipsitt, L. P., and Kaye, H. Olfactory responses and adaptation in the human neonate. *Journal of Comparative and Physiological Psychology,* 1963, *56,* 73-77.

Eriksen, C. W. Discrimination and learning without awareness: A methodological survey and evaluation. *Psychological Review,* 1960, *67,* 279-300.

Esper, E. A. *A history of psychology.* Philadelphia: Saunders, 1964.

Essman, W. B., and Alperin, H. Single trial conditioning: Methodology and results with mice. *Psychological Reports,* 1964, *14,* 731-740.

Estes, W. K. An experimental study of punishment. *Psychological Monographs,* 1944, *57* (Whole No. 263).

Estes, W. K. Component and pattern models with Markovian interpretations. In R. Bush and W. Estes (Eds.), *Studies in mathematical learning theory.* Stanford: Stanford University Press, 1959. Pp. 9-52.

Estes, W. K., and Hopkins, B. L. Acquisition and transfer in pattern-vs.-component discrimination learning. *Journal of Experimental Psychology,* 1961, *4,* 322-328.

Estes, W. K., and Skinner, B. F. Some quantitative properties of anxiety. *Journal of Experimental Psychology,* 1941, *29,* 390-400.

Evans, S. M. Non-associative avoidance learning in *Nereid polychaetes. Animal Behaviour,* 1966a, *14,* 102-106.

Evans, S. M. Non-associative behavioural modifications in the polychaete *Nereis diversicolor. Animal Behaviour,* 1966 b, *14,* 107-119.

Exner, S. Zur Kenntniss von der Wechselwirkung der Erregungen in Centralnervensystems. *Pflügers Archiv für die Gesamte Physiologie des Menschen und der Tiere,* 1882, *28,* 487-506.

Fadeyeva, V. K. *Methodology of experimental investigation of higher nervous activity in man (child, adult, normal and abnormal)*. Moscow: Medgiz, 1960.

Fanardzhan, V. V. (1958) Quoted by Sergeyev, 1964a, and read by Razran; reference not available at this time.

Farber, I. E. The things people say to themselves. *American Psychologist*, 1963, *18*, 185-197.

Fatt, P. Biophysics of junctional transmission. *Physiological Review*, 1954, *34*, 674-710.

Fayziyev, S. *Unconditioned and natural-conditioned salivary reflexes in Romanov and Karakul sheep*. Leningrad: Author, 1957.

Fayziyev, S. Unconditioned salivary reactions in Karakul sheep in ontogeny. In V. V. Chernigovsky (Ed.), *Physiological bases of complex behavior*. Moscow: Akademiya Nauk SSSR, 1963. Pp. 182-184.

Feather, B. Human salivary conditioning: A methodological study. In G. A. Kimble (Ed.), *Foundations of conditioning and learning*. New York: Appleton-Century-Crofts, 1967. Pp. 117-143.

Fechner, G. T. *Elemente der Psychophysik*. Leipzig: Breitkopf, 1860.

Fechner, G. T. *Vorschule der Aesthetic*. II. Leipzig: Breitkopf, 1876.

Fedorov, L. N. The effect of unusual strong stimuli on a dog of excitatory type of nervous system. *Trudy Fiziologicheskikh Laboratorii imeni I. P. Pavlova*, 1927, *2*(1), 25-36.

Fedorov, V. K. The soporific action of weak electrical stimulation applied cutaneously in a dog and its special effect upon the locus of stimulation. *Trudy Fiziologicheskikh Laboratorii imeni I. P. Pavlova*, 1933, *5*, 199-212.

Fedorov, V. K., and Yakovleva, V. V. Analysis of the physiological mechanism of experimental neuroses. *Trudy Fiziologicheckikh Laboratorii imeni I. P. Pavlova*, 1949, *15*, 364-385.

Fedoseyev, P. N. (Ed.) *Philosophical problems of higher nervous activity and psychology*. Moscow: Akademiya Nauk SSSR, 1963.

Fedotov, Yu. P. Action of painful stimuli on reflex activity of the spinal cord. I: Effect of painful stimuli on reflex chronaxie. *Fiziologichesky Zhurnal SSSR imeni I. M. Sechenova*, 1950a, *36*, 166-175.

Fedotov, Yu. P. Action of painful stimuli on reflex action of the spinal cord. III: Effect of painful stimuli on the patellar reflex. *Fiziologichesky Zhurnal SSSR imeni I. M. Sechenova*, 1950b, *36*, 436-444.

Fedotov, Yu. P. The effect of painful stimulation on spinal reflexes. IV: Changes of warmth thresholds of the flexor reflexes and some motor manifestations after painful stimuli. *Fiziologichesky Zhurnal SSSR imeni I. M. Sechenova*, 1951, *37*, 69-74.

Fedotov, Yu. P. The effect of a painful stimulus on conditioned salivary reflexes in dogs. *Fiziologichesky Zhurnal SSSR imeni I. M. Sechenova*, 1954, *40*, 673-680.

Fehr, F. S., and Stern, J. A. Heart rate conditioning in the rat. *Journal of Psychosomatic Research*, 1965, *8*, 441-453.

Ferster, C. B. Control of behavior in chimpanzees and pigeons by time out from positive reinforcer. *Psychological Monographs*, 1958, *72* (Whole No. 461).

Ferster, C. B., and DeMyer, M. K. The development of performances in autistic children in an automatically controlled environment. *Journal of Chronic Disorders*, 1961, *13*, 312-345.

Ferster, C. B., and Skinner, B. F. *Schedules of reinforcement*. New York: Appleton-Century-Crofts, 1957.

Field, W. S., and Abbott, W. (Eds.) *Information storage and neural control.* Springfield, Ill.: Charles C Thomas, 1963.

Fields, P. E. Contributions to visual figure discrimination in the white rat. *Journal of Comparative Psychology,* 1931, *11*, 327-366.

Fifkova, E. Cortical-hippocampal interrelation of the spread of [Leăo] depression. *Gagrskiye Besedy,* 1968, *5*, 144-158.

Filby, Y., and Appel, J. B. Variable-interval punishment during variable-interval reinforcement. *Journal of the Experimental Analysis of Behavior,* 1966, *9*, 521-527.

Filiminov, I. N. Phylogeny and ontogeny of the nervous system. In I. N. Filiminov, (Ed.), *Handbook of neurology.* Vol. 1, Book 1. *Phylogeny and ontogeny of the nervous system.* Moscow: Medgiz, 1959. Pp. 9-89.

Filiminov, I. N. Architecture and localization of functions in the cerebral cortex. In I. N. Filiminov (Ed.), *Handbook of neurology.* Vol. 1, Book 2. *Neural cytoarchitecture.* Moscow: Medgiz, 1960. Pp. 153-167.

Fink, J. B., and Patton, R. M. Decrement of a learned drinking response accompanying changes in several stimulus characteristics. *Journal of Comparative and Physiological Psychology,* 1953, *46*, 23-37.

Firsov, L. A. Conditioned motor reflexes to chains of stimuli in young chimpanzees. *Zhurnal Vysshey Nervnoy Deyatel'nosti imeni I. P. Pavlova,* 1955, *5*, 247-254.

Fitzwater, M. E., and Reisman, M. N. Comparison of forward, simultaneous, backward and pseudoconditioning. *Journal of Experimental Psychology,* 1952, *44*, 211-214.

Fleure, H. J., and Walton, C. Notes on the habits of some sea anemones. *Zooligischer Anzeiger,* 1907, *31*, 212-220.

Florovsky, G. B. On the mechanism of reflex salivary action. *Bulletin de l'Academie des Sciences, St. Petersbourg,* 1917, *17*, 119-136.

Flyoss, D. A., Krushinsky, L. V., Molodkina, L. N., and Ochinskaya, E. I. Regulation of complex animal behavior (extrapolative reflexes) by means of psychotropic agents. In V. N. Chernigovsky (Ed.), *Physiological bases of complex forms of behavior.* Moscow: Akademiya Nauk SSSR, 1963. Pp. 34-36.

Forbes, A., and Mahan, C. Attempts to train the spinal cord. *Journal of Comparative and Physiological Psychology,* 1963, *56*, 36-40.

Franzisket, L. Gewöhnheitsbildung und bedingte Reflexe bei Rückenmarksfröschen. *Zeitschrift für Vergleichende Physiologie,* 1951, *33*, 142-178.

Franzisket, L. Characteristics of instinctive behavior and learning in reflex activity of the frog. *Animal Behaviour,* 1963, *11*, 318-324.

Friedman, M. P. Transfer effects and response strategies in pattern-versus-component discrimination learning. *Journal of Experimental Psychology,* 1966, *71*, 420-428.

Friedman, M. P., and Gelfand, H. Transfer effects in discrimination learning. *Journal of Mathematical Psychology,* 1964, *1*, 204-214.

Frolov, S. A. *Afferent effects of the integument and cavity of the gastrum on the functions of the salivary glands.* Ivanovo: Author, 1951. (Thesis)

Frolov, Yu. P. Transformation of trace conditioned reflexes into trace conditioned inhibitors through simultaneous conditioned reflexes. *Trudy Fiziologicheskikh Laboratorii imeni I. P. Pavlova,* 1926, *1*(2-3), 279-286.

Fromer, R. Conditioned vasomotor responses in the rabbit. *Journal of Comparative and Physiological Psychology,* 1963, *56*, 1050-1055.

Fulton, G. F. *Physiology of the nervous system.* London and New York: Oxford University Press, 1943.

Furawaka, T., Fukami, Y., and Asada, Y. A third type of inhibition in the Mauthner cells of goldfish. *Journal of Neurophysiology*, 1963, *26*, 759-774.

Furawaka, T., and Furshpan, E. J. Two inhibitory mechanisms in the Mauthner neurones of goldfish. *Journal of Neurophysiology*, 1963, *26*, 140-176.

Furness, W. H. Observations on the mentality of chimpanzees and orang-utan. *Proceedings of the American Philosophical Society*, 1916, *55*, 281-289.

Fursikov, D. S., Gurevich, M. O., and Zalmanzon, A. N. (Eds.) *Higher nervous activity*. Moscow: Kommunisticheskaya Akademiya, 1929.

Gakel, L. B. Neuroses in man. In S. N. Davidenkov (Ed.), *Handbook of neurology*. Vol. 6. *Neuroses, epilepsy and narcolepsy*. Moscow: Medgiz, 1960. Pp. 44-212.

Galambos, R., and Morgan, C. T. The neural basis of learning. In J. Field, H. W. Magoun, and V. E. Hall (Eds.), *Handbook of physiology*. Vol. 3. Baltimore: Waverly Press, 1960. Pp. 1471-1499.

Galambos, R., and Sheatz, G. S. An electroencephalographic study of classical conditioning. *American Journal of Physiology*, 1962, *203*, 173-184.

Galambos, R., Sheatz, G., and Vernier, V. G. Electrophysiological correlates of a conditioned response in cats. *Science*, 1956, *123*, 376-377.

Galeano, C., Roig, J. A., Segundo, J. P., and Sommer-Smith, J. A. Alternate applications of tone and subcutaneous stimulus in the cat. I. Effect of tone cessation. *Abstracts of Communications, XXI International Congress of Physiological Sciences*, Buenos Aires, August 9-15, 1959. P. 101.

Galton, F. Psychometric experiment. *Brain*, 1879-1880, *2*, 149-162.

Gambaryan, L. S. *Problems of the physiology of the motor analyzer*. Moscow: GIZ, 1962. (English translation, Bethesda, Md.: National Library of Medicine, 1963.)

Gantt, W. H. The origin and development of nervous disturbances experimentally produced. *American Journal of Psychiatry*, 1942, *98*, 475-481.

Gantt, W. H. Experimental basis for neurotic behavior. *Psychosomatic Medicine Monographs*, 1944, *3*, No. 3-4.

Gantt, W. H. *Physiological bases of psychiatry*. Springfield, Ill.: Charles C Thomas, 1958.

Garcia, J., Ervin, F. R., Yorke, C. H., and Koelling, R. A. Conditioning with delayed vitamin injection. *Science*, 1967, *155*, 716-718.

Garcia, J., Kimmeldorf, D. J., and Koelling, R. A. Conditioned aversion to saccharin resulting from exposure to gamma radiation. *Science*, 1955, *122*, 157-158.

Gardner, R. A., and Gardner, B. T. Teaching sign language to a chimpanzee, *Science*, 1969, *165*, 664-672.

Garner, R. L. *Apes and monkeys, their life and language*. Boston: Ginn, 1900.

Gayet, R., and Guillaummie, M. Recherches sur les inhibition réflexes de la sécretion pancréatique par stimulation des nerfs sensitifs. *Compte Rendu des Séances de la Societé de Biologie, Paris*, 1933, *112*, 1058-1062.

Gelber, B. Investigation of the behavior of paramecium aurelia: I. Modification of behavior after training with reinforcement. *Journal of Comparative and Physiological Psychology*, 1952, *45*, 58-65.

Gellerman, L. W. Form discrimination in chimpanzees and two-year-old children. I. Form (triangularity) per se. *Journal of Genetic Psychology*, 1933, *42*, 3-27.

Gershuni, G. V. The study of aware (sensory) and unaware (subsensory) reactions evoked by external stimuli. *Izvestiya Akademii Nauk SSSR, Seriya Biologicheskaya*, 1945, 210-228.

Gershuni, G. V. Interrelation of awareness and conditioned reflexes. *Fiziologichesky Zhurnal SSSR imeni I. M. Sechenova,* 1946, *32,* 43-47.

Gershuni, G. V. Study of subsensory reaction in sense-organ activities. *Fiziologichesky Zhurnal SSSR imeni I. M. Sechenova,* 1947, *33,* 393-412.

Gershuni, G. V. The study of sensations and conditioned reflexes in auditory stimulation. *Trudy Fiziologicheskogo Instituta imeni I. P. Pavlova,* 1949a, *4,* 19-24.

Gershuni, G. V. Interaction of reflex reactions to external stimuli and sensations in the sense organs of man. *Fiziologichesky Zhurnal SSSR imeni I. M. Sechenova,* 1949b, *35,* 541-560.

Gershuni, G. V. Quantitative studies of the action range of subsensory auditory stimulation. *Problemy Fiziologicheskoy Akustiki,* 1950, *2,* 29-36.

Gershuni, G. V. Characteristics of conditioned galvanic skin reflexes and alpharhythm blocking in subsensory and supersensory auditory stimulations in man. *Zhurnal Vysshey Nervnoy Deyatel'nosti imeni I. P. Pavlova,* 1955, *5,* 665-676.

Gershuni, G. V. Studies of the activity of the auditory analyzer through various reactions. *Zhurnal Vysshey Nervnoy Deyatel'nosti imeni I. P. Pavlova,* 1957, *7,* 13-24.

Gershuni, G. V. (Ed.) *Problems of the physiology of sensory systems (a review).* Moscow, Nauka, 1966.

Gershuni, G. V., Alekseyenko, N. Yu., Arapova, A. A., Klaas, Yu. A., Maruseva, A. M., Obraztsova, G. A., and Solovtsova, A. P. Disruption of activity of sense organs in some neural functions during "aerial" contusion. *Voyenno-Meditzinsky Sbornik,* 1945, No. 2, 98-192.

Gershuni, G. V., Avakyan, R. V., Baru, A. V., and Mironova, L. M. Sound discrimination and temporal recruitment. In E. M. Kreps (Ed.), *The evolution of function.* Moscow: Nauka, 1964. Pp. 66-75.

Gershuni, G. V., and Korotkin, I. I. Subsensory conditioned reflexes to auditory stimuli. *Doklady Akademii Nauk SSSR,* 1947, *57,* 417-420.

Gershuni, G. V., Kozhevnikov, V. A., Maruseva, A. M., Avakyan, R. V., Radionova, E. A., Altman, J. A., and Soroko, V. I. Modifications in electrical responses of the auditory system in different states of higher nervous activity. In H. H. Jasper and G. D. Smirnov (Eds.), The Moscow Colloquium on Electroencephalography of Higher Nervous Activity, *Electroencephalography and Clinical Neurophysiology,* 1960, Supplement 13, 115-125.

Gershuni, G. V., Kozhevnikov, V. A., Maruseva, A. M., and Chistovich, L. A. Characteristics of the formation of temporary connections to unaware auditory stimuli in man. *Byulleten' Eksperimental'noy Biologii i Meditsiny,* 1948, *26*(3), 205-209.

Gibson, J. J. *The senses considered as perceptual systems.* Boston: Houghton Mifflin, 1966.

Gibson, J. J., and Gibson, E. J. Perceptual learning: Differentiation or enrichment? *Psychological Review,* 1955, *62,* 33-40.

Gifford, E. W. California kinship terminologies. *University of California Publications in American Archaeology and Ethnology,* 1922, *18,* 1-285.

Gilden, L., Vaughan, H. G., and Costa, L. D. Summated human EEG potentials with voluntary movements. *Electroencephalography and Clinical Neurophysiology,* 1966, *20,* 433-438.

Ginetsinsky, A. G. (Ed.) *Problems of the evolution of physiological functions.* Moscow: Akademiya Nauk SSSR, 1958.

Ginetsinsky, A. G. (Ed.) *The evolution of physiological functions.* Moscow: Akademiya Nauk SSSR, 1960.

Giurgea, C. Dinamica elabrarii connexiuni temporare prin excitarea directa a scoartei cerebrale. *Studii şi Cercetări de Fiziologie si Neurologie,* 1953, *4,* 41-49.

Glanzer, M. Stimulus satiation: An explanation of spontaneous alternation and related phenomena. *Psychological Review,* 1953, *60,* 257-268.

Gliedman, L. H., and Gantt, W. H. The effects of reserpine and chlorpromazine on orienting behavior and retention of conditioned reflexes. *Southern Medical Journal,* 1956, *49,* 880-889.

Gnedenko, B. V. *Textbook of theory of probability.* Moscow: GIZ, 1950.

Goldstein, K. *Language and language disturbances.* New York: Grune and Stratton, 1948.

Goleva, N. G. Unconditioned respiratory reflexes in foxes. In *Problems of comparative physiology and pathology of higher nervous activity.* Leningrad: Medgiz, 1955. Pp. 76-85.

Golubeva, E. L. Conditioned motor reflexes in guinea pig neonates. *Arkhiv Biologicheskikh Nauk,* 1939, *54*(4), 132-142.

Goodson, F. E., and Brownstein, A. Secondary reinforcing and motivating properties of stimuli contiguous with shock onset and termination. *Journal of Comparative and Physiological Psychology,* 1955, *48,* 381-386.

Gormezano, I., and Moore, J. W. Classical conditioning. In M. H. Marx (Ed.), *Learning: Processes.* New York: Macmillan, 1970. Pp. 121-203.

Gorská, T., and Jankovká, E. The effect of deafferentation on instrumental (Type II) conditioned reflexes in dogs. *Acta Biologiae Experimentalis,* 1961, *21,* 219-234.

Gorská, T., Jankovká, E., and Kozak, W. The effect of deafferentation on the instrumental (Type II) cleaning reflex in cats. *Acta Biologiae Experimentalis,* 1961, *21,* 207-218.

Gos, M. Le psychisme de la moelle épinière. *Bulletin de la Societé Royale de Science de Liége,* 1932, *4,* 95-97.

Gos, M. Les réflexes conditionnels chez l'embryon d'oiseau. *Bulletin de la Societé Royale de Science de Liége,* 1933, No. 4-5, 194-199; No. 6-7, 246-250.

Gossette, R. L., and Brown, H. R. The scaling of relative task difficulty across spatial, brightness, and form successive discrimination reversal (SDR) problems with capuchin monkeys. *Psychonomic Science,* 1967, *9,* 1-2.

Granit, R. (Ed.) *Nobel Symposium I. Muscular afferents and motor control.* New York: Wiley, 1966.

Granit, R., and Phillips, C. G. Excitatory and inhibitory processes acting upon individual Purkinje cells of the cerebellum in cats. *Journal of Physiology,* 1956, *133,* 520-547.

Grant, D. A. The pseudo-conditioned eyelid response. *Journal of Experimental Psychology,* 1943a, *32,* 139-149.

Grant, D. A. Sensitization and association in eyelid conditioning. *Journal of Experimental Psychology,* 1943b, *32,* 201-212.

Grant, D. A. A sensitized eyelid reaction related to the conditioned eyelid response. *Journal of Experimental Psychology,* 1945, *35,* 393-402.

Grant, D. A., and Adams, J. K. "Alpha" conditioning in the eyelid. *Journal of Experimental Psychology,* 1944, *34,* 136-142.

Grant, D. A., and Dittmer, D. G. A tactile generalization gradient for a pseudo-conditioned response. *Journal of Experimental Psychology,* 1940, *26,* 404-412.

Grant, D. A., and Hilgard, E. R. Sensitization as a supplement to association in eyelid conditioning. *Psychological Bulletin,* 1940, *37,* 478-479.

Grant, D. A., and Meyer, H. F. The formation of generalized response sets during repeated electric shock stimulation. *Journal of General Psychology,* 1941, *24,* 21-38.

Grant, D. A., and Schneider, D. Intensity of the CS and strength of conditioning. I. The conditioned eyelid response. *Journal of Experimental Psychology,* 1948, *38,* 690-696.

Grant, D. A., and Schneider, D. Intensity of the CS and strength of conditioning. II. The conditioned galvanic skin response to an auditory stimulus. *Journal of Experimental Psychology,* 1949, *39,* 35-40.

Gray, J. A. Stimulus intensity dynamism. *Psychological Bulletin,* 1965, *63,* 180-196.

Grechushnikova, L. S. EEG changes in motor dominance produced by fading rhythmic stimulation. *Trudy Instituta Vysshey Nervnoy Deyatel'nosti imeni I. P. Pavlova, Seriya Fiziologicheskaya,* 1962, *7,* 33-38.

Green, P. C. Learning, extinction, and generalization of conditioned responses by young monkeys. *Psychological Reports,* 1962, *10,* 731-738.

Greene, W. A., and Kimmel, H. D. Habituation of large and small GSRs. *Psychological Reports,* 1966, *19,* 587-591.

Greenspoon, J. The reinforcing effect of two spoken sounds on the frequency of two responses. *American Journal of Psychology,* 1955, *68,* 409-416.

Grether, W. F. Pseudo-conditioning without paired stimulation encountered in attempted backward conditioning. *Journal of Comparative Psychology,* 1938, *25,* 91-96.

Grice, G. R., and Hunter, J. J. Stimulus intensity effects depend upon the type of experimental design. *Psychological Review,* 1964, *71,* 247-256.

Grigoryan, V. Z. Effect of electroconvulsive shock on higher nervous activity in rats. *Zhurnal Vysshey Nervnoy Deyatel'nosti imeni I. P. Pavlova,* 1954, *4,* 282-288.

Grings, W. W. Preparatory set variables in classical conditioning. *Psychological Review,* 1960, *67,* 243-252.

Grings, W. W. Compound stimulus transfer in human classical conditioning. Paper read at Conference on Classical Conditioning, McMaster University, May 12, 1969.

Grings, W. W., and Kimmel, H. D. Compound stimulus transfer for different sense modalities. *Psychological Reports,* 1959, *5,* 253-260.

Grings, W. W., and Lockhart, R. A. Effects of "anxiety lessening" instructions and differential set development on the extinction of GSR. *Journal of Experimental Psychology,* 1963, *66,* 292-299.

Grings, W. W., and Lockhart, R. A. Problems of magnitude measurement with multiple GSRs. *Psychological Reports,* 1965, *17,* 979-982.

Grings, W. W., and Lockhart, R. A. Galvanic skin response during avoidance learning. *Psychophysiology,* 1966, *3,* 29-34.

Grings, W. W., Lockhart, R. A., and Dameron, L. I. Conditioning autonomic responses of mentally subnormal individuals. *Psychological Monographs,* 1962, *76,* (39, Whole No. 558).

Grings, W. W., and O'Donnell, D. E. Magnitude of response to compounds of discriminated stimuli. *Journal of Experimental Psychology,* 1956, *52,* 354-359.

Grings, W. W., and Shmelev, V. N. Changes in GSR to a single stimulus as a result of training of a compound stimulus. *Journal of Experimental Psychology,* 1959, *58,* 129-133.

Grings, W. W., Uno, T., and Feibiger, J. Component to compound stimulus transfer. *Psychonomic Science,* 1965, *3,* 63-64.

Grundfest, H. Evolution of conduction in the nervous system. In *Evolution of nervous control from primitive organisms to man.* Washington: American Association for the Advancement of Science, 1959. Pp. 43-86.

Grundfest, H., Reuben, J. P., and Rickles, W. H. The electrophysiology and pharmacology of lobster neuromuscular responses. *Journal of General Physiology,* 1959, *42,* 1301-1323.

Guseva, E. G. The study of experimental neurosis by alimentary and defensive methods. *Trudy Instituta Fiziologii imeni I. P. Pavlova,* 1956, *5,* 25-49.

Guth, S. L. Pattern effects with compound stimuli. *Journal of Comparative and Physiological Psychology,* 1967, *63,* 480-485.

Guthrie, E. R. *The psychology of learning.* New York: Harper, 1935.

Guthrie, E. R. Association by contiguity. In S. Koch (Ed.), *Psychology: A study of a science* Vol. 2. New York: McGraw-Hill, 1959, Pp. 158-195.

Guttman, W., and Kalish, H. I. Discriminability and stimulus generalization. *Journal of Experimental Psychology,* 1956, *51,* 79-88.

Gvozdev, A. N. *Problems of studying speech in children.* Moscow: Akademiya Pedagogicheskikh Nauk RSFSR, 1961.

Hadamand, J. *The psychology of invention in the mathematical field.* Princeton, N.J.: Princeton University Press, 1945.

Haecker, V. Über Lernversuche bei Axolotln. *Archiv für die Gesamte Psychologie* 1912, *25,* 1-35.

Hagbarth, K. E., and Kugelberg, E. The plasticity of the human abdominal skin reflex. *Brain,* 1958, *81,* 305-318.

Hagiwara, S., and Morita, H. Electrotonic transmission between two nerve cells in a leech. *Journal of Neurophysiology,* 1962, *25,* 721-731.

Haith, M. M. The response of the human newborn to visual stimuli. *Journal of Experimental Child Psychology,* 1966, *3,* 235-243.

Hake, D. F., and Azrin, N. H. An apparatus for delivering pain-shock to monkeys. *Journal of the Experimental Analysis of Behavior,* 1963, *6,* 297-298.

Hamburger, V., and Balaban, M. Observations and experiments on spontaneous rhythmical behavior in the chick embryo. *Developmental Biology,* 1963, *7,* 533-545.

Harlow, H. F. Forward conditioning, backward conditioning, and pseudo-conditioning in the goldfish. *Journal of Genetic Psychology,* 1939, *55,* 49-58.

Harlow, H. F. The formation of learning sets. *Psychological Review,* 1949, *56,* 51-65.

Harlow, H. F., Harlow, M. K., and Meyer, D. K. Learning motivated by a manipulation drive. *Journal of Experimental Psychology,* 1950, *40,* 228-234.

Harlow, H. F., and Toltzien, F. Formation of pseudo-conditioned responses in the cat. *Journal of General Psychology,* 1940, *23,* 367-375.

Harper, R. J., Anderson, C., Christenson, C. C., Clifford, M., and Hunka, S. M. *The cognitive process: Readings.* Englewood Cliffs, N.J.: Prentice-Hall, 1964.

Harris, J. D. Forward conditioning, backward conditioning, pseudoconditioning, and adaptation to the conditioned stimulus. *Journal of Experimental Psychology,* 1941, *28,* 491-502.

Harris, J. E., and Whiting, H. P. Structure and functions in the locomotor system of the dogfish embryo. *Journal of Experimental Biology,* 1954, *31,* 501-524.

Hartley, D. *Various conjectures on the perception, motion, and generation of ideas* (1746). (Translated from the Latin by R. E. A. Palmer.) Los Angeles: William Andrews Clark Memorial Library of the University of California, 1959.

Hartley, D. Observations on man, his frame, his duty and his expectations. London: Johnson, 1749.

Hartline, H. K., Wagner, H. G., and Ratliff, F. Inhibition in the eye of the Limulus. Journal of General Physiology, 1956, 39, 651-673.

Hayes, C. The ape in our house. New York: Harper, 1951.

Hearst, E., Beer, B., Galambos, R., and Sheatz, G. S. Some electrophysiological correlates of conditioning in the monkey. Electroencephalography and Clinical Neurophysiology, 1960, 12, 137-152.

Hebb, D. O. The organization of behavior. New York: Wiley, 1949.

Hebb, D. O. Heredity and environment in mammalian behavior. British Journal of Animal Behavior, 1953, 1, 43-47.

Hebb, D. O. A textbook of psychology. Philadelphia: Saunders, 1958.

Hebb, D. O. A textbook of psychology (2nd ed.). Philadelphia: Saunders, 1966.

Hefferline, R. F., Keenan, B., and Hartford, R. A. Escape and avoidance conditioning in human subjects without their observation of the response. Science, 1959, 130, 1338-1339.

Hernandez-Peón, R. Neurophysiological correlates of habituation and other manifestations of plastic inhibition (internal inhibition). In H. H. Jasper and G. D. Smirnov (Eds.), The Moscow Colloquium on Electroencephalography of Higher Nervous Activity, Electroencephalography and Clinical Neurophysiology, 1960, Supplement 13, 101-114.

Hernandez-Peón, R., Scherer, H., and Jouvet, M. Modification of electrical activity in cochlear nucleus during attention in unanaesthesized cats. Science, 1956, 123, 331-332.

Hilgard, E. R. The relationship between the conditioned response and conventional learning. Psychological Bulletin, 1937, 34, 61-102.

Hilgard, E. R. An algebraic analysis of conditioned discrimination in man. Psychological Review, 1938, 45, 472-496.

Hilgard, E. R. Psychology after Darwin. In S. Tax (Ed.), Evolution after Darwin. Vol. II. The evolution of man. Chicago: University of Chicago Press, 1960, Pp. 269-287.

Hilgard, E. R., and Bower, G. H. Theories of learning. New York: Appleton-Century-Crofts, 1966.

Hilgard, E. R., and Marquis, D. G. Conditioning and learning. New York: Appleton-Century, 1940.

Hinde, R. A. Factors governing the changes in strength of a partially inborn response, as shown by the mobbing behaviour of the chaffinch. II. The waning of the response. Proceedings of the Royal Society, Series B, 1954, 142, 331-358.

Hinde, R. A. Animal behaviour. A synthesis of ethology and comparative psychology. New York: McGraw-Hill, 1966.

Hobhouse, L. T. Mind in evolution. New York: Macmillan, 1901.

Hodos, W., and Valenstein, E. S. Motivational variables affecting the rate of behavior maintained by intracranial stimulation. Journal of Comparative and Physiological Psychology, 1960, 53, 502-508.

Hoffeld, D. R., Kendall, S. B., Thompson, R. F., and Brogden, W. J. Effects of amount of preconditioning training upon the magnitude of sensory preconditioning. Journal of Experimental Psychology, 1960, 59, 198-204.

Hoffeld, D. R., Thompson, R. F., and Brogden, W. J. Effect of stimuli time relations during preconditioning training upon the magnitude of sensory preconditioning. Journal of Experimental Psychology, 1958, 56, 437-442.

von Holst, E., and von Saint Paul, U. On the functional organization of drives. *Animal Behaviour*, 1963, *11*, 1-20.

Holt, E. B. *Animal drive and the learning process*. New York: Holt, 1931.

Holz, W. C., and Azrin, N. H. Interactions between the discriminative and aversive properties of punishment. *Journal of the Experimental Analysis of Behavior*, 1962a, *5*, 229-234.

Holz, W. C., and Azrin, N. H. Recovery during punishment by intense noise. *Psychological Reports*, 1962b, *11*, 655-657.

Holz, W. C., and Azrin, N. H. Conditioning human verbal behavior. In W. K. Honig (Ed.), *Operant Behavior: Areas of research and application*. New York: Appleton-Century-Crofts, 1966. Pp. 790-826.

Honig, W. K. (Ed.) *Operant Behavior: Areas of research and application*. New York: Appleton-Century-Crofts, 1966a.

Honig, W. K. The role of discrimination training in the generalization of punishment. *Journal of the Experimental Analysis of Behavior*, 1966b, *9*, 377-384.

Honig, W. K., and Slivka, R. M. Stimulus generalization of the effects of punishment. *Journal of the Experimental Analysis of Behavior*, 1964, *7*, 21-25.

Horridge, G. A. Analysis of the rapid response of *Nereis* and *Harmothoe* (*Annelida*). *Proceedings of the Royal Society, Series B*, 1959, *150*, 245-262.

Horridge, G. A. Learning leg position by the ventral nerve cord in headless insects. *Proceedings of the Royal Society, Series B*, 1962a, *157*, 33-52.

Horridge, G. A. Learning of leg positions by headless insects. *Nature* (London), 1962b, *193*, 697-698.

Horridge, G. A. The electrophysiological approach to learning in isolatable ganglia. *Animal Behaviour*, 1965, *13* (Supplement 1), 163-182.

Hovey, H. B. Associative hysteresis in marine flatworms. *Physiological Zoology*, 1929, *2*, 322-333.

Hovland, C. I. Inhibition of reinforcement and phenomena of experimental extinction. *Proceedings of the National Academy of Science*, 1936, *22*, 430-433.

Hoyle, G. Neurophysiological studies on "learning" in headless insects. In J. E. Treherne and J. W. Beament (Eds.), *The physiology of the insect central nervous system*. New York: Academic Press, 1965. Pp. 204-232.

Hrbek, J. Discussion. In H. H. Jasper and G. D. Smirnov (Eds.), The Moscow Colloquium on Electroencephalography of Higher Nervous Activity. *Electroencephalography and Clinical Neurology*, 1960, Supplement 13, 86-88.

Hubel, D. H., and Wiesel, T. N. Receptive fields of single neurones in the cat's striate cortex. *Journal of Physiology* (London), 1959, *148*, 574-591.

Hubel, D. H., and Wiesel, T. N. Integrative action in the cat's lateral geniculate body. *Journal of Physiology* (London), 1961, *155*, 385-398.

Hubel, D. H., and Wiesel, T. N. Receptive fields, binocular interaction and functional architecture in the cat's visual cortex. *Journal of Physiology* (London), 1962, *160*, 106-154.

Hubel, D. H., and Wiesel, T. N. Receptive fields of cells in striate cortex of very young visually inexperienced kittens. *Journal of Neurophysiology*, 1963, *26*, 994-1002.

Hughes, J. R. Post-tetanic potentiation. *Physiological Review*, 1958, *38*, 91-113.

Hull, C. L. A functional interpretation of the conditioned reflex. *Psychological Review*, 1929, *36*, 498-511.

Hull, C. L. Mind, mechanism, and adaptive behavior. *Psychological Review*, 1937, *44*, 1-32.

Hull, C. L. Explorations in the patterning of stimuli conditioned to the GSR. *Journal of Experimental Psychology,* 1940, *27,* 95-110.

Hull, C. L. *Principles of behavior.* New York: Appleton-Century-Crofts, 1943.

Hull, C. L. Stimulus intensity dynamism (V) and stimulus generalization. *Psychological Review,* 1949, *56,* 67-76.

Hullett, J. W., and Homzie, M. J. Sensitization effect in the classical conditioning of *Dugesia dorotocephala. Journal of Comparative and Physiological Psychology,* 1966, *62,* 227-230.

Humphrey, G. The effect of sequences of indifferent stimuli on a reaction of the conditioned response type. *Journal of Abnormal and Social Psychology,* 1928, *22,* 194-212.

Humphrey, G. *The nature of learning in its relation to the living system.* New York: Harcourt, Brace, 1933.

Humphrey, G. *Directed thinking.* New York: Dodd Mead, 1948.

Humphreys, L. G. Measures of strength of conditioned eyelid responses. *Journal of General Psychology,* 1943, *29,* 101-111.

Hunt, E. L. Establishment of conditioned responses in chick embryos. *Journal of Comparative and Physiological Psychology,* 1949, *42,* 107-117.

Hunt, H. F., and Brady, J. V. Some effects of punishment and intercurrent anxiety on a simple operant. *Journal of Comparative and Physiological Psychology,* 1955, *48,* 305-310.

Hunter, W. S. Conditioning and extinction in the rat. *British Journal of Psychology,* 1935, *26,* 135-148.

Hunter, W. S., and Hudgins, C. V. Voluntary activity from the standpoint of behaviorism. *Journal of General Psychology,* 1934, *10,* 198-204.

Hydén, H. Activation of nuclear RNA in neurons and glia in learning. In D. P. Kimble (Ed.), *Learning, remembering, and forgetting.* Vol. I. *The anatomy of memory.* Palo Alto, Calif.: Science and Behavioral Books, 1965. Pp. 170-239.

Hydén, H. Biochemical aspects of learning. In K. H. Pribram (Ed.), *On the biology of learning.* New York: Harcourt, Brace and World, 1969. Pp. 97-125.

Isaacs, W., Thomas, J., and Goldiamond, I. Application of operant conditioning to reinstate verbal behavior in psychotics. *Journal of Speech and Hearing Disorders,* 1960, *25,* 8-12.

Ison, J. R. Experimental extinction as a function of number of reinforcements. *Journal of Experimental Psychology,* 1962, *64,* 314-317.

Itina, N. A. Physiological characteristics of the lymph heart muscles in tadpoles. *Fiziologichesky Zhurnal SSSR imeni I. M. Sechenova,* 1958, *44,* 121-127.

Ivanov-Smolensky, A. G. Experimental neuroses in dogs upon differentiation of complex stimuli. *Trudy Fiziologicheskikh Laboratorii I. P. Pavlova,* 1927a, *2*(1), 125-139.

Ivanov-Smolensky, A. G. Studying the grasping reflex in children. *Mediko-Biologichesky Zhurnal,* 1927b, No. 2, 33-41.

Ivanov-Smolensky, A. G. On the method of examining the conditioned food reflexes in children and in mental disorders. *Brain,* 1927c, *50,* 138-141.

Ivanov-Smolensky, A. G. *Method of studying conditioned reflexes in man (child and adult, normal and abnormal).* Leningrad: GIZ, 1928a.

Ivanov-Smolensky, A. G. Basic forms of conditioned- and unconditioned-reflex activity of man and their anatomical substrata. *Zhurnal Nevropatologii i Psikhiatri imeni S. S. Korsakova,* 1928b, *21,* 229-245.

Ivanov-Smolensky, A. G. The mechanisms of the linkages of conditioned bonds in the cortex of the large hemispheres of the child. *Pediatriya* (Moscow), 1929, *13*, 233-239.

Ivanov-Smolensky, A. G. Remarks about studying the basic mechanisms of conditioned-reflex activity in children. *Trudy Laboratorii Fiziologii Vysshey Nervnoy Deyatel'nosti Rebyonka,* 1930, *2*, 7-10.

Ivanov-Smolensky, A. G. (Ed.) *Experimental studies of higher nervous activity in children.* Moscow: GIZ, 1933.

Ivanov-Smolensky, A. G. *Essays on the patho-physiology of the higher nervous activity according to I. P. Pavlov and his school.* Moscow: Foreign Languages Publishing House, 1934. (In English)

Ivanov-Smolensky, A. G. Experimental studies of the interaction of direct and symbolic projections in man's cortex. *Arkhiv Biologicheskikh Nauk,* 1935a, *38*(1), 59-79.

Ivanov-Smolensky, A. G. Experimental study of the child's higher nervous activity. *Journal of Physiology (USSR),* 1935b, *19*, 149-155.

Ivanov-Smolensky, A. G. *Pavlov's teachings and pathological physiology.* Moscow: Akademiya Meditsinskikh Nauk SSSR, 1952.

Ivanov-Smolensky, A. G. *Ways of interaction of experimental and clinical cerebral pathophysiology.* Moscow: Meditsina, 1965.

Ivanov-Smolensky, A. G., and Shurpe, E. Yu. (Eds.) *The study of higher nervous activity in children.* Moscow: GIZ, 1934.

Iwama, K. Delayed conditioned reflex in man and brain waves. *Tohoku Journal of Experimental Medicine,* 1950, *52*, 53-62.

Jacobovitz, L. A., and Miron, M. S. (Eds.) *Readings in the psychology of language.* Englewood Cliffs, N.J.: Prentice-Hall, 1967.

Jacobson, E. Electrical measurements of neuromuscular states during mental activities: IV. Evidence of contraction of specific muscles during imagination. *American Journal of Physiology,* 1930, *95*, 703-712.

Jacobson, E. Electrophysiology of mental activities. *American Journal of Psychology,* 1932, *44*, 677-694.

James, W. *The principles of psychology.* New York: Holt, 1890. 2 vols.

James, W. T., and McFarlane, J. A study of form discrimination in the opposum. *Journal of Psychology,* 1966, *64*, 193-198.

Janet, P. *Les médications psychologiques; études historiques, psychologiques et cliniques sur les méthodes de la psychothérapie.* Paris: Alcan, 1919. (English translation: *Psychological healing: A historical and clinical study.* New York: Macmillan, 1925.)

Janis, I. L., Kaye, D., and Kirschner, P. Facilitating effects of "eating while reading" on responsiveness to persuasive communication. *Journal of Personality and Social Psychology,* 1965, *1*, 181-186.

Janos, O., Papoušek, H., and Dittrichová, J. The effect of age upon various aspects of higher nervous activity in the first months of life. *Activitas Nervosa Superior,* 1963, *4*, 407-410.

Jasper, H. H., and Shagass, C. Conditioning of occipital alpha rhythm in man. *Journal of Experimental Psychology,* 1941, *28*, 373-388.

Jasper, H. H., and Smirnov, G. D. (Eds.) The Moscow Colloquium on Electroencephalography of Higher Nervous Activity. *Electroencephalography and Clinical Neurophysiology,* 1960, Supplement 13.

Jennings, H. S. Studies on reactions to stimuli in unicellular organisms. IX. On the behavior of fixed infusoria (*Stentor* and *Vorticella*) with special reference to the modifiability of protozoan reactions. *American Journal of Physiology,* 1902, *8,* 23-60.

Jennings, H. S. Modifiability in behavior. I. Behavior of sea-anemones. *Journal of Experimental Zoology,* 1905, *2,* 447-473.

Jennings, H. S. *Behavior of the lower organisms.* New York: Columbia University Press, 1906.

John, E. R. High nervous function: Brain function and learning. *Annual Review of Physiology,* 1961, *23,* 451-484.

John, E. R. Some speculation on the psychophysiology of mind. In J. M. Scher (Ed.), *Theories of the mind.* New York: Free Press of Glencoe, 1962. Pp. 80-121.

John, E. R. *Mechanisms of memory.* New York: Academic Press, 1967.

John, E. R., and Killam, K. F. Electrophysiological correlates of avoidance conditioning in the cat. *Journal of Pharmacology and Experimental Therapy,* 1959, *125,* 252-274.

John, E. R., and Killam, K. F. Studies of electrical activity of the brain during differential conditioning in cats. In J. Wortis (Ed.), *Recent advances in biological psychiatry.* New York: Grune and Stratton, 1960a. Pp. 138-140.

John, E. R., and Killam, K. F. Electrophysiological correlates of differential approach-avoidance conditioning in cats. *Journal of Nervous and Mental Disorders,* 1960b, *136,* 183-201.

John, E. R., Leiman, A. L., and Sachs, E. An exploration of the functional relationship between electroencephalographic potentials and differential inhibition. *Annals of the New York Academy of Science,* 1961, *92,* 1160-1182.

Jones, J. E. Contiguity and reinforcement in relation to CS-US intervals in classical conditioning. *Psychological Review,* 1962, *69,* 176-186.

Jost, A. Die Assoziationsfestigkeit in ihrer Abhängigkeit von der Verteilung der Widerholungen. *Zeitschrift für Psychologie,* 1897, *14,* 436-472.

Kaada, B. R., and Bruland, H. Blocking of the cortically induced behavioral attentiveness (orienting) response by chlorpromazine. *Psychopharmacology,* 1960, *1,* 372-388.

Kalinin, P. I. Changes in bioelectric cortical action when the dominant cortical center is reinforced by afferent stimulation. In E. A. Asratyan (Ed.), *Neural mechanisms of conditioned-reflex activity.* Moscow: Akademiya Nauk SSSR, 1963a. Pp. 200-205.

Kalinin, P. I. Electrophysiological studies of interaction of cortical and subcortical structures in producing motor dominance. In *Electrophysiology of the nervous system.* Rostov-on-Don, 1963b. Pp. 176-177.

Kalinin, P. I., and Khan-Shen, L. The role of the reticular formation of the midbrain and thalamus in producing motor dominance. *Trudy Instituta Vysshey Nervnoy Deyatel'nosti imeni I. P. Pavlova, Seriya Fiziologicheskaya,* 1962, *7,* 57-68.

Kamin, L. J. Backward conditioning and the conditioned emotional response. *Journal of Comparative and Physiological Psychology,* 1963, *56,* 517-519.

Kamin, L. J. Temporal and intensity characteristics of the conditioned stimulus. In W. F. Prokasy (Ed.), *Classical conditioning: A symposium.* New York: Appleton-Century-Crofts, 1965. Pp. 118-147.

Kamin, L. J., and Brimer, C. J. The effects of intensity of conditioned and unconditioned stimuli on a conditioned emotional response. *Canadian Journal of Psychology,* 1963, *17,* 194-198.

Kamin, L. J., and Schaub, R. E. Effects of conditioned stimulus intensity on the conditioned emotional response. *Journal of Comparative and Physiological Psychology,* 1963, *56,* 502-507.

Kaminsky, S. D. The problem of experimental neuroses. II: Experimental neuroses in *macaques. Arkhiv Biologicheskikh Nauk,* 1939, *53*(2-3), 89-100.

Kant, I. *Anthropologie in pragmatischer Hinsichts angefasst.* Konigsberg: Nicolovius, 1798.

Kaplan, I. I., and Ukhtomsky, A. A. Sensory and motor dominance in spinal frogs. *Russky Fiziologichesky Zhurnal,* 1923, *6,* 71-88.

Kappers, C. U. A. Weitere Mitteilungen über Neurobiotaxis. Die Selektivität der Zellenwanderung. Die Bedeutung Synchronischer Reizwandshaft. *Folia Neurobiologica,* 1907, *1,* 507-534.

Kapustnik, O. P., and Fadeyeva, V. K. Extinction of conditioned reflexes in children 5 to 12 years of age. *Trudy Laboratorii Fiziologii Vysshey Nervnoy Deyatel'nosti Rebyonka,* 1930, *2,* 19-41.

Karamyan, A. I. *The evolution of functions of the cerebellum and cerebrum.* Leningrad: Medgiz, 1956.

Karamyan, A. I., and Sergeyev, B. F. Stages in development of conditioned reflex activity in the phylogeny of vertebrates. In E. Sh. Ayrapet'yants (Ed.), *Central and peripheral mechanisms of nervous activity.* Yerevan: Akademiya Nauk ASSR, 1966. Pp. 209-223.

Karamyan, A. I., Sergeyev, B. F., and Sollertinskaya, T. N. The formation of temporary connections through the association of "indifferent" stimuli in reptiles. *Zhurnal Vysshey Nervnoy Deyatel'nosti imeni I. P. Pavlova,* 1964, *14,* 626-634.

Karlova, A. N. Orienting reflexes in young children. *Zhurnal Vysshey Nervnoy Deyatel'nosti imeni I. P. Pavlova,* 1959, *9,* 37-44.

Karsh, E. R. Effects of number of rewarded trials and intensity of punishment on running speed. *Journal of Comparative and Physiological Psychology,* 1962, *55,* 44-51.

Kasatkin, N. I. *Development of higher nervous activity in early childhood.* Moscow: Medgiz, 1951.

Kasatkin, N. I. Early conditioned reflexes. *Zhurnal Vysshey Nervnoy Deyatel'nosti imeni I. P. Pavlova,* 1952, *2,* 572-581.

Kasatkin, N. I. (Ed.) *From simple to complex.* Moscow: Nauka, 1964.

Kasatkin, N. I., Mirozyants, N. S., and Khokhitva, A. P. Conditioned orienting reflexes in infants during the first year of life. *Zhurnal Vysshey Nervnoy Deyatel' nosti imeni I. P. Pavlova,* 1953, *3,* 192-202.

Kasherininova, N. A. *Contributions to the study of salivary conditioned reflexes to tactile stimuli in dogs.* St. Petersburg: Military Medical Academy, 1908. (Thesis)

Kasyanov, V. M. Bilateral characteristics of the cerebral hemispheres of dogs in experimental neurosis. *Zhurnal Vysshey Nervnoy Deyatel'nosti imeni I. P. Pavlova,* 1967, *17,* 64-69.

Katz, M. S., and Deterline, W. A. Apparent learning in the paramecium. *Journal of Comparative and Physiological Psychology,* 1958, *51,* 243-248.

Kaye, H. The conditioned Babkin reflex in human newborns. *Psychonomic Science,* 1965, *2,* 287-288.

Kaye, H., and Levin, G. R. Two attempts to demonstrate tonal suppression of nonnutritive sucking in neonates. *Perceptual and Motor Skills,* 1963, *17,* 521-522.

Kecen, J. D. Operant conditioning of unconscious blinking. *Symposium 4, XVIII International Congress of Psychology,* Moscow, 1966, 147-153.

Keen, R. E., Chase, H. H., and Graham, F. K. Twenty-four hour retention by neonates of a habituated heart rate response. *Psychonomic Science,* 1965, *2,* 265-266.

Kekcheyev, K. Kh. Conditioned sensory reflexes. *Trudy Ob'yedinennoy Sessii, Posvyashchennoy 10-letiyu so Dnya Smerti I. P. Pavlova,* 1948, 249-252.

Kelleher, R. T. Discrimination learning as a function of reversal and nonreversal shifts. *Journal of Experimental Psychology,* 1956, *49,* 153-157.

Keller, F. S., and Schoenfeld, W. N. *Principles of psychology.* New York: Appleton-Century-Crofts, 1950.

Kellogg, W. N. Communication and language in the home-raised chimpanzee. *Science,* 1968, *162,* 423-427.

Kellogg, W. N., Deese, J., Pronko, N. H., and Feinberg, M. An attempt to condition the chronic spinal dog. *Journal of Experimental Psychology,* 1947, *37,* 99-117.

Kellogg, W. N., and Kellogg, L. A. *The ape and the child: A study of environmental influence on early behavior.* New York: McGraw-Hill, 1933.

Kellogg, W. N., Pronko, N. H., and Deese, J. Spinal conditioning in dogs. *Science,* 1946, *103,* 49-50.

Kel'man, Kh. B. The effects of the cerebral cortex on splenic movement. *Byulleten' Vsesoyuznogo Instituta Experimental'noy Meditsiny imeni A. M. Gorkogo,* 1935, No. 5, 13-14.

Kel'man, Kh. B. The effects of the cerebral cortex on splenic movements. Neurohumoral connections. In K. B. Bykov (Ed.), *VIEM Collected papers,* 1937, *3,* 7-15.

Kendler, H. H., and D'Amato, M. F. A comparison of reversal shifts and nonreversal shifts in human concept formation behavior. *Journal of Experimental Psychology,* 1955, *49,* 165-174.

Kendler, H. H., and Kendler, T. S. Vertical and horizontal processes in problem solving. *Psychological Review,* 1962, *69,* 1-16.

Kendler, T. S. Verbalization and optional reversal shifts among kindergarten children. *Journal of Verbal Learning and Verbal Behavior,* 1964, *3,* 428-436.

Kendler, T. S., and Kendler, H. H. Reversal and nonreversal shifts in kindergarten children. *Journal of Experimental Psychology,* 1959, *58,* 56-60.

Kendler, T. S., and Kendler, H. H. Optional shifts of children as a function of number of training trials on the initial discrimination. *Journal of Experimental Child Psychology,* 1966, *3,* 216-224.

Kendler, T. S., Kendler, H. H., and Learned, B. Mediated responses to size and brightness as a function of age. *American Journal of Psychology,* 1962, *75,* 571-586.

Kendler, T. S., Kendler, H. H., and Wells, D. Reversal and nonreversal shifts in nursery school children. *Journal of Comparative and Physiological Psychology,* 1960, *53,* 83-88.

Kerr, N., Myerson, L., and Michael, J. A procedure for shaping vocalization in a mute child. In L. P. Ullman and L. Krasner (Eds.), *Case studies of behavior modification.* New York: Holt, 1965. Pp. 366-370.

Key, B. J., and Bradley, P. B. The effect of drugs on conditioned arousal responses. *Electroencephalography and Clinical Neurophysiology,* 1959, *11,* 841.

Key, B. J., and Bradley, P. B. The effects of drugs on conditioning and habituation to arousal stimuli in animals. *Psychopharmacology,* 1960, *1,* 451-462.

Khananshvili, M. M. New data on the differentiation of spatial conditioned reflexes. *Yezhegodnik, Instituta Experimental'noy Meditziny,* 1956, 36-40.

Khananshvili, M. M. The mechanism of action of aminazine on higher nervous activity. *Farmacologiya i Toksikdogiya,* 1960, *4,* 915-921.

Kharchenko, P. D. *Delayed conditioned reflexes.* Kiev: Kiev University Press, 1960.

Khekht, K. Linkage mechanisms of conditioned reflexes of the second order. *Doklady Akademii Nauk SSSR*, 1957, *113*, 1383-1386.

Khodorov, B. I. The effect of the conditioned defense reflex on the magnitude of the unconditioned in dogs. *Zhurnal Vysshey Nervnoy Deyatel'nosti imeni I. P. Pavlova*, 1954, *4*, 852-861.

Khodorov, B. I. Action of conditioned stimulus preceded by the unconditioned stimulus. *Zhurnal Vysshey Nervnoy Deyatel'nosti imeni I. P. Pavlova*, 1955, *5*, 61-69.

Khodzhava, Z. I. *The problem of habit in psychology.* Tbilisi: Akademiya Nauk GSSR, 1960.

Kimble, D. P., and Ray, R. S. Reflex habituation and potentiation in *Rana pipiens*. *Animal Behaviour*, 1965, *13*, 530-533.

Kimble, G. A. *Hilgard and Marquis' Conditioning and Learning.* New York: Appleton-Century-Crofts, 1961.

Kimble, G. A. Classical and instrumental conditioning: One process or two? In *Symposium 4, XVIII International Congress of Psychology,* Moscow, 1966. Pp. 55-65.

Kimble, G. A. (Ed.) *Foundations of conditioning and learning.* New York: Appleton-Century-Crofts, 1967a.

Kimble, G. A. Attitudinal factors in eyelid conditioning. In G. A. Kimble (Ed.), *Foundations of conditioning and learning.* New York: Appleton-Century-Crofts, 1967b. Pp. 642-659.

Kimmel, H. D. Amount of conditioning and intensity of conditioned stimulus. *Journal of Experimental Psychology,* 1959, *58*, 283-288.

Kimmel, H. D. Adaptation of the GSR under repeated applications of a visual stimulus. *Journal of Experimental Psychology,* 1964, *68*, 421-422.

Kimmel, H. D. Instrumental inhibitory factors in classical conditioning. In W. F. Prokasy (Ed.), *Classical conditioning.* New York: Appleton-Century-Crofts, 1965. Pp. 148-171.

Kimmel, H. D. Instrumental conditioning of autonomically mediated behavior. *Psychological Bulletin,* 1967, *67*, 337-345.

Kimmel, H. D., and Goldstein, A. J. Retention of habituation of the GSR to visual and auditory stimulation. *Journal of Experimental Psychology,* 1967, *73*, 401-404.

Kimmel, H. D., and Hill, F. A. Operant conditioning of the GSR. *Psychological Reports,* 1960, *7*, 555-562.

Kimmel, H. D., Hill, F. A., and Fowler, R. L. Intersensory generalization in compound classical conditioning. *Psychological Reports,* 1962, *11*, 631-636.

Kimmel, H. D., Hill, F. A., and Morrow, M. Strength of GSR and avoidance conditioning as a function of CS intensity. *Psychological Reports* 1962, *11*, 103-109.

Kintsch, W., and Witte, R. S. Concurrent conditioning of bar press and salivation responses. *Journal of Comparative and Physiological Psychology,* 1962, *55*, 963-968.

Kleshchov, S. V. Ratio of sounds as conditioned reflex stimuli. *Trudy Fiziologicheskikh Laboratorii I. P. Pavlova,* 1933, *5*, 213-218.

Kleshchov, S. V. Inhibitory conditioned reflexes to a ratio of tones. *Trudy Fiziologicheskikh Laboratorii imeni I. P. Pavlova,* 1944, *11*, 21-30.

Klimova, V. I. The characteristics of components of some orienting reactions. In L. G. Voronin, A. N. Leont'yev, A. R. Luria, E. N. Sokolov, and O. S. Vinogradova (Eds.), *The orienting reflex and orienting-investigatory activity.* Moscow: Akademiya Pedagogicheskikh Nauk RSFSR, 1958. Pp. 76-80.

Klyavina, M. P. Conditioned-reflex generalization in animal embryos, neonates and early postnatal periods. In *Theses, 3rd Scientific Conference on Evolutionary Physiology Dedicated in Memory of Academician L. A. Orbeli.* Leningrad, 1961. Pp. 93-94.

Knapp, H. D., Taub, E., and Berman, A. J. Effect of deafferentiation on a conditioned avoidance response. *Science*, 1958, *128*, 842-843.

Koffka, K. *The growth of mind*. London: Kegan, 1924.

Koffka, K. Bemerkungen zur Denk-psychologie. *Psychologische Forschung*, 1927, *9*, 163-184.

Koffka, K. *Principles of gestalt psychology*. New York: Harcourt, Brace, 1935.

Kogan, A. B. *The use of electroencephalography in subcortical studies*. Rostov-on-Don, 1936.

Kogan, A. B. *Electrophysiological studies of the central mechanisms of some complex reflexes*. Moscow: Akademiya Meditsinskikh Nauk SSSR, 1949.

Kogan, A. B. Electrophysiological indices of central inhibition. *Gagrskiye Besedy*, 1956, *2*, 377-403.

Kogan, A. B. *Fundamentals of the physiology of higher nervous activity*. Moscow: Vysshaya Shkola, 1959.

Kogan, A. B. Structural foundations of the nature of the temporary connections of the conditioned reflex. *Gagrskiye Besedy*, 1960, *3*, 191-212.

Kogan, A. B. Chemistry, structure and function of cortical neurones. *Gagrskiye Besedy*, 1963, *4*, 59-85.

Kogan, A. B. Physiological mechanism of irradiation of neural processes in the cerebral cortex. *Zhurnal Vysshey Nervnoy Deyatel'nosti imeni I. P. Pavlova*, 1965, *15*, 963-970.

Kogan, A. B. Probability organization of physiological mechanisms of higher analysis. *Zhurnal Vysshey Nervnoy Deyatel'nosti imeni I. P. Pavlova*, 1970, *20*, 403-412.

Köhler, W. Intelligenprufung an Anthropoiden. *Abhandlungen der Preussischen Academie der Wissenchaften, Physische-Mathematische Klasse*, No. 1, 1917.

Köhler, W. *Die physische Gestalten in Ruhe and in stationarer Zustand*. Braunschweig: Vieweg, 1920.

Köhler, W. Zur theorie des sukzessivvergleich der Zeitfehler. *Psychologische Forschung*, 1923, *4*, 115-175.

Köhler, W. *The mentality of apes*. New York: Harcourt, Brace, 1925.

Köhler, W., and Held, R. The cortical correlate of pattern vision. *Science*, 1949, *110*, 414-419.

Kolmogorov, A. N., *Theory of transformation of information*. Moscow: Akademiya Nauk SSSR, 1956.

Kolmogorov, A. N. *The possible and impossible of cybernetics*. Moscow: Akademiya Nauk SSSR, 1963.

Kol'tsova, M. M. The rise and development of the second-signal system in the child. *Trudy Fiziologicheskogo Instituta imeni I. P. Pavlova*, 1949, *4*, 49-102.

Kol'tsova, M. M. *Formation of higher nervous activity in children*. Moscow: Medgiz, 1958.

Kol'tsova, M. M. Development of systematicity as a basis of the process of generalization. *Zhurnal Vysshey Nervnoy Deyatel'nosti imeni I. P. Pavlova*, 1960, *10*, 167-172.

Kol'tsova, M. M. The role of temporary connections of the associative type in the development of systematicity. *Zhurnal Vysshey Nervnoy Deyatel'nosti imeni I. P. Pavlova*, 1961a, *11*, 39-41.

Kol'tsova, M. M. Development of systematicity as a basis of generalization. *Zhurnal Vysshey Nervnoy Deyatel'nosti imeni I. P. Pavlova*, 1961b, *11*, 56-59.

Kol'tsova, M. M. The interaction of different types of temporary connections in the formation of conditioned reflexes to ratios of stimuli. *Zhurnal Vysshey Nervnoy Detatel'nosti imeni I. P. Pavlova,* 1961c, *11,* 636-641.

Kol'tsova, M. M Comparative role of different analyzers in the formation of the higher nervous activity of children. In S. A. Sarkisov (Ed.), *Structure and function of analyzers in human ontogeny.* Moscow: Medgiz, 1961d.

Kol'tsova, M. M. Characteristics of the formation of systems of temporary connections in the second-signal system. *Zhurnal Vysshey Nervnoy Deyatel'nosti imeni I. P. Pavlova,* 1962, *12,* 450-455.

Kol'tsova, M. M. Conditions of formation of systematicity at different functional levels of children's nervous activity. *Zhurnal Vysshey Nervnoy Deyatel'nosti imeni I. P. Pavlova,* 1963, *13,* 626-630.

Kol'tsova, M. M. (Ed.) *Materials for a symposium on man's systems of signals.* Leningrad: Nauka, 1965a.

Kol'tsova, M. M. Development of the signalling function of words. In M. M. Kol'tsova (Ed.), *Materials for symposium on man's system of signals.* Leningrad: Nauka, 1965b. Pp. 71-80.

Kol'tsova, M. M. *Generalization as a function of the brain.* Leningrad: Nauka, 1967.

Konorski, J. *Conditioned reflexes and neuron organization.* New York: Cambridge University Press, 1948a.

Konorski, J. The problem of internal inhibition. *Trudy Ob'yedinennoy Sessii Posvyashchennoy 10-letiyu so Dnya Smerti I. P. Pavlova,* 1948b. Pp. 225-229.

Konorski, J. The study of a case of aphasia. In I. P. Pavlov, *Wednesdays,* 1949, Vol. 2, pp. 468-475.

Konorski, J. Discussion. In J. F. Delafreshaye (Ed.), *Brain mechanisms and learning.* Springfield, Ill.: Charles C Thomas, 1961. P. 112.

Konorski, J. Some problems concerning the mechanism of instrumental conditioning. *Acta Biologiae Experimentalis,* 1964, *24*(2), 59-72.

Konorski, J. *Integrative activity of the brain. An interdisciplinary approach.* Chicago: University of Chicago Press, 1967.

Konorski, J. Postscript to "On a particular form of conditioned reflexes." *Journal of the Experimental Analysis of Behavior,* 1969, *12,* 189.

Konorski, J., and Lawická, W. Physiological mechanism of delayed reactions. *Acta Biologiae Experimentalis,* 1959, *19,* 175-196.

Konorski, J., and Miller, S. Podstawy fiziologichnej teorji ruchow nabytych [Physiological principles of a theory of acquired reflexes]. *Medycina Doswiadczalna i Spoleczna,* 1933, *16,* 95-107; 234-298.

Konorski, J., and Miller, S. Conditioned reflexes of the motor analyzer. *Trudy Fiziologicheskikh Laboratorii I. P. Pavlova,* 1936, *6*(1), 119-288.

Konorski, J., and Miller, S. On two types of conditioned reflex. *Journal of General Psychology,* 1937, *16,* 264-272.

Konradi, G. P. Differentiation and interaction of active conditioned reflexes based on different unconditioned reflexes. *Trudy Fiziologichesky Laboratorii I. P. Pavlova,* 1932, *4,* 60-101.

Kopnin, P. V., and Vilnitsky, M. B. (Eds.) *Problems of thinking and modern science.* Moscow: Mysl', 1964.

Korotkin, I. I. The physiological mechanism of so-called "relations" in higher nervous activity. *Fiziologichesky Zhurnal SSSR imeni I. M. Sechenova,* 1938, *14,* 696-714.

Korotkin, I. I. Some factors aiding the formation of subsensory conditioned reflexes to auditory stimuli. *Doklady Akademii Nauk SSSR*, 1947, *57*, 529-531.

Korotkin, I. I. Methodology of studying conditioned eyelid reflexes in man. *Fiziologichesky Zhurnal SSSR imeni I. M. Sechenova*, 1949, *35*, 467-471.

Kostyuk, P. G. *The two-neuron reflex*. Moscow: Medgiz, 1959.

Kostyuk, P. G. Characteristics of polysynaptic excitation and inhibition of single motor neurones. *Fiziologichesky Zhurnal SSSR imeni I. M. Sechenova*, 1960a, *46*, 398-407.

Kostyuk, P. G. Plasticity of synaptic connections. *Gagrskiye Besedy*, 1960b, *3*, 83-110.

Kovach, J. K., and Hess, E. H. Imprinting: Effects of painful stimulation upon the following response. *Journal of Comparative and Physiological Psychology*, 1963, *56*, 461-464.

Kovalev, A. G., Stepanov, A. A., and Shabalin, C. N. *Psikhologiya*. Moscow: Prosvescheniye, 1966.

Kovalgin, V. M. *The problem of sensation and the reflex theory*. Minsk: Akademiya Nauk BSSR, 1959.

Kozak, W., MacFarlane, W. W., and Westerman, R. A. Long-lasting reversible changes in the reflex responses of chronic spinal cats to touch, heat, and cold. *Nature* (London), 1962, *193*, 171-173.

Kozhevnikov, V. A., and Maruseva, A. M. Electroencephalographic studies of the formation of temporal connections to unaware stimuli in man. *Izvestiya Akademii Nauk SSSR, Seriya Biologicheskaya*, 1949, No. 5, 560-569.

Krachkovskaya, M. V. Reflex changes in leucocyte count of newborn infants in relation to food intake. *Zhurnal Vysshey Nervnoy Deyatel'nosti imeni I. P. Pavlova*, 1959, *9*, 205-211.

Krasner, L., and Ullmann, L. P. (Eds.) *Research in behavior modification and implications*. New York: Holt, Rinehart and Winston, 1965.

Krasnogorsky, N. I. An experiment in artificial conditioned reflexes in young children. *Russky Vrach*, 1907, *36*, 1245-1246.

Krasnogorsky, N. I. *Inhibition and localization of the cutaneous and the motor analyzers in the cerebrum of dogs*. St. Petersburg: Military Medical Academy, 1911. (Thesis)

Krasnogorsky, N. I. Über die grundmechanismus der arbeit der Grosshirnrinde bei kinder. *Jahrbuch für Kinderkheilkunde*, 1913, *78*, 374-398.

Krasnogorsky, N. I. On the method of studying the motor conditioned reflexes in children. *Trudy Obshchestva Russkikh Fiziologov*, 1929, *2*, 8-9.

Krasnogorsky, N. I. Bedingte und unbedingte reflexe im kindesalter und ihre bedeutung für die klinik. *Ergebnisse der inneren Medizin und Kinderheilkunde*, 1931, *39*, 613-730.

Krasnogorsky, N. I. The reflection of direct conditioned connections in cortical symbolic projections. *Trudy Laboratorii Fiziologii i Patofizologii Vysshey Nervnoy Deyatel'nosti Rebyonka*, 1934, *4*, 436-450.

Krasnogorsky, N. I. *Study of higher nervous activity of man and animals*. Moscow: Medgiz, 1954.

Krasnogorsky, N. I. *Higher nervous activity of children*. Leningrad: Medgiz, 1958.

Krauklis, A. A. *Conditioned-reflex regulation of nervous activity*. Riga: Akademiya Nauk LSSR, 1960.

Krech, D. Heredity, environment, brain and problem solving. *Voprosy Psikhologii*, 1966 (3), 39-43.

Krech, D., and Crutchfield, R. S. *Theory and problems of social psychology.* New York: McGraw-Hill, 1948.

Krechevsky, I. (Krech, D.) "Hypotheses" in rats. *Psychological Review,* 1932, *39,* 516-532.

Kreps, E. M. The reactions of Ascidians to external stimuli. *Arkhiv Biologicheskikh Nauk,* 1925, *25*(4-5), 197-226.

Kreps, E. M. The possibility of forming a conditioned reflex when the unconditioned precedes the indifferent stimulus. *Trudy Fiziologicheskikh Laboratorii I. P. Pavlova,* 1933, *5,* 20.

Kreps, E. M. (Ed.) *The evolution of functions.* Moscow: Nauka, 1964.

Krestovnikov, A. N. Essential conditions for the formation of conditioned reflexes. *Trudy Obshchestva Russkikh Vrachey v St. Peterburge,* 1913, *80,* 205-213.

Krestovnikov, A. N. The essential conditions for the formation of conditioned reflexes. *Izvestiya Petrogradskogo Nauchnogo Instituta imeni P. F. Lesgafta,* 1921, *3,* 197-240.

Kries, J. V. Über die Natur gewisser mit den psychischen Vorgangen verknüpfter Gehirnzustande. *Zeitschrift für Psychologie,* 1895, *8,* 1-33.

Kroeber, A. L., and Kluckhohn, C. Culture: A critical review of concepts and definitions. *Papers of the Peabody Museum of American Archaeology and Ethnology,* Harvard University, 1952, *47,* No. 1.

Krushinsky, L. V. Extrapolative reflexes as elementary bases of judgment activity in animals. *Doklady Akademii Nauk SSSR,* 1958a, *121,* 762-765.

Krushinsky, L. V. Extrapolative reflexes in birds. *Uchenyye Zapiski Moskovskogo Ordena Lenina Gosudarstvennogo Universiteta imeni M. V. Lomonosova,* 1958b, No. 197. *Ornitologiya,* 145-159.

Krushinsky, L. V. Biological significance of extrapolative reflexes in animals. *Zhurnal Obshchey Biologii,* 1958c, *19,* 155-167.

Krushinsky, L. V. The study of extrapolative reflexes in animals. *Problemy Kibernetiki,* 1959, No. 2, 229-292.

Krushinsky, L. V. *Formation of animal behavior: Normal and abnormal.* Moscow: Moscow University, 1960. (English translation: New York: Consultants', 1962.)

Krushinsky, L. V. Comparative-physiological studies of extrapolative reflexes in animals. In *Theses, 3rd Scientific Conference on Evolutionary Physiology in Memory of Academician L. A. Orbeli.* Leningrad: 1961. P. 112.

Krushinsky, L. V., Flyoss, D. A., Molodkina, L. N., Ochinskaya, E. I., and Popova, N. P. Extrapolative reflexes as a factor in the evolution of behavior of animals. In *Theses, 4th Scientific Conference on Evolutionary Physiology in Memory of Academician L. A. Orbeli.* Leningrad: 1965. Pp. 160-161.

Krushinsky, L. V., Flyoss, D. A., Molodkina, L. N., Popova, N. P., and Ochinskaya, E. I. Extrapolative reflexes in different species of animals and their role in learning. In *Theses, 10th All-Union Congress of the Pavlov Physiological Society.* Yerevan: Nauka, 1964. P. 431.

Krushinsky, L. V., Molodkina, L. N., and Popova, N. P. Extrapolative reflexes in different species of animals and their relation to conditioned reflexes. In V. N. Chernigovsky (Ed.), *Physiological bases of complex forms of behavior.* Moscow: Akademiya Nauk SSSR, 1963. P. 19.

Krushinsky, L. V., Molodkina, L. N., Popova, N. P., Svetukhina, V. M., and Mats, V. N. Special-information associations as a basis of some complex forms of animal behavior. In A. D. Slonim (Ed.), *Complex forms of behavior.* Moscow-Leningrad: Nauka, 1965. Pp. 58-63.

Kryazhev, V. Ya. Experimental neurosis on the basis of emotional shock. *Fiziologichesky Zhurnal SSSR imeni I. M. Sechenova*, 1945, *31*, 236-259.

Kuczka, H. Verhaltensphysiologische Untersuchungen über die Wischhandlung der Erdkröte (*Bufo bufo L.*). *Zeitschrift für Tierpsychologie*, 1956, *13*, 185-207.

Kuenzer, P. P. Verhaltensphysiologische Untersuchungen über des Zucken des Regenwurms. *Zeitschrift für Tierpsychologie*, 1958, *15*, 31-49.

Kuffler, S. W., and Edwards, J. E. Mechanism of gamma-aminobutyric acid (GABA) action and its relation to synaptic inhibition. *Journal of Neurophysiology*, 1958, *21*, 589-610.

Kuffler, S. W., and Katz, B. Inhibition at nerve-muscle junction in Crustacea. *Journal of Neurophysiology*, 1946, *9*, 337-346.

Kugelmas, S., Hakerem, G., and Mantgiaris, L. A paradoxical conditioning effect in the human pupil. *Journal of General Psychology*, 1969, *80*, 115-127.

Kukuyev, L. A. Evolution of the nucleus of the motor analyzer and subcortical ganglia. *Zhurnal Vysshey Nervnoy Deyatel'nosti imeni I. P. Pavlova*, 1953, *3*, 765-773.

Kukuyev, L. A. Characteristics of subcortical formations of the motor analyzer in man. In S. A. Sarkisov and N. S. Preobrazhenskaya (Eds.), *Development of the central nervous system*. Moscow: Medgiz, 1959.

Kukuyev, L. A. Development of motor analyzer in man. In S. A. Sarkisov (Ed.), *Structure and function of analyzers in human ontogeny*. Moscow: Medgiz, 1961. Pp. 257-263.

Külpe, O. *Grundriss der psychologie auf experimentelle Grundlage dargestelt*. Leipzig: Englemann, 1893. (English translation by E. B. Titchener, New York: Macmillan, 1895.)

Külpe, O. Versuche über Abstraktion. In F. Schumann (Ed.), *Bericht über den 1-sten Kongress für experimentelle Psychologie*, Giessen, April, 1904. Leipzig: Barth, 1904. Pp. 56-58.

Külpe, O. Über die moderne Psychologie des denkens. *Internationale Monatschrift für Wissenschaft, Kunst und Technik*, 1912, *12*, 1069-1110.

Kuo, Z. Y. *The dynamics of behavior development. An epigenetic view*. New York: Random House, 1967.

Kupalov, P. S. Conditioned neurotic reflexes. *Arkhiv Biologicheskikh Nauk*, 1941, *61*(3), 3-14.

Kupalov, P. S. Physiological studies of higher manifestations of animal activities. *Klinicheskaya Meditzina (Moskva)*, 1946, *12*, 3-4.

Kupalov, P. S. Certain problems of the physiology of higher nervous activity. In *Communications, XX International Congress of Physiologists*, Brussels. Moscow: Akademiya Nauk SSSR, 1956. Pp. 45-46.

Kupalov, P. S. Experimental neuroses. In S. N. Davidenkov (Ed.), *Handbook of neurology*. Vol. 6. *Neuroses, epilepsy and narcolepsy*. Moscow: Medgiz, 1960. Pp. 9-43.

Kupalov, P. S. Developmental perspective of the reflex and reflex activity. In P. N. Fedoseyev (Ed.), *Philosophical problems of the physiology of higher nervous activity and psychology*. Moscow: Akademiya Nauk SSSR, 1963. Pp. 106-155.

Kupalov, P. S. *Situational [positional] conditioned reflexes in normal and pathological dogs*. Moscow: Meditsina, 1964.

Kupalov, P. S., and Gantt, W. H. Interrelations of intensities of conditioned stimuli and magnitudes of conditioned reflexes. *Trudy Fiziologichesky Laboratorii I. P. Pavlova*, 1928, *2*, 1-12.

Kuznetsova, G. D. The dominance of swallowing and formation of a conditioned reflex based on it. *Trudy Vysshey Nervnoy Deyatel'nosti imeni I. P. Pavlova, Seriya Fiziologicheskaya,* 1959, *3,* 1-18.

Kuznetsova, G. D. Changes in steady cortical potentials upon constant current anode stimulation. In E. A. Asratyan (Ed.), *Neural mechanisms of conditioned-reflex activity.* Moscow: Akademiya Nauk SSSR, 1963. Pp. 182-189.

Ladygina-Kots, N. N. *A study of cognitive abilities of chimpanzees.* Moscow: GIZ, 1923. (Published also in German.)

Ladygina-Kots, N. N. *Adjustive motor habits of macaques under experimental conditions.* Moscow: Darwin Museum, 1929.

Ladygina-Kots, N. N. *Infant chimpanzee and human child: Instincts, emotions, play, habits and expressive movements.* Moscow: Darwin Museum, 1935.

Ladygina-Kots, N. N. *Psychic development in the evolution of organism.* Moscow: Sovetskaya Nauka, 1958.

Ladygina-Kots, N. N. *Constructive and tool-using activities of higher apes.* Moscow: Akademiya Nauk SSSR, 1959.

Lagutina, N. I. The structure of orienting reflexes. In L. G. Voronin, A. N. Leont'yev, A. R. Luria, E. N. Sokolov, and O. S. Vinogradova (Eds.), *The orienting reflex and orienting-investigatory activity.* Moscow: Akademiya Pedagogicheskikh Nauk RSFSR, 1958. Pp. 80-86.

Lagutina, N. I., and Batuyev, A. S. The role of the frontal lobes in mechanisms of conditioned reflexes. In *Theses, 21st Conference on Problems of Higher Nervous Activity.* Moscow-Leningrad: Nauka, 1966. Pp. 172-173.

Landa, L. N. *Algorithmization in teaching.* Moscow: Prosveshcheniye, 1966.

Landis, D., and Solley, C. M. Classical conditioning to a negative afterimage. *Psychological Record,* 1965, *15,* 553-560.

Lange, N. Beitrage zur Theorie der sinnlichen Aufmerksamkeit und der aktiven Apperception. *Philosophische Studien,* 1888, *4,* 390-422.

Lange, N. N. *Psikhologiya.* St. Petersburg: Mir, 1914.

Larrabee, M. G., and Bronk, D. W. Long-lasting effects of activity on ganglionic transmission. *American Journal of Psychology,* 1938, *123,* 126.

Larrabee, M. G., and Bronk, D. W. Prolonged facilitation of synaptic excitation in sympathetic ganglia. *Journal of Neurophysiology,* 1947, *10,* 139-154.

Lashley, K. S. *Brain mechanisms and intelligence.* Chicago: University of Chicago Press, 1929a.

Lashley, K. S. Learning: I. Nervous mechanisms in learning. In C. Murchison (Ed.), *The foundations of experimental psychology.* Worcester, Mass.: Clark University Press, 1929b.

Lashley, K. S. Cerebral control versus reflexology: A reply to Professor Hunter. *Journal of General Psychology,* 1931, *5,* 3-20.

Lashley, K. S. The mechanism of vision: V. Preliminary studies of the rat's capacity for detailed vision. *Journal of General Psychology,* 1938, *18,* 123-193.

Lashley, K. S. In search of the engram. In *Symposium of the Society for Experimental Biology IV.* Cambridge University, The University Press, 1950. Pp. 454-482.

Lashley, K. S. The problem of serial order in behavior. In L. A. Jeffries (Ed.), *Cerebral mechanisms in behavior: The Hixon Symposium.* New York: Wiley, 1951. Pp. 112-146.

Lashley, K. S., Chow, K. K., and Semmes, J. An examination of the electrical field theory of cerebral integration. *Psychological Review,* 1951, *58,* 123-136.

Lashley, K. S., and Wade, M. The Pavlovian theory of generalization. *Psychological Review,* 1946, *53,* 72-87.

Lazarus, R. S., and McCleary, R. A. Autonomic discrimination without awareness: A study of subception. *Psychological Review,* 1951, *38,* 113-122.

Leão, A. A. P. Spreading depression of activity in the cerebral cortex. *Journal of Neurophysiology,* 1944, *7,* 359-390.

Leeper, R. Cognitive processes. In S. S. Stevens (Ed.), *Handbook of experimental psychology.* New York: Wiley, 1951. Pp. 730-751.

Lehner, G. F. J. A study of the extinction of unconditioned reflexes. *Journal of Experimental Psychology,* 1941, *29,* 435-456.

Lehrman, D. S. A critique of Konrad Lorenz's theory of instinctive behavior. *Quarterly Review of Biology,* 1953, *28,* 337-363.

Lehrman, D. S., Hinde, R. A., and Shaw E. (Eds.) *Advances in the study of behavior.* New York and London: Academic Press, 1965.

Lekishvili, V. P. The effect of collision of alimentary and defensive reflexes on cardiac action. *Trudy Instituta Fiziologii imeni I. P. Pavlova,* 1954, *3,* 303-315.

LeLord, G. Étude chez l'animal et chez l'homme d'un mode d'association spécifique, distinct du conditionnement classique, l'acquisition libre. *Acta Biologiae Experimentalis,* 1966, *27,* 379-405.

Lenneberg, E. H. *Biological foundations of language.* New York: Wiley, 1967.

Leont'yev, A. N. *Problems of mental development.* Moscow: Akademiya Pedagogicheskikh Nauk RSFSR, 1959.

Leont'yev, A. N. *Theory of verbal activity: Problems of psycholinguistics.* Moscow: Nauka, 1968.

Leont'yev, A. N., Luria, A. R., and Smirnov, A. A. Foreword. In M. Cole and I. Maltzman (Eds.), *A handbook of contemporary Soviet psychology.* New York: Basic Books, 1969. Pp. v-vii.

Lethlean, A. K. Habituation in the rat spinal cord—a triggered process. *Federation Proceedings,* 1965, *24*(2), 517.

Lewis, D. J., and Adams, H. E. Retrograde amnesia from conditioned competing responses. *Science,* 1963, *141,* 516-517.

Li, C. L., and Chou, C. N. Cortical intracellular synaptic potentials and direct cortical stimulation. *Journal of Cellular and Comparative Physiology,* 1962, *60,* 1-16.

Lichtenstein, F. E. Studies of anxiety: I. The production of a feeding inhibition in dogs. *Journal of Comparative and Physiological Psychology,* 1950, *43,* 16-29.

Liddell, H. S. The experimental neurosis and the problem of mental disorder. *American Journal of Psychiatry,* 1938, *94,* 1035-1943.

Lindsley, D. B. Emotion. In S. S. Stevens (Ed.), *Handbook of experimental psychology.* New York: Wiley, 1951. Pp. 473-516.

Lipsitt, L. P. Learning in the first year of life. In L. P. Lipsitt and C. C. Spiker (Eds.), *Advances in child development and behavior.* Vol. 1. New York: Academic Press, 1963. Pp. 147-195.

Lipsitt, L. P., and Kaye, H. Conditioned sucking in the human newborn. *Psychonomic Science,* 1964, *1,* 29-30.

Lisina, M. I. Some ways of transforming involuntary into voluntary reactions. *Doklady Akademii Pedagogicheskakh Nauk RSFSR,* 1957, No. 1, 85-87.

Lisina, M. I. The role of orientation in the transformation of involuntary into voluntary reactions. In L. G. Voronin, A. N. Leont'yev, A. R. Luria, E. N. Sokolov, and O. S. Vinogradova (Eds.), *The orienting reflex and orienting-investigatory activity*. Moscow: Akademiya Pedagogicheskikh Nauk RSFSR, 1958. Pp. 338-344.

Lisina, M. I. Quoted in A. V. Zaporozhets, *Development of voluntary movements*. Moscow: Akademiya Pedagogicheskikh Nauk RSFSR, 1960. Pp. 70-89.

Livanov, M. N. Rhythmic stimuli and their interrelations in the cortex. *Fiziologichesky Zhurnal SSSR imeni I. M. Sechenova*, 1940, *25*, 172-193.

Livanov, M. N. Electrophysiological studies of higher nervous activity. In *The teachings of I. P. Pavlov and theoretical and practical medicine*. Moscow: Ministerstvo Zdravokhraneniya, 1951. Pp. 124-141.

Livanov, M. N. Electrophysiological studies of conditioned-reflex connections. *Trudy 15-go Soveshchaniya no Probleman Vysshey Nervnoy Deyatel'nosti Posvyashchennogo 50-letiyu Ucheniya Adademika I. P. Pavlova*, 1952, 248-261.

Livanov, M. N. Electrophysiological studies of the formation of conditioned reflexes. *Gagrskiye Besedy*, 1960a, *3*, 111-147.

Livanov, M. N. Concerning the establishment of temporary connections. Results of electrophysiological investigations. In H. H. Jasper and G. D. Smirnov (Eds.), The Moscow Colloquium on Electroencephalography of Higher Activity, *Electroencephalography and Clinical Neurophysiology*, 1960b, Supplement 13, 185-198.

Livanov, M. N. Neurokinetics. In V. N. Chernigovsky (Ed.) *Problems of contemporary neurophysiology*, Moscow: Nauka, 1965a. Pp. 37-71.

Livanov, M. N. Inhibition in neuronal systems of the cortex. In E. A. Asratyan (Ed.), *Reflexes of the brain*. Moscow: Nauka, 1965b. Pp. 64-71.

Livanov, M. N., Korol'kova, I. A., and Frenkel', G. M. Electrophysiological studies of higher nervous activity. *Zhurnal Vysshey Nervnoy Deyatel'nosti imeni I. P. Pavlova*, 1951, *1*, 521-538.

Livanov, M. N., and Polyakov, K. L. Electrical processes in the cerebral cortex of a rabbit during the formation of a conditioned defense reflex to a rhythmic stimulus. *Izvestiya Akademii Nauk SSSR, Seriya Biologicheskaya*, 1945, *3*, 286-307.

Livanov, M. N., and Ryabinovskaya, A. M. Localization of electrical changes in the rabbit's cortex during the formation of conditioned defense reflexes to rhythmic stimuli. *Trudy Ob'yedinennoy Sessii Posvyashchennoy 10-letiyu so Dnya Smerti I. P. Pavlova*, 1948, 229-237.

Lloyd, D. P. C. Reflex action in relation to pattern and peripheral sources of afferent stimulation. *Journal of Neurophysiology*, 1943, *6*, 111-119.

Lloyd, D. P. C. Post-tetanic potentiation of response in monosynaptic reflex pathways of the spinal cord. *Journal of General Physiology*, 1949, *33*, 147-170.

Lockhart, R. A. Dominance and contiguity as interactive determinants of autonomic conditioning. *Dissertation Abstracts*, 1966a, 27B, 317.

Lockhart, R. A. Temporal conditioning of the GSR. *Journal of Experimental Psychology*, 1966c, *71*, 438-466.

Lockhart, R. A., and Grings, W. W. Comments on "An analysis of GSR conditioning." *Psychological Review*, 1963, *70*, 562-564.

Lockhart, R. A., and Grings, W. W. Interstimulus interval effects on GSR discrimination conditioning. *Journal of Experimental Psychology*, 1964, *67*, 209-214.

Loeb, J. *Comparative physiology of the brain and comparative psychology*. New York: Putnam, 1900.

Logan, F. A. A note on stimulus intensity dynamism (V). *Psychological Review*, 1954, *61*, 77-80.

Longo, N., and Bitterman, M. E. The effect of partial reinforcement with spaced practice on resistance to extinction in fish. *Journal of Comparative and Physiological Psychology,* 1960, *53,* 169-172.

Lopatin, N. G., and Chesnokova, E. G. Formation of a stereotype of alimentary conditioned reflexes in the honeybee (*Apis millifera L.*). In V. N. Chernigovsky (Ed.), *Physiology and pathology of higher nervous activity.* Moscow: Nauka, 1965. Pp. 107-110.

Lorens, S. A., and Darrow, C. W. Eye movements, EEG, GSR, and EKG during mental multiplication. *Electroencephalography and Clinical Neurophysiology,* 1962, *14,* 739-746.

Lorenté de Nó, R. La corteza cerebral del ratón. *Trabajos del Laboratorio de Investigaciones Biológicas de la Universidad de Madrid,* 1922, *14,* 41-78.

Lorenté de Nó, R. Studies on the structure of the cerebral cortex. *Journal für Psychologie und Neurologie,* I: 1933, *45,* 381-438; II: 1934, *46,* 113-177.

Lorenz, K. Der Kumpan in der Umwelt des Vogels. *Journal für Ornithologie,* 1935, 137-413.

Lorenz, K. Vergleichende Verhaltensforschung. *Zooligischer Anzeiger,* 1939, Vol. 12, Supplement 2, 69-102.

Lorenz, K. *King Solomon's ring.* New York: Cromwell, 1952.

Lorenz, K. *Man meets dog.* Boston: Houghton Mifflin, 1955.

Lubbock, J. *Ants, bees and wasps.* New York: Appleton, 1882.

Luciani, L., and Sippelli, G. *Le localizzazioni funzionali del cervello.* Napoli: Vallardi, 1885.

Lukas, F. *Psychologie der niedersten Tiere. Eine Untersuchung über die ersten Spuren psychischen Leben im Tierreiche.* Wien: Braumuller, 1904.

Lukina, E. V. Interaction of innate and acquired reactions in birds. *Trudy Instituta Fiziologii imeni I. P. Pavlova,* 1953, *2,* 340-346.

Luria, A. R. *The nature of human conflict.* New York: Liveright, 1932.

Luria, A. R. (Ed.) *Problems of higher nervous activity of the normal and abnormal child.* Moscow: Akademiya Pedagogicheskikh Nauk RSFSR, Vol. 1, 1956; Vol. 2, 1958.

Luria, A. R. *The regulatory development of the role of speech.* New York: Liverright, 1961.

Luria, A. R. *The human brain and psychic (mental) processes.* Moscow: Akademiya Pedagogicheskikh RSFSR, Nauk, 1963.

Luria, A. R., and Vinogradova, O. S. An objective investigation of the dynamics of semantic systems. *British Journal of Psychology,* 1959, *50,* 89-105.

Lyakh, G. S. Articulatory and auditory mimicry in the first months of life. *Zhurnal Vysshey Nervnoy Deyatel'nosti imeni I. P. Pavlova,* 1968a, *18,* 831-835.

Lyakh, G. S. Characteristics of conditioned connections in mimo-articulatory and auditory components of speech stimuli in the first year of life. *Zhurnal Vysshey Nervnoy Deyatel'nosti imeni I. P. Pavlova,* 1968b, *18,* 1069-1071.

Lyan, Chi-an. Interaction of cortical centers of conditioned and unconditioned reflexes. *Zhurnal Vysshey Nervnoy Deyatel'nosti imeni I. P. Pavlova,* 1959, *9,* 578-584.

Lyan, Chi-an. Role of intensity relations between neural centers of associated stimulation in the formation of conditioned reflexes. *Trudy Instituta Vysshey Nervnoy Deyatel'nosti imeni I. P. Pavlova, Seriya Fiziologicheskiya,* 1962a, *7,* 155-161.

Lyan, Chi-an. The problem of "direct" and "reverse" conditioned connections in associated stimulation. *Trudy Instituta Vysshey Nervnoy Deyatel'nosti imeni I. P. Pavlova, Seriya Fiziologicheskaya,* 1962b, *7,* 163-167.

Lyan, Chi-an. A situational motor reflex in the formation of a conditioned food reflex to an electric shock in dogs. *Trudy Instituta Vysshey Nervnoy Deyatel'nosti imeni I. P. Pavlova, Seriya Fiziologicheskaya,* 1962c, *7,* 169-176.

Lynn, R. *Attention, arousal and the orientation reaction.* New York: Pergamon Press, 1966.

MacCorquodale, K., and Meehl, P. E. Preliminary suggestions as to a formalization of expectancy theory. *Psychological Review,* 1953, *60,* 55-63.

Machtinger, D. I. The influence of a prolonged homogeneous diet on conditioned and unconditioned reflexes in children. *Fiziologichesky Zhurnal SSSR imeni I. M. Sechenova,* 1933, *16,* 421-428.

Magoun, H. W. Recent contributions to the electrophysiology of learning. *Annals of the New York Academy of Science,* 1961, *92,* 818-829.

Maier, N. R. F. Reasoning in white rats. *Comparative Psychology Monographs,* 1929, *6*(29), 1-93.

Maier, N. R. F. Reasoning in humans: I. On direction. *Journal of Comparative Psychology,* 1930, *10,* 115-143.

Maier, N. R. F. Reasoning in humans: II. The solution of a problem and its appearance in consciousness. *Journal of Comparative Psychology,* 1931, *12,* 181-194.

Maier, N. R. F. Age and intelligence in rats. *Journal of Comparative Psychology,* 1932a, *13,* 1-6.

Maier, N. R. F. The effect of cerebral destruction on reasoning and learning in rats. *Journal of Comparative Psychology,* 1932b, *13,* 45-75.

Maier, N. R. F. An aspect of human reasoning. *British Journal of Psychology,* 1933, *24,* 144-155.

Maier, N. R. F. Reasoning in children. *Journal of Comparative Psychology,* 1936, *21,* 357-366.

Maier, N. R. F. Reasoning in rats and human beings. *Psychological Review,* 1937, *44,* 365-378.

Maier, N. R. F., and Schneirla, T. C. *Principles of animal psychology.* New York: McGraw-Hill, 1935.

Makarov, P. O. The latent period of interoceptive sensations. *Doklady Akademii Nauk SSSR,* 1949, *66,* 521-524.

Makarov, P. O. A study of interoception in human subjects. *Uchenyye Zapiski Leningradskogo Universiteta, Seriya Biologicheskaya,* 1950a, *22*(123), 345-368.

Makarov, P. O. Pre-excitation and presentation. *Uchenyye Zapiski Leningradskogo Universiteta, Seriya Biologicheskaya,* 1950b, *22*(123), 369-399.

Makarov, P. O. *The neurodynamics of man.* Leningrad: Medgiz, 1959.

Makarov, P. O. Changes in excitability, liability and brain rhythm during the formation of temporary connections. *Gagrskiye Besedy,* 1960, *3,* 299-321.

Malakhovskaya, I. B. Development of specialized movements in postnatal periods in rabbits. In *Theses, 3rd Scientific Conference on Evolutionary Physiology in Memory of Academician L. A. Orbeli.* Leningrad: 1961. Pp. 126-127.

Malinovsky, O. V. Conditioned reflexes of the second-order in primates. *Trudy Instituta Fiziologii imeni I. P. Pavlova,* 1952, *1,* 205-212.

370 · Mind in Evolution

Malinovsky, O. V. Formation of temporary connections between indifferent stimuli. *Trudy Instituta Fiziologii imeni I. P. Pavlova,* 1953, *2,* 335-339.

Maltzman, I. Thinking: From a behavioristic point of view. *Psychological Review,* 1955, *62,* 275-286.

Maltzman, I. Theoretical conceptions of semantic conditioning and generalization. In T. R. Dixon and P. L. Horton (Eds.), *Verbal behavior and general behavior theory.* Englewood Cliffs, N. J.: Prentice-Hall, 1968. Pp. 291-339.

Mandler, G. From association to structure. *Psychological Review,* 1962, *69,* 415-427.

Mandler, G., and Kaplan, W. K. Subjective evaluation and reinforcing effect of a verbal stimulus. *Science,* 1956, *224,* 582-583.

Marbe, K. *Experimentell-psychologie Untersuchungen über das Urteil.* Leipzig: Engelmann, 1901.

Markov, A. A. *The calculus of probability.* St. Petersburg: Imperatorskaya Akademiya Nauk, 1900.

Marsh, J. T., McCarthy, D. A., Sheatz, G., and Galambos, R. Amplitude changes in evoked auditory potentials during habituation and conditioning. *Electroencephalography and Clinical Neurophysiology,* 1961, *13,* 224-234.

Martin, E. GSR conditioning and pseudoconditioning. *British Journal of Psychology,* 1962, *53,* 365-371.

Marukhanyan, E. V. The effect of the duration and intensity of a conditioned electroshock stimulus upon the magnitude of conditioned food and acid reflexes. *Zhurnal Vysshey Nervnoy Deyatel'nosti imeni I. P. Pavlova,* 1954, *4,* 684-691.

Marx, M. H. (Ed.) *Learning: Theories.* New York: Macmillan, 1970.

Masserman, J. H. *Behavior and neurosis.* Chicago: University of Chicago Press, 1964.

Masserman, J. H., and Prechtl, C. Neurosis in monkeys: A preliminary report of experimental observations. *Annals of the New York Academy of Science,* 1953, *56,* 253-265.

Mateer, F. *Child behavior. A critical and experimental study of young children by the method of conditioned reflexes.* Boston: Badger, 1918.

Max, L. W. An experimental study of the motor theory of consciousness: I. Critique of earlier studies. *Journal of General Psychology,* 1934, *11,* 112-127.

Max, L. W. An experimental study of the motor theory of consciousness: III. Action-current responses in deaf mutes during sleep, sensory stimulation and dreams. *Journal of Comparative Psychology,* 1935, *12,* 469-486.

Max, L. W. An experimental study of the motor theory of consciousness: IV. Action-current responses in the deaf during awakening, kinesthetic imagery and abstract thinking. *Journal of Comparative Psychology,* 1937, *24,* 301-344.

Mayer, A., and Orth, J. Zur qualitativen Untersuchung der Association. *Zeitschrift für Psychologie,* 1901, *26,* 1-13.

Mayorov, F. P. Overstraining of inhibition as a cause of experimental neurosis. *Trudy Fiziologicheskikh Laboratorii imeni I. P. Pavlova,* 1938, *8,* 349-359.

McConnell, J. V. Comparative physiology: Learning in invertebrates. *Annual Review of Physiology,* 1966, *28,* 107-136.

McDougall, W. *Physiological psychology.* London: Dent, 1905.

McGeoch, J. A. The vertical dimensions of mind. *Psychological Review,* 1936, *43,* 107-130.

McGeoch, J. A., and Irion, A. L. *The psychology of learning.* New York: Longmans, Green, 1952.

McGuigan, F. J. (Ed.) *Thinking: Studies of covert language responses.* New York: Appleton-Century-Crofts, 1966.

McNamara, H. J., Solley, C. M., and Long, J. Effects of punishment (electric shock) upon perceptual learning. *Journal of Abnormal and Social Psychology*, 1958, *57*, 91-98.

Meinecke, G. Einige technische Konstruktsionsaufgaben und deren Lösungsmethoden. *Archiv. für die gesamte Psychologie*, 1934, *92*, 249-254.

Meinong, A. *Über die Erfahrungsgrundlagen unseres Wissens.* Berlin: Springer, 1906.

Menzies, R. Conditioned vasomotor responses in human subjects. *Journal of Psychology*, 1937, *4*, 75-120.

Meshchersky, R. M. Cortical modification or afferent firing through the lateral geniculate body. In E. A. Asratyan (Ed.), *Reflexes of the brain.* Moscow: Nauka, 1965. Pp. 295-296.

Meshchersky, R. M. The role of corticofugal influences in effecting dominance and conditioned reflexes. *Zhurnal Vysshey Nervnoy Deyatel'nosti imeni I. P. Pavlova,* 1966, *16*, 14-17.

Messer, A. Experimentall-psychologische Untersuchungen über das Denken. *Archiv für die Gesamte Psychologie,* 1906, *8*, 1-224.

Meyer, M. *The fundamental laws of human behavior.* Boston: Badger, 1911.

Meyer, M. Some nonsense about the common path. *Psychological Review,* 1925, *32*, 431-442.

Mikhelson, N. I., and Yurman, M. N. The study of conditioned reflexes based on different unconditioned reflexes. Irradiation of extinctive inhibition. In D. S. Fursikov, M. O. Gurevich, and A. N. Zalmanzon (Eds.), *Higher nervous activity.* Moscow: Kommunisticheskaya Akademiya, 1929. Pp. 211-231.

Miller, G. A., Galanter, E., and Pribram, K. *Plans and the structure of behavior.* New York: Holt, 1960.

Miller, J. The effect of facilitatory and inhibitory attitudes on eyelid conditioning. Unpublished doctoral dissertation, Yale University, 1939. (Abstract in *Psychological Bulletin,* 1939, *36,* 577-578.)

Miller, N. E. Comments on multiple-process conceptions of learning. *Psychological Review,* 1951, *58,* 375-381.

Miller, N. E. Liberalization of basic S-R concepts: Extensions to conflict behavior, motivation and learning. In S. Koch (Ed.), *Psychology: A study of a science.* Vol. 2. *General systematic formulations, learning, and special processes.* New York: McGraw-Hill, 1959. Pp. 196-292.

Miller, N. E. Learning resistance to pain and fear: Effects of overlearning, exposure, and rewarded exposure in context. *Journal of Experimental Psychology,* 1960, *60,* 137-145.

Miller, N. E. Chemical coding of behavior in the brain. *Science,* 1965, *148,* 328-338.

Miller, N. E. Learning of visceral and glandular responses. *Science,* 1969a, *163,* 434-445.

Miller, N. E. Skeletal learning, visceral learning and homeostatis. In V. V. Parin (Ed.), *System organization of physiological functions. Collected contributions dedicated to the 70th birthday of Academician P. K. Anokhin.* Moscow: Meditsina, 1969b. Pp. 363-372.

Miller, N. E., and Kessen, M. C. Reward effects of food via stomach fistula compared with those of food via mouth. *Journal of Comparative and Physiological Psychology,* 1952, *45,* 555-564.

Miller, N. E., Roberts, W. W., and Delgado, J. M. R. *Learning motivated by electrical stimulation of the brain.* Motion picture shown at the 61st Annual Convention of the American Psychological Association, Cleveland, Ohio, September 4-9, 1953.

Miller, N. E., and Senf, G. Evidence for positive induction in instrumental conditioning. In E. Sh. Ayrapet'yants (Ed.), *Central and peripheral mechanisms of nervous activity.* Yerevan: Akademiya Nauk, ArSSR, 1966.

Miller, N. E., and Stevens, S. S. Agitated behavior of rats during experimental extinction and a curve of spontaneous recovery. *Journal of Comparative Psychology,* 1936, *21,* 205-232.

Miller, S., and Konorski, J. Sur une forme particulière des réflexes conditionnels. *Compte Rendu des Séances de la Societé de Biologie,* Paris, 1928, *99,* 1155.

Milleryan, E. A., and Tkachenko, V. G. The effect of practice on the magnitude of the spatial discrimination. In B. G. Anan'yev and B. F. Lomov (Eds.), *Problems of spatial and temporal perception.* Leningrad: 1961. Pp. 33-35.

Milstein, V., and Stevens, J. R. Verbal and conditioned avoidance learning during abnormal EEG discharge. *Journal of Nervous and Mental Disorders,* 1961, *132,* 50-60.

Miyata, Y., and Hamano, K. Can the autonomic response be trained through the operant paradigm? *Humanities Review,* Kwansei Gakuin University, 1967, *18,* 1-18.

Mogenson, G. J. An attempt to establish secondary reinforcement with rewarding brain stimulation. *Psychological Reports,* 1965, *16,* 163-167.

Moiseyeva, N. A. Effects of mechanoreceptors of the gastrointestinal canal on higher nervous activity. *Trudy Instituta Fiziologii imeni I. P. Pavlova,* 1952, *1,* 93-102.

Molodkina, L. N. Stability of directional movement of a food stimulus disappearing from the sight of cats. In *Theses, 21st Conference on Problems of Higher Nervous Activity.* Moscow-Leningrad: Nauka, 1966. P. 208.

Moore, A. U. Conditioning and stress in the newborn lamb and kid. In W. H. Gantt (Ed.), *Physiological bases of psychiatry.* Springfield, Ill.: Charles C Thomas, 1958. Pp. 270-297.

Moore, T. V. The process of abstraction. *University of California Publications in Psychology,* 1910, *1,* 72-197.

Morgan, C. L. *Animal life and intelligence.* Boston: Ginn, 1891.

Morgan, C. L. *Introduction to comparative psychology.* New York: Scribner's, 1894.

Morrell, F. Electrophysiological contributions to the neural basis of learning. *Physiological Review,* 1961a, *41,* 443-494.

Morrell, F. Effect of anodal polarization on the firing pattern of single cortical cells. *Annals of the New York Academy of Science,* 1961b, *92,* 860-876.

Morrell, F. *Information storage in nerve cells.* In W. S. Field and W. Abbott (Eds.), Information storage and neural control. Springfield, Ill.: Charles C Thomas, 1963. Pp. 189-229.

Morrell, F., and Naitoh, P. Effect of cortical polarization on a conditioned avoidance response. *Experimental Neurology,* 1962, *6,* 597-523.

Moscovitch, A., and LoLordo, V. M. Role of safety in the Pavlovian backward fear conditioning procedure. *Journal of Comparative and Physiological Psychology,* 1968, *66,* 673-678.

Motokawa, K. Electroencephalogram of man in the generalization and differentiation of conditioned reflexes. *Tohoku Journal of Experimental Medicine,* 1949, *50,* 225-235.

Mowrer, O. H. Preparatory set (expectancy)—a determinant in motivation and learning. *Psychological Review,* 1938, *45,* 62-91.

Mowrer, O. H. The psychologist looks at language. *American Psychologist,* 1954, *9,* 660-694.

Mowrer, O. H. *Learning theory and behavior.* New York: Wiley, 1960a.

Mowrer, O. H. *Learning theory and symbolic behavior.* New York: Wiley, 1960b.

Müller, G. E., and Pilzecker, A. Experimentelle Beitrage zur Lehre von Gedächtniss. *Zeitschrift für Psychologie,* 1900. Erganzungsband No. 1.

Murphy, G. *Personality: A biosocial approach to origins and structure.* New York: Harper, 1947.

Mysyashchikova, S. S. The extinction of vegetative reactions during the stimulation of the peripheral apparatus of various analyzers. In K. M. Bykov (Ed.), *Problems of the physiology of interoception.* Moscow: Akademiya Nauk SSSR, 1952. Pp. 411-427.

Nagaty, M. O. The effect of reinforcement on closely following S-R connections. I. The effect of a backward conditioning procedure on the extinction of conditioned avoidance. *Journal of Experimental Psychology,* 1951a, *42,* 239-246.

Nagaty, M. O. The effect of reinforcement on closely following S-R connections. II. Effect of food reward immediately preceding performance of an instrumental conditioned response on extinction of that response. *Journal of Experimental Psychology,* 1951b, *42,* 333-340.

Narbutovich, I. O. The possibility of forming a conditioned reflex when the unconditioned defense stimulus precedes the indifferent stimulus. *Trudy Fiziologicheskikh Laboratorii I. P. Pavlova,* 1940, *9,* 371-390.

Narbutovich, I. O., and Podkopayev, N. A. The conditioned reflex as an association. *Trudy Fiziologicheskikh Laboratorii I. P. Pavlova,* 1936, *6*(2), 5-25.

Natadze, R. G. Set action in imagination. In A. S. Prangishvili and Z. I. Khodzava (Eds.), *Experimental studies of the psychology of set.* Tbilisi: Akademiya Nauk GSSR, 1958. Pp. 243-294.

Natashvili, A., Veshapeli, N., Abdushelishvili, M., Gogitidze, E., Dzhorbenadze, A., Tsibadze, D., Tvaladze, G., Sakvarelidze, S., and Zhgenti, V. Microcephalic girl "Peeta" and her clinical and morphological characteristics. In *Problems of neurophysiology and behavior, dedicated to I. Beritashvili (J. S. Beritoff).* Tbilisi: Akademiya Nauk SSR, Gruzinsky Filial, 1936. Pp. 454-501.

Naumova, T. S. Electrical activity of a dominant cortical center during reflex reactions to sounds. *Fiziologichesky Zhurnal SSSR imeni I. M. Sechenova,* 1956, *42,* 361-364.

Nemtsova, O. L. The capacity of cerebral cortex to receive stimulation during the action of the unconditioned stimulus. In P. K. Anokhin (Ed.), *Problems of higher nervous activity.* Moscow: Akademiya Meditinskikh Nauk, 1949. Pp. 186-195.

Nesmeyanova, T. N. The inhibition of the motor reflex in spinal dogs under conditions of chronic experimentation. *Fiziologichesky Zhurnal SSSR imeni I. M. Sechenova,* 1957, *42,* 281-288.

Nezhdanova, Z. A. The formation of conditioned reflexes when the unconditioned stimulus precedes the indifferent stimulus. *Trudy Fiziologichesky Laboratorii imeni I. P. Pavlova,* 1940, *9,* 353-359.

Nicholls, M. F., and Kimble, G. A. Effects of instructions upon eyelid conditioning. *Journal of Exprimental Psychology,* 1964, *67,* 400-402.

Nikolaeff, P. N. Contribution a l'analyse des réflexes conditionnels complexes. *Archives des Sciences Biologiques, St. Petersbourg,* 1911, *16,* 411-444.

Nishizawa, S. Some acquired properties of the backward CS paired with an electric shock as US: The effects of fluctuated US-duration upon a certain secondary property of the backward CS in the rat. *Annual Review of Animal Psychology,* 1962, *12*(2), 83-92.

Nissen, H. W. Phylogenetic comparison. In S. S. Stevens (Ed.), *Handbook of experimental psychology*. New York: Wiley, 1951. Pp. 347-386.

Nissen, H. W. Axes of behavioral comparison. In A. Roe and G. G. Simpson (Eds.), *Behavior and evolution*. New Haven: Yale University Press, 1958. Pp. 183-205.

Norakidze, V. D. Temperament and fixation of set. In A. S. Prangishvili and Z. I. Khodzhava (Eds.), *Experimental studies of the psychology of set*. Tbilisi: Akademiya Nauk GSSR, 1958. Pp. 347-356.

Norakidze, V. D. *General psychology of sports*. (In Georgian.) Tbilisi: Tsodna, 1959.

North, A. J., and Stimmel, D. T. Extinction of an instrumental response following a large number of reinforcements. *Psychological Reports, 1960, 6,* 227-234.

Notterman, J. M. Force emission during bar pressing. *Journal of the Experimental Analysis of Behavior, 1959, 58,* 341-347.

Notterman, J. M., and Mintz, D. E. *Dynamics of response*. New York: Wiley, 1965.

Novikova, A. A. The physiological mechanism of the formation of conditioned reflexes to relations. *Fiziologichesky Zhurnal SSSR imeni I. M. Sechenova,* 1938, *24,* 831-843.

Novikova, L. A. Electrophysiological investigation of speech kinesthesis. In B. G. Anan'yev, A. N. Leont'yev, A. R. Luria, N. A. Menchenskaya, S. L. Rubinshteyn, and B. M. Teplov Eds.), *Materials for the Conference on Psychology*. Moscow: Akademiya Pedagogicheskikh Nauk, 1957. Pp. 337-351.

Novikova, L. A., and Farber, D. A. Electrophysiological studies of the connections of auditory and visual analyzers in the presence of dominant foci in the cerebral cortex of the rabbit. *Fiziologichesky Zhurnal SSR imeni I. M. Sechenova,* 1956, *42,* 341-350.

Novikova, L. A., Rusinov, V. S., and Semiokhina, A. F. Electrophysiological analysis of cortical linkage functions of the cortex in presence of a dominant center. *Zhurnal Vysshey Nervnoy Deyatel'nosti imeni I. P. Pavlova,* 1952, *2,* 844-861.

Novikova, L. A., and Sokolov, E. N. The study of electroencephalograms of motor and galvanic skin reactions in orienting and conditioned reflexes in man. *Zhurnal Vysshey Nervnoy Deyatel'nosti imeni I. P. Pavlova,* 1957, *7,* 363-373.

Obraztsova, G. A. *Problems of the ontogeny of higher nervous activity*. Moscow: Nauka, 1964.

Ochs, S. The nature of spreading depression in neural networks. In C. C. Pfeifer and J. R. Smythies (Eds.), *International Review of Neurobiology* Vol. 4. New York: Academic Press, 1962. Pp. 1-69.

Ohrbach, J., and Miller, M. Visual performance of infra-human primates reared in an intermittently illuminated room. *Vision Research,* 1969, *9,* 713-716.

Okhnyanskaya, L. G. A study of the conditioned respiratory-vasomotor reflex. Respiration as the stimulus of vasomotor action. *Fiziologichesky Zhurnal SSSR imeni I. M. Sechenova,* 1953, *39,* 610-613.

Olds, J. Differentiation of reward systems in the brain by self-stimulation techniques. In E. R. Ramsey and D. S. Doherty (Eds.), *Electrical studies on the unanesthetized brain*. New York: Hoeber, 1960. Pp. 17-51.

Olds, J., and Milner, P. Positive reinforcement produced by electrical stimulation of septal area and other regions of rat brain. *Journal of Comparative and Physiological Psychology,* 1954, *47,* 419-427.

O'Leary, J. Structure of the area striata of the cat. *Journal of Comparative Neurology,* 1941, *25,* 131-164.

Omelyansky, V. L. (Ed.) *Volume dedicated to the 75th birthday of Academician I. P. Pavlov.* Leningrad: GIZ, 1925.

Oniani, T. V., Naneyshvili, T. L., Koridze, M. G., and Abzianidze, E. V. Neurophysiological mechanisms of delayed reactions. *Fiziologichesky Zhurnal SSSR imeni I. M. Sechenova,* 1969, *55,* 658-663.

Orbeli, L. A. Problems of evolutionary physiology. *Arkhiv Biologicheskikh* 1941, *61*(1), 43-55.

Orbeli, L. A. The application of the principle of evolution to the physiology of the central nervous system. *Uspekhi Sovremennoy Biologii,* 1942, *15*(3), 257-272.

Orbeli, L. A. The second-signal system. *Fiziologicheskikh Zhurnal SSSR, imeni I. M. Sechenova,* 1947, *33,* 675-687.

Orbeli, L. A. *Problems of higher nervous activity.* Moscow: Akademiya Nauk SSSR, 1949.

Orbeli, L. A. The dialectical method in the physiology of the nervous system. *Fiziologichesky Zhurnal SSSR imeni I. M. Sechenova,* 1950, *36,* 5-18.

Orbeli, L. A. (Ed.) *Materials for evolutionary physiology.* Moscow: Akademiya Nauk SSSR, 1956-1958. 4 Vols.

Orbeli, L. A. Basic problems and methods of evolutionary physiology. In D. A. Biryukov (Ed.), *Evolution of functions of the nervous system.* Leningrad: Medgiz, 1958. Pp. 7-17.

Oreshuk, F. A. Comparative physiology of associative connections. *Fiziologichesky Zhurnal SSSR imeni I. P. Pavlova,* 1950, *36,* 425-428.

Orlov, V. V. *The psychophysiological problem.* Perm: Perm University, 1966.

Osgood, C. E. *Method and theory in experimental psychology.* New York: Oxford University Press, 1953.

Osgood, C. E. On understanding and creating sentences. *American Psychologist,* 1963, *18,* 735-751.

Osgood, C. E., Suci, G. I., and Tannenbaum, P. H. *The measurement of meaning.* Urbana: University of Illinois Press, 1957.

Ostrogorsky, S. A. *An obscure point in the innervation of the salivary glands.* St. Petersburg: Stasyulevich, 1894.

Pakovich, B. I. The summation reflex in situations of conditioned reflexes. In E. A. Asratyan (Ed.), *Neural mechanisms of conditioned-reflex activity.* Moscow: Akademiya Nauk SSSR, 1963. Pp. 206-230.

Palladin, A. Formation of laboratory conditioned reflexes to sums of stimuli. *Trudy Obshchestva Russkikh Vrachey v St. Peterburge,* 1906, *73,* 393-401.

Panferov, Yu. K. Chained conditioned reflexes in children. In *Theses, 2nd All-Union Congress of Physiology.* Leningrad: 1926. Pp. 153-156.

Papoušek, H. A method of studying conditioned food reflexes in infants under six months of age. *Zhurnal Vysshey Nervnoy Deyatel'nosti imeni I. P. Pavlova,* 1959, *9,* 143-147.

Papoušek, H. Conditioned food reflexes in infants. I. Experimental conditioned sucking reflexes. *Československá Pediatrie,* 1960a, *15,* 861-872.

Papoušek, H. Conditioned motor food reflexes in infants. II. A new experimental method of investigation. *Československá Pediatrie,* 1960b, *15,* 981-988.

Papoušek, H. Conditioned head rotation reflexes in infants in the first months of life. *Acta Paediatrica,* 1961, *50,* 565-570.

376 · Mind in Evolution

Papoušek, H. The development of higher nervous activity in children in the first half year of life. In P. H. Mussen (Ed.), European research in cognitive development. *Monographs of the Society for Research in Child Development,* 1965, *30*(2), 102-111.

Papoušek, H. Experimental studies of appetitional behavior in human newborn and infants. In H. W. Stevenson, E. H. Hess, and H. L. Rheingold (Eds.), *Early Behavior: Comparative and developmental approaches.* New York: Wiley, 1967a.

Papoušek, H. Conditioning during early postnatal development. In I. Brackbill and G. G. Thompson (Eds.), *Behavior in infancy and early childhood: A book of readings.* New York: Free Press, 1967b. Pp. 259-274.

Papoušek, H. Genetics and child development. In J. N. Spuhler (Ed.), *Genetic diversity and human behavior.* Chicago: Aldine, 1967c. Pp. 171-186.

Papoušek, H. Elaborations of conditioned head-turning. Paper read at XIX International Congress of Psychology, London, July 28, 1969.

Papoušek, H., and Bernstein, P. The functions of conditioning stimulation in human neonates and infants. Paper read at Conference on Functions of Stimulation in Early Postnatal Development, London, November 13-17, 1967.

Parin, V. V. (Ed.) *Problems of the physiology and pathology of the central nervous system in animal and human ontogeny.* Moscow: Medgiz, 1961.

Parin, V. V. (Ed.) *System organization of physiological functions. Collected contributions dedicated to the 70th birthday of Academician P. K. Anokhin.* Moscow: Meditsina, 1969.

Parks, E. R. The orientation reaction as a mediator in sensory preconditioning. Unpublished doctoral dissertation, University of Nebraska, 1963.

Parks, E. R. The orientation reaction as a mediator of sensory preconditioning. *Psychonomic Science,* 1968, *11,* 11-12.

Patrick, C. Creative thought in poets. *Archives of Psychology,* New York, 1935, No. 178.

Patrick, C. Creative thought in artists. *Journal of Psychology,* 1937, *4,* 35-73.

Pauperova, G. F. Formation of a secondary exteroceptive conditioned reflex on the basis of a primary interoceptive one. In K. M. Bykov (Ed.), *Problems of the physiology of interoception.* Moscow: Akademiya Nauk SSSR, 1952. Pp. 437-442.

Pavlov, I. P. Reflex inhibition of salivary secretion. *Trudy Sankt-Peterburgskago Obshchestva Yestestvoispytateley,* 1877, *8,* 84-87.

Pavlov, I. P. *Lectures on the work of the main digestive glands.* St. Petersburg: Kushneroff, 1897.

Pavlov, I. P. Experimental psychology and psychophysiology of animals. *Izvestia Voyenno-Meditsinskoy Akademii,* 1903, *7*(2), 109-121.

Pavlov, I. P. Sur la sécrétion psychique des glandes salivaire (phénomènes nerveux complexes dans le travail de glandes salivaires). *Archives Internationales de Physiologie,* 1904, *1,* 119-135.

Pavlov, I. P. Scientific study of so-called psychical processes of higher animals. (Thomas Huxley Lecture) *Lancet,* 1906, *84*(2), 911-915.

Pavlov, I. P. Basic laws of the work of the cerebral cortex. *Trudy Obshchestva Russkikh Vrachey v Sankt-Peterburge,* 1911, *78,* 175-187.

Pavlov, I. P. *Twenty years of objective study of higher nervous activity (behavior) of animals. Conditioned reflexes. A collection of articles, lectures, and addresses.* Moscow: GIZ, 1923.

Pavlov, I. P. The latest successes of the objective study of higher nervous activity. *Izvestiya Petrogradskogo Nauchnogo Instituta imeni P. F. Lesgafta,* 1924, *8,* 43-52.

Pavlov, I. P. Derniers résultats des recherches sur le travail des hémisphères cérébraux. *Journal de Psychologie,* 1926a, *23,* 501-510.

Pavlov, I. P. Type de système nerveux a prédominance des processus inhibiteurs. *Journal de Psychologie,* 1926b, *23,* 1012-1018.

Pavlov, I. P. *Lectures on the work of the large hemispheres of the brain.* Moscow-Leningrad: GIZ, 1927a.

Pavlov, I. P. *Conditioned reflexes: An investigation of the physiological activity of the cerebral cortex* (translation by C. V. Anrep of Pavlov, 1927a). London: Oxford University Press, 1927b.

Pavlov, I. P. Certain problems of the physiology of the cerebral cortex. *Proceedings of the Royal Society, Series B,* 1928a, *103,* 97-110.

Pavlov, I. P. *Lectures on conditioned reflexes: Twenty-five years of objective study of higher nervous activity (behavior) of animals.* (Translated, with additions, by W. H. Gantt, from Pavlov, 1923). New York: International Publishers, 1928b.

Pavlov, I. P. Physiology of higher nervous activity. *Priroda,* 1932a, Nos. 11-12, 1139-1156.

Pavlov, I. P. The reply of a physiologist to psychologists. *Psychological Review,* 1932b, *39,* 91-127.

Pavlov, I. P. *Twenty years of objective study of higher nervous activity (behavior) of animals. A collection of articles, lectures and addresses,* (5th ed.). Leningrad: Lenmedizdat, 1932c.

Pavlov, I. P. Essai d'une interprétation physiologique de l'hystèrie. *L'encéphale,* 1933, *28,* 288-295.

Pavlov, I. P. Conditioned reflexes. *Bol'shaya Meditzinskaya Entsiklopedia,* Vol. 33, pp. 431-446. Moscow: Meditsina, 1936a.

Pavlov, I. P. Physiological mechanism of so-called voluntary movements. *Trudy Fiziologicheskikh Laboratorii I. P. Pavlova,* 1936b, *4*(6), 115-118.

Pavlov, I. P. *Lectures on conditioned reflexes.* Vol. 2. *Conditioned reflexes and psychiatry* (translated by W. H. Gantt). New York: International Publishers, 1941.

Pavlov, I. P. *Wednesdays: Protocols and stenograms of physiological colloquia.* Moscow-Leningrad: Akademiya Nauk SSSR, 1949. 3 vols.

Pavlov, I. P. *Collected works.* Moscow: Akademiya Nauk SSSR, 1951. 5 vols.

Pavlov, I. P. *Clinical Wednesdays: Stenograms of sessions in neurological and psychiatric clinics.* Moscow-Leningrad: Akademiya Nauk SSSR, 1954-1957. 3 vols.

Pavlov, I. P. *Selected works.* Moscow: Foreign Languages Publishing House, 1955. (In English)

Pavlova, A. M. Can a conditioned reflex be formed when the unconditioned stimulus precedes the indifferent stimulus? *Trudy Fiziologicheskikh Laboratorii I. P. Pavlova,* 1933, *5,* 21-31.

Pavlygina, R. A. Formation of a dominant center in the hypothalamus and study of its characteristics. *Trudy Instituta Vysshey Nervnoy Deyatel'nosti imeni I. P. Pavlova, Seriya Fiziologicheskaya,* 1956, *2,* 124-138.

Pavlygina, R. A. Cortical centers of excitation with "single tetanized contractions." *Trudy Instituta Vysshey Nervnoy Deyatel'nosti imeni I. P. Pavlova, Seriya Fiziologicheskaya,* 1962, *7,* 39-48.

Pavlygina, R. A. Trace phenomena in states of dominance. *Zhurnal Vysshey Nervnoy Deyatel'nosti imeni I. P. Pavlova*, 1967, *17*, 505-512.

Pavlygina, R. A., and Pozdnyakova, R. A. Formation of dominant centers in the motor analyzer of the cortex with pulsating currents. *Trudy Instituta Vysshey Nervnoy Deyatel'nosti imeni I. P. Pavlova, Seriya Fiziologicheskaya*, 1960, *5*, 49-57.

Peastral, A. Studies in efficiency: Semantic generalization in schizophrenia. Unpublished doctoral dissertation, University of Pennsylvania, 1961.

Peckham, G. W., and Peckham, E. G. Some observations on the mental powers of spiders. *Journal of Morphology*, 1887, *1*, 383-419.

Penfield, W. Speech, perception and the uncommitted cortex. In J. C. Eccles (Ed.), *Brain and conscious experience*. New York: Springer-Verlag, 1966. Pp. 217-237.

Penfield, W. Conscious memory and man's conditioned reflexes. In K. H. Pribram (Ed.), *On the biology of learning*. New York: Harcourt Brace, 1969. Pp. 129-168.

Penfield, W., and Jasper, H. H. *Epilepsy and the functional anatomy of the human brain*. Boston: Little, Brown, 1954.

Penfield, W., and Perot, P. The brain's record of auditory and visual experience. A final summary and discussion. *Brain*, 1963, *86*, 595-696.

Penfield, W., and Roberts, L. *Speech and brain mechanisms*. Princeton: Princeton University Press, 1959.

Pennypacker, H. S., and Cook, W. A. Acquisition and extinction of the conditioned eyelid response in the squirrel monkey as functions of CS-US intervals. *Psychological Reports*, 1967, *20*, 1235-1243.

Pereltsvayg, I. *Materials on the study of conditioned reflexes*. St. Petersburg: Military Medical Academy, 1907. (Thesis)

Perkins, C. C., Jr. The relation between conditioned stimulus intensity and response strength. *Journal of Experimental Psychology*, 1953, *46*, 225-231.

Perry, R. B. *General theory of value*. New York: Longmans, Green, 1926.

Petropavlovsky, V. P. Method of conditioned muscle tonus and attempts at its extinction. *Mediko-Biologichesky Zhurnal*, 1927, *2*, 43-57.

Petropavlovsky, V. P. The methodology of conditioned motor reflexes. *Fiziologichesky Zhurnal SSSR imeni I. M. Sechenova*, 1934, *17*, 217-225.

Petrov, S. A. Dynamic stereotype effects on individual stimuli in different sequential positions. *Trudy Fiziologicheskikh Laboratorii I. P. Pavlova*, 1941, *10*, 332-336.

Petrova, M. K. *The study of the irradiation of excitatory and inhibitory processes*. St. Petersburg: Military Medical Academy, 1914. (Thesis)

Petrova, M. K. Different types of internal inhibition in difficult conditions. *Trudy Fiziologicheskikh Laboratorii I. P. Pavlova*, 1924, *1*(1), 61-70.

Petrova, M. K. Curing experimental neuroses in dogs. *Arkhiv Biologicheskikh Nauk*, 1925, *25*(1-3), 3-16.

Petrova, M. K. Pathological deviations of the excitatory and inhibitory processes during difficult confrontation. *Trudy Fiziologicheskikh Laboratorii I. P. Pavlova*, 1926, *1*(2-3), 199-211.

Petrova, M. K. The prevalence of the inhibitory action of the unconditioned stimulus when it precedes the indifferent stimulus. *Trudy Fiziologicheskikh Laboratorii I. P. Pavlova*, 1933, *5*, 49-79.

Petrova, M. K. Experimental neuroses. *Uspekhi Sovremmennoy Biologii*, 1939, *11*(3), 509-529.

Pfaffmann, C. De gustibus. *American Psychologist*, 1965, *20*, 21-33.

Piaget, J. *Le language et la pensée chez l'enfant.* Neuchatel and Paris: Delachaut, 1923.

Piaget, J. Pensée egocentrique et pensée sociocentrique. *Cahiers Internationales Sociologie,* 1951, *10,* 34-49.

Pieron, H. L'adaptation aux obscurations répetées comme phénomène de mémoire chez les animaux inferieurs. La loi de l'oubli chez la limnée. *Archives de Psychologie, Geneve,* 1910, *9,* 39-50.

Pieron, H. Recherches experimentales sur la phénomènes de mémoire. *Année Pyschologique,* 1913, *19,* 91-193.

Pieron, H. *L'évolution de la mémoire.* Paris: Costes, 1920.

Pimenev, P. P. *A new group of conditioned reflexes.* St. Petersburg: Voyenno-medizinskaya Akademiya, 1907. (Thesis)

Platonov, K. I. *The formation of associated motor reflexes to simultaneous auditory and visual stimuli in human subjects.* St. Petersburg: Military Medical Academy, 1912. (Thesis)

Platt, W., and Baker, B. A. The relation of the scientific "hunch" to research. *Journal of Chemical Education,* 1931, *8,* 1969-2002.

Podkopayev, N. A. What happens in the cells (centers) of the indifferent and the conditioned stimuli during the action of the unconditioned stimulus? *Trudy Fiziologicheskikh Laboratorii I. P. Pavlova,* 1928, *2*(2), 81-86.

Podsosennaya, L. S. Dominance with fading electrodermal stimulation and its effect on conditioned defense reflexes. *Trudy Instituta Vysshey Nervnoy Deyatel'nosti imeni I. P. Pavlova, Seriya Fiziologicheskaya,* 1956, *2,* 139-145.

Polikanina, R. I. Extinction of the orienting reflex to a rhythmic auditory stimulus in premature infants. *Zhurnal Vysshey Nervnoy Deyatel'nosti imeni I. P. Pavlova,* 1966, *16,* 813-829.

Polikanina, R. I., and Sergeyeva, L. N. Biolectric brain activity and reactions to external stimuli in premature neonates. *Zhurnal Vysshey Nervnoy Deyatel'nosti imeni I. P. Pavlova,* 1965, *15,* 722-732.

Polikanina, R. I., and Sergeyeva, L. N. Development of extinctive inhibition in early ontogenesis of children. *Zhurnal Vysshey Nervnoy Deyatel'nosti imeni I. P. Pavlova,* 1967, *17,* 228-239.

Polivannaya, M. F. Extinctive inhibition in chickens. In *Theses, 4th Scientific Conference on Evolutionary Physiology in Memory of Academician L. A. Orbeli.* Leningrad: 1965. Pp. 219-220.

Polivannaya, M. F., and Kharchenko, P. D. Differential inhibition of chickens in ontogeny. *Zhurnal Vysshey Nervnoy Deyatel'nosti imeni I. P. Pavlova,* 1965, *15,* 1129-1132.

Polosukhin, A. P. The effects of emotional and conditioned-reflex stimuli on the volume of the spleen in ontogeny. *Byulleten' Eksperimental'noy Biologii i Meditsiny,* 1938, *5*(2), 162-164.

Polyakov, G. I. Five structural characteristics of man's cortex and functional interrelations among neurons. *Arkhiv Anatomii Gistologii i Embriologii,* 1953, *30*(5), 48-63.

Polyakov, G. I. The ratio of main types of neurons in man's cerebral cortex. *Zhurnal Vysshey Nervnoy Deyatel'nosti imeni I. P. Pavlova,* 1956, *6,* 461-478.

Polyakov, G. I. *Origin of reflex mechanisms of the brain.* Moscow: Meditsina, 1964.

Polyakov, G. I. *Principles of neuronal organization of the brain.* Moscow: Moscow University, 1965.

Polyakov, G. I., and Sarkisov, S. A. Cortical neuronal and interneuronal connections. In S. A. Sarkisov, I. N. Filiminov, and N. S. Preobrazhenskaya (Eds.), *Cytoarchitechture of man's cortex.* Moscow: Medgiz, 1949. Pp. 102-119.

Ponomarev, Ya. Y. *The psychology of creative thinking.* Moscow: Akademiya Pedagogicheskikh Nauk RSFSR, 1960.

Popova, N. S. Certain characteristics of the formation of conditioned reflexes to visual and auditory stimuli (free-movement method). *Zhurnal Vysshey Nervnoy Deyatel'nosti imeni I. P. Pavlova,* 1960, *10,* 80-87.

Porter, J. M. Backward conditioning of the eyelid response. *Journal of Experimental Psychology,* 1938, *23,* 403-410.

Postman, L. Association theory and perceptual learning. *Psychological Review,* 1955, *62,* 438-466.

Postman, L., and Sassenrath, J. The automatic action of verbal rewards and punishments. *Journal of General Psychology,* 1961, *65,* 109-136.

Povorinsky, Yu. A. *Methods of studying conditioned motor reflexes with verbal reinforcement.* Leningrad: Medgiz, 1954.

Poznanskaya, N. B. Dermal sensitivity to visible and infrared radiation. *Fiziologichesky Zhurnal SSSR imeni I. M. Sechenova,* 1938, *24,* 774-783.

Prangishvili, A. S. *Studies in the psychology of set.* Tbilisi: Metsniyerba, 167.

Prangishvili, A. S., and Khodzhava, Z. I. (Eds.) *Experimental studies of a psychology set.* Tbilisi: Akademiya Nauk GSSR, Vol. 1, 1958; Vol. 2, 1963.

Pratusevich, Yu. M. *Verbal stimuli in children.* Moscow: GIZ, 1960.

Pratusevich, Yu. M. *Mental fatigue in school children.* Moscow: Meditsina, 1964.

Pravda, April 9, 1966.

Prazdnikova, N. V. Methods of studying conditioned food-motor reflexes in fish. *Zhurnal Vysshey Nervnoy Deyatel'nosti imeni I. P. Pavlova,* 1953a, *3,* 464-468.

Prazdnikova, N. V. Conditioned food-motor reflexes and conditioned inhibition in fish. *Trudy Instituta Fiziologii imeni I. P. Pavlova,* 1953b, *2,* 370-383.

Prazdnikova, N. V. Conditioned-reflex activity of fish with multiple applications of the stimulus. *Trudy Instituta Fiziologii imeni I. P. Pavlova,* 1959, *8,* 186-193.

Prazdnikova, N. V. Individual variations in higher nervous activity of fish. *Zhurnal Vysshey Nervnoy Deyatel'nosti imeni I. P. Pavlova,* 1960, *10,* 464-467.

Prazdnikova, N. V. Delayed conditioned reflexes in fish. *Trudy Instituta Fiziologii imeni I. P. Pavlova,* 1962, *10,* 273-283.

Prechtl, H. F. R. The directed head-turning response and allied movements of the human body. *Behaviour,* 1958, *13,* 212-242.

Prechtl, H. F. R. Problems of the behavioral studies in the newborn infant. In D. S. Lehrman, R. A. Hinde, and E. Shaw (Eds.), *Advances in the study of behavior.* New York: Academic Press, 1965. Pp. 75-98.

Premack, D. Reversibility of the reinforcement relation. *Science,* 1962, *136,* 255-257.

Premack, D. Reinforcement revisited: A structural view. In M. R. Jones (Ed.), *Nebraska Symposium on Motivation: 1963.* Lincoln: University of Nebraska Press, 1963. Pp. 113-150.

Premack, D. Reinforcement theory. In D. Levine (Ed.), *Nebraska Symposium on Motivation: 1965.* Lincoln: University of Nebraska Press, 1965. Pp. 123-188.

Pressman, Ya. M. An attempt to form a conditioned reflex with children when the reinforcement precedes the signal. In A. G. Ivanov-Smolensky (Ed.), *Studies of higher forms of the neurodynamics of children.* Moscow: GIZ, 1934. Pp. 131-136.

Pressman, Ya. M., and Tveritskaya, I. N. Quantitative characteristics of the summation [pseudoconditioned] reaction. *Zhurnal Vysshey Nervnoy Deyatel'nosti imeni I. P. Pavlova,* 1969, *19,* 566-573.

Pressman, Ya. M., and Tveritskaya, I. N. The relation of the summation reaction and the conditioned reflex. *Zhurnal Vysshey Nervnoy Deyatel'nosti imeni I. P. Pavlova,* 1970, *20,* 569-577.

Pribram, K. H. The frontal lobes of primates. In V. V. Parin (Ed.), *System organization of physiological functions. Collected contributions dedicated to the 70th birthday of Academician P. K. Anokhin.* Moscow: Meditsina, 1969. Pp. 375-384.

Priestley, J. *Letters to a philosophical unbeliever.* Birmingham, 1787.

Prokasy, W. F. ₍Ed.) *Classical conditioning.* New York: Appleton-Century-Crofts, 1965.

Prokasy, W. F., and Ebel, H. C. GSR conditioning and sensitization as a function of intertrial intervals. *Journal of Experimental Psychology,* 1964, *67,* 113-119.

Prokasy, W. F., and Ebel, H. C. Three distinct components to the classically conditioned GSR in human subjects. *Journal of Experimental Psychology,* 1967, *73,* 247-256.

Prokasy, W. F., Hall, J. F., and Fawcett, J. T. Adaptation, sensitization, forward and backward conditioning, and pseudoconditioning of the GSR. *Psychological Reports,* 1962, *10,* 103-106.

Promptov, A. N. Stereotyped species behavior and its formation in wild birds. *Doklady Akademii Nauk SSSR,* 1940, *27,* 171-175.

Promptov, A. N. Conditioned reflex components of instinctive activities in birds. *Fiziologichesky Zhurnal SSSR imeni I. M. Sechenova,* 1946, *32,* 48-62.

Promptov, A. N. *Outline of problems of biological adaptation of sparrows.* Moscow: Akademiya Nauk SSSR, 1956.

Prosser, C. L., and Hunter, W. S. The extinction of startle responses and spinal reflexes in the white rat. *American Journal of Physiology,* 1936, *117,* 609-618.

Pshonik, A. T. The role of the cortex in the formation of cutaneous algesic awareness. In *Theses, 11th Conference on Problems of Physiology.* Leningrad: 1946. P. 55.

Pshonik, A. T. Cortical factors in presensory reflexes. In *Theses, 13th Conference on Problems of Physiology.* Leningrad: 1948a. Pp. 82-85.

Pshonik, A. T. The role of the cortex in extero- and interoceptive conditioned reflexes. In *Theses, Scientific Psychosomatic Conference.* Leningrad: 1948b. Pp. 29-31.

Pshonik, A. T. The problem of interaction between exteroceptive and interoceptive stimuli. In K. M. Bykov (Ed.), *Problems of corticovisceral physiology.* Moscow: Akademiya Nauk SSSR, 1949a. Pp. 255-269.

Pshonik, A. T. More about vasomotor neuroses. *Sovetskaya Meditsina,* 1949b, No. 9, 22-23.

Pshonik, A. T. *The cerebral cortex and the receptor functions of the organism.* Moscow: GIZ, 1952.

Puni, A. Ts. (Ed.) *Problems of the psychology of sports.* Moscow: Fizkultura, 1955.

Puni, A. Ts. *Outlines of the psychology of sports.* Moscow: Fizkultura, 1959.

Purpura, D. P. Discussion of Danilewsky, Wedensky and Ukhtomsky. In M. A. B. Brazier (Ed.), *The central nervous system and behavior.* New York: Josiah Macy, Jr. Foundation, 1959. P. 161.

Rabinovich, M. Yu. Organization of cortical mechanisms of linkages of conditioned motor connections. *Zhurnal Vysshey Nervnoy Deyatel'nosti imeni I. P. Pavlova,* 1967, *17,* 3-14.

Rabinovich, M. Yu., and Kopytova, F. V. The effects of associated polarization of the cortical motor zones with auditory stimulation. *Zhurnal Vysshey Nervnoy Deyatel'nosti imeni I. P. Pavlova,* 1969, *19*, 329-354.

Rachlin, H. Recovery of responses during mild punishment. *Journal of the Experimental Analysis of Behavior,* 1966, *9*, 251-263.

Rakhimov, K. Innate and natural-conditioned food reflexes in ontogeny of ruminants. *Opyt Izucheniya Regulatsii Fiziologicheskikh Funktsii,* 1958, *4*, 124-132.

Ramón y Cajal, S. (Ed.) *El sistema nervioso del hombre y de los vertebrados.* Madrid, 1897-1898.

Ramón y Cajal, S. *Histologie du système nerveux de l'homme et des vertébres.* Vol. II. Paris: Malone, 1911.

Ratner, S. C., and Miller, K. R. Classical conditioning in earthworms, *Lumbricus terrestris. Journal of Comparative and Physiological Psychology,* 1959, *52*, 102-105.

Rayevsky, A. N. *The psychology of speech in Soviet psychological science. 1917-1957.* Kiev: Kiev University, 1958.

Raytses, V. S. Changes in the analytico-synthetic activity of dogs during visceral pathology. In *Theses, 20th Conference on Problems of Higher Nervous Activity.* Moscow-Leningrad: Akademiya Nauk SSSR, 1963. P. 203.

Razenkov, I. P. Changes in excitatory processes of a dog's cortex under difficult conditions. *Trudy Fiziologicheskikh Laboratorii I. P. Pavlova,* 1925, *1*(1), 83-97.

Razran, G. Review of V. M. Bekhterev's *General principles of human reflexology,* 3rd ed. (Leningrad: GIZ, 1926). *Journal of Philosophy,* 1927, *24*, 355-357.

Razran, G. Theory of conditioning and of related phenomena. *Psychological Review,* 1930, *37*, 225-243.

Razran, G. Conditioned responses in children. *Archives of Psychology,* New York, 1933a, *23* (Whole No. 148).

Razran, G. Conditioned responses in animals other than dogs. *Psychological Bulletin,* 1933b, *30*, 261-324.

Razran, G. Conditioned withdrawal responses in adult human subjects. *Psychological Bulletin,* 1934, *31*, 111-143.

Razran, G. Conditioned responses: An experimental study and a theoretical analysis. *Archives of Psychology,* New York, 1935, *28* (Whole No. 190).

Razran, G. Attitudinal control of human conditioning. *Journal of Psychology,* 1936, *2*, 327-337.

Razran, G. Studies in configural conditioning: VII. Ratios and elements in salivary conditioning to various musical intervals. *Psychological Record,* 1938a, *2*, 370-376.

Razran, G. Music, art, and the conditioned response. *Psychological Bulletin,* 1938b, *35*, 532. (Abstract)

Razran, G. Conditioning away social bias by the luncheon technique. *Psychological Bulletin,* 1938c, *36*, 693. (Abstract)

Razran, G. Studies in configural conditioning: I. Historical and preliminary experimentation. *Journal of General Psychology,* 1939a, *21*, 307-330.

Razran, G. Studies in configural conditioning: II. The effect of subjects' attitudes and of task-sets upon configural conditioning *Journal of Experimental Psychology,* 1939b, *24*, 95-105.

Razran, G. Studies in configural conditioning: III. The factors of similarity, proximity, and continuity in configural conditioning. *Journal of Experimental Psychology,* 1939c, *24*, 202-210.

Razran, G. Studies in configural conditioning: IV. Gestalt organization and configural conditioning. *Journal of Experimental Psychology*, 1939d, *7*, 3-16.

Razran, G. Studies in configural conditioning: VI. Comparative extinction and forgetting of pattern and of single-stimulus conditioning. *Journal of Experimental Psychology*, 1939e, *24*, 432-438.

Razran, G. Extinction, spontaneous recovery, and forgetting. *American Journal of Psychology*, 1939f, *52*, 100-102.

Razran, G. Decremental and incremental effects of distracting stimuli upon the salivary CRs of 24 adult human subjects. *Journal of Experimental Psychology*, 1939g, *24*, 647-652.

Razran, G. A simple technique for controlling subjective attitudes in salivary conditioning of adult human subjects. *Science*, 1939h, *89*, 160-162.

Razran, G. A quantitative study of meaning by a conditioned salivary technique (semantic conditioning). *Science*, 1939i, *90*, 89-91.

Razran, G. The nature of the extinctive process. *Psychological Review*, 1939j, *46*, 264-297.

Razran, G. The law of effect or the law of qualitative conditioning. *Psychological Review*, 1939k, *46*, 445-463.

Razran, G. Conditioning and attitudes. *Journal of Experimental Psychology*, 1939l, *24*, 215-226.

Razran, G. Studies in configural conditioning: V. Generalization and transposition. *Journal of General Psychology*, 1940a, *56*, 3-11.

Razran, G. Conditioned response changes in rating and appraising sociopolitical slogans. *Psychological Bulletin*, 1940b, *37*, 481. (Abstract)

Razran, G. Determinants of the consolidation (memorial generalization-differentiation) or "Praegnanz" of conditioned preferences. *Psychological Bulletin*, 1940c, *37*, 564.

Razran, G. Sentential and propositional generalizations of salivary conditioning to verbal stimuli. *Science*, 1949a, *109*, 447-448.

Razran, G. Semantic and phonetographic generalization of salivary conditioning to verbal stimuli. *Journal of Experimental Psychology*, 1949b, *39*, 642-652.

Razran, G. Some psychological factors in the generalization of salivary conditioning to verbal stimuli. *American Journal of Psychology*, 1949c, *62*, 247-256.

Razran, G. Attitudinal determinants of conditioning and of generalization of conditioning. *Journal of Experimental Psychology*, 1949d, *39*, 820-829.

Razran, G. Stimulus generalization of conditioned responses. *Psychological Bulletin*, 1949e, *46*, 337-365.

Razran, G. Reply to Grice's "Comments on Razran's discussion of stimulus generalization." *Psychological Bulletin*, 1951, *48*, 153-155.

Razran, G. Experimental semantics. *Transactions of the New York Academy of Science*, 1952, *14*, 171-177.

Razran, G. The conditioned evocation of attitudes (cognitive conditioning?). *Journal of Experimental Psychology*, 1954, *48*, 278-282.

Razran, G. Conditioning and perception. *Psychological Review*, 1955a, *62*, 83-95.

Razran, G. A note on the use of the terms conditioning and reinforcement. *American Psychologist*, 1955b, *10*, 173-174.

Razran, G. A note on second-order conditioning—and secondary reinforcement. *Psychological Review*, 1955c, *62*, 327-332.

Razran, G. Partial reinforcement of salivary CRs in adult human subjects: Preliminary study. *Psychological Reports,* 1955d, *1,* 409-416.

Razran, G. Operant vs. classical conditioning. *American Journal of Psychology,* 1955e, *68,* 489-490.

Razran, G. A direct laboratory comparison of Pavlovian conditioning and traditional associative learning. *Journal of Abnormal and Social Psychology,* 1955f, *51,* 649-652.

Razran, G. Extinction re-examined and re-analyzed: A new theory. *Psychological Review,* 1956a, *63,* 39-52.

Razran, G. Backward conditioning. *Psychological Bulletin,* 1956b, *53,* 55-69.

Razran, G. Avoidant vs. unavoidant conditioning and partial reinforcement in Russian laboratories. *American Journal of Psychology,* 1956c, *59,* 127-129.

Razran, G. The dominance-contiguity theory of the acquisition of classical conditioning. *Psychological Bulletin,* 1957, *54,* 1-46.

Razran, G. Transliteration of Russian. *Science,* 1959a, *129,* 1111-1113.

Razran, G. *A bibliography of Soviet experiments in interoceptive conditioning and unconditioned interoception.* (145 +326 titles). Bethesda, Md.: National Institutes of Health, 1959b.

Razran, G. The observable unconscious and the inferrable conscious in current Soviet psychophysiology: Interoceptive conditioning, semantic conditioning, and the orienting reflex. *Psychological Review,* 1961a, *68,* 81-147.

Razran, G. Recent Soviet phyletic comparisons of classical and of operant conditioning: Experimental designs. *Journal of Comparative and Physiological Psychology,* 1961b, *54,* 357-365.

Razran, G. Discussion. Pavlovian Conference on Higher Nervous Activity. *Annals of the New York Academy of Science,* 1961c, *92,* 1069-1072.

Razran, G. Raphael's "idealess" behavior. *Journal of Comparative and Physiological Psychology,* 1961d, *54,* 366-367.

Razran, G. *The conditioning of attitudes.* Cincinnati, Ohio: Sound Seminars, Behavioral and Social Sciences, 1962. (Now owned by McGraw-Hill, Inc., New York).

Razran, G. Russian physiologists' psychology and American experimental psychology. *Psychological Bulletin,* 1965a, *62,* 42-65.

Razran, G. The psychopathology of interoceptive stimulation. In J. Zubin and P. Hoch (Eds.), *The psychopathology of perception.* New York: Grune and Stratton, 1965b. Pp. 62-82.

Razran, G. Evolutionary psychology: Levels of learning—and perception and thinking. In B. Wolman (Eds.), *Scientific psychology: Principles and approaches.* New York: Basic Books, 1965c. Pp. 207-253.

Razran, G. Empirical codification and specific theoretical implications of compound-stimulus conditioning: Perception. In W. Prokasy (Ed.), *Classical conditioning.* New York: Appleton-Century-Crofts, 1965d. Pp. 215-233.

Razran, G. Classical and instrumental conditioning. *Zhurnal Vysshey Nervnoy Deyatel'nosti imeni I. P. Pavlova,* 1968a, *18,* 407-412.

Razran, G. Pavlov, Ivan Petrovich. In *International Encyclopedia of Social Sciences.* Vol. XI. New York: Macmillan, 1968b. Pp. 481-487.

Razran, G. Higher nervous activity and the dynamics of esthetic affectivity and perception. In V. V. Parin (Ed.), *System organization of physiological functions. Collection of contributions dedicated to the 70th birthday of Academician P. K. Anokhin.* Moscow: Meditsina, 1969. Pp. 384-397.

Reid, R. L. A test of sensory pre-conditioning in pigeons. *Quarterly Journal of Experimental Psychology*, 1952, *4*, 49-56.

Reid, T. *Works*. Vol. 2. *Essays on the intellectual powers of man.* Charleston, S.C.: Etheredge, 1813. (First published in 1785.)

Rensch, B., and Döhl, J. Wahlen zwischen zwei überschaubaren Labyrinthwegen durch einen Schimpansen. *Zeitschrift für Tierpsychologie*, 1968, *25*, 216-231.

Rescorla, R. A. Predictability and number of pairings in Pavlovian fear conditioning. *Psychonomic Science*, 1966, *4*, 383-384.

Rescorla, R. A., and Solomon, R. L. Two-process learning theory: Relationship between Pavlovian conditioning and instrumental learning. *Psychological Review*, 1967, *64*, 151-182.

Resolutions of the 1962 Moscow All-Union Conference on the Philosophical Problems of the Physiology of Higher Nervous Activity and Psychology. *Zhurnal Vysshey Nervnoy Deyatel'nosti imeni I. P. Pavlova*, 1962, *12*, 980-983; *Voprosy Psikhologii*, 1962, *8*(4), 1-8; A. N. Fedoseyev (Ed.), *Philosophical problems of the physiology of higher nervous activity and psychology.* Moscow: Akademiya Nauk SSSR, 1963. Pp. 755-762.

Retzlaff, E. A. A mechanism for excitation and inhibition of Mauthner's cells in teleost: A histological and neurophysiological study. *Journal of Comparative Neurology*, 1957, *107*, 209-226.

Revusky, S. H. Aversion to sucrose produced by contingent X-radiation. *Journal of Comparative and Physiological Psychology*, 1968, *65*, 17-22.

Rheingold, H. I., and Stanley, W. Developmental psychology. *Annual Review of Psychology*, 1963, *14*, 1-28.

Riess, B. F. Semantic conditioning involving the galvanic skin reflex. *Journal of Experimental Psychology*, 1940, *26*, 238-240.

Riess, B. F. Genetic changes in semantic conditioning. *Journal of Experimental Psychology*, 1946, *36*, 143-152.

Rikman, V. V. Disturbance of the normal action of a dog upon application of strong external stimuli. *Trudy Fiziologicheskikh Laboratorii I. P. Pavlova*, 1928a, *3*(1), 19-34.

Rikman, V. V. Stimulus intensity and conditioned reflexes. *Trudy Fiziologicheskikh Laboratorii I. P. Pavlova*, 1928b, *2*(2), 137-148.

Rikman, V. V. Traces of defensive reflexes as an analogue of traumatic neuroses. *Trudy Fiziologicheskikh Laboratorii I. P. Pavlova*, 1932, *4*, 102-167.

Rite, R. Ya. The effects of the unconditioned reflex upon the conditioned reflex. *Trudy Fiziologicheskikh Laboratorii I. P. Pavlova*, 1928, *2*(2), 87-94.

Robinson, E. W. A preliminary experiment on abstraction in a monkey. *Journal of Comparative Psychology*, 1933, *16*, 231-236.

Rodgers, W. L., Melzack, R., and Segal, J. R. "Tail flip response" in goldfish. *Journal of Comparative and Physiological Psychology*, 1963, *56*, 917-923.

Rodieck, R. W. Receptive fields in the cat retina: A new type. *Science*, 1967, *157*, 9-92.

Rodieck, R. W., and Stone, J. Analysis of receptive cells of the cat ganglion cells. *Journal of Neurophysiology*, 1963, *28*.

Rodnick, E. H. Characteristics of delayed and trace conditioned responses. *Journal of Experimental Psychology*, 1937, *20*, 409-425.

Roe, A., and Simpson, G. A. (Eds.) *Behavior and evolution.* New Haven: Yale University Press, 1958.

Roff, M. A factorial of tests in the perceptual area. *Psychometric Monographs*, 1952, No. 8.

Roginsky, G. Z. Comparative psychology of lower monkeys. *Trudy Instituta Mozga*, 1939, *11*, 99-105.

Roginsky, G. Z. *Habits and beginnings of intellectual activities in anthropoids (chimpanzees)*. Leningrad: LGU, 1948.

Rohrer, J. H. A motivational state resulting from non-reward. *Journal of Comparative and Physiological Psychology*, 1949, *42*, 476-485.

Roig, J. A., and Sommer-Smith, J. A. Atenuacion especifica del sobressalto provacado par excitation nerviosa central. *Annales de la Facultad de Medicina, Universidad de Montevideo*, 1959, *44*, 410-413.

Roitback (Roytbak), A. I. Critique of the Eccles hypothesis. *Fiziologichesky Zhurnal SSSR imeni I. M. Sechenova*, 1945, *40*, 239-243.

Roitback, A. I. Dendrites and the process of inhibition. *Gagrskiye Besedy*, 1956, *2*, 165-187.

Roitback, A. I. Electrical manifestations in the neural center of the conditioned stimulus. *Trudy Instituta Fiziologii GSSR*, 1958, *11*, 120-154.

Roitback, A. I. Electrical phenomena in the cerebral cortex during the extinction of orientation and conditioned reflexes. In H. H. Jasper and G. D. Smirnov (Eds.), The Moscow Colloquium on Electroencephalography of Higher Nervous Activity. *Electroencephalography and Clinical Neurophysiology*, 1960a, Supplement 13, 91-100.

Roitback, A. I. Some oscillographic data on the formation of temporary connections. *Gagrskiye Besedy*, 1960b, *3*, 150-187.

Rokotova, N. A. Formation of temporary connections in dogs between traces of "indifferent" stimuli. *Trudy Instituta Fiziologii imeni I. P. Pavlova*, 1952, *1*, 35-42.

Rokotova, N. A. Physiological mechanisms of temporary connections among "indifferent" stimuli. *Zhurnal Vysshey Nervnoy Deyatel'nosti imeni I. P. Pavlova*, 1954, *4*, 516-525.

Romanes, G. J. *Animal intelligence*. London: Kegan Paul, 1882.

Ross, D. M. The behavior of sessile coelenterates in relation to some conditioning experiments. *Journal of Animal Behavior*, 1965, Supplement 1, 43-53.

Ross, D. M., and Sutton, L. Inhibition of the swimming response by food and nematocyst discharge during swimming in the sea anemones *Stomphia coccinea*. *Journal of Experimental Biology*, 1964, *41*, 751-757.

Rossman, J. *The psychology of the inventor*. Washington: Inventors Publishing Co., 1931.

Rowland, V. Differential electroencephalographic response to conditioned auditory stimuli in arousal from sleep. *Electroencephalography and Clinical Neurophysiology*, 1957, *7*, 585-594.

Rubinshteyn, S. L. (Ed.) *Thinking and means of studying it*. Moscow: Akademiya Nauk SSSR, 1958.

Rubinshteyn, S. L. *Principles and ways of development of psychology*. Moscow: Akademiya Nauk SSSR, 1959.

Rubinshteyn, S. L. (Ed.) *Thinking and principles of analysis, synthesis and generalization: Experimental Studies*. Moscow: Akademiya Nauk SSSR, 1960.

Ruger, H. The psychology of efficiency. *Archives of Psychology*, New York, 1910, No. 15.

Rushforth, N. B. Behavioral studies of the coelenterate *Hydra pirardi Brien*. *Animal Behaviour*, 1965 (Supplement 1), 30-42.

Rushforth, N. B., Krohn, I. T., and Brown, L. K. Behavior in hydra: Inhibition of the contraction responses of *Hydra pirardi*. *Science*, 1964, *139*, 760-761.

Rusinov, V. S. An electrophysiological analysis of the connection function in the cerebral cortex in the presence of a dominant center. In *Communications, XIX International Congress of Physiologists.* Moscow: Akademiya Nauk SSSR, 1953. Pp. 147-150.

Rusinov, V. S. Electrophysiological studies of dominant foci in the higher portions of the central nervous system. In *Communications, XX International Congress of Physiologists.* Moscow: Akademiya Nauk SSSR, 1956. Pp. 350-353.

Rusinov, V. S. Electrophysiological studies of stationary excitatory centers in the central nervous system. *Zhurnal Vysshey Nervnoy Deyatel'nosti imeni I. P. Pavlova,* 1958, *8,* 473-481.

Rusinov, V. S. Stationary excitation and changes in steady cortical potentials in dominance and formation of conditioned reflexes. *Zhurnal Vysshey Nervnoy Deyatel'nosti imeni I. P. Pavlova,* 1961, *9,* 776-794.

Rusinov, V. S. Electrophysiological studies during the formation of a temporary connection. In *Proceedings, XXII International Congress of Physiologists.* Amsterdam: Excerpta Medica, 1962. Pp. 882-887.

Rusinov, V. S. Constant-current anodal polarization of the motor area of the cortex and motor dominance. *Zhurnal Vysshey Nervnoy Deyatel'nosti imeni I. P. Pavlova,* 1965a, *15,* 217-228.

Rusinov, V. S. From dominance to inhibition. In E. A. Asratyan (Ed.), *Reflexes of the brain.* Moscow: Nauka, 1965b. Pp. 127-138.

Rusinov, V. S. The study of experimental and clinical excitatory foci. In V. N. Chernigovsky (Ed.), *Problems of contemporary neurophysiology.* Moscow: Nauka, 1965c. Pp. 73-99.

Rusinov, V. S. Foci of excitation in the central nervous system and their functional significance. In E. Sh. Ayrapet'yants (Ed.), *Central and peripheral mechanisms of nervous action.* Yerevan: Akademiya Nauk ArSSR, 1966. Pp. 373-383.

Rusinov, V. S., and Rabinovich, M. Yu. Electroencephalographic researches in the laboratories and clinics of the Soviet Union. *Electroencephalography and Clinical Neurophysiology,* 1958, Supplement 8, 1-36.

Rusinov, V. S., and Smirnov, G. D. Quelques données sur l'étude électroencéphalographique de l'activité nerveuse supérieure. *Electroencephalography and Clinical Neurophysiology,* 1957, Supplement 6, 9-23.

Ryabinina, M. A. Dominant centers in rabbits' cortex produced by means of pressure. *Trudy Instituta Nysshey Nervnoy Deyatel'nosti imeni I. P. Pavlova, Seriya Fiziologicheskaya,* 1958, *3,* 42-49.

Ryabinina, M. A. The significance of various cortical layers in the formation of a dominant center with a constant current. *Trudy Instituta Vysshey Nervnoy Deyatel'nosti imeni I. P. Pavlova, Seriya Fiziologicheskaya,* 1961, *6,* 211-221.

Ryantseva, T. N. Significance of an antecedent conditioned reflex in the formation of a conditioned reflex in white rats. *Trudy Instituta Vysshey Nervnoy Deyatel' nosti imeni I. P. Pavlova, Seriya Fiziologicheskaya,* 1955, *1,* 55-66.

Sakhiulina, G. T. Electroencephalograms of dogs in some complex forms of conditioned reflex activity. *Electroencephalography and Clinical Neurophysiology,* 1960, Supplement 13, 211-220.

Sakhiulina, G. T., and Lyubchinsky, E. B. Stable electrophysiological correlates of conditioned food-securing reflexes. *Zhurnal Vysshey Nervnoy Deyatel'nosti imeni I. P. Pavlova,* 1968, *18,* 555-564.

Salzinger, K., and Pisoni, S. Reinforcement of affect responses of schizophrenics during the clinical interview. *Journal of Abnormal and Social Psychology,* 1958, *57,* 84-90.

Samsonova, V. G. Some characteristics of the interaction of the first and second systems in the formation of conditioned reactions to visual stimuli of low intensity. *Zhurnal Vysshey Nervnoy Deyatel'nosti imeni I. P. Pavlova,* 1953, *3,* 689-703.

Sapir, E. *Language: An Introduction to the study of speech.* New York: Harcourt Brace, 1921.

Sarkisov, S. A. *Structural characteristics of cortical neuronal connections in the cortex.* Moscow: Akademiya Meditsinskikh Nauk SSSR, 1948.

Sarkisov, S. A. (Ed.) *The structure and function of analyzers in human ontogeny.* Moscow: Medgiz, 1961.

Sarkisov, S. A., and Bogolepov, N. N. *Electromicroscopy of the brain.* Moscow: Meditsina, 1967.

Sarkisov, S. A., Filiminov, I. N., and Preobrazhenskaya, N. S. (Eds.) *Cytoarchitecture of man's cortex.* Moscow: Medgiz, 1949.

Sarkisov, S. A., and Preobrazhenskaya, N. S. (Eds.) *Development of the central nervous system. Phylogeny and ontogeny of the cortex and subcortical formations.* Moscow: Medgiz, 1959.

Savich, A. A. *Further materials on the problems of the effects of food reflexes on one another.* St. Petersburg: Military Medical Academy, 1913. (Thesis)

Scarborough, B. B., Whaley, D. L., and Rogers, J. G. Saccharin avoidance behavior instigated by X-irradiation in backward conditioning paradigms. *Psychological Reports,* 1964, *14,* 475-481.

Schaeffer, A. A. Habit formation in frogs. *Journal of Animal Behavior,* 1911, *1,* 309-335.

Schapiro, S., and Yukovich, K. R. Early experience effects upon cortical dendrites: A proposed model for development. *Science,* 1970, *167,* 292-294.

Schastny, A. I. Bioelectric changes in the muscles of dogs' limbs during the formation of conditioned defensive reflex. *Doklady Akademii Nauk SSSR,* 1956, *107,* 350-351.

Schiff, J. M. *Lezioni di fiziologia sperimentale sul sistema nervosa encefalico.* Firenze: March, 1864-1865.

Schneirla, T. C. A consideration of some conceptual trends in comparative psychology. *Psychological Bulletin,* 1952, *49,* 559-597.

Schneirla, T. C. Interrelationship of the "innate" and the "acquired" in instinctive behavior. *In L'instinct dans les comportment des animaux et de l'homme.* Paris: Mason, 1956. Pp. 387-452.

Schneirla, T. C. Aspects of stimulation in approach-withdrawal processes underlying vertebrate behavioral development. In D. S. Lehrman, R. A. Hinde, and Evelyn Shaw (Eds.), *Advances in the study of behavior.* Vol. 1. New York: Academic Press, 1965. Pp. 1-74.

Schoenfeld, W. N. Editorial. Some old work for modern conditioning theory. *Conditional Reflex,* 1966, *1,* 219-223.

Schroff, E. Über Gestaltauffassung bei Kindern in Alter von 6 vis 14 Jahren. *Psychologische Forschung,* 1928, *11,* 235-266.

Schumann, F. Eine Beobachtung über Zussamenfassung von Gesichtsseindurcken zu Einheiten. *Zeitschrift für Psychologie,* 1900, *23,* 1-32.

Schuster, C. R., and Brady, J. V. The discriminative control of a food-reinforced operant by interoceptive stimulation. *Zhurnal Vysshey Nervnoy Deyatel'nosti imeni I. P. Pavlova,* 1964, *14,* 448-458.

Sears, R. R. Effect of optic lobe ablation on the visuomotor behavior of goldfish. *Journal of Comparative Psychology,* 1934, *17,* 233-265.

Sears, R. R., and Cohen, L. H. Hysterical anaesthesia, analgesis, and asteriognosis. *Archives of Neurology and Psychiatry, New York,* 1939, *29,* 260-271.

Sechenov, I. M. Reflexes of the brain. *Meditsinsk Vestnik,* 1863, *3,* 461-484; 493-512.

Sechenov, I. M. By whom and how should psychology be studied? *Vestnik Yevropy,* 1873, No. 2, 124-138.

Sechenov, I. M. Elements of thought. *Vestnik Yevropy,* 1878, No. 2, 39-107; 457-533.

Sechenov, I. M. Object-thought and reality. In D. Anuchin (Ed.), *Pomoshch golod-. ayushchim.* Moscow: Russkiye Vedomsti, 1892. Pp. 193-209.

Sechenov, I. M. *Selected works.* Moscow: Medgiz, 1935. (In English and German)

Sechenov, I. M. *Selected physiological and psychological works.* Moscow: Foreign Languages Publishing House, 1952-1956. (In English)

Sedlaček, G. Mechanisms of development of specialized reflexes. I. The unconditioned role of specialized reflexes. *Activitas Nervosa Superior,* 1961a, *3,* 263-266.

Sedlaček, G. Mechanisms of development of specialized reflexes. II. The role of specialized reflexes as conditioned stimuli. *Activitas Nervosa Superior,* 1961b, *3,* 267-275.

Sedlaček, G. Mechanisms of development of specialized reflexes. III. Mechanisms of the activation of the centers of specialized reflexes. *Activitas Nervosa Superior,* 1962a, *14,* 17-23.

Sedlaček, G. Mechanisms of development of specialized reflexes. IV. The role of signal factors. *Activitas Nervosa Superior,* 1962b, *4,* 24-27.

Sedlaček, G. Temporary connections in chick embryos. *Physiologia Bohemoslovenika,* 1962c, *11*(4), 300-306.

Sedlaček, G. Notes on the characteristics of the temporary connections in chick embryos. *Physiologia Bohenoslovenika,* 1962d, *11*(4), 307-312.

Segundo, J. P., Galeano, C., Sommer-Smith, J. A., and Roig, J. A. Behavioral and EEG effects of tones "reinforced" by cessation of painful stimuli. In J. F. Delafreshaye (Ed.), *Brain mechanisms and learning.* Springfield, Ill.: Charles C Thomas, 1961. Pp. 265-291.

Segundo, J. P., Roig, J. A., and Sommer-Smith, J. A. Conditioning of cortical formation effects. *Electroencephalography and Clinical Neurophysiology,* 1959, *11,* 471-484.

Seidel, R. J. An investigation of mediation in preconditioning. *Journal of Experimental Psychology,* 1958, *56,* 220-225.

Seidel, R. J. A review of sensory preconditioning. *Psychological Bulletin,* 1959, *56,* 58-73.

Sellars, R. W. *The philosophy of physical realism.* New York: Macmillan, 1932.

Selz, O. *Über die Gesetze des geordnetan Denkverlaufs.* Stuttgart: Spemann, 1913.

Selz, O. *Zur Psychologie des produktiven Denkens und des Irrtums.* Bonn: Cohen, 1922.

Serebrinnikov, S. S. Digestion and painful stimuli. I. Work of gastric glands. *Fiziologichesky Zhurnal SSSR imeni I. M. Sechenova,* 1932a, *15,* 301-313.

Serebrinnikov, S. S. Digestion and painful stimuli. II. Work of pancreas. *Fiziologichesky Zhurnal SSSR imeni I. M. Sechenova,* 1932b, *15,* 330-334.

Serebrinnikov, S. S. The effect of strong (painful) stimuli on the work of the digestive apparatus. III. Salivary secretion. *Fiziologichesky Zhurnal SSSR imeni I. M. Sechenova,* 1939a, *27,* 316-321.

Serebrinnikov, S. S. The effect of strong (painful) stimuli on the work of the digestive apparatus. IV. Gastric secretions. *Fiziologichesky Zhurnal SSSR imeni I. M. Sechenova,* 1939c, *27,* 322-330.

Serebrinnikov, S. S. The effect of strong (painful) stimuli on the work of the digestive apparatus. VI. Bile secretions. *Fiziologichesky Zhurnal SSSR imeni I. M. Sechenova,* 1939c, *27,* 464-465.

Sereysky, M. Ya. *Problems of the clinic and therapy of psychic illness,* 1946. (Quoted by Grigoryan, 1954, and seen by Razran, but not available at this time.)

Sergeyev, B. F. The mechanism of temporary connections among so-called indifferent stimuli. *Doklady Akademii Nauk SSSR,* 1955, *101,* 771-774.

Sergeyev, B. F. Formation of inhibitory connections between so-called indifferent stimuli. *Doklady Akademii Nauk SSSR,* 1956, *107,* 346-349.

Sergeyev, B. F. Temporary connections between "indifferent" stimuli in the ontogeny of puppies. In N. I. Kasatkin and M. G. Zaks (Eds.), *Materials on evolutionary physiology.* Vol. 4. Moscow: Akademiya Nauk SSSR, 1960. Pp. 83-90.

Sergeyev, B. F. The localization of inhibition in the extinction of conditioned reflexes to chains of stimuli. *Zhurnal Vysshey Nervnoy Deyatel'nosti imeni I. P. Pavlova,* 1961a, *11,* 609-673.

Sergeyev, B. F. Formation of temporary connections between "indifferent" stimuli in birds. *Zhurnal Vysshey Nervnoy Deyatel'nosti imeni I. P. Pavlova,* 1961b, *11,* 956-959.

Sergeyev, B. F. Formation of temporary connections in lancelets. *Zhurnal Vysshey Nervnoy Deyatel'nosti imeni I. P. Pavlova,* 1962, *12,* 757-761.

Sergeyev, B. F. The physiology of the parietal lobes of the dog's cortex. *Zhurnal Vysshey Nervnoy Deyatel'nosti imeni I. P. Pavlova,* 1963, *13,* 104-111.

Sergeyev, B. F. The structure of temporary connections in lower chordates. *Zhurnal Vysshey Nervnoy Deyatel'nosti imeni I. P. Pavlova,* 1964a, *14,* 904-910.

Sergeyev, B. F. Associative temporary connections in the phylogeny of vertebrates. In *Theses, 10th All-Union Congress of the Pavlov Physiological Society.* Moscow: Nauka, 1964b. Pp. 263-264.

Sergeyev, B. F. Electrophysiological analysis of formation of temporary connections of the association type in lower vertebrates. *Zhurnal Vysshey Nervnoy Deyatel'nosti imeni I. P. Pavlova,* 1965a, *15,* 425-432.

Sergeyev, B. F. Comparative study of the physiology of memory. In *Theses, 4th Scientific Conference on Evolutionary Physiology in Memory of Academician L. A. Orbeli.* Leningrad: 1965b. Pp. 234-235.

Sergeyev, B. F. *Evolution of associative temporary connections.* Moscow: Akademiya Nauk SSSR, 1967.

Seward, J. P. Conditioning mechanisms. In M. H. Marx (Ed.), *Learning: Theories.* New York: Macmillan, 1970. Pp. 93-107.

Seward, J. P., and Seward, G. H. The effect of repetition on reactions to electric shock with special reference to the menstrual cycle. *Archives of Psychology,* New York, 1934, *25,* No. 168.

Seward, J. P., Uyeda, A. A., and Olds, J. Resistance to extinction following self-stimulation. *Journal of Comparative and Physiological Psychology,* 1959, *52,* 294-299.

Seward, J. P., Uyeda, A. A., and Olds, J. Reinforcing effect of brain stimulation on run-way performance as a function of interval between trials. *Journal of Comparative and Physiological Psychology,* 1960, *53,* 224-227.

Shamarina, N. M., and Nesmeyanova, T. N. Experimental transformation of spinal reflex action. *Fiziologichesky Zhurnal SSSR imeni I. M. Sechenova,* 1953, *39,* 601-609.

Shapiro, M. M. Temporal relationship between salivation and lever pressing with differential reinforcement of low rates. *Journal of Comparative and Physiological Psychology,* 1962, *55,* 567-571.

Shapiro, M. M., and Miller, T. M. On the relationship between conditioned and discriminative stimuli and between instrumental and consummatory responses. In W. F. Prokasy (Ed.), *Classical conditioning.* New York: Appleton-Century-Crofts, 1965. Pp. 269-301.

Sharpless, S., and Jasper, H. H. Habituation of the arousal reaction. *Brain,* 1956, *79,* 655-680.

Shastin, N. R. Conditioned preparatory stimuli. *Acta Universtatis Voronozhensis,* 1925, 146-151.

Shaw, J. A., and Thompson, R. F. Dependence of evoked cortical association responses on behavioral variables. *Psychonomic Science,* 1964, *1,* 153-154.

Sheffield, F. D. Relation between classical conditioning and instrumental learning. In W. F. Prokasy (Ed.), *Classical conditioning.* New York: Appleton-Century-Crofts, 1965. Pp. 302-322.

Sheffield, F. D., Roby, T. B., and Campbell, B. A. Drive reduction versus consummatory behavior as determinants of reinforcement. *Journal of Comparative and Physiological Psychology,* 1954, *47,* 349-354.

Shemyakin, F. N. Thought and speech. *Izvestiya Akademii Pedagogicheskakh Nauk RSFSR,* 1960, No. 113.

Shenger-Krestovnikova, N. R. Differentiation of visual stimuli and their limits in the visual analyzer of the dog. *Izvestiya Petrogradskogo Nauchnogo Instituta imeni P. F. Lesgafta,* 1921, *3,* 1-41.

Shepeleva, V. K. Mobility of neural processes in wild animals. *Doklady Akademii Nauk SSSR,* 1954, *95,* 451-456.

Sherrington, C. S. Decerebrate rigidity, and reflex coordination of movements. *Journal of Physiology* (London), 1898a, *22,* 319-332.

Sherrington, C. S. Experiments in examination of the peripheral distribution of the fibers of the posterior roots of some spinal nerves. *Philosophical Transactions of the Royal Society in London,* 1898b, *90,* 49-186.

Sherrington, C. S. On certain spinal reflexes in the dog. *Journal of Physiology,* 1904, *31,* 17-19.

Sherrington, C. S. *The integrative action of the nervous system.* New York: Macmillan, 1906.

Shichko, G. A. Formation of temporary connections through association of several indifferent stimuli. *Zhurnal Vysshey Nervnoy Deyatel'nosti imeni I. P. Pavlova,* 1959, *9,* 519-525.

Shichko, G. A. *The second-signal system and its physiological mechanisms.* Leningrad: Meditsina, 1969.

Shirkova, G. I. Conditioned motor reflexes to a simultaneous complex of stimuli in lower primates. *Zhurnal Vysshey Nervnoy Deyatel'nosti imeni I. P. Pavlova,* 1951, *1,* 716-721.

Shkol'nik-Yarros, E. G. The morphology of the visual analyzer. *Zhurnal Vysshey Nervnoy Deyatel'nosti imeni I. P. Pavlova,* 1954, *4,* 289-304.

Shkol'nik-Yarros, E. G. Efferent pathways of the visual cortex. *Zhurnal Vysshey Nervnoy Deyatel'nosti I. P. Pavlova,* 1958, *8,* 123-136.

Shkol'nik-Yarros, E. G. Differences between the neurons of the visual cortex in dogs and rabbits. In S. A. Sarkisov and N. S. Preobrazhenskaya (Eds.), *Development of central nervous system. Phylogeny and ontogeny of the cortex and subcortical formations.* Moscow: Medgiz, 1959. Pp. 169-184.

Shmavonian, B. M. Methodological study of vasomotor conditioning in human subjects. *Journal of Comparative and Physiological Psychology,* 1959, *52,* 315-321.

Shnirman, A. K. The possibility of forming an associated motor reflex through "retro-signal" associations. *Novoye v Refleksologii i Fiziologi Nervnoy Sistemy,* 1925, *1,* 218-243.

Shorokhova, E. V. *The study of thinking in Soviet psychology.* Moscow: Nauka, 1966.

Shurrager, P. S., and Culler, E. Phenomena allied to conditioning in the spinal dog. *American Journal of Physiology,* 1938, *123,* 186-187.

Shurrager, P. S., and Culler, E. Conditioning in the spinal dog. *Journal of Experimental Psychology,* 1940, *26,* 133-159.

Shurrager, P. S., and Shurrager, H. C. Converting a spinal CR into a reflex. *Journal of Experimental Psychology,* 1941, *29,* 217-224.

Shustin, I. A. Vocal reactions in animals as a signalling activity. *Trudy Fiziologicheskogo Instituta imeni I. P. Pavlova,* 1949, *4,* 103-112.

Shvarts, L. A. The problem of words as conditioned stimuli. *Byulleten' Eksperimental'noy Biologii i Meditsiny,* 1954, *38*(12), 15-18.

Shvarts, L. A. Conditioned reflexes to verbal stimuli. *Voprosy Psikhologii,* 1960, *6*(1), 86-98.

Shvets, T. B. Two-way character of conditioned temporary connections between the motor and visual analyzers (changes in steady potentials of the cortex in the rabbit). *Zhurnal Vysshey Nervnoy Deyatel'nosti I. P. Pavlova,* 1965, *15,* 23-29.

Silver, C. A., and Meyer, D. R. Temporary factors in sensory preconditioning. *Journal of Comparative and Physiological Psychology,* 1954, *47,* 57-59.

Singh, S. D. Conditioned emotional response in the rat. *Journal of Comparative and Physiological Psychology,* 1959, *52,* 574-578.

Siqueland, E. R., and Lipsitt, L. P. Conditioned head-turning in human newborns. *Journal of Experimental Child Psychology,* 1966, *3,* 356-376.

Skinner, B. F. Two types of conditioned reflex and a pseudo type. *Journal of General Psychology,* 1935, *12,* 66-77.

Skinner, B. F. Two types of conditioned reflex: A reply to Konorski and Miller. *Journal of General Psychology,* 1937, *16,* 272-279.

Skinner, B. F. *The behavior of organisms.* New York: Appleton-Century, 1938.

Skinner, B. F. "Superstition" in the pigeon. *Journal of Experimental Psychology,* 1950, *38,* 168-172.

Skinner, B. F. *Science and human behavior.* New York: Macmillan, 1953.

Skinner, B. F. *Verbal behavior.* New York: Appleton-Century-Crofts, 1957.

Skinner, B. F. *Cumulative record.* New York: Appleton-Century-Crofts, 1959.

Skipin, G. V. Physiological mechanism of so-called voluntary movements. *Zhurnal Vysshey Nervnoy Deyatel'nosti imeni I. P. Pavlova,* 1951, *1,* 922-925.

Skipin, G. V. Generalization mechanisms of conditioned reflexes (linkage functions in higher regions of the central nervous system). *Zhurnal Vysshey Nervnoy Deyatel'nosti imeni I. P. Pavlova,* 1952, *2,* 501-508.

Slobin, D. I. Soviet psycholinguistics. In N. O'Connor (Ed.), *Present-day Russian psychology: A symposium by seven authors.* Oxford, England: Pergamon Press, 1966. Pp. 109-150.

Slonim, A. D. *Fundamentals of general ecological physiology of mammals.* Moscow: Akademiya Nauk SSSR, 1961.

Slonim, A. D. *Special ecological physiology of mammals.* Moscow: Akademiya Nauk, SSSR, 1962.

Slucki, H., Ádám, G., and Porter, R. W. Operant of an interoceptive stimulus in Rhesus monkeys. *Journal of the Experimental Analysis of Behavior,* 1965, *8,* 405-414.

Small, W. S. Notes on the psychic development of the young white rat. *American Journal of Psychology,* 1899, *11,* 80-100.

Smirnov, A. A., Leont'yev, A. N., Rubinshteyn, S. L., and Teplov, B. M. *Psikhologiya.* Moscow: Uch Ped GIZ, 1956.

Smith, D. E. P. and Hochberg, J. E. The effects of punishment (electric shock) on figure-ground perception. *Journal of Psychology,* 1954, *38,* 83-87.

Smith, D. M. *Mammalian learning and behavior.* Philadelphia: Saunders, 1965.

Smith, F., and Miller, G. A. (Eds.) *The genesis of language: A psycholinguistic approach,* Cambridge: M.I.T. Press, 1966a.

Smith, F., and Miller, G. A. Introduction. In F. Smith and G. A. Miller (Eds.), *The genesis of language: A psycholinguistic approach.* Cambridge: M.I.T. Press, 1966b. Pp. 1-13.

Smith, M. P., and Buchanan, G. Acquisition of secondary reward as associated with shock reduction. *Journal of Experimental Psychology,* 1954, *48,* 123-126.

Smith, O. A., and Stebbins, W. C. Conditioned blood flow and heart rate in monkeys. *Journal of Comparative and Physiological Psychology,* 1965, *59,* 432-435.

Snapper, A. G., Schoenfeld, W. N., and Locke, B. Adrenal and thymus weight loss in the food-deprived rat produced by random ratio punishment schedules. *Journal of Comparative and Physiological Psychology,* 1966, *62,* 65-70.

Snarsky, A. T. *Analysis of normal work of the salivary glands in dogs.* St. Petersburg: Military Medical Academy, 1901. (Thesis)

Sokolov, E. N. *Perception and the conditioned reflex.* Moscow: Moscow University, 1958a.

Sokolov, E. N. The orienting reflex, its structure and mechanism. In L. G. Voronin, A. N. Leont'yev, A. R. Luria, E. N. Sokolov, and O. S. Vinogradova (Eds.), *The orienting reflex and orienting-investigatory activity.* Moscow: Akademiya Pedagogicheskikh Nauk RSFSR, 1958b. Pp. 111-120.

Sokolov, E. N. (Ed.), *The orienting reflex and problems of higher nervous activity.* Moscow: Akademiya Pedagogicheskikh Nauk RSFSR, 1959a.

Sokolov, E. N. The orienting reflex. In E. N. Sokolov (Ed.), *The orienting reflex and problems of higher nervous activity.* Moscow: Akademiya Pedagogicheskikh Nauk RSFSR, 1959b. Pp. 5-50.

Sokolov, E. N. Modelling in the central nervous system of man and animals. *Gagrskiye Besedy,* 1963, *4,* 183-202.

Sokolov, E. N. (Ed.), *The orienting reflex and problems of normal and pathological reception.* Moscow: Prosveshicheniye, 1964a.

Sokolov, E. N. The orienting reflex as a regulator of information. In E. N. Sokolov (Ed.), *The orienting reflex and problems of normal and pathological reception.* Moscow: Prosveshicheniye, 1964b. Pp. 3-20.

394 · *Mind in Evolution*

Sokolov, E. N. Neuronal mechanisms of "habituation" as simplest forms of conditioned reflexes. *Zhurnal Vysshey Nervnoy Deyatel'nosti imeni I. P. Pavlova,* 1965, *15,* 249-259.

Sokolov, E. N. The inhibitory conditioned reflex at a single-neurone level. *Gagrskiye Besedy,* 1968, *5,* 311-318.

Sokolov, V. A. Conditioned reflexes in snails *Physa acuta. Vestnik Leningrad University,* 1959, No. 9, 82-86.

Sokolova, A. A. Electrical activity in the visual and motor cortical areas of rabbits when the dominant motor area is reinforced by visual stimuli. *Zhurnal Vysshey Nervnoy Deyatel'nosti imeni I. P. Pavlova,* 1958, *10,* 593-601.

Sokolova, A. A. Electrical cortical and subcortical activity in rabbits during cortical dominance. *Zhurnal Vysshey Nervnoy Deyatel'nosti imeni I. P. Pavlova,* 1959, *9,* 759-767.

Sokolova, A. A., and Sek-Bu, K. Electrophysiological study of dominant centers in rabbits' cortex produced by polarization. *Zhurnal Vysshey Nervnoy Deyatel' nosti imeni I. P. Pavlova,* 1957, *7,* 135-145.

Solley, C. M., and Murphy, G. *Development of the perceptual world.* New York: Basic Books, 1960.

Solomon, R. L. Punishment. *American Psychologist,* 1964, *19,* 239-253.

Solomon, R. L., and Turner, L. H. Discriminative classical conditioning paralyzed by curare can later control discriminative avoidance responses in normal state. *Psychological Review,* 1962, *69,* 202-219.

Solomon, R. L., and Wynne, L. C. Traumatic avoidance learning: The principle of anxiety conservation and partial irreversibility. *Psychological Review,* 1954, *61,* 353-385.

Soloveychik, D. I. Disturbance of normal activity of the cerebral cortex through changes of usual regime. *Trudy Fiziologicheskikh Laboratorii I. P. Pavlova,* 1928a, *2*(2), 61-80.

Soloveychik, D. I. The excitability of the cortical cells during the action of the unconditioned stimuli. *Trudy Fiziologicheskikh Laboratorii I. P. Pavlova,* 1928b, *2*(2), 95-114.

Sovetov, A. N. The role of associative (parietal) cortical areas of dogs in conditioned-reflex activity. *Zhurnal Vysshey Nervnoy Deyatel'nosti imeni I. P. Pavlova,* 1967, *17,* 51-63.

Sovetov, A. N., and Chernigovsky, V. N. Mobility of basic neural processes in the cortical portion of the interoceptive analyzer. *Zhurnal Vysshey Nervnoy Deyatel' nosti imeni I. P. Pavlova,* 1959, *9,* 63-69.

Spence, K. W. *Behavior theory and conditioning.* New Haven: Yale University Press, 1956.

Spence, K. W. Reinforcement and non-reinforcement in simple learning. In K. W. Spence (Ed.), *Behavior theory and learning: Selected papers.* Englewood Cliffs, N. J.: Prentice-Hall, 1960.

Spence, K. W. Cognitive factors in the extinction of the conditioned eyelid response in humans. *Science,* 1963, *140,* 1224-1225.

Spence, K. W., and Beechcroft, R. S. Differential conditioning and level of anxiety. *Journal of Experimental Psychology,* 1954, *48,* 399-403.

Spence, K. W., and Platt, J. P. UCS intensity and performance in eyelid conditioning. *Psychological Bulletin,* 1966, *65,* 1-10.

Spencer, H. *The principles of psychology.* London: Longmans, 1855.

Speransky, A. D. The effect of intense destructive stimuli on a dog of an inhibitory nervous system. *Trudy Fiziologicheskikh Laboratorii I. P. Pavlova,* 1927, *2*(1), 3-24.

Spevack, A. A., and Suboski, M.D. A confounding of conditioned suppression in passive avoidance: ECS effects. *Psychonomic Science,* 1967, *9,* 23-24.

Spevack, A. A., and Suboski, M. D. Retrograde effects of electroconvulsive shock on learned responses. *Psychological Bulletin,* 1969, *72,* 66-76.

Spooner, A., and Kellogg, W. N. The backward conditioning curve. *American Journal of Psychology,* 1947, *60,* 321-334.

Staats, C. K., and Staats, A. W. Meaning established by classical conditioning. *Journal of Experimental Psychology,* 1957, *54,* 74-80.

Staats, C. K., and Staats, A. W. Attitudes established by classical conditioning. *Journal of Abnormal and Social Psychology,* 1958, *57,* 37-40.

Stanley, W. C., Cornwell, A. C., Poggiani, C., and Trattner, C. Conditioning in the neonatal puppy. *Journal of Comparative and Physiological Psychology,* 1963, *56,* 211-214.

Stein, L. Habituation and stimulus novelty: A model on classical conditioning *Psychological Review,* 1966, *73,* 352-356.

Stevens, S. S. (Ed.) *Handbook of experimental psychology.* New York: Wiley, 1951.

Stol'nikov, Ya. Salivation upon faradization of *N. ischiadici. Trudy Obshchestva Russkikh Vrachey v St. Peterburge,* 1875-1876, 271-278.

Stolz, S. B. Vasomotor response in human subjects: Conditioning and pseudoconditioning. *Psychonomic Science,* 1965, *2,* 181-182.

Stone, J., and Fabian M. Specialized receptive cells in the cat's retina. *Science,* 1966, *152,* 1277-1279.

Storms, L. H., and Boroczi, G. Effectiveness of fixed ratio punishment and durability of its effects. *Psychonomic Science,* 1966, *5*(11), 1133-1134.

Storms, L. H. Boroczi, G., and Broen, W. E. Punishment inhibits an instrumental response in hooded rats. *Science,* 1962, *135,* 1133-1134.

Storms, L. H., Boroczi, G., and Broen, W. E. Effects of punishment as a function of strain of rat and duration of shock. *Journal of Comparative and Physiological Psychology,* 1963, *56,* 1022-1026.

Stroganov, V. V. Extinction of reflexes (conditioned) with reinforcement upon repetition of homogeneous stimuli. *Trudy Fiziologicheskikh Laboratorii imeni I. P. Pavlova,* 1929, *3*(2-3), 103-116.

Stroganov, V. V. The effects of the center of unconditioned stimuli upon that of conditioned stimuli. *Trudy Fiziologicheskikh Laboratorii imeni I. P. Pavlova,* 1940, *9,* 360-370.

Stroganov, V. V. The effect of the first link of a dynamic stereotype on the excitatory state of the cortex in the course of one experimental regime. *Trudy Fiziologicheskogo Instituta imeni I. P. Pavlova,* 1949, *3,* 32-41.

Struchkov, M. N. Direct connections and feedback in conditioned food reflexes. *Zhurnal Vysshey Nervnoy Deyatel'nosti imeni I. P. Pavlova,* 1969, *19,* 18-25.

Suboski, M. D., Spevack, A. A., Litner, J., and Beaumaster, E. Effects of ECS following one-trial discriminated avoidance conditioning. *Neurophysiologia,* 1969, *7,* 67-68.

Suchman, R. G., and Trabasso, T. Color and form preference in young children. *Journal of Experimental Child Psychology,* 1966, *3,* 177-187.

Supin, A. Y. Possible neurophysiological mechanisms of internal inhibition. *Zhurnal Vysshey Nervnoy Deyatel'nosti imeni I. P. Pavlova,* 1969, *19,* 100-109.

Suvorov, N. F. Experimental neuroses upon collision of conditioned reflexes to direct cortical stimulations. *Trudy Instituta Fiziologii imeni I. P. Pavlova*, 1962a, *10*, 114-122.

Suvorov, N. F. Experimental neuroses upon collision of conditioned reflexes to direct cortical and subcortical stimulations. *Trudy Instituta Fiziologii imeni I. P. Pavlova*, 1962b, *10*, 123-131.

Svetukhina, V. M. Cytoarchitecture of the precoronary and frontal lobes in carnivores. In S. A. Sarkisov and N. S. Preobrazhenskaya (Eds.), *Development of the central nervous system. Phylogeny and ontogeny of the cortex and subcortical formations.* Moscow: Medgiz, 1959. Pp. 115-138.

Svetukhina, V. M. Progressive evolution and differentiation of cytoarchitecture in birds. In *Theses, 3rd Scientific Conference on Evolutionary Physiology in Memory of Acadamician L. A. Orbeli.* Leningrad: 1961. Pp. 168-169.

Svetukhina, V. M., Krushinsky, L. V., Mats, V. N., and Molodkina, L. N. Characteristics of the morphology of the brain of birds in relation to mastery of extrapolative reflexes. In V. N. Chernigovsky (Ed.), *Physiological bases of complex forms of behavior.* Moscow: Akademiya Nauk SSSR, 1963. P. 74.

Switzer, S. A. Backward conditioning of the eyelid reflex. *Journal of Experimental Psychology*, 1930, *13*, 76-97.

Syrensky, V. I. Motor disturbances upon ablation of frontal lobes. *Yezhegodnik, Institut Experimental'noy Meditziny*, 1960, 44-46.

Syrensky, V. I. The significance of certain head and body positions in correct differentiation of conditioned auditory reflexes in free movement experiment. *Byulleten' Experimental'noy Biologii i Meditsiny* 1962a, *7*, 6-10.

Syrensky, V. I. Spatial disposition of conditioned reflexes in the formation of conditioned motor reflexes. *Zhurnal Vysshey Nervnoy Deyatel'nosti imeni I. P. Pavlova*, 1962b, *5*, 862-866.

Szentágothai, J. Possible histological basis of inhibition. In E. A. Asratyan (Ed.), *Reflexes of the brain.* Moscow: Nauka, 1965. Pp. 178-185.

Szymanski, J. S. Modification of the innate behavior of cockroaches. *Journal of Animal Behavior*, 1912, *2*, 81-90.

Tagiyev, S. K. Synthesis of two different conditioned reflexes into a chain in fishes, pigeons and rabbits. *Zhurnal Vysshey Nervnoy Deyatel'nosti imeni I. P. Pavlova*, 1958, *8*, 404-409.

Tanzi, E. I fatti e le induzine nell' odierne istologia del sistema nervosa. *Rivista Sperimentale di Freniatria e Medicina*, 1893, *19*, 419-472.

Tauc, L. Interaction non-synaptique entre deux neurones adjacent du ganglion abdominal de l'Aplysie. *Comptes Rendus Hebdomadaires de Séances de l'Académie des Sciences*, Paris, 1959, *248*, 1857-1859.

Tauc, L., and Gerschenfeld, H. M. Cholinergic transmission mechanisms for both excitation and inhibition in molluscan central synapses. *Nature* (London), 1961, *192*, 366-367.

Thomas, D. R., Berman, D. L., Serendensky, G. E., and Lyons, J. Information value and stimulus configuring as factors in conditioned reinforcement. *Journal of Experimental Psychology*, 1968, *76*, 181-189.

Thompson, R. F. The neural basis of stimulus generalization. In D. I. Mostofsky (Ed.), *Stimulus generalization.* Stanford, Calif.: Stanford University Press, 1965. Pp. 154-178.

Thompson, R. F., and Kramer, R. F. Role of association cortex in sensory preconditioning. *Journal of Comparative and Physiological Psychology,* 1965, *60*(2), 186-191.

Thompson, R. F., and Spencer, W. A. Habituation: A model phenomenon. *Psychological Review,* 1966, *73*, 16-43.

Thorndike, E. L. Animal intelligence: An experimental study of the associative processes in animals. *Psychological Monographs,* 1898, *2*, No. 8.

Thorndike, E. L. *Animal intelligence.* New York: Macmillan, 1911.

Thorndike, E. L. *Educational psychology.* Vol. II. *The psychology of learning.* New York: Teachers College, Columbia University, 1913.

Thorndike, E. L. *Human Learning.* New York: Appleton-Century, 1931.

Thorndike, E. L. A theory of the action of after-effects of a connection upon it. *Psychological Review,* 1933, *40*, 434-439.

Thorndike, E. L. *The psychology of wants, interests, and attitudes.* New York: Appleton-Century-Crofts, 1935

Thorndike, E. L., and Rock, I. T. Learning without awareness of what is being learned or intent to learn it. *Journal of Experimental Psychology,* 1934, *17*, 1-19.

Thornton, G. L. The effect of stimulus intensities upon sensory preconditioning. *Proceedings of the Iowa Academy of Science,* 1956, *63*, 620-626.

Thorpe, W. H. *Learning and instinct in animals.* London: Methuen, 1950.

Thorpe, W. H. Ethology and the coding problem in germ cell and brain. *Zeitschrift für Tierpsychologie,* 1963, *20*, 529-551.

Thurstone, L. L. *Primary mental abilities.* Chicago: University of Chicago Press, 1944.

Timofeyev, N. N. Method of studying interoceptive conditioned reflexes in fish. *Fiziologichesky Zhurnal SSSR imeni I. M. Sechenova,* 1955, *41*, 289-291.

Tinbergen, N. *The study of instinct.* Oxford: Clarendon, 1951.

Tinbergen, N. Behavior, systematics, and natural selection. In S. Tax (Ed.), *Evolution after Darwin.* Vol. 1. Chicago: University of Chicago Press, 1960. Pp. 595-613.

Titchener, E. B. *Lectures on the experimental psychology of the thought processes.* New York: Macmillan, 1909.

Titchener, E. B. *Textbook of psychology.* New York: Macmillan, 1910.

Tolman, E. C. *Purposive behavior in animals and men.* New York: Appleton-Century-1932.

Tolman, E. C. Sign-gestalt or conditioned reflex? *Psychological Review,* 1936, *43*, 258-281.

Tolman, E. C. The determiners of behavior at a choice point. *Psychological Review,* 1938, *45*, 1-41.

Tolman, E. C. Cognitive maps in rats and men. *Psychological Review,* 1948, *55*, 189-208.

Tolman, E. C. Performance vectors and the unconscious. In *Proceedings, 14th International Congress of Psychology,* Montreal, 1954. Amsterdam: North-Holland Publishing Co., 1955. Pp. 31-40.

Tolman, E. C. Principles of purposive behavior. In S. Koch (Ed.), *Psychology: A study of a science.* Vol. 2. *General systematic formulations, learning, and special processes.* New York: McGraw-Hill, 1959. Pp. 92-157.

Tolochinov, I. F. Contributions a l'étude de la physiologie et de la psychologie des glands salivaires. *Comptes rendu des Congrès de naturalistes et médecins du Nord, tenu a Helsingfors,* July 7-12, 1903a, 41-43.

Tolochinov, I. F. Original application of the method of conditioned reflexes to the study of the action of the cerebral cortex in dogs. *Nevrologichesky Vestnik,* 1903b, *19*, 410-445.

Tolochinov, I. F. Basic manifestation of conditioned salivary reflexes and original development of their method. St. Petersburg: *Author,* 1912a.

Tolochinov, I. F. Original development of the method of conditioned reflexes and use of the term "conditioned reflex." *Russky Vrach,* 1912b, *11*, 1277-1282.

Toporkova, L. A. The formation of conditioned respiratory reflexes to simultaneous and successive complex stimuli in cats. *Zhurnal Vysshey Nervnoy Deyatel'nosti imeni I. P. Pavlova,* 1961, *11*, 718-722.

Tracy, H. C. The development of motility and behavior reactions in toadfish (*Opsanus tau*). *Journal of Comparative Neurology,* 1926, *40*, 253-369.

Trapold, M. H., Homzie, M., and Rutledge, E. Backward conditioning and UCR latency. *Journal of Experimental Psychology,* 1964, *67*, 387-391.

Traugott, N. N. *Disturbances of interactions of the signal systems.* Moscow-Leningrad: Akademiya Nauk SSSR, 1957.

Tsaio, Ch. Transswitching short- into long-delay conditioned reflexes. *Zhurnal Vysshey Nervnoy Deyatel'nosti imeni I. P. Pavlova,* 1959, *9*, 585-592.

Turner, L. H., and Solomon, R. L. Human traumatic avoidance learning: Theory and experiments on the operant-respondent distinction and failures to learn. *Psychological Monographs,* 1962, *76* (Whole No. 559).

XXIII Congress of the Communist Party of the USSR, March 29-April 8, 1966. Stenographic Record. Moscow: Politicheskaya Literatura, 1966. 2 vols.

Ukhtomsky, A. A. Dominance as a working principle of neural centers. *Russky Fiziologichesky Zhurnal,* 1923a, *6*, 31-45.

Ukhtomsky, A. A. Instinct and dominance. *Nauchnyye Izvestiya Smolenskogo Universiteta,* 1923b, 99-101.

Ukhtomsky, A. A. Dominance and the integral image. *Vrachebnaya Gazeta,* 1924, No. 2, 26-29.

Uktomsky, A. A. The principle of dominance. *Novoye v Refleksologii i Fiziologi Nervnoy Sistemy,* 1925, *1*, 60-80.

Ukhtomsky, A. A. The excitatory state in dominance. *Novoye v Refleksologii i Fiziologi Nervnoy Sistemy,* 1926, *2*, 4-15.

Ukhtomsky, A. A. Dominance as a factor of behavior. *Vestnik Kommunisticheskoy Akademii,* 1927, *22*, 215-241.

Ukhtomsky, A. A. Excitation, fatigue, inhibition. *Fiziologichesky Zhurnal SSSR imeni I. M. Sechenova,* 1934, *17*, 1114-1127.

Ukhtomsky, A. A. The great physiologist (in memory of I. P. Pavlov). *Priroda,* 1936, No. 3, 10-14.

Ukhtomsky, A. A. Conditioned reflection of action. *Fiziologichesky Zhurnal SSSR imeni I. M. Sechenova,* 1938, *25*, 767-768.

Ukhtomsky, A. A. *The dominant.* Moscow: Nauka, 1966.

Ukhtomsky, A. A., and Vinogradov, M. I. The inertia of dominance. In V. L. Omelyansky (Ed.), *Volume celebrating the 75th birthday of Academician I. P. Pavlov.* Leningrad: GIZ, 1924. Pp. 47-53.

Ullmann, L. P., and Krasner, L. *Case studies in behavior modification.* New York: Holt, Rinehart and Winston, 1965.

Underwood, B. J., and Schulz, R. W. *Meaningfulness and verbal learning.* Philadelphia: J. B. Lippincott, 1960.

Undeutsch, U. Die Aktuelgenese in ihrer allgemeinpshycologischen und ihrer characterologischen Bedeutung. *Scientia,* 1942, *72,* 37-42.

Uno, T. The effects of awareness and successive inhibition on interoceptive and exteroceptive conditioning of the GSR. *Psychophysiology,* in press.

Usiyevich, M. A. The nervous system of a dog solving a difficult task. *Trudy Fiziologicheskikh Laboratorii imeni I. P. Pavlova,* 1938, *8,* 315-320.

Usnadze, D. Uber die Gewichtstauschung und ihre Analoga. *Psychologische Forschung,* 1931, *14,* 366-380.

Usnadze, D. N. *Basic principles of the theory of set.* Tbilisi: Akademiya Nauk GSSR, 1950.

Uzhdavini, E. R. Inherited food reflexes in puppies. *Opyt Izucheniya Regulatsii Fiziologicheskikh Funktsii,* 1958, *4,* 112-123.

Uzhdavini, E. R., and Shepeleva, V. K. *Outline of the development of innate behavior.* Moscow: Nauka, 1966.

Varga, M. E. The role of intensity relations in functioning of two-way conditioned connections. *Zhurnal Vysshey Nervnoy Deyatel'nosti imeni I. P. Pavlova,* 1955, *5,* 723-731.

Varga, M. E. Physiological significance of precedence of the signal stimulus in conditioned-reflex action. *Zhurnal Vysshey Nervnoy Deyatel'nosti imeni I. P. Pavlova,* 1958, *8,* 710-716.

Varga, M. E., and Pressman, Ya. M. Certain characteristics of conditioned-reflex connections in pairing so-called indifferent stimuli. In L. G. Voronin, A. N. Leont'yev, R. R. Luria, E. N. Sokolov, and O. S. Vinogradova (Eds.), *The orienting reflex and orienting-investigatory activity.* Moscow: Akademiya Pedagogicheskikh Nauk RSFSR, 1958. Pp. 33-40.

Varga, M. E., and Pressman, Ya. M. Some functional characteristics of forward and reverse conditioned-reflex connections. In E. A. Asratyan (Ed.), *Neural mechanisms of conditioned-reflex activity.* Moscow: Akademiya Nauk SSSR, 1963. Pp. 3-18.

Varga, M. E., and Pressman, Ya. M. Forward and reverse conditioned connections. In E. Sh. Ayrapet'yants (Ed.), *Central and peripheral mechanisms of neural activity.* Yerevan: Akademiya Nauk ArSSR, 1966. Pp. 139-152.

Vasileva, O. N. Interrelation between unconditioned and conditioned defensive reflexes in backward sequences. *Zhurnal Vysshey Nervnoy Deyatel'nosti imeni I. P. Pavlova,* 1957, *7,* 389-397.

Vasilevskaya, N. E. Interoceptive conditioned reflexes of the second order. *Doklady Akademii Nauk SSSR,* 1948, *61,* 161-164.

Vasilevskaya, N. E. The formation of second-order interoceptive conditioned reflexes with exteroceptive reinforcement. *Nauchny Byulleten' Leningradskogo Grosudarstvennogo Universiteta,* 1950, No. 26, 21-23.

Vatsuro, E. G. *Study of the higher nervous activity of anthropoids (chimpanzees).* Moscow: Medgiz, 1948.

Vatsuro, E. G. Dominant afferentation in higher nervous activity. *Fiziologichesky Zhurnal SSSR imeni I. M. Sechenova,* 1949, *35,* 535-540.

Vatsuro, E. G. *Pavlov's views of higher nervous activity.* Moscow: Akademiya Nauk SSSR, 1952.

Vatsuro, E. G. Some general loss of higher nervous activity (behavior) in animals. *Zhurnal Vysshey Nervnoy Deyatel'nosti imeni I. P. Pavlova,* 1961, *11,* 1012-1018.

Vatsuro, E. G. *Conditioned reflexes to specific food stimuli.* Leningrad: Meditsina, 1967.

Vedayev, F. P. Comparative physiology of conditioned reflexes to complex stimuli. *Zhurnal Vysshey Nervnoy Deyatel'nosti imeni I. P. Pavlova,* 1956, *6,* 786-793.

Vedayev, F. P., and Karmanova, I. G. Comparative physiology of the orienting reflex. In L. G. Voronin, A. N. Leont'yev, A. R. Luria, E. N. Sokolov, and O. S. Vinogradova (Eds.), *The orienting reflex and orienting-investigatory activity.* Moscow: Akademiya Pedagogicheskikh Nauk RSFSR, 1958. Pp. 201-204.

Verplanck, W. S. The control of the content of conversation: Reinforcement of statements of opinion. *Journal of Abnormal and Social Psychology,* 1955, *51,* 668-676.

Vinogradov, N. V. The emergence of new connections in the inhibition regions of the cortex. *Trudy Fiziologicheskikh Laboratorii I. P. Pavlova,* 1933, *5,* 33-48.

Vinogradova, O. S. The dynamics of the orienting reflex in the process of the formation of conditioned connections. In L. G. Voronin, A. N. Leont'yev, A. R. Luria, E. N. Sokolov, and O. S. Vinogradova (Eds.), *The orienting reflex and orienting-investigatory activity.* Moscow: Akademiya Pedagogicheskikh Nauk RSFSR, 1958. Pp. 40-47.

Vinogradova, O. S. The role of the orienting reflex in the formation of conditioned connections in man. In E. N. Sokolov (Ed.), *The orienting reflex and problems of higher nervous activity.* Moscow: Akademiya Pedagogicheskikh Nauk RSFSR, 1959. Pp. 86-160.

Vinogradova, O. S. *The orienting reflex and its neurophysiological mechanisms.* Moscow: Akademiya Pedagogicheskikh Nauk RSFSR, 1961.

Vinogradova, O. S. Dynamic classification of the reactions of single neurones of the hippocampus to sensory stimuli. *Zhurnal Vysshey Nervnoy Deyatel'nosti imeni I. P. Pavlova,* 1965, *15,* 500-512.

Vinogradova, O. S. The study of habituation in single neurones of the caudate nucleus in rabbits. *Zhurnal Vysshey Nervnoy Deyatel'nosti imeni I. P. Pavlova,* 1968, *18,* 671-680.

Vinogradova, O. S., and Eysler, N. A. The manifestations of verbal connections in recording vascular reactions. *Voprosy Psikhologii,* 1959, *4*(2), 101-116.

Vinogradova, O. S. Konovalov, V. F., and Semyonova, T. P. Neuronal correlates of the extinction of the orienting reflex in different regions of the brain. *Voprosy Psikhologii,* 1969, *15*(1), 46-59.

Vinogradova, O. S., and Lindsley, D. E. Single-neurone extinctions of reactions to sensory stimuli in the unanesthetized visual cortex of the rabbit. *Zhurnal Vysshey Nervnoy Deyatel'nosti imeni I. P. Pavlova,* 1963, *13,* 207-217.

Vinogradova, O. S., and Sokolov, E. N. Characteristics of the dynamics of specific and nonspecific reaction in repeated applications of stimuli. In E. N. Sokolov (Ed.), *The orienting reflex and problems of normal and pathological reception.* Moscow: Prosveshicheniye, 1964. Pp. 173-184.

Vladimirov, G. E. Functional biochemistry of the brain. *Fiziologichesky Zhurnal SSSR imeni I. M. Sechenova,* 1953, *39,* 3-16.

Vladimirov, G. E. Biochemical changes in the brain during inhibition. *Gagrskiye Besedy,* 1957, *2,* 345-374.

Vogler, R. E. Awareness and the operant conditioning of a cooperative response. *Journal of Psychology,* 1968, *69,* 117-127.

Volkova, V. D. On certain characteristics of the formation of speech reflexes to speech stimuli. *Fiziologichesky Zhurnal SSSR imeni I. M. Sechenova,* 1953, *39,* 540-548.

Volkova, V. D. Quoted in N. I. Krasnogorsky, *Studies of the higher nervous activity of animals and children.* Moscow: Medgiz, 1954. Pp. 478-480.

Volkova, V. D. The effect of caffein and adrenalin on situational [positional] conditioned reflexes. *Yezhegodnik, Institut Experimental'noy Meditziny,* 1961, 31-40.

Volkova, V. D., and Kudryavtseva, N. N. The effects of antiphein on salivary and situational [positional] reflexes. In *Pharmacology of new sedatives.* Moscow: Medgiz, 1962. Pp. 159-162.

Volokhov, A. A. *Laws of ontogenesis of higher nervous activity in light of evolution.* Moscow: Akademiya Nauk SSSR, 1951.

Volokhov, A. A. Problems of comparative study of nervous activity in ontogenesis. In A. G. Ginetsinsky (Ed.), *Evolution of physiological functions.* Moscow: Akademiya Nauk SSSR, 1960. Pp. 52-62.

Volokhov, A. A. *Outline of the physiology of the nervous system.* Leningrad: Meditsina, 1968.

Voronin, L. G. Development of unconditioned and conditioned reactions in newborn macaques. *Fiziologichesky Zhurnal SSSR imeni I. M. Sechenova,* 1948a, *34,* 333-338.

Voronin, L. G. *Analysis and synthesis of complex stimuli in normal and in brain-damaged dogs: An experimental study.* Moscow: Akademiya Meditsinskikh Nauk, 1948b.

Voronin, L. G. *Analysis and synthesis of complex stimuli in higher animals.* Leningrad: Medgiz, 1952.

Voronin, L. G. Summary of comparative-physiological studies of higher nervous activity. *Izvestiya Akademii Nauk SSSR, Seriya Biologicheskaya,* 1954a, 5, 122-134.

Voronin, L. G. More about speed of formation of conditioned reflexes. *Zhurnal Vysshey Nervnoy Deyatel'nosti imeni I. P. Pavlova,* 1954b, *4,* 756-767.

Voronin, L. G. *Comparative physiology of higher nervous activity.* Moscow: Moscow University, 1957.

Voronin, L. G. Some results of comparative-physiological investigations of higher nervous activity. *Psychological Bulletin,* 1962, *59,* 161-195.

Voronin, L. G. *Lectures on the physiology of higher nervous activity.* Moscow: Vysshaya Shkola, 1965.

Voronin, L. G. Comparative physiology of conditioned reflexes. *Zhurnal Vysshey Nervnoy Deyatel'nosti imeni I. P. Pavlova,* 1967, *17,* 869-879.

Voronin, L. G. Ivan Petrovich Pavlov and contemporary cerebral physiology. *Zhurnal Vysshey Nervnoy Deyatel'nosti imeni I. P. Pavlova,* 1969, *19,* 914-920.

Voronin, L. G., Karas', A. Ya., Tushmalova, N. A., and Khoncheva, N. M. Types of acquired reactions in invertebrates. *Uspekhi Sovremmennoy Biologii,* 1967, *64,* 2(5), 312-332.

Voronin, L. G., Leont'yev, A. N., Luria, A. R., Sokolov, E. N., and Vinogradova, O. S. (Eds.) *The orienting reflex and orienting-investigatory activity.* Moscow: Akademiya Pedagogicheskikh Nauk RSFSR, 1958.

Voronin, L. G., and Sokolov, E. N. Cortical mechanisms of the orienting reflex and its relation to the conditioned reflex. In H. H. Jasper and G. D. Smirnov (Eds.), The Moscow Colloquium on Electroencephalography of Higher Nervous Activity, *Electroencephalography and Clinical Neurophysiology,* 1960, Supplement, 13, 335-340.

Voronin, L. G., and Yordanis, K. A. Interrelation of inhibitory and excitatory processes in complex motor conditioned activity. *Zhurnal Vysshey Nervnoy Deyatel'-nosti imeni I. P. Pavlova,* 1961, *11,* 71-74.

Voss, J. E. (Ed.) Approaches to thought. Columbus, Ohio: Charles E. Merrill, 1969.

Voyevodina, O. N. The effect of small doses of roentgen radiation on situational [positional] conditioned reflexes. *Yezhegodnik, Institut Experimental'noy Meditziny,* 1960, 492-496.

Voznaya, A. I. Conditioned-reflex activity in young puppies. In *Theses, 20th Conference on Problems of Higher Nervous Activity.* Moscow-Leningrad: Akademiya Nauk SSSR, 1963. P. 59.

Voznaya, A. I. Positive functional connections among simultaneous complexes of conditioned stimuli. In *Theses, 21st Conference on Problems of Higher Activity.* Moscow-Leningrad: Nauka, 1966. P. 77.

Vulfson, S. G. *The work of the salivary glands.* St. Petersburg: Military Medical Academy, 1898. (Thesis)

Vvedensky, N. E. *The relation between stimulation and excitation in tetanus.* St. Petersburg: 1886.

Vygotsky, L. S. *Thought and language.* Moscow: Sovgiz, 1934.

Vygotsky, L. S. *Selected psychological studies.* Moscow: Akademiya Pedagogicheskikh Nauk RSFSR, 1954.

Vygotsky, L. S. *Development of higher psychic functions.* Moscow: Akademiya Pedagogicheskikh Nauk RSFSR, 1960.

Wagner, A. R. Conditioned frustration as a learned drive. *Journal of Experimental Psychology,* 1963, *66,* 142-148.

Wagner, A. R. Frustration and Punishment. In R. N. Haber (Ed.), *Current research in motivation.* New York: Holt, Rinehart and Winston, 1966. Pp. 229-239.

Wagner, G. On some movements and reactions of *Hydra. Quarterly Journal of Microscopical Science,* 1905, *48,* 585-622.

Walker, E. G. Eyelid conditioning as a function of intensity of conditioned and unconditioned stimulus. *Journal of Experimental Psychology,* 1960, *59,* 303-311.

Walter, W. G., Cooper, R., Aldridge, V. J., McCallum, W. C., and Winter, A. L. Contingent negative variation: An electric sign of sensorimotor association and expectancy in the human brain. *Nature* (London), 1964, *203,* 380-384.

Walter, W. G., Cooper, R., McCallum, C., and Cohen, J. The origin and significance of the contingent negative variation or "expectancy wave." *Electroencephalography and clinical Neurophysiology,* 1965, *18,* 720-729.

Wanatabe, A., and Bullock, T. A. Modulation of activity of one neurone by subthreshold slow potentials in another cardiac ganglion. *Journal of General Physiology,* 1960, 1031-1045.

Warden, C. J., Jenkins, T. N., and Warner, L. H. *Comparative psychology.* New York: Ronald Press, 1935. 3 Vols.

Warren, J. M. Oddity learning set in cats. *Journal of Comparative and Physiological Psychology,* 1960, *53,* 433-434.

Warren, J. M., and Baron, A. The formation of learning sets by cats. *Journal of Comparative and Physiological Psychology,* 1956, *49,* 227-231.

Warren, J. M., and Kimball, H. Transfer relations in discrimination learning by cats. *Journal of Comparative and Physiological Psychology,* 1959, *52,* 336-338.

Washburn, M. F. *The animal mind.* New York: Macmillan, 1908.

Washburn, M. F. *Movement and mental imagery.* Boston: Houghton Mifflin, 1916.

Watson, J. B. *Psychology from the standpoint of a behaviorist.* Philadelphia: J. B. Lippincott, 1919.

Watson, J. B. The unverbalized in human behavior. *Psychological Review,* 1924, *31,* 273-280.

Watson, J. B. *Behaviorism.* New York: W. W. Norton, 1925.

Watson, J. B. The myth of the unconscious. A behavioristic explanation. *Harper's Monthly Magazine,* 1927, *155,* 502-508.

Watson, J. B. The heart or the intellect? *Harper's Monthly Magazine,* 1928, *156,* 345-353.

Watt, H. J. Experimentelle Beitrage zu einer Theorie des Denkens. *Archiv für Gesamte Psychologie,* 1905, *4,* 289-436.

Wells, M. J. Early learning in sepia. *Symposium of the Zoological Society, London,* 1962a, *8,* 149-169.

Wells, M. J. *Brain and behavior in cephalopods.* Stanford, Calif.: Stanford University Press, 1962b.

Wells, M. J. Learning and movements in octopuses. *Animal Behaviour,* 1965 (Supplement 1), *13,* 115-128.

Wells, M. J. Sensitization and evolution of associative learning. In *Symposium on Neurobiology of Invertebrates.* Budapest: Akadémiai Kiadó, 1967, Pp. 391-411.

Wells, M. J., and Wells, J. Tactile discrimination and the behavior of blind octopus. *Pubblicazioni della Stazione Zoologica de Napoli,* 1956, *28,* 94-126.

Werner, H., and Wapner, S. Toward a general theory of perception. *Psychological Review,* 1952, *59,* 324-338.

Wertheimer, M. Experimentelle Studien über das Sehen von Bewegung. *Zeitschrift für Psychologie,* 1912, *61,* 161-205.

Wertheimer, M. *Über Schlusprozesse in produktiven Denken.* Berlin-Leipzig: de Gruyter,1920.

Wertheimer, M. Untersuchungen zur Lehre von der Gestalt. *Psychologische Forschung,* 1923, *4,* 301-350.

Wertheimer, M. *Drei Abhandlungen zur Gestalttheorie.* Erlangen: Philosophishe Akademie, 1925.

Wertheimer, M. *Productive thinking.* New York: Harpers, 1945.

Wertheimer, Michael. Psychomotor coordination of auditory and visual space at birth. *Science,* 1961, *134,* 1962.

Westerman, R. A. Somatic inheritance of habituation of responses to light in planarians. *Science,* 1963, *140,* 676-677.

Wheeler, W. M. *Ants: Their structure, development and behavior.* New York: Columbia University Press, 1910.

Wickens, D. D. Conditioning to complex stimuli. *American Psychologist,* 1959, *14,* 180-188.

Wickens, D. D. Compound conditioning in humans and cats. In W. F. Prokasy (Ed.), *Classical conditioning.* New York: Appleton-Century-Crofts, 1965. Pp. 323-339.

Wickens, D. D., Born, D. G., and Wickens, C. D. Response strength to a compound conditioned stimulus and its elements as a function of the element interstimulus interval. *Journal of Comparative and Physiological Psychology,* 1963, *56,* 727-731.

Wickens, D. D., Cross, H. A., and Morgan, R. M. CS termination and the response strength acquired by elements of a stimulus complex. *Journal of Experimental Psychology,* 1959, *58,* 363-368.

Wickens, D. D., Gehman, R. S., and Sullivan, S. N. The effect of differential onset time in the conditioned response strength to elements of a stimulus complex. *Journal of Experimental Psychology,* 1959, *58,* 85-93.

Wickens, D. D., Nield, A. F., and Wickens, C. D. Habituation of the GSR and of breathing disturbances in the cat. *Psychonomic Science,* 1966, *6,* 325-326.

Wickens, D. D., and Snide, J. D. The influence of the nonreinforcement of a component of a complex stimulus on resistance to extinction of the complex itself. *Journal of Experimental Psychology,* 1955, *42,* 197-200.

Wickens, D. D., and Wickens, C. D. Study of conditioning in the neonates. *Journal of Experimental Psychology,* 1940, *26,* 94-102.

Wickens, D. D., and Wickens, C. D. Some factors related to pseudoconditioning. *Journal of Experimental Psychology,* 1942, *31,* 518-526.

Williams, D. R. Classical conditioning and incentive motivation. In W. F. Prokasy (Ed.), *Classical conditioning.* New York: Appleton-Century-Crofts, 1965. Pp. 340-357.

Wilson, V. J. Post-tetanic potentiation of polysynaptic reflexes of the spinal cord. *Journal of General Psychology,* 1955, *39,* 197-206.

Windle, W. F. The genesis of somatic behavior in mammalian embryos. *Journal of Physiology,* 1936, *87,* 31-33P.

Windle, W. F. *Physiology of the fetus: Origin and extent of function in prenatal life.* Philadelphia: Saunders, 1940.

Windle, W. F. The genesis of somatic behavior in mammalian embryos. *Physiological Zoology,* 1944, *17,* 247-260.

Windle, W. F., Minear, W. L., Austin, M. F., and Orr, W. D. The origin and early development of somatic behavior in the albino rat. *Physiological Zoology,* 1935, *8,* 156-185.

Witte, S. Failure to obtain pseudoconditioning in a shuttlebox. *Psychonomic Science,* 1965, *3,* 375-376.

Wodinsky, J., and Bitterman, M. E. Discrimination-reversal in fish. *American Journal of Psychology,* 1957, *70,* 569-576.

Wodinsky, J., and Bitterman, M. E. Resistance to extinction in the fish after extensive training with partial reinforcement. *American Journal of Psychology,* 1960, *73,* 429-434.

Wokoon, F. W. The effect of stimulus intensity in sensory preconditioning. Unpublished doctoral dissertation, University of Nebraska, 1959.

Wolfle, H. M. Time factors in conditioning finger withdrawal. *Journal of General Psychology,* 1930, *4,* 372-378.

Wolfle, H. M. Conditioning as a function of the interval between the conditioned and the original stimulus. *Journal of General Psychology,* 1932, *7,* 80-103.

Wolpe, J. *Psychotherapy by reciprocal inhibition.* Stanford, Calif.: Stanford University Press, 1958.

Woodbury, C. B. The learning of stimulus patterns by dogs. *Journal of Comparative Psychology,* 1943, *35,* 29-40.

Woodworth, R. S. Imageless thought. *Journal of Philosophy,* 1906, *3,* 701-707.

Woodworth, R. S. A revision of imageless thought. *Psychological Review,* 1915, *22,* 1-27.

Woodworth, R. S. *Experimental psychology.* New York: Holt, 1938.

Woodworth, R. S., and Schlosberg, H. *Experimental psychology.* New York: Holt, 1954.

Woodworth, R. S., and Sells, S. B. An atmosphere effect in formal syllogistic thinking. *Journal of Experimental Psychology,* 1935, *18,* 451-460.

Wundt, W. M. *Grundriss der Psychologie*. Leipzig: Engelmann, 1896. (English translation by C. H. Judd, 1897.)

Yelshina, M. A., Zimkin, N. V., and Moreva, Z. E. Formation of motor defensive reflexes in rats when the unconditioned stimulus precedes the conditioned stimulus. *Zhurnal Vysshey Nervnoy Deyatel'nosti imeni I. P. Pavlova*, 1955, *5*, 881-891.

Yerkes, R. M. Formation of habits in the turtle. *Popular Science Monthly*, 1901, *58*, 519-525.

Yerkes, R. M. Habit formation in the green crab, *Carcinus granulatus*. *Biological Bulletin*, 1902, *3*, 241-244.

Yerkes, R. M. Inhibition and reinforcement of reaction in the frog, *Rana clamitans*. *Journal of Comparative Neurology and Psychology*, 1904, *14*, 124-137.

Yerkes, R. M. Animal psychology and criteria of the psychic. *Journal of Philosophy*, 1905a, *2*, 141-149.

Yerkes, R. M. The sense of hearing in frogs. *Journal of Comparative Neurology*, 1905b, *15*, 279-304.

Yerkes, R. M. *The dancing mouse*. New York: Macmillan, 1907.

Yerkes, R. M. *Introduction to psychology*. New York: Holt, 1911.

Yerkes, R. M. The intelligence of earthworms. *Journal of Animal Behavior*, 1912, *2*, 332-352.

Yerkes, R. M. The mental life of monkeys and apes. *Behavior Monographs*, 1916a, *3*, 1-145.

Yerkes, R. M. Ideational behavior of monkeys and apes. *Proceedings of the National Academy of Science*, 1916b, *2*, 639-642.

Yerkes, R. M. The mind of a gorilla. *Genetic Psychology Monographs*, 1927a, *2*, 1-193.

Yerkes, R. M. The mind of a gorilla. II. Mental development. *Genetic Psychology Monographs*, 1927b, *2*, 375-551.

Yerkes, R. M. The mind of a gorilla. III. Memory. *Comparative Psychology Monographs*, 1928, *5*, No. 24.

Yerkes, R. M., and Coburn, C. A. A study of the behavior of the pig *Sus Scrofa* by the multiple choice method. *Journal of Animal Behavior*, 1915, *5*, 185-225.

Yerkes, R. M., and Huggins, G. E. Habit formation in the crawfish, *Cambrus affinis*. *Psychological Review*, 1903, *Monograph Supplement*, No. 17 (Harvard Studies I), 565-577.

Yerkes, R. M., and Learned, B. W. *Chimpanzee intelligence and its vocal expression*. Baltimore: Williams and Wilkins, 1925.

Yerkes, R. M., and Yerkes, A. W. *The great apes*. New Haven: Yale University Press, 1929.

Yerkes, R. M., and Yerkes, D. N. Concerning memory in the chimpanzee. *Journal of Comparative Psychology*, 1928, *8*, 237-271.

Yerofeyeva, M. N. *Electrical stimulation of the skin of the dog as a conditioned salivary stimulus*. St. Petersburg, 1912. (Thesis)

Yerofeyeva, M. N. Additional data on nocuous conditioned reflexes. *Izvestiya Petrogradskogo Nauchnogo Instituta imeni P. F. Lesgafta*, 1921, *3*, 69-73.

Yevdokimov, S. A., and Zaklyakova, V. N. Recording apparatus of the eyelid reflex in children. *Zhurnal Vysshey Nervnoy Deyatel'nosti imeni I. P. Pavlova*, 1962, *12*, 354-357.

Yoshi, N., and Hockaday, W. J. Conditioning of frequency-characteristic repetitive electroencephalographic response with intermittent photic stimulation. *Electroencephalography and Clinical Neurophysiology*, 1958, *10*, 487-502.

Young, J. Z. Growth and plasticity in the nervous system. *Proceedings of Royal Society, Series B*, 1951, *139*, 18-37.

Young, J. Z. Responses of untrained octopuses to various figures and the effect of removal of the vertical lobe. *Proceedings of Royal Society, Series B*, 1958, *149*, 463-483.

Young, J. Z. Extinction of unrewarded responses in Octopus. *Pubblicazione della Stazione Zoologica de Napoli*, 1959, *31*(2), 225-247.

Young, J. Z. Unit processes in the formation of representations in the memory of Octopus. *Proceedings of the Royal Society of London, Series B*, 1960, *153*, 1-17.

Young, M. L., and Harlow, H. F. Solution by Rhesus monkeys of a problem involving the Weigl principle using the oddity method. *Journal of Comparative Psychology*, 1943, *35*, 205-217.

Zachar, J., and Zacharová, D. Mechanisms of Leăo's spreading cortical depression. *Physiologia Bohemoslovenika*, 1961, *10*, 341-348.

Zachar, J., and Zacharová, D. *Mechanismus vzniku siriacesja kortikálnej depresie.* (The mechanism of the origin of spreading cortical depression.) Bratislava: Slovenska Akademia Vied a Umeni, 1963.

Zakharzhevsky, V. B. Changes in chemoreceptors of the intestine upon collision of alimentary and defensive reflexes. *Trudy Instituta Fiziologii imeni I. P. Pavlova*, 1960, *9*, 350-359.

Zaklyakova, V. N. The functional roles of the auditory and motor analyzers in the generalization of the first- and second-order systems. *Zhurnal Vysshey Nervnoy Deyatel'nosti imeni I. P. Pavlova*, 1963, *13*, 980-986.

Zaklyakova, V. N. Comparative role of direct and verbal reinforcement in formation of stereotypes. In M. N. Kol'tsova (Ed.), *Materials for symposium on man's system of signals*. Leningrad: 1965. Pp. 49-52.

Zalmanzon, A. N. Conditioned defense reflexes during local poisoning of the cortical motor centers with strychnine and cocaine. In D. S. Fursikov, M. O. Gurevich, and A. N. Zalmanzon (Eds.), *Higher nervous activity*. Moscow: Kommunisticheskaya Akademiya, 1929a. Pp. 39-48.

Zalmanzon, A. N. Specialization of alimentary and defensive conditioned reflexes paired with similar conditioned stimuli. In D. S. Fursikov, M. O. Gurevich, and A. N. Zalmanzon (Eds.), *Higher nervous activity*. Moscow: Kommunisticheskaya Akademiya, 1929b. Pp. 191-220.

Zaporozhets, A. V. *Development of voluntary movements*. Moscow: Akademiya Pedagogicheskikh Nauk RSFSR, 1960.

Zborovskaya, I. I. Characteristics of differential conditioning of components in complex successive reflexes. *Fiziologichesky Zhurnal SSSR imeni I. M. Sechenova*, 1949, *35*, 263-269.

Zbroźyna, A. W. The conditioned cessation of eating. *Bulletin de l'Académie Polonaise des Sciences, Série de Sciences Biologique*, 1957, *5*(7-8), 261-265.

Zbroźyna, A. W. On the conditioned reflex of the cessation of the act of eating. I. Establishment of the conditioned cessation reflex. *Acta Biologiae Experimentalis*, 1958a, *18*, 137-162.

Zbroźyna, A. W. On the conditioned reflex of cessation of the act of eating. II. Differentiation of the act of eating. *Acta Biologiae Experimentalis*, 1958b, *18*, 163-193.

Zbroźyna, A. W. On the conditioned reflex of the cessation of the act of eating. *Acta Biologiae Experimentalis*, 1959, *19*, 249-255.

Zeiner, A., and Grings, W. W. A replication with emphasis on conceptualization by subject. *Journal of Experimental Psychology*, 1968, *76*, 238-241.

Zelgeym, A. P. *Work of the salivary glands before and after transection of nn. glossopharingei i linguales.* St. Petersburg: Military Medical Academy, 1904. (Thesis)

Zeliony, G. P. *The reactions of dogs to auditory stimuli.* St. Petersburg: Military Medical Academy, 1907. (Thesis)

Zeliony, G. P. A new conditioned reflex (cessation of a sound). *Kharkovsky Meditsinky Zhurnal,* 1908, *5,* 1-15.

Zeliony, G. P. Contributions a l'analyse des excitants complexes des réflexes conditionnels. *Archives de Sciences Biologiques,* 1910a, *15,* 437-453.

Zeliony, G. P. Über die Reaktion der Katze auf Tonreize. *Zentralblatt für Physiologie,* 1910b, *23,* 762-767.

Zeliony, G. P. Procéde technique pour l'étude des réflexes musculaires conditionnels. *Compte Rendu des Séances de la Societé de Biologie, Paris,* 1913a, *75,* 659-660.

Zeliony, G. P. Contributions a l'étude des réflexes conditionnels. *Compte Rendu des Séances de la Societé de Biologie, Paris,* 1913b, *75,* 661-662.

Zeliony, G. P. A new method of studying the reactions of animals to external stimuli. *Russky Fiziologichesky Zhurnal,* 1918, *1,* 128-138.

Zeliony, G. P., Vysotsky, N., Dobrotina, G., Irzhanskaya, K., Medyakov, F., Naumov, S., Poltyrev, S., and Tuntsova, E. Forms and means of forming associated reflexes. In *Transactions of the 6th All-Union Congress of Physiologists, Biochemists, and Pharmacologists.* Tbilisi: 1937. Pp. 165-171.

Zenkevich, L. A. Outline of the evolution of the motor apparatus in animals. *Zhurnal Obshchey Biologii,* 1944, *5,* 129-161.

Zevald, R. G. Different forms of behavior in the ontogeny of dogs. In *Theses, 21st Conference on Higher Nervous Activity.* Leningrad: Nauka, 1966. P. 127.

Zimny, G. H., and Schwabe, N. W. Stimulus change and habituation of the orienting response. *Psychophysiology,* 1965, *2,* 103-115.

Zonova, A. V. Differentiation of spectral colors of equal brightness by infants in the first half year of life. In N. I. Kasatkin (Ed.), *From simple to complex.* Moscow: Nauka, 1964a. Pp. 56-58.

Zonova, A. V. Color vision in infants of the first years of life. In N. I. Kasatkin (Ed.), *From simple to complex.* Moscow: Nauka, 1964b. Pp. 135-153.

Zubkov, A. A., and Polikarpov, G. G. Conditioned reflexes in coelenterates. *Uspekhi Sovremmennoy Biologii,* 1951, *32*(5), 301-302.

AUTHOR INDEX

SUBJECT INDEX

See also Alpha conditioning, Habituation, Pseudoconditioning.
Sensory preconditioning, 186-207, 252-255
  adults, 195-198
  amblystoma, 198
  American and Soviet experiments compared, 201-207
  apes, 205
  axolotls, 198
  baboons, 194-195, 200, 201, 204
  bats, 198, 200
  birds, 187, 198, 200, 201, 205
  carnivores, 200, 201
  cats, 192-194, 202-203, 204
  children, 186, 201, 205
  chimpanzees, 198
  cognition vs. orienting interpretations, 205-207
  and configuring, compared, 221-223
  dogs, 186, 187-192, 200-201, 204, 205
  fish, 198, 205
  frogs, 198
  guinea pigs, 187
  hedgehogs, 198
  human infants (orienting reaction), 198
  insectivores, 200
  man, 201, 204
  mice, 198
  monkeys, 205
  orienting reactions and consciousness, 252-255
  and perceptual learning, 252-253
  polecats, 198, 205
  primates, 201
  puppies, 200, 201
  rabbits, 187, 205
  rats, 201-202
  salamander, 198
  sensation vs. perception, 253-254
  Sergeyev's generalizations, 198-201
  Soviet experiments, 186-201
  turtles, 205
Sheep (wild), unlearned learning, 20
Snails:
  classical motor conditioning, 134-135
  habituation, 45
Spontaneous-operant behavior. *See* Operant behavior.
Stimulus satiation, 30. *See also* Habituation.
Subception, 225-226. *See also* Perception.
Subjective reports, 12, 14-15
Superstitious behavior, 87

Symboling, 270-307
  adults, 277
  children, 277, 302-304
  college students, 277, 278-279
  definition, 276-277
  dominance over percepts, 283-284
  experimental distinction of symbols and sememes, 276-277
  human infants, 298-301
  mediation (the Kendlers), 304-305
  ontogeny of, 297-305
  vs. perceiving and conceiving, 270-276
  retarded children, 277
  schizophrenics, 277
  and verbalization, 302-304
Symbols, 276-277
Thinking, 284-290
  chimpanzees, 273-276
  college students (semantic generalization), 286-287
  definition, 22, 284-285
  and imagery, 285-286
  microcephalic child, 276
  modern experiments, 286-287
  neo-behavioristic approach, 289-290
  phenomenological approach, 288-289
  physiological meaning, 287-288
  unconscious thinking, 288
  See also Conceiving, Symboling.
Turtles:
  configuring, 209, 210-211
  habituation, 45
  sensory preconditioning, 198
Two-way conditioning, 99-101
  and backward conditioning, 101
  dogs, 99-100
  and dominance view, 100
  modifying reaction and modified reaction, 100-101
Ukhtomsky's dominance principle, 24-26, 75-78, 312-313
Verbal reports, and classical conditioning, 139
Verbalization, reinforcement of, 176-181
Willing, 292-296
  conditioning pupillary contractions to words and thoughts, 292
  electroencephalographic accompaniments, 293, 307
  vasomotor conditioning and cognition, 292
  voluntary control, 293-296
    vs. conditioned control, 293, 307
Worms: